Word Study in Action

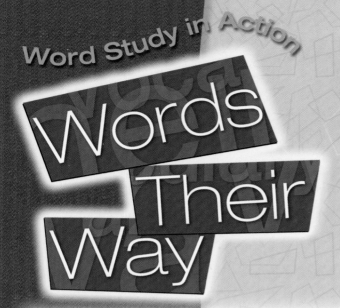

Implement the *Words Their Way*™ Philosophy Today!

Words Their Way: Word Study in Action brings together all the resources that you need to successfully teach your students to read.

By teaching with this program, you can:

- Meet Reading First requirements by delivering a balanced, hands-on approach to phonics and word study.

- Develop phonemic awareness, phonics, vocabulary, and spelling in just 15-20 minutes a day through focused instruction.

- Engage students in grouping sounds, words, and pictures into specific categories with photographic picture cues and full-color design.

Celebration Press

Pearson Learning Group

Provides an easy-to-use weekly lesson plan for each sort.

Day 1 Introduce the sort using the *Big Book of Rhymes.*

Sort 8: Word Families -op, -ot, -og

One Hot Day
One hot day a dog and hog
Saw a frog hop on a log.
Dog and Hog like the spot
To sit and rest when it is hot.
Frog said, "I know what to do!"
Then Dog and Hog hopped in, too.

Day 2 Practice the sort in the *Word Study Notebook.*

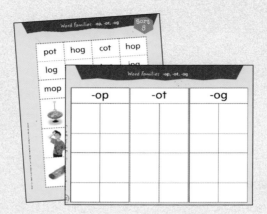

Word Families -op, -ot, -og

-op	-ot	-og

Day 3 Find words in context with the *Words Their Way Library.*

LOST in the FOG

And they did.

"Lost!" said the dog.
"Oh, no!" said the frog.
"Help!" said the hog.

Day 4 Apply the skill in the *Word Study Notebook.*

Write on the lines words that rhyme with hop, hot, and hog.

hop	hot	hog

Day 5 Complete the sort using fun games from the *Teachers Resource CD With Games and Sorts.*

Words Their Way Classroom Package (Basic)	Words Their Way Library	Words Their Way Classroom Package + Library
Level K 0-7652-6738-1	Level K 0-7652-6742-X	Level K 0-7652-6730-6
Level A 0-7652-6739-X	Level A 0-7652-6743-8	Level A 0-7652-6731-4
Level B 0-7652-6740-3	Level B 0-7652-6744-6	Level B 0-7652-6732-2
Level C 0-7652-6741-1	Level C 0-7652-6745-4	Level C 0-7652-6733-0
Level D 0-7652-7633-X		
Level E 0-7652-7634-8		

PEARSON
Learning Group

Inspire.
Achieve.
All Ways.

Customer Service
PH: 1-800-321-3106
FX: 1-800-393-3156
www.pearsonlearning.com

C129 6/06

From the best-selling authors of *Words Their Way* comes a word study book for English Learners. Donald Bear, Marcia Invernizzi, Shane Templeton, Francine Johnston, along with new author Lori Helman – a word study expert and English learner specialist – proudly present

Words Their Way with English Learners

One reality of today's classrooms is the limited help available to teachers supporting English learners' literacy skills. The educators and researchers who developed *Words Their Way* understand this challenge. Based on the same solid research, *Words Their Way with English Learners* helps you determine what your students bring with them from their home languages, where their instruction in English orthography should begin, and how best to move these students through their development and help them master their new language.

Features

You'll find guidance for evaluating students' language needs, research-based suggestions for targeting instruction, and hands-on word study activities geared specifically to the English learner.

- Chapters 1 through 3 introduce you to the stages of spelling and reading development, the assessments to use, and the best ways to organize your classroom and your day for word study.
- Chapters 4 through 7 are organized around the developmental levels of your English learners. Each chapter helps you focus instruction where students can best benefit, and provides a rich bank of classroom-proven word study activities to engage your students, motivate them, and improve their oral and written abilities in English.
- A robust appendix at the back of the book contains all the assessment tools necessary to get word study underway. You'll also find word lists in Spanish, Chinese, Korean, Vietnamese, and Arabic; picture and word sorts; and game templates to advance word study instruction in diverse K-8 classrooms.

Words Their Way™ with English Learners
Word Study for Phonics, Vocabulary, and Spelling Instruction

Donald R. Bear • Lori Helman • Shane Templeton
Marcia Invernizzi • Francine Johnston

Words Their Way Companion Volumes

Words Their Way: Word Study for Phonics, Vocabulary, and Spelling Instruction is the cornerstone to any plan for implementing word study in the classroom. It provides a plan of action for motivating your students and engaging them in literacy at the word level. It gives you a hands-on method for targeting instruction to each student's zone of proximal development.

How can you make this a part of your curriculum?

Five companion volumes are available, each targeted to the needs of an individual stage of spelling development. Each of these stage-specific companions provides a complete curriculum of reproducible sorts and detailed directions. You'll find extensive background notes about the features of study and step-by-step directions on how to guide a sorting lesson. Organizational tips and follow-up activities extend lessons through weekly routines.

Letter and Picture Sorts for Emergent Spellers
Teachers in Pre-K through Grade 1 will find ready-made sorts as well as rhymes and jingles crafted specifically for emergent spellers.

Word Sorts for Letter Name-Alphabetic Spellers
Primarily for students in Kindergarten through Grade 3, black-line masters include picture sorts for beginning sounds, word families with pictures and words, and word sorts for short vowels.

Word Sorts for Within Word Pattern Spellers
Teachers of Grades 1 through 4 will find reproducible sorts that cover the many vowel patterns.

Word Sorts for Syllables and Affixes Spellers
This text includes sorts for syllables and affixes spellers in Grades 3 through 8.

Word Sorts for Derivational Relations Spellers
Teachers in Grades 5 through 12 will find upper-level word sorts that help students build their vocabulary as well as spelling skills.

All *Words Their Way* products can be ordered online at www.allynbaconmerrill.com

Unlock the Full Potential of *Words Their Way*
With Professional Development from Pearson Achievement Solutions

Your staff will gain the skills and strategies they need to boost student spelling, word attack skills, vocabulary, fluency, and reading comprehension using word study.

Our *Words Their Way* professional development program brings the activities and instructional word games of the book to life, training teachers to use word study in their classrooms to increase student literacy.

Professional Development for *Words Their Way*
- Explores strategies for the five developmental phases of spelling discussed in the book: Emergent, Letter Name-Alphabetic, Within Word Pattern, Syllables and Affixes, and Derivational Relations
- Helps educators group students based on results of spelling inventories
- Offers strategies for teachers with students learning English as a second language
- Identifies key classroom management strategies for successful grouping for word study

Professional development for *Words Their Way* is available as a three- or five-day institute. Both programs explore the five stages of spelling and student assessments. The five-day training covers the student spelling assessments in more depth, prepares educators to use word study with English learners, and provides classroom management strategies. After the institute, teachers receive onsite support from a Pearson Achievement Solutions consultant to help them as they incorporate word study into their instruction.

To learn more, call **800-348-4474** and select **option 4**, or visit **www.PearsonAchievementSolutions.com/de1v**

Words Their Way professional development program aligns with the standards and requirements set forth in the Reading First Initiative.

Words Their Way™

Words Their Way™

Word Study for Phonics, Vocabulary, and Spelling Instruction

Fourth Edition

Donald R. Bear
University of Nevada, Reno

Marcia Invernizzi
University of Virginia

Shane Templeton
University of Nevada, Reno

Francine Johnston
University of North Carolina at Greensboro

PEARSON
Prentice Hall

Upper Saddle River, New Jersey
Columbus, Ohio

Library of Congress Cataloging-in-Publication Data

Words their way: word study for phonics, vocabulary, and spelling instruction/Donald
Bear . . . [et al.]. — 4th ed.
    p. cm.
  Includes bibliographical references and index.
  ISBN 0-13-223968-X
 1. Word recognition.   2. Reading—Phonetic method.   3. English language—Orthography
and
spelling. I. Bear, D. (Donald)
  LB1050.44.B43 2008
  372.63'2—dc22

                                      2007004014

Vice President and Executive Publisher: Jeffery W. Johnston
Senior Editor: Linda Ashe Bishop
Senior Development Editor: Hope Madden
Senior Production Editor: Mary M. Irvin
Senior Editorial Assistant: Laura Weaver
Design Coordinator: Diane C. Lorenzo
Cover Designer: Ali Mohrman
Cover Image: Hope Madden
Illustrator: Francine Johnston
Production Manager: Pamela D. Bennett
Director of Marketing: David Gesell
Marketing Manager: Darcy Betts Prybella
Marketing Coordinator: Brian Mounts

This book was set in Palatino by Carlisle Communications, Ltd. It was printed and bound
by Edwards Brothers, Inc. The cover was printed by Phoenix Color Corp.

Photo Credits: All photos by Hope Madden/Merrill

Pearson Education Ltd.
Pearson Education Singapore Pte. Ltd.
Pearson Education Canada, Ltd.
Pearson Education—Japan

Pearson Education Australia Pty. Limited
Pearson Education North Asia Ltd.
Pearson Educacíon de Mexico, S.A. de C.V.
Pearson Education Malaysia Pte. Ltd.

                                  10 9 8
ISBN-13: 978-0-13-223968-4
ISBN-10:   0-13-223968-X

This book is dedicated to the memory of our teacher, Edmund H. Henderson.

Donald R. Bear
Marcia Invernizzi
Shane Templeton
Francine Johnston

Preface

I see and I forget. I hear and I remember. I do and I understand.

Confucius

Through word study, students examine, manipulate, and categorize words. When teachers use this practical, hands-on way to study words with students, they create tasks that focus students' attention on critical features of words—sound, pattern, and meaning.

Words Their Way is a developmentally driven instructional approach providing an integrated way to teach phonics, vocabulary, and spelling to improve literacy skills. Using a systematic approach to word study, guided by an informed interpretation of spelling errors and other literacy behaviors, *Words Their Way* offers a teacher-directed, child-centered plan for vocabulary growth and spelling development. Step by step, the chapters in this text explain and model exactly how to provide effective word study instruction. The keys to this research-based approach are knowing your students' literacy progress, organizing for instruction, and implementing word study. New to this edition are supportive media components that, together with this manageable text, provide you all the tools you need to carry out word study instruction that will motivate and engage your students and help them succeed in literacy learning.

Knowing Your Students

After Chapter 1 provides you with the foundational information on word study and the research in orthography and literacy development that led to this word study approach, Chapter 2 integrates assessment and evaluation into the process. Thoroughly revised, Chapter 2 presents a clear, streamlined vision of assessment and evaluation, walking you step by step through the process of determining your students' instructional level and focusing your word study instruction appropriately.

Characteristics Charts in Chapters 4 through 8 help you pinpoint information to guide your decision making about each student in each stage of development.

Word Study with English Learners sections in each chapter provide targeted guidance to help students master English. This fully revised and expanded material will help you organize and adapt instruction to meet the needs of students whose first language is not English.

 Media Integration. *Words Their Way Word Study Resources CD: Assessment Planning and Additional Interactive Word Sorts* contains computerized assessments to gauge students' developmental levels. Included on this CD are three key elements of assessment that will help you plan for developmentally appropriate instruction:

- Primary Spelling Inventory Feature Guide and Classroom Composite
- Elementary Spelling Inventory Feature Guide and Classroom Composite
- Upper Level Spelling Inventory Feature Guide and Classroom Composite

After you administer the spelling inventories with your primary, elementary, or upper-level students, you will be able to compile a Feature Guide on the CD for each of your students. Feature Guides are records of individual performance on the spelling inventories that guide you to identifying students' instructional levels. Once entered into the program, feature guide information data will automatically feed into a classroom composite record. The classroom composite will identify which students have similar instructional needs, allowing you to plan wisely and effectively for word study grouping.

In addition to the feature guides and classroom composites, the Assessment Resources CD houses additional spelling inventories, error guides, and a classroom organization chart. You'll find:

- Primary Spelling Inventory Error Guide
- Elementary Spelling Inventory Error Guide
- Spelling by Stage Organizational Chart
- Qualitative Spelling Checklist
- Emergent Class Record
- Word Feature Inventory
- McGuffey Qualitative Spelling Inventory
- Content Area Spelling Inventories
- Spanish Spelling Inventory and Analysis
- Kindergarten Spelling Inventory and Analysis

Organizing for Instruction

A thoroughly revised Chapter 3 clearly outlines the best and most effective ways to organize word study for classroom instruction. In addition, *Word Study Routines and Management* sections in every chapter give you practical guidance on managing and implementing word study in primary, elementary, and upper-level classrooms.

Media Integration.   *Words Their Way DVD Tutorial: Planning for Word Study in K–8 Classrooms* reinforces and illustrates classroom organization and management, as outlined in Chapter 3. The classroom footage will lead you through daily instruction, assessment, organization and grouping, and adapting instruction for English learners. Classroom footage examines:

- Assessment and Evaluation
- Classroom Organization
- Word Sorting
- Emergent Stage
- Letter Name–Alphabetic Stage
- Within Word Pattern Stage
- Syllables and Affixes Stage
- Derivational Relations Stage

Implementing Word Study

Once you've assessed your students' development based on the tools provided in Chapter 2 and the Assessment Resources CD, and you've used Chapter 3 to form leveled groups and develop routines for word study, the information and materials in Chapters 4 through 8 and the Appendix will guide your instruction. Chapters 4 through 8 explore the characteristics of each particular stage, from the emergent learner through the advanced reader and writer in the derivational relations stage of spelling development. Each of these chapters covers the research and principles that drive instruction and the most appropriate sequence and instructional pacing. You'll find the word study instruction in phonics, spelling, and vocabulary development best suited to learners in each developmental stage.

In addition, Chapters 4 through 8 present myriad word study activities, including concept sorts, word sorts, literature ideas, and games for each developmental level, focusing instruction where it is needed to move students into the next stage of development. Each rich bank of word study activities promises to engage your students, motivate them, and improve their literacy skills. The activities sections have shaded tabs for your convenience, creating a handy classroom resource.

The Appendix at the back of the book contains all the assessment instruments described in Chapter 2, as well as the word sorts, sound boards, and game templates you'll need to get your own word study instruction underway. Here you will find all the reproducible materials in one place. The Appendix pages are perforated for your convenience.

Media Integration.   *Words Their Way Word Study Resources CD: Assessment Planning and Additional Interactive Word Sorts* provides more than just assessments. You'll also find hundreds of *additional* word and picture sorts, games and templates, and interactive *Create Your Own* software for each developmental stage, as well as robust coverage of word study appropriate for students whose first language is Spanish.

Companion Volumes

We believe that the hands-on word sorting approach to word study is an invaluable literacy tool for you and your students. Broaden your word study understanding and instruction with the variety of additional materials available. Each stage-specific companion volume provides a complete curriculum of reproducible sorts and detailed directions for the teacher. Purchase any of the following valuable professional resources at **www.allynbaconmerill.com**:

- *Words Their Way with English Learners: Word Study for Phonics. Vocabulary, and Spelling Instruction,* by Donald R. Bear, Lori Helman, Shane Templeton, Marcia Invernizzi, and Francine Johnston
- *Words Their Way: Letter and Picture Sorts for Emergent Spellers,* by Donald R. Bear, Marcia Invernizzi, Francine Johnston, and Shane Templeton
- *Words Their Way: Word Sorts for Letter Name–Alphabetic Spellers,* by Francine Johnston, Donald R. Bear, Marcia Invernizzi, and Shane Templeton
- *Words Their Way: Word Sorts for Within Word Pattern Spellers,* by Marcia Invernizzi, Francine Johnston, Donald R. Bear, and Shane Templeton
- *Words Their Way: Word Sorts for Syllables and Affixes Spellers,* by Francine Johnston, Marcia Invernizzi, Donald R. Bear, and Shane Templeton
- *Words Their Way: Word Sorts for Derivational Relations Spellers,* by Shane Templeton, Francine Johnston, Donald R. Bear, and Marcia Invernizzi.

Acknowledgments

We would like to thank the reviewers of our manuscript for their careful consideration and comments: Cathy Blanchfield, California State University, Fresno; Stephanie Collom, Fresno Unified School District; Lori Helman, University of Minnesota; and Maria J. Meyerson, University of Nevada, Las Vegas.

We would like to thank the following teachers for their classroom-tested activities: Cindy Aldrete-Frazer, Tamara Baren, Margery Beatty, Telia Blackard, Janet Bloodgood, Cindy Booth, Karen Broaddus, Wendy Brown, Janet Brown Watts, Fran de Maio, Allison Dwier-Seldon, Marilyn Edwards, Ann Fordham, Mary Fowler, Erika Fulmer, Elizabeth Harrison, Esther Heatley, Lisbeth Kling, Rita Loyacono, Barry Mahanes, Carolyn Melchiorre, Darrell Morris, Colleen Muldoon, Liana Napier. Katherine Preston, Brenda Riebel, Leslie Robertson, Geraldine Robinson, Elizabeth Shuett, Jennifer Sudduth, and Charlotte Tucker.

Brief Contents

Contents

Classroom Tools

CHAPTER 6

Word Study for Transitional Learners in the Within Word Pattern Stage 169

CHAPTER 7

Word Study for Intermediate Readers and Writers: The Syllables and Affixes Stage 202

CHAPTER 8

Word Study for Advanced Readers and Writers: The Derivational Relations Stage 230

APPENDICES

Developmental Word Knowledge

The Braid of Literacy

Literacy is like a braid of interwoven threads. The braid begins with the intertwining threads of oral language and stories. As children experiment with putting ideas on paper, a writing thread is entwined as well. As children move into reading, the threads of literacy begin to bond. Students' growing knowledge of spelling or **orthography**—the correct sequences of letters in the writing system—strengthens that bonding. The size of the threads and the braid itself become thicker as orthographic knowledge grows. See Figure 1-1.

During the primary years, children acquire word knowledge in a fundamentally aural way from the language that surrounds them. Through listening to and talking about life experiences and stories, children develop a rich speaking vocabulary. As they have opportunities to talk about and to categorize their everyday experiences, children begin to make sense of their world and to use language to negotiate and describe it.

As children observe parents, siblings, and caregivers writing for many purposes, they begin to experiment with pen and paper, gradually coming to understand the forms and functions of written language. The first written words students learn are usually

FIGURE 1-1   Braid of Literacy

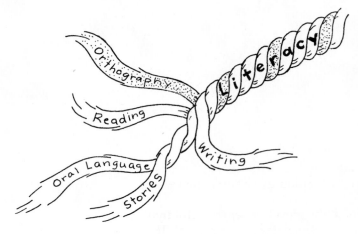

their own names, followed by those of significant others. Words such as *Mom, cat, dog,* and phrases like *I love you* represent people, animals, and ideas dear to their lives.

As students mature as readers and writers, print becomes a critical medium for conceptual development. When purposeful reading, writing, listening, and speaking take place, vocabulary is learned along the way. Even more words are acquired when they are explicitly examined to discover the orthographic relationships among them and how these relationships represent sounds, patterns, and meanings.

The aim of this book is to demonstrate how an exploration of orthographic knowledge can lead to the lengthening and strengthening of the literacy braid. To do this, teachers must know a good deal about the way in which these threads join to create this bond so that they can direct children's attention to "words their way."

There are similarities in the ways learners of all ages expand their knowledge of the world. It seems that humans have a natural interest to find order, to compare and contrast, and to pay attention to what remains the same despite minor variations. Infants learn to recognize Daddy as the same Daddy with or without glasses, with or without a hat or whiskers. Through such daily interactions, we categorize our surroundings. Our students expand their vocabularies by comparing one concept with another. Gradually, the number of concepts they analyze increases, but the process is still one of comparing and contrasting. They may first call anything with four legs a dog until they attend to the features that distinguish dogs, cats, and cows, and later terriers, Labrador retrievers, border collies, and greyhounds. In the process they learn the vocabulary to label the categories.

Word study, as described in this book, occurs in hands-on activities that mimic basic cognitive learning processes: comparing and contrasting categories of word features and discovering similarities and differences within and between categories. For example, students often misspell words that end with the /k/ sound, spelling the word *snake* as *SNACK* or even *SNACKE*. By sorting words that end in *ck* and *ke* into two groups, as the student is doing in Figure 1-2, students discover the invariant pattern that goes with each (*ck* only follows a short vowel). The system is laid bare when words are sorted into categories.

FIGURE 1-2   Student Sorting Words

track, ack

During word study, words and pictures are sorted in routines that require children to examine, discriminate, and make critical judgments about speech sounds, spelling patterns, and meanings. Just as *Math Their Way* (Baretta–Lorton, 1968) uses concrete manipulatives to illustrate principles of combining and separating, so *Words Their Way,* uses concrete pictures and words to illustrate principles of similarity and difference.

Invented Spellings: A Window into Developing Word Knowledge

Students have probably been inventing their own spelling ever since paper and pencil have been available, but it was not until the early 1970s that research by Charles Read (1971) and Carol Chomsky (1971) took a serious look at young children's spelling attempts. Their work introduced the world of literacy to the notion of **invented spelling.** Read understood that preschooler's attempts were not just random displays of ignorance and confusion. To the contrary, his linguistic analysis showed that invented spelling provides a window into a child's developing word knowledge (Read, 1971, 1975). Read's research uncovered a systematic, phonetic logic to preschoolers' categorizations of English speech sounds. At about the same time, Edmund Henderson and his colleagues at the University of Virginia had begun to look for similar logic in students' spellings across ages and grade levels (Beers & Henderson, 1977; Gentry, 1981; Henderson, Estes, & Stonecash, 1972). Read's findings provided these researchers with the tools they needed to interpret the errors they were studying. The Virginia spelling studies corroborated and extended Read's findings upward through the grades and resulted in a comprehensive model of developmental word knowledge (Henderson, 1990; Templeton & Bear, 1992a; Templeton & Morris, 1999). The power of this model lies in the diagnostic information contained in students' spelling inventions that reveal their current understanding of how written words work (Invernizzi, Abouzeid, & Gill, 1994).

Henderson and his students not only studied the development of children's spelling, but also devised an instructional model to complement that development. They determined that an informed analysis of students' spelling attempts can cue timely instruction in phonics, spelling, and vocabulary that is essential to move students forward in reading and writing. By using students' invented spellings as a guide, teachers can differentiate efficient, effective instruction in phonics, spelling, and vocabulary. We call this instruction **word study.**

WHY IS WORD STUDY IMPORTANT?

Becoming fully literate is absolutely dependent on fast, accurate recognition of words and their meanings in texts, and fast, accurate production of words in writing so that readers and writers can focus their attention on making meaning. Letter-sound correspondences, phonics, spelling patterns, high-frequency-word recognition, decoding, word meaning, and other attributes are the basis of written word knowledge. Designing a word study program that explicitly teaches students necessary skills and engages their interest and motivation to learn about how words work is a vital aspect of any literacy program. Indeed, how to teach students these basics in an effective manner has sparked controversy among educators for nearly two hundred years (Balmuth, 1992; Smith, 2002; Mathews, 1967).

Many phonics, spelling, and vocabulary programs are characterized by explicit skill instruction, a systematic scope and sequence, and repeated practice. However, much of the repeated practice consists of rote drill, so students have little opportunity to manipulate word concepts or apply critical thinking skills. Although students need explicit skill instruction within a systematic curriculum, it is equally true that "teaching is not telling" (James, 1958).

Students need hands-on opportunities to manipulate word features in a way that allows them to generalize beyond isolated, individual examples to entire groups of words that are spelled the same way (Juel & Minden-Cupp, 2000). Excelling at word recognition, spelling, and vocabulary is not just a matter of memorizing isolated rules and definitions. The best way to develop fast and accurate perception of word features is to engage in meaningful reading and writing, and to have multiple opportunities to examine those same words out of context. The most effective instruction in phonics, spelling, and vocabulary links word study to the texts being read, provides a systematic scope and sequence of word-level skills, and provides multiple opportunities for hands-on practice and application. In a sense, word study teaches students how to look at words so that they can construct an ever-deepening understanding of how spelling works to represent sound and meaning. We believe that this word study is well worth 10 to 15 minutes of instruction and practice daily.

What Is the Purpose of Word Study?

The purpose of word study is twofold. First, students develop a *general* knowledge of English spelling. Through active exploration, word study teaches students to examine words to discover generalizations about English spelling. They learn the regularities, patterns, and conventions of English orthography needed to read and spell. This general knowledge is conceptual in nature and reflects what students understand about the nature of our spelling system. Second, word study increases *specific* knowledge of words—the spelling and meaning of individual words.

General knowledge is what we access when we encounter a new word, when we do not know how to spell a word, or when we do not know the meaning of a specific word. The better our knowledge of the system, the better we are at decoding an unfamiliar word, spelling correctly, or guessing the meaning of a word. For example, if you have knowledge of short vowels and consonant blends, you would have no trouble attempting the word *crash* even if you have never seen it or written it before. The spelling is unambiguous, like so many single-syllable short-vowel words. Knowledge of how words that are similar in spelling are related in meaning, such as *compete* and *competition*, makes it easier to understand the meaning of a word like *competitor*, even if it is unfamiliar. Additional clues offered by context also increase the chances of reading and understanding a word correctly.

To become fully literate, however, we also need specific knowledge about individual words. The word *rain*, for example, might be spelled *rane*, *rain*, or *rayne*—all are orthographically and phonetically plausible. However, only specific knowledge will allow us to remember the correct spelling. Likewise, only specific knowledge of the spelling of *which* and *witch* makes it possible to know which witch is which! The relationship between specific knowledge and knowledge of the system is reciprocal; that is, each supports the other. Ehri (1992) expressed this idea in the following manner.

> What students store in memory about specific words' spellings is regulated in part by what they know about the general system. Learners who lack this knowledge are left with rote memorization which takes longer and is more easily forgotten. Similarly, what students learn about the orthographic system evolves in part from the accumulation of experiences with specific word spellings. (p. 308)

The purpose of word study, then, is to examine words in order to reveal consistencies within our written language system and to help students master the recognition, spelling, and meaning of specific words.

WHAT IS THE BASIS FOR DEVELOPMENTAL WORD STUDY?

Word study evolves from three decades of research exploring developmental aspects of word knowledge with children and adults (Henderson, 1990; Henderson & Beers, 1980; Templeton & Bear, 1992a). This line of research has documented the convergence of certain kinds of spelling errors that tend to occur together in clusters and reflect students' confusion over certain recurring orthographic principles. These "clusters" of errors have been described in relationship to the types of errors noted, specifically (1) errors dealing with the alphabetic match of letters and sound (*BAD* for *bed*), (2) errors dealing with letter patterns (*SNAIK* for *snake*,) and (3) errors dealing with words related in meaning (*INVUTATION* for *invitation*). The same cluster types of errors have been observed among students with learning disabilities and dyslexia (Sawyer, Lipa-Wade, Kim, Ritenour, & Knight, 1997; Worthy & Invernizzi, 1989), students who speak in nonstandard dialects (Cantrell, 1990), and students who are learning to read in different alphabetic languages (Helman, 2004; Bear, Templeton, Helman, & Baren, 2003; Yang, 2004). Longitudinal and cross-grade-level research in developmental spelling has shown that this developmental progression occurs for all learners of written English in the same direction and varies only in the rate of acquisition (Invernizzi & Hayes, 2004). The scope and sequence of word study instruction is based on research investigating the linguistic logic underlying students' spelling as they progress in literacy.

Word study also comes from what we have learned about the orthographic structure of written words. Developmental spelling researchers have examined the three layers of English orthography (Figure 1-3) in relation to the historical evolution of English spelling as well as developmental progressions from alphabet to pattern to meaning among learners of English. Each layer builds on the one before, and in mature readers and writers, there is interaction among the layers.

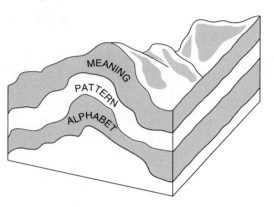

FIGURE 1-3   Three Layers of English Orthography

Alphabet

Our spelling system is **alphabetic** because it represents the relationship between letters and sounds. In the word *sat*, each sound is represented by a single letter; we blend the sounds for /s/, /a/, and /t/ to read the word *sat*. In the word *chin*, we still hear three sounds, even though there are four letters, because the first two letters, *ch*, function like a single letter, representing a single sound. So we can match letters—sometimes singly, sometimes in pairs—to sounds from left to right and create words. This **alphabetic layer** in English spelling is the first layer of information at work.

The alphabetic layer of English orthography was established during the time of Old English, the language spoken and written by the Anglo-Saxons in England between the Germanic invasions of the sixth century c.e. and the conquest of England by William of Normandy in 1066. Old English was remarkably consistent in letter–sound correspondence and used the alphabet to systematically represent speech sounds. The long vowels were pronounced close to the way they are in modern Romance languages today. The simplicity and consistency of the grapheme–phoneme correspondence in Old English were such that, armed with a phonetic guide to letters and sounds, modern readers can still read Abbot Aelfric's *Lord's Prayer* similar to the way Aelfric himself may have recited it over a thousand years ago (Henderson, 1990).

The history of the alphabetic layer reflected in the story of Old English is relevant to teachers today because beginners spell like little Saxons as they begin to read and write (Henderson, 1981). Armed with only a rudimentary knowledge of the alphabet and letter sounds, beginning spellers of all backgrounds use their alphabet knowledge quite literally. They rely on the sound embedded in the names of the letters to represent the sounds they are trying to represent (Read, 1971). This strategy works quite well for consonants when the names do, in fact, contain the correct corresponding speech sounds (*Bee, Dee, eF, eS*, etc). It works less well for letters that have more than one sound (C, G), and it does not work at all for consonants with names that do not contain their corresponding speech sounds (W: *double you*; Y: *wie*; and H: *aitch*). Short-vowel sounds are particularly problematic for novice spellers because there is no single letter that "says" the short-vowel sound. As a result, beginning readers choose a vowel whose pronounced name is closest by place of articulation to the targeted short-vowel sound (Beers & Henderson, 1977; Read, 1975). For example, a beginning reader might spell BAD for *bed*, or *bad*.

Pattern

What about words like *cape, bead,* and *light*? If we spelled these words with single letters, they would look like *cap, bed,* and *lit;* but of course these spellings already represent other words. The **pattern layer** therefore overlies the alphabetic layer. English does not have a single sound for each letter under all conditions. Single sounds are sometimes spelled with more than one letter or are affected by other letters that do not stand for any sounds themselves. When we look beyond single letter–sound match-ups and search for **patterns** that guide the groupings of letters, however, we find surprising consistency (Hanna, Hanna, Hodges, & Rudorf, 1966).

Take, for example, the *-ape* in *cape;* we say that the final *-e* makes the preceding vowel letter, *a*, stand for a long vowel sound. The *e* does not stand for a sound itself, but it plays an important role. The *-ape* group of letters therefore follows a pattern: when you have a vowel, a consonant, and a silent *-e* in a single syllable, this letter grouping forms a pattern that usually will function to indicate a long vowel. We refer to this pattern as the consonant-vowel-consonant-silent e (CVCe) pattern—one of several high frequency, long-vowel patterns.

The notion of pattern helps us talk more efficiently about the alphabetic layer as well. In a CVC pattern (*sat, chin, crash*), note that, regardless of how many consonant letters are on either side of the single vowel, the fact that there is but one vowel letter in that pattern means it will usually stand for a short vowel sound.

Words of more than one syllable also follow spelling patterns. These patterns are described with the same V and C symbols and also relate to the vowel sound within each syllable. Let's consider two of the most common syllable patterns. First is the VCCV pattern, such as in *robber* (the pattern is vowel and consonant to the left of the syllable break and consonant and vowel to the right). When we have this pattern, the first vowel is usually short. Second is the VCV syllable pattern, as in *robot, pilot,* and *limit.* This pattern will usually signal that the first vowel is long, but as in the case of *limit*, the first vowel also can be short. Overall, knowledge about patterns within single syllables, and syllable patterns within words, will be of considerable value to students in both their reading and their spelling.

Where did these patterns originate? The simple letter–sound consistency of Old English was overlaid by a massive influx of French words after the Norman Conquest in 1066. Because these words entered the existing language through bilingual Anglo-Norman speakers, some of the French pronunciations were adopted, too. Also, because the scribes who wrote the new words were biliterate, they applied French orthographic conventions to the spelling of some English words as well. Old English was thus overlaid with the vocabulary and spelling traditions of the ruling class, the Norman French. This complex interaction of pronunciation change on top of the intermingling of French and English spellings led to a proliferation of different vowel sounds represented by different vowel patterns. The extensive repertoire of vowel patterns today is attributable to this period of history, such as the various pronunciations of the *ea* vowel digraph in words like *bread, thread, great, break, meat,* and *clean.* To be sure, this merging of oral and written traditions disrupted the relatively consistent relationship between letters and sounds that existed in Old English. However, this second tier was superimposed on the alphabetic foundation— creating a pattern layer in which letter combinations reflected roughly the language of origin (Invernizzi & Hayes, 2004). It is uncanny that students moving out of the beginning phase spell like little Anglo-Normans when they write *taste* as *taist*, or *leave* as *leeve*.

Meaning

The third layer of English orthography is the **meaning layer.** When students learn that groups of letters can represent meaning directly, they will be much less puzzled when encountering unusual spellings. Examples of these units or groups of letters are prefixes, suffixes, Greek roots, and Latin stems.

As one example of how meaning functions in the spelling system, think of the prefix *re-*; whether we hear it pronounced "ree" as in *rethink* or "ruh" as in *remove*, its spelling stays the same because it directly represents meaning. Why is *composition* not spelled *compusition* since the second vowel sounds more like /uh/ than *o*? It is related in meaning to *compose*. The spelling of the second vowel in the related words, *compose* and *composition*, stays the same even though the pronunciation of the second syllable is different. Likewise, the letter sequence *photo* in *photograph*, *photographer*, and *photographic* signals spelling–meaning connections among these words, despite the changes in sounds that the letter *o* represents.

How did Greek roots like *photo* enter into English orthography? The explosion of knowledge and culture during the Renaissance required a new, expanded vocabulary to accommodate the growth in learning that occurred during this time. Classical roots and stems had the potential to meet this demand for meaning. Greek roots could be compounded or combined (e.g., *autograph* and *autobiography*) and prefixes and suffixes were added to Latin stems (*spectator, spectacular, inspect*). So, to the orthographic record of English history was added a third layer of meaning that built new vocabulary from elements that came from classical Greek and Latin. The spelling/meaning relations inherent in words brought into English during the Renaissance have important implications for vocabulary instruction today as students move through the intermediate grades and beyond (Templeton, 1991). As students explore how spelling visually preserves the semantic relationships among derivationally related words (e.g., *bomb* and *bombard*), vocabulary and spelling instruction become closely related. Chomsky and Halle (1968) used the word *muscle* to show how the seemingly arbitrary spelling of some words is, in reality, central to understanding the meaning of related words (*muscle*, from the Latin *musculus, muscular, musculature*). The silent *c* in the word *muscle* represents a **morphemic** aspect of written English that preserves its etymological history.

Organizing the phonics, spelling, and vocabulary curriculum according to historical layers of alphabet, pattern, and meaning provides a systematic guide for instruction and places the corpus of words to be studied in an evolutionary progression that mirrors the orthographic system itself. Anglo-Saxon words, the oldest words in English, are among the easiest to read and the most familiar. Words like *sun, moon, day*, and *night* are high-frequency, "earthy" words that populate easy reading materials in the primary grades. Anglo-Saxon words survive in high-frequency prepositions, pronouns, conjunctions, and auxiliary verbs (e.g., *have, was, does*) although the pronunciation is now quite different. More difficult Norman French words of one and two syllables—words like *chance, chamber, royal, guard*, and *conquer*—appear with great frequency in books suitable for the elementary grades. The most difficult words in English—words like *calculate, maximum, cumulus, nucleus, hemisphere, hydraulic*, and *rhombus*—are of Latin and Greek origin and appear most often in student reading selections in the middle grades and beyond. Thus, the history of English spelling reflects the frequency of written words as well as the appropriateness of studying certain kinds of words over others in relation to the learner (Henderson, 1992).

Alphabet, pattern, and meaning represent three broad principles of written English and form the layered record of orthographic history. Students' spelling attempts mirror the richness and complexity of this history. As students learn to read and write, they appear to literally reinvent the system as it was itself invented. As shown in Figure 1-4, beginners invent the spellings of simple words quite phonetically, just as the Anglo-Saxons did in 1000 C.E. As students become independent readers, they add a second layer of complexity by using patterns, much as the Norman French did in the latter part of the 14th century. Notice the overuse of the silent *-e* at the end of all of Antonie's words, much like Geoffrey Chaucer's! Intermediate and advanced readers invent conventions for joining syllables and morphemes, as was done during the Renaissance when English was first introduced to a Greco and Latinate vocabulary (Henderson, 1990). As Figure 1-4 shows, both Julian and Elizabeth I struggled with issues relating to consonant doubling where syllables meet.

What Students Need to Learn to Read and Spell English

Students discover the basic principles of spelling—alphabet, pattern, and meaning— when they read and write purposefully and are also provided with explicit, systematic word study instruction by knowledgeable teachers. Word study should give students the experiences they need to progress through these layers of information.

FIGURE 1-4   Historical Development of English Orthography: Sound, Pattern, and Meaning from Past to Present Adapted from "Using Students' Invented Spellings as a Guide for Spelling Instruction that Emphasizes Word Study" by M. Invernizzi, M. Abouzeid, & T. Gill, 1994, *Elementary School Journal, 95*(2), p. 158. Reprinted by permission of The University of Chicago Press.

The Historical Development of Spelling		
	Anglo-Saxon	**Letter Name-Alphabetic**
Alphabet	WIF (wif) TODAEG (today) HEAFONUM (heaven) **(Lord's Prayer, 1000)**	WIF (wife) TUDAE (today) HAFAN (heaven) **(Tawanda, age 6)**
	Norman French	**Within Word Patterns**
Pattern	YONGE (young) SWETE (sweet) ROOTE (root) CROPPE (crops) **(Chaucer, 1440)**	YUNGE (young) SWETE (sweet) ROOTE (root) CROPPE (crop) **(Antonie, age 8)**
	Renaissance	**Syllables & Meaning**
Meaning	DISSCORD (discord) FOLOWE (follow) MUSSIKE (music) **(Elizabeth I, 1600)**	DISSCORD (discord) FOLOWE (follow) MUSSIC (music) **(Julian, age 14)**

- For students who are experimenting with the alphabetic match of letters and sounds, teachers can contrast aspects of the writing system that relate directly to the representation of sound. For example, words spelled with short *e* (*bed, leg, net, neck, mess*) are compared with words spelled with short *o* (*hot, rock, top, log, pond*).
- For students experimenting with pattern, teachers can contrast patterns as they relate to vowels. For example, words spelled with *ay* (*play, day, tray, way*) are compared with words spelled with *ai* (*wait, rain, chain, maid*).
- For students experimenting with conventions of syllables, affixes, and other meaning units, teachers can contrast the stability of base words, roots, and affixes (prefixes and suffixes) across variations. Students can see that words with similar meanings are often spelled the same, despite changes in pronunciation. For example, *admiration* is spelled with an *i* because it comes from the word *admire.*

WORD STUDY IS DEVELOPMENTAL

When we say word study is developmental, we mean that the study of word features must match the level of word knowledge of the learner. Word study is not a one-size-fits-all program of instruction that begins in the same place for all students within a grade level. One unique quality of word study, as we describe it, lies in the critical role of differentiating instruction for different levels of word knowledge. Research spanning over 20 years has established how students learn the specific *features* of words as well as the *order* in which they learn them. Knowledgeable educators have come to know that word study instruction must match the needs of the child. This construct, called **instructional level,** is a powerful delimiter of what may be learned. Simply put, we must teach where the child "is at." To do otherwise results in frustration or boredom and little learning in either case. Just as in learning to play the piano students must work through book A, then book B, and then book C, learning to read and spell is a gradual and cumulative process. Word study begins with finding out what each child already knows and then starting instruction there.

One of the easiest ways to know what students need to learn is to look at the way they spell words. Students' spellings provide a direct window into how they think the system works. By interpreting what students do when they spell, educators can target a specific student's "zone of proximal development" (Vygotsky, 1962) and plan word study instruction that this student is conceptually ready to master. Further, by applying basic principles of child development, educators have learned how to engage students in learning about word features in a child-centered, developmentally appropriate way. When students are instructed within their own zone of proximal development—studying "words their way"—they are able to build on what they already know, to learn what they need to know next, and to move forward. With direct instruction and ongoing support, word features that were previously omitted or confused become amalgamated into an ever-increasing reading and writing vocabulary.

The Development of Orthographic Knowledge

Developmental spelling research describes students' growing knowledge of words as a continuum or a series of chronologically ordered stages or phases of word knowledge. In this book, we use the word *stage* as a metaphor to inform instruction. In reality, students grow in conceptual knowledge of the three general layers of information, and of specific word features, along a continuum and there is often an overlap in the layers and features students understand and use.

Students move hierarchically from easier, one-to-one correspondences between letters and sounds, to more difficult, abstract relationships between letter patterns and sounds, to even more sophisticated relationships between meaning units (**morphology**) as they relate to sound and pattern. Stages are marked by broad, qualitative shifts in the types of spelling errors students make as well as changes in the way they read words. It is not the case that students abandon sound once they move to the use of patterns, or abandon patterns once they move to the use of morphology. Rather, the names of the stages capture the key understandings that distinguish them among the layers of English orthography and among the levels of students' general knowledge of the orthography (Bryant, Nunes, & Bindman, 1997; Ehri, 1997, 2006; Templeton, 2002, 2003).

Because word study is based on students' level of orthographic knowledge, the word study activities presented in this book are arranged by stages of spelling. Knowing each student's stage of spelling will determine your choices of appropriate word study activities. This chapter presents an overview of these stages (see Figure 1-5), which guides you to the instructional chapters.

Teachers can use the guidelines discussed in this chapter and the assessment procedures described in Chapter 2 to determine the spelling stages of their students. By conducting regular spelling assessments, perhaps three times a year, teachers can track students' progress and development. An important prerequisite, however, is to know the continuum of orthographic development.

FIGURE 1-5   Spelling and Reading Stages, Grade Levels, and Corresponding Instructional Chapters

For each stage, students' orthographic knowledge is defined by three functional levels that are useful guides for knowing when to teach what (Invernizzi et al., 1994):

1. What students do correctly—an independent or easy level
2. What students use but confuse—an instructional level where instruction is most helpful
3. What is absent in students' spelling—a frustration level where spelling concepts are too difficult

By studying the stages of spelling development, it becomes obvious what sequence word study should take. In Vygotskian terms (1962), focus on the student's zone of proximal development by determining what the student uses but confuses. In this way, you will learn which orthographic features and patterns to explore, because this is where instruction will most benefit the student.

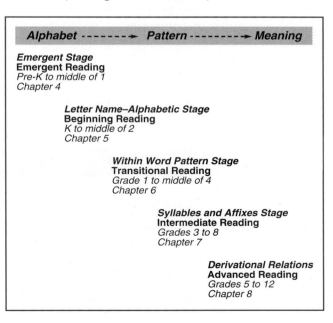

Alphabet - - - - - - - ➤ Pattern - - - - - - - ➤ Meaning

Emergent Stage
Emergent Reading
Pre-K to middle of 1
Chapter 4

Letter Name–Alphabetic Stage
Beginning Reading
K to middle of 2
Chapter 5

Within Word Pattern Stage
Transitional Reading
Grade 1 to middle of 4
Chapter 6

Syllables and Affixes Stage
Intermediate Reading
Grades 3 to 8
Chapter 7

Derivational Relations
Advanced Reading
Grades 5 to 12
Chapter 8

STAGES OF SPELLING DEVELOPMENT

Henderson described a developmental stage model of spelling acquisition after a decade of work at the University of Delaware and later at the University of Virginia (1981). He and his students examined the specific features students use to spell when they write. The discovery of Read's work (1971) in the linguistic arena helped Henderson and his students make sense of the spellings they had collected. Henderson and his students also found that students' spelling errors are not just random mistakes. Building on Read's discoveries, Henderson unearthed an underlying logic to students' errors that changed over time, moving from using but confusing elements of sound to using but confusing elements of pattern and meaning (Henderson et al., 1971). Subsequently, similar developmental changes in spelling have been observed across many groups of students, from preschoolers (Templeton & Spivey, 1980), through adults (Bear, Truex, & Barone, 1989; Worthy & Viise, 1996), as well as across socioeconomic levels, dialects, and other alphabetic languages (Cantrell, 2001; Yang, 2005). In addition, the analysis of students' spelling has been explored by other researchers independently (e.g. Bissex, 1980; Treiman, 1985; Ehri, 1992; Richgels, 1995, 2001).

By 1974, Henderson had formulated a description of increasingly sophisticated phases, or stages, of orthographic knowledge. Since then, he and his students have refined the description of these stages and reworked the labels to reflect their changing understanding of developmental word knowledge and to represent most appropriately what occurs at each level. For example, the label "syllable juncture" was broadened to include affixes. Table 1-1 displays the names of the stages currently in use compared to previous labels used by Henderson and his students at the University of Virginia. The stage names describe students' spelling behavior and make it easier to remember the basic strategies that students use to read and spell.

Stage I: Emergent Spelling

The *Words Their Way* DVD explores the characteristics of the emergent stage as it looks at implementing word study with all emergent spellers, including English learners.

Emergent spelling encompasses the writing efforts of children who are not yet reading conventionally, and in most cases have not been exposed to formal reading instruction. Emergent spellers typically range in age from 0 to 5 years, although anyone not yet reading conventionally is in this stage of development. Most toddlers and preschoolers are emergent spellers, as are most kindergartners and even some first graders at the beginning of the year. Emergent spelling may range from random marks to legitimate letters that bear a relationship to sound. However, most of the emergent stage is decidedly **prephonetic.**

Emergent spelling may be divided into a series of steps or landmarks. In the early emergent stage, students may produce large scribbles that are basically drawings. The movement may be circular, and children may tell a story while they draw. At the earliest points in this stage, there are no designs that look like letters, and the writing is undecipherable from the drawing. As you can see in Figure 1-6A, Haley has drawn large

TABLE 1-1 Stages of Spelling Development		
Current Stage Name	**Henderson's Stages (1990)**	**Original Stage Names (Virginia Spelling Studies)**
Emergent	Preliterate	Prephonetic
Letter Name–Alphabetic	Early Letter Name	Semi-Phonetic
	Letter Name	Phonetic
Within Word Pattern	Within Word	Transitional
Syllables & Affixes	Syllable Juncture	Correct
Derivational Relations	Derivational Constancies	

FIGURE I-6   **Early Emergent Writing** Adapted with permission from Bloodgood, J.R (1996).

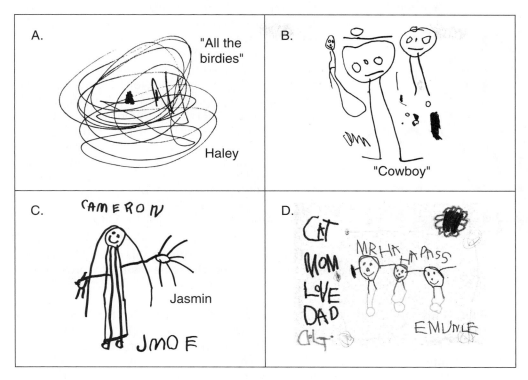

scribble-like circles and simply called it writing, asserting that it says, "All the little birdies." There is little order to the direction in Haley's production; it goes up, down, and around, willy-nilly.

Gradually and especially when sitting next to other children or adults who write, children begin to use something that looks like script to "tell" about the picture. In the middle of the emergent stage, pretend writing is separate from the picture, although there is still no relationship between letters and sound. Writing may occur in any direction but is generally linear. In Figure 1-6B, the child labeled his drawing to the left of the picture as "Cowboy."

Throughout the emergent stage, children begin to learn letters, particularly the letters in their own names, and begin to pay attention to the sounds in words. Toward the end of the emergent stage, their writing starts to include the most prominent or salient sounds in a word. The ability to make a few letter-sound matches is evident in Figure 1-6C, where *Jasmin* is spelled JMOE. The movement from this stage to the next stage hinges on learning the **alphabetic principle:** Letters represent sounds in a systematic way, and words can be segmented into sequences of sound from left to right. Toward the end of emergent spelling, students start to memorize some words and write them repeatedly, such as the *cat, Mom, love,* and *Dad* in Figure 1-6D.

Stage II: Letter Name–Alphabetic Spelling

The **letter name–alphabetic spelling stage** is the second stage in the developmental model and encompasses that period of time during which students are formally taught to read, typically during the kindergarten and first-grade years and extending into the middle of second grade. Most letter name–alphabetic spellers are between the ages of 5 and 8 years, although a beginning reader at age 55 also can be a letter name–alphabetic

Watch the *Words Their Way* DVD to witness the way word study motivates letter name–alphabetic spellers.

FIGURE 1-7 Early Letter Name–Alphabetic Spelling: Ellie's Note to Her Sister, Meg—"When Are You Coming?"

speller (Bear, 1989; Viise, 1996). The name of this stage reflects students' dominant approach to spelling; that is, they use the *names* of the letters as cues to the sound they want to represent (Read, 1975). In Ellie's early letter–name alphabetic spelling shown in Figure 1-7, she used the letter *y* to represent the /w/ sound at the beginning of the word *when*, because the first sound in the pronounced letter name Y (wie) matches the first sound in the word *when*. The letter name for N includes the "en" sound to finish off the word *when*. Charles Read (1975) coined the term "letter name spelling" based on this predominant strategy of using letter names to represent speech sounds. Ellie used R and U to represent the entire words *are* and *you*, another early letter name strategy.

We divide this letter name–alphabetic stage into early, middle, and late periods because of the rapid and dramatic growth during this time. Throughout this stage, students learn to segment the sounds or **phonemes** within words and to match the appropriate letters or letter pairs to those sequences.

Early letter name–alphabetic spelling. Students who are early in the letter name–alphabetic stage apply the alphabetic principle primarily to consonants as Ellie did in Figure 1-7. Often, students spell the first sound and then the last sound of single-syllable words. For example, *when* may be spelled Y or YN. The middle elements of syllables, the vowels, are usually omitted. Typically, only the first sound of a two-letter consonant blend is represented, as in FT for *float*. Early letter name–alphabetic writing often lacks spacing between words, which makes it hard to decipher unless you know something about the writer's message. This type of writing is **semiphonetic** because only some of the phonemes are represented.

When early letter name–alphabetic students use the alphabetic principle, they find matches between letters and the spoken word by how the sound is made or articulated in the mouth. For example, students may confuse the /b/ sound and /p/ sound because they are made with the lips in the same way except for one feature: In making the /b/, the vocal chords vibrate to produce a **voiced** sound. An early letter name–alphabetic speller might spell the word *pat* as BT.

FIGURE 1-8 Middle to Late Letter Name–Alphabetic Spelling: Kaitlyn's Farewell Note to her First Grade Teacher

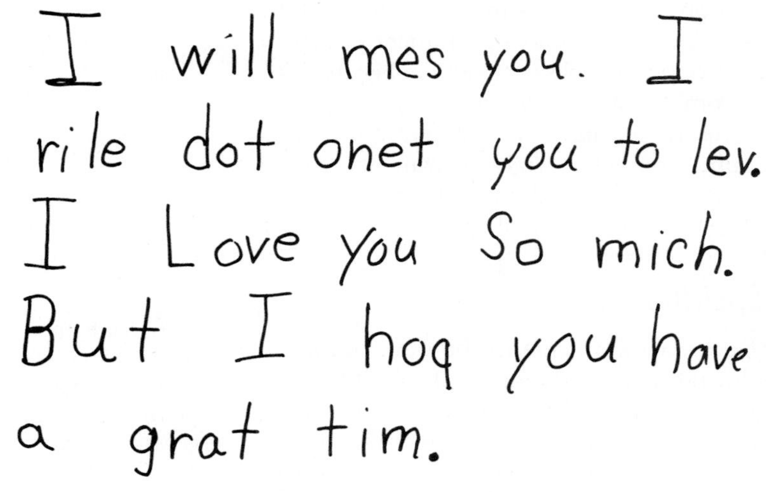

I will mes you. I rile dot onet you to lev. I Love you So mich. But I hoq you have a grat tim.

Middle to late letter name–alphabetic spelling. In her note in Figure 1-8, Kaitlyn shows mastery of most beginning and ending consonants. She spells many high-frequency words correctly, such as *will, love, have,* and *you,* but also makes spelling errors typical of a student in the middle letter name–alphabetic stage. What separates her from the early letter name speller is her consistent use of vowels. Long vowels, which "say their name," appear in *tim* for *time* and *hop* for *hope,* but silent letters are not represented. Short vowels are used but confused, as in *miss* spelled as *mes* and *much* as *mich.*

In the middle letter name–alphabetic stage, students are also learning to segment both sounds in a consonant blend and begin to represent the blends correctly, as in *GRAT* for *great*. Kaitlyn has also correctly represented the ch digraph in *much*. Because middle letter name–alphabetic spellers can segment and represent most of the sound sequences heard within single-syllable words, their spelling is described as **phonetic.**

By the end of this stage, late letter name-alphabetic spellers are able to consistently represent most regular short-vowel sounds, digraphs, and consonant blends because they have full **phonemic segmentation**. The letters *n* and *m* as in *bunk* or *lump* are referred to as **preconsonantal nasals** (nasals that come before a consonant) and are generally omitted by students throughout this stage when they spell them as *BUK* or *LUP*. Kaitlyn omitted the nasal in her spelling of *don't* as *DOT* and used an interesting strategy to get the *n* in *want* by spelling it as *one + t*. Henderson (1990) recognized that the correct spelling of the preconsonantal nasal was a reliable and important watershed event that heralds the onset of the next stage of orthographic knowledge. By the end of the stage, students have mastered the alphabetic layer of English orthography and will now begin to use but confuse silent long-vowel markers such as the silent *-e* in the spelling of *rain* as *RANE*.

Stage III: Within Word Pattern Spelling

The *Words Their Way* DVD explores the organization and implementation of word study with within word spellers, focusing in detail on English learners in this stage.

Students entering the **within word pattern spelling stage** can read and spell many words correctly because of their automatic knowledge of letter sounds and short-vowel patterns. This level of orthographic knowledge typically begins as students transition to independent reading toward the end of first grade, and expands throughout the second and third grades, and even into the fourth grade. Although most within word pattern spellers typically range in age from 7 to 10 years, many adult, low-skilled readers remain in this stage. Regardless, this period of orthographic development lasts longer than the preceding one, because the vowel pattern system of English orthography is quite extensive.

The within word pattern stage begins when students can correctly spell most single-syllable, short-vowel words correctly as well as consonant blends, digraphs, and preconsonantal nasals. Because these basic phonics features have been mastered, within word pattern spellers work at a more abstract level than letter name–alphabetic spellers (Zutell, 1994). They move away from the linear, sound-by-sound approach of the letter name–alphabetic spellers and begin to include patterns or chunks of letter sequences. Within word spellers can think about words in more than one dimension; they study words by sound and pattern simultaneously. As the name of this stage suggests, within word pattern spellers take a closer look at vowel patterns within single-syllable words (Henderson, 1990). They are sometimes referred to as transitional spellers because they are transitioning from the alphabetic layer to the meaning layer of English orthography through patterns.

Kim's writing in Figure 1-9 is that of an early within word pattern speller. She spells many short-vowel and high-frequency words correctly such as *hill, had, them, girl,* and *won*. She also spells some common long vowel patterns correctly in CVCe words like *time* and *game*. Kim hears the long vowel sound in words like *team, goal,* and *throw,* but she selects the wrong pattern, spelling them as *TEME, GOWL,* and *THROWE*. She omits the silent *e* in *cones*. These are good examples of how Kim is using but confusing long vowel patterns.

During the within word pattern stage, students first study the common long-vowel patterns (long *-o* can be spelled with *o*–consonant–*e* as in *joke*, *oa* as in *goal*, and *ow* as in *throw*) and then less common patterns such as the VCC pattern in *cold* and *most*. The most difficult patterns are **ambiguous vowels** because the sound is neither long nor short and the same pattern may represent different sounds, such as the *ou* in *mouth, cough, through,* and *tough*. These less common and ambiguous vowels

FIGURE 1-9   Early Within Word Pattern Spelling: Kim's Soccer Game

My teme won the scoer game. I was the boll girl. We had to use cons for the gowl. Evre time the boll wintdowe Hill I Had to Throwe them a nother boll.

FIGURE 1-10   Syllables and Affixes Spelling: Xavier's Account of his Summer Adventures

> We went out west last sumer. We drove a littel camper bus. We stoped in alot of Nashal Parks and went hikeing in the mountins. It was relly cool.

may persist as misspellings into the late part of the within word pattern stage.

Although the focus of the within word pattern stage is on the pattern layer of English orthography, students must also consider the meaning layer to spell and use **homophones** such as *bear* and *bare, deer* and *dear, hire* and *higher*. Sound, pattern, and meaning must be considered when spelling homophones. This introduces the spelling-meaning connection explored in the next two stages of spelling development.

Stage IV: Syllables and Affixes Spelling

 Watch the *Words Their Way* DVD to see how teacher Ryan Ichanberry organizes for instruction with his syllables and affixes spellers.

The **syllables and affixes stage** is typically achieved in the upper elementary and middle school grades, when students are expected to spell many words of more than one syllable. This represents a new point in word study when students consider spelling patterns where syllables meet and meaning units such as affixes (prefixes and suffixes). Students in this fourth stage are most often between 9 and 14 years, though many adults with poor literacy skills may be found in this stage.

In Figure 1-10, a fourth-grader in the early syllables and affixes stage has written about his summer vacation. Xavier spelled most one-syllable short- and long-vowel words correctly (*went, west, drove, hike*). Many of his errors are in two-syllable words and fall at the place where syllables and affixes meet. Xavier has used—but confused—the conventions for preserving vowel sounds when adding an **inflected ending** in *stopped* and *hiking*, spelled as *STOPED* and *HIKEING*. The principle of doubling the consonant at the **syllable juncture** to keep the vowel short is used in *LITTEL* for *little*, but is lacking in his spelling of *summer* as *SUMER*. Syllable juncture patterns include the **open first syllable** in *hu-mor* (V/CV usually signals a long vowel in the first syllable) and **closed** first syllable in *sum-mer* and *cam-per* (VC/CV usually signals a short vowel sound in the first syllable). **Unaccented** final syllables give students difficulty, as shown in Xavier's spellings of *LITTEL* for *little* and *MOUNTIN* for *mountain*.

Toward the end of the syllables and affixes stage, students grapple with affixes that change the meaning of the word. They may misspell affixes, such as in *desloyal* for *disloyal,* or *carefull* for *CAREFUL*. By studying base words and affixes as meaning units, these students anticipate the next stage, derivational relations, where they study the spelling–meaning connections of related words (Templeton, 2004). By studying base words and derivational affixes, students learn about English spelling at the same time they enrich their vocabularies.

Stage V: Derivational Relations Spelling

View the *Words Their Way* DVD to see how assessment, word study routines, and classroom organization look with derivational relations spellers.

The **derivational relations spelling stage** is the last stage in the developmental model. Although some students may move into the derivational stage as early as grade 4 or 5, most derivational relations spellers are found in middle school, high school, and college. This stage continues throughout adulthood, when individuals continue to read and write according to their interests and specialties. This stage of orthographic knowledge is known as *derivational relations* because this is when students examine how words share common derivations and related base words and word roots. They discover that the meaning and spelling of parts of words remain constant across different but derivationally related words (Henderson & Templeton, 1986; Henry, 1988; Schlagal, 1989; Templeton, 1983). Word study in this stage builds on and expands knowledge of a wide vocabulary, often of Greek and Latin origin.

Early derivational relations spellers like Kaitlyn (Figure 1-11) spell most words correctly. However, some of her errors reflect a lack of knowledge about derivations. For example, *favorite* is spelled *FAVERITE* and does not show its relationship to *favor*, and *different* is spelled *DIFFRENT* and lacks a connection to *differ*. Her errors on final suffixes, such as the *-sion* in *division* and the *-ent* in *ingredients* are also very typical of students in this stage.

Frequent errors have to do with the **reduced vowel** in derivationally related pairs. For example, the vowel sound in the second syllable of the word *competition* is reduced to a **schwa** sound, as in *com-puh-ti-tion*. Students in the earlier part of the derivational relations stage might spell *competition* as *COMPUTIION* or *COMPOTITION* or even *COMPITITION*. A student who misspells *competition* may see the cor-

FIGURE 1-11 Derivational Relations Spelling: Kaitlyn's 6th Grade Math Journal Reflection

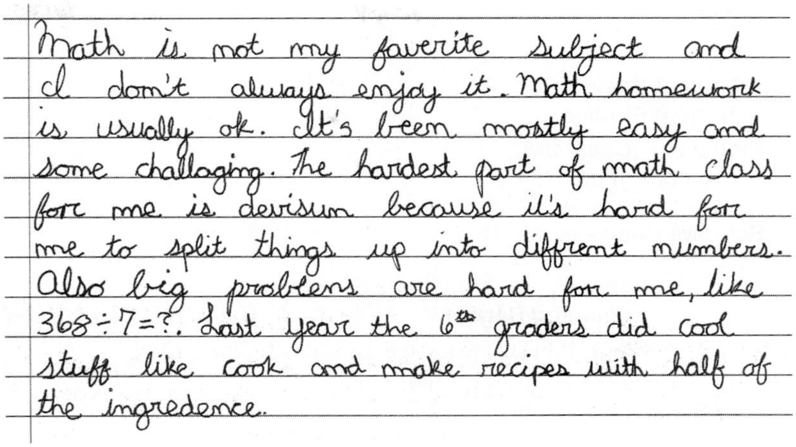

Math is not my faverite subject and I don't always enjoy it. Math homework is usually ok. It's been mostly easy and some challaging. The hardest part of math class fore me is devisiun because it's hard for me to split things up into diffrent numbers. Also big problems are hard for me, like $368 \div 7 = ?$. Last year the 6th graders did cool stuff like cook and make recipes with half of the ingredence.

rect spelling more easily by going back to a base or root, as in *compete*, where the long vowel gives a clear clue to spelling. Knowing that the word *competition* is derivationally related to the word *compete* will help these students spell the derived form correctly.

Students' spelling errors often have to do with using but confusing issues of consonant doubling in **absorbed prefixes**, the convention of changing the last consonant of a prefix to the first consonant of the root word (e.g., *in + mobile = immobile*). For example, they may spell *immobile* as *IMOBILE* or *correspond* as *CORESPOND*. Other aspects of affixation students negotiate in the latter part of the derivational relations stage involve changing adjectives to nouns (*brilliant* to *brilliance*; *adolescent* to *adolescence*), and it is not uncommon to find students using but confusing these derivational endings (e.g., *ADOLESCANCE* for *adolescence*; *BRILLENCE* for *brilliance*).

The logic inherent in this lifelong stage can be summed up as follows: "Words that are related in meaning are often related in spelling as well, despite changes in sound" (Templeton, 1979, 1983, 2004). Spelling–meaning connections provide a powerful means for expanding vocabulary.

THE SYNCHRONY OF LITERACY DEVELOPMENT

The scope and sequence of word study instruction that is presented in Chapters 4 through 8 is based on research that has described the developmental relationship between reading and spelling behaviors. When teachers conduct word study with students, they are addressing learning needs in all areas of literacy because development in one area relates to development in other areas. This harmony in the timing of development has been described as the **synchrony** of reading, writing, and spelling development (Bear, 1991b; Bear & Templeton, 1998). All three advance in stage-like progressions that share important conceptual dimensions.

Working independently, other researchers have described a remarkably similar progression of reading phases that cover the range from prereading to highly skilled, mature reading (Chall, 1983; Ehri, 1997; Frith, 1985; Juel, 1991; Spear-Swerling & Sternberg, 1997). There is converging evidence that reading, writing, and spelling development are integrally related. Figure 1-12 compares other researchers' descriptions of reading development to the spelling stages.

Individuals may vary in their rate of progress through these stages, but most tend to follow the same order of development. The synchrony that is observed makes it possible to bring together reading, writing, and spelling behaviors to assess and plan differentiated instruction that addresses students' developmental pace of instruction.

FIGURE 1-12 Spelling and Reading Stages

Alphabet ──────────────────────▶ **Pattern** ──────────────────────▶ **Meaning**

Emergent Spelling
Emergent Reader

Prereading *(Chall, 1983)*
Logographic *(Frith, 1985)*
Prealphabetic *(Ehri, 1997)*
Selective Cue *(Juel, 1991)*

     Letter Name–Alphabetic Spelling
     Beginning Reader

     Stage 1: Initial Reading & Decoding *(Chall, 1983)*
     Alphabetic *(Frith, 1985)*
     Partial-to-Full Alphabetic *(Ehri, 1997)*
     Phonetic Cue *(Spear-Swerling & Sternberg, 1997)*

          Within Word Pattern Spelling
          Transitional Reader

          Stage 2: Confirmation & Fluency *(Chall, 1983)*
          Orthographic *(Frith, 1985)*
          Consolidated Alphabetic *(Ehri, 1997)*
          Automatic Word Recognition *(Spear-Swerling & Sternberg, 1997)*

               Syllables and Affixes Spelling
               Intermediate Reader

               Stage 3: Reading to Learn *(Chall, 1983)*
               Strategic Reading *(Spear-Swerling & Sternberg, 1997)*

                    Derivational Relations Spelling
                    Advanced Reader

                    Stage 4: Multiple Viewpoints *(Chall, 1983)*
                    Stage 5: Construction & Reconstruction *(Chall, 1983)*
                    Proficient Adult Reading *(Spear-Swerling & Sternberg, 1997)*

The following discussion centers on this overall progression with an emphasis on the synchronous behaviors of reading and writing with spelling.

Emergent Readers

During the emergent stage, the child may undertake reading and writing in earnest, but adults will recognize their efforts as more pretend than real. Students may write with scribbles, letterlike forms, or random letters that have no phonetic relationship to the words they confidently believe they are writing. These students may "read" familiar books from memory using the pictures on each page to cue their recitation of the text. For this reason, Chall (1983) called this stage of development *pre-reading*. Emergent readers may call out the name of a favorite fast food restaurant when they recognize its logo or identify a friend's name because it starts with a *t*, but they are not systematic in their use of any particular cue. During the emergent stage, children lack an understanding of the alphabetic principle or show only the beginning of this understanding. Ehri (1997) designated this as the *prealphabetic phase*; children's use of logos led Frith (1985) to name it the *logographic stage*. Juel (1991) uses the term *selective cue* to describe how children select nonalphabetic visual cues like the two *o*s in *look* to remember a word.

During the emergent stage, children can become quite attached to selected letters that they notice in their name. Upon entering preschool, Lee noticed that other children's names on their cubbies used some of the same letters that she used in her name. Perplexed and somewhat annoyed, she pointed to the letters that were also in her name. "Hey, that's MY letter!" she insisted. Children in the emergent stage also begin to see selected letters in their names in environmental print. Walking around the grocery store, Lee pointed to the box of Cheer detergent and said, "Look, Mommy! There's my name!" Lee's special relationship with the letters in her name is a living embodiment of the prealphabetic, logographic, and selective–cue strategy these researchers describe.

Beginning Readers

The understanding of the alphabetic nature of our language is a major hurdle for readers and spellers. The child who writes *light* as *LT* has made a quantum conceptual leap, having grasped that there are systematic matches between sounds and letters that must be made when writing. The early letter name–alphabetic speller is a beginning reader who has moved from pretend reading to real reading and begun to use systematic letter sound matches to identify and store words in memory. Just as early attempts to spell words are partial, so, too, beginning readers initially have limited knowledge of letter sounds as they identify words by phonetic cues. Ehri (1997) describes these readers and writers as being in the *partial alphabetic* phase. The kinds of reading errors students make during this phase offer insights into what they understand about print. Using context as well as partial consonant cues, a child reading about good things to eat might substitute *candy* or even *cookie* for *cake* in the sentence, "The cake was good." Readers in this stage require much support in the form of predictable, memorable texts.

As readers and writers acquire more complete knowledge of letter sounds in the later part of the letter name–alphabetic stage, they will include, but often confuse, vowels in the words they write and read. Students who spell *BAD* for *bed* may make similar vowel errors when they read *hid* as *had* in "I hid the last cookie." These students resemble Ehri's (1997) *full alphabetic* readers who begin to use the entire letter string to decode and store sight words. Nevertheless, the reading of letter name–alphabetic spellers is often disfluent and word by word, unless they have read the passage before or are otherwise familiar with it (Bear, 1992). If you ask such spellers to read silently, the best they can do is to whisper. They need to read aloud to vocalize the letter sounds. Readers in this stage continue to benefit from repeated readings of predictable texts, but also from the reading of text with many phonetically regular words. These "decodable" texts support the development of decoding strategies and the acquisition of sight words (Juel & Roper-Schneider, 1985; Mesmer, 2006). Not surprisingly, Chall (1983) referred to this stage as a period of *initial reading and decoding* when students are "glued to print."

Transitional Readers

Transitional readers and spellers move into the within word pattern spelling stage when single letter–sound units are consolidated into patterns or larger chunks and other spelling regularities are internalized. Longitudinal research on spelling development has identified the progressive order in which students appear to use these larger chunks. After automating basic letter sounds in the **onset** position (initial consonants, consonant blends, and consonant digraphs), students focus on the vowel and what follows (Ganske, 1994; Invernizzi, 1985, 1992; Viise, 1996). Short-vowel **rimes** are learned first with consonant blends in the context of simple word families or **phonograms** such as *h-at*, *ch-at*, or *fl-at*. These chunks come relatively easily in the letter name–alphabetic stage, probably as a result of their frequency in one-syllable words. Once the rime unit is solidified as a chunk, students appear to use but confuse the various long-vowel patterns of English (Invernizzi, 1992). Other stage models of reading acquisition describe this chunking phenomenon as an *orthographic* stage in which readers use progressively higher-order units of word structures to read and spell (Chall, 1983; Frith, 1985; Gibson, 1965). Ehri and McCormick (1998) call this the *consolidated alphabetic phase* in which students' reading is supported by familiarity with frequently occurring letter pattern units.

From the beginning to the end of this stage, students move from needing support materials and techniques to being able to pick from various texts and reading them independently—from the Sunday comics to easy chapter books such as *Freckle Juice* and *Superfudge*, both by Judy Blume, and *Ramona the Pest*, by Beverly Cleary. With easy, independent-level material, students stop fingerpointing and, for the first time, read silently (Bear, 1982; Henderson, 1990). Their reading moves from halting word-by-word reading to more expressive phrasal reading, and they can read fluently at their instructional level (Zutell & Rasinski, 1989). During this stage, students integrate the knowledge and skills acquired in the previous two stages, so Chall (1983) described this stage as one of *confirmation and fluency*. Advances in word knowledge affect students' writing, too. Their sizable sight word vocabulary allows them to write more quickly and with greater detail. Writing and reading speeds increase significantly between the letter name–alphabetic stage and the transitional within word pattern stage (Bear, 1992; Invernizzi, 1992).

Intermediate and Advanced Readers

Two additional stages of word knowledge characterize **intermediate** and **advanced readers:** syllables and affixes and derivational relations as shown in Figure 1-13. These two periods of literacy development are generally accompanied by the ability to solve abstract problems and to reflect metacognitively on experiences. Students operating within the meaning layer of English orthography have relatively automatic word recognition, and thus their minds are free to think as rapidly as they can read. They can use reading as a vehicle for learning new information from texts, and their vocabulary grows with their reading experience. Intermediate and advanced readers are also fluent writers. The content of their writing displays complex analysis and interpretation, and reflects a more sophisticated, content-oriented vocabulary.

Syllable and affix spellers read most texts with good accuracy and speed, both orally and silently. For these students, success in reading and understanding is related to familiarity and experience with the topic being discussed. Students in this intermediate stage acquire, through plenty of practice, a repertoire of reading styles that reflects their experience with different genres. They may obsess on reading fantasy or historical fiction and voraciously consume all of the books in a series, such as the Harry Potter books by J. K. Rowling or *His Dark Materials* by Philip Pullman. The same is true for writing. Students who are in this stage of word knowledge delight in writing persuasive essays, editorials, poetry, or their own versions of fantasy or realistic fiction.

Derivational relations spellers have a broader experience base that allows them to choose among a variety of reading styles to suit the text and their purposes for reading. They read according to their own interests and needs and they seek to integrate their knowledge with the knowledge of others. The same picture is evidenced in their writing. With purpose and practice, derivational relations students develop and master a variety of writing styles.

These two stages of word knowledge correspond roughly to Chall's (1983) *multiple viewpoints* and *construction and reconstruction* stages. Others refer to this period as one during which students learn to become *strategic readers* and ultimately become *proficient adult readers* (Spear-Swerling & Sternberg, 1997). Still others lump these two stages of reading together as the *automatic* stage (Gough & Hillinger, 1980), even though much is still not automatic. Syllable and affixes spellers continue to struggle with issues such as how to pronounce the name of the main character in *Caddie Woodlawn*, sometimes calling her "Cadie." Derivational relations spellers may have seen the word *segue* in print but never have heard it pronounced, and read it as *seck* or *seck-que*. Vocabulary and word use plays a central role in the connections that intermediate and advanced readers forge

FIGURE I-13   The Synchrony of Literacy Development From *The Synchrony of Literacy Development: A Guide to Instruction* by D. Bear, 1998.

Layers of the Orthography

ALPHABET/SOUND

PATTERN

MEANING

Reading and Writing Stages:

	Emergent	Beginning	Transitional	Intermediate	Advanced
	Pretend read	Read aloud, word-by-word, fingerpoint reading	Approaching fluency, phrasal, some expression in oral reading. Wright Brothers of reading	Read fluently, with expression. Develop a variety of reading styles. Vocabulary grows with experience reading.	
	Pretend write	Word-by-word writing, writing moves from a few words to paragraph in length	Approaching fluency, more organization, several paragraphs	Fluent writing, build expression and voice, experience different writing, styles and genre, writing shows personal problem solving and personal reflection.	

Spelling Stages:

	Emergent →			Letter Name- Alphabetic →			Within-Word Pattern →			Syllables and Affixes →			Derivational Relations →		
	Early	Middle	Late	Early	Middle	Late	Early	Middle	Late	Early	Middle	Late	Early	Middle	Late

Examples of spellings:

	Emergent Early	Emergent Middle	Emergent Late	LN Early	LN Middle	LN Late	WW Early	WW Middle	WW Late	SA Early	SA Middle	SA Late	DR Early	DR Middle	DR Late
bed	 [drawing]	MST	E	bd	bad		*bed*								
ship	[drawing]	TFP	S	sp	sep		*ship*								
float	[drawing]	SMT	F	ft	fot	flot	flowt	floaut	flote / *float*						
train	[drawing]	FSMP	G	jin	jan	tan / chran	teran	traen	trane / *train*						
bottle			B	bt	botl	bodol	botel	botal		bottel	*bottle*				
cellar			S	slr	salr	celr	seler	celer	seler	celer	seller	*cellar*			
pleasure			P	pjr	plasr	plager	plejer	pleser	pleser	plesher	plesour		plesure	*pleasure*	
confident										confadent	confedent	confednet	confedent	confident	*confident*
opposition										opasishan	opasishan	oppasishion	opositian	oposision	*opposition*

between reading and writing. From adolescence on, most of the new vocabulary students learn—except perhaps for slang—comes from reading and reflects new domains of content-specific knowledge that students explore (Beck, McKeown, & Kucan, 2002). Studying spelling–meaning connections is central to maximizing this vocabulary growth (Templeton, 1979, 1992).

Research to Support the Synchrony of Spelling and Reading

Significant correlations between spelling and various measures of word recognition and decoding have been reported. For example, Ehri (2000) reviewed six correlational studies in which students of various ages (first grade through college) were asked to read and spell words and reported correlations ranging from .68 to .86. In other studies, spelling measures have accounted for as much as 40% to 60% of the variance in oral reading measures (Zutell, 1992; Zutell & Rasinki, 1989). Intervention studies exploring the added value of supplemental spelling instruction have repeatedly found that students who receive additional spelling instruction perform better on reading tasks such as oral reading, silent reading comprehension, and other reading-related measures in addition to spelling (Berninger et al., 1998; Goulandris, 1992; Graham, Harris, & Chorzempa, 2002; McCandliss, Beck, Sandak, & Perfetti, 2003). Notably, Perfetti (1997) observed that practice at spelling helps reading more than practice at reading helps spelling.

Students' spelling attempts also provide a powerful medium for predicting reading achievement (Cataldo & Ellis, 1988). Morris and Perney (1984) found that first graders' invented spellings were a better predictor of end-of-grade reading than a standardized reading readiness test. In a two-year study following students from first through third grade, Ellis and Cataldo (1992) reported spelling to be the most consistent predictor of reading achievement. Sawyer et al. (1997) reported that a child's score on a developmental spelling inventory (Ganske, 1999) was a more powerful predictor of decoding than phonemic awareness tasks such as segmentation. Moreover, the spelling inventory identified the exact word elements students had already mastered and those currently under negotiation. Thus, establishing levels of development in spelling and reading has enormous potential for guiding instruction.

INTEGRATED PHONICS, SPELLING, AND READING INSTRUCTION

Henderson (1981) devised the concept of **word study** because he was convinced that understanding how children learned to spell words could also provide insight on how they read them. He believed that children's growing word knowledge encompassed phonological, syntactic, semantic, and orthographic information, and that categorizing written words enabled them to sort out the relationships among these linguistic sources. Henderson's instructional approaches (for example, *word sorts, word hunts, writing sorts*) were shaped by his belief that both linguistic and orthographic aspects of written words were critical factors in learning to read and write. His work, and the work of his colleagues and students, demonstrated that written word knowledge is developmental and advances progressively and in synchrony in relation to cognitive development, exposure to print, and instruction.

Figure 1-13 presents an integrated model of how reading, writing, and spelling progress in synchrony. In parent-teacher conferences, teachers might refer to this figure in discussing each student's development when they share his or her writing or show a collection of books that illustrates the range of instructional reading levels that correspond to the developmental levels in the figure. Parents can better understand where their children are along the developmental continuum and across reading, writing, and spelling by looking at the described behaviors and the spelling samples.

Word study activities in this book are organized around this model. If you can identify your students by the stages of reading, writing, and spelling, then you will know which chapters contain the activities that are most relevant to their development, as shown in Figure 1-5 on page 9.

As described throughout this chapter, developmental spelling theory suggests that invented spelling is a window into a child's knowledge of how written words work and can be used to guide instruction. Specific kinds of spelling errors at particular levels of orthographic knowledge reflect a progressive differentiation of word elements that determine how quickly students can read words and how easily they can write them. Insight into students' conceptual understanding of these word elements helps teachers direct their efforts as students learn to read and spell.

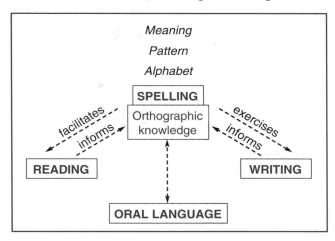

FIGURE 1-14   Word Study: Reading and Writing

In this book, we suggest that orthographic knowledge plays a central role in a comprehensive language arts program that links reading and writing. Word knowledge accumulates as students develop orthographic understandings at the alphabetic level, the pattern level, and the meaning level in overarching layers of complexity. Our complete understanding of phonics, word recognition, spelling, vocabulary, and even the grammar of words (syntax) is part of our word knowledge. Reading provides the corpus of words and defines the parameters of what may be studied. Through word study, students learn how the spelling system, or orthography, works to represent sound, pattern, and meaning. Writing then exercises that word knowledge. Figure 1-14 illustrates the theory of developmental word knowledge and shows how word study links reading and writing.

WHERE DO I BEGIN WORD STUDY?

Students acquire word knowledge implicitly as they read and write, and also through explicit instruction orchestrated by the teacher. However, it is impossible to know exactly what to teach and when to teach it until we have a living child before us. An informed interpretation of students' reading and writing attempts shows us which words they can read and spell, and of those, which they might learn more about. There is more to pacing instruction than plugging students into a sequence of phonics or spelling features. Instructional *pacing* must be synonymous with instructional *placing*. That is, we must fit our instruction to what our students are using but confusing. How do we know what they are using but confusing? A good deal of what students know about orthography is revealed in their invented spellings produced in uncorrected writing. In addition, teachers can elicit inventions by using the spelling assessments described in the next chapter. Spelling inventories described in the next chapter can be used to select the content of word study instruction for phonics, spelling, and vocabulary.

WORDS THEIR WAY

To help students explore and learn about words their way, instruction must be sensitive to two fundamental tenets:

1. Students' learning of phonics, spelling, and vocabulary is based on their developmental or instructional level.
2. Students' learning is based on the way they are naturally inclined to learn: through comparing and contrasting word features and discovering consistencies.

When these two tenets are honored, students learn *their* way—building from what is known about words to what is new. Rather than rote memorization activities designed only to ensure repeated mechanical practice, word study encourages active exploration and examination of word features that are within a student's stage of literacy development. Word study is active, and by making judgments about words and sorting words according to similar features, students construct their own understandings about how the features work. Active, thoughtful practice helps students internalize word features and become automatic in using what they have learned.

Table 1-2 summarizes the characteristics of each stage of development to help you understand the reading and writing context for the word study instruction that is appropriate for each stage. After learning in Chapter 2 how to assess the developmental word knowledge of your students, the remaining chapters offer more detail about planning word study instruction for each stage of development.

TABLE 1-2 Developmental Stages, Characteristics, and Word Study Instruction

I. Emergent Stage—Chapter 4

Characteristics
1. Scribbles letters and numbers
2. Lacks concept of word
3. Lacks letter-sound correspondence or represents most salient sound with single letters
4. Pretends to read and write

Reading and Writing Activities
1. Read to students and encourage oral language activities
2. Model writing using dictations and charts
3. Encourage pretend reading and writing

Word Study Focus
1. Develop oral language with concept sorts
2. Play with speech sounds to develop phonological awareness
3. Plan activities to learn the alphabet
4. Sort pictures by beginning sound
5. Encourage fingerpoint memory reading of rhymes, dictations, and simple pattern books
6. Encourage invented spelling

II. Letter Name–Alphabetic Stage—Chapter 5

Early Letter Name–Alphabetic
Characteristics
1. Represents beginning and ending sounds
2. Uses letter names to invent spellings
3. Has rudimentary or functional concept of word
4. Reads word by word in beginning reading materials

Reading and Writing Activities
1. Read to students and encourage oral language activities
2. Secure concept of word by plenty of reading in predictable books, dictations, and simple rhymes
3. Record and reread individual dictations
4. Label pictures and write in journals regularly

Word Study Focus
1. Collect known words for word bank
2. Sort pictures and words by beginning sounds

TABLE 1-2 *Continued*

3. Study word families that share a common vowel
4. Study beginning consonant blends and digraphs
5. Encourage invented spelling

Middle to Late Letter Name–Alphabetic Stage
Characteristics
1. Correctly spells initial and final consonants and some blends and digraphs
2. Uses letter names to spell vowel sounds
3. Spells phonetically, representing all salient sounds in a one-to-one, linear fashion
4. Omits most silent letters and preconsonantal nasals in spelling (*bop* or *bup* for *bump*)
5. Fingerpoints accurately and can self-correct when off track
6. Reads aloud slowly in a word-by-word manner

Reading and Writing Activities
1. Read to students
2. Encourage invented spellings in independent writing, but hold students accountable for features and words they have studied
3. Collect two- to three-paragraph dictations that are reread regularly
4. Encourage more expansive writing and consider some simple editing procedures for punctuation and high-frequency words

Word Study Focus
1. Sort pictures and words by different short vowel word families
2. Sort pictures and words by short vowel sounds and CVC patterns
3. Continue to examine more difficult consonant blends with pictures and words
4. Study preconsonantal nasals and digraphs at the end of words
5. Sort pictures comparing short and long vowel sounds
6. Collect known words for word bank (up to 200)

III. Within Word Pattern Stage—Chapter 6

Characteristics
1. Spells most single-syllable, short vowel words correctly
2. Spells most beginning consonant digraphs and two-letter consonant blends
3. Attempts to use silent long vowel markers
4. Reads silently and with more fluency and expression
5. Writes more fluently and in extended fashion
6. Can revise and edit

Reading and Writing Activities
1. Continue to read aloud to students
2. Guide silent reading of simple chapter books
3. Write each day, writers' workshops, conferencing, and publication

Word Study Focus
1. Complete daily activities in word study notebook
2. Sort words by long- and short-vowel sounds and by common long-vowel patterns
3. Compare words with *r*-influenced vowels,
4. Explore less common vowels, diphthongs (*oi, oy*), and other ambiguous vowels (*ou, au, ow, oo*)
5. Examine triple blends and complex consonant units such as *thr, str, dge, tch, ck*
6. Explore homographs and homophones

IV. Syllables and Affixes—Chapter 7

Characteristics
1. Spells most single-syllable words correctly
2. Makes errors at syllable juncture and in unaccented syllables
3. Reads with good fluency and expression
4. Reads faster silently than orally
5. Writes responses that are sophisticated and critical

Continued

TABLE 1-2 *Continued*

Reading and Writing Activities
1. Plan read-alouds and literature discussions
2. Include self-selected or assigned silent reading of novels of different genres
3. Begin simple note taking and outlining skills, and work with adjusting reading rates for different purposes
4. Explore reading and writing styles and genres

Word Study Focus
  1. Examine plural endings
  2. Study compound words
  3. Study consonant doubling and inflected endings
  4. Study open and closed syllables and other syllable juncture issues
  5. Explore syllable stress and vowel patterns in the accented syllable, especially ambiguous vowels
  6. Focus on unaccented syllables such as *er* and *le*
  7. Explore unusual consonant blends and digraphs (*qu, ph, gh, gu*)
  8. Study base words and affixes
  9. Focus on two-syllable homophones and homographs
10. Join spelling and vocabulary studies; link meaning and spelling with grammar and meaning
11. Explore grammar through word study
12. Sort and study common affixes (prefixes and suffixes)
13. Study stress or accent in two-syllable words

V. Derivational Relations—Chapter 8

Characteristics
1. Has mastered high frequency words
2. Makes errors on low frequency, multisyllabic words derived from Latin and Greek
3. Reads with good fluency and expression
4. Reads faster silently than orally
5. Writes responses that are sophisticated and critical

Reading and Writing Activities
1. Include silent reading and writing, exploring various genres
2. Develop study skills, including textbook reading, note taking, adjusting rates, test taking, report writing, and reference work
3. Focus on literary analysis

Word Study Focus
1. Focus on words that students bring to word study from their reading and writing
2. Join spelling and vocabulary studies; link meaning and spelling with grammar and meaning
3. Examine common and then less common roots, prefixes, and suffixes (e.g., *ion*)
4. Examine vowel and consonant alternations in derivationally related pairs
5. Study Greek and Latin word roots and stems
6. Focus on abstract Latin suffixes (*ence/ance; ible/able; ent/ant*)
7. Learn about absorbed or assimilated prefixes
8. Explore etymology, especially in the content areas
9. Examine content-related foreign borrowings

Getting Started: The Assessment of Orthographic Development

2

Effective teaching cannot begin until you understand what students already know about words and what they are ready to learn. This chapter presents an informal assessment process that will enable you to:

- Find out what particular orthographic features students know and what they need to study.
- Identify students' developmental stage of word knowledge or instructional level
- Group students for instruction
- Monitor students' growth in word knowledge over time.

This informal assessment process includes observations of student writing and reading as well as the administration of spelling inventories.

INFORMAL OBSERVATIONS TO ASSESS ORTHOGRAPHIC KNOWLEDGE

Observe Students' Writing

Teachers have daily opportunities to observe students as they write for a variety of purposes. These observations help to reveal what students understand about words. The following example demonstrates what you might learn about a kindergartner's literacy development. Sarah called this her "first restaurant review." Although it appears to be a menu, she posted it on the wall the way she had seen reviews posted in restaurants.

What Sarah Wrote	How She Read What She Wrote
1. CRS KAM SAS	First course, clam sauce
2. CRS FESH	Second course, fish
3. CRS SAGATE	Third course, spaghetti
4. CRS POSH POPS	Fourth course, Push Pops

This writing tells a lot about Sarah: She sees a practical use for writing and she enjoys displaying her work. She has a good grasp of how to compose a list and she is even beginning to understand menu planning!

When we look for what Sarah knows about spelling, we see that she represents many consonant sounds and some digraphs (the *sh* in *fish* and *push*), but blends are incomplete (as in *KAM* for *clam*). She has placed a vowel in all but one syllable; however, she is using but confusing short vowels. In spelling *fish* as *FESH*, Sarah uses a vowel, but she confuses *e* and *i*. In the word *course*, spelled as *CRS*, the letter *r* represents the /r/ and the vowel sound. According to the sequence of development presented in Chapter 1, Sarah is considered a middle letter name–alphabetic speller who would benefit from activities described in Chapter 5.

In Figure 2-1, we see a writing sample from Jake, an older student. The writing is readable because many words are spelled correctly and the others are close approximations. When we look for what Jake knows, we see that he has mastered most consonant relationships—even the three-letter blend in *scraped*—but not the complex *tch* unit in *STITCHES*. Most long and short vowels are correctly represented, however, as in *had, have, went, cone, home,* and *day.* When we look for what Jake uses but confuses, we see that he inserts an extra vowel where none are needed when he spells *chin* as *CHIAN* and he omits some vowel markers where they are needed in his spelling of *cream* as *CREM*. He has spelled the *r*-controlled vowel in *tired* as *TIRD* and the ambiguous vowel in *bought* as *BOUT*. Based on the vowel errors, Jake would be considered a within word pattern speller and would benefit from activities in Chapter 6. We will take another look at Jake's word knowledge when we look at his spelling on an inventory later in this chapter.

Student writings, especially unedited rough drafts, are a goldmine of information about their orthographic knowledge.

FIGURE 2-1   Jake's Writing Sample

My Accident

Last year I scrapped my chian. I was shacking and my mom was too. My Dad met us at the docters offises. And I had to have stiches. Then my Dad bout me an ice crem cone. And we went home. I didn't go to school the nexs day. I was to tird.

Many teachers keep a variety of student writing samples to document students' needs and growth over time. Relying entirely on writing samples has drawbacks, however. Some students are anxious about the accuracy of their spelling and will only use words they know how to spell. Others will use resources in the room, such as word walls, dictionaries, and the person sitting nearby. Using these resources, students' writing may overestimate what they really know. On the other hand, when students concentrate on getting their ideas on paper, they may not pay attention to the spelling and thus make excessive errors. Some students write freely with little concern about accuracy and need to be reminded to use what they know. Knowing your students through daily observations will help you to determine not only their orthographic knowledge but also their habits and dispositions.

The Qualitative Spelling Checklist found on the CD-ROM that accompanies this text can be used to determine a student's developmental spelling stage from his or her writing.

Observe Students' Reading

Important insights into orthographic knowledge are also made when we observe students reading. As you read in Chapter 1, a close relationship exists between reading and spelling, described as the synchrony of development (Figure 1-13). Students' reading and spelling are related but are not mirror images because the processes differ slightly. In reading, words can be recognized with many types of textual supports, so the ability to read words correctly lies a little ahead of students' spelling accuracy (Bear & Templeton, 2000). For example, within word pattern spellers, who are also transitional readers, may read many two-syllable words like *shopping* and *bottle* correctly, but might spell those same words as *SHOPING* and *CATEL*. Spelling is a conservative measure of what students know about words in general. If students can spell a word, then we know they can read the word. It seldom works the other way around except in the very early stages, when students might generate spellings they don't know how to read (Rayner, Foorman, Perfetti, Pesetsky, & Seidenburg, 2001). When students consult reference materials such as a spell checker or dictionary, the spelling task becomes a reading task; we all know the phenomenon of being able to recognize the correct spelling if we just see it.

We can expect to hear particular reading errors at different instructional levels. Like spelling errors, reading errors show us what students are using but confusing when they read. Teachers who understand students' developmental word knowledge will be in a good position to interpret students' reading errors and to make decisions about the appropriate prompt to use (Brown, 2003). A student who substitutes *bunny* for *rabbit* in the sentence, "The farmer saw a rabbit," is probably a beginning reader and an early letter name–alphabetic speller. The student uses the picture to generate a logical response, not knowledge about sound–symbol correspondences. For students at this partial alphabetic or semiphonetic stage, drawing attention to the first sound can teach them to use their consonant knowledge. The teacher might point to the first letter and say, "Can that word be bunny? It starts with an R. What would start with /rrrrr/?

Further in development, assessments of oral reading substitutions show a different level of word knowledge. A transitional reader who substitutes *growled* for *groaned* in the sentence, "Jason groaned when he missed the ball," is probably attending to several orthographic features of the word. The student appears to use the initial blend *gr, the vowel o,* and the *-ed* ending to come up with a word that fits the meaning of the sentence. Because this student has vowel knowledge, a teacher might direct the student's attention to the *oa* pattern and ask him to try it again.

Our response to reading errors and our expectations for correcting such errors depend on a number of factors, one of which is knowing where students are developmentally. For example, it would be inappropriate to ask students in the early letter name–alphabetic stage to sound out the word *flat,* or even to look for a familiar part within the word in the hope that they might use their knowledge of *-at* words by analogy.

Emergent and early letter name–alphabetic spellers may be able to use the beginning letters and sounds of words as clues, but frequently must also turn to context clues to read the words on the page (Adams, 1990; Biemiller, 1970; Johnston 2000). However, students in the latter part of the letter name–alphabetic stage could be expected to sound out *flat* because they know something about blends and short vowels. Having students read at their instructional levels means that they can read most words correctly and when they encounter unfamiliar words in text, their orthographic knowledge, combined with context, will usually help them read the words.

Although observations made during writing and reading provide some insight into students' development, assessments should also include an informal qualitative spelling inventory. Together, reading, writing, and spelling inventories provide a rich collection of information to understand students' knowledge of orthography. Use the developmental model in Figure 1-13 by reading from top to bottom across the literacy behaviors of reading, spelling, and writing. Look for corroborating evidence to place students' achievement along the developmental continuum. This model helps to generate expectations for student development using an integrated literacy approach. A student's reading behaviors should be in synchrony with his or her range of writing behaviors.

QUALITATIVE SPELLING INVENTORIES

What Are Spelling Inventories?

Spelling inventories consist of lists of words specially chosen to represent a variety of spelling features or patterns at increasing levels of difficulty. The words in spelling inventories are designed to assess students' knowledge of key spelling features that relate to the different spelling stages. The lists are not exhaustive in that they do not test all spelling features; rather, they include orthographic features that are most helpful in identifying a stage and planning instruction. Students take an inventory as they would a spelling test. The results are then analyzed to obtain a general picture of their development.

The first inventories were developed under the leadership of Edmund Henderson at the University of Virginia. One of the best known early inventories is the McGuffey Qualitative Inventory of Word Knowledge (Schlagal, 1992). This inventory consists of eight graded lists and is described in more detail later in the chapter. Many of Henderson's students developed simpler inventories that consisted of a continuous list of words sampling a range of spelling features characteristic of each stage (Bear, 1982; Ganske, 1999; Invernizzi, 1992; Invernizzi, Meier, & Juel, 2003; Morris, 1999; Viise, 1994). The same developmental progression has been documented through the use of these inventories with learning disabled students (Invernizzi & Worthy, 1989), students identified as dyslexic (Sawyer, Wade, & Kim, 1999), and functionally literate adults (Worthy & Viise, 1996). Spelling inventories have also been developed and researched for other alphabetic languages (Temple, 1978; Gill, 1980; Yang, 2004).

Spelling inventories not only offer information about students' spelling stages and their knowledge of orthographic features, but also offer information about their reading. Studies show that scores on these inventories are consistently related and predict reading achievement at all age levels from kindergartners through adult learners (Bear, Truex, & Barone, 1989; Bear, Templeton, & Warner, 1991; Edwards, 2003; Ehri 2000; Ellis & Cataldo, 1992; Morris, Nelson, & Perney, 1986).

Table 2-1 shows a collection of spelling checklists, inventories, scoring guides, and classroom organization forms that may be used with a broad range of students in preschool, primary, intermediate, and secondary classrooms and with Spanish-speaking students. In this chapter, we will focus on three of these: The Primary Spelling Inventory (PSI), the Elementary Spelling Inventory (ESI), and the Upper Level Spelling Inventory (USI). These can be found in Appendix A.

All assessments are available on the accompanying Assessment CD-ROM.

TABLE 2-1   Words Their Way Spelling Assessments

Spelling Inventories	Grade Range	Developmental Range
Primary Spelling Inventory (p. 266)	K–3	Emergent to late within word pattern
Elementary Spelling Inventory (p. 270)	1–6	Letter name to early derivational relations
Upper Level Spelling Inventory (p. 273)	5–12	Within word pattern to derivational relations

Additional Resources on the Words Their Way Word Study Resources CD-ROM

Qualitative Checklist	K–8	All stages
Emergent Class Record	Pre-K–K	Emergent to letter name–alphabetic
Kindergarten Spelling Inventory (KSI)	Pre-K–K	Emergent to early letter name–alphabetic
McGuffey Spelling Inventory	1–8	All stages
Viise's Word Feature Inventory (WFI)	K–12+	Letter name to derivational relations
Content Area Spelling Inventories in Biology,		Within word pattern to derivational relations
Geometry, and U.S. History	9–12	
Spanish Spelling Inventory	1–6	Emergent to syllables and affixes

Use of Inventories

Spelling inventories are quick and easy to administer and score, and they are reliable and valid measures of what students know about words. Many teachers find these spelling inventories to be the most helpful and easily administered literacy assessment in their repertoire. Use of these spelling inventories requires four basic steps summarized here and discussed in detail in the sections that follow.

1. Select a spelling inventory based on grade level and students' achievement levels. Administer the inventory much as you would a traditional spelling test, but do not let students study the words in advance.
2. Analyze students' spellings using a **feature guide** provided in Appendix A and on the CD-ROM. You might also analyze the results globally after you have had experience understanding qualitative scoring. This analysis will help you identify what orthographic features students know and what they are ready to study.
3. Organize groups using a **classroom composite form** and/or the **spelling by stage form.** These will help you plan instruction for developmental groups.
4. Monitor overall progress by using the same inventory several times a year. Weekly spelling tests will also help you assess students' mastery of the orthographic features they study.

Error Guides can also be used to analyze spelling. You'll find these on the CD-ROM that accompanies this text.

SELECT AND ADMINISTER A SPELLING INVENTORY

Select an Inventory

The best guide to selecting an inventory is the grade level of the students you teach. However, you may find that you need an easier or harder assessment depending on the range of achievement in your classroom. Table 2-1 is a guide to making your selection. Specific directions are provided in Appendix A for each inventory, but the administration is similar for all of them.

Some teachers begin with the same list for all students and after 10 or 20 words, shift to small-group administration of segments from other lists. For example, a second grade

The Words Their Way DVD walks you through selecting, administering, and evaluating inventories for instructional purposes.

teacher may begin with the Primary Spelling Inventory, and decide to continue testing a group of students who spelled most of the words correctly using the Elementary Spelling Inventory. A key point to keep in mind is that students must generate a number of errors for you to determine a spelling stage.

1. Primary spelling inventory. The Primary Spelling Inventory (PSI) (see Appendix A page 266) consists of a list of 26 words that begins with simple CVC words (*fan, pet*) and ends with inflected endings (*clapping, riding*). It is recommended for kindergarten through early third grade because it assesses features found from the emergent stage to the late within word pattern stage. The PSI has been used widely along with the accompanying feature guide and is a reliable scale of developmental word knowledge. The internal consistency is highly reliable as demonstrated by alpha coefficients over .90 (Invernizzi, 2005; Johnston, 2003).

For kindergarten or with other emergent readers, you may only need to call out the first five words. In an early first grade classroom, call out at least 15 words so that you sample digraphs and blends; and use the entire list of 25 words for late first, second, and third grades. If any students spell more than 20 words correctly, you may want to use the Elementary Spelling Inventory. This is likely to happen in third grades classes, where some students are moving into the syllables and affixes stage.

2. Elementary spelling inventory. The Elementary Spelling Inventory (ESI), presented in Appendix A on page 270, is a list of 25 increasingly difficult words that begins with *bed* and ends with *opposition*. It surveys a range of features throughout the elementary grades (first through sixth) and can be used to identify students up to the derivational relations stage. If a school or school system wants to use the same inventory throughout the elementary grades to track growth over time, this inventory is a good choice. By second grade, most students can try to spell all 25 words, but be ready to discontinue testing for any students who are visibly frustrated or are misspelling five in a row.

A strong relationship between scores on the ESI teachers' stage analysis, and standardized reading and spelling test scores has been observed. The words in this list present a reliable scale of developmental word knowledge. In Guttman Scalogram analyses, the ESI's coefficients of reproducibility was .92 for the first half, and .91 for the second, and its coefficient of scalability was .76 for the first half and .63 for the second half. (Bear, 1982, 1992)

3. Upper level spelling inventory. The Upper Level Spelling Inventory (ULI), found in Appendix A on page 275, can be used in upper elementary, middle, and high school. This list is also used to assess the orthographic knowledge of older students at the college and university levels as well as among students in general equivalency diploma (GED) programs. The words in this list were chosen because they help identify, more specifically than the ESI, what students in the syllables and affixes and derivational relations stages are doing in their spelling. For efficiency, this inventory combines the former Intermediate and Upper Level Inventory into one list of 31 words. These words are arranged in order of difficulty from *switch* to *irresponsible*. The internal consistency of the ULI is highly reliable with alpha coefficients over .90. With normally achieving students, you can administer the entire list, but stop giving the USI to students who have misspelled five of the first eight words—the words that assess spelling in the within word pattern stage. The teacher should use the ESI with these students to identify within word pattern features that need instruction.

Prepare Students for the Inventory

Unlike weekly spelling tests, these inventories are not used for grading purposes and students should not study the particular words either before or after the inventory is administered. Set aside 20 to 30 minutes to administer an inventory. Ask students to number a paper as they would for a traditional spelling test. For younger children, you may want to prepare papers in advance with one or two numbered columns. (Invariably, a few younger students write across the page from left to right.) Very young children should have an alphabet strip on their desks for reference in case they forget how to form a particular letter.

Students must understand the reason for taking the inventory so they will do their best. They may be nervous, so be direct in your explanation:

> *I am going to ask you to spell some words. You have not studied these words and will not be graded on them. Some of the words may be easy and others may be difficult. Do the best you can. Your work will help me understand how you are learning to read and write and how I can help you.*

Teachers often tell students that as long as they try their best in spelling the words, they will earn an A for the assignment. Once these things are explained, most students are able to give the spelling a good effort. You can conduct lessons like the one described in Box 2-1 to prepare younger students for the assessment or to validate the use of invented spelling during writing. Lessons like these are designed to show students how to sound out words they are unsure of how to spell.

Sometimes it is easier to create a relaxed environment working in small groups, especially with kindergarten and first grade students. Children who are in second grade and older are usually familiar with spelling tests and can take the inventory as a whole class. If any students appear upset and frustrated, you may assess them at another time, individually, or use samples of their writing to determine an instructional level.

Copying can be a problem when students are working close together. Sometimes students copy because they are accustomed to helping each other with their writing or because they lack confidence in their own spelling. Students in the earlier stages of development often enunciate the sounds in the word orally or spell them aloud, which can give cues to those around them. Some students will try to copy if they feel especially concerned about doing well on a test. Creating a relaxed atmosphere with the explanation suggested above can help overcome some of the stress students feel. Seat students to minimize the risk of copying or give them cover sheets. Some teachers give students manila folders to set upright around their paper to create a personal workspace. There will be many opportunities to collect corroborating information, so there is no reason to be upset if primary students copy. If it is clear that a student has copied, make a note to this effect after collecting the papers and administer the inventory individually at another time.

Call the Words Aloud

Pronounce each word naturally without drawing out the sounds or breaking it into syllables. Leave this for students to do. Say each word twice and use it in a sentence if the context will be helpful to the student in knowing what word is being called. For example, use *cellar* in a sentence to differentiate it from *seller*. Sentences are provided with the word lists in the Appendix. For most words, however, saying every word in a sentence is time-consuming and may even be distracting.

Move around the room as you call the words aloud to monitor students' work and observe their behaviors. Look for words you cannot read due to poor handwriting. Without making students feel that something is wrong, it is appropriate to ask them to rewrite the word or to read the letters in the words that cannot be deciphered. Students who write in cursive and whose writing is difficult to read can be asked to print.

Occasionally, if there is time, students are asked to take a second try at spelling words about which they may have been unsure. Through this reexamination, students show their willingness to reflect on their work. These notations and successive attempts are additional indicators of the depth of students' orthographic knowledge.

BOX 2-1 *Spelling the Best We Can: Lessons to Encourage Students to Spell*

To help young students feel more comfortable attempting to spell words, conduct a few lessons either in small groups or with the whole class using the theme "How to Spell the Best We Can." You might do this to prepare young students for taking the inventory or to encourage students to invent spellings during writing. If you want students to produce quality writing, they need to be willing to take risks in their spelling. Hesitant writers who labor over spelling or avoid using words they can't spell lose the reward of expressing themselves.

A Discussion to Encourage Invented Spelling

"We're going to do a lot of writing this year. We will write nearly every day. We will write stories and write about what we see and do. When we want to write a word, and we don't know how to spell it, what might we do?" Student responses usually include:

"Ask the teacher."
"Ask someone."
"Look it up."
"Skip it."

If no one suggests the strategy of listening for sounds, you can tell your students, "Write down all the sounds you hear when you say the word and spell it the best you can."

Spell a Few Words Together

"Who has a word they want to spell?"

Following a lesson on sea life, a student may offer, "Sea turtle."

"That's a great one. Can we keep to the second word, *turtle?*" Assuming that they agree, ask students to say the word *turtle*. Encourage them to say it slowly, stretching out the sounds and breaking it into two syllables (TURRR—TLLLLLE). Model how to listen for the sounds and think about the letters that spell those sounds: "Listen. T-t-t-turtle. What's the first sound at the beginning of *turtle?* What letter do we use to spell that /t/ sound."

"Turtle. T."

On the board or an overhead transparency, write a *T*. Then ask a few students what the next sounds are that they "hear" and "feel."

Depending on the level of the group, you may generate a range of possible spellings: *TL, TRTL, TERDL,* and *TERTUL.*

Finally, talk about what to do if the student can only figure out one or two sounds in a word. "Start with the sound at the beginning. Write the first letter and then draw a line." Here, write *T* with a line: T _____.

Occasionally, a student will be critical about another student's attempt: "That's not the right way to spell it!" Be careful to handle this criticism firmly. You might say: "The important thing is that you have written your word down, and that you can reread what you have written." Remind students that they are learning; there will be times when they do not know how to spell a word and it is okay to spell it the best they can. Encourage them by saying, "You will see your writing improve the more you write. At the end of the year, you will be surprised by how much more you can write."

Model Spelling Strategies Over Time

One lesson to discuss spelling will not suffice, so plan to conduct similar lessons over time. Of course, if you do interactive writing activities in which you "share the pen" (described on page 126–127 in Chapter 4), you will model the spelling process every time you write together. Keep in mind the following points.

- Have students reread their writing to be sure that they can read what they have written and to add to or correct their spelling efforts.
- In addition to sounding out words, model other self-help strategies such as looking at a word wall posted in the room using simple beginning dictionaries, or checking word banks.
- Value your students' efforts to spell words, but also push them constantly to listen for additional sounds and to use what they have been taught.

Know When to Stop

As you walk around the room or work with a small group, scan students' papers and watch for misspellings and signs of frustration to determine whether to continue with the list. With younger students who tire quickly, you might stop after they spell the first five words if they did not spell any correctly. Older students in groups can usually take an entire inventory in about 20 minutes, and it is better to err on the side of too many words than too few. Rather than being singled out to stop, some students may prefer to "save face" by attempting every word called out to the group even when working at a frustration level. In Figure 2-2, you will see where Jake missed more than half the words on the inventory but continued to make good attempts at words that were clearly too difficult for him. However, his six errors in the first fifteen words identify him as needing work on vowel patterns, and testing could have been discontinued at that point. Sometimes teachers are required to administer the entire list in order to have a complete set of data for each child. In this case, tell students that the words will become difficult but to do the best they can.

FIGURE 2-2   Jake's Spelling Inventory

Jake		September 8 9/25	
1. bed		14. caryes	carries
2. ship		15. martched	marched
3. when		16. showers	shower
4. lump		17. bottel	bottle
5. float		18. faver	favor
6. train		19. rippin	ripen
7. place		20. selar	cellar
8. drive		21. pleascher	pleasure
9. brite	bright	22. forchunate	fortunate
10. shoping	shopping	23. confdant	confident
11. spoyle	spoil	24. sivulise	civilize
12. serving		25. opozishun	opposition
13. chooed	chewed		

HOW TO SCORE AND ANALYZE SPELLING INVENTORIES

Once you have administered the inventory, collect the papers and set aside time to score and analyze the results. Scoring the inventories is more than marking words right or wrong. Instead, each word has a number of orthographic "features" that are scored separately. For example, a student who spells *when* as *wen* knows the correct short vowel and ending consonant and gets points for knowing those features even though the spelling is not correct. The feature guides will help you score each word in this manner. This analysis provides *qualitative* information regarding what students know about specific spelling features and what they are ready to study next.

Watch the Assessment portion of the *Words Their Way* DVD for a step-by-step guide to scoring and analyzing spelling inventories.

Establishing a Power Score

Begin by marking the words right or wrong. It is helpful to write the correct spelling beside the misspelled words as was done in the sample of Jake's spelling in Figure 2-2. This step focuses your attention on each word and the parts of the words that were right and wrong (key to the qualitative feature analysis). Scoring in this way also makes it easier for other teachers and parents to understand students' papers. Calculate a raw score or power score (9 words correct on Jake's paper in Figure 2-2). This will give you a rough estimate of the student's spelling stage.

Previous research on grade-level spelling lists such as The McGuffey Spelling Inventory revealed a relationship between the power score (total number of words correct) and the quality of spelling errors that students committed (Morris, Nelson, & Perney,

1986; Schalgal, 1989; Henderson, 1990). The relationship between power scores and specific features is also germane to single-list, spelling-by-stage spelling assessments such as the ones in this book. The ESI, for example, consists of groups of words containing spelling features negotiated in successive spelling stages. In Figure 2-2, for example, you can see that the first five words Jake spelled tap easy spelling features such as beginning and ending consonant sounds, short vowels (*bed, ship, when*), consonant digraphs (*ship, when*), preconsonantal nasals (*lump*), and consonant blends (*float*)—all features acquired during the letter name–alphabetic stage. He would be considered "independent" at this stage.

His spelling of the word *float* transitions into the next set of words, all tapping long-vowel patterns (*float, train, place, drive,* and *bright*)—the primary features acquired during the within word pattern stage of spelling development. Although Jake spells the first four long-vowel pattern words correctly, he commits his first error in this set on the word *bright* (*BRITE*). Because Jake spells most of the long-vowel pattern words correctly (*float, train, place, drive*) and one incorrectly (*BRITE*), we can say that he needs only a brief review of long vowel patterns.

The next five words tap late within word pattern and early syllables and affixes features as well as other vowel patterns including diphthongs (*spoil*), schwa-plus-r (*serving*), and lower-frequency vowel patterns (*chewed*) in addition to a variety of inflections (*serving, chewed, carries,* and *marched*). We see Jake *using but confusing* these features, getting some of them right (*serving*) and others wrong (*SPOYLE, CHOOED, CARYES, MARTCHED*), so this set, would be considered Jake's instructional range. However, the final ten words tapping syllable and affixes features (*showers, bottle, favor, ripen, cellar*) and derivational relations features (*pleasure, fortunate, confident, civilize,* and *opposition*), were all misspelled by Jake. Because he got all the words wrong, we can determine that these two stages represent Jake's frustration level.

In planning instruction for Jake, we analyze the features he uses but confuses on his instructional level—within word pattern. Table 2-2 lists the power scores on the three major inventories in *Words Their Way* in relation to estimated stages and their breakdown by early, middle, or late stage designations. As can be seen, Jake's power score of 9 on the ESI places him in the late within word pattern stage as described above.

The Assessment Database on the Words Their Way CD gives you an electronic format for scoring student feature guides, storing that information, and using it to inform grouping.

Scoring the Feature Guides

Feature guides help analyze student errors and confirm the stage designations suggested by the power score. The feature guides that accompany each inventory are included in Appendix A. Jake's spellings are used as an example in Figure 2-3 to guide you in the scoring process. Follow these steps to complete the feature guide.

TABLE 2-2   Power Scores and Estimated Stages

Inventory	Emergent	Letter Name			Within Word Pattern			Syllables & Affixes			Derivational Relations		
		E	M	L	E	M	L	E	M	L	E	M	L
PSI	0	0	2	6	8	13	17	22					
ESI		0	2	3	5	7	9	12	15	18	20	22	
USI					2	6	7	9	11	18	21	23	27

FIGURE 2-3   Jake's Feature Guide for Elementary Spelling Inventory

Words Their Way Elementary Spelling Inventory Feature Guide

Student's Name **Jake Fisher**   Teacher **T. Atkinson**   Grade **5**   Date **September**

Words Spelled Correctly: **9** /25   Feature Points: **43** /62   Total: **52** /87   Spelling Stage: **Late Within Word Pattern**

SPELLING STAGES →	EMERGENT LATE	LETTER NAME—ALPHABETIC EARLY	MIDDLE	MIDDLE	LATE	WITHIN WORD PATTERN EARLY	MIDDLE	LATE	SYLLABLES AND AFFIXES EARLY	MIDDLE	LATE / DERIVATIONAL EARLY	DERIVATIONAL MIDDLE		
Features →	Consonants Initial	Consonants Final	Short Vowels	Digraphs	Blends	Long Vowels	Other Vowels	Inflected Endings	Syllable Junctures	Unaccented Final Syllables	Harder Suffixes	Bases or Roots	Feature points	Words Spelled Correctly
1. bed	b ✓	d ✓	e ✓										3	1
2. ship	p ✓	p ✓	i ✓	sh ✓									3	1
3. when			e ✓	wh ✓									2	1
4. lump	l ✓		u ✓		mp ✓								3	1
5. float		t ✓			fl ✓	oa ✓							3	1
6. train		n ✓			tr ✓	ai ✓							3	1
7. place					pl ✓	a-e ✓							2	1
8. drive		v ✓			dr ✓	i-e ✓							3	1
9. bright					br ✓	igh i-e							1	
10. shopping			o ✓	sh ✓				pping					2	
11. spoil					sp ✓		oi oy						1	
12. serving							er ✓	ving ✓					2	1
13. chewed				ch ✓			ew oo	ed ✓					2	
14. carries							ar ✓	ies	rr				1	
15. marched				ch ✓			ar ✓	ed ✓					3	
16. shower				sh ✓			ow ✓			er ✓			3	
17. bottle									tt ✓	le			1	
18. favor									v ✓	or			1	
19. ripen									p	en				
20. cellar									ll	ar ✓			1	
21. pleasure											ure	pleas ✓	1	
22. fortunate							or ✓				ate ✓	fortun	2	
23. confident											ent	confid		
24. civilize											ize	civil		
25. opposition											tion	pos		
Totals	7/7	5/5	5/5	6/6	7/7	4/5	5/7	3/5	2/5	2/5	1/5	1/5	43	9

1. Make a copy of the appropriate feature guide for each student and record the date of testing. The spelling features are listed in the second row of the feature guide and follow the developmental sequence observed in research.
2. Look to the right of each word to check off each feature of the word that is represented correctly. For example, because Jake spelled *bed* correctly, there is a check for the beginning consonant, the final consonant, and the short vowel for a total of three feature points. Jake also gets a point for spelling the word correctly and that is recorded in the far right column. For the word *bright*, which he spelled as *BRITE*, he gets a check for the blend but not for the spelling pattern of *igh*. Notice Jake's feature guide in Figure 2-3 and how the vowel patterns Jake substituted have been written in the space beside the vowel feature to show that Jake is using but confusing these patterns. Every feature in every word is not scored, but the features sampled are key to identifying the stages of spelling.
3. After scoring each word, add the checks in each column and record the total score for that column at the bottom as a ratio of correct features to total possible features. (Adjust this ratio and the total possible points if you call fewer than the total.) Notice how Jake scored seven out of eight under digraphs and blends, and four out of five under long-vowel patterns. Add the total feature scores across the bottom and the total words spelled correctly. This will give an overall total score that can be used to rank order students and to compare individual growth over time.

Common Confusions in Scoring

To assure consistency in scoring students' spelling, these guidelines for scoring common confusions are presented. Letter reversals, such as writing *b* as *d*, are not unusual in young spellers, but questions often arise about how to score them. Reversals should be noted, but in the qualitative analysis, reversals should be seen as the letters they were meant to represent. These might be considered handwriting errors rather than spelling errors. For example, a **static reversal** such as the *b* written backwards in *bed* or the *p* written backwards in *ship*, should be counted as correct. There is space in the boxes of the feature analysis to make note of these reversals. Record what the student did, but add the check to give credit for representing the sound. Letter reversals occur with decreasing frequency through the letter name–alphabetic stage.

Confusions can also arise in scoring **kinetic reversals** when the letters are present but out of order. For example, beginning spellers sometimes spell the familiar consonant sounds and then tag on a vowel at the end (e.g., *FNA* for *fan*). This can be due to their extending the final consonant sound or to repeating each sound in the word *fan* and extracting the short *a* after having already recorded the *FN*. In cases like this, give credit for the consonants and the vowels. However, the bonus point for correct spelling is not given.

Early beginning spellers sometimes spell part of the word and then add random strings of letters to make it look longer (e.g., *FNWZTY* for *fan*). Older students will sometimes add vowel markers where they are not needed (as in *FANE* for *fan*) or will include two possibilities when in doubt (as in *LOOKTED* for *looked* or *TRAINE* for *train*). In these cases, students should get credit for what they represent correctly. In the case of *FANE* for *fan* or *TRAINE* for *train*, the student would get credit for the vowel feature, but would not get the extra point for spelling the word correctly. In general, give students credit when in doubt and make a note of the strategy they might be using. Such errors offer interesting insights into their developing word knowledge.

Identifying Features for Instruction

The feature guide should be used to determine appropriate instruction. Looking across the feature columns from left to right, instruction should begin at the point where a student first makes two or more errors on a feature. Consider the totals along the bottom of

Jake's feature guide. Ask yourself what he knows and what he is using but confusing. His scores indicate that he has mastery of consonants and short vowels, so he does not need instruction there. Jake only missed one of the digraphs long vowel patterns and these can be considered an acceptable score. However, he missed two of the other vowel patterns, so this is the feature that needs attention during instruction.

As you can see in the total scores in Figure 2-3, there will be overlaps of features across columns. We can see this when Jake spells five of the other vowel patterns as well as more advanced features. Instructionally, there is good reason to take a step back and review. In Jake's case, we might expect that a few weeks of long-vowel review might be all that is needed before he moves on to other vowel patterns. If Jake had missed more of the long-vowel patterns, we would expect him to need more time to study them.

Determine a Developmental Stage

The continuum of features at the top of the feature guide shows gradations for each developmental level. A student who has learned to spell most of the features relevant to a stage is probably at the end of that stage. Conversely, if a student is beginning to use the key elements of a stage, but still has some misspellings from the previous stage, the student is at an early point in that new stage. Tables in each instructional chapter (Chapters 4–8) provide additional information about how to determine where students are within each stage (early, middle, late). These gradations make the assessment of orthographic knowledge more precise than simply an overall stage designation, which will be useful in designing a word study curriculum.

Developmental stages should be circled in the shaded bar across the top that lists the stages. For example, Jake spelled all of the short- and most long-vowel features correctly, and he was also spelling some of the words in the other-vowels category, so Jake is at least in the middle of the within word pattern stage. This has been circled in the top row. These stage designations can be used to complete the Spelling-by-Stage form described below that will help you create instructional groups. Knowing the student's developmental stage is a guide to the instructional chapter for word study. In Jake's case, refer to Chapter 6 for activities.

Colleagues who teach together may not always agree on a student's stage. The gradations within each stage clarify the distance between ratings and make it possible to resolve scoring differences between raters. For example, a teacher who may have noted that a student is in the late letter name–alphabetic stage is quite close to a teacher who has determined that the student is an early within word pattern stage speller.

You do not need to make the discrimination within stages too weighty a decision. When it comes to planning instruction, take a step backwards to choose word study activities at a slightly easier level than the stage determination may indicate. It is easier to introduce students to sorting routines when they are working with familiar features and known words.

Spelling inventory results should be compared to what we learn about students' orthographic knowledge in terms of their reading and writing. Referring back to Jake's writing in Figure 2-1, we see similar strengths and weaknesses. His mastery of short vowels and his experimentation with long-vowel and other vowel patterns is what we would expect of a student in the middle to late within word pattern stage of spelling. When Jake reads he may confuse words like *through* and *thought*. These errors in word identification will be addressed in word study when he examines other vowel patterns. His spelling inventory, writing sample, and reading errors offer corroborating evidence that we have identified his developmental stage and the features that need attention.

Some students are out of synchrony in their development, such as the student who is notoriously bad at spelling but is a capable reader. When there is a mismatch between reading and spelling development, you can help improve spelling and obtain synchrony by pinpointing the stage of spelling development and then providing instruction that addresses the student's needs. Using these assessments and the developmental model, you can create individual educational plans for students and plan for small-group instruction accordingly.

Sample Practice

The spelling samples of five students in Box 2-2 can be used to practice analyzing student spellings and determining a developmental stage if you do not have a class of children to assess or if you want to try analyzing a broad spectrum of responses. Make a copy of the ESI feature guide for each student. Determine both the developmental stage of the speller and the place you would start instruction. After you are finished, check the results at the bottom of the page. Were you close in the stages you selected? If you scored the spelling in terms of three gradations within a stage, you may find that although your assessment may differ by a stage name, it is possible that the difference is just one gradation.

USING CLASSROOM PROFILES TO GROUP FOR INSTRUCTION

Your spelling analysis as discussed in the previous section will pinpoint students' instructional levels and the features that are ripe for instruction. In most classrooms, there will be a range in students' word knowledge. For example, in a second grade class there will be students in the letter name–alphabetic stage who need to study short vowels and consonant blends while others are in the syllables and affixes stage and ready to study two-syllable words. After analyzing students individually, you can create a classroom profile by recording the individual assessments on a single chart.

We present two ways to record information about the class: the classroom composite to group students by features and the spelling-by-stage classroom organization chart to group students by developmental levels. These charts show you the instructional groups at a glance. Before we discuss them, however, let us consider the importance of grouping for instruction in word study.

Why Group?

Grouping for instruction is a challenge for teachers and there are reasons to be suspicious of homogeneous or ability grouping. There may be stigmas associated with grouping and sometimes the lower ability groups receive inferior instruction (Stanovich, 1986; Allington, 1983). However, students benefit from developmentally appropriate instruction. Experience has shown that when students study a particular orthographic feature, it is best if they are in groups with students who are ready to study the same features. For example, it is difficult to study long-vowel patterns when some of the students in the group still need work on digraphs or blends and may not even be able to read the words. When students are taught at their instructional levels in spelling (even when instruction is below grade level), they will make more progress than when they are put in materials that are too difficult for them (Morris, Blanton, Blanton, Nowacek, & Perney, 1995).

Many teachers organize three and sometimes four small groups by instructional level for reading. Word study can be incorporated in these small-group reading lessons, especially in the lower grades where students work with words under the teacher's

BOX 2-2   Assessment Check

Examples of Students' Spelling in September

	Greg	*Jean*	*Reba*	*Alan*	*Mitch*
Grade	1	1	2	3	3
bed	bd	bed	bed	bed	bed
ship	sp	sep	ship	ship	ship
when	yn	whan	when	when	when
lump	lp	lop	lump	lump	lump
float	fot	flot	flote	flote	float
train		tran	trane	train	train
place		plac	plais	place	place
drive		driv	drive	drive	drive
bright		brit	brite	brigt	bright
shopping		sopng	shopen	shoping	shopping
spoil			spoal	spoale	spoil
serving			serving	serveing	serving
chewed			chud	choued	chewed
carries			cares	carres	carries
marched			marcd	marched	marched
shower				shouer	shower
bottle				bottel	bottle
favor				favir	favor
ripen				ripen	ripen
cellar				seller	celler
pleasure					pleshur
fortunate					forchenet
confident					confedent
civilize					civilize
opposition					oposition

Results:
- Greg—early letter name–alphabetic
  - Review consonants, study short vowel word families, digraphs, and blends
- Jean—middle letter name–alphabetic
  - Study short vowels
- Reba—middle within word pattern
  - Study long vowel patterns
- Alan—late within word pattern
  - Study long vowels and other vowel patterns
- Mitch—early derivational relations
  - Study roots and unaccented final syllables

supervision and then complete other activities at their desks or work stations. In other classes, especially in the upper grades, word study may occur at a separate time of the day, but still two to four groups are needed to meet students' needs.

Groups should be fluid, and if a student is frustrated or not challenged by the activities, then groups should be reorganized. There are many literacy activities in which students are not grouped by developmental level, as in writing workshops, science, social studies, and the many small-group projects related to units of study.

Classroom Composite Chart

After administering an inventory and completing a feature analysis form for each student, transfer the individual scores in the last row of the form to a classroom composite chart (Figure 2-4) to get a sense of the group as a whole. The following steps will help you do this.

1. Begin by stapling each student's spelling test and his or her feature guide together.
2. Sort student papers by the power score (or number of words correct) or by the total feature score and record students' names from top to bottom on the composite form on the basis of this rank order.
3. Next, record each student's scores from the bottom row of his or her feature guide in the row beside his or her name on the composite chart.
4. Highlight cells in which students are making more than one error on a particular feature and column. For example, a student who spells all but one of the short vowels correctly has an adequate understanding of short vowels and is considered to be at an independent level. However, students who misspell two or three of the short vowels need more work on that feature. Highlighted cells indicate a need for sustained instruction on a feature. Do not highlight cells where students score a zero because they are not using but confusing that feature and it is at their frustration level. Focus instead on features to the left of zero that need attention first.
5. Look for instructional groups. If you rank order your students before completing the composite chart, you can find clusters of highlighted cells that can be used to assign students to developmental stages and word study groups. For example, the fifth grade class composite in Figure 2-4 shows that many students fall under the syllables and affixes stage of development because this is where they are making two or more spelling errors (students 3 through 16). John, Patty, and Maria, who missed more than two words in vowel patterns, might join this group or might go in a lower group, but should be carefully monitored. A smaller group of students fall under the middle-to-late within word pattern stage (students 17 through 25) and should begin word study by looking at single-syllable word patterns for long vowels and then other vowel patterns. One student (Mike) needs individualized help, beginning with short vowels as well as digraphs and blends. At the upper end of the class composite are two children in the derivational relations stage who should be further assessed with the USI to gather more information about particular features to study.

Spelling-by-Stage Classroom Organization Chart

When you know students' development stage, you can also form groups using the spelling-by-stage classroom organization chart on page 42 (see Figure 2-5). Many teachers find this easier to use than a class composite when planning groups. Refer to the stage circled in the shaded bar with the developmental stages for each student's feature guide. Students' names are recorded underneath a spelling stage on the chart, differentiating among those who are early, middle, or late. (To determine early, middle, and late designations, refer to the tables in each chapter for further information.) Once the names are entered, begin to look for groups. In each of the classroom examples in Figure 2-5, three or four groups have been circled.

You can see different ways to organize word study instruction in the three classroom profiles presented in Figure 2-5. The first profile is of a first grade class with many emergent spellers. The four circled groups suggested for this class are also the teacher's reading groups.

In the third grade and sixth grade examples, you can see where teachers have used arrows to reconsider the group placement of a few students. Inventory results are considered along with other observations of students' reading or writing. The arrows indicate students who might place slightly higher or lower as the groups take shape. Some

FIGURE 2-4 Example of Classroom Composite

Words Their Way Elementary Spelling Inventory Classroom Composite

Teacher _Freedman_ School _Kidel Elementary_ Grade _5_ Date _September_

SPELLING STAGES →	EMERGENT LATE	LETTER NAME–ALPHABETIC			WITHIN WORD PATTERN			SYLLABLES AND AFFIXES			DERIVATIONAL RELATIONS			
		MIDDLE		LATE	EARLY	MIDDLE	LATE	EARLY	MIDDLE	LATE	EARLY	MIDDLE		
Students' Name	Consonants	Short Vowels	Digraphs	Blends	Long Vowels	Other Vowels	Inflected Endings	Syllable Junctures	Unaccented Final Syllables	Harder Suffixes	Bases or Roots	Correct Spelling	Total Rank Order
Possible Points	7	5	6	7	5	7	5	5	5	5	5	25	86
1. Stephanie	7	5	6	7	5	7	5	5	5	4	3	23	82
2. Andi	7	5	6	7	5	7	5	4	4	3	2	21	76
3. Henry	7	5	6	7	5	7	5	4	3	3	2	20	74
4. Molly	7	5	6	7	5	7	4	4	3	2	2	20	72
5. Jasmine	7	5	6	7	5	7	3	3	3	2	2	19	69
6. Maria H.	7	5	6	7	5	7	3	3	2	3	2	19	69
7. Mike	7	5	6	7	5	6	3	3	2	2	1	17	64
8. Lee	7	5	6	7	5	6	2	2	1	2	1	15	59
9. Beth	7	5	6	7	5	7	2	2	1	1	2	14	59
10. Gabriel	7	5	6	7	5	6	2	2	1	1	2	14	59
11. Yamel	7	5	6	7	4	6	2	2	1	1	0	12	54
12. John	7	5	6	7	3	5	2	2	1	1	0	10	53
13. Elizabeth	7	5	6	7	4	6	2	2	1	0	0	11	51
14. Maria R.	7	5	6	7	3	4	2	2	1	0	0	11	47
15. Patty	7	5	6	7	3	5	2	2	1	0	0	11	47
16. Sarah	7	5	6	7	4	4	2	1	0	1	0	9	46
17. Jared	7	5	6	7	2	3	1	1	1	1	0	9	43
18. William	7	5	6	7	3	3	2	0	1	0	0	8	42
19. Steve	7	5	6	7	3	3	2	1	0	0	0	8	42
20. Anna	7	5	6	6	4	3	1	1	0	0	0	8	42
21. Nicole W.	7	5	6	6	3	3	1	1	0	0	0	8	39
22. Robert	7	5	5	7	3	3	2	0	0	0	0	6	38
23. Celia	7	4	6	6	2	3	1	0	0	0	0	7	36
24. Jim	7	5	5	6	2	2	1	0	0	0	0	7	36
25. Nicole R.	7	4	5	6	2	3	2	0	0	0	0	7	36
26. Mike	7	3	4	5	1	0	1	0	0	0	0	4	25
Highlight for instruction*		1	1	1	12	13	22	16	15	13	10		

*Highlight students who miss more than 1 on a particular feature; they will benefit from more instruction in that area.

41

42

FIGURE 2-5 Examples of Spelling-by-Stage Classroom Organization Charts

First-Grade Spelling-by-Stage Classroom Organization Chart

SPELLING STAGES→	EMERGENT			LETTER NAME—ALPHABETIC			WITHIN WORD PATTERN			SYLLABLES & AFFIXES			DERIVATIONAL RELATIONS		
	EARLY	MIDDLE	LATE	EARLY	MIDDLE	LATE	EARLY	MIDDLE	LATE	EARLY	MIDDLE	LATE	EARLY	MIDDLE	LATE

Gerald, Buck, Tammy, Milo, Brandi
Doug, Felicia 7, Kristy, Jennifer, Matthew
Danielle, Brad, Brandon, Jerrilynn 5
Jon 5, Shann, J.J.
Jennifer, Luis
Jona 6
Adam
Carita
Reyhe

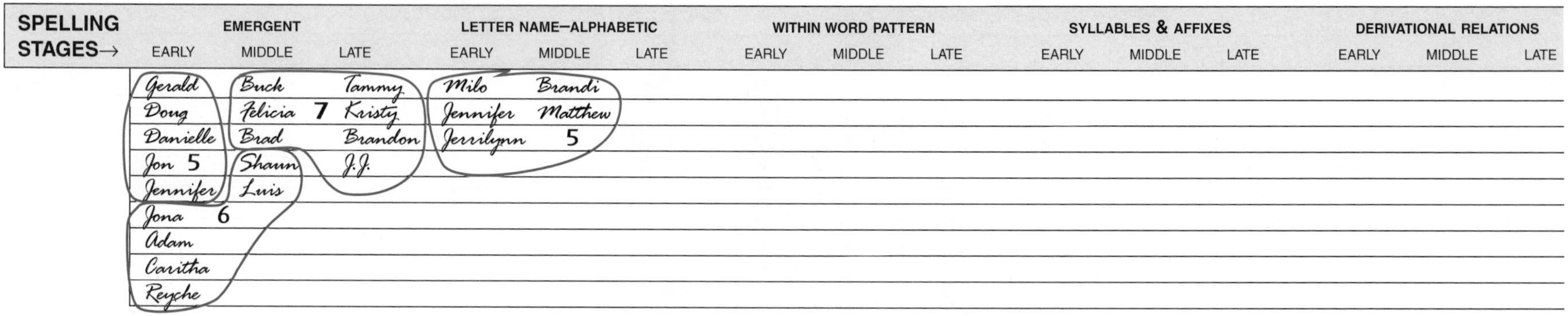

Third-Grade Spelling-by-Stage Classroom Chart

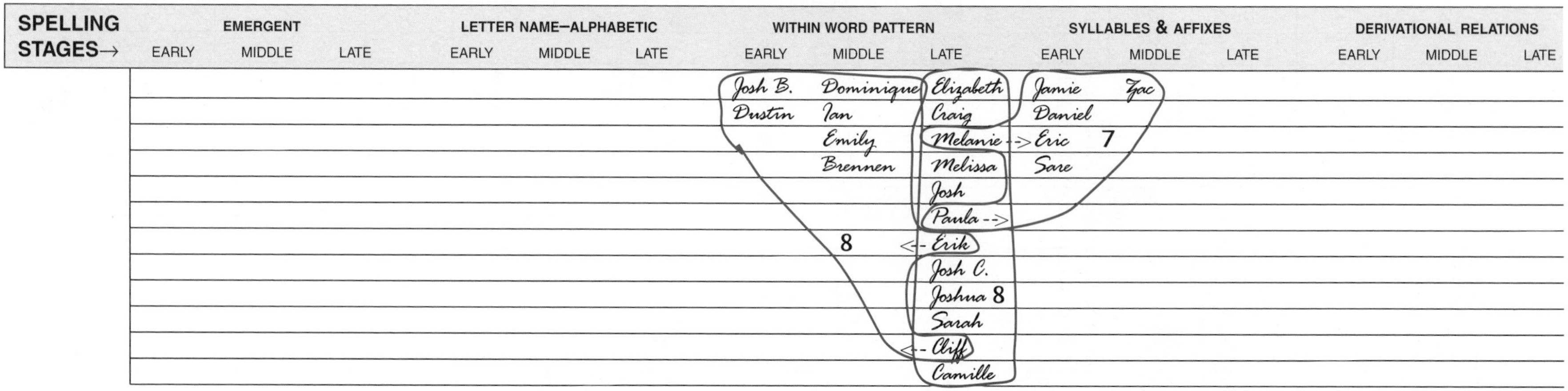

SPELLING STAGES→	EMERGENT			LETTER NAME—ALPHABETIC			WITHIN WORD PATTERN			SYLLABLES & AFFIXES			DERIVATIONAL RELATIONS		
	EARLY	MIDDLE	LATE	EARLY	MIDDLE	LATE	EARLY	MIDDLE	LATE	EARLY	MIDDLE	LATE	EARLY	MIDDLE	LATE

Josh B., Dominique, Elizabeth, Jamie, Zac
Dustin, Ian, Craig, Daniel
Emily, Melanie -> Eric 7
Brennen, Melissa, Sara
Josh
Paula ->
8
<- Erik
Josh C.
Joshua 8
Sarah
<- Ali
Camille

Sixth-Grade Spelling-by-Stage Classroom Organization Chart

SPELLING STAGES→	EMERGENT			LETTER NAME—ALPHABETIC			WITHIN WORD PATTERN			SYLLABLES & AFFIXES			DERIVATIONAL RELATIONS		
	EARLY	MIDDLE	LATE	EARLY	MIDDLE	LATE	EARLY	MIDDLE	LATE	EARLY	MIDDLE	LATE	EARLY	MIDDLE	LATE

Victoria, Juan 3, Mike
Jon, Elizabeth --> Nicole, Phong, Sean, Steve, Desiree
<-- Arceha, Ray, Mario, Sheri, Eric
9, Scott, Christa, 5, Mary
Don, Jonna 6, 11
<-- Rashid, Heather
Esther

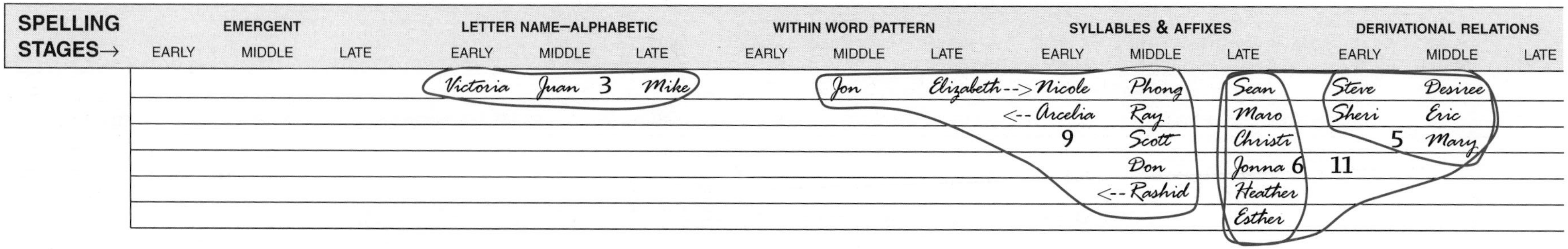

of the group placement decisions are based on social and psychological factors related to self-esteem, leadership, and behavior dynamics.

The teacher in the sixth grade classroom could consider running two groups at the upper levels, or combine them as one group. The three students in the letter name–alphabetic stage will need special attention because they are significantly behind for sixth graders. Ideally, these students will have additional instruction with a literacy specialist or in a tutoring program to review and practice activities that are appropriate for the letter name–alphabetic spelling stage.

Factors to Consider When Organizing Groups

The classroom composite chart and the spelling-by-stage classroom organization chart help to determine word study groups for instruction. Groups of six to eight students make it easier for students to listen to each other, and for you to observe how they sort. While students work on different features and with different words, they can still work side by side during many of the follow-up word study routines that occur after the initial small-group discussion. Different schemes for managing class, group, and individual sorts are discussed in Chapter 3.

When there is a wide range of achievement and decisions are made in forming groups, some students may not be placed exactly at their developmental stage. Consider that your best spellers are not likely to be hurt with grade-level word study activities that might be easy for them. However, your less able spellers are most likely to suffer if they are working at a frustration level where they will not make progress.

In many classrooms, there are students at each end of the developmental continuum who, in terms of word study and orthographic development, are outliers. For example, Zac in the third grade class in Figure 2-5 is the only student in the middle syllables and affixes stage and it is impractical to place him in a group by himself. He has been placed in the closest group for instruction. The teacher may ask Zac to work with a different, more difficult set of words that share the same features that the early syllables and affixes spellers are studying, such as harder words with open and closed syllables. Less advanced students, such as Jon in the sixth grade class in Figure 2-5, may work with a partner who can help him read and sort the group's words, such as one-syllable words with long-vowel patterns. English language learners also benefit from sorting with partners who clarify the pronunciation and meaning of the words.

MONITORING PROGRESS OVER TIME

How Often to Assess

Students may be given the same spelling inventory several times during the year to assess progress and to determine if changes need to be made in groups or instructional focus. You can even use the same paper several times if you fold back the results from the previous time and ask students to record their latest effort in the next column. In Figure 2-6, you will see Benny's spelling inventory results at three different times across the first grade year recorded on the same form. He has made noticeable progress across the year, moving from early letter name–alphabetic spelling to within word pattern. However, don't expect such dramatic progress in one year beyond the primary grades. Some students will take two years to master the within word

FIGURE 2-6   Samples of Benny's Spelling Errors at Three Times in First Grade

	September	January	May
1. fan	FNA	fan	fane
2. pet	PT	pat	pet
3. dig	DKG	deg	dig
4. hope	HOP	hop	hope
5. wait	YAT	wat	wayt
6. sled	SD	sed	sled
7. stick	SK	stek	stike
8. shine	HIN	shin	shine

pattern stage. Therefore, teachers in upper elementary, middle school, and high school may find that assessing students only at the beginning and end of the year is enough.

Using the same spelling inventory each time is recommended. This enables you to compare the same words. In Benny's inventory results, we can track the qualitative changes in his spelling over time. Don't be too surprised if students sometimes spell a word correctly one time and later spell the same word incorrectly. Because students are sometimes inventing a spelling for a word that they do not have stored in memory, they may invent it correctly one time and not the next. Or they might master short-vowel sound matches but later use but confuse silent vowel markers as Benny did in his spelling of *fan* as FANE.

Remember that you should not have students directly study the words on the inventory, although they may naturally show up in word study activities that you plan. If students study the lists in advance, assessment results will be inflated and you will lose valuable diagnostic information. Using the same inventory more than three or four times a year may also familiarize students with the words enough to inflate the results.

Setting Expectations for Student Progress

Spelling assessments are used to identify students' developmental stages, to determine the features that need instruction, and to form and reform instructional groups. At the same time, teachers need to set goals and objectives for student growth within grade levels. While it true that all students do not develop at the same rate despite the very best instruction, it is helpful to articulate end-of-grade expectations in terms of stages of development. (See Table 2-3.) Teachers should know the typical range of development within grade levels so that they can provide additional instruction and intervention for students who lag below that range. Teachers should also know where students must be at the end of the year if they are to succeed in subsequent grades and meet state standards in reading and writing.

Share Spelling Inventories with Parents and Other Teachers

Spelling inventories are valuable artifacts to add to students' portfolios and can be used in parent conferences to discuss individual needs and progress. Benny's parents should be able to appreciate the growth he has made over his first grade year, as shown in Figure 2-6). It is reassuring for parents to see that their students' earlier invented spellings give way to correct spellings. Benny has made good progress moving from early letter name–alphabetic spelling to early within word pattern spelling across the year. In looking at the end-of-grade expectations chart in Table 2-3, we see that Benny is right on target.

Unlike some literacy skills, spelling results are very visible, and with a little explanation parents can understand how you are using spelling errors to plan instruction. Parents who are accustomed to seeing their children bring home lists of spelling words

TABLE 2-3   Spelling Stage Expectations by Grade Levels

Grade Level	Typical Spelling Stage Ranges Within Grade	End-of-Year Spelling Stage Goal
K	Emergent—Letter Name–Alphabetic	Middle Letter Name–Alphabetic
1	Late Emergent—Within Word Pattern	Early Within Word Pattern
2	Late Letter Name—Early Syllables & Affixes	Late Within Word Pattern
3	Within Word Pattern—Syllables & Affixes	Early Syllables and Affixes
4	Within Word Pattern—Syllables & Affixes	Middle Syllables and Affixes
5	Syllables & Affixes—Derivational Relations	Late Syllables and Affixes
6 +	Syllables & Affixes—Derivational Relations	Derivational Relations

taken from thematic units and content materials are sometimes a little dismayed when they see word lists designed for their children's developmental level. In one case, second graders were given words like *butterfly, chrysalis,* and *caterpillar* to memorize for a test each week. When those children had a teacher the next year who designed word study based on a spelling inventory, the parents thought the words (*drew, flew, blow, snow*) were too easy and that their children were not being challenged enough. The teacher responded by explaining the spelling inventory and showing parents the results. The parents then understood and appreciated that the teacher was teaching their children *how to spell* and not just *assigning them words* to memorize and forget.

In many schools, literacy specialists meet with teachers in grade-level meetings to review inventory results, discuss grouping, and plan for word study instruction. Some schools use spelling inventory results to help identify students who might benefit from intervention services. The end-of-grade level expectations chart in Table 2-3 can be useful in this regard. Often spelling inventories are administered at all grade levels and each year the results are put in students' permanent records and serve as an important part of the school's cumulative literacy assessment. Next year's teachers and specialists have access to these records and can use them to place students and plan instruction.

Weekly and Review Spelling Tests

We recommend weekly tests at most grade levels as a way to monitor mastery of the studied features and to send a message to students and parents alike that students are accountable for learning to spell the words they have sorted and worked with in various activities all week. Ideally students will be very successful on these weekly tests when they are appropriately placed for instruction. If they are missing more than a few words, it may mean that they need to spend more time on a feature or that they are not ready to study the feature and should work on easier features first. You may also want to periodically give a review test—without asking students to study in advance—to test for retention. Simply select a sample of words from previous lessons and call them aloud as you would for any spelling test.

OTHER ASSESSMENT TOOLS

The Assessment CD-ROM includes several other assessment forms that teachers find useful as an alternative or supplement to the inventories.

Qualitative Spelling Checklist

When you look at students' writing in their journals or at the first drafts of their reports and stories, you can use the Qualitative Spelling Checklist to verify what types of orthographic features students have mastered and what types of features they are using but confusing. The checklist offers examples of spelling errors students make and matches these errors to stages of spelling. Through a series of 20 questions, you check off the student's progress through the stages. Consider what features are used consistently, often, or not at all. The checklist is set up to be used at three different points and can serve as a record of progress over time.

Emergent Class Record

The Emergent Class Record is used to assess daily writing or spelling inventory results of pre-K or kindergarten children, or other emergent spellers. Making a copy of the PSI feature guide for each student may seem like a waste of paper when the most that many will represent are a few initial and final consonants. The Emergent Class Record can be used as an alternative with the entire class recorded on one form. It captures the prephonetic writing progression (from random marks to letters) that is missing on the other feature guides and covers the range from emergent through letter name–alphabetic spelling that would be expected in many kindergarten classes at the beginning of the year.

Kindergarten Spelling Inventory

The Kindergarten Spelling Inventory (KSI) has been used widely with thousands of children as part of Virginia's Phonological Assessment and Literacy Screening (PALS) (Invernizzi, Juel, Swank, & Meier, 2006). Five three-phoneme words have been carefully chosen after extensive research. Each of the five words is scored for the number of phonemes represented in the students' spelling. A feature guide is provided, but unlike the feature guides described so far, students get credit for identifying phonemes and representing those sounds with phonetically logical letters, even if those letters are actually incorrect. As a result, the KSI is a reliable measure of phonemic awareness development, letter-sound correspondences, and the gradual development of conventional spelling (Invernizzi, Justice, Landrum, & Booker, 2005).

The McGuffey Spelling Inventory

The McGuffey Qualitative Inventory of Word Knowledge (QIWK) (Schlagal, 1992) is useful for conducting individual testing and for obtaining grade-level information. The inventory spans grades 1 through 8 with from 20 to 30 words in each level. Instructional spelling levels are found when a student's power score falls above 50% but below 90% on a graded list (Morris, Blanton, Blanton, & Perney, 1995; Morris, Nelson, & Perney, 1986). After administering the grade-level list, you will need to give an easier list (if students fell below 50%) or a harder one (if students scored above 50%).

The McGuffey Inventory is especially useful when teachers want to use a longer and more detailed spelling list and when they want to report spelling achievement in terms of grade levels. The words in these lists present plenty of opportunities to observe a student's spelling across a variety of features. For example, a teacher may want to obtain a fuller assessment of prefixes, suffixes, and roots. Levels 5 and 6 would offer a large number of derivational words with prefixes and suffixes words to analyze.

Because a feature guide has not been developed for the McGuffey Inventory, you must analyze errors yourself to determine what features and patterns students know and what they are using but confusing.

Viise's Word Feature Inventory

The Word Feature Inventory (WFI) list is a spelling list developed by Neva Viise (Viise, 1996; Worthy & Viise, 1996). The WFI is divided into four achievement levels corresponding to four of the five stages of developmental word knowledge: letter name–alphabetic, within word pattern, syllables and affixes, and derivational relations. The words on each level are divided into groups of five, each subgroup probing the student's treatment of a specific word feature such as short vowel, consonant blend, long vowel pattern, and so on. An assessment of students' spellings of the words on this list will indicate the features which have already been mastered and will pinpoint the level at which instruction must begin.

Content Area Spelling Inventories

Spelling inventories have been developed for Biology, Geometry, and US History. These content area inventories give teachers an indication as to how well students will be able to read related materials and, at the same time, provide some insights into the student's conceptual background knowledge and vocabulary. The words students are asked to spell for content area inventories are the key vocabulary words for the course. Students who score well tend to do better than students who are unable to spell many words correctly (Bear, Templeton, & Warner, 1991). After writing the words, teachers ask students to put a star beside words whose meaning they know. This serves as a record to track student's vocabulary growth in the particular content area.

ASSESSING SPELLING AMONG STUDENTS WHO SPEAK OTHER LANGUAGES

To obtain a complete understanding of the word knowledge of students who are English language learners, we study what students know about literacy in their primary or first language. A spelling inventory in students' spoken language can indicate what their literacy levels might be and, specifically, show what orthographic features they already understand. Students speaking different languages make many similar spelling errors, confusing sounds that are different from English by just one feature. Consequently, students can study some of the same features together even though their primary languages are not the same. *Words Their Way with English Learners* discusses spelling development, assessment, and instruction among English learners in depth (Bear, Helman, Invernizzi, Templeton, & Johnston, 2007).

Spanish Spelling Inventory

Many students in the United States speak Spanish and may read in Spanish. A Spanish Spelling Inventory developed by Lori Helman and the accompanying scoring guide is included on the Assessment CD-ROM. This 25-word inventory covers the range of instructional levels that have been observed in Spanish (Bear, Templeton, Helman, & Baren, 2003; Helman, 2004). Comparing students' spelling on an inventory in their first language with their spelling in English, the second language, will show the confusions some students experience.

English Learners Use What They Know: The Spelling of English Learners

Research in the English spelling acquisition of students who speak a different primary language shows that bilingual learners use knowledge of their primary language to spell words in their second language (Fashola, Drum, Mayer, & Kang, 1996; Nathenson-Mejia, 1989; Zutell & Allan, 1988: Yang, 2004; Shen & Bear, 2003). For example, Spanish speakers take the 22 sounds of Spanish and match them to the roughly 44 sounds of English.

By assessing their orthographic knowledge in their first language and English, teachers can observe whether students are applying the rules of phonology and orthography from the written form of their primary language to English or vice-versa (Helman, 2004; Estes & Richards, 2002).

Bear, Templeton, Helman, & Baren (2003) have identified which English consonant sounds are problematic for Spanish speakers. For students who speak Spanish, a variety of substitutions can be traced to the influence of Spanish on students' spelling. For example, a student who speaks Spanish might spell *that* as *DAT* and *ship* as *CHAP* because the digraphs *th* and *sh* do not exist in Spanish. The silent *h* in Spanish can be spelled with a *j*, so *hot* may be spelled *JAT*. Spellers use the nearest equivalents in their attempts to spell English. Short *-a, -e, -i,* and *-u* do not occur in Spanish, and the sound we call short *o* is spelled with the letter *a* so we can expect many confusions about how to represent these short vowel sounds.

The impact of a student's knowledge of spoken Spanish on English spelling can be seen in the spelling sample from Rosa, a second grader in Figure 2-7. Several of Rosa's

The Assessment Database on the *Words Their Way* CD contains a Spanish inventory and assessments to help you adapt word study instruction for your students whose first language is Spanish.

FIGURE 2-7   Rosa's Spelling

1.	bed	bed
2.	ship	shep
3.	when	wan
4.	lump	lamp
5.	float	flowt
6.	train	trayn
7.	place	pleays
8.	drive	Kids
9.	bright	brayt
10.	shopping	shapen
11.	spoil	spoyo
12.	serving	sorven
13.	chewed	shod
14.	carries	cares
15.	marched	marsh
16.	shower	showar
17.	cattle	cadoto
18.	favor	fayvr
19.	ripen	raypn
20.	cellar	sallar

spellings follow the logical substitutions that are seen in English-speaking students in the letter name–alphabetic stage, that is, *SHEP* for *ship* and *WAN* for *when*. Other errors make good sense in relation to her knowledge of Spanish. For example, given that there is no short *u* in Spanish, her substitution of *LAMP* for *LUMP* is understandable. We find the substitution of *sh* for the *ch* in *chewed* spelled as *SHOD*. The *ay* in three of her spellings shows that Rosa is trying to find a spelling for the long *i*. The long *i* is really two vowels (a diphthong), and the *y*, pronounced as a long *e* in Spanish, is used to spell the second half of the long *i*, as in *eye-ee*. In *spoil* as *SPOYO*, Rosa seems to be using the /y/ sound as in *yes* to help spell /oil/.

The Influences of Students' Primary Languages: The Developmental Spelling of English Learners

As Rosa's spelling illustrates, English learners' invented spellings are logical and interesting. Look for spelling errors that may be explained by students' primary languages or their dialects. For example, one teacher learned about the influence of different Indian dialects when she noticed confusions of /p/ sounds for words that began with an *f*, and students who substituted /sh/ sounds for words with *s*. Another teacher noted that her Korean students consistently confused the sounds for *r* and *l* in English. In their native language, /r/ and /l/ are not different sounds and are represented with the same letter in Hangul (Yang, 2005).

As you listen to the speech and oral reading of English language learners, notice the influences of students' first languages on their pronunciation. Through observing students' other languages, teachers can better understand their literacy development in English. Look in each of the instructional chapters for specific guidance on the interrelatedness of students' home languages and English. For example, Chapter 4 includes a discussion of English language learning and concept sorts, and Chapter 5 and 6 discuss the way students' dialects are observed in their spelling of vowel sounds.

CONCLUSION

Looking at a child's spelling gives us a window into that child's word knowledge, the information he or she uses to read and write words. The word *assessment* comes from the Latin word *assidere*—to sit beside. Spend some time sitting beside your students and looking through the window that their spellings provide. Learn to assess what they know about how words work by administering one of the spelling inventories provided in this book, or on the *Words Their Way Assessment CD*.

You may refer to the developmental sequence inside the front and back covers, as well as the detailed sequences of word study in Chapters 4 through 8, for the specific types of features to explore in word study activities. Remember that the inventories only sample the most common features. At each stage there is a considerable body of knowledge that students should master before they move on to the next stage.

Organizing for Word Study: Principles and Practices

3

Once you have ascertained the developmental level of each of your students as described in Chapter 2, you are ready to organize your classroom for word study. In this chapter we will describe for you the basic activities for word study, how to create and organize materials, and how to set up weekly routines that will facilitate effective and efficient word study. We will address related issues such as expectations for editing and grading before ending with a review of guiding principles and a table of resources. To illustrate the details that make up this chapter, let us first visit the classroom of Mrs. Zimmerman as she introduces a group of her students to *r*-influenced vowels.

Earlier in the year, Mrs. Zimmerman assessed her third graders and divided them into three instructional groups for word study. On Mondays she meets with each group for about 15 to 20 minutes to go over the words, model the word sort for the week, and help her students make discoveries about the particular group of words she has chosen. After getting her students started on independent reading and journal writing, Mrs. Zimmerman calls her first group together on the carpet. She has a set of words written on cards that she lays out for everyone to see. She begins by saying, "Let's read over these words to be sure everyone knows how to read them and what they mean. After discussing *mare*, which Julio defines as a "mother horse," she picks up *bear* and *bare* and

FIGURE 3-1A   Mrs. Zimmerman's Sound Sort

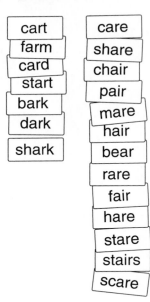

reads both. "Who remembers what words like these are called? That's right, they are homophones." She holds up *bear* and asks who knows what it means.

"It's an animal and I saw one last summer when we went camping," offers Shannon.

"What about this *bare*?" asks Mrs. Zimmerman, as she holds up the word. Rayshad explains that it means "having no hair, like being bald."

"Right," says Mrs. Zimmerman, "or you might go barefooted without shoes. There is another set of homophones here. Can anyone find them?" Mason finds *hair* and *hare* and again they talk about the meaning of each. They recall that they have heard the word *hare* in the story *The Hare and the Tortoise*, which they read during a unit on fables.

Mrs. Zimmerman continues the lesson by saying, "We are going to begin today by thinking about the sound in these words. I am going to put *cart* here as one of our key words and *care* over here for the other. Listen to the middle sounds in each: caaarrrt, caaarrrre." Then she picks up the word *farm*. "Does the middle sound like *cart* or *care*? Right! We will put it under *cart*. How about *chair*? Does the middle sound like *cart* or *care*?" After sorting several more words, Mrs. Zimmerman hands out the rest of the word cards and calls on students to read and sort each word by its vowel sound. After sorting all the words, the students read the words down each column to verify that they all have the same sound in the middle. The final sort by sound looks like Figure 3-1A.

Next, Mrs. Zimmerman directs her students' attention to the spelling patterns of the words. "How are all the words in the first column alike?" she asks. Lisa replies that they all have an *a* and *r* in them. "That's right," says Mrs. Zimmerman, "and what about the words under *care*?" William volunteers that they all have an *ar* also, but sometimes there is an *e* at the end or an *i* in the middle. "Can we put these words into two separate categories?" asks Mrs. Zimmerman. "What shall we use as headers?" The students agree to keep *care* as one header and to use *chair* for the other. Mrs. Zimmerman passes out the rest of the word cards and students take turns placing each word under *care* or *chair*.

"I have an oddball!" calls out Tan, and she places the word *bear* off to the right.

"I am glad you caught that," says Mrs. Zimmerman. "Why is it an oddball?"

"It is the only one with an *ea*," explains Tan.

After sorting the words as shown in Figure 3-1B, Mrs. Zimmerman asks her students to tell her how the words in each column are alike, and they read the words

FIGURE 3-1B   Mrs. Zimmerman's Pattern Sort

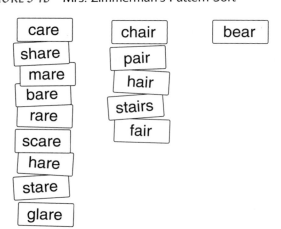

once more to verify that they all have the same sound as well as the same pattern. Mrs. Zimmerman then asks her students if the patterns remind them of other words they have studied. Brian points out that *ai* and *a* with an *e* on the end are patterns that go with long *-a*. "Are these long *-a* words?" probes Mrs. Zimmerman. "Listen: caaaare, chaaair." The children agree that they can hear the sound of /a/ in those words. "What about the *a* in *cart*? Does that sound like an *a*?" asks Mrs. Zimmerman. This time there is some discussion as students come to the conclusion that they cannot even hear a vowel! Mrs. Zimmerman tells the students that over the next few weeks they will look at more words with an *r* after the vowel and they should keep these ideas in mind.

Before they return to their seats, Mrs. Zimmerman gives each student a handout of word cards to cut apart for sorting independently at their seats. She reminds them to sort by sound and then by pattern as they did in their final group sort. Two volunteers agree to illustrate the homophones for the class homophone dictionary. After Mrs. Zimmerman meets with her next word study group, she quickly checks in with each student to look at his or her sort. As she moves around the room, she asks individual students to read a column of words and explain how they are alike. On Tuesday she will ask all her students to sort their words once more and then to write the words by categories in word study notebooks. On other days they will work with partners to sort and to find more words that fit the sound and/or pattern. On Friday, Mrs. Zimmerman assesses all three groups at one time by calling out a word in turn for each group to spell.

Watch the Classroom Organization section on the *Words Their Way* DVD to learn specifics about organization for word study, then see how these ideas play out in each developmental stage.

THE ROLE OF WORD SORTING

Throughout this textbook you will see many examples of games and activities, but the simple process of sorting words into categories, like the word sort described in Mrs. Zimmerman's class, is the heart of word study. Categorizing is the fundamental way that humans make sense of the world. It allows us to find order and similarities among various objects, events, ideas, and words that we encounter. When students sort words, they are engaged in the active process of searching, comparing, contrasting, and analyzing. Word sorts help students organize what they know about words and to form generalizations that they can then apply to new words they encounter in their reading (Gillet & Kita, 1979).

Because sorting is such a powerful way to help students make sense of words, we will take some time here to discuss it in depth. We recommend this same categorization routine for students in all stages who are studying a variety of word features. At first, emergent and beginning readers learn to pay attention to sounds at the beginning of words by sorting pictures. By the time they are transitional readers, reading their first *Frog and Toad* books (by A. Lobel), students benefit from sorting written words by vowel patterns. In later grades, students enhance their spelling by sorting words by prefixes and suffixes. In middle school and high school, students sort words by Greek and Latin stems and roots that share common meanings. As children progress in word knowledge, they learn how to look at and think about words differently.

Word sorting offers the best of both constructivist learning and teacher-directed instruction. The teacher begins by "stacking the deck" with words that can be contrasted by sound, pattern, or meaning. In the process of sorting, students have an opportunity to make their own discoveries and form their own generalizations about how the English spelling system works. Notice that Mrs. Zimmerman avoids telling the students any rules or generalizations herself, but instead leads them to some tentative conclusions through careful questioning. Over the next few weeks, they will continue to explore *r*-influenced vowels through a series of sorts and will discover that *r* often "robs" the vowel of the sounds we normally associate with it. Rather than simply memorizing 20 words each week for a spelling test, students have the opportunity to construct their own word knowledge that they can apply to reading and writing. As a result, word study develops positive attitudes about word learning. Through sorting, students acquire and integrate new word knowledge that is extended and refined through the activities we describe. In addition to learning how to spell, read, understand, and use new words, students develop productive habits of mind (Marzano, 1992).

Picture and word sorting differ from other phonics programs in some important ways. First, word sorts are interesting and fun for students because they are hands-on and manipulative. The process of sorting requires students to pay attention to words and to make logical decisions about their sound, pattern, and/or meaning as they place each one in a column. Consider the ancient proverb: "I hear and I forget, I see and I remember, I do and I understand." Word sorts help students learn by doing (Morris, 1982).

Second, students work with words or the names of pictures that they can already pronounce. In this way, sorting words from the known to the unknown and as children sort through a stack of cards, they concentrate on analyzing the sounds or patterns within each word. This is not possible if students cannot first name the words. Because learning to spell involves making associations between the spelling of words and their pronunciations, it is important that children know and can already pronounce most of the words to be sorted.

A third way in which sorting differs is that sorting is **analytic**, whereas many phonics programs take a **synthetic** approach. In both approaches, students are taught letter-sound correspondences. However, in a synthetic approach, students are expected to sound out unknown words phoneme by phoneme, sometimes every word in a sentence! This makes reading tedious and can detract from meaning and engagement. Rather than building up from the phoneme to the word, in a synthetic approach, sorting builds on known words and then examines their parts. Analytic phonics supports the synthetic skill necessary to decode new words when reading and to encode words when writing.

A fourth way in which sorts differ from most phonics and spelling programs is that sorting does not rely on rote memorization, or the recitation of rules prior to an understanding of the underlying principles. During sorting, students determine similarities and differences among targeted features as they utilize higher level critical thinking skills to make categorical judgments. When students make decisions about whether the middle vowel sound in *cat* sounds more like the medial vowel sound in *map* or *top*, independent analysis and judgment are required. Memorization *is* necessary to master the English spelling system. One simply must remember that the animal is spelled *bear* and the adjective is spelled *bare*, but memorization is easier when served by knowledge and understanding of the principles of English spelling. Likewise, rules are a useful mnemonic for concepts already understood.

Efficiency is a fifth reason why sorts are effective and offer more concentrated practice than most phonics programs. Sorting doubles or triples the number of examples children study, and they study them in a shorter amount of time. Phonics workbooks may have only five to ten examples per page, and most of these exercises ask children to fill in the blank or color their choices from the answers provided. It takes an average first grader 10 to 20 minutes to complete such a workbook activity—time that could be better spent reading. In contrast, sorting a stack of 15 to 25 cards takes only a few minutes and the same stack can be used for a variety of sorting activities throughout the week. Compare the number of examples in Figure 3-2 to see the difference. The efficiency of sorting also makes it more cost effective. Picture and word cards can be reused indefinitely, and the low cost of preparing sorts for word study instruction leaves a larger chunk of the budget for children's books.

Finally, because of the simplicity of sorting routines, teachers find it easier to differentiate instruction among different groups of learners. Sorting is infinitely adaptable and the process involved in categorizing word features lends itself to cooperative learning.

One central goal of word study is to teach students how to spell and decode new words and to improve their word recognition speed in general. To accomplish this goal, we teach our students how to examine words to learn the regularities that exist in the spelling system. Word recognition and decoding, phonics and spelling are two sides of the same word knowledge coin. Picture sorts and word sorts are designed to help students learn how and where to look at words.

TYPES OF SORTS

There are three basic types of sorts that reflect the three layers of English orthography: sound, pattern, and meaning. In addition, there are variations of these sorts that students can do under the teacher's direction, with a partner, or by themselves for additional practice. In this section we describe all of these.

FIGURE 3-2   Picture Sorting Offers More Practice Than Traditional Worksheets

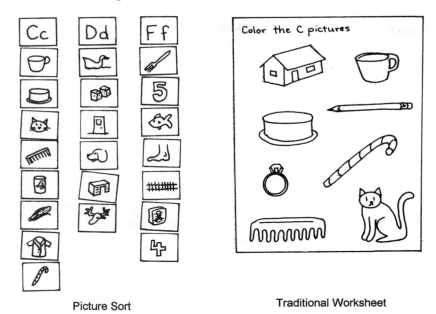

Picture Sort   Traditional Worksheet

Sound Sorts

Sound is the first layer of English orthography that students must negotiate to make sense of the alphabetic nature of English spelling. Pictures are naturally suited for sound sorts: the picture begs to be named, yet there is no printed form of the word for reference. As students sort each picture, they must pay attention to the phonemes contained in the word. Printed words, too, can be sorted for sound, as Mrs. Zimmerman did using the key words *cart* and *care*. Students may sort by rhyme, by the number of syllables, and even by syllable stress when they compare such words as *pro' duce* versus *pro duce'*. There are several basic kinds of sound sorts.

Picture sorts.   Picture sorting is particularly suited for students in the emergent, letter name–alphabetic, and early within word pattern stages of spelling development who do not have extensive reading vocabularies. Picture sorts can be used to develop **phonological awareness,** the ability to identify and categorize various speech sounds such as rhyme and alliteration. Picture sorts can also be used to teach **phonics,** the consistent relationship between letters and sounds. At different points in development, students sort pictures by initial sounds, consonant blends or digraphs, rhyming families, or vowel sounds.

   Teachers first model picture sorts, such as the one shown above in Figure 3-2, as they work with students who are learning initial consonants. Working as a group they say the names of the pictures as they place them under the letters they need to associate with the initial sound. At the end of this guided activity, students work independently to sort similar sets of pictures into the same categories. For variety, small objects can be used instead of pictures.

Words sorts.   Words sorts can also draw students' attention to sound, and because sound is the first aspect of a word a speller has for reference, these sound sorts are very important. For example, only after the long -*a* in *tape* is identified can the speller consider which of several spelling patterns might be used (*taip* or *tape?*). Mrs. Zimmerman began with a sound sort when she met with her group for the first time to introduce the weekly sort. This laid an important foundation for the pattern sort that followed. Not all word sorts involve a sound contrast, but many do.

Blind sorts.   When students are asked to sort words by sound, the printed form of the word can sometimes "give away" the category (as when short -*a* words are compared with short -*u*). In a blind sort, a key word or picture for each sound is established; the teacher or a partner shuffles the word cards, and then calls the words aloud without showing them. The student indicates the correct category by pointing to or naming the key word that has the same sound. The response can be checked and corrected immediately when the printed word is revealed and put in place. A variation of the blind sort is a **blind writing sort**, where the students must write each word under the correct key word before seeing the word. In a blind writing sort, students must rely on the sound they hear in the word, as well as their memory for the letters associated with it, cued by the key word at the top of the column. This is what spelling is all about. Blind writing sorts are an established weekly routine in many classrooms. Some teachers conduct them in a group using the overhead projector, saying the word aloud and letting the students write it before they lay the word down to be checked. This sort is important for students who should attend less to the visual patterns and more to the sounds. Blind writing sorts can help identify what words need more attention and can serve as a pretest for the final assessment. Blind writing sorts, however, should only be used after plenty of word sorts, so students have an opportunity to see the printed form and examine the orthography first.

Blind sorts are a good way to increase the time students practice and also encourage cooperative learning. Students enjoy working with and learning from each other. The task is well defined and the time spent is productive when teachers have taken the time to teach children how to work together through modeling and role-play.

Pattern Sorts

When students use the printed form of the word they can sort by the visual patterns formed by groups of letters or letter sequences. Letter name–alphabetic spellers sort their words into groups that share the same **word families** or **rime** (*hat, rat, pat; ran, fan, tan*). Students in the within word pattern stage sort their words into groups by vowel patterns (*wait, train, mail, pain* versus *plate, take, blame*). Syllables and affixes spellers sort words into groups by the pattern of consonants and vowels at the syllable juncture (*button, pillow, ribbon* versus *window, public, basket*). More advanced spellers will sort word pairs by patterns of constancy and change across derivationally related words (e.g., *divine–divinity, mental–mentality*).

Pattern sorts often follow a sound sort as we saw in the lesson with Mrs. Zimmerman. The words under *care* were subdivided into two pattern groups: words spelled with *air* and words spelled with *are*. One fundamental tenet for pattern sorts is to sort first by sound and then by pattern. Because certain patterns go with certain categories of sound, students must be taught to first listen for the sound and then to consider alternative ways to spell that sound. When students sort by sound and by pattern, they discover those alternatives as well as the small number of words that do not fit the more common patterns.

Sometimes a new feature is best introduced with a pattern sort to reveal a related sound difference. Consider the words in Figure 3-3 that have been sorted by the final *ch* or *tch* pattern. The final sound in all the words is the same, so a sound sort would not help to differentiate their spelling. However, now that the words are sorted by the final consonant patterns, read down each column to see if you notice anything about the vowel sounds within each column. What did you discover? *Tch* is associated with the short-vowel sound and *ch* is associated with the long-vowel sound. Exceptions are *rich* and *such*, and they should be moved to a new column of oddballs or exceptions and remembered as such.

Because pattern sorts depend on the visual array of letters within printed words, picture sorts are not appropriate. However, pictures can be placed at the top of the sorting

The word sorting Application on the *Words Their Way* CD contains hundreds of additional picture and word sorts.

columns in place of key words. Using key pictures to head a column forces students to think about sound while they are learning about patterns.

Although pictures cannot teach patterns, it is sometimes a good idea to mix a few pictures into a pattern word sort. Because it is easier to sort words by their visual pattern, students can lose sight of the fact that certain patterns go with certain sounds. By mixing a few pictures in with a stack of word cards, students are challenged to be flexible in their word analysis and capitalize on the pattern-to-sound regularities of English spelling.

Word sorts. Word sorts using printed word cards are the mainstay of pattern sorts and are useful for all students who have a functional sight word vocabulary. Key words containing the pattern under study are used to label each category and students sort word cards by matching the pattern in each word to the pattern in the key word at the top of the column. Recurring patterns are often represented as an abbreviated code that stands for the pattern of consonants and vowels in the feature of study. The letter *C* represents consonants; the letter *V* represents vowels. The abbreviation *CVC* may be used as a column header for recurring patterns of short vowel words such as *cat, stop,* or *ship,* while *CVVC* may be used as a column header for the recurring pattern in long-vowel words such as *rain, coat, suit,* or *green.*

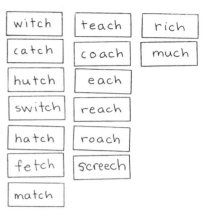

FIGURE 3-3 Word Sort by Final *ch* and *tch* Patterns

witch	teach	rich
catch	coach	much
hutch	each	
switch	reach	
hatch	roach	
fetch	screech	
match		

Meaning Sorts

Students will learn that meaning also influences the spelling of words, and so sometimes the focus of a sort is on meaning. The two major types of meaning sorts are concept sorts and meaning sorts related to spelling. The earliest sorts by meaning are picture concept sorts that do not involve spelling. Meaning sorts related to spelling include (a) homophone and homograph sorts, and (b) roots, stems, and affix sorts.

Concept sorts. Sorting pictures or words by concepts or meaning is a good way to link vocabulary instruction to students' conceptual understanding. Concept sorts are appropriate for all ages and stages of word knowledge and should be used regularly in the content areas. Mathematical terms, science concepts, and social studies vocabulary words all can be sorted into conceptual categories for greater understanding.

Concept sorts can be used for assessing and building background knowledge before embarking on a new unit of study. A science unit on matter, for example, might begin by having children categorize the following words into groups that go together: *steam, wood, air, ice cube, rain, metal, glue, paint, plastic, smoke, milk,* and *fog.* A discussion of the reasons behind their conceptual groupings is most revealing! As the unit progresses, this sort can be revisited and used for teaching core concepts and vocabulary. Having students categorize examples under the key words *solid, liquid,* and *gas* will help them sort out the essential characteristics for each state of matter. Concept sorts are great for dealing with new words in novels, too. While reading *Stuart Little* (by E. B. White), a group of Mrs. Birckhead's third graders sorted some of the vocabulary they encountered as follows:

Weather Words	**Boat Terms**	**Birds**
squall	rigging	henbird
mist	bow	vireo
breeze	stern	wren
brisk	schooner	beak
ominous	helm	breast
cloudy	mainmast	
sunshiny	capsize	

The creative possibilities for concept sorts are endless. They can be used as advanced organizers for anticipating new reading, they can be revisited and refined after reading, and they can be used to organize ideas before writing. Concept sorts are even useful for teaching grammar. Words can be sorted by parts of speech.

Concept picture sorts are particularly useful for English language learners. Without knowing the English terms, they can sort pictures of a dog, a cat, a duck, and so on into an animal category. These can be contrasted with pictures of a flower, a tree, a cornfield, a pumpkin, and so on—all examples of plants. English vocabulary is expanded as students repeat the sort, naming each picture and category with help from a teacher or peer.

Spelling-meaning sorts.   Students see that meaning influences the spelling of words when they first encounter sound-alike pairs like *by* and *buy*, or *to* and *too*. Words that sound alike but are spelled differently are called **homophones.** Students enjoy homophones because they are interesting and it makes such sense that words with different meanings take a different spelling pattern. When teachers teach homophones through word sorting, students expand their vocabularies and learn about spelling patterns at the same time, as demonstrated by the discussion of *bare* in Mrs. Zimmerman's class. The study of homographs also provides a prime opportunity for vocabulary enrichment. **Homographs** are words that are spelled the same but are pronounced differently depending on their part of speech: We *record* our sorts so that we will have an ongoing *record* of them. By sorting homographs into grammatical categories by part of speech, students enrich their vocabulary while learning how to pay attention to syllable stress.

Advanced spellers learn how words that are related in meaning often share similar spellings. This spelling-meaning connection in derivationally related words provides a rich arena for meaning sorts that build on Greek and Latin elements. Spellers who are learning derivational relations will sort words by similarities in roots and stems such as the *spect* in *spectator, spectacle, inspect*, and *spectacular* versus the *port* in *transport, import, portable*, and *port-o-john*.

Approaches to Sorting

There are two basic approaches to sorting: teacher-directed approaches to sorting and student-centered approaches to sorting. In classrooms where word study is flourishing, both teacher-directed and student-centered approaches are used judiciously for different purposes.

Teacher-directed closed sorts.   Most introductory word sort tasks are teacher-directed or **closed sorts.** In closed sorts, teachers define the categories and model the sorting procedure (Gillet & Kita, 1979). For example, in a beginning-sound phonics sort, the teacher isolates the beginning sound to be taught and explicitly connects it to the letter that represents it using a **key word** to designate the categories. The teacher might think aloud like this: "Shhhhhoe, shhhhell. I hear the same sound at the beginning of *shoe* and *shell*, so I am going to put the picture of the shell under the key word *shoe*. They both begin with /sh/, the sound made by the letters *sh*." After modeling several words this way, the teacher gradually releases the task to the students' control as they replicate the process. As they work, teachers and students discuss the characteristics of the words in each column. Students may then sort independently or collaboratively in pairs under the teacher's guidance. This practice is carefully monitored and corrective feedback is provided.

Student-centered open sorts.   Student-centered or **open sorts** are particularly useful after students are already accustomed to sorting and are quite adept at finding commonalties among words. In open sorts, students create their own categories with the set of words.

These sorts are more diagnostic in nature because they reveal what students know about examining the orthography when they work independently. Open sorts provide an opportunity for students to test their own hypotheses and they often come up with unexpected ways to organize words. For example, when given the words shown in Figure 3-3, some students sort by the final patterns (*tch* or *ch*), others sort by the vowel sounds (long and short), and others sort by rhyming words. These open sorts are interesting for the teacher to observe and to discover what students already understand or misunderstand. Some of the most productive discussions about orthography come when students explain *why* they sorted the way they did in an open sort. As students become sorting pros, they begin to anticipate the teacher-directed closed sorts. In many classrooms, students are given their words for the week on Monday morning, and they sort their words independently in anticipation of the categories they will be sorting later in teacher-directed groups.

Variations of Sorts

Variations of teacher-directed and student-centered picture and word sorts serve different instructional purposes. Directed instruction through explicit teaching, problem solving by hypothesis testing, connecting word study to reading and writing, building speed and automaticity—all are important instructional goals, and for each, there is a sort. Writing sorts, word hunts, blind sorts, and speed sorts will be described in relation to their instructional purpose. These sorts differ greatly from traditional phonics, spelling, or vocabulary instruction. Sorting activities develop productive habits of looking and thinking about word attributes. They give students plenty of individual practice and experience manipulating and categorizing words until they can sort quickly and accurately.

1. Guess My Category.　When children are comfortable with sorts, you can introduce any new area of study with a collection of objects, words, or pictures with an activity called Guess My Category. In this sort you do not label or describe the categories in advance. Rather, it will be the job of your students to decide how the things in each category are alike. You begin by sorting two or three pictures or words into each group. When you pick up the next picture or word, invite someone to guess where it will go. Continue doing this until all the pictures or words have been sorted. Try to keep the children who have caught on to the attributes of interest from telling the others until the end.

Guess My Category is particularly useful for exploring content-specific vocabulary and stimulates creative thinking. You could give small groups sets of words or pictures that might be grouped in a variety of ways. Ask each group to come up with their own categories working together. Allow them to have a miscellaneous group for those things that do not fit the categories they establish. After the groups are finished working, let them visit each other's sorts and try to guess the categories that were used. For example, pictures of animals might be sorted into groups according to body covering, habitat, or number of legs.

2. Writing sorts.　Writing words as a study technique for spelling is well established. Undoubtedly the motoric act reinforces the memory for associating letters and patterns with sounds and meanings. However, the practice of assigning students to write words five or more times is of questionable value because it can become simply mindless copying. Where there is no thinking, there is no learning. Writing words into categories demands that students attend to the sound and/or the pattern of letters and to think about how those characteristics correspond with the established categories cued by the key word, picture, or pattern at the top of the column. Writing sorts encourage the use of analogy as students use the key word as a clue for the spelling of words that have the same sound, pattern, or meaning.

Start by writing key words to label each category. The words are then written down in the appropriate categories as seen in Figure 3-4. Students can do this individually by copying a sort they have done with word cards or by turning over one word at a time

FIGURE 3-4   Word Study Notebook

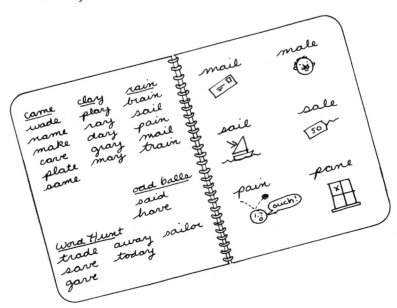

from their collection and writing it down. Even better, the teacher might appoint some-one to call the words aloud for the student to write and then to immediately show the word to check the spelling and placement in a blind writing sort. Teachers can do this with a group, partners can do it with each other, and parents can do it at home. Writing sorts are also an instructionally sound way to construct spelling tests. Key words are written and then students write and sort the words as they are called. They can get credit for putting the word in the right category as well as for spelling the word correctly.

3. Word hunts.   Students do not automatically make the connection between spelling words and reading words. Word hunts help students make this important connection. In **word hunts,** students hunt through their reading and writing for words that are ad-ditional examples of the sound, pattern, or meaning unit they are studying. They see, for example, the many short -*a* words or that -*le* is much more common at the end of words than -*el*. Some patterns are found in virtually every text again and again, whereas others are harder to find; thus, word hunts are more appropriate for some features than others.

Before students are expected to do word hunts, the teacher should model word hunting. This can be done with a portion of text copied onto chart pages, copies of text on overhead transparencies, a big book, or simply a book being used for instruction. Working line by line, teachers demonstrate how to locate words that fit the categories under study and how to record those words into categories. After the teacher demon-stration, students return to familiar texts to hunt for other words that contain the same features. These words are then added to written sorts under the corresponding key word. See Figure 3-4 for words added to the long -*a* categories at the bottom of the note-book page. It is important that students not confuse skimming for word patterns with reading for meaning. The teacher asks the students to use familiar books or already-read portions of the books they are currently reading.

Word hunts can be conducted in small groups, with partners, or individually for seatwork or homework. Figure 3-5 shows how students have gathered around a large sheet of paper on which key words have been written. Students skim and scan pages of books that they have already read, looking for words that match the key words accord-ing to the feature under study. Much discussion may ensue as to whether a word

Watch Leta Robenstine and her small group of second graders conduct a word hunt on the Letter Name–Alphabetic section of the *Words Their Way* DVD.

FIGURE 3-5 Cooperative Group Word Hunt

proof
stood
spoil
toy
school
room
roof
shoot
look
good
cook
oil
boy

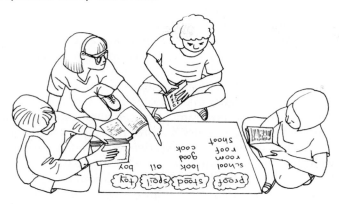

contains the spelling feature in question. Often students consult the dictionary, particularly to resolve questions of stress, syllabication, or meaning.

Figure 3-6 shows an example of a word hunt conducted on a chart summary by a small group of students in Mrs. Fitzgerald's third grade class during a unit on folktales. After working with long *-o* and short *-o* in word study, students found and charted more words from *The Three Billy Goats Gruff.* After this sound sort, students sorted the words by orthographic patterns and organized them in their word study notebooks.

Five words, including *gobble,* were added to the short *-o* column.

Groaned and *goat* were added to the *oa* column.
Home was added to the *o*–consonant–*e* column.
Troll was added to the *o*–consonant–consonant column.
Meadow was added to the *ow* column.
A new pattern of open, single, long *-o* spellings was discovered with *so, go,* and *over.*

FIGURE 3-6 Word Hunt in Story Summary

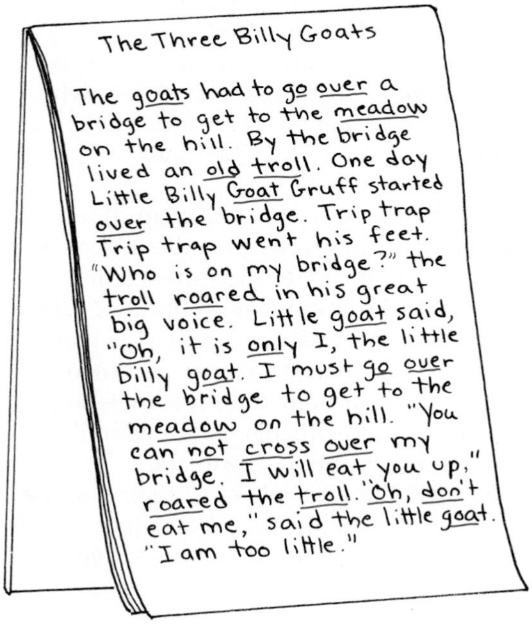

The Three Billy Goats
The goats had to go over a bridge to get to the meadow on the hill. By the bridge lived an old troll. One day Little Billy Goat Gruff started over the bridge. Trip trap Trip trap went his feet. "Who is on my bridge?" the troll roared in his great big voice. Little goat said, "Oh, it is only I, the little billy goat. I must go over the bridge to get to the meadow on the hill." "You can not cross over my bridge. I will eat you up," roared the troll. "Oh, don't eat me," said the little goat. "I am too little."

This word hunt in *The Three Billy Goats Gruff* summary added more examples for students to consider and created new categories. Word hunts connect word study to other literacy contexts and can also extend the reach to more difficult vocabulary such as *meadow* and *gobble*. With these words, students are able to generalize the pattern within one-syllable words to two-syllable words. Word hunts provide a step up in word power!

When conducting word hunts with emergent to beginning readers, teachers should have children scan texts that are guaranteed to contain the phonics features targeted in their search. Many core reading programs provide **phonics readers** that are simple books organized around specific phonics features that repeat in the text. Many other companies create such books for emergent readers that contain recurring phonics elements books as well. Two examples are *Ready Readers*® by Pearson Learning Group and the phonics readers by Creative Teaching Materials. Although such text may not be the heart of your reading program, they offer children a chance to put into practice what they are learning about words and to see many words at the same time that work the same way.

4. Brainstorming.   While word hunts can extend the number of examples to consider, students can also supply additional examples through brainstorming. Brainstorming might be considered a word hunt through one's own memory. The teacher asks for more words that rhyme with *cat*, words that describe people ending in /er/, or words that have *spire* as a root. Word hunts through current reading materials are just not as productive when it comes to some features. It is unlikely, for example, that a word hunt would turn up many words with the Latin stem *spire,* but students may be able to brainstorm derived words they already know, such as *inspire* or *perspire*. Words brainstormed by students can be added to established categories listed on the board, a chart, or a word study notebook.

Brainstorming can also be used to introduce a sort. The teacher may ask students for words that have particular sounds, patterns, or roots and write them on the board. The teacher might write words in categories as they are given, as in a Guess My Category sort, or categories might be determined by discussion. These words might then be transferred to word study sheets for weekly word-sorting routines. After one student raised a question about why the word *receive* had an *e* on the end when it already had the *ei,* Mrs. Zimmerman asked her students to think of other words that ended in either *ve* or *v.* After listing their brainstormed words on the board, students sorted them into two groups—those that had a long-vowel sound and needed the *e* to mark the vowel (*stove, alive, cave*) and those that did not (*give, love, achieve*). After awhile, students realized that there were no words that ended in plain *v*. There was always an *e* after *v*, whether the vowel needed it or not. *Luv,* as in the diapers, became the only oddball.

5. Repeated individual and buddy sorts.   To become fluent readers, students must achieve fast, accurate recognition of words in context. The words they encounter in context are made of the same sounds, patterns, and meaning units they examine out of context, in word study. One of the best ways to build accuracy and **automaticity** in word recognition is to build fast, accurate recognition of these spelling units. To meet that goal, it is necessary to have students do a given picture or word sort more than one time. Repeated individual sorts are designed for just that—repeated sorting. Just as repeated reading of familiar texts builds fluency, repeated individual sorts provide a student with the necessary practice to build automaticity. In Mrs. Zimmerman's class, students sort individually after the group lesson, again on Tuesday, and then with a partner on Wednesday. They are also expected to take their words home to sort several days a week. All this adds up to sorting the same words five to seven times throughout the week.

To accomplish repeated sorting throughout the week, have your students take turns sorting a collection of pictures or words and then talking to each other about what they discover. Partners can work together to complete blind sorts or blind writing sorts. One partner calls the words while the other writes, and then the partners switch roles. Blind sorts are a good way to prepare for tests, especially the writing sort format.

FIGURE 3-7 Draw and Label Activity

6. Speed sorts. Once students have become accurate with a particular sort, you might consider using **speed sorts.** These sorts are motivating and develop fluency and automacity (Samuels, 1988). Speed sorting is no different than ordinary word sorting except that students time themselves using a stopwatch. Students can be paired with other students to time each other and learn to chart their progress. We recommend not pitting students against each other in a competitive mode, however; instead, students should compare their speed with their own earlier speeds and work toward individual improvement.

Some teachers have found that students are highly motivated to practice their sorts in preparation for a **beat-the-teacher speed sort** that takes place later in the week. The teacher circulates from group to group and sorts the word cards while being timed. The group members then try to beat this time.

7. Draw and label / cut and paste. Drawing is particularly useful for teaching emergent and letter name–alphabet spellers initial consonant sounds, as it encourages them to brainstorm other words that begin with the same sounds. Some teachers provide special drawing and labeling paper that has been divided into columns headed by a key letter (see Figure 3-7). Each column is divided into boxes so that students can see where to draw, how big to draw, and how many to draw. Students brainstorm other words that start with the same sound, illustrate the word in a box under the appropriate key letter and picture, and then label the picture with their best writing. Students are held accountable for spelling the word study feature correctly, but they are encouraged to invent the rest if they do not know how to spell the entire word.

A variation of the draw and label activity is the **cut and paste** activity, which is like a word hunt using pictures instead of written words and is appropriate for emergent and letter name–alphabetic spellers. Students hunt through old catalogs and magazines for pictures beginning with a certain sound and then cut out the pictures to paste them in the appropriate column. They then label the pictures as indicated. Pictures that have been used for sorting can also be pasted on a sheet of paper and labeled.

Drawing and labeling are good activities at a variety of levels to demonstrate the meaning of words. The multiple meanings of a word like *block* might be illustrated as a toy, a section of a neighborhood, and a sports play. Homophones like *bear* and *bare* are made more memorable through drawings and creating an ongoing class homophone book, as shown in Figure 3-8, is a popular activity. Even advanced spellers in the derivational relations stage might illustrate the meaning of words like *spectacles, spectators,* and *inspector.*

GUIDELINES FOR PREPARING AND INTRODUCING WORD SORTS

Now that we have described the rationale for sorting and a variety of ways to sort, we will focus on some guidelines for preparing and conducting a teacher-directed sort.

FIGURE 3-8   Class Homophone Book

Preparing Your Word Sorts

After identifying spelling stages and grouping students for instruction, you must decide on what orthographic features to study and prepare collections of words or pictures for sorting. The particular feature you choose to study (initial consonant sounds, short-vowel sounds, consonant doubling, etc.) should be based on what you see students using but confusing in their writing and other diagnostic information such as that derived from a spelling inventory. The upcoming chapters in this book will provide information about orthographic features to study within each stage. No matter what the feature is, when preparing word lists for sorting, it is best to collect sets of words that offer a contrast between at least two sounds, patterns, or meaning categories. Compare *b* to *s*, compare short *-a* to short *-i*, compare words that double the final consonant before adding *-ing* with those that do not. By carefully setting up contrasts in a collection of words, you are stacking the deck for students' discoveries as they sort.

You can utilize several resources to help prepare sorts. Chapters 4 through 8 have suggestions for each stage and the Appendices provide pictures and word lists as well as examples of sorts. In addition, the CD-ROM that accompanies this book offers picture and word sorts. We suggest these as a starting point for eventually creating your own sorts. Only you can be sure of what words your students can already read and thus use for sorting. It is unlikely that any prepared collection of sorts or sequence of study will be just right for your students.

The following additional resources are also valuable.

1. Prepared picture and word sorts: The *Words Their Way* companion volumes provide a complete curriculum for each stage, with prepared sorts and spell checks for each unit.

2. Prepared word lists: Valuable references include the *WTW* Appendix, *The Reading Teacher's Book of Lists* (Fry & Kress, 2006), and *The Spelling Teacher's Book of Lists* (Phoenix, 1996).

3. Dictionaries: Special dictionaries such as the *Scholastic Rhyming Dictionary* (Young, 1994) lists words by rimes and vowel patterns. Regular dictionaries are good for finding words with such beginning features as blends, digraphs, and prefixes. Online dictionaries and those on CD-ROM can be used to search for internal spelling patterns such as vowel digraphs or root words. To search for an internal pattern, you usually use an asterisk or a question mark before or after the pattern. Using a question mark as in ??ar? or ?ar?? would yield five-letter words with *ar* in the middle. Using an asterisk, as in *ar*, would yield all the words in the dictionary with *ar* in them.

Some dictionary Web sites have excellent vocabulary enrichment activities such as a "word of the day" with information about the origins and use of the word. Take some time to explore sites like those listed here:

- http://www.yourdictionary.com
- http://www.wordcentral.com
- www.allwords.com

4. Spelling books: The spelling features introduced across grade levels in basal phonics and spelling programs generally follow the same progression of orthographic features that are outlined in Chapters 4 through 8 of this textbook. One difference is that basal phonics or spelling programs often present only one sound or spelling pattern at a time in lists that offer no contrasts. For example, one unit may be on words ending with the /j/ phoneme spelled with the *tch* pattern (*patch, itch, fetch,* etc.). Without a contrast in vowel sound, students are not able to discover that the final /j/ phoneme in single syllable words is spelled with the *tch* pattern (*match, pitch, scotch*) or the *ch* pattern (*coach, teach, pooch*) depending on the medial vowel sound: short, long, or other. One solution to this is to cull words from successive units in the basal program to create word sorts with categorical contrasts. For example, *short-vowel* words from Unit 7 using the *tch* pattern (*fetch, hitch*) might be contrasted with the *long-vowel* words in Unit 8 using the *ch* pattern (*peach, roach*).

Preparing Your Sorts for Cutting and Storing

Word study does not require great monetary investment because the basic materials are already available in most classrooms. Access to a copier and plenty of unlined paper will get you well on your way. Copies of word sheets or picture sheets like those in Figure 3-9 can easily be created by hand using the templates and pictures in this textbook or by using the "Tables" format on the computer and setting all margins at 0 inches. The copies are given to students to cut apart for sorting activities. Asking students to quickly scribble over the backside of their paper before cutting, using colors different from their neighbors, will help them identify words that end up lost on the floor. Students quickly learn the routine of cutting words apart, sorting them into categories, and storing them in an envelope or plastic bag that is reused each week. Sometimes the cut-up words and pictures are kept and later combined with new words or pictures the following week; sometimes they are pasted into a notebook or onto paper, and sometimes they may be simply discarded. Creating these sheets of pictures or words is the first task teachers must tackle.

Modeling the categorization procedure you want your students to use is important, so think about how you will do this. In small groups, you may simply use the same cutout words your students will be using as you model on a table or on the floor. For larger groups you may want to model sorts on the chalkboard or whiteboard, with an overhead transparency using cut-up transparencies of the words, or with large word cards in a pocket chart. Large picture cards can be made by enlarging the pictures in this book and pasting them on cardstock. Some schools have chart-maker copiers that easily enlarge pictures. Magnetic tape can be attached to the back of pictures and word cards for sorting on a metal chalk-board.

FIGURE 3-9   Sample Word Study Handouts

FIGURE 3-10 Students Can Complete Sorts Independently Using Classification Folders

You may also want to make your own special set of pictures for sorting by copying the pictures in Appendix C onto cardstock and coloring them. Laminating the cardstock is optional, as the material is quite durable. A set of these pictures can be stored by beginning sounds or by vowel sounds in library pockets or in envelopes. They can then be used for small group work or for individual sorting assignments. For example, you may find that you have one student who needs work on digraphs. You can pull out a set of *ch* and *sh* pictures, mix them together, and then challenge the student to sort them into columns using the pocket as a header. The **sound boards** in Appendix B can be copied, cut apart, and used to label the picture sets. It might be useful to have several of these picture sets, especially for resource teachers who work with individual children or small groups. Resource teachers may also want to create word card sets that can be stored in envelopes and reused from year to year to reduce paper consumption.

Word study does not require dramatic changes to the physical setup of most classrooms. Storage space is needed for the word or picture sheets, large word cards, and games you create, but most of these can be stored in folders in a filing cabinet. Word study notebooks might be stored in a common area such as a plastic file box or tub to make it easy for the teacher to access them when checking student work.

Many teachers use manila file folders to hold materials and to help students sort their words or pictures into categories as shown in Figure 3-10. Classification folders are divided into three to five columns with key words or pictures for headers glued in place. Words or pictures for sorting are stored in the folder in library pockets or plastic bags and students sort directly on the open folder into the columns. Laminating makes the sorting surface slippery, so you may not want to do that unless you anticipate heavy use. Once the folders have been developed, teachers can individualize word study fairly easily by pulling out the folders that target the exact needs of their students. When there is little room in a class for centers, teachers use these folders as a place to store activities that students can take back to their desks for seatwork.

FIGURE 3-11 Follow-the-Path Game for Initial Consonants

Ball starts with a B.

Preparing Word Study Games for Extension and Practice

Games are appealing for children and encourage them to practice in more depth and apply what they have learned in a new situation. This book contains many ideas for the creation of games, and you will want to begin making these to supplement the basic word or picture sorts as you have time. Look for generic games in the activity section of each chapter first, as many of them can be used with a variety of word features you will study across the year. For example, the follow-the-path game being played by the boys in Figure 3-11 can be laminated before labeling the spaces and then new letters substituted as they become the focus of study. Label the spaces with a washable overhead projector pen. Over time you can create more specific games.

TABLE 3-1 Word Study Materials		
From the Supply Room	**From the Bookstore**	**From the Copy Room**
copy paper for sorts	student dictionaries	photocopied picture cards
cardstock	rhyming dictionary	photocopied word cards
word study notebooks	etymological dictionary	student sound boards
manila folders	homophone books	poster sound boards
gameboard materials	alphabet books	
spinners and dice	phonics readers	
storage containers		
library pockets		
chart paper		
stop watches		

Preparing Your Space for Sorting

Classroom space is needed for group work, individual work, and partner work. Separate areas for word sorting and discussion are needed to convene a group on the floor or at tables in one part of the classroom while other children continue to work at their desks or in other areas of the room. Students' desks provide a surface for individual word sorting. In addition, centers or workstations can be set up where students work individually or with a partner to sort or play a game. A stopwatch is needed for speed sorts and can be placed in the word study center. Many teachers also post chart-size sound boards in this area. Table 3-1 summarizes what you might need, depending on the age and range of developmental word knowledge in your classroom.

Teacher-Directed Word Study Lesson Plan

The teacher-directed sort is the most commonly used approach to introduce a new sort to a group and provides a model of direct instruction that is explicit and systematic, yet sensitive to individual variation. It is described in detail here, but it is only one model. As you and your students become more comfortable with sorting routines, you might also choose to begin with an open sort or with a Guess My Category sort. The teacher-directed sort follows a four-step process: (a) demonstrate, (b) sort and check, (c) reflect, and (d) extend (see Figure 3-12).

The word sorting segment of the Words Their Way DVD clarifies the lesson plan. You'll see how teachers carry out the four part plan across classes and developmental levels.

Demonstrate: Introduce the sort using key pictures or words

1. Look over the words or pictures for ones that are potentially difficult to identify or that may be unfamiliar to students. You should name the pictures ("This is a picture of a yard") and pronounce the words, define them, and use them in a sentence. ("Does

FIGURE 3-12   Word Study Lesson Plan Format

Demonstrate	Introduce sort, use key words or pictures
Sort and check	Individually or with a partner
Reflect	Compare and declare
Extend	Introduce and assign activities to complete at seats, in centers, or at home: sorts, games, cut and paste, word study notebook, word charts

anyone know what a hutch is? Pet rabbits often live in hutches"). Do not make reading words or naming the pictures into a guessing game. Tell your students the names of the pictures immediately. (Your English Language Learners will especially benefit from this discussion of vocabulary!)

2. Next establish the categories. An open-ended question such as, "What do you notice about these words?" or "How might we sort these words?" can be used to get students thinking about categories. If you have stacked the deck with words that share common patterns or sounds and if your students are familiar with categorizing, then they should notice common features fairly quickly. If they do not, then define the categories for them directly as Mrs. Zimmerman did with the two *r*-influenced vowel sounds in *cart* and *care*.

3. Use letter cards, key pictures, key words, or pattern cues such as CVC as column headers. If you are working with sounds, you can emphasize or elongate them by stretching them out. If you are working with patterns, you can think aloud as you point out the spelling pattern. If you are working with syllables, affixes, or derivational relations, you can explicitly point out the unit you are using to compare and contrast.

4. Shuffle the rest of the cards and say, for example, "We are going to listen for the sound in the middle of these words and decide if they sound like *map* or like *duck*. I'll do a few first. Here is a rug. Ruuuuug, uuuug, uuuuuuh. *Rug* has the /*uh*/ sound in the middle, so I'll put it under *duck*, uuuuck, uuuuh. Here is a flag. Flaaaaag, aaaag, aaaa. I'll put *flag* under *maaaap*. *Flag* and *map* both have the /ă/ sound in the middle; the /ă/ sound is made by the vowel letter *a*."

5. After modeling several words, turn the task over to students. Display the rest of the pictures or words, pass them out, or continue to hold them up one at a time. Students even enjoy the anticipation of turning over a word in the stack when it is their turn. Students should name or read the word aloud and then place it in the correct category. If students make a mistake at the very beginning, correct it immediately. Simply say: "*Sack* would go under *map*. Its middle sound is /a/." Then model the phoneme segmentation process for isolating the medial vowel: /s/ /a/ /k/.

Sort and check: Individually or with a partner.   After students have completed the first sort under your guidance, immediately ask them to shuffle and sort again, but this time cooperatively or independently. Unless your students are in the last two levels of word knowledge (syllables and affixes or derivational relations), ask them to name each word or picture aloud as they sort. If someone does not know what to call a picture, tell the student immediately. If someone cannot read a word, discard it or lay it aside to consider later. During the second, repeated sort, do not correct your students, but when they are through, have them name the words or pictures in each column to check themselves. If there are misplaced cards students fail to find, tell how many and in which column, and ask students to find them.

Reflect: Compare and declare.   At the end of the sort, have students verbalize what the words or pictures in each column have in common. The best way to initiate such a discussion is to say, "What do you notice about the words in each column?" Guide them to consider sound, pattern, and meaning with open-ended questions such as, "How are the sounds in these words alike? What kind of pattern do you notice? Are any of these words similar in meaning?" Avoid telling rules, but help students shape their ideas into statements, such as, "All of these words have the letter *u* in the middle and have the /*uh*/ sound" or, "The words with an *e* on the end have the /a/ sound in the middle." During the reflection part of the lesson, students are asked to declare their knowledge about sound, pattern, and meaning.

Extend: Activities to complete at seats, in centers, or at home.   After the group demonstration, sorting, and reflection, students participate in a number of activities described earlier that reinforce and extend their understanding. They continue to sort a number of times individually and with partners. They hunt for similar words. They draw and label pictures, add to word charts, complete word study notebooks, and play games.

Making Sorts Harder or Easier

The difficulty of sorts can be adjusted in several ways:

1. Increasing the number of contrasts in the sort provides more challenge. If children are young or inexperienced, starting with two categories is a good idea. As they become adept at sorting into two groups, step up to three categories and then four. Even after working with four categories or more, however, you may want to go back to fewer categories when you introduce a new concept.

2. Another way to make sorts easier or harder is by the contrasts you choose. It is easier to compare the sounds for /b/ and /s/ than for /b/ and /p/, for example, because the letter names *b* and *s* are made in different parts of the mouth. Likewise, it is easier for students to learn the short sound for *i* when it is contrasted with the short sound of *a* or *o* than with *e*. Start with obvious contrasts, then move to finer distinctions.

3. The difficulty of sorts can also be increased or decreased by the actual words you choose as examples within each category. For example, adding words with blends and digraphs (*black, chest, trunk*) to a short-vowel sort can make those words more challenging. Ideally, children should be able to read all of the words in a word sort. In reality, however, this may not always be the case. The more unfamiliar words in a given sort, the more difficult that sort will be. This caveat applies to both being able to read the word and knowing what the word means. A fifth grader studying derivational relations will need easier words to study than a tenth grader, simply because the fifth grader will have a more limited vocabulary. If there are unfamiliar words in a sort, try to place them toward the end of the deck so that known words are the first to be sorted. When new words come up, encourage your students to compare the new spelling with the known words already sorted in the columns to arrive at a pronunciation.

4. Finally, adding a miscellaneous or an oddball column and including "exception" words that do not fit the targeted letter-sound or pattern feature can increase the difficulty of a sort.

Oddballs.   Oddballs, words that are at odds with the consistencies within each category, will inevitably turn up in word hunts and should be deliberately included in teacher-developed sorts. The word *have*, for example, would be an oddball in a short *-a* versus long *-a* vowel sort. The vowel sound of the *a* in *have* is short, yet it appears to be spelled with a long-vowel pattern. Oddballs are often high frequency words such as *have, said, was*, and *again*. Such words become memorable from repeated usage, but are also memorable because they are odd. They stand out in the crowd. Such words should be included in the sorts you prepare, but not too many. One to three oddballs per sort are plenty, so that they do not overwhelm the regularity you want students to discover.

The oddball category is also where students may place words if they are simply not sure about the sound they hear in the word. This often happens when students say words differently due to dialectical or regional pronunciations that vary from the "standard" pronunciation. For example, one student in Wise County, Virginia, pronounced the word *vein* as *vine* and was correct in placing *vein* in the oddball column as opposed to the long *-a* group. To this student, the word *vein* was a long *-i*. Sometimes students detect subtle variations that adults may miss. Students often put words like *mail* and *sail* in a different sound category than *maid, wait*, and *paid*, because the long *-a* sound is slightly different before liquid consonants like *r* and *l*. *Mail* may sound more like /*may-ul*/.

Dealing with mistakes.   Mistakes are part and parcel of learning, but not all mistakes are dealt with in the same way. As described in the preceding guidelines for sorting, mistakes made early on in a sort should probably be corrected immediately. Sometimes, however, it is useful to find out why a student sorted a picture or word in a particular way. Simply asking, "Why did you put that there?" can provide further insight into a student's word knowledge. If mistakes are made during the second sort, your students will learn more if you guide them to finding and correcting the mistake on their own. You might say, "I see one word in this column that doesn't fit. Start at the top of the column and see if you can figure out which one it is." If students are making a lot of mistakes, it may indicate a need to take a step back or to make the sort easier.

Once you are familiar with the basic word study lesson plan, you are ready to organize your classroom for differentiating word study to meet the needs of all your students.

ORGANIZATION OF WORD STUDY INSTRUCTION

What does a word study classroom look like? How can you differentiate instruction within a heterogeneous classroom? How much time does it take? What exactly do students do on different days? These questions and more about organizing for word study are answered in the sections that follow.

Weekly Routines, Schedules, and Management Plans

Once you have prepared your word lists and introduced your students to basic sorting procedures, it is time to set up a weekly schedule and to develop predictable routines. There are many ways to organize word study. Some teachers conduct word study lessons as part of their reading groups. Other teachers work with two to three separate word study groups and may rotate their students from **circle time** with the teacher to individual **seat work** and workstation or **center times.** Still others use a block of time that incorporates differentiated word study. There may also be time set aside for teachers to conference individually with students in a largely independent workshop routine. In all settings, the focus of word study should be on active inquiry and problem solving where students are engaged in their own learning. When scheduling word study in your classroom, consider the following.

1. *Develop a familiar weekly routine with daily activities.*   Routines will save you planning time, ease transitions, and make the most of the time you devote to word study. Weekly schedules described in this chapter will give you ideas about how to create your own schedules. Include homework routines as well. When parents know what to expect every evening, they are more likely to see that the work gets done.

2. *Schedule time for group work with the teacher.*   Students at the same developmental level should work with a teacher for directed word study. During this time, teachers model new sorts, guide practice sorts, and lead students in discussions that stimulate thinking and further their understanding. Chapter 2 offers assessment-driven guidelines for grouping students for instruction.

3. *Keep it short.*   Word study should be a regular part of daily language arts, but it need not take up a great deal of time. Teacher-led introductory lessons may take 15 to 20 minutes, but subsequent activities should last only about 10 minutes a day and do not require a lot of supervision once students understand the routines. Word study can fit easily into odd bits of time during the day. Children can play spelling games right before lunch or sort their words one more time before they pack up to go home. Our favorite short activity is a quick word hunt through already-read pages following the guided reading lesson—searching for and sharing words from the reading that fit the same categories under study.

4. *Plan time for students to sort independently and with partners.*   Students need time to sort through words on their own and make decisions about their attributes. Teachers

build this independent work into seatwork, center activities, and group games. Word study also lends itself nicely to many cooperative activities and fosters critical thinking. Thinking together in pairs and in groups allows students to learn from each other. The ability to recognize the logic in the explanations of their partners' sorts helps all students in the group compare the similarities and differences among the various words. Working together, students more easily form generalizations and gather orthographic support for their new insights.

Word Study as an Extension of the Reading Group

Because spelling development and reading development are so closely aligned, it makes good sense for word study instruction to occur as an extension of the reading group whenever possible. Not only does this format make sense organizationally, but it has a lot of theoretical integrity, too, as orthographic knowledge is central to both reading and writing. You can move quite seamlessly from the reading lesson into the word study lesson by asking students to look back through certain pages to find words that contain the feature you are about to introduce. For example, if you are about to introduce a word sort comparing two or more ways of spelling the long -*a* sound, you might have your students skim back through the first three pages of the selection they just finished looking for words with a long -*a* sound. Record their contributions on a chart or dry-erase board, and categorize them into columns as you do so. Invariably, someone will supply a word that doesn't have a long -*a* sound, but this fortuitous situation will allow you to review and clarify the phoneme under study. Your students will probably find many of the long -*a* spelling patterns in words like *day, eight, snake, great,* and *away,* and they may fall for a number of oddballs, too—words like *have* and *said* that contain a common long -*a* spelling pattern but not the long -*a* sound. This culling of reading vocabulary for further word study may be all that is accomplished on this introductory day. On subsequent days you will demonstrate a word sort and have your students repeat the sort. Additional word study activities might be assigned during group time that will be completed as seatwork or for homework. This organizational set-up is efficient and integrates word study into the total reading and language arts program.

Separate WS groups in a circle-seat-center format. Figure 3-13 shows a five-day schedule that accommodates the four-step word study lesson plan for three groups rotating through a circle-seat-center instructional plan.

FIGURE 3-13   Circle-Seat-Center Morning Schedule

		9:00–9:25	9:25–9:30	9:30–9:55	9:55–10:00	10:00–10:25	
Whole Class Review of Schedule & Activities	Group 1	Circle	Evaluation and Break	Seat	Evaluation and Break	Center	Evaluation and Break
	Group 2	Center		Circle		Seat	
	Group 3	Seat		Center		Circle	Whole Class Activities

The circle-seat-center plan works well if your word study groups are separate from the reading groups. The teacher introduces a new sort during circle time to a group of students who are at the same developmental level. Half of the remaining students work independently or in buddy pairs at their desks or tables while the other half works at stations or literacy centers. After about 10–15 minutes, the groups rotate. Students who were at the centers join the teacher at the circle table, students who were working at their seats go to the centers, and students who had been with the teacher return to their seats to work independently or with buddies. Counting transition time, three word study groups rotate through all three instructional formats in about an hour. A second slightly longer rotation occurs also for reading groups. This organization scheme works well in schools where the entire morning is devoted to reading and language arts.

Word Study Block

In this assessment driven approach to phonics, spelling, and vocabulary, students study different word features during word study. All students may cut and sort their words at the same time, but the words they are sorting and the word features they are categorizing are different. Across the five days of the week, students during this block of time will: (1) sort, check, and discuss their words (See Figure 3-20 for scheduling teacher led groups), (2) write their words into columns in their word study notebook, (3) search for and record additional words that contain the same feature in the books they have been reading and the stories and reports they have been writing, (4) engage in speed sorts, blind sorts, and word study games, and (5) take a weekly spell check. This organizational plan works well for teachers who prefer everyone to be doing the same thing at the same time, yet allows for differentiation of instruction within the word study block.

Word Study in a Readers' Workshop Environment or Resource Room (Upper El/Secondary)

Reading and the English language arts are often taught in a readers' workshop environment in the upper grades. In this situation, students may be reading self-selected books within given choices related to the curriculum, such as genre, theme, or author studies. The classroom may make use of literature circles (Daniels, 2002) or book clubs (Raphael, Pardo, Highfield, & McMahon, 1997), or the teacher may have different groups of students come together for explicit instruction on the use of particular comprehension or writing strategies, or to introduce a particular word feature. The workshop environment allows teachers to meet individually with groups and individuals to provide direct instruction in word study and feedback as necessary. Learning or reading resource rooms also contain a wide range of students who are working individually on diagnosed needs. In these more complex classrooms, it is often desirable for word study to be scheduled through individual student contracts or assignment plans. Weekly contracts are particularly useful at the secondary level. Students contract in advance to complete a certain amount of work in different areas, and to turn in that work by a certain date. Figure 3-14 shows a sample student contract for a high school English class. Note the word study requirement in item 4. Student contracts "spell out" exactly what is expected of students in terms of assignments and how much they have to do to earn various grades.

An important decision that a teacher makes is how to schedule word study activities over the course of a week. Teachers can either schedule word study as an extension of the reading group, or separately in a circle, seat, and center rotation; or, they can adapt a block of time to differentiate instruction. Many teachers in the upper grades prefer the more flexible approach that student contracts afford to accommodate a workshop or resource environment. As you consider the management of your word study instruction,

FIGURE 3-14 Sample Student Contract

Name: Jerry Garcia	Contract Period: 10/14 – 10/25		Work Due by: 10/25
Assignment:	Deliverable:	Points Worth	Points Earned
1. Independent Reading Title: _____	5 Reading log entries: 1/2 page each, covering pages _____ to _____	5 pts per entry	_____
2. Participation in _____ Group Reading Lesson. Title/Date: _____ _____ _____	1 Written summary per lesson (minimum of 1 page per summary)	5 pts per summary	_____
3. Leader of Group Reading Lesson: Title/Date: _____	• Before reading book or background • During reading questions (stopping points marked with sticky notes) • After reading reflection and revisit	5 pts each before, during, after	_____
4. Complete Word Study Lesson. Your feature: long-to-short vowel sound changes in related words. (ex. mine → mineral)	• Sort, check, record and reflect (written reflection below columns) • 3 speed sorts (times recorded) • Word hunts (find at least 5 additional words) • Blind written sort • Spell check	5 pts per step	_____

5. Writing/Grammar
Your Focus:
Explications of Story Structure
Title: _____
	• 2 Page Story explication that includes:
	  – setting
	  – tone
	  – characters
	  – problem
	  – major events
	  – resolution
	  – theme, moral, message, or purpose
		5 pts per story element	_____

Comments:			

it might be helpful to see how these various organizational schemes play out across the days of the week. In the following section, we revisit these formats in greater depth and in grade-level contexts. In the following examples, all of the teachers begin with a directed word study session in which they introduce the categories.

FIGURE 3-15   Betty Lee's Weekly Schedule of Word Study with Pictures

Betty Lee's Schedule				
Monday	**Tuesday**	**Wednesday**	**Thursday**	**Friday**
Picture Sorting	Drawing and Labeling	Cutting and Pasting	Word Hunts Word Banks	Games

The classroom organization section of the *Words Their Way* DVD provides examples of these schedules in classroom contexts.

A Weekly Schedule for Students in the Primary Grades

Betty Lee, a first grade teacher from Montgomery County, Maryland, organized her word study program around a circle-seat-center rotation format (see Figure 3-13). Betty Lee's plan works well for children who are in the emergent to early letter name–alphabetic stages, where sorting is done with pictures. Betty Lee introduced her spelling concepts with a picture sort at circle time, working with about a third of the class who were at the same developmental level. A second third of the class worked at their seats, drawing and labeling pictures of words they recalled from a previous lesson. The remaining students were stationed at different centers where they worked at cutting and pasting or playing word study games with a partner. These activities can be organized in a 5-day routine as summarized in Figure 3-15 and described in the following paragraphs, or this routine can be shortened into a 3-day plan for students who are reviewing and need to move more quickly. Figure 3-16 shows a student's pocket folder that can be used at this level to keep materials organized and guide students to the daily routines. Students can keep their cutout pictures in the envelope until they are pasted down or discarded. Each folder has a sound board (one of three sound charts that can be found in Appendix B) to use as a reference and a record of progress. Students can simply color the boxes lightly with crayon to indicate that they have worked with that sound.

Monday—Picture Sort. The teacher models the categorization routine using picture cards and helps students recognize the sounds and letters they are studying. Sound categories are established using a letter card and a key picture that is used repeatedly to help students develop a strong association between the beginning sound of the word and the letter that represents it. Each picture is named and compared with the key picture to listen for sounds that are the same. The sort might be repeated several times in the circle as a group or with partners. During their center or seat time, students do the same picture sort again on their own or with a partner.

FIGURE 3-16   Pocket Folder for Organizing Materials

Tuesday—Draw and Label. Students sort again at their seats or in the literacy centers and then extend the feature through drawing and labeling activities. The example in Figure 3-7 on page 61 shows a student's recall of initial consonants. Students are encouraged to write as much of the word as they can, using invented spelling to label their drawing. Teachers can use these spellings to judge student progress in hearing and representing sounds.

Wednesday—Cut and Paste. After sorting again, children make judgments and extend their understanding to other examples when they look through old catalogs and magazines for pictures that begin with a particular sound. These pictures are cut out, pasted into categories or into an alphabet book (see Chapter 4), and labeled. Children who have photocopies of picture sorts might paste these into categories and label them. This takes less time than looking through magazines, but it is also less challenging. Large retail store catalogs are particularly useful because the index is arranged alphabetically. Teachers can tear out several pages and place them in a folder for students to look through as they search for pictures to cut and paste and then label.

Thursday—Word and Picture Hunts. Children apply what they have learned as they look for more words through word hunts, word bank activities, and other tasks. Children can reread nursery rhymes and jingles and circle words that begin with the same sounds they have been categorizing all week. These words are added to their sorts. (Word bank activities are described in more detail in Chapter 5.) Students can also go for word hunts in alphabet books or beginning dictionaries. Keep a variety on hand to teach students rudimentary research skills. Their findings can be recorded as an additional draw and label activity.

Friday—Game Day and Assessment. Children delight in the opportunity to play board or card games and other games in which the recognition, recall, and judgment of spelling features are applied. Assessment at this level is primarily informal as the teacher watches for automaticity and accuracy during sorting and how well students label pictures or use initial sounds in writing.

A Weekly Schedule for Students in the Elementary and Middle Grades

The next schedule works well for children who are readers and able to spell entire words. Sorting words in a variety of contexts and completing assignments in a word study notebook comprise most of the schedule summarized in Figure 3-17.

FIGURE 3-17   Two Schedules for Students Who Sort Words

Weekly Schedule for Students in the Primary and Elementary Grades				
Monday	**Tuesday**	**Wednesday**	**Thursday**	**Friday**
Introduce Sort in Group	Re-sort and Write Sort	Buddy Sort Writing Sort	Word Hunt	Testing and Games
Monday	**Tuesday**	**Wednesday**	**Thursday**	**Friday**
Introduce Sort in Group	Speed Sort with Partner	Word Hunts in Trade Books	Speed Sort with Teacher	Testing
Word Study Notebook Assignments Throughout the Week				

FIGURE 3-18   Expectations for Word Study Notebooks

Word Study Notebooks

Weekly activities for this notebook include:
1. Written sorts
2. Draw and label
3. Sentences
4. Words from word hunts

You are expected to:
1. Use correct spelling of assigned words
2. Use complete sentences
3. Use your best handwriting
4. Make good use of word study time

You will be evaluated in this manner:
* Excellent work
√ Good work but could be improved
R You need to redo this assignment

Word study notebooks provide a built-in, orderly record of activities and progress. Many teachers grade the notebooks as part of an overall spelling grade. Figure 3-18 is a list of the expectations and grading criteria used by Kathy Gankse when she taught fourth grade. This chart can be reproduced and pasted inside the cover of the notebook. Composition books with stiff cardboard covers and sewn pages last all year. Below is a list of possible assignments to be completed in the notebook. You may want to make some "required" activities, such as writing the sort, and some "choice" activities, such as draw and label. There is no need to do all every week and some are more valuable at times than others.

1. *Write word sorts.*   Students write the words into the same categories developed during hands-on sorting. Key words are used as headers for each column.
2. *Select 5-10 words to draw and label.*   Even older students enjoy the opportunity to illustrate words with simple drawings that reveal their meanings. Encourage students to think about multiple meanings of even simple words like *park* or *yard*.
3. *Change a letter (or letters) to make new words.*   Initial letter(s), or orthographic units, might be substituted to create lists of words that rhyme. For example, starting with the word *black*, a student might substitute other consonant blends or digraphs to generate *stack, quack, track, shack,* and so on.
4. *Select 5–10 words to use in sentences.*   This is important as children begin the study of homophones, inflected words (*ride, rides, riding*), and roots and suffixes where meaning is an issue.
5. *Record words from word hunts in trade books and response journals.*   Students add these words to the written sorts in their notebooks.

FIGURE 3-19   Students Gather with Weekly Word Lists for an Introductory Sort

Monday—Introduce the Sort. Many teachers pass out the set of words for the week on Monday morning so students can cut them apart in preparation for group work; other teachers pass out the handouts during group time (as shown in Figure 3-19). Some teachers may not hand them out until after the group sort to keep students' attention on one set of words. Each group in the class has different words, depending on the students' stage of development.

The teacher-directed introductory lesson should include demonstration, sorting, checking, and reflecting, as described on pages 65–67. Students are then sent back to their seat to repeat the sort and may be assigned the task of sorting again for homework. The teacher then repeats this procedure with the next group, focusing on a different feature.

Tuesday—Practice the Sort and Write It. On Tuesday, students sort again. This might be done at their seats: everyone sorts his or her own collection of words for 5 or 10 minutes as the teacher circulates and asks students to read the words and declare their categories. Or it might be done group by group, as students bring their words to sort under the teacher's supervision in a brief session or as part of a guided reading group. Students are assigned a writing sort for seatwork or for homework. Speed sorts might also be planned for Tuesday. Students can be paired up for speed sorts, and follow a posted schedule of times and partners. Throughout the day, partners go back to the "sorting table" at 10-minute intervals to sort their word cards for accuracy and speed. One child times the other with a stopwatch kept at the table and then checks for correctness against an answer sheet. Partners return to their seats to complete work in word study notebooks and pick up where they left off with other assignments.

Wednesday—Blind Sorts and Writing Sorts. On Wednesday, students work in pairs to do blind sorts as described earlier in this chapter. After each partner has led the sort, the pair might do a blind writing sort in which partners take turns calling words aloud for the other to write into categories. This can also be a homework assignment in which the parents call the words aloud.

Thursday—Word Hunts. Word hunts are conducted in groups, with partners, or individually. All students in the class can be engaged in this at the same time by convening in their respective groups. The teacher circulates from group to group to comment and listen in on students' discussions. The teacher asks group members to provide reasons for the agreed-upon groupings. After this activity, the word hunt is recorded in each member's word study notebook. For homework that night, students find additional examples to add to their notebooks from the books they are reading at home.

Friday—Assessment and Games. A traditional spelling test format can be used for assessment. If you have two or three groups, simply call one word in turn for each group. This may sound confusing, but children will recognize the words they have studied over the week and rarely lose track. It is not necessary to call out every word studied during the week (10 words may be enough) and teachers may even call out some bonus or transfer words that were not among the original list to see if students can generalize the orthographic principles to new words. In this way, the discriminating orthographic feature is emphasized, as opposed to rote memorization of a given list of words. It is particularly effective to conduct the spelling test as a writing sort, having students write each word as it is called out into the category where it belongs. One point can be awarded for correct category placement, and one point for correct spelling. Spelling tests conducted as writing sorts reinforce the importance of categorization and press students to generalize from the specific word to the system as a whole. Although games can be played anytime, Fridays might be reserved for them as a reward for doing their best on the spelling test.

Friday completes the cycle for the week. Results of the Friday test and observations made during the week influence the teacher's plans for the next week. The teacher may decide that students need to revisit a feature, compare it with another feature, or move on to new features. Group membership may also change depending on a given child's pace and progress.

If you do not want to take a large block of time on Monday to do all the introductions, you can spread them across the week by meeting with other groups on Tuesday and Wednesday while Monday's group works independently in an "offset" schedule (see Figure 3-20). In this schedule, students with the least ability get the most practice, but everyone does similar activities by Thursday and Friday.

FIGURE 3-20   "Offset" Weekly Plan

	Monday	Tuesday	Wednesday	Thursday	Friday
Lowest Group	Meet with teacher Sort again at seats	Sort again and write sort for homework	Partner work	Word hunts blind sort writing sort for homework	Assessment games
Middle Group		Meet with teacher Sort and write sort at home	Partner work	Word hunts blind sort writing sort for homework	Assessment games
Highest Group		Sort words independently Write sort and reflect	Meet with teacher Partner work if time	Word hunts blind sort writing sort for homework	Assessment games

A Weekly Schedule for Students in the Secondary Grades

Secondary students often change classes every 50 minutes, or if they have block scheduling, every 1 hour and 40 minutes. Either way, the constraints of periods or blocks limit the way word study is conducted. Because secondary English classes are not usually as heterogeneous as elementary classrooms, students are more likely to have similar word study needs. Still, the typical secondary English teacher plans instruction for students in at least two different stages of word knowledge. The range of word knowledge and the limited amounts of time make for a challenge.

One way to organize word study instruction in secondary classrooms is through the use of contracts or individualized assignment plans, as described above. In individual assignment plans, students agree to participate in a set number of word sorts, writing sorts, and word hunts each week. Some teachers find that a two-week cycle works better. In this case students have more time to work with a set of words and word hunts can go on for days instead of taking time on a particular day. If students are in the late syllables and affixes stage or the derivational relations stage, it is less important for them to physically sort word cards. Instead, sorts can be conducted in writing, using a worksheet format. Here, students write the words listed at the top or bottom of the sheet into the appropriate category. All of the other word study activities may also be conducted as paper-and-pencil tasks and organized in a word study section of a three-ring binder.

Introducing a Class to Sorting and Starting Your Weekly Routines

For students who are not familiar with the process of cutting, setting up categories, and sorting, and for teachers who are hesitant about implementing a brand new organizational scheme, we recommend a series of introductory lessons over a period of a week or two to gradually transition into a fully differentiated word study routine.

At first, begin with whole-class sorts that will be relatively easy for everyone in the class, and then model some of the routines you will want your students to use such as cutting, drawing, labeling, the writing sorts, and word hunts. Teaching your students how to do all of this may take a few minutes every day for a few weeks, but it will be well worth the investment. Once routines are well established, you can begin to work with small groups of students as other students work independently or with partners using the now-familiar routines. Shari Neilson and Tamara Barren suggest the following steps below to ease yourself into the word study routines described above.

Week 1, day 1: Introduce a concept sort (20 minutes).   Model sorting objects or pictures into two categories: Those that fit and those that don't (Example: animals, not animals or mammals, not mammals). Talk through the sort as students watch. Be interactive; ask them where they think the next one will go, or if they know why you are sorting the way you are.

Week 1, day 2: Repeat the sort from day 1 (15 minutes).   Sort the same words or pictures with a different category (Example: birds, mammals). Call on students to come up to the overhead or pocket chart to sort and talk them through the thinking process. Model a written explanation of the sort when the sort is complete.

Week 1, day 3: Open concept sort in small groups (20 minutes).   Form groups of 3–4 students. Give each group a collection of objects, pictures, or words for a concept sort. Have each group work together to sort into categories of their choice and then share their ideas with the whole class. Use some of the following language to promote critical thinking:

"Explain why you sorted the way you did."
"How did you decide your column title?"
"One of the things I heard while you were sorting was. . . ."
"Were there any words that were hard to sort? Why?"

Week 1, day 4: Introduce closed sort (20 minutes).   Give the criteria for the new sort and suggest headers for each category. Students sort and copy their sort onto chart paper. Students dictate or write one or two sentences to explain the reasoning behind their sorts.

Week 2, day 1: Sound sort.   Collect 15–20 pictures or words that fit into one of two categories of sound (e.g., two different initial consonant sounds, two different short-vowel sounds, two different syllable stress patterns, etc.). Include a few words or pictures that will go into a miscellaneous category. Lay out the pictures or words in random order. Establish the categories: "Pictures that sound like *ball* at the beginning will go over here, under the picture of the ball and the letter *B*, etc." Model the process of sorting and think aloud about the reason for the sorts. Next, have students come to the overhead and repeat the process.
     When the columns are complete, say: "Let's check to be sure." Read down each column of pictures or words. Ask: "What do we know about the pictures (or words) in this column? How are they different from the ones in the other column? Why didn't these words fit?" Create a class chart of the sort and model how to write a sentence or two about what it reveals. If students have sorted pictures, have them brainstorm additional things that could go in each category and draw a picture to record it.

Week 2, day 2: Introduce the word study folder or notebook.   Repeat the sort from the week before. Discuss the sort with your students: "What did we notice about each category? What did we learn about words from this sort?" Students should write the sorts into columns with an explanatory sentence at the bottom of the sort. Circulate among students as they are writing their explanatory sentence and encourage accuracy, completeness, and neatness. Students who have sorted pictures can be asked to draw two pictures for each category.

Week 2, days 3 and 4: Introduce buddy sorts (10 minutes).   Demonstrate the blind sort. Lay down the key words from the day before. Call the word aloud and call on someone to identify the category. Pair up students to repeat the sort with a buddy. On a different day, demonstrate how to do a speed sort by timing a buddy with a stop watch. Because the idea is for students to beat their own time, not their partner's, each student will sort twice—once to establish a baseline speed, and a second time to try to beat it.

Week 2, day 5: Whole class picture or word hunt (20 minutes).   Review the chart and discuss the categories once again. Ask students to find additional pictures or words that will fit into the same categories using preselected pages from magazines. If students are looking for words, they will search for them in books they have already read or on a chart like the one in Figure 3-6. In groups, students cut out the pictures that will fit, or write the words. After 10 minutes, suspend this activity so that students can share what they find. Students can paste the pictures, or write the additional words into the appropriate columns on their paper or notebook from the previous day.

Week 3, day 1: Differentiate your sorts.   Divide your students into two or three groups. Pass out sets of three *different* sheets of picture or word sorts that have not yet been cut—a different sheet for each group. Tell students to use a magic marker or crayon to draw three vertical lines down the back side of their paper to distinguish their word cards from others. Next, have students cut out the sort. Kindergarten and first grade students will need instruction on how to hold and move the scissors. Older students can be shown shortcuts such as folding the sheet in half and cutting along the lines. Once you have shown students how to mark and cut out their own sort sheet, you are ready to repeat the steps from the previous week.

Week 3, days 2–5: Introduce classroom management.   In the last few days of this third week, you will repeat the same routines from the previous week in the classroom management format you design. Now is the time to teach students how to work in small groups or buddy pairs while you work directly with just one group. By now you should be well on your way to implementing assessment-driven, differentiated word study instruction.

INTEGRATING WORD STUDY INTO READING, WRITING, AND THE LANGUAGE ARTS CURRICULUM

The weekly schedules described herein provide examples of how to integrate spelling instruction into the language arts classroom. These routines are central to both reading and writing. Students return again and again to trade books they have already read to analyze the reading vocabulary. Word study should be integrated into other studies as well. Poetry lessons begin with reference to a word study lesson on syllable stress. In a writing lesson, students discuss comparative adjectives from a previous word study lesson that focused on words ending in -er. During a lesson on parts of speech, students are asked to sort their week's spelling words into categories of nouns, verbs, and adjectives. Whatever scheduling scheme you choose, your sequence of activities must fit comfortably within your reading/writing/language arts block of instruction.

The features and strategies that students learn during word study should also be applied to decoding strategies during reading and to spelling strategies during writing. If students get stuck on a word while reading, prompt them with a word study cue. Cover up part of the word with your finger to highlight the specific orthographic unit. You can also point out the similarity between the orthographic features in that particular word to the spelling features they have been sorting. The more frequently you make connections between word study and decoding strategies, the more often your students will use them. This is equally true for writing, and many teachers use the features students are categorizing during word study for targeted proofreading.

Selecting Written Word Study Activities: A Caveat Regarding Tradition

There are many long-standing activities associated with spelling that teachers often assign their students, such as writing words five times, writing them in alphabetical order, and copying definitions of words from the dictionary. Think critically about whether assignments like these fulfill the purpose of spelling instruction—which is not only to learn the spellings of particular words, but also to learn generalizations about the spelling system itself and to cultivate a curiosity about words. Writing a word five times can be a rote, meaningless activity, whereas writing words into categories requires the recognition of common spelling features and the use of judgment and critical thinking. Writing words in alphabetical order may teach alphabetization, but it will not teach anything about spelling patterns. Alphabetizing words might be assigned occasionally as a separate dictionary skill, and children will be more successful at it when they can first sort their word cards into alphabetical order before writing them. Students do need to associate meanings with the words they are studying, particularly in upper-level word study when dealing with syllables and affixes and derivational relations. It is reasonable to ask students to look up the meanings of a few words they do not know or to find additional meanings for words, but asking students to write the definitions of long lists of words they already know is disheartening and not likely to encourage dictionary use.

Writing words in sentences can also be overdone. You might allow students to choose 5–10 words (out of 20–25) each week to write sentences in their word study notebooks. This is a more reasonable assignment than writing 25 isolated sentences with the weekly spelling list. Writing just a few sentences per day encourages the application of word use and meaning. Many teachers use sentence writing to work on handwriting, punctuation, and grammar (see expectations in Figure 3-17). Writing sentences is more useful for some features than others. For example, sentences will help students show that they understand homophones or the tense of verb forms when studying inflected endings such as *-ed* and *-ing*.

Be wary of other traditional assignments that take up time and may even be fun, but have little value in teaching children about spelling. Activities such as hangman, word searches, and acrostics may keep students busy, but they impart little or no information about the English spelling system. Spelling bees reward those children who are already good spellers and eliminate early the children who need practice the most. Word study can be fun, but make good use of the time spent on it and do not overdo it. Remember that word study activities should be short in duration so that students can devote most of their attention and time to reading and writing for meaningful purposes.

Word Study Homework and Parental Expectations

Classrooms are busy places and many teachers find it difficult to devote a lot of time to word study. Homework can provide additional practice time, and parents are usually pleased to see that spelling is part of the curriculum. A letter sent home, such as the one shown in Figure 3-21, is a good way to encourage parents to become involved in their children's spelling homework. Parents are typically firm believers in the importance of spelling because it is such a visible sign of literacy, and many are even taking political action to see it reinstated. Unfortunately, invented spelling is often a scapegoat because parents, politicians, and even some teachers unfairly associate the acceptance of invented spelling with lack of instruction and an "anything goes" expectation regarding spelling accuracy in children's writing at all grade levels. Communicate clearly to parents that their children will be held accountable for what they have been taught. Homework assignments help them see what is being taught in phonics and spelling.

FIGURE 3-21   Parent Letter

Dear Parents,

Your child will be bringing home a collection of spelling words weekly that have been introduced in class. Each night of the week your child is expected to do a different activity to ensure that these words and the spelling principles they represent are mastered. These activities have been modeled and practiced in school, so your child can teach you how to do them.

Monday   Remind your child to *sort the words* into categories like the ones we did in school. Your child should read each word aloud during this activity. Ask your child to explain to you why the words are sorted in a particular way—what does the sort reveal about spelling in general? Ask your child to sort them a second time as fast as possible. You may want to time them.

Tuesday   Do a *blind sort* with your child. Lay down a word from each category as a header and then read the rest of the words aloud. Your child must indicate where the word goes without seeing it. Lay it down and let your child move it if he or she is wrong. Repeat if your child makes more than one error.

Wednesday   Assist your child in doing a *word hunt,* looking for words in a book they have already read that have the same sound, pattern, or both. Try to find two or three for each category.

Thursday   Do a *writing sort* to prepare for the Friday test. As you call out the words in a random order your child should write them in categories. Call out any words your child misspells a second or even third time.

Thank you for your support. Together we can help your child make valuable progress!

Sincerely,

Teacher Name

Expectations for Editing and Accuracy in Children's Written Work

Invented spellings free children to write even before they can read during the emergent stage, and children should be free to make spelling approximations when writing rough drafts at all levels. Invented spellings also offer teachers diagnostic information about what children know and what they need to learn. But that does not mean that teachers do not hold children accountable for accurate spelling. Knowing where children are in terms of levels of development and knowing what word features they have studied enable teachers to set reasonable expectations for accuracy and editing. Typical third graders in the within word pattern stage can be expected to spell words like *jet, flip,* and *must,* but it would be unreasonable to expect them to spell multisyllabic words like *leprechaun* or *celebration.* Just as students are gradually held more and more accountable for conventions of writing such as commas and semicolons, so, too, they are gradually held more accountable for spelling accuracy. Understanding of how spelling develops over time enables teachers to have reasonable expectations for the class and for individuals within the class. Teachers also need to direct students to a range of spelling resources and help students learn to use them.

When teachers work with students in small groups, they often use chart paper to make lists of words that are then posted around the room. Words listed on the walls call attention to the richness and power of a versatile vocabulary. Sometimes these charts chronicle discussions of content studies, and sometimes they focus on the specific study of words: happy words, sad words, holiday or seasonal words, homophones, homographs, synonyms, and antonyms. They all provide a ready reference for writing.

Learning to use resources such as word walls (Cunningham, 2004), word banks, personal dictionaries, sound boards, and dictionaries should be a part of the word study curriculum. Even first graders can use simple dictionaries appropriate for their level to look up some special words, and they can be encouraged to refer to their own individual word banks for words.

However, that does not mean you could expect them to look up all the words they need to use. A study by Clarke (1988) found that first graders who were encouraged to use invented spellings wrote more and could spell as well at the end of the year as first graders who had been told how to spell the words before writing. This suggests that children are not marred by their own invented spellings or perseverate with errors over time. However, unless teachers communicate that correct spelling is valued, students may develop careless habits.

Many teachers wonder when they should make the shift from allowing children to write in invented spelling to demanding correctness. The answer is "from the start." Teachers must hold students accountable for what they have been taught. What they have not been taught can be politely ignored. For example, if a child has been taught the sound-to-letter correspondences for *b, m, r,* and *s,* the teacher would expect the child to spell these beginning sounds correctly; however, if the child has not yet been taught the short-vowel sounds, these should be allowed to stand as invented spellings. Because the sequence for phonics and spelling instruction is cumulative and progresses linearly from easier features such as individual letter sounds to harder features such as Latin-derived *-tion, -sion,* and *-cian* endings, there will always be some features that have not yet been taught. Thus, children (and adults!) will always invent a spelling for what they do not yet know.

Spelling Tests and Grades

Some teachers are expected to assign grades for spelling, or spelling may be part of an overall language arts or writing grade. Ideally such a grade should include more than an average of Friday test scores (which should all be high when children are working on words at their instructional level). Table 3-2 offers a more holistic assessment using a form that can be adapted for any grade level. Some teachers may wish to add a section for students to rate themselves. This one might be used with students in upper elementary grades who can be expected to spell most words correctly.

TABLE 3-2   Grading Form for Word Study

Name	Grading Period		
	Excellent Effort	**Good Effort**	**Needs Improvement**
Weekly Word Study			
Word sorts			
Word study notebook			
Partner work			
Final tests			
Editing Written Work			
Spells most words right			
Finds misspelled words to correct			
Assists others in editing work			
Uses a variety of resources to correct spelling			
A = Excellent work in most areas B = Good work in most areas C = Needs improvement in most areas Recommended Grade _____ Comments:			

TEN PRINCIPLES OF WORD STUDY INSTRUCTION

A number of basic principles guide the kind of word study described in *Words Their Way*. These principles set word study apart from many other approaches to the teaching of phonics, spelling, or vocabulary.

   1. *Look for What Students Use But Confuse.*   Students cannot learn things they do not already know something about. This is the underlying principle of Vygotsky's (1962) **zone of proximal development (ZPD)** and the motivating force behind the assessment described in Chapter 2. By analyzing invented spellings, a zone of proximal development may be identified and instruction can be planned to address features the students are using but confusing, instead of those they totally neglect (Invernizzi, Abouzeid, & Gill, 1994). Take your cue from the students. Teachers look to see what features are consistently present and correct to determine what aspects of English orthography the students already know. By looking for features that are used inconsistently, teachers determine those aspects of the orthography currently under negotiation. These are the features to target in word study instruction.

   2. *A Step Backward Is a Step Forward.*   Once you have identified students' stages of developmental word knowledge and the orthographic features under negotiation, take a step backward and build a firm foundation. Then, in setting up your categories, contrast something new with something that is already known. It is important to begin word study activities where students will experience success. For example, students in the within word pattern stage who are ready to examine long-vowel patterns begin by sorting words by short-vowel sounds, which are familiar, and long-vowel sounds, which are being introduced for the first time. Then they move quickly to sorting by pattern. A step backward is the first step forward in word study instruction.

   3. *Use Words Students Can Read.*   Because learning to spell involves achieving a match between the spoken language and the orthography, your students should examine words that they can readily pronounce. Dialect does not alter the importance of this basic principle of word study. Whether one says "hog" or "hawg," it is still spelled *hog*. The consistency is in the orthography, and it is your job as the teacher to make those consistencies explicit. It is easier to look across words for consistency of pattern when the words are easy for students to pronounce. Known words come from any and all sources that students can read: language experience stories, recent readings, poems, phonics readers, and even old spelling books collecting dust on the shelf. As much as possible, choose words to sort that students can read out of context.

   4. *Compare Words "that do" with Words "that don't."*   To learn what a Chesapeake Bay retriever looks like, you have to see a poodle or a bulldog, not another Chesapeake Bay retriever. What something *is* is also defined by what it is *not*; contrasts are essential to students' building of categories. Students' spelling errors suggest what contrasts will help them sort out their confusions. For example, a student who is spelling *stopping* as *stoping* will benefit from a sort in which words with double consonants before adding *-ing* are contrasted with those that do not, as in Figure 3-22.

   5. *Sort by Sound and Sight.*   Students examine words by how they sound and how they are spelled. Both sound and visual pattern are integrated into students' orthographic knowledge. Too often, students focus on visual patterns at the expense of how words are alike in sound. The following sort illustrates the way students move from a sound sort to visual pattern sort. First, students sorted by the differences in sound between hard *-g* and soft *-g*. Then students subdivided the sound sort by orthographic patterns. See what you can discover from this sort.

FIGURE 3-22 Doubling Sort: Comparing Words "That Do" with Words "That Don't"

hopping	raining
planning	cleaning
skipping	nailing
batting	reading
hugging	sleeping
	peeling
	feeling

First Sort by Sound of *G*		**Second Sort by Pattern**		
Soft	*Hard*	*dge*	*ge*	*g*
edge	bag	edge	cage	bag
cage	twig	judge	huge	twig
huge	slug	badge	stage	slug
judge	drug	lodge	page	flag
stage	leg			drug
badge	flag			leg
page				
lodge				

6. ***Begin with Obvious Contrasts.***   When students begin the study of a new feature, teachers choose key words or pictures that are distinctive. For example, when students first examine initial consonants, teachers do not begin by contrasting *m* with *n*. They share too many features to be distinct to the novice: They are both nasals and visually similar. It is better to begin by contrasting *m* with something totally different at first—*s*, for example—then work toward finer distinctions as these categorizations become quite automatic. Move from general, gross discriminations to more specific ones.

Likewise, be wary of two-syllable words for beginners, even if only picture cards are used. *Banana* may start with a *b*, but the first /n/ sound is stressed or pronounced the loudest, and some beginners will be confused.

7. ***Don't Hide Exceptions.***   Exceptions arise when students make generalizations. Do not hide these exceptions. By placing so-called irregular words in a miscellaneous or oddball category, new categories of consistency frequently emerge. For example, in looking at long-vowel patterns, students find these exceptions: *give, have,* and *love*; yet it is no coincidence that they all have a *ve*. They form a small but consistent pattern of their own. True exceptions do occasionally occur and become memorable by virtue of their rarity.

8. ***Avoid Rules.***   Rules with many exceptions are disheartening and teach children nothing. They may have heard the long-vowel rule, "When two vowels go walking, the first one does the talking," but this rule is frequently violated in words like *head, boot,* or *soil.* Learning about English spelling requires students to consider sound and pattern simultaneously to discover consistencies in the orthography. This requires both reflection and continued practice. Students discover consistencies and make generalizations for themselves. The teacher's job is to stack the deck and structure categorization tasks to make these consistencies explicit and to instill in students the habit of looking at words, asking questions, and searching for order. Rules are useful mnemonics if you already understand the underlying concepts at work. They are the icing on the cake of knowledge. But memorizing rules is not the way children make sense of how words work. Rules are no substitute for experience.

9. ***Work for Automaticity.***   Accuracy in sorting is not enough; accuracy *and* speed are the ultimate indicators of mastery. Acquiring automaticity in sorting and recognizing orthographic patterns leads to the fluency necessary for proficient reading and writing. Your students will move from hesitancy to fluency in their sorting. Keep sorting until they do.

10. ***Return to Meaningful Texts.***   After sorting, students need to return to meaningful texts to hunt for other examples to add to the sorts. These hunts extend their analysis to more words and more difficult vocabulary. For example, after sorting one-syllable words into categories labeled *cat, drain,* and *snake,* a student added *tadpole, complain,* and *relate.* Through a simple word hunt, this child extended the pattern-to-sound consistency in one-syllable words to stressed syllables in two-syllable words.

These 10 principles of word study boil down to one golden rule of word study instruction: *Teaching is not telling* (James, 1958). In word study, students examine, manipulate, and categorize words. Teachers stack the deck and create tasks that focus students' attention on critical contrasts. Stacking the deck for a discovery approach to word study is not the absence of direct instruction. On the contrary, a systematic program of word study, guided by an informed interpretation of spelling errors and other literacy behaviors, is a teacher-directed, child-centered approach to vocabulary growth and spelling development. The next five chapters will show you exactly how to provide effective word study instruction.

Words Their Way Word Study Resources

Words Their Way DVD Tutorial: Planning for Word Study in K-8 Classrooms	The DVD that accompanies this text prepares you for word study by examining successful classroom instruction—from assessment to organization to implementation across grade levels. You'll hear teachers explain the process, watch students master skills, and see how a successful word study approach is established and managed.

Words Their Way Word Study Resources CD: Assessment Planning and Additional Interactive Word Sorts	Manage your classroom assessments electronically with the CD ROM that accompanies this text. You'll also find alternate inventories, additional evaluation forms, and hundreds of additional sorts and games. Choose from the sorting and game template options to create and print your own hands-on activities.
Words Their Way with English Learners: Word Study for Phonics, Vocabulary, and Spelling Instruction by D. Bear, L. Helman, M. Invernizzi, S. Templeton, and F. Johnston	Based on the same research and following the same manageable format as the core text, this companion volume focuses on using word study to enhance literacy learning for English learners. You'll find guidance for evaluating students' language needs, research-based suggestions for targeting instruction, and hands-on word study activities geared specifically to the English learner.

Words Their Way Companion Volumes

Each of the following stage-specific companion volumes provides a complete curriculum of reproducible sorts and detailed directions for the teacher. You'll find extensive background notes about the features of study and step-by-step directions on how to guide the sorting lesson. Organizational tips and follow-up activities extend lessons through weekly routines.

Letter and Picture Sorts for Emergent Spellers by D. Bear, F. Johnston, M. Invernizzi	Teachers in Pre-K through Grade 1 will find ready-made sorts as well as rhymes and jingles crafted specifically for emergent spellers.

Word Sorts for Letter Name–Alphabetic Spellers by F. Johnston, M. Invernizzi, D. Bear, and S. Templeton	Primarily for students in Kindergarten through Grade 3, black line masters include picture sorts for beginning consonants, diagraphs and blends, word families with pictures and words, and word sorts for short vowels.
Word Sorts for Within Word Pattern Spellers by M. Invernizzi, F. Johnston, D. Bear, and S. Templeton	Teachers of Grades 1 through 4 will find reproducible sorts that cover the many vowel patterns.

Word Sorts for Syllables and Affixes Spellers by F. Johnston, M. Invernizzi, and D. Bear	This text includes sorts for syllables and affixes spellers in Grades 3 to 8.
Word Sorts for Derivational Relations Spellers by F. Johnston, D. Bear, and M. Invernizzi	Teachers in Grades 5–12 will find upper level word sorts that help students build their vocabulary as well as spelling skills.

All *Words Their Way* products can be ordered online at www.allynbaconmerrill.com

4 Word Study for Learners in the Emergent Stage

T his chapter presents an overview of the literacy development that occurs during the emergent stage, a period in which young children imitate and experiment with the forms and functions of print. Emergent readers are busy orchestrating the many notes and movements essential to literacy: directionality, the distinctive features of print, the predictability of text, and how all of these correlate with oral language. The emergent stage lies at the beginning of a lifetime of learning about written language.

Early emergent students do not read or spell conventionally and they score 0 on spelling inventories because they have very tenuous understandings of how units of speech and units of print are related. Nevertheless, children are developing remarkable insights into written language, and with the help of caregivers and teachers they learn a great deal during what has sometimes been called the **preliterate stage** (Henderson, 1990). Before we go into a thorough description of the emergent stage, we will visit a classroom where 23 kindergartners explore literacy under the guidance of their teacher, Mrs. Singh.

During a unit on animals, Mrs. Singh shared the big book, *Oh, A-Hunting We Will Go*, by John Langstaff. This book is based on the traditional song, "Oh, a-hunting we will go, a-hunting we will go. We'll catch a fox and put him in a box and then we'll let him go." The pattern repeats with various animals and places substituting for *box* and *fox*. After reading several pages, Mrs. Singh began pausing to allow her students to guess the name of the place using their sense of rhyme and picture cues. When several students sang out that the *whale* would be put in a *bucket,* Mrs. Singh pointed to the word *pail* on the page and said, "Could that word be *bucket?* What does *bucket* start with? Listen: *b-b-b-bucket.* What does this word start with?"

In this fashion, Mrs. Singh introduced a new book with her children as they enjoyed the silliness of the rhymes and pictures. In the process she drew her students' attention to letters and sounds and modeled directionality and fingerpointing as she read. After enjoying the big book version, she planned a number of follow-up activities to further develop emergent literacy skills.

Mrs. Singh created a chart with the first five lines of patterned text and posted it in the room for children to read from memory. She also wrote each of the first five lines on sentence strips and placed them in order in a pocket chart. After the children had read the lines several times chorally, Mrs. Singh passed out the strips. As a group they put the sentences back in order by comparing them to the chart. Another day, word cards for *fox, box, catch, go,* and *we* were held up one by one as volunteers came up to find the words on the chart or sentence strips. Mrs. Singh observed carefully to see which children were beginning to point accurately as they recited. She made sure the book, chart, strips, and words were left out where everyone could practice freely with them during the day.

Most of the students in Mrs. Singh's class were studying initial consonants. In previous lessons they had compared words that started with *s* and *m.* Now they looked for words that started with *b* and *f* on the five-line chart and found *fox* and *box.* Mrs. Singh wrote those words on cards as the key words for a picture sort. She brought out a collection of pictures that started with *b* and *f* and put up a picture of a box and fox as headers in a pocket chart. After naming all the pictures, she modeled how to sort several by beginning sound before inviting the children to take turns sorting the rest. This sort was repeated by the group, and on subsequent days all the children had a number of opportunities to sort on their own, to hunt for more pictures in alphabet books and magazines, and to draw and label pictures with those sounds. After the students compared the sounds for *b* and *f* in several ways, the pictures were combined with *m* and *s,* which had been studied previously, for a four-category sort. The students worked with all four letters and sounds for several days before moving on to a new contrast.

Watch the Emergent section of the *Words Their Way* DVD to see students in this stage succeeding through word study.

Mrs. Singh used a core book as the basis for teaching a variety of emergent literacy skills in a developmentally appropriate fashion. Her word study activities address issues critical to emergent literacy in the context of shared reading and playful language lessons.

FROM SPEECH TO PRINT: MATCHING UNITS OF SPEECH TO PRINT

Learning to read and spell is a process of matching oral and written language structures at three different levels: (a) the global level, at which the text is organized into phrases and sentences, (b) the level of words within phrases, and (c) the level of sounds and letters within syllables. For someone learning to read, there is not always an obvious match between spoken and written language at any of these levels. Mismatches occur because of the inflexible nature of print and the flowing stream of speech it represents. Learning to make the match between speech and print is a gradual process, but essential to learn how to read.

The Phrase and Sentence Level

In oral language, the global level is characterized as **prosodic.** This is the "musical" level of language, usually consisting of phrases. Within these phrases, speakers produce and listeners hear intonation contours, expression, and tone of voice, all of which communicate ideas and emotions. For example, a rising note at the end of a statement often indicates a question; precise, clipped words in a brusque tone may suggest anger or irritation. Oral language is a direct form of communication accompanied by gestures and facial expressions that takes place in a shared context. Written language is an indirect form of communication and must contain complete, freestanding messages to make meaning clear. Punctuation and word choice are the reader's only cues to the emotions and intent of the writer. Written language tends to be more formal and carefully constructed, using recognizable structures and literacy devices such as "happily ever after" to cue the reader. When children learn to read, they must match the prosody of their oral language to these more formal structures of written language.

Words in Phrases

A second level of structures that students negotiate are the units of meaning called **words.** In print, words are clearly set off with spaces between a string of letters. In speech, words are not distinct; there is not a clear, separable unit in speech that equates perfectly to individual words. For example, the phrase "once upon a time" represents a single idea composed of four words and five syllables. Because of this, when children try to match their speech to print, they often miss the mark, as Lee does in her elephant story in Figure 4-4. It takes practice and instruction to match words in speech to written words (Morris, 1980; Roberts, 1992).

This mismatch of meaning units between speech and print is most clearly illustrated through an instrument called a spectrograph. This acoustic representation of speech reveals a surprising thing: Humans do not speak in words! There are no demarcations for individual words when a person is talking. The only break in a spectrograph coincides with phrases and pauses for breathing. These breaks always occur between syllables. *Word* is a term specific to print, and according to Malinowski (1952), cultures that have no written language have no word for *word*. This remarkable state of affairs creates an enormous challenge for individuals learning to read.

Sounds in Syllables

Sounds and letters make up the third level of analysis. In learning to read, students must segment the sounds or **phonemes** within syllables. In speech, the phonemes (consonants and vowels) are interconnected and cannot be easily separated (Liberman & Shankweiler, 1991). Yet the alphabet and letter sounds must be understood as discrete units that match in systematic ways. This is the basis for the alphabetic principle that is essential for learning to read and spell English.

CHARACTERISTICS OF THE EMERGENT STAGE OF READING AND SPELLING

Some emergent children may have well-developed language skills and know a great deal about stories and books; others may not. It is not necessary for children to develop a certain amount of oral language *before* learning the alphabet or seeing printed words tracked in correspondence to speech. To withhold these essential components of the learning-to-read process would hold them in double jeopardy. Not only would they be behind in language and story development, but they also would be behind in acquiring the alphabetic principle. Children can develop oral language, learn about stories, *and* learn about words, sounds, and the alphabet simultaneously as teachers model reading and writing and encourage children to imitate and experiment.

Emergent Reading

The reading of the emergent child is actually pretend reading, or reading from memory. Both are essential practices for movement into literacy. **Pretend reading** is basically a paraphrase or spontaneous retelling at the global level which children produce while turning the pages of a familiar book. In pretend reading, children pace their retelling to match the sequence of pictures and orchestrate dialogue and the voice and cadence of written language (Sulzby, 1986).

Memory reading is more exacting than pretend reading and involves an accurate recitation of the text accompanied by pointing to the print in some fashion. Reading from memory helps children coordinate spoken language with print at the level of words, sounds, and letters. Emergent children's attempts to touch individual words while reading from memory are initially quite inconsistent and vague. Children gradually acquire **directionality** and realize that they should move left to right, top to bottom, and end up on the last word on the page. However, the units that come in between are a blur until the systematic relationship between letters and sounds is understood. The ability to fingerpoint or track accurately to words in print while reading from memory is a phenomenon called **concept of word.** It is a watershed event that separates the emergent reader from the letter name–alphabetic beginning reader (Flanigan, 2006; Morris, 1981; Morris, Bloodgood, Lomax, & Perney, 2003).

When children lack a concept of word, word boundaries are also obscured in their writing, even if some phoneme–grapheme correspondences have been made. Note how the words all run together in Figure 4-1. Words gradually begin to evolve as distinct entities with their boundaries defined by beginning and ending sounds and fingerpointing becomes more exact. Children's early letter name–alphabetic writing provides evidence of this understanding as illustrated in Figure 4-2.

Emergent readers are in what Ehri (1997) calls the prealphabetic phase of reading. They may actually learn to identify a few words such as their name and the names of friends and families, and they might identify signs in their environment, but their strategy is to look for nonalphabetic cues such as the shape of a stop sign. They may call out the name of a favorite fast food restaurant when they recognize its logo or identify a large retail store because it starts with a big red *K*, but they are not systematic in their selection of any particular cue. During the emergent stage, children lack an understanding of the alphabetic principle or show only the beginning of this understanding.

FIGURE 4-1   Late Emergent Writing Without Word Boundaries

"I like housekeeping"

Emergent Writing

The child's first task as a writer is to discover that scribbling can represent something and, thereafter, to differentiate drawing from writing and representation from communication. The child must come to realize that a drawing of a flower does not actually say "flower." Writing is necessary to communicate the complete message. The top row of Figure 4-3 presents a progression of drawings and their accompanying utterances that show a clear differentiation between picture and writing.

FIGURE 4-2   Early Letter Name–Alphabetic Spelling with Word Boundaries

"I like housekeeping"

FIGURE 4-3   The Evolution of Emergent Writing

Random Marks	Representational Drawing	Drawing Distinct from Writing
	"This is my sister."	"A flower for my Mom."
Mock Linear or Letter Like	Symbol Salad	Partial Phonetic
"A note for Daddy."	"Macaroni"	"cat" / "baby" / "I love you"

There are many similarities between infant talk and emergent writing. When babies learn to talk, they do not begin by speaking in phonemes first, then syllables, words, and finally phrases. In fact, it is quite the opposite. They begin by cooing in phrasal contours, approximating the music of their mother tongue. Likewise, children begin to write by approximating the broader contours of the writing system; they begin with the linear arrangement of print. This kind of pretend writing has been called "mock linear" (Clay, 1975; Harste, Burke, & Woodward, 1983). The bottom row of Figure 4-3 shows the movement from mock linear writing (bottom left) to real writing (bottom right) that uses letters to represent speech sounds. When babies move into what is conventionally recognized as baby talk, they give up their melodious cooing to concentrate on smaller segments, usually stressed syllables. "Dat!" is hardly as fluid as cooing "Ah-ha-ah-ha," but these awkward exclamations will be smoothed out in time. Likewise, global knowledge of writing and letterforms is temporarily abandoned as children concentrate their attention on the specifics of letter formation and the representation of the most salient sounds of speech. Such attention sometimes leads children to spit out parts of words on paper, often using single consonants to stand for entire syllables as in Figure 4-1. The message is often indecipherable because children do not understand the purpose or need for spaces and they tend to run their syllables and words together on paper.

Here is where the similarity between spoken and written language breaks down. Humans do not actually talk in words, and there is no such thing as an isolated phoneme. Both words and phonemes are artifacts of print and do not naturally coincide with acoustic realities such as syllables. Children become aware of them as a consequence of learning to read and write. The concepts of word and phoneme must be taught; both will emerge as children gradually acquire the alphabetic principle and coordinate the units of speech with printed units on the page.

THE EMERGENT STAGE: FROM SCRIBBLES TO INVENTED SPELLING

There are dramatic changes as children develop across the emergent stage that can be characterized as early, middle, and late emergent writing behaviors. Like emergent reading, early emergent writing is largely pretend. Regardless of most children's culture or where they live, this pretend writing occurs spontaneously wherever writing is encouraged, modeled, and incorporated into play (Ferreiro & Teberosky, 1982). In the early emergent stage, children learn to hold a pencil, marker, or crayon and to make marks on paper (or windows, walls, or floors!) These marks are best described as scribbles that lack directionality and may not serve a communicative function. Sometime during this early emergent stage, scribbles evolve into more representational drawings and children learn that print is distinct from drawings, as can be seen in the right-hand box of the top row of Figure 4-3. This frame shows the drawing as distinct from the writing, which is assigned a specific message: "A flower for my Mom."

In the middle emergent stage, children begin to approximate the most global contours of the writing system: the top-to-bottom and linear arrangement. They experiment with letter-like forms that resemble the separate circles and lines of manuscript writing or the connected loops of cursive. As letters of the alphabet and numbers are learned, they begin to show up in random strings or a "symbol salad," as in the spelling of *macaroni* in Figure 4-3. The child may identify his or her efforts as writing and announce that it is a "note for Daddy." Parents may be challenged at this point when children come to them with their pretend writing and say, "Read this to me, Mommy" or "What does this say?" What is exciting and significant is that young children recognize that print carries a message that can be read by others.

By the end of the emergent stage, children are beginning to use letters to represent speech sounds in a systematic way, as shown in the last box in Figure 4-3. These partially phonetic invented spellings represent a number of critical insights and skills. First, to invent a spelling, children must know some letters—not all, but enough to get started. Second, children must know how to form or write some of the letters they know. Third, children must know that letters represent sounds. Again, they do not have to know all of the letter sounds; indeed, if they know the names of the letters, they might use those as substitutes. Fourth, children must attend to the sounds within syllables and match those sound segments to letters. This ability to divide syllables into the smallest units of sound is called **phonemic awareness.** To invent a spelling, a child must have some degree of phonemic awareness and some knowledge of letter sounds. By the time children gain insight into all four of these aspects of sound and print, they are at the end of the emergent stage. See the table on the next page.

As emergent readers learn their letters and sounds, they use their alphabetic knowledge to represent the units of sound they perceive. If children are able to discern only the most **salient,** or outstanding, sound, then they usually will put down only one letter: *D* for *dog,* *S* for *mouse,* *N* for *and,* or *N* for *mitten.* Until terms about language segments like "beginning sound" are sorted out, emergent children rely on the feel of their mouths as they analyze the speech stream. Say the phrase "once upon a time" aloud. Say it again while paying attention to what your tongue and lips are doing. The tongue touches another part of the mouth only for the /s/ sound of *once,* the /n/ sound of *upon,* and the /t/ sound of *time.* The lips touch each other twice: for the /p/ sound in the middle of *upon* and for the /m/ sound at the end of *time.* It is not surprising, therefore, that Lee wrote "once upon a time" as 1SPNTM in Figure 4-4. Late emergent spellers pay attention to those tangible points of an utterance where one part of the mouth touches another, or to the most forcefully articulated sounds that make the most vibration or receive the most stress. If some letters are known, they will be matched to these salient sounds accordingly. When literacy development has occurred in a balanced environment, phonemic awareness and the ability to invent a spelling go hand in hand, so much so that it is

Characteristics of Emergent Spelling

	What Students Do Correctly	What Students Use but Confuse	What Is Absent
Early Emergent 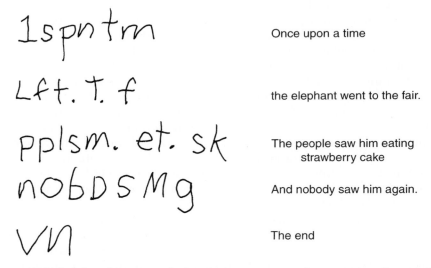	Mark on the page Hold the writing implement	Drawing and scribbling for writing	Letters Directionality
Middle Emergent	Linear movement across page Clear distinction between writing and drawing Letter-like forms	Letters and numbers Random strings of letters Directionality	Phonemic awareness Sound–symbol correspondences
Late Emergent SKP for *housekeeping* D for *duck*	Consistent directionality Use of letters Some letter–sound matches	Substitutions of letters that sound, feel, and look alike: B/P, D/B Salient phonemes	Complete sound–symbol correspondences Spacing between words

FIGURE 4-4   Lee's Elephant Story

1spntrn   Once upon a time

Lft. T. f   the elephant went to the fair.

pplsm. et. sk   The people saw him eating
                                     strawberry cake

nobDSMg   And nobody saw him again.

VN   The end

possible to track the development of phonemic awareness by counting the number of sounds represented in student's invented spelling.

Figure 4-4 illustrates Lee's phonemic analysis of words and phrases in her elephant story relative to her knowledge of the alphabet and letter sounds. As children begin to achieve a concept of word, they become more able to pay attention to sounds that correspond to the beginning and the end of word units. Such children will usually put down one or two letters, as in *F* for *fair* or *TM* for *time*. If children know how to write their letters, their invented spelling will reflect their degree of phonemic awareness. As the spellings in Lee's elephant story depict, the phonemes represented are always the most salient, but the most salient are not always at the beginning of a word; she spelled *went* as *T* and *him* as *M*. Notice her confusion with word boundaries and how she tries to help herself with periods.

The goal of phonemic awareness instruction for emergent readers is to help them classify the sounds they know into categories that coincide with printed word boundaries—beginnings and ends. When letter names are coordinated with word boundaries in a consistent fashion, the student is no longer an emergent speller. Spelling that honors word boundaries consistently is early letter name–alphabetic.

Teaching students the names of the alphabet letters and the sounds they represent is absolutely essential during the emergent stage, but children do not have to get them all straight before they begin to read and write. As with oral language learning, written language learning involves forming and testing hypotheses as new bits of knowledge are perceived and internalized; and, like the incessant chatter of the growing child, it is the extensive practice in approximating the writing system that extends the child's reach. Pretend writing and pretend reading must come first, and as they evolve, real reading and real writing are likely to follow (Chomsky, 1971; Goulandris, 1992).

Early Literacy Learning and Instruction

To move from emergent to beginning reading, students must have many opportunities to see and experiment with written language. They must see their own spoken language transcribed into print, and they must be supported in making the speech-to-print match by choral recitation and fingerpoint memory reading. They must be encouraged to write, even if this writing is little more than scribbles. The most important condition for emergent literacy to blossom is the opportunity to practice, and children's approximations must be encouraged and celebrated.

Emergent children will write, or pretend to write, well before they learn to read, provided they are encouraged to do so. The trick in developmental literacy instruction is how to give that encouragement. The mere act of leaving one's mark on paper has been called the "fundamental graphic act" (Gibson & Yonas, 1968)—an irresistible act of self-fulfillment. As the teacher, you have to do little more than provide immediate and ready access to implements of writing (markers, crayons, pencils, chalk) and provide a visible role model by drawing and writing yourself. Creating a conducive environment for writing also helps: a grocery store play area where grocery lists are drawn and labeled; a restaurant where menus are offered and orders are written; a block center with cardboard shapes for making signs; a writing center with a variety of paper, alphabet stamps, and markers. Outfitted and supported accordingly, writing will happen spontaneously without formal instruction and well before children can spell or properly compose (Strickland & Morrow, 1989).

Emergent reading instruction consists of modeling the reading process as teachers read aloud from enlarged texts like big books and charts. This is accompanied by talk about where one begins to read on the page and where one goes after that, and demonstrations of left-to-right directionality and the return sweep at the end of each line: conventions of written language known as *concepts of print*. Of course, all the talk and demonstration in the world will not substitute for hands-on practice. Early literacy instruction includes lots of guided practice with fingerpointing to familiar texts. In the process, pretend or memory reading gradually becomes real reading.

The reading materials best suited for emergent readers are simple predictable books, familiar nursery rhymes, poems, songs, jump rope jingles, and children's own talk written down. Familiarity with songs and rhymes helps bridge the gap between speech and print and cultivates the sense that what can be sung or recited can be written or read. Recording children's own language in the form of picture captions and dictated **language experience** stories also nurtures the notion that print is talk written down. The ownership that comes with having one's own experiences recorded in print is a powerful incentive to explore the world of written language.

Useful techniques for fostering early literacy development include rebuilding familiar rhymes and jingles with sentence strips in pocket charts and matching word cards to individual words on the sentence strips as an explicit way to direct attention to words in print. Sorting objects, pictures, and words by beginning sounds draws attention to letter–sound correspondences. But reading and rereading are the techniques of choice.

As is true with all of the stages of word knowledge described in this book, the best way to create a reader is to make reading happen, even if it is just pretend.

Through these activities, the word study instruction for the emergent reader must aim toward the development of five main components of the learning-to-read process:

1. Vocabulary growth and concept development
2. Phonological awareness
3. Alphabet knowledge
4. Letter–sound knowledge
5. Concept of word in print

These five components constitute a comprehensive "diet" for early literacy learning and instruction (Invernizzi, 2002). If all five components are addressed on a daily basis, no matter how far along the emergent continuum a child may be, conventional reading and writing should inevitably follow.

COMPONENTS OF EARLY LITERACY LEARNING

This section examines the wondrous ways in which emergent spellers analyze speech and apply it to what they know about print. Bear in mind, however, that emergent understandings of how units of speech correspond to units of print operate within a larger context of concept, language, and vocabulary growth (Snow, 1983). For this reason, we will first look at emergent vocabulary growth and concept development. Then we will describe the other components of early literacy learning.

Vocabulary Growth and Concept Development

A flourishing child who is 4 or 5 years old has acquired a working oral vocabulary of over 5,000 words (Justice, 2006) and most children have learned an average of 13,000 by the time they enter kindergarten. The child has mastered the basic subject–verb–object word order of the English language, and may take great delight in the silliness of word sounds and meanings. Many children have learned to recite the days of the week, and some, the months of the year. But to assume that these children need no further experience with the vocabulary of time is to stunt their conceptual understanding of the larger framework of time—how days, weeks, months, and years relate to one another. Ask some precocious 5-year-olds to name the months of the year, and 9 out of 10 will name the seasons instead. Ask kindergartners to tell you what season of the year December falls in, and many will no doubt tell you "Christmas." These are the answers from children who know the names of the days, the months, and the seasons, but do not fully understand the relationships among them.

Young children use many words whose meanings they do not fully comprehend (Carey, 2001). Their knowledge of words is only partially formed by the information gleaned from their few years of life. To extend their partial understandings of words, and to acquire new word meanings, children must have language experiences, such as conversations and being read to, that allow them to add new information to their existing store of word knowledge.

Language differences.   Children come to school having had very different language experiences (Biemiller & Slonim, 2001). In a classic study, it was estimated that some children had heard three million more words than other children (Hart & Risley, 1995). A well developed vocabulary is an essential part of school success (Cunningham & Stanovich, 2003) and vocabulary instruction needs to be a part of instruction for students at all ages (Biemiller, 2001, 2004). Multiple examples, repeated use, and student interaction are ingredients that are part of vocabulary learning (Beck, McKeown, & Kucan,

2002). There are many ways to encourage children to talk so that they can exercise their vocabularies. Basic concept-development tasks are a surprisingly simple way to provide such experiences, and they are a good way for English learners to be engaged and involved in verbal interactions (Bear & Helman, 2004).

Concept sorts.   The human mind appears to work by using a compare-and-contrast categorization system to develop concepts and attributes. The sorting activities appropriate for emergent readers build on and reinforce this natural tendency. By stacking the deck with familiar objects, ideas, animals, and things, teachers can devise sorting tasks to help children differentiate and expand existing concepts and labels for those concepts.

One bright 5-year-old knew about tables, chairs, sofas, beds, ovens, refrigerators, microwaves, and blenders; but in her mind, these were all undifferentiated "things in a house." Simply by sorting these items into two different categories—tables, chairs, sofas, and beds; and refrigerators, ovens, microwaves, and blenders—she was able to differentiate the characteristics of *furniture* from those of *appliances*. In this way her concept of things in a house was refined to include new concepts and vocabulary.

Read-alouds play a critical role in the development of vocabulary and concepts. Books provide background knowledge that some children may not have experienced. For example, books about seasons, weather, transportation, and how seeds grow provide basic vocabulary and information, both of which are essential to comprehending written texts. After listening to Ruth Heller's book, *Chickens Aren't the Only Ones,* children might be provided picture cards to sort into groups: birds, mammals, and reptiles. In this way children build upon a simple conceptual understanding of where eggs come from to include other attributes of the animal kingdom. Concept sorts based on daily life experiences and information gleaned from books develop and expand children's understandings of their world and their language to talk about it. For example, during a unit on animals, a teacher could introduce children to a concept sort such as the one shown in Figure 4-5.

The concept sorts described in the activities section of this chapter are all variations on the theme of categorization tasks. In addition to basic sorting, concept-development activities are generally followed by draw-and-label or cut-and-paste procedures. As always, we recommend having children write at every possible opportunity during or following the concept sorts. As a culminating activity for a unit on animals, one teacher helped her children create their own books in which they drew pictures of their favorite animals. Many of her children were able to label these pictures or write briefly about the animals with either pretend writing or invented spelling. Her children's efforts ranged from scribbles and random letters to readable approximations found in the next step of development such as I LIK THE LINS N TGRS.

The pictures used in concept sorts may be words that are new to students, and they need to be directly taught. It will be important to talk about the meaning of the word and to use the words repeatedly each time they are used in sorting. For example, when sorting birds and animals, it may be a good time to stop and talk about the meaning of the word *claw* or *hoof*. English learners will need to learn the names of more common objects, like *cup*. Students are requested to say the names of the pictures as they sort, and this provides additional practice saying and hearing others pronounce new words.

Adults need to engage children in conversation and they should also encourage children to talk to each other to increase their verbal activity and the number of times they will use new terms. There are many strategies to use to introduce, contextualize, and exercise vocabulary. When new words are introduced, children should be asked to repeat them and say them in phrases and sentences: "The little bear *hustled* after

FIGURE 4-5   Concept Sort with Farm Animals and Zoo Animals

his mother (from *Blueberries for Sal* by Robert McCloskey). Say the word *hustle*. What do you think it means? Would you hustle to catch the bus? Would you hustle fast or hustle slow? Tell your partner how you would fill in this sentence: I hustled to _____."
Beck, McKeown, and Kucan (2002) describe how to plan repeated exposure to words in different contexts to help students learn the meaning and use of new vocabulary.

An activity described by McCabe (1996) is "tell a story to get a story." The teacher tells a simple two- to three-sentence story and then asks the children if they know a similar story: "Has anything like that happened to you?" Children then tell their own story to the teacher or a peer.

Phonological Awareness

The ability to pay attention to, identify, and reflect on various sound segments of speech is known as **phonological awareness**. It is the umbrella term for a range of understandings about speech sounds, including syllables, rhyme, and a sense of alliteration. Phonemic awareness is a subcategory of phonological awareness that is quite difficult to achieve. It refers to the ability to identify and reflect on the smallest units of sound: individual phonemes. The ability to segment *sit* or *thick* into three sounds (/s/-/i/-/t/ or /th/-/i/-/ck/) is an example of phonemic awareness. Phonemic awareness develops gradually over time and has a reciprocal relationship to learning about print and the alphabetic code. Children who have phonemic awareness learn to read more easily than children who do not. At the same time, instruction in alphabet recognition, letter sounds, and concept of word increases a child's phonemic awareness (Morris, Bloodgood, Lomax, & Perney, 2003).

Children can hear and use individual phonemes easily at a tacit level—they can talk and can understand when others talk to them. Bringing tacit, subconscious awareness of individual phonemes to the surface to be examined consciously and explicitly is a critical goal of emergent literacy instruction. Conscious awareness is necessary to learn an alphabetic writing system because letters represent individual sounds.

A certain amount of phonological awareness is critical to reading success, and participation in phonological awareness activities has a positive influence on beginning reading, especially when these activities coincide with word study instruction (Ball & Blachman, 1988). Newer research suggests that phonological awareness develops concurrently with students' growing understanding of how the spelling system works to represent sound (Stahl & McKenna, 2001). While children do need a certain amount of phonological awareness to grasp the alphabetic nature of English, awareness of beginning sounds will get them started. Thereafter, phonological awareness, word recognition, decoding, and spelling will continue to develop in a symbiotic fashion. Growth in one area stimulates growth in another (Ehri, 2006; Perfetti, Beck, Bell, & Hughes, 1987).

Phonological awareness activities in preschool and primary classrooms can be fun oral and written language activities that benefit all students. Classroom teachers should include some of the instructional components that have been identified as successful and effective (Adams, Foorman, Lundberg, & Beeler, 1998; Blachman, 1994; Lundberg, Frost, & Peterson, 1988; Smith et al., 1995). Students should work with sound units that closely approximate their level of word knowledge and incorporate letters and print when working with sounds. Early emergent readers need to participate in phonological awareness activities that focus attention on syllables and rhyming words while middle emergent readers learn alliteration by sorting pictures that begin with the same sound.

By the end of the emergent stage, children should learn to segment **onsets** (initial consonant sounds) and **rimes** (the vowel and what follows). In the word *mat, m* is the onset and *at* is the rime; in *track, tr* is the onset and *ack* is the rime.) Onsets and rimes are more accessible to emergent readers than are individual phonemes within words (Goswami & Mead, 1992). The ability to separate an onset from a rime and to match it with other onsets that begin with the same sound is the beginning of phoneme awareness (Kaderavek & Justice, 2004). Matching that onset to a letter of the alphabet enables emergent readers to locate words in context and to begin to spell (Ehri, 1998; Murray, 1998; Morris et al., 2003).

FIGURE 4-6 Odd-One-Out with Rhyming Words

Rhymes and jingles. Rhyme awareness activities are an easy, natural way for children to play with words and to begin to focus on speech sounds. Songs, jingles, nursery rhymes, and poems fill children's ears with the sounds of rhyme. Many children develop a sense of rhyme easily, whereas others need more structured activities that draw their attention specifically to rhyming words. The easiest activity is to talk about the rhyming words in favorite and familiar books and poems. Some books and poems lend themselves to an activity in which you simply pause and let the children supply the second rhyming word in a couplet. When picture books such as *Oh, A-Hunting We Will Go* or *Is Your Mama a Llama?* by Deborah Guarina are used, children have the support of the illustrations to help them out. Some other favorite rhyming books are listed in the activities section at the end of this chapter.

Rhyming book read-alouds can be followed by picture sorts for rhymes. For example, a rhyming sort extension to *Oh, A-Hunting We Will Go* is to match up pictures of animals and the places they will go (fox/box, mouse/house, goat/boat, etc.) To make it easier for beginners, lay out just two pictures that rhyme and one that does not. This odd-one-out setup shown in Figure 4-6 enables children to identify more readily the two rhyming pictures. They have only to pick up an animal and the rhyming object.

Songs are naturally full of rhythm and rhyme and hold great appeal for children. Several songs recorded by Raffi, a popular singer and songwriter for children, are particularly well suited for language play. Rhyme is featured prominently in the song "Willoughby Wallaby Woo" from the taped collection *Singable Songs for the Very Young* (Raffi, 1976). The song features a rhyme starting with *W* for everyone's name. After hearing the song played several times, children can begin to sing it using the names of their classmates around the circle, perhaps passing along a stuffed elephant to add to the fun. The song can be changed to focus on alliteration by holding up a particular letter to insert in front of every word. *B,* for example, would result in "Billaby Ballaby Boo," and *F* would produce "Fillaby Fallaby Foo."

As children become more adept at listening for rhymes, they can play a variety of categorization and matching games. Traditional games such as Bingo, Lotto, and Concentration are always winners in which picture cards are matched to other picture cards that rhyme. More ideas for rhyming games and activities can be found later in this chapter.

Alliteration and beginning sounds. **Alliteration** refers to a series of two or more words that begin with the same sound. Activities that play with alliteration focus children's attention on the beginning sounds that mark word boundaries in print. This awareness of beginning sounds supports children as they learn to separate the speech stream into individual words. A number of activities help promote children's understanding of beginning sounds, starting with ABC books such as *Dr. Seuss's ABC*, which celebrates alliteration in the famous Seuss style.

Beginning-sound segmentation games can be played with puppets or stuffed animals that have a funny way of talking. The puppet teaches the children how to isolate the initial phoneme from the remaining portion of the word. The children are then asked to repeat what the puppet said. The children get to manipulate the puppet themselves as they segment words given to them by the teacher. For example, Pat the Puppet first says "p–ig," and the students repeat by saying "p–ig." Then the teacher says "pick" and asks the students to say the word like Pat the Puppet would say it in "puppet talk." The children respond with "p–ick" (Treiman, 1985).

Riddles such as "I Spy" or "I'm Thinking of Something" can be used here, too. The hints given by the teacher should accentuate the initial sound. "This thing I'm thinking of begins with /mmmmm/. This thing is small and gray. It is an animal." As the children respond "mouse" or "mole," the teacher asks them to exaggerate the beginning sound. As children become proficient at playing this game, they create their own riddles. Always encourage students to emphasize the beginning sounds of the words they guess as the answer to the riddles.

Children must become aware that speech can be divided into smaller segments of sound before they will advance in literacy and they must also learn some of the terminology used to talk about these sounds. Without this insight, instruction in phonics or letter–sound correspondences will have little success. Children have no trouble hearing sounds, but directions such as "Listen for the first sound" may mystify them. In response to the question "What sound does *cow* start with?" one puzzled child tentatively replied, "Moo?" Without a stable concept of word, "first" is a relative notion. Phonological awareness activities at the emergent level should help students attend to sounds and learn to label and categorize these sounds in various ways.

Alliteration or beginning-sound awareness is further developed as children sort pictures by beginning sound under a corresponding letter, an activity that will be described shortly. At this point, oral language activities, designed to teach phonological awareness, cross over into the learning of letter–sound correspondences and this is known as **phonics.** Phonological awareness does not have to precede or follow alphabet knowledge or other components of emergent literacy instruction. Awareness of sounds is heightened by print, and thus is a reciprocal, ongoing by-product of the learning-to-read process. Although phonological awareness is essential, phonological awareness activities need not be conducted as isolated tasks, nor do they need to take up a lot of time. According to some estimates, an entire year of phonemic awareness instruction should not exceed 20 hours (Armbruster, Lehr, & Osborn, 2001).

Assessing Phonological Awareness

The research on the development of phonological awareness identifies two sound units significantly related to reading outcomes: (a) rhyme awareness, and (b) individual phoneme awareness (Swank, 1991; Yopp, 1988). The pictures in Appendix C may be used to assess these two categories of speech sounds by using a matching or "odd-one-out" procedure. For example, after being presented with pictures of a mop, a top, and a bed, children can be asked to find the one that doesn't belong—"the odd one out." Alternatively, using a matching task format for beginning sounds, children can be asked to pick up the ones that begin with the same sound after being given picture choices such as a bed, a ship, and a boat. Phonological awareness tasks similar to these have been scientifically validated by Invernizzi and her colleagues (Invernizzi, Juel, Swank, & Meier, 2006) with thousands of children screened in Virginia with PALS assessments at the preschool and kindergarten levels.

Alphabet Knowledge

Among the reading readiness skills that are traditionally studied, the one that appears to be the strongest predictor of later reading success on its own is letter naming (Snow, Burns, & Griffin, 1998). There is a great deal to learn about the alphabet. Letters have names, a set sequence, sounds, upper and lower case forms, and they must be written in particular ways. Directional orientation is vital. In the three-dimensional world, a chair is a chair whether you approach it from the front or from the back, whether you approach it from the left or from the right. Not so with letters: A *b* is a *b* and a *d* is a *d*. Print is one of the few things in life where direction makes a difference.

Many letter names share similar sounds. The letter name *B* (bee), for example, shares the vowel sound of the letter name *E*, as do *P*, *D*, *T*, *C*, *G*, *V*, and *Z*. There are visual similarities as well. There are verticals with circles in *p*, *q*, *d*, and *b*. Verticals and horizontals intersect in *T*, *L*, *H*, *F*, *E*, and *I*. Intersecting diagonals are shared by *K*, *A* (which also share parts of letter name sounds), *M*, *N*, *V*, *W*, *X*, and *Z*. Even movements overlap in the formation of letters: the up-down-up-down motion is basic to *M*, *N*, *W*, and *V*; a circular movement is required of *B*, *C*, *D*, *G*, *O*, *P*, *Q*, *R*, *U*, and *S*; and the direction of these movements hinges critically on where one begins on the page. (See Clay, 1975 and Ehri & Roberts, 2006 for a detailed discussion of the acquisition of distinctive features of letters.)

Students in the emergent stage appear to practice these distinctive features on their own, provided they are given a model. First efforts at a global level mimic the kinds of letters children know best, such as the letters in their own name. Meanwhile, letters that share distinctive visual features will continue to be confused for some time; *N* may be mistaken for *Z*, *E* for *F*, and so forth. Provided with the incentive to practice and the means to do so, emergent children will rehearse letter names, practice letter writing, and match uppercase to lowercase with delight.

Learning the names of the letters is an important first step toward learning the sounds associated with the letters. Most of the letters have names that include a sound commonly associated with it and can serve as a mnemonic device for remembering the sound. *B* (bee), *K* (kay), and *Z* (zee) have their sounds at the beginnings of their names, while *F* (eff), *L* (ell), and *S* (ess) have their sounds at the end. The names of the vowels are their long sounds. Only *H* (aitch), *W* (doubleyou), and the consonant *Y* (wie) have no beginning-sound association and these letters are often the most difficult to learn. Letter names serve as the first reference point many children use when writing and explain some of the interesting invented spelling they create during the letter name–alphabetic stage discussed more in the next chapter.

Most mainstream, middle-class children take five years to acquire this alphabet knowledge at home and in preschool. Magnetic letters on the refrigerator door, alphabetic puzzles, and commercial alphabet games are staples in many middle-class homes (Adams, 1990). Truly advantaged youngsters also have attentive parents at the kitchen table modeling letter formation and speech segmentation as they encourage their child to write a grocery list or a note to Grandma using invented spelling. Yet many of these children also require the direct instruction provided by formal schooling to fully understand the complexity of the alphabet. The best way to share five years of accumulated alphabet knowledge with those who have not been privy to this information is to teach it directly, in as naturalistic, fun, and gamelike a manner as possible (Delpit, 1988). The word study activities described in the next section are designed to do just that.

Alphabet games and matching activities. The alphabet is learned the same way that concepts and words for concepts are learned—through active exploration of the relationships between letter names, the sounds of the letter names, their visual characteristics, and the motor movement involved in their formation. By noting the salient, stable characteristics of *B* in many contexts and across many different fonts, sizes, shapes, and textures, a rudimentary concept of *B* is formed (see Figure 4-7). Every new encounter with *B* adds new attributes to the concept of the letter.

FIGURE 4-7   Different Print Styles

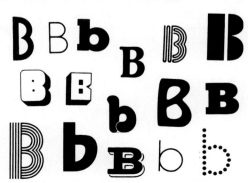

Many alphabet activities begin with the child's name, building it with letter tiles, cutting it out of play dough, or matching it letter for letter with a second set. Writing or copying their own name and the names of other family members or friends is alluring to emergent writers and is a great introduction to the alphabet as well as to writing. Letters take on personalities: *K* is Katie's letter and *T* is Tommy's letter.

The alphabet games and activities described at the end of this chapter are designed to develop all aspects of alphabet knowledge including letter naming, letter recognition (both uppercase and lowercase), letter writing, and letter sounds. Many traditional games such as Bingo and Concentration can be adapted to learn the alphabet. A writing component can be added to many of these games to incorporate letter formation, an important and often neglected component of early literacy instruction.

Assessing alphabet knowledge.   To determine how much instruction is needed in the area of learning letters, teachers need to use a variety of tasks. Students may be asked to point to and recite the letters in order as a first step. Watch out for how they handle LMNOP: sometimes it becomes one letter! Both capital and lowercase letters should also be presented in random order to assess letter recognition. Letter production is easily assessed by calling letters aloud, in or out of order, for students to write. According to research conducted with hundreds of thousands of kindergarteners in the Commonwealth of Virginia, kindergarteners should be able to recognize and name a minimum of 12 lowercase letters (presented in random order) in the fall of the year, and nearly all of them by the end of kindergarten (Invernizzi, Juel, Swank, & Meier, 2006).

Letter–Sound Knowledge

During the emergent stage, children learn their letters, attend to speech sounds, and begin to make connections between letters and sounds. Toward the end of the emergent stage, many children will begin producing partial phonetic spellings that contain one or two letters for each syllable (see Figure 4-3). Picture-sorting by beginning sounds secures these tentative efforts and moves children along in acquiring more knowledge of letter–sound correspondences through a game-like, manipulative phonics activity.

Some teachers choose *M* and *S* for students' first consonant contrast because both letters have **continuant sounds** that can be isolated and elongated without undue distortion (*mmmmoon* and *ssssun*). The sounds also feel very different in the mouth in terms of how they are articulated, which makes it easier for children to judge the categories while sorting. The sound for *B*, /b/, cannot be elongated or isolated without adding a vowel to it (buh), but it is still fairly easy to learn, perhaps because it has a distinctive feel as the lips press together. However, to contrast *B* and *P* in an early sort would be confusing because they are both articulated the same way (Purcell, 2002). The only difference between them is that the sound for /b/ causes the vocal chords to vibrate and /p/ does not. Try placing two fingers on your larynx and feel the difference in **voiced** /b/ and **unvoiced** /p/.

Groups of letter sounds that share the same place of articulation in the mouth are shown in each row of Table 4-1. Read across each row and then down each column,

TABLE 4-1   *Pronunciation Chart of Consonant Sounds*

Unvoiced	Voiced	Nasals	Other	Place of Articulation
p	b	m		lips together
wh	w			lips rounded
f	v			teeth and lips
th (the)	th (thin)			tip of tongue and teeth
t	d	n	l	tip of tongue and roof of mouth
s	z		r	tongue and roof of mouth
sh			y	sides of tongue and teeth
ch	j			sides of tongue and roof of mouth
k	g	ng		back of tongue and throat
h				no articulation—breathy sound

paying attention to how the sounds are produced. Understanding something about articulation may seem unnecessarily complicated, but it explains so many of the interesting things children do in their invented spellings during the emergent and letter name–alphabetic stages. Use the chart to see the logic in the invented spelling JP for *chip,* VN for *fan,* and PD for *pet.* In each case the substitutions vary only because one is voiced and the other is unvoiced. Otherwise, they are articulated exactly the same way.

Knowledge of articulation also helps teachers make decisions about setting up picture sorts. The letters in each row will feel very much alike and are best not contrasted in the very first letter-sound sorts. Remember the sixth principle of word study: Begin with obvious contrasts!

English language learners will be unfamiliar with many of the sounds of English and they will substitute sounds and letters closest to their primary languages and alphabets. Many English learners will not articulate some sounds for awhile, but their substitutions are logical. For example, Spanish speakers may use the letter v to represent the /b/ sound. The logic behind the misspellings of English learners are discussed in Chapter 2 and in more detail in Chapter 5.

Guidelines for beginning sound picture sorts.   There are a number of other things to keep in mind when organizing sorts for beginning letter-sounds.

1. *Start with meaningful text.* Choose several sounds to contrast that represent key words from a familiar rhyme, patterned book (such as *Oh, A-Hunting We Will Go*), or dictation. One advantage of teacher-directed word study over packaged programs is that teachers can integrate phonics and the variety of printed materials used in emergent classrooms.

2. *Make sorts easier or harder as needed.* Start with two obvious contrasts, then add one or two for up to four categories. Look for fast and accurate picture sorting before moving on. Be ready to drop back to fewer categories if a child has difficulty.

3. *Use a key picture and a letter as headers.* Children should associate the letter and the sound. The headers may be letters or words selected from familiar text. Suggested key pictures can be found on the sound boards in Appendix B. Whatever key word you use, be consistent and use the same one every time.

4. *Begin with teacher-directed sorts.* Discuss both the sound and the letter name, and model the placement of two or three pictures in each category. Be explicit about why you sort the way you do. Say, for example, "Foot, fffoot, ffffox. *Foot* and *fox* start with the same sound, *ffff.* I will put *foot* under the letter *F.*" Over time, as children catch on to what it is they are to attend to, you can use fewer directives. Figure 4-8 shows how this sort would look after several pictures are sorted. Pictures to use for sorting can be found in Appendix C. These can be enlarged to use for group modeling.

5. *Use sets of pictures that are easy to name and sort.* Introduce the pictures to be sure that children know what to call them. Use pictures that are easy to identify and do not start with consonant blends or digraphs. Single-syllable words are better than two-syllable words because they have fewer sounds that need attention.

6. *Correct mistakes on the first sort but allow errors to wait on subsequent sorts.* Show children how to check their sorts by naming the pictures down the columns, emphasizing the beginning sounds. Then ask if there are any pictures that need to be changed. Ask children to check their own work using the same process and praise them when they find

FIGURE 4-8   Sound Sort for Comparing *B* and *F*

their own errors. If they do not, prompt them by saying, "There is a picture in this row that needs to be changed. Can you find it?"

7. *Vary the group sorting.* Start by putting out all the pictures face up and let children choose one that they feel confident in naming and sorting correctly. Ask them to name the picture and the letter by saying "_____ begins with the _____ sound and goes under the letter _____." Another time pass out the pictures and call on children to come up and sort the card they were given. Then turn the pictures face down in a stack or spread them out on the floor and let children turn over the picture they will sort. Children enjoy the anticipation of not knowing which picture they will get.

8. *Plan plenty of time for individual practice.* After group modeling and discussion, put sets of pictures in centers or create copies of picture sets for children to cut apart for more sorting. Sheets of pictures for sorting can be created by copying pictures from this book, cutting them apart, and pasting them in a mixed-up fashion on a template.

9. *Plan follow-up activities.* Cut and paste, draw and label, and word hunts through familiar chart stories, nursery rhymes, or little books are helpful follow-up activities. They require children to recognize, or recall, the same beginning sounds, and to judge whether they fit the category.

10. *Encourage invented spelling.* In the process of inventing spellings, children exercise their developing phonemic awareness and letter–sound knowledge in a meaningful activity (NRP, 2000; Snow, Burns & Griffin, 1998; Clarke, 1988).

To get students started, demonstrate how to use letters to represent the sounds in words in group activities like The Morning Message described in the activity section. Asking young children to "write a story" may loom as an impossible task when their concept of a story is a picture book! Asking them to label their drawings or to write just a sentence about something is a good way to get writing started.

Assessing letter sound knowledge. Observing children's efforts to write using invented spelling is a good way to determine if they are matching letters to sounds. The Emergent Class Record found on the Assessment CD-ROM will help you analyze children's writing across the emergent stage. A simple five-word spelling assessment such the Kindergarten Spelling Inventory (KSI), also found on the CD-ROM, is particularly appropriate for late emergent spellers. You might also use the first few words from the Primary Spelling Inventory (PSI). Longitudinal research indicates that kindergarten children should be able to provide at least four letter sounds in the fall of the year, and at least 20 letter sounds in the spring. Students who know fewer than this will need additional instruction to succeed in formal reading instruction (Invernizzi, Justice, Landrum, & Booker, 2005). Letter sounds can also be assessed in a matching task in which children circle the picture that starts with the sound prompted by a particular letter.

Concept of Word in Print

All the phonological awareness, alphabet, and letter–sound knowledge in the world will not help children learn to read if they cannot match what they say to the words on the page. Emergent readers do not have a concept of word in print. What they point to as they recite may not coincide with printed word units at all. Like the babbling infant imitating the intonation contours of speech, the preliterate child points in a rhythmic approximation of the memorized text with little attention to word boundaries or even, perhaps, direction on the page. Prior to achieving a concept of word, in text emergent children, as well as emergent adults, have great difficulty identifying individual phonemes within words (Morais, Cary, Alegria, & Bertelson, 1979). There is an interaction between alphabetic knowledge, the ability to match speech to print, and phonemic awareness (Flanigan, 2006; Morris, Bloodgood, Lomax, & Perney, 2003; Tunmer, 1991).

FIGURE 4-9   Trying to Match Voice to Print

Through the teachers' demonstrations, children's fingerpointing behaviors change. Left-to-right movement becomes habitualized, though children may not routinely use letter or word units to guide their tracking. As white spaces are noted and much talk about words is introduced, children begin to track rhythmically across the text, pointing to words for each stressed beat. For example, when tracking the traditional five-word ditty "Sam, Sam, the baker man," they may point four times: Sam/Sam/the-baker/man. An article (*the, a, an*) may be treated as part of the noun that follows it.

As children become aware that print has something to do with sound, their fingerpointing becomes more precise and changes from a gross rhythm to a closer match with syllables. This works well for one-syllable words, but not so well for words of two or more syllables. When they track "Sam, Sam, the baker man," they may now point six times: Sam/Sam/the/ba/ker/man. When they pronounce "ker," the second syllable of *baker*, they point to the next word, *man*. Figure 4-9 illustrates the phenomenon of getting off track on two-syllable words.

Later, as children learn the alphabet and the sounds associated with the letters, beginning sounds will anchor the children's fingerpointing more directly to the memorized recitation: They realize that when they say the word *man*, they need to have their finger on a word beginning with an *m*. If they do not, then they must start again. These self-corrections herald the onset of a concept of word in print. Figure 4-10 shows the progression of fingerpointing accuracy in relation to children's writing development during this emergent to early letter name–alphabetic stage of word knowledge.

Fingerpoint reading and tracking words.   The best way for children to achieve a concept of word is to have them point to the words as they reread familiar text and to draw their attention to letters and sounds when they get off track. These texts might be picture captions, dictated experience stories, poems, songs, simple patterned books, or excerpts from a favorite story printed on sentence strips or chart paper. Once these texts become familiar, children can be encouraged to read them from memory, pointing to each word as it is spoken. In this way, children learn how to find the words on the page—an important prerequisite to learning how to identify those words.

Rhythmic texts are particularly appealing but may throw children off in their tracking, and eventually a move to less rhythmic, less predictable texts may be in order (Cathey, 1991). No matter what the source of text, the important thing from a word study point of view is to focus on individual words within the text. Fingerpointing, repeated

Watch the Emergent section of the *Words Their Way* DVD to see kindergarden teacher Anne Noel's Emergent Spellers practice fingerpoint memory reading

FIGURE 4-10   Voice-to-Print Match in Relation to Spelling Development. *Source:* Focus on research: Development of word knowledge as it relates to reading, spelling, and instruction. *Language Arts,* *69,* 6, 444–453. Adapted with permission from Gill (1992).

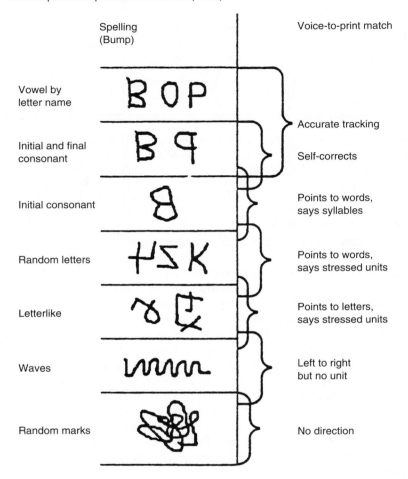

reading, cut-up sentences, and word-card matching activities call attention to words and their letter–sound features.

One of the easiest ways to help children make connections between speech and print is to write captions beneath the pictures they draw. First have the children draw a picture of their favorite toy or Halloween costume and encourage them to include as much detail as possible. While they are finishing their drawings, walk around and ask each child to tell something about his or her picture. Choose a simple phrase or sentence that the child speaks, and write it verbatim beneath the picture (see Figure 4-11). Say each word as you write it, drawing attention to the sounds and letters. Read the caption by pointing to each word. Ask the child to read along with you and then to read it alone while pointing. Later, the child may attempt to reread the caption to a buddy.

Like picture captions, spoken or dictated accounts of children's experiences also help them link speech to print. This approach has traditionally been referred to as the **language experience approach,** or LEA (Hall, 1980; Henderson, 1981; Nessel & Jones, 1981; Stauffer, 1980). Field trips, cooking activities, playground episodes, and class pets provide opportunities for shared experiences in which the children's own

FIGURE 4-11   Drawing with Dictated Caption

language abounds. Students' observations and comments can then be written next to each child's name as shown in Figure 4-12. When the dictation is completed, it should be read and reread many times. In this format, attention to words and to their boundaries will be highlighted in a meaningful context. For example, children may be asked to locate their own name in the dictated account or to find a word that starts with the same letter as their own name. Each child should get his or her own copy of the dictation so he or she can practice fingerpointing while reading chorally in the group and from memory. A second copy of the dictation can be cut apart into sentence strips or individual words to match back to the original.

Assessing concept of word.   Concept of word is easily assessed by asking children individually to point to the words in a familiar piece of text such as a nursery rhyme. "One, Two, Buckle My Shoe" or "Humpty Dumpty" work well because they have words of more than one syllable. Observe how children parse their oral language and how they point to the page using the descriptors in Figure 4-10. You can also ask children to name words that you point to in context: "Can you tell me what this word is?" Or you can ask them to find a word: "Can you show me the word *wall?*" Observe their strategies. Do they reread an entire line to identify the word? Or do they identify it quickly? Probe for their strategies by asking, "How did you find that word?" or "How did you know that word?" They may tell you that the word started with a *W* and then you will know that they are using their developing letter–sound knowledge.

FIGURE 4-12   Dictated Language Experience Chart

> The Fire Station
> Amanda said, "We went to the fire station yesterday."
> Jason said, "We rode on a big orange bus."
> Clint said, "I liked the ladder truck. It was huge!"
> D. J. said, "The firemen told us how to be safe."
> Beth said, "Firemen wear big boots and a mask."

WORD STUDY ROUTINES AND MANAGEMENT

The research in emergent literacy suggests that a comprehensive approach to instruction and early intervention is the most effective (Pressley, 2006). A comprehensive approach includes five essential literacy activities: *Read To, Read With. Write With, Word Study, and Talk With (RRWWT)*. During *read to* time, teachers read aloud literature that offers exposure to new vocabulary and literary language. During *read with* time, children engage in shared reading and rereading of familiar texts. When teachers model how to write by stretching out the sounds in words and matching them to letters, they are *writing with* children and children will, in turn, write for themselves. *Word study* includes direct instruction in phonological awareness, the alphabet, and letter sounds. Finally, a comprehensive program provides students with ample opportunities to *talk with* teachers and peers about the books and experiences they have shared.

Combining these activities into a cohesive RRWWT routine is important so that the activities and materials flow together in a logical way and serve multiple purposes. Recall once more how Mrs. Singh introduced an engaging core book and used it to draw attention to letters and sounds, to offer children practice tracking familiar text, and to sort pictures by rhyme and beginning sounds.

Emergent Literacy Daily Management Plan

As a kindergarten teacher, Terri Purcell developed a management plan with small groups of students. In Ms. Purcell's school, kindergarten class sizes were reduced through parallel scheduling. Half of each class went to "specials," such as PE, art, or music, while the other half stayed with Ms. Purcell for teacher-directed literacy instruction. Scheduling in this way reduced the size of the kindergarten class by half and resulted in a 40-minute block each day. The word study portion is a variation of Betty Lee's plan for emergent to early letter name–alphabetic spellers discussed in Chapter 3.

Literacy instruction began and ended each day with a whole group *read with* lesson in which the children were introduced to new reading materials and they reread familiar books, poems, and jingles. After a word study lesson, students practiced the sort in small groups or buddy pairs. Later the sort was placed in *word study* centers for more practice. This plan is easily adaptable to early intervention programs in which teachers work with small, rotating groups of three to four students. Table 4-2 summarizes the instructional activities.

Alphabet and letter sounds.   Students followed a set routine. They started by pointing to the letters on the alphabet strip as they sang the ABC song. This was often followed by an uppercase and lowercase matching activity, or a beginning sound sort where students sorted picture cards or objects. After they sorted, checked, and reflected, they did cut-and-paste, draw-and-label, or word hunt activities.

Word awareness or concept of word.   To develop concept of word students reread as they pointed to familiar patterned stories, poems, songs, and their individual sentences from group experience charts. Familiar, two-to-four-line rhymes were stored in students' own **personal readers,** discussed in more detail in the next chapter. They also rebuilt these familiar texts with sentence strips and word cards. They then located specific words in context that matched the word cards they had been given. This required them to reread very carefully to note the beginning letter of each word.

Phonological awareness and language play.   To develop phonological awareness students worked with rhyme or alliteration and listened for beginning or ending sounds as

TABLE 4-2   Instructional Activities for Emergent Learners

Word Study Component	Time	Activity	Observations
Alphabet & Letter Sounds	10–12 min	**ABC Tracking:** **Letter Recognition & Letter Sounds:** **Writing for Sounds:**	• Track letters accurately? • Identify letters? • Identify sounds? • Sort correctly? • Sort automatically? • Can write letter/sound?
Concept of Word (COW)	10 min	**Text title:** _____ **Book/Song/Rhyme/Poem** **COW activity:**	• Text was easy/hard to track? # of times reread: _____ • Describe fingerpointing:
Phonological Awareness (PA) & Language Play	10 min	**PA focus:** Syllables/Rhyme/Beginning Sounds/ Ending Sound **Literacy focus:** Word/Sentence/Beginning Sound/ Ending Sound **PA Activity:**	• PA task was easy/hard/just right? • Record observations:
Concept & Vocabulary	15 min	**Book title:** _____ **Targeted Concepts or Semantic Category:** **Targeted Words:** **Activity:**	• Describe students' talk:

Thanks to Mary Fowler and Colleen Muldoon

they listened to a rhyming book, and played games like Concentration, described at the end of this chapter. Ms. Purcell often incorporated print into these phonological awareness activities as she found that a concrete referent helped the children attend to the sounds.

Concepts and vocabulary development.   An important part of Ms. Purcell's daily plan was getting her students to talk and to listen to others talk, so she encouraged lots of oral language interaction. Ms. Purcell involved her students in talk before, during, and after her whole group read-alouds, and she planned activities to extend their conceptual understanding of ideas and vocabulary. She had students talk about the cover of a book, making predictions about what the book would be about. During reading, she paused in selected places where students were asked to evaluate their initial predictions, to make new predictions, and to justify those predictions. Ms. Purcell would also pause to talk about vocabulary that might be new for her students (Juel et al., 2003) and invited questions and comments in the form of an interactive read-aloud (Barrentine, 1996). Concept sorts, like those described in the activity section that follows, often concluded these daily sessions and stimulated meaningful conversation.

Write with activities.   Ms. Purcell often worked with her children to compose group experience stories, letters to classroom visitors, and other forms of writing. She modeled how to segment sentences into words and words into sounds and how to match sounds to letters. Sometimes she wrote for the children and sometimes she would share the pen and invite them to do the writing under her supervision in the form of shared writing (McKenzie, 1985) or interactive writing (Button, Johnson, & Furgeson, 1996). Her students were also encouraged to write for themselves each day in a simple journal and to label drawings.

> Create your own sorts by choosing pictures to drop into the templates available on the CD-ROM.

The word study activities described in the following section are designed to help you establish RRWWT routines and, in so doing, meet the literacy needs of your emergent learners. As you read through them, see which activities might fit in the lesson plan in Table 4-3.

Activities for Emergent Readers

This section provides specific activities arranged by these categories: concept development, phonological awareness, alphabet knowledge, letter–sound knowledge, and concept of word. Within each category the activities are roughly in order of increasing difficulty. However, as noted earlier in this chapter, it is not the case that concept sorts must precede sound awareness, which in turn must precede alphabet. In reality, these develop simultaneously during the emergent years and many activities cut across the categories. Some of the games are generic to all stages of developmental word knowledge as indicated by the adaptable symbol used throughout the book.

> You'll find even more activities for Emergent spellers in the Emergent section of the Word Sorting Application on the *Words Their Way* CD. Create your own activities, games, and manipulatives and print them or save them to your hard drive to use again and again.

CONCEPT DEVELOPMENT

The activities for concept development are all variations on the theme of categorization tasks. In addition to basic sorting tasks, activities are generally followed by draw-and-label and cut-and-paste procedures as discussed in Chapter 3. We recommend having children write at every possible opportunity during or following the concept sorts. Categories and examples can be labeled with invented spellings.

Adaptable
for Other
Stages

Beginning with Children's Books and Concept Sorts 4-1

Books make great beginnings for concept sorts. Here are just a few examples to get you started.

Materials

Gregory the Terrible Eater (by Marjorie Sharmat) tells the story of a young goat who wants to eat real food while his parents constantly urge him to eat "junk food." In this case, the goats' favorite foods really are junk from the local dump: tires, tin cans, old rags, and so on. Collect real objects or pictures of items suggested by the story, for example, fruits, vegetables, newspaper, shoelaces, spaghetti, and pieces of clothing.

Procedures

1. After enjoying this story together, the children can be introduced to a concept sort. Gather the children on the rug, around a large table or pocket chart, and challenge them to group the items by the things Gregory liked and the things he disliked.
2. After deciding where everything should go, ask the students to describe how the things in that category are alike. Decide on a key word or descriptive phrase that will label each category. *Real food* and *junk food* are obvious choices, but your children might be more inventive. As you print the selected key words on cards, model writing for the children. Say each word slowly and talk about the sounds you hear in the words and the letters you need to spell them. Each child in the group might also be given a card and asked to label one of the individual items using invented spelling.
3. Plan time for individual sorting. Keep the items and key word cards available so that children will be free to redo the sort on their own or with a partner at another time, perhaps during free time or center time.
4. Draw-and-label or cut-and-paste activities should follow the sorting. This may be done as a group activity, in which case a section of a bulletin board or a large sheet of paper is divided into two sections and labeled with the key words. If children work independently, each child can be given a sheet of paper folded into two sections. The children might be asked to draw items or they might be given a collection of magazines or catalogs to search for pictures to cut out and paste into the correct category (seed catalogs are great for fruits and vegetables). Again, they can be encouraged to use invented spelling to label the pictures.

Extensions

Gregory the Terrible Eater serves as an excellent introduction to the study of healthy eating. The same pictures the children have drawn or cut out can serve as the beginning pictures for categories such as meats, grains, fruits and vegetables, and dairy products.

Variations

Other books will also serve as the starting point for concept sorts of many kinds. Here are just a few suggestions.

Noisy Nora by Rosemary Wells—sort pictures that suggest noisy activities or objects with pictures that suggest quiet activities.

The Country Mouse and the City Mouse by Jan Brett and various authors—sort pictures of things you would see in the country and things you would see in the city.

Alexander and the Wind-Up Mouse by Leo Lionni—sort pictures of real animals and toy or imaginary animals.

Amos and Boris by William Steig—sort pictures of things that Amos would see on the land and things that Boris would see in the ocean.

Is It Red? Is It Yellow? Is It Blue? by Tana Hoban—one of many books that suggest sorting objects and pictures by color.

My Very First Book of Shapes by Eric Carle—one of many books that lead into a sorting activity based on shapes.

Paste the Pasta and Other Concrete Concept Sorts 4-2

Adaptable for Other Stages

Categorizing pasta by size, shape, and color is a good hands-on activity that introduces the idea of sorting to young children. Ann Fordham developed this sort at the McGuffey Reading Center. Many early childhood curricula include the study of pattern, but being able to categorize by particular attributes must come first. It is difficult for young children to stay focused on a single attribute of interest. They may begin sorting by color and then switch to shape in midstream. They will need many activities of this kind, sorting real, concrete objects that have different features.

Materials

You will need three to six types of pasta that vary in size and shape. You may find pasta of various colors or you can dye your own by shaking the pasta in a jar with a tablespoon of alcohol and a few drops of food coloring. Lay it out on newspaper to dry. If you dye your own, make sure that any one color has a variety of shapes and sizes. Two or three colors are enough. Children can sort onto paper divided into columns as shown in Figure 4-13 or simply into piles.

FIGURE 4-13 Paste the Pasta

Procedures

1. Prepare a mixture of the dried pasta and give each child a handful and a sorting paper.
2. Begin with an open sort in which you invite the students to come up with their own way of grouping. This will give you an opportunity to evaluate which of the children understand attribute sorting and who will need more guidance. Ask the children to share their ideas and show their groups. Discuss the different features or attributes by which they can sort.
3. Ask them to re-sort using a category different from their first one. You might end this activity by letting the students glue the pasta onto their paper by categories and label their chosen sorts.

Variations

There is no end to the concrete things you can sort with your students as you explore the different features that define your categories. Here are some suggestions.

Children—male/female, hair color, eye color, age, favorite color
Shoes—girls'/boys', right/left, tie/Velcro/slip-on
Mittens and gloves—knit/woven, right/left
Coats—short/long, button/zip, hood/no hood
Buttons—two holes/four holes/no holes, shapes, colors, size
Bottle caps—size, color, plastic/metal, plain/printed, ribbed/smooth
Lunch containers—boxes/bags, plastic/metal/nylon
Legos©—color, shape, number of pegs, length
Blocks—shape, color, size
Toys—size, color, purpose, hardness
Food—sweet, sour, bitter, salty, fruits, vegetables, grains

All My Friends Photograph Sort 4-3

Another example of an open-ended sort involves guessing each other's categories. Pat Love, from Hollymead Elementary School, Charlottesville, Virginia, developed this idea.

Materials

You can use photocopies of the children's school photographs made into a composite sheet or take digital pictures of your students and cut and paste them into sheets printed from a computer. The students will also need a sheet of construction paper to divide into columns for sorting.

Procedures

1. Brainstorm with the children some of the ways that the pictures might be grouped (hair length, hair color, clothing, boys/girls, facial expressions).
2. Have students work in groups to sort by these or other categories they discover. After pasting their pictures into the columns on their paper, each group can hold up their effort and ask the others in the class to guess their categories. The category labels or key words should then be written on the papers.

Variations

Photographs from home may be sorted according to places (inside/outside, home/vacation, holidays, and so forth), number of people in the photograph (adults, sisters, brothers), number of animals in the photograph, seasons (by clothing, outside trees/plants), age, and so forth.

   As children learn to recognize their classmates' names, have them match the names to the pictures. Later, these names may be sorted by beginning letter and then placed under the corresponding letter of an ABC wall strip to form a graph.

THEMATIC UNITS AS A STARTING POINT FOR CONCEPT SORTS

Teachers of young children often organize their curriculum into thematic units of study. Such units frequently lend themselves to concept sorts, which will review and extend the understandings central to the goals of the unit. Here are some examples.

Animal Unit 4-4

Adaptable for Other Stages

The study of animals particularly lends itself to concept sorts and can be used as a way of introducing a unit. Lay out a collection of plastic animals or animal pictures and ask students to think of ways that they can be grouped together. Such an open sort will result in many different categories based on attributes of color, number of legs, fur or feather coat, and so on. A lively discussion will arise as students discover that some animals will go in different categories.

   The direction you eventually want this activity to go will depend on the goal of your unit. If you are studying animal habitats, then you will eventually guide the children to sorting the animals by the places they live. If you are studying classes of animals, then the students must eventually learn to sort them into mammals, fish, amphibians, and birds. If you are focusing on the food chain, your categories may be carnivores, herbivores, and omnivores.

Transportation Unit 4-5

Another open sort involves a unit on transportation. A collection of toy vehicles (planes, boats, cars, and trucks) can be laid on the floor or table and the children invited to think of which ones might go together. Encourage them to think up a variety of possibilities that will divide everything into only two or three categories. After each suggestion, sort the vehicles by the identified attributes, and write the key words on a chart or chalkboard. Some possibilities include plastic/metal, big/little, old/new, one color/many colors, windows/no windows, wheels/no wheels, and land/air/water.

After exploring this open sort thoroughly, have the children select the suggestion they liked the best. They can then be given construction paper to label their categories and draw or cut out pictures for each. As always, encourage them to label the pictures and the categories with invented spelling as shown in Figure 4-14.

FIGURE 4-14   Transportation Draw and Label

Variations

Other concept sorts might be developed along the same lines. The following list of categories represents some that are frequently confused by preschool, kindergarten, and first grade children.

> real, imaginary
> smooth, rough
> kitchen tools, office tools, shop tools
> plastic, wood, metal
> hard, soft

PLAY WITH SOUNDS TO DEVELOP PHONOLOGICAL AWARENESS

Phonological awareness consists of an array of understandings about sounds that include a sense of rhyme, alliteration, syllables, phonemic segmentation, and blending. Rhyme and alliteration are easier than others for emergent learners and many activities for developing these are included here. There are also some activities in this section for syllable sense, segmenting, and blending, but they are also addressed as part of other activities such as The Morning Message (4-36) and Start with Children's Names (4-18).

Begin with Rhyme in Children's Books 4-6

Filling children's heads with rhyme is one of the easiest and most natural ways to focus their attention on the sounds of the English language. Books written with rhyme provide one way to do this.

Materials

Many of the books enjoyed by children in the emergent stage feature rhymes. Here are just a few.

> Ahlsberg, J., & Ahlsberg, A. (1978). *Each peach pear plum: An "I spy" story.* New York: Scholastic.
> Cameron, P. (1961). *I can't, said the ant.* New York: Putnam Publishing.
> Crews, D. (1986). *Ten black dots.* New York: Greenwillow.

Degan, B. (1983). *Jamberry*. New York: Harper.

Florian, D. (1987). *A winter day*. New York: Scholastic; (1990). *A beach day*. New York: Greenwillow.

Guarina, D. (1989). *Is your mama a llama?* Illustrated by Steven Kellogg. New York: Scholastic.

Hennessy, B. G. (1989). *The missing tarts.* Illustrated by T. C. Pearson. New York: Scholastic.

Macmillan, B. (1990). *One sun*. New York: Holiday House; (1991). *Play day*. New York: Trumpet.

Slate, J. (1996). *Mrs. Bindergarten gets ready for kindergarten*. New York: Scholastic.

Strickland, P., & Strickland, H. (1994). *Dinosaur roar!* New York: Scholastic.

Walton, R. (1998). *So many bunnies: A bedtime ABC and counting book*. New York: Scholastic.

Procedures

1. As you read books with rhyme aloud, pause to allow the children to guess the rhyming word. *I Can't, Said the Ant* is an old favorite that invites student participation with each line cued by an illustration.

2. Some rhyming books are so repetitive and simple that children can easily memorize them and read them on their own. *Play Day* and *One Sun*, by Bruce Macmillan, are some of the simplest rhyming books available. They feature "hinkpink" rhymes such as *white kite* or *bear chair* with a vivid photograph to cue the child's response. Douglas Florian has written a series of books, including *A Beach Day* and *A Winter Day*, that feature only two or three words on a page. These books can also be used to introduce concept sorts in which summer/winter and city/country can be contrasted. After hearing these books read aloud two or three times, young children may be able to recite the words or track the print successfully for themselves and will get great satisfaction from the feeling that they can read.

Match and Sort Rhyming Pictures 4-7

After reading rhyming books aloud, you can follow up with an activity that has the children sorting or matching rhyming pictures.

Materials

Rhyming pictures are available commercially or you can create your own. The Appendix of this book contains pictures grouped by initial sounds and by vowels. These can be copied, colored lightly, and glued to cards to make sets for sorting. The list on page 280 of Appendix C will help you find rhyming sets. You can create sets of matching pairs or sets of three or more pictures that can be sorted by rhyme.

Procedures

1. Display a set of pictures and model how to sort them by rhyme. Say something like this: "*Boat* rhymes with *coat*, so I will put it with the picture of the coat. Can you find two pictures that rhyme?" To make it easier for beginners, put out three pictures at a time: two pictures that rhyme and one that does not. Name the pictures and ask children to find the two that rhyme: "Listen. *Boat, train, coat*. Which pictures rhyme?"

2. After sorting pictures as a group, put the pictures in a center for children to match on their own or create a rhyming sort handout so that each child can have his or her own sort.

Variations

Set up two or more categories and lead the children in sorting pictures by rhyming sound. For example, lay down *cat* and *bee* as headers and sort other pictures in turn under the correct header.

Invent Rhymes 4-8

Nonsense rhymes and books with rhyme and word play are a delightful way to cultivate awareness of sounds. Word play directs children's attention to the sounds of the English language and can stimulate them to invent their own words. Jan Slepian and Ann Seidler's *The Hungry Thing* tells of a creature who comes to town begging for food but has trouble pronouncing what he wants: *shmancakes* (pancakes), *feetloaf* (meatloaf), and *hookies* (cookies) are among his requests. It is only a small boy who figures out what he wants. After reading the book, children can act it out. As each takes the part of the Hungry Thing, they must come up with a rhyming word for the food they want: *blizza, bandwich, smello*? The story continues in *The Hungry Thing Returns*.

Making up one's own rhymes is likely to come after the ability to identify rhymes. Thinking up rhyming words to make sense in a poem is quite an accomplishment, requiring a good sense of rhyme and an extensive vocabulary. Children need supported efforts to create rhymes, and a good place to start is pure nonsense. No one was a greater master of this than Dr. Seuss. *There's a Wocket in My Pocket* takes readers on a tour of a young boy's home in which all kinds of odd creatures have taken up residence. There is a *woset* in his closet, a *zlock* behind the clock, and a *nink* in the sink. After reading this to a group, ask children to imagine what animal would live in their cubby, under the rug, or in the lunchroom. Their efforts should rhyme, to be sure, but anything will do: a *rubby, snubby,* or *frubby* might all live in a cubby.

Patterned text can also be used to create rhymes. The rhyming pattern in *Ten Black Dots* by Donald Crews can be extended to 11, 12, and so on: "Twelve dots can make ice cream cones or the buttons to dial a _____." In the supportive framework of a familiar patterned sentence, children are likely to be more successful at creating their own rhymes.

Use Songs to Develop a Sense of Rhyme and Alliteration 4-9

Earlier we mentioned how appropriate works by the singer/songwriter Raffi are for young children. Teaching these songs by Raffi can lead to inventive fun with rhymes and sounds, and some are available as books.

> "Apples and Bananas" (from *One Light, One Sun*)
> "Spider on the Floor" (from *Singable Songs for the Very Young*)
> "Down by the Bay" (also available as a book, from *Singable Songs for the Very Young*)

Another song that features names, rhyme, and alliteration is "The Name Game," originally sung by Shirley Ellis. It has apparently passed into the oral tradition of neighborhood kids and may be known by some children in your class. Sing the song over and over, substituting the name of a different child on every round. Here are two examples:

> *Sam Sam Bo Bam, Banana Fanna Bo Fam, Fee Fi Mo Mam, Sam!*
> *Kaitlyn Kaitlyn Bo Baitlyn, Banana Fanna Bo Faitlyn, Fee Fi Mo Maitlyn, Kaitlyn!*

Lend an ear to the playground songs and chants your children already know and encourage them to share them with you. Generations of children have made up variations of "Miss Mary Mack Mack Mack" and a new generation with a taste for rap is

Emergent Stages

creating a whole new repertoire. You can take an active role in teaching these jingles to your students—or letting them teach them to you! Write them down to become reading material. Here are some printed sources of traditional chants and jingles.

Cole, J. (1989). *Anna Banana: 101 jump-rope rhymes*. New York: Scholastic.

Cole, J., & Calmenson, S. (1990). *Miss Mary Mack and other children's street rhymes*. Illustrated by Alan Tiegreen. New York: Morrouno.

Schwartz, A. (1989). *I saw you in the bathtub*. New York: HarperCollins.

Sierra, J., & Sweet, M. (2005). *Schoolyard rhymes: Kids own rhymes for rope jumping, hand clapping, ball bouncing, and just plain fun*. New York: Knopf.

Yolan, J. (1992). *Street rhymes from around the world*. New York: Wordsong.

RHYMING GAMES

There are many commercially made games and computer software programs that feature rhyming words. The two games described here are easy to make and are based on familiar formats.

Adaptable for Other Stages

Rhyming Bingo 4-10

Materials

Prepare enough Bingo gameboards for the number of children who will participate (small groups of three to five children are ideal). An appropriate gameboard size for young children is a 6-by-6-inch board divided into nine 3-by-3 squares; for older students, the gameboard can be expanded to a 4-by-4 or 5-by-5-array. Copy sets of pictures from Appendix C and form rhyming groups such as those listed on page 280. Paste all but one of each rhyming group in the spaces on the gameboards and then laminate them for durability. Each gameboard must be arranged differently.

Prepare a complementary set of cards on which you paste the remaining picture from each rhyming group. These will become the deck from which rhyming words are called aloud during the game. You will need some kind of marker to cover the squares on the gameboard. These may be as simple as 2-inch squares of construction paper, plastic chips, bottle caps, or pennies.

Procedures

1. Each child receives a gameboard and markers to cover spaces.
2. The teacher or a designated child is the caller who turns over cards from the deck and calls out the name of the picture.
3. Each player searches the gameboard for a picture that rhymes with the one that has been called out. Players can cover a match with a marker to claim the space.
4. The winner is the first player to cover a row in any direction, or the first player to fill his or her entire board.

Rhyming Concentration 4-11

Materials

This game for two or three children is played like the traditional Concentration or the more current Memory game. Assemble a collection of six to ten rhyming pairs from the pictures in Appendix C. Paste the pictures on cards and laminate for durability. Be sure the pictures do not show through from the backside.

Procedures

1. Shuffle the pictures and then lay them facedown in rows.
2. Players take turns flipping over two pictures at a time. If the two pictures rhyme, the player keeps the cards to hold to the end of the game. The player who makes a match gets another turn.
3. The winner is the child who has the most matches at the end of the game.

Variations

This can be adapted to use with beginning sounds. Put letters on one set of cards and paste a picture of something that begins with that letter on another.

Beginning-Middle-End: Find Phonemes in Sound Boxes 4-12

Phonemic segmentation is best developed as teachers model writing and as children try to invent spellings, but at times you want to give some added emphasis to phonemic segmentation using sound boxes. Originally developed by Elkonin (1973), sound boxes serve as a concrete way to demonstrate how words are made of smaller pieces called *sounds* (or *phonemes*). Here is a variation developed by Erica Fulmer, a reading specialist, who has created a song she and her children sang as they tried to find the location of each sound in the word.

Materials

You will need large letter cards and a three-pocket holder such as the one shown in Figure 4-15.

Procedures

1. Place the letters needed to spell a three-letter word in the pocket backwards so the children cannot see the letters. Announce the word, such as *sun*. Choose words from a familiar book, poem, or dictation when possible. Words that start with continuant sounds such as |m|, |s|, or |f| work well because they can be said slowly.
2. Sing the song to the tune of "Are You Sleeping, Brother John?"

   Beginning, middle, end; beginning, middle, end
   Where is the sound? Where is the sound?
   Where's the ssss in sun? Where's the ssss in sun?
   Let's find out. Let's find out.

3. Children take turns coming forward to pick the position and check by turning the letter card.

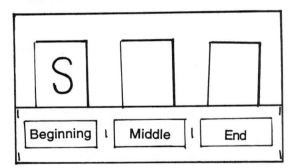

FIGURE 4-15 Sound Boxes

It's in the Bag—A Phoneme Blending Game 4-13

Materials

You will need a paper bag (gift bags are attractive) and an assortment of small objects collected from around the classroom, from outside, or from home: chalk, pen, paper clip, tack, key, rock, stick, and so on. You might use a puppet to add interest.

Procedures

Lay out a dozen or so objects and name them with the children. Explain that you will use them to play a game. Introduce the puppet. The puppet will name an object in the bag, saying it very slowly, and the children will guess what it is saying.

Variations

Use objects or pictures related to a topic of study. For example, if you are teaching a unit on animals, you could put toy animals or pictures of farm animals in the bag. This can be a sensory activity by letting children reach into the bag, figure out an object by touch, and then say it slowly for the other children to guess. Objects that begin with the same beginning sounds can also be put into the bag to sort.

Incorporate Phonological Skills into Daily Activities 4-14

Teachers of emergent children can incorporate sound play into many daily activities and routines.

1. *Lining up, taking attendance, or calling children to a group:* Call each child's name and then lead the class in clapping the syllables in the name. Announce that everyone whose name has two syllables can line up, then one syllable, three, and so on. Say each child's name slowly as it is called. Make up a rhyme for each child's name that starts with a sound of interest: Billy Willy, Mary Wary, Shanee Wanee, and so on. Substitute the first letter in everyone's name with the same letter: Will, Wary, Wanee, Wustin, and so on.
2. *During read-alouds:* Pause to let children fill in a rhyming word, especially on a second or third reading. If they have trouble, say the first sound for them with a clue: "It rhymes with *whale* and starts with /p/." Draw attention to a long word by repeating it and clapping the syllables: "That's a big word! Let's clap the syllables: hip-po-pot-a-mus, five syllables!" You might also pause while reading and say a key word very slowly before asking the children to repeat it fast: "The next day his dad picked him up in a red . . . jeeeep. What's that? A jeep, right." You might point to the letters as you do this.

There are many other published resources on the topic of phonological awareness and what teachers can do to facilitate it. The following are particularly worthwhile.

Adams, M.J., Foorman, B.A., Lundberg, I., & Beweler, T. (1998). *Phonemic awareness in young children.* Baltimore, MD: Paul H. Brookes Pub. Co.

Blevins, W. (1997). *Phonemic awareness activities for early reading success.* New York: Scholastic.

Ericson, L., & Juliebo, M. F. (1998). *The phonological awareness handbook for kindergarten and primary teachers.* Newark, DE: International Reading Association.

Fitzpatrick, J. (1998). *Phonemic awareness: Playing with sounds to strengthen beginning reading skills.* Cypress, CA: Creative Teaching Press.

Opitz, M.F. (2000). *Rhymes and reasons: Literature and language play for phonological awareness.* Portsmouth, NH: Heinemann.

Yopp, H.K., & Yopp, R.E. (2000). *Oo-pples and boo-noo-noos.* Portsmouth, NH: Heinemann.

ALPHABET ACTIVITIES AND GAMES

The following activities are designed to develop all aspects of alphabet knowledge, including letter recognition (both uppercase and lowercase), letter naming, letter writing, and letter sounds. You may notice that these activities address more than one letter at a time: For children who have not cut their teeth on alphabet letters and picture books, one letter per week is not enough. We must teach more than one letter at a time.

Begin with Alphabet Books 4-15

Share alphabet books with a group as you would other good literature and plan follow-up activities when appropriate. Some books are suitable for toddlers and merely require the naming of the letter and a single accompanying picture, such as Dick Bruna's *B Is for Bear*. Others, such as Graeme Base's *Animalia,* will keep even upper elementary children engaged as they try to name all the things that are hidden in the illustrations. Look for alphabet books, such as the ones listed here, to draw children's attention to beginning sounds through alliteration.

Base, G. (1986). *Animalia*. New York: Harry Abrams.
Bayor, J. (1984). *A: My name is Alice*. Illustrated by Steven Kellogg. New York: Dial.
Berenstain, S., & Berenstain, J. (1971). *The Berenstain's B book*. New York: Random House.
Cole, J. (1993). *Six sick sheep: 101 tongue twisters*. New York: Morrow.
Seuss, Dr. (1963). *Dr. Seuss's ABC*. New York: Random House.

Many ABC books can be incorporated into thematic units, such as Jerry Pallotta's ABC books featuring insects and animals, or Mary Azarian's *A Farmer's Alphabet*. Some alphabet books present special puzzles, such as Jan Garten's *The Alphabet Tale*. Children are invited to predict the upcoming animal by showing just the tip of its tail on the preceding page. Following is a list of some outstanding ABC books for school-age children.

Anglund, J. W. (1960). *In a pumpkin shell*. (Alphabet Mother Goose). San Diego, CA: Harcourt Brace, Jovanovich.
Anno, M. (1975). *Anno's alphabet*. New York: Crowell.
Azarian, M. (1981). *A farmer's alphabet*. Boston: David Godine.
Baskin, Leonard. (1972). *Hosie's alphabet*. New York: Viking Press.
Ernst, L. C. (1996). *The letters are lost*. New York: Scholastic.
Fain, K. (1993). *Handsigns: A sign language alphabet*. New York: Scholastic.
Falls, C. B. (1923). *ABC book*. New York: Doubleday.
Gág, W. (1933). *The ABC bunny*. Hand lettered by Howard Gág. New York: Coward-McCann.
Hague, K. (1984). *Alphabears: An ABC book*. Illustrated by Michael Hague. New York: Holt, Rinehart & Winston.
Horenstein, H. (1999). *Arf! Beg! Catch! Dogs from A to Z*. New York: Scholastic.
McPhail, D. (1989). *David McPhail's animals A to Z*. New York: Scholastic.
Musgrove, M. (1976). *Ashanti to Zulu: African traditions*. Illustrated by Leo and Diane Dillon. New York: Dial.
Owens, M. B. (1988). *A caribou alphabet*. Brunswick, ME: Dog Ear Press.
Pallotta, J. (1989). *The yucky reptile alphabet book* (1991); *The dinosaur alphabet book*. Illustrated by Ralph Masiello. New York: Bantam Doubleday, Dell. (There are many more in this series.)
Shannon, G. (1996). *Tomorrow's alphabet*. Illustrated by Donald Crews. New York: Greenwillow.
Thornhill, J. (1988). *The wildlife A-B-C: A nature alphabet book*. New York: Simon & Schuster.

Alphabet Book Follow-Ups 4-16

Procedures

1. Discuss the pattern of the books, solve the puzzle, and talk about the words that begin with each letter as you go back through the books a second time.
2. Focus on alliteration by repeating tongue twisters and creating a list of words for a particular letter. Brainstorm other words that begin with that letter, and write them under the letter on chart paper.

Emergent Stages

3. Make individual or class alphabet books. You might decide on a theme or pattern for the book. Refer back to the alphabet books you have read for ideas. One idea might be a noun-verb format, for example: ants attack, bees buzz, cats catch, and dogs doze.
4. Look up a particular letter you are studying in several alphabet books or a picture dictionary to find other things that begin with that sound. This is an excellent introduction to using resource books.

FIGURE 4-16   Chicka Chicka Boom Boom Board

Chicka Chicka Boom Boom Sort 4-17

Martin and Archambault's *Chicka Chicka Boom Boom* is a great favorite and provides a wonderful way to move from children's books to alphabet recognition and letter–sound activities. After reading this delightful book with her children, Pat Love demonstrates how to match foam "Laurie Letters," one at a time, to the letters printed in the book. Pat's boom boards (see Figure 4-16) can be used for sorting letters and pictures by beginning sounds. Other teachers have created a large coconut tree on the side of their filing cabinet so that children can act out the story and match uppercase and lowercase forms using magnetic letters.

Start with Children's Names 4-18

Names are an ideal point from which to begin the study of alphabet letters because children are naturally interested in their own names and their friends' names. We like the idea of a "name of the day" (Cunningham, 2005) so much better than a "letter of the week," because many more letters are covered in a much shorter time!

Materials

Prepare a card for each child on which his or her name is written in neatly executed block letters. Put all the names in a box or can. Have additional blank cards ready to be cut apart as described. A pocket chart is handy for displaying the letters.

Procedures

1. Each day, with great fanfare, a name is drawn and becomes the name of the day. The teacher begins with a very open-ended question: "What do you notice about this name?" Children will respond in all sorts of ways depending upon what they know about letters: "It's a short name." "It has three letters." "It starts like Taneesh's name." "It has an *O* in the middle."
2. Next children chant or echo the letters in the name as the teacher points to each one. A cheer led by the teacher is lots of fun:

   Teacher: "Give me a *T*."   Children: "T"
   Teacher: "Give me an *O*."   Children: "O"
   Teacher: "Give me an *M*."   Children: "M"
   Teacher: "What have we got?"   Children: "Tom!"

3. On an additional card, the teacher writes the name of the child as the children recite the letters again. Then the teacher cuts the letters apart and hands out the

letters to children in the group. The children are then challenged to put the letters back in order to spell the name correctly. This can be done in a pocket chart or on a chalkboard ledge and repeated many times. The cut-up letters are then put into an envelope with the child's name and picture on the outside. The envelope is added to the name puzzle collection. Children love to pull out their friends' names to put together.

4. All the children in the group should attempt to write the featured name on individual whiteboards, on chalkboards, or on pieces of paper. This is an opportunity to offer some handwriting instruction as you model for the children. Discuss the details of direction and movement of letter formation as the children imitate your motions.

5. Each day the featured name is added to a display of all the names that have come before. Because they are displayed in a pocket chart, they can be compared to previous names and used for sorting activities.

   Sort the names by the number of letters or syllables.

   Sort the names that share particular letters; for example, find all the names with an *e* in them.

   Sort the names that belong to boys and girls.

   Sort the names by alphabetical order.

6. Create a permanent display of the names and encourage children to practice writing their own and their friends' names. If you have a writing center, you might put all the names on index cards in a box for reference. Children can be encouraged to reproduce names not only by copying the names with pencils, chalk, and markers, but also with rubber stamps, foam cutout letters, link letters, or letter tiles. The display of children's names becomes an important reference tool during writing time.

One Child's Name 4-19

Learning the letters in one name is a good starting point for children in the early emergent stage. For them, the following activity is valuable.

FIGURE 4-17   Brandon's Name Puzzle

1. Spell out a child's name with letter cards, tiles, foam, or plastic letters using both uppercase and lowercase.

2. Spell it with uppercase letters in the first row and ask the child to match lowercase letters in the row below, as shown in Figure 4-17. Ask children to touch and name each letter. Scramble the top row and repeat.

3. Play Concentration with the set of uppercase and lowercase letters needed to spell a child's name.

Alphabet Scrapbook 4-20

Materials

Prepare a blank book for each child by stapling together sheets of paper. (Seven sheets of paper folded and stapled in the middle is enough for one letter per page.) Children can use this book in a variety of ways (see Figure 4-18).

1. Practice writing uppercase and lowercase forms of the letter on each page.

2. Cut out letters in different fonts or styles from magazines and newspapers and paste them into their scrapbooks.

Emergent Stages

FIGURE 4-18   Alphabet Scrapbook

3. Draw and label pictures and other things that begin with that letter sound.
4. Cut and paste magazine pictures onto the corresponding letter page. These pictures, too, can be labeled.
5. Add sight words as they become known to create a personal dictionary.

The Alphabet Song and Tracking Activities 4-21

Every early childhood classroom should have an alphabet strip or chart at eye level. Too often these strips are put up out of the children's reach. The best locations for the strips are desktops or tabletops for easy reference. Here are activities that make active use of these charts.

Materials

Commercial or teacher-made alphabet strips for both wall display and for individual children.

Procedures

1. Learn the ABC song to the tune of "Twinkle, Twinkle, Little Star." Sing it many times!
2. Model pointing to each letter as the song is sung or the letters are chanted. Then ask the children to fingerpoint to the letters as they sing or chant.
3. When students know about half of the alphabet, they can work on putting a set of letter cards, tiles, or linking letters in alphabetical order. Use uppercase or lowercase letters, or match the two (see Figure 4-19). Keep an ABC strip or chart nearby as a ready reference.

FIGURE-4-19   Alphabet Link Letters

Adaptable for Other Stages

Alphabet Eggs 4-22

Materials

Create a simple set of puzzles designed to practice the pairing of uppercase and lowercase letters. On poster board, draw and cut out enough 4-inch egg shapes for each letter in the alphabet. Write an uppercase letter on the left half and the matching lowercase letters on the right portion. Cut the eggs in half using a zigzag line (see Figure 4-20). Make each zigzag slightly different so the activity is self-checking. Students should say the letters to themselves and put the eggs back together by matching the upper-case and lowercase form.

FIGURE 4-20   Alphabet Eggs

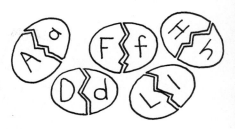

Variations

There are many other shapes that can be cut in half for matching. In October, for example, pumpkin shapes can be cut into two and in February, heart shapes can be cut apart the same way. There is no end to matching possibilities. Acorn caps can be matched to bottoms, balls to baseball gloves, frogs to lily pads, and so on. These matching sets can also be created to pair letters and a picture that starts with that letter, rhyming words, contractions, homophones, and so on.

Alphabet Concentration 4-23

Adaptable for Other Stages

This game works just like Concentration with rhyming words as described in Activity 4-11. Create cards with uppercase and lowercase forms of the letters written on one side. Be sure they cannot be seen from the backside. Use both familiar and not-so-familar letters. Do not try this with all 26 letters at once, or it may take a long time to complete; 8 to 10 pairs are probably enough.

Variations

To introduce this game or to make it easier, play it with the cards face up. As letter sounds are learned, matching consonant letters to pictures that begin with that letter sound can change the focus of this game.

Letter Spin 4-24

Adaptable for Other Stages

Alison Owier-Seldon created this fast-paced game to practice upper and lower case letter recognition.

Materials

Make a spinner with six to eight spaces, and label each space with a capital letter. If you laminate the spinner before labeling, you can reuse it with other letters. Write the letters with a grease pencil or nonpermanent overhead transparency pen. Write the lowercase letters on small cards, creating five or six cards for each letter (see Figure 4-21). See Appendix F for tips on making a spinner.

Procedures

1. Lay out all the lowercase cards face up.
2. Each player in turn spins and lands on an uppercase letter. The player then picks up one card that has the corresponding lowercase form, orally identifying the letter.
3. Play continues until all the letter cards have been picked up.
4. The winner is the player with the most cards when the game ends.

Variations

Students can be asked not only to name but also to write the uppercase and lowercase forms of the letter after each turn. This game can be adapted to any feature that involves matching—letters to sounds, rhymes, vowel patterns, and so on.

Emergent Stages

FIGURE 4-21   Letter Spin Game

Alphabet Cereal Sort 4-25

Materials

For this sorting activity created by Janet Brown Watts, you will need a box of alphabet cereal—enough to give each child a handful. Prepare a sorting board for each child by dividing a paper into 26 squares. Label each square with an uppercase or lowercase letter.

FIGURE 4-22   Cereal Sort

A	B	C ⓒ ⓒ	D ✏	E	F ✗	G
H ω	I	J	K K	L	M	N
O ⓞⓞ ⓞⓞ	P	Q	R ρ	S	T ✗	U
V ∨	W	X ✗	Y	Z z		

g ωⓞⓑη

Procedures

1. Allow the children to work individually or in teams to sort their own cereal onto their papers (see Figure 4-22). Discard (or eat) broken or deformed letters.
2. After the children are finished, they can count the number of letters in each category (e.g., A-8, B-4). This could become a graphing activity.
3. Eat the cereal! (Or glue it down.)

Variations

Have the children spell their names or other words using the cereal.

Sort Letters with Different Print Styles 4-26

Children need to see a variety of print styles before they will be readily able to identify their ABCs in different contexts. Draw children's attention to different letter forms wherever you encounter them. Environmental print is especially rich in creative lettering styles. Encourage the children to bring in samples from home—like the big letters on a bag of dog food or cereal—and create a display on a bulletin board or in a class big book.

Materials

Cut out different styles of letters from newspapers, catalogs, magazines, and other print sources. You can also search your computer fonts and print out letters in the largest size possible. Cut the letters apart, mount them on small cards, and laminate for durability. Use both capitals and lowercase, but avoid cursive styles for now (see Figure 4-23).

Procedures

1. After modeling the sort with a group of children, place the materials in a center where the children can work independently.
2. Avoid putting out too many different letters at one time—four or five are probably enough, with 8 to 12 variations for each.

Variations

If you have created alphabet scrapbooks (Activity 4-21), children can paste in samples of different lettering styles.

FIGURE 4-23 Sorting Letters with Different Print Styles

Emergent Stages

TEACHING BEGINNING SOUNDS

Specific guidelines for creating and using picture sorting for initial sounds are described earlier in this chapter and general guidelines are presented in Chapter 3. Picture and word sorts are at the heart of word study and the procedures will be revisited throughout this book. Games can be used to review beginning sounds after children have already practiced categorizing targeted sounds in basic picture-sorting activities.

Use Books to Enhance Beginning Sounds 4-27

Because alphabet books often include one or more examples of words that start with a targeted letter, they are a natural choice to use when teaching beginning sounds. Such books can be used to introduce an initial sound, or they can be used as a resource for a word hunt as children go searching for more words that start with targeted letters. Watch out for the choices authors and artists sometimes make, however. The *C* page may have words that start with the digraph *ch (chair)*, hard *c (cat)*, and soft *c (cymbals)*. Children will eventually need to sort out these confusions, but not at this time.

Soundline 4-28

This activity, contributed by Leslie Robertson, can be used to focus on letter matching or letter–sound correspondences.

Adaptable for Other Stages

Materials

You will need rope, clothespins, markers, tagboard, glue, pictures, scissors, and laminating film.

Procedures

1. Write uppercase and lowercase letters on the top of the clothespins.
2. Glue a picture beginning with each letter on a square of tagboard and laminate.
3. Students can match the picture card to the clothespin and hang it on the rope (see Figure 4-24).

FIGURE 4-24   Soundline

Adaptable
for Other
Stages

Letter Spin for Sounds 4-29

This is a good game to review up to eight beginning sounds at a time. It is a variation of the letter spin described in Activity 4-24.

Materials

You will need a spinner divided into four to eight sections and labeled with beginning letters to review. You will also need a collection of picture cards that correspond with the letters, with at least four pictures for each letter. Follow the procedures for the letter spin activity.

Procedures

1. Lay out all the pictures face up.
2. Two to four players take turns spinning. The player can select one picture that begins with the sound indicated by the spinner. The next player spins and selects one picture. If there are no more pictures for a sound, the player must pass.
3. Play continues until all the pictures are gone. The winner is the one with the most pictures at the end.

Variations

A large cube could be used like a die instead of a spinner.

Sort Objects by Sounds 4-30

Rule off a large sheet of poster board into squares and label each one according to the initial sounds you want to review. Collect miniature toys and animals or small objects (a button, bell, box, rock, ring, ribbon, etc.) that begin with the sounds of interest. Children are asked to sort the objects into the spaces on the board.

Adaptable
for Other
Stages

Initial Consonant Follow-the-Path Game 4-31

This game is simple enough that even preschoolers can learn the rules and it can be used throughout the primary grades to practice a variety of features. You will see this game adapted in many ways in Chapters 5 and 6.

Materials

You will need to copy the two halves of a follow-the-path gameboard found in Appendix F. To make the game in a folder that can be easily stored, paste each half on the inside of a manila folder (colored ones are nice) leaving a slight gap between the two sides in the middle (so the folder can still fold). Add some color and interest with stickers or cutout pictures to create a theme such as "Trip to the Pizza Parlor" or "Adventures in Space."

Label each space on the path with one of the letters you want to review, using both uppercase and lowercase forms (see Figure 4-25). Sets of three to six letter sounds at a time work best. Reproduce a set of picture cards that correspond to the letters. Copy them on cardstock or glue cutout pictures to cards. You will need two to four game pieces to move around the board. Flat ones like bottle caps or plastic disks store well. Store the pictures and playing pieces in a labeled plastic zip-top bag inside the folder.

FIGURE 4-25   Follow-the-Path Game

Procedures

1. Turn the picture cards facedown in a stack. Players go in alphabetical order.
2. Each player draws a picture in turn and moves the playing piece to the next space on the path that is marked by the corresponding beginning consonant.
3. The winner is the first to arrive at the destination.

HELP CHILDREN ACQUIRE A CONCEPT OF WORD

When children are learning about letters and sounds at the same time they are finger-point reading from memory, there is a complementary process at work. Learning one will give logic and purpose to learning the other. Fingerpoint reading to familiar rhymes and pattern books is the best way to achieve a concept of word.

Rhymes for Reading 4-32

After playing with the sounds in rhyming songs and jump rope jingles, an important further step is to let the children see and interact with the printed form. Here is an example making use of a classic fingerplay which children will quickly be able to read from memory.

FIGURE 4-26   Rhymes for Reading

Materials

Record the words to a well-known jingle such as "I had a little turtle" on a sheet of 24-inch-wide chart paper—big enough for all to see (see Figure 4-26). Some teachers have special pointers (imaginative variations include the rib bone of a cow and the beam of a flashlight), but a finger will do fine when the chart is at eye level.

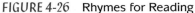

There was a little turtle.

He lived in a box.

He swam in the water.

He climbed on a rock.

Procedures

1. Teach the children the words to the song, if you know it. Sing it repeatedly until everyone knows it well.
2. Display the words to the song and model for the children how to point to the words as they are said. Invite children to take their own turn at tracking the words as they or their classmates chant the words.

3. Make smaller copies of the text and photocopy them so that every child can get his or her own finger on the print. Modeling with a large chart for a group is only a starting point. Nothing beats individual practice. Copies of familiar songs and poems can be left posted in the room and small copies can be put into personal readers (described in Chapter 5).

Cut-Up Sentences 4-33

Write sentences or phrases from a familiar piece of text on a sentence strip. Sentences might come from a book or a poem the group has read together, such as the turtle rhyme in the previous activity. The sentences can then be used in the group to rebuild the text in order using a pocket chart. Individual copies of text can be cut apart so that each child gets to practice.

A further step is to ask the students to cut apart the words in the sentence and then challenge them to reconstruct the sentence. Hand out scissors and call out each word as the children cut it off. The spaces between words are not obvious to emergent children so be prepared to model for them. Demonstrate how to find the words in order to rebuild the sentence: "What letter would you expect to see at the beginning of *swam?*" Leave the word cards and model sentence strips with a pocket chart in a center for children to practice in their spare time. Put individual words into an envelope with the sentence written on the outside (see Figure 4-27). These can be sent home with the children to reassemble for homework. They can also be pasted down under a drawing done by the child.

FIGURE 4-27   Cut-Up Sentences

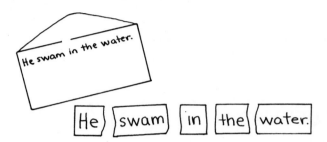

Be the Sentence 4-34

Children can also rebuild familiar sentences by pretending to be the words themselves. Write a familiar sentence on a chart or on the board. Start with short sentences such as "Today is Monday" or "I love you." Then write each word from the sentence on a large card. Give each word to a child, naming it for him or her. "Stephanie, you are the word *Monday;* Lorenzo, you are the word *is.*" Ask the children to work together to arrange themselves into the sentence. Have another child read the sentence to check the direction and order. Try this again with another group of children and then leave the words out for children to work with on their own.

Pull It All Together as You Share the Pen 4-35

The act of writing for children offers teachers the opportunity to model the use of the alphabet, phonemic segmentation, letter–sound matching, concept of word, and conventions such as capitalization and punctuation all in the context of a meaningful group activity. As the teacher writes on the chalkboard, chart paper, or an overhead transparency, children see their own ideas expressed in oral language transformed into print.

During interactive writing, children share the pen and are invited to come forward to add a letter, a word, or a period. Such writing can take place any time of the day and for any reason—for example, to list class rules, to make a shopping list, to record observations from a field trip, to create a new version of a familiar text, or to list questions for a classroom visitor. The following activity is a favorite form of group writing in which the teacher and children compose sentences that report on daily home and school events that are of importance to the class.

The Morning Message 4-36

Each morning the teacher talks with the entire group to discover bits of news that can be part of the morning message. In preschool or early kindergarten, this may be only one sentence, but over time, it can grow to be as long as the teacher and children desire.

Materials

You will need a large sheet of chart paper or a chalkboard with markers or a chalk, and white tape for covering mistakes.

Procedures

1. Chat with children informally, sharing news from home or the classroom. Select a piece of news to record in the form of a single sentence such as "We will go to PE."
2. Recite the sentence together with the children to decide how many words it contains, holding up a finger for each word. Then draw a line for each word on the board or chart (see Figure 4-28).
3. Repeat each word, emphasizing the sounds as they are written, and invite the group to make suggestions about what letters are needed: "The first word we need to write is *we*. Wwwwwweeeeee. What letter do we need for the first sound in *wwweee?*" A child might suggest the letter *Y*. "The name of the letter *Y* does start with that sound. Does anyone have another idea?" Every letter in every word need not be discussed at length. Focus on what is appropriate for the developmental level of your students.

FIGURE 4-28 Morning Message

4. You can do the writing in the beginning, but as children learn to write their letters you can share the pen. White tape is used to cover any mistakes made on paper. Let children take turns writing, usually just one child per letter or word at this level.
5. Model and talk about concepts of print such as left to right, return sweep, capitalization, punctuation, and letter formation. Clap the syllables in longer words, spelling one syllable at a time.
6. After each sentence is completed, read it aloud to the group, touching each word. If your sentence contains a two- or three-syllable word, touch it for every syllable, helping children see how it works. Invite children to fingerpoint as they read.
7. The morning message should be left up all day. Some children may want to copy it or you might want to use it for the cut-up sentence or be-the-sentence activities described earlier.
8. A collection of all the morning messages for a week can be sent home on Friday as a summary of class news that children will have a good chance of proudly reading to their parents.

Variations

Give each child a lap-sized white board, chalkboard, or clipboard so everyone can participate in listening for sounds, handwriting, and use of punctuation.

The word study activities for the emergent stage promote concept and vocabulary development, awareness of sounds, concept of word, and the alphabetic principle. These activities spring from and return to children's books and are extended through writing. Once children achieve a concept of word in print and can segment speech and represent beginning and ending consonant sounds in their spelling, they are no longer emergent, but beginning readers. This is also when they move into the next stage of spelling, the letter name–alphabetic stage. Word study for the letter name–alphabetic speller/ beginning reader is described in Chapter 5.

Word Study for Beginners in the Letter Name–Alphabetic Stage

The letter name–alphabetic stage of literacy development is a period of beginnings. Students begin to read and write in a conventional way. That is, they begin to learn words and actually read text, and their writing becomes readable to themselves and others. However, this period of literacy development needs careful scaffolding because students know how to read and write only a small number of words. The chosen reading materials and activities should provide rich contextual support. In word study, the earliest sorts are pictures; later, students work with words in families and words known by sight. In the following discussion of reading and writing development and instruction, we look closely at the support teachers provide and the way word knowledge develops during this stage. Word study for letter name–alphabetic spellers helps beginners (a) acquire a sight vocabulary through reading and word banks, (b) construct phonics generalizations through picture and word sorts, and (c) create ever more sophisticated, if not completely accurate, spellings as they write. Before we examine this stage of word knowledge and provide guidelines for word study instruction, let us visit the first grade classroom of Mr. Richard Perez.

During the first weeks of school, Mr. Perez observed his first graders as they participated in reading and writing activities and he used the Primary Spelling Inventory described in Chapter 2 to collect samples of their spelling for analysis. Like most first

TABLE 5-1   Spellings of Three First Graders

Word	Cynthia	Tony	Maria
fan	FN	fan	fan
pet	PD	pat	pet
dig	DK	dkg	deg
wait	YAT	wat	wat
sled	SD	sd	sad
stick	SK	sek	stik
shine	CIN	sin	shin

grade teachers, Mr. Perez has a range of ability in his classroom, so he manages three instructional groups for reading and word study and uses students' spellings as a guide to appropriate phonics instruction. Mr. Perez meets with each group daily for guided reading. Some days he uses part of that group time for teacher-directed word study.

Cynthia is a typical student in the early letter name–alphabetic group who writes slowly, often needing help sounding out a word and confusing consonants such as *y* and *w* and *d* and *t* as shown in Table 5-1. The results of her writing efforts are limited primarily to single consonants with few vowels. Cynthia has memorized the words to jingles such as "Five Little Monkeys Jumping on the Bed," but frequently gets off track when she tries to point to the words as she reads. Mr. Perez decides to take a step back with this group and plans a review of beginning sounds. Each Monday he introduces a set of four initial consonants such as *b, m, r,* and *s*. After modeling the sort and practicing it in the group, he gives each student a handout of pictures to be cut apart for individual sorting practice, as shown in Figure 5-1A. The next day the students sort the pictures again and Mr. Perez observes how quickly and accurately they work. On subsequent days of the week during seat work time or center time, the students draw and label pictures beginning with those sounds, paste and label pictures, and do word hunts (follow-up routines described in Chapter 3).

FIGURE 5-1   Word Study Handouts for Letter Name–Alphabetic Spellers in Three Different Instructional Groups

A. Beginning Consonant Sort

Bb	Mm	Rr	Ss

B. Word Family Sort

cat	man	can
rat	fan	hat
pan	sat	pat
that	tan	bat
van	mat	than
fat	ran	

C. Short-Vowel Sort

cap	pig	hot
sit	hat	shop
ship	stop	fast
camp	fish	lock
mad	job	will
him	trap	not
got	that	pin

Each day when Mr. Perez meets with Cynthia's group, they read chart stories, jingles, and big books with predictable texts. To help the students in this group develop a sight vocabulary, Mr. Perez started a **word bank** for each child. He wrote words the students could quickly identify on small cards for their collection. The students add new words several times a week and review their words on their own or with classroom volunteers.

Tony is part of a large group in the middle letter name–alphabetic stage who has beginning and ending consonants under good control, but shows little accuracy when spelling digraphs and blends as shown in Table 5-1. He is using but confusing vowels in some words. Tony points to the words as he reads "Five Little Monkeys" and immediately self-corrects if he gets off track on words with more than one syllable such as *jumping* and *mama*. Mr. Perez decides to introduce the digraphs *sh, ch, th,* and *wh* using picture sorts, and then begins the study of word families such as *at* and *an* using word cards. He knows that Tony and the other students in that group can read words such as *cat, can,* and *man,* and that these words serve as the basis for the study of other words in the same family. Mr. Perez takes 10 minutes in group time to introduce new word families. The children then receive their own set of words (Figure 5-1B) to cut apart for sorting, and work alone and with partners to practice the sort, write and illustrate the words, and play follow-up games.

Maria represents a third group of students in the late letter name–alphabet stage who use single consonants accurately, as well as many digraphs and blends, as shown in Table 5-1. This group uses short vowels with more accuracy. Maria can read some books independently and is quickly accumulating a large sight vocabulary simply from doing lots of reading. Mr. Perez reviews different-vowel word families for several weeks, making an effort to include words with digraphs and blends, but he soon discovers that word families are too easy and decides to move to the study of short vowels in nonrhyming words. Each Monday he introduces a collection of words that can be sorted by short vowels into three or four groups. This group also receives a handout of words, as shown in Figure 5-1C, to cut apart and use for sorting. They learn to work in pairs for buddy sorts, writing sorts, word hunts, and games on other days of the week.

LITERACY DEVELOPMENT OF LETTER NAME–ALPHABETIC STUDENTS

Letters have both names and sounds. Students typically learn the names of the letters first and then use them to spell. This phenomenon accounts for the name of the letter name–alphabetic stage. Spellers in this group operate in the first layer of English—the alphabetic layer. They understand that words can be segmented into sounds and that letters of the alphabet must be matched to these sounds in a systematic fashion. At first these matches may be limited to the most **salient** or prominent sounds in syllables, usually the beginning and ending consonants. By the middle of this stage, students include a vowel in each stressed syllable and they spell short vowels by matching the way they articulate the letter names of the vowels. By the end of the letter name–alphabetic stage, students have learned how to spell many words with short vowels correctly. The following table summarizes the characteristics of students in the early, middle, and late letter name–alphabetic stage.

Watch the Letter Name–Alphabetic section of the *Words Their Way* DVD to see how word study is implemented with this stage of learner.

Reading and Writing in the Letter Name–Alphabetic Stage

Students who are in the letter name–alphabetic stage of spelling have recently acquired a **concept of word**—the ability to track or fingerpoint read a memorized text without getting off track on a two-syllable word.

Characteristics of Letter Name–Alphabetic Spelling

	What Students Do Correctly	What Students Use but Confuse	What Is Absent
Early Letter Name–Alphabetic B, BD for *bed* S, SP for *ship* YN for *when* L, LP for *lump* FT for *float* G, J, GF, JF, GV, for *drive*	Represent most salient sounds, usually beginning consonants Directionality Use most letters of the alphabet Partial spelling of consonant blends and digraphs Spell some known sight words correctly: *the, is*	Letter name sound matches Consonants based on manner and point of articulation (j/dr, b/p) Concept of word is rudimentary, gets off track on two syllable words Spaces between words	Vowels Complete blends and digraphs
Middle Letter Name–Alphabetic BAD for *bed* SEP or SHEP for *ship* LOP for *lump* FOT for *float* GRIV for *drive*	All of the above plus: Spell beginning and ending consonants Spell frequently occurring short-vowel words: *cat, dog* Concept of word is fully developed	Short vowels by point of articulation Consonant blends and digraphs	Silent letters Preconsonantal nasals
Late Letter Name–Alphabetic *bed ship* *lump* STEK for *stick* FLOT for *float* DRIV for *drive* BAKR for *baker*	All of the above plus: Spell many short-vowels and most consonant blends and digraphs Spell frequently occurring long-vowel words: *like, come*	Some short vowels still confused Substitutions of common short vowels for ambiguous vowels: COT for *caught* Preconsontantal nasals Affricate blends (dr, tr)	Most long-vowel markers or silent vowels Vowels in unstressed syllables

Concept of word.   There are two levels of concept of word to consider in this stage: rudimentary and full concept of word (Bear & Barone, 1998; Flanigan, 2006; Morris, 1981; Morris et al., 2003). The movement from no concept of word in the emergent stage, when students cannot point accurately, and, in this stage, from rudimentary to full concept of word, completes the picture of how we view beginning reading and the way students acquire sight words through reading, word banks, and word study.

Students with a rudimentary concept of word are able to point and track to the words of a memorized text using their knowledge of consonants as clues to word boundaries. However, they get off track with two syllable words and when they are asked to find words in what they read, they are slow and hesitant. They may return to the beginning of the sentence or line to get a running start with memory as a support to read and locate the requested word. Students with a rudimentary concept of word are able to acquire a few words from familiar stories and short dictations that they have reread several times. In word study, students with a rudimentary concept of word are in the early part of the letter name–alphabetic stage: they study beginning consonants and ending consonants, and blends and digraphs through same-vowel word families. With a rudimentary concept of word, students' sight vocabulary grows slowly (15–60 words). Pictures are mixed with known words in sorting.

Students with a full concept of word can fingerpoint read accurately, and if they get off track they can quickly correct themselves without starting all over. When asked to find words in the text, they are able to identify them immediately or nearly immediately. They acquire many sight words after several rereadings of familiar text. Students with a full concept of word pick up with the study of different-vowel word families and then examine individual short vowels and the consonant-vowel-consonant pattern (CVC) for short vowels, including short vowel words containing beginning and ending consonant blends. With an expanding sight word vocabulary, sorts rely more on words than pictures.

Reading fluency. All beginning readers read slowly, except when they read well-memorized texts, and they are often described as word-by-word readers (Bear, 1989, 1991b). They do not remember enough words, nor do they know enough about orthography to read words quickly enough to permit fluent reading or writing. Often beginning readers' reading rates are painfully slow. For example, a beginning reader may read at fewer than 50 words per minute.

Most beginning readers point to words when they read, and they read aloud to themselves. This helps them to keep their place and to buy processing time. While they hold the words they have just read in memory, they read the next word, giving them time to fit the words together into a phrase. Silent reading is rarely evidenced. If you visit a first grade classroom during "sustained silent reading" (SSR) or during "drop everything and read" (DEAR), you are likely to hear a steady hum of voices. Disfluency, fingerpointing, and reading aloud to oneself are natural reading behaviors to look for in beginning readers.

There is a similar pattern of disfluency in beginning writing because students often write words slowly, sound by sound (Bear, 1991a). In the previous, emergent stage of development, writers are often unable to read what they have written because they lack or have limited letter-to-sound correspondences. Students in the letter name–alphabetic stage can usually read what they write depending on how completely they spell, and their writing is generally readable to anyone who understands the logic of their letter name–alphabetic strategy.

Vocabulary learning. Beginning readers' vocabularies continue to grow with oral language interactions, and the quality and quantity of vocabulary growth is dependent on the richness and frequency of verbal interactions with peers and adults. Adult input should include the teacher's commenting on and making observations about words throughout the day and the teacher's readalouds—both narrative and informational. Teachers can make words interesting in many ways, and in so doing help their students become "wordsmiths"—kids who are curious about words, their sounds, their meanings, their usage. This type of attitude toward words raises students' **word consciousness** or word awareness, which is a critical aspect of vocabulary growth (Stahl & Nagy, 2006). For beginning readers, several words from a readaloud can be highlighted and discussed throughout the week. Estimates vary, but most children can add on average 10–15 new words a week to their vocabularies (Biemiller, 2005).

Most beginning readers and writers are not able to grow their meaning vocabularies through wide reading because the texts they are learning to negotiate do not contain a large number of words whose meanings they do not know. English learners, however, often learn new vocabulary as they acquire phonics skills and new sight words, and by learning the names of pictures they use in sorts.

Pictures and known words are used in concept sorts to expand children's vocabulary and to encourage rich verbal interactions. For example, letter name–alphabetic spellers can discuss forms of transportation with pictures of airplanes, tractors, trucks, bicycles, horses, and trains in addition to sight words related to transportation, which may include words like *cars, feet,* and *road.* Combinations of known words and pictures are used as a platform for concept sorts that encourage verbal interaction and vocabulary development. Teachers should model and use the language of comparison/contrast: "bigger than, smaller than, not as large as," and so forth. This explicit attention to language helps children "unpack" what they tacitly know about the concepts underlying the labels, and becomes part of their own discussions about words and concepts.

Supporting Beginning Literacy Learning

Letter name–alphabetic spellers need support to make reading happen. Support can come from two sources: the text and the teacher. Support from the text comes from its degree of predictability and familiarity. Predictability means a student can predict what is coming up next because of certain recurring elements. A rhyming pattern may repeat: "Five little monkeys jumping on the bed, one fell off and bumped his head." A refrain may recur: "Have you seen my cat?" (Carle, 1987). A cumulative sequence may recur: "This is the cat that caught the rat that ate the malt that lay in the house that Jack built." Or specific words and spelling patterns may recur: "The cat sat on the mat. The dog sat on the mat. The goat sat on the mat" (Wildsmith, 1982).

Familiarity makes the text predictable as well. Familiarity with the subject, the language, and the words supports students as they read. Text becomes familiar when students have heard it, recited it, sung it, or because they have read it or heard it many times. Texts also become familiar when the words are about an event experienced firsthand by the students, as in student dictations created using the **language experience approach** (LEA).

Support from the teacher comes from the many ways a teacher may scaffold the reading experience. For example, the teacher may provide a book introduction (Clay, 1991) that uses the language of the text and anticipates difficult words and concepts. A teacher may read the text aloud and then encourage students to read in unison (**choral reading**) or immediately after the teacher reads (**echo reading**). A tension lies between these two forms of support. The more predictable a text is, the less support is needed from the teacher. Conversely, the less support provided from recurring elements of text, the more scaffolding is needed from the teacher. Because early letter name–alphabetic spellers require support when they read, we often call these beginners "support readers." As students develop as readers, they need less support from either teacher or text and they benefit from reading text that is not so predictable.

Support readers do not recognize many words by sight. As partial alphabetic readers (Ehri, 1997), they know something about consonants, but they lack the vowel knowledge needed to sound out words or store words completely in memory. In the familiar rhyming book *Five Little Monkeys Jumping on the Bed* by Eileen Christelow (1989), beginning readers can point to the words using their memory for the rhyming pattern and their knowledge of beginning sounds /f/, /l/, /m/, /j/, and /b/. The word *monkeys* might be recognized out of context by virtue of several letters in the word (*mk* or *my* perhaps). In another context, however, these partial phonetic cues alone will not suffice. *Monkeys* might be confused with *Mike* or *many.* Partial information about the alphabetic code is not enough to support unerring word recognition. Support reading must be accompanied by systematic word study.

Influences on Development in the Letter Name–Alphabetic Stage

Students in the letter name–alphabetic stage provide a wonderful example of how learners construct knowledge in an attempt to make sense of the world of print. Without knowing much about orthography, students carefully analyze the sound system more vigorously than do adults, and they make surprisingly fine distinctions about the way sounds and words are formed in the mouth. They match segmented sounds to the letter names of the alphabet in ways that may seem curious and random to the uninformed adult.

Students in the letter name–alphabetic stage use their knowledge of the actual names of the letters of the alphabet to spell phonetically or alphabetically. For example, students in the early letter name–alphabetic stage are likely to spell the word *jeep* as *GP*, selecting *g* as the first letter because of its name (gee) and *p* for the final letter because its letter name (pee) offers a clear clue to the sound it represents. According to letter name logic, there is no need to add the vowel because it is already part of the letter name for *g*. Sometimes early letter name–alphabetic spellers do include vowels, especially when they spell long vowels that "say their name." For example, students might spell *jeep* as *GEP*. During the early part of this stage spelling is largely consonantal, but as phonemic awareness improves by the middle part of this stage, students' spellings gradually include more vowels.

Some letter names do not cue students to the sounds they represent. For example, the letter name for *w* is "double u" and the name for *h* is "aitch." Neither offers a clue to the sound it represents. However, the name for *h* does end with the /ch/ sound and when you say the name of the letter *y* you can feel your lips moving to make the shape of the /wuh/ sound. Consequently, early letter name–alphabetic spellers may spell *witch* as *YH*. Read through the letter names in Table 5-2 to see what the letter names offer students in terms of sound matches. Most consonants do offer a clue to the sound they represent either at the beginning (b̲ee) or the end (ef̲) of the letter name.

How Consonant Sounds Are Articulated in the Mouth

Understanding something about phonetics (the science of sounds) will help us understand and appreciate what young spellers are doing. When they spell, letter name–alphabetic students rely not only on what they hear in the letter names, but also on how the letters are articulated, or formed in the mouth. For example, when students try to spell the *dr* in *drive*, they are misled in their spelling by the similarity between *dr* and *jr*, and they may spell *drive* as *JRV*. Say *drive* and *jrive*. Do they sound and feel alike? Linguists call these sounds **affricates,** made by forcing air through a small closure at the roof

TABLE 5-2 Names of the Letters of the Alphabet

A ay	H aitch	O oh	V vee
B bee	I ie	P pee	W doubleyoo
C see	J jay	Q kyoo	X ecks
D dee	K kay	R are	Y wie
E ee	L el	S es	Z zee
F ef	M em	T tee	
G gee	N en	U yoo	

of the mouth to create a feeling of friction (*friction*, *affricatives*—see the meaning connection?). English has several other letters and letter combinations that create the affricate sound and these are often substituted for each other: *j, g, ch, dr, tr,* and the letter name for *h* (aitch). Try saying *jip, chip, trip,* and *drip* several times and you will see why young spellers confuse these affricates.

The voiced and unvoiced consonant pairs discussed in Chapter 4 and listed in Table 4-2 accounts for other confusions experienced by letter–name alphabetic spellers. They may spell *brave* as BRAF, or *oven* as OFN. Both *v* and *f* are articulated exactly the same, but one is **voiced** and the other is **unvoiced.** When voiced phonemes are created, vocal chords vibrate. You can feel this if you place your fingers on your larynx as you say the words *van* and *fan*. One implication for instruction is that students in the letter name–alphabetic stage benefit from saying the words aloud as they are sorting so that they can feel the sound differences. Another implication is that initial teaching of these sounds should avoid contrasting voiced and unvoiced pairs: b/p, d/t, g/k, z/s, v/f, and j/ch (Purcell, 2002), but once most consonant sounds are mastered children may need to focus attention on these finer distinctions. This is especially true for English learners for whom the fine contrasts may be new or unusual in their primary languages.

Vowels in the Letter Name–Alphabetic Stage

Vowels pose special problems for letter name–alphabetic spellers who rely on the name of letters and how a sound feels in the mouth. Try saying the word *lip*. You can feel the initial consonant as your tongue curls up toward your palate and you can feel the final consonant as it explodes past your lips, but did you feel the vowel? Unlike the consonants—articulated by tongue, teeth, lips, and palate—the vowels are determined by more subtle variations in the shape of the mouth and the vibration of the vocal cords.

Vowels are elusive but central to every syllable humans speak. Try to say a consonant such as *b*. What vowels did you attach to the *b*? If you said the letter name (bee), then you would have said the long -*e* vowel. If you said the sound associated with *b*, /buh/, you attached the **schwa** sound—/uh/. Now try to say a /b/ sound without a vowel. Try to whisper *b* and cut your breath short in a whisper. The whisper is as close as you come to separating the vowel from the consonant sound. (There are some consonants that are easier to say without a vowel; these are the **continuant** sounds: /f/, /l/, /m/, /n/, /r/, /s/, /v/, and /z/.)

Studies in acoustical phonetics have demonstrated that vowels are like musical tones, and without the music of the vowel, the consonants become just noise—clicks and snaps and nothing like speech. Because vowels are so closely wedded to the consonants around them, spellers in the early letter name–alphabetic stage have difficulty separating vowels from consonants. It is as if the consonant were the proverbial squeaky wheel; at first, the consonants seem to demand more attention than the vowel and are more easily examined.

Talking About Vowels

The difference in the medial vowel sounds can be described linguistically as **tense** and **lax.** The vocal cords are tense when producing the long -*a* sound (*ate*), but relax a bit in producing the short -a sound (*at*). The vowels we call "long-a" are no longer in duration than short vowels, but the terms are holdovers from classical Latin. Although these terms may not be the most accurate terms linguistically, they are more common than *tense* and *lax* and teachers understand each other when they are used. The simplest way to talk about vowels is probably the best. Descriptions like "in the middle" may suffice to draw students' attention to the vowels at first, but students have no trouble learning *long vowel* and *short vowel* and such terms make word study discussions easier.

How Vowels Are Articulated in the Mouth

Over the course of the letter name–alphabetic stage, students become adept at fully segmenting words into phonemes, including the medial vowel, and they use the alphabetic principle to represent each sound with a letter. Long vowels say their letter name, so the letter choices are obvious. Students spell *line* as *LIN*, *rain* as *RAN*, and *boat* as *BOT*. Perhaps what is most interesting about invented spelling in the letter name–alphabetic stage is the way students spell the short vowels. They turn to the names of the letters, but find no clear letter–sound matches for the short-vowel sounds. For example, there is no letter name that says the short *-i* sound in *bit* or the /uh/ sound in *cup*. Very early letter name–alphabetic spellers might use *f* (ef) or *s* (ess) for short *-e*, but they seldom do. Instead, spellers throughout the letter name–alphabetic stage use their knowledge of the alphabet to find the letter name closest to the place of articulation of the short-vowel sound they are trying to write.

You may have never analyzed sounds at this level, so let's take a moment to consider the vowels and where and how sounds are made in the vocal tract. In Figure 5-2, the vowels are placed to mimic the general area where speakers can feel their place of articulation. Vowels are subtly differentiated by the shape of the mouth, the openness of the jaw, and the position of the tongue while the word is being said. They are all voiced because it is impossible to articulate a vowel sound without vibrating the vocal chords. Compare the vowels in this figure by saying the following words in sequence several times:

beet bit bait bet bat bite but bot ball boat book boot

Do you feel how the production of the vowels moves from high in the front of the oral cavity (*beet*) to low in the oral cavity (*bite*) to the back of the oral cavity (*bot*), down the front, back, and up (*boot*)? Contrast the rounded vowel in *boot* with the way your lips feel when you say the high front vowel sounds in *beet* or *bit*.

The way a word is pronounced may vary by dialect. For example, many people say *caught* and *cot* the same way. Some native speakers of English pronounce *bought, bore, roof,* and *stalk* with different vowels. Teachers must be aware of dialectical differences when students sort and talk about words. These differences do not interfere with word

FIGURE 5-2   Vowels in the Mouth

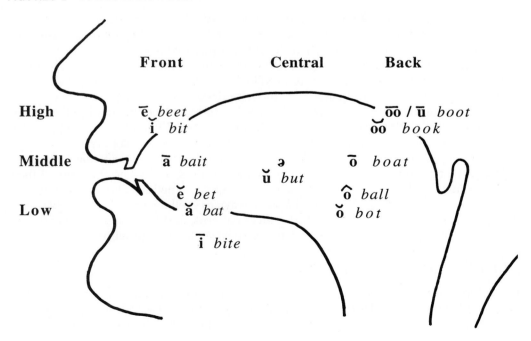

study and learning to spell, but an awareness of these differences enhances word study. Everyone speaks a dialect, but we all learn to read and write the same orthography.

A Letter Name Strategy to Spell Short Vowels

Students in the letter name–alphabetic stage use their knowledge of letter names and the feel of the vowels as they are produced in the vocal tract to spell *bet* as BAT. Without being consciously aware that they are doing this, letter name–alphabetic spellers spell short vowels with the letter name closest in articulation to that short vowel. There are five letter names from which to choose: *a, e, i, o,* and *u*. How would an alphabetic speller spell the word *bed*? What letter name is closest to the short -*e* sound in *bet*? Try saying *bet–beet* and *bet–bait* to compare how the short-vowel sounds and the long vowel or letter names feel in your mouth. Repeat the pairs several times and pay attention to how the mouth is shaped. The short -*e* sound is closer in place of articulation to the long -*a* or letter name for *a* than it is to the letter name for *e*. Students might spell *ship* as *shep* for a similar reason: the short -*i* sound is closer in place of articulation to the letter name for *e* than the letter name for *i*. (If you look back at Figure 5-2, you will see how short -*i* and long -*e* are both high front vowels, while the long -*i* is a low front vowel.) Short -*a* poses little problem for spellers because the letter name for *a* is already close in place of articulation. This is a good reason to teach it first. However, because short -*e* is close to short -*a*, these pairs are not good contrasts for first introducing short vowels.

The wondrous aspect of these letter name substitutions for short vowels is that they are so predictable. Read (1975) found that nearly all students go through a period of time when they substitute the short vowels with other letter names closest in articulation. The following chart will help you remember how the letter names of vowels are substituted for the short-vowel sounds beginning readers try to spell.

Invented Spelling	**Logical Vowel Substitution**
BAT for *bat*	None, short -*a* is close to *a*
BAT for *bet*	*a* for short -*e*
BET for *bit*	*e* for short -*i*
PIT for *pot*	*i* for short -*o*
POT for *put*	*o* for short -*u*

Through word study, students in the letter name–alphabetic stage learn to spell short-vowel words correctly and they see that short vowels follow a specific pattern, a **consonant-vowel-consonant (CVC)** pattern. Regardless of how many consonant letters are on either side of the single vowel (*cat, clap, clack*), one vowel letter in the middle signals the short-vowel sound. The CVC pattern is introduced in the late letter name–alphabetic stage and is contrasted with long-vowel patterns in the within word pattern stage.

As they mature and learn more sight words, students face the ambiguities of **homographs,** words that are spelled the same but pronounced differently. For example, students in the letter name–alphabetic stage may spell *bent, bet, bat,* and *bait* the same way: BAT. The burden of so many homographs is a catalyst for students to change, a good problem. Letter name–alphabetic spellers are also readers, and when they reread their own spelling of *bait* as BAT, a word that they know spells something else, they experience disequilibrium. This forces them to find other ways to spell a word like *bait*. When students are able to spell these basic short-vowel patterns, and they begin to experiment with long-vowel patterns, they have entered the next spelling stage: within word pattern.

Other Orthographic Features

In addition to short vowels, students work through four other features during the letter name–alphabetic stage: (1) consonant digraphs, (2) consonant blends, (3) preconsonantal nasals, and (4) influences on the vowel from certain surrounding consonants.

Consonant digraphs and blends.   Letter name–alphabetic spellers take some time to learn consonant digraphs and blends. A **digraph** is two letters that make a single sound. The word *digraph* ends with a digraph, the *ph* that stands for the single sound of */f/*. Digraphs are easier than blends and can be taught right along with other beginning consonants because they represent a single phoneme. The most commonly recognized digraphs have an *h* as the second letter of the pair. Digraphs include the bold letters in **th**in, fi**sh**, ea**ch**, **wh**en, **ph**one.

A **consonant blend** is slightly different. A blend is a spelling unit (sometimes called a *consonant cluster*) of two or three consonants that retain their identity when pronounced. The word *blend* contains two blends: *bl* and *nd*. Each of the sounds in a blend can still be heard, but they are tightly bound and not easily segmented into individual phonemes, which makes blends difficult for students to spell accurately. The *t* in the *st* blend may be omitted in *stick*, as in the spellings *SEK* or *SEC*. Blends can occur at the beginning or end of words and are represented by the bold letters in the following words: **bl**ack, **cl**ap ju**st**, li**sp**, ma**sk**.

Preconsonantal nasals.   Some blends are more subtle than others. The nasal sounds associated with *m, n,* and *ng,* are made by air passing through the nasal cavity in the mouth. **Preconsonantal nasals** come right before a final consonant, such as the *m* in *jump* or the *n* in *pink*. Try saying *bad, ban,* and then *band*. You cannot feel the *n* in *band* because it passes out through the nose, but it is definitely there! Preconsonantal nasals are often omitted during the letter name–alphabetic stage (*jump* may be spelled *JOP* and *pink* may be spelled *PEK*). When students begin to spell words with preconsonantal nasals correctly, they are usually at the end of the letter name–alphabetic stage.

Consonant influences on the vowel.   The letters *r, w,* and *l* influence the vowel sounds they follow. For example, the vowel sounds in words like *bar, ball,* and *saw* are not the same as the short-vowel sounds in *bat* and *fast*. They cannot be called short *-a*, yet all of these words have the CVC pattern. The *w* often has an effect on vowels that follow it in words such as *want, was, wash, word,* and *war*. The consonant sounds */r/* and */l/* are known in linguistics as **liquids** because they roll around in the mouth and have vowel-like qualities. Both can change the pronunciation of the vowel they follow. These spellings are often known as *r*-influenced or *r*-controlled and *l*-influenced or *l*-controlled.

R-influenced vowels can be difficult to spell by sound alone. For example, *fur, her,* and *sir* have the same vowel sound yet are spelled three different ways. *R*-influenced vowels that follow a CVC pattern (*car, for*) are examined during the late letter name–alphabetic stage and can be compared with short vowels in word sorts. Students might also contrast consonant blends with an *r* (*fr, tr, gr*) and *r*-influenced vowels (e.g., *from–form, grill–girl, tarp–trap*) as a way to compare exactly where the *r* falls.

WORD STUDY INSTRUCTION FOR THE LETTER NAME–ALPHABETIC STAGE

The focus for word study in the letter name–alphabetic stage begins with initial consonants and continues through consonant digraphs, blends, and the study of short vowels. Word study during this stage makes use of pictures and known words from students' reading and word banks. This section discusses the sequence of word study throughout the letter name–alphabetic stage, presents ways to build a sight-word vocabulary and the use of word banks, and offers some tips for how to lead group sorting activities.

Sequence and Pacing of Word Study

Initially, students use beginning consonants in their writing, so this is the place to begin word study in the early letter name–alphabetic stage. As their ability to segment phonemes becomes more complete, they begin to use but confuse short vowels and consonant blends in the middle to late letter name stage. This is the time to study those features. When students begin to use long-vowel patterns in their spelling, they are ready to examine long-vowel word patterns and move on to the next stage. Table 5-3 summarizes the sequence of word study in this stage. Table 5-1 will help you identify whether students are in the early, middle, or late part of the stage.

Although there is a predictable pattern of development, the exact sequence and pace will not be precisely the same for every student. There are three factors to consider.

1. *Student development.* Because students always use known words in word study, phonics instruction during this stage is constrained by students' sight vocabularies. Teachers may need to spend different lengths of time on phonics features with different students. For this reason, membership in word study groups must be fluid.
2. *Urgency.* There is no time to waste. Teachers must set as fast a pace as possible during the letter name–alphabetic stage because success in beginning reading depends on learning the basic phonics elements that are covered in this stage.
3. *Curriculum.* School districts and schools may specify through core curriculum guides *what* phonics features should be studied. Some core programs specify *when* in the year a phonics feature should be taught. You will probably find the scope and sequence of what is taught will be similar to the order presented here. We may differ on the exact order of presentation, e.g., which consonants should be taught first. Based on a developmental approach, teachers can be assured that all the phonics features are covered. The sequence we recommend is outlined in Table 5-3.

Balancing the three factors described above is a challenging task. We will offer ideas about how to address each phonics feature appropriate for the letter name–alphabetic stage and how to know when to move on to the next area of word study instruction.

Sight Word Learning, Word Banks, and Personal Readers

Sight words are the basis of word sorts, and collecting and monitoring sight word learning is an important effort during this stage. We define **sight words** as any words that are

TABLE 5-3	Scope and Sequence of Word Study in the Letter Name–Alphabetic Stage
Early	Review all initial consonants with picture sorts and known words from the word bank.
	Contrast specific consonants that students confuse.
	Introduce digraphs and blends in picture sorts.
	Introduce short vowels in same-vowel word families using pictures and words.
Middle	Study short vowels in mixed-vowel word families.
	Include digraphs and blends in the study of word families.
	Use pictures and words in the study of blends and digraphs as needed.
Late	Study short vowels in CVC words outside of word families.
	Review digraphs and blends in CVC words, especially those producing an affricate sound (*tr, dr, sh, ch*).
	Study preconsonantal nasals in short vowel words.
	Introduce *r*-influenced vowels spelled with *ar* and *or*.

stored completely enough in memory to be recognized consistently in and out of context. Sight words will include many high-frequency words, but are not limited to them. Any word can be a sight word. Acquiring a sight vocabulary is critical for progress in reading. Automatic word recognition makes it possible to read fluently and to devote attention to comprehension rather than to figuring out unknown words. A sight vocabulary also provides a corpus of known words from which students can discover generalizations about how words work.

What students know about particular words during this time may only be partial. For example, as they read, early letter name–alphabetic spellers may substitute *leopard* for *lion* in a story about big cats at the zoo. From such errors, it appears that they are attending to beginning letters for cues. This is also evident in the way they spell during this time. *Lion* might be spelled as *ln*. Ehri (1997) has described these readers as "partial alphabetic," because their letter-sound knowledge is not automatic or complete and they use only partial letter-sound cues—usually consonant cues—to identify and spell words. Students will acquire sight words slowly during the early letter name–alphabetic period and they will need frequent exposure to those words. Examining words out of context makes a difference in how well they learn those words (Ehri & Wilce, 1980) and how many words they learn over time (Johnston, 1998, 2000). Word banks and personal readers are described as a context for sight word learning and word study.

A **word bank** is a collection of words gathered from the texts that students have been reading and rereading (Stauffer, 1980). The words are lifted out of context and written on small cards and collected over time. These words are reviewed regularly, and words that have been forgotten are matched back to their counterpart in context or discarded. Sometimes we are asked why students need to review words they already know. The answer is, they do not know them the same way more mature readers do; they know them only partially and tentatively. Letter name–alphabetic students may confuse *ran* and *run*, *stop* and *ship*, *lost* and *little*. They may get *gingerbread* every time because it is the only long word they have that starts with *g*, but when you ask them to spell it (*gnrbrd*) you get a better idea of what they really know about that word.

Regular review of word bank words encourages students to look more thoroughly at words and to note individual letter-sound correspondences. As they study initial sounds, students can be asked to find words in their word bank that have those same sounds. This will help them make connections between the pictures they sort and the words they read. Later in the letter name–alphabetic stage, the word bank becomes a source of known words to be used in word sorts. It is crucial that students work with known words because it is easier to look across known words for similarities and differences in sounds and letters. There is an added burden in word study if students must labor to pronounce the words before analyzing their orthographic features and their relationships to other words.

The words in a word bank come from many sources: students' preprimer readers, rhymes, leveled books, dictations, small group experience charts, and poems that they read and reread. By using words that come from familiar readings and by numbering the stories and rhymes and the word cards, students can be encouraged to return to the primary source to find a forgotten word and to match the word bank card to its counterpart in print.

Personal readers, shown in Figure 5-3, contain copies of familiar rhymes and jingles, or selected passages from simple books that students can read independently or with some support from a teacher or partner (Bear, Caserta-Henry, & Venner, 2004). They may also contain copies of group or individual dictations. Students are enormously proud of their personal readers and they reread them many times before taking them home to read some more. The stories in the personal readers are numbered, and the date they are

FIGURE 5-3   Personal Reader with Word Bank

introduced is recorded. Personal readers are an ideal place for students to collect words for their word banks. They can simply underline the words they know best and these words can then be transferred to small cards. A number can be written on each word card that matches the numbered stories.

In Figure 5-3, the student's word bank is a plastic bag that can be stored in the personal reader. You can also see that little leveled books can fit inside the front pocket. The personal reader also contains a page that lists the words in the student's word bank. A reduced soundboard (see Appendix B) of consonant sounds is included for a student reference in word study and writing.

Word banks increase slowly and steadily. At first, students do not have enough words in their banks to use them much for sorting. Gradually, word banks increase to 50 words, and then there are plenty of words for many sorts. When the word bank contains at least 200 words and the student is at the end of the letter name–alphabetic stage, the word bank can be discontinued.

Word banks take extra work but are well worth the effort, particularly for students in the beginning of this stage who are not making good progress in reading. Word banks promote sight word development and growing word knowledge. They are also motivating for students because they offer tangible evidence of their growing word knowledge (Johnston, 1998). Guidelines for making and using word banks, individual dictations, and group experience charts can be found in the first part of the activities section of this chapter.

The Study of Beginning Sounds

FIGURE 5-4   Initial Consonant Picture and Word Sort

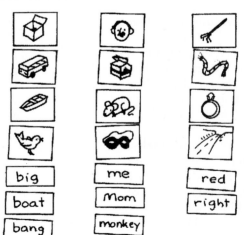

Word study for students in the early letter name–alphabetic stage starts with a review of initial consonant sounds. Sorts give students an opportunity to compare pictures based on how they "sound at the beginning." Figure 5-4 is an example of a sort that started with pictures and then included sight words from the students' word banks. Pictures to use for sorts can be found in Appendix C. Chapter 4 offers suggestions for how to plan and carry out picture sorts for initial consonants as well as games for further practice. Chapter 3 describes follow-up activities such as sort-and-paste and draw-and-label.

Mr. Perez, whom we met at the beginning of this chapter, was wise in deciding to take a step back to firm up Cynthia's understandings of consonants. Many students benefit from a fast-paced review of consonants at the beginning of first grade to clear up lingering confusions or to secure tentative letter-sound matches. There is no particular order to the sequence of beginning sounds, but starting with frequently occurring initial consonants where the contrasts or differences are clear both visually and phonologically is recommended. Many teachers have found the following sequence to be effective.

B	M	R	S
T	G	N	P
C	H	F	D
L	K	J	W
Y	Z	V	

Some students may only have a few lingering confusions with certain letter-sounds based on letter name confusions (*y* and *w*, for example) or voiced and unvoiced pairs (*b* and *p*, for example). They will benefit from sorts designed to address these confusions. English language learners might also need sorts that address the confusions that arise because of sounds that are missing or different in their native language. There's more about this later in the chapter.

Picture sorts with initially occurring short vowels can also be included here as a way to introduce those letter-sound correspondences. Pictures for these beginning short vowels can be found in Appendix C, after the beginning consonant pictures.

A few ending consonants might be introduced and studied with picture sorts, but once students have developed enough phonemic awareness to attend to final sounds, most of them can easily use their knowledge of letter-sound matches to spell those final consonants as well. Some students may have a few remaining confusions even when they are in control of most consonant matches, but do not hesitate to move on if they are beginning to represent vowels in their invented spellings. Beginning consonants are reviewed and ending consonants are targeted in same-vowel word families. English language learners may need more sorts with final consonant sounds.

The study of digraphs and blends. After students know their beginning consonant sounds, they are ready to learn about initial consonant digraphs and blends. The goal is to not only master letter-sound correspondences, but also to help students see these two-letter combinations as single orthographic units in the CVC pattern.

Beginning Digraphs. The digraphs to be studied in the letter name stage are *ch, sh, th,* and *wh*. (*Ck* is sometimes considered a digraph, but it only comes at the end of short vowel words and cannot be studied with pictures. *Ph* is a digraph that occurs in many words derived from Greek, and is best studied later). The study of digraphs begins with pictures that can be found in Appendix C. There are several things to consider when setting up sorting contrasts for digraphs. First, consider the confusions students show us in their invented spellings. Some students substitute *j* for *ch* as they spell words like *chin* as *IN* or they may confuse the letter name of *h* (aitch) with *ch* and spell *chin* as *HN*. These affricate confusions suggest that a good sort to study *ch* might include pictures that start with *ch, c,* and *h*. *Th* might be compared to single *t, sh* to single *s,* and *ch* to single *c*. Note, however, that it would be difficult to sort pictures by *w* and *wh* because many words beginning with *wh* do not have a distinctive sound. (Which witch was which?) Compare *wh* to *th, sh,* and *ch* in a culminating digraph sort. Possible contrasts for digraphs include:

1. *c / ch / h*
2. *s / sh / h*
3. *sh / ch*
4. *t / th / h*
5. *ch / sh / th*
6. *wh / sh / th / ch*

Beginning Blends. Beginning consonant blends come in three major groups:

S blends (*sc, sk, sl, sn, sm, sp, st, sw*)
R blends (*br, cr, dr, fr, gr, pr, tr*)
L blends (*bl, cl, fl, gl, pl, sl*)

The easiest group of blends is the *s* blends because *s* is a continuant (*/sssss/*) and because, with the exception of *sl*, the *s* blends do not contain the "slippery" *l* or *r*. Other initial blends include *tw* and *qu*. (In *qu*, the *u* is a consonant representing the */w/* sound.) Three-letter blends (*spr, str, squ, thr, shr*) are less common and studied in the within word pattern stage.

The study of beginning consonant blends starts by contrasting a single initial consonant with its blend because this is the problem students show us when they spell *sled* as *SED*. Pictures that begin with *st* may be contrasted with pictures that begin with *s* for spellers such as Tony who spell *stick* as *SEK*. After studying several blends in this fashion, it is best to pick up the pace and introduce other blends in groups. Some suggested contrasts are listed as follows, but once students catch on to how blends work and learn to segment and blend the individual sounds in a consonant blend, they may move quickly through a sequence of study or skip some contrasts altogether.

Suggested contrasts for beginning blends include:

1. *st / s / t*
2. *sp / s / p*
3. *st / sp / sk / sm*
4. *sl / sn / sc / sw*
5. *bl / b / l*
6. *gl / pl / bl / cl*
7. *tr / t / r*
8. *dr / r / r*
9. *gr / tr / dr / pr*
10. *bl / br / gl / gr*
11. *cl / cr / fl / fr*
12. *k / qu / tw*

The procedures and routines for the study of digraphs and blends are the same as for other beginning sound sorts described in Chapter 4. Pictures needed for the study of digraphs and blends can be found in Appendix C. Chapter 3 describes follow-up activities such as draw and label, which are appropriate for digraphs and blends. Many of the games described for beginning consonants in Chapter 4 and in this chapter can be easily adapted to review digraphs and blends.

Students in the early part of the letter name–alphabetic stage are not expected to acquire great fluency or accuracy in spelling and sorting consonant blends and digraphs because they will be revisited throughout the stage. Research (Johnston, 2003) shows that blends, digraphs, and short vowels all begin to appear in children's spellings about the same time, so there should be some interplay between these features in the instructional sequence as shown in Table 5-4. Consonant blends and digraphs that create an affricate sound (*tr, dr, ch*) will have to be revisited throughout this stage because their sounds are so similar (*chip, trip, drip*).

Final blends (*st, sp, sk, ft, pt, lt, lf,* and *lp*) are not studied with pictures due to a lack of examples, but should be included toward the end of the stage in the study of short-vowel words. Other ending blends like *rd, rt, rp*, that include an *r* are studied with *r*-influenced vowels.

Preconsonantal nasals are also studied at the end of the letter name stage. They include *mp, nt, nd,* and *nk*. We include *ng* as well and it may be studied as a word family as there are many words spelled with *ang, ing, ong,* and *ung*. Appendix E has lists of words by families and you will find words with preconsonantal nasals among them. Many children find this feature particularly difficult and will need explicit routines for making words with and without the nasal, changing *rag* into *rang*, or *hung* into *hug*, for example. Building, blending, and extending described in the activity section can be adapted for this.

The Study of Short Vowels

Once letter name–alphabetic spellers have a solid, if not complete, mastery of beginning and ending consonant sounds, they are ready for the study of medial short vowels. If

TABLE 5-4   Possible Pace and Sequence of Word Family Study

Introductions	Moderate Pace	Fast Pace / Review
Same-Vowel Word Families		
at family with pictures and words	*at* and *an*	*at, an, ad, ap*
an and *ad* with pictures and words	*ag, ad, ap*	*ip, ig, in, it*
ap and *ag* with pictures and words	*ip, ig, in, ill*	*ug, ut, un, ub*
op, ot, and *og* with pictures and words	*op, ot, og*	
ip, ig, ill with pictures and words	*ug, ut, un, ub*	
ug, ut, un		
ed, et, eg, ell		
Mixed-Vowel Word Families	Include words with blends and digraphs	
at, ot, it	*at, ot, ag, og*	*am, im, um*
an, en, in, un	*an, en, un*	*ag, ig, eg, ug, og*
ad, ed, ab, ob	*ip, ap, op, up*	*all, ell, ill*
ap, ip, op, up	*ack, ock, ick, uck*	*ack, ock, ick, uck*
ag, eg, ig, og, ug	*ang, ing, ung, ong*	*ink, ank, unk*
all, ill, ell	*ink, ank, unk*	
ack, ock, ick, uck	*ish, ash, ush*	
ish, ash, ush		
ang, ing, ong, ung		
ank, ink, unk		

vowels are still missing or used only occasionally in students' invented spellings, start the study of vowels with same-vowel word families or **phonograms.** Once students are using (though still confusing) short vowels consistently, they can be asked to compare short vowels in word sorts that examine the CVC pattern across a variety of vowels. Refer again to Table 5-2 and 5-3 to see how to use students' spellings for planning instruction during this stage.

Word families offer an easy and appealing way to introduce the issue of vowels early on in this stage. Students are supported in their first efforts to analyze the vowel because the vowel and the ending letter(s) are presented as a chunk or pattern. In linguistic terms, the **rime** consists of the vowel and what follows. What comes before the vowel is the **onset.** Examples of onset-rime breaks are *m-an*, *bl-and*, *m-at*, and *th-at*. Dividing words into onsets and rimes is easier and more natural for students than dividing them into individual phonemes (Treiman, 1985).

The study of word families makes sense for several other reasons. First, 37 rimes can be used to generate 500 different words that students encounter in primary reading materials (Wylie & Durrell, 1970). In addition, these same rimes will be familiar chunks in thousands of multisyllabic words: the *an* chunk can be found in *canyon, incandescent,* and *fantastic.* Second, vowel sounds are more stable within families than across families (Adams, 1990; Wylie & Durrell, 1970). For example, the word *dog* is often presented as a short *-o* word in phonics programs; but in some regions of the United States, it is pronounced more like *dawg.* If you say it that way, then you probably pronounce *fog* as *fawg, frog* as *frawg,* and *log* as *lawg.* In the study of word families, the actual pronunciation of the short vowel does not matter; it is the *-og* chunk that is examined and compared.

Knowing that students in the early letter name stage have trouble isolating and attending to the medial vowel, it is a good idea to compare word families that share the same vowel before contrasting different vowels. This supports students' first efforts to read and spell those words. What they really must attend to are the beginning and ending consonants in order to sort and spell the words. The study of same-vowel word families serves to review those features. In sorting words like *mat* and *man*, for example, students must attend to the final consonant more than any place else.

There is no particular order to the study of word families, but starting with short -*a* families (*at*, *an*, *ad*, *ap*, *ack*) seems to be a good choice because these words abound in early reading materials, and students are likely to already know several words from these families by sight. In addition, short -*a* is the least likely short vowel to be confused when students try to make matches based on letter names and place of articulation.

Move quickly, however, to comparing words that have different vowels. The difference between *mitt*, *met*, and *mat* lies in the medial vowel and it is through such contrasts that students are forced to attend to the vowel sound itself. Students in the middle letter name stage should be ready to study mixed-vowel word families. Words with blends and digraphs should be included after they have been studied with picture sorts. For example, the *ag* family can be expanded to include *flag*, *brag*, *drag*, *shag*, and *snag*.

Table 5-4 suggests contrasts and a sequence for the study of word families under three possible pacing guides. However, it is offered only as a model from which to plan your own course of study. Consider the words that your students have in their word banks and the kinds of words they encounter in their reading. If you are reading a story with lots of short -*u* words, then study a few short -*u* families. You will find lists of words for each family in Appendix C to complete your sorts, and Appendix D has preplanned sorts that can simply be written into the template provided on page 376. Look in the short vowel pictures and the chart of rhyming words in Appendix C to create word family sorts with pictures.

Introducing word families with pictures.   Here are the steps to follow when introducing a word family sort with pictures (see Figure 5-5).

FIGURE 5–5   Same-Vowel Word Family Sort with Pictures

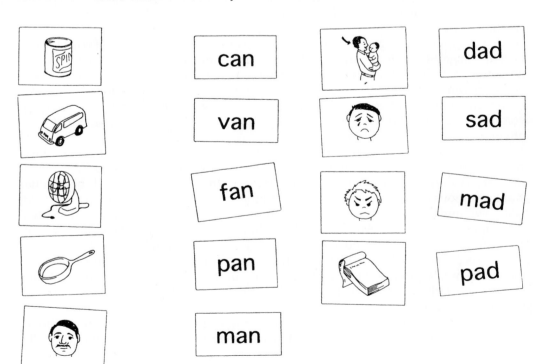

1. Lay out all the *pictures* and start with a rhyming sort. Put down pictures as headers for each column (*can* and *dad*) and then pick up another picture: "*Van*. Does *van* rhyme with *can* or *dad*? I will put it under the *van*." Model several and then have students help you finish the sort. Name all the pictures in each column and talk about how they rhyme.
2. Lay out the *word cards*. Name a header such as *can* and say: "Who can find the word *can*? What letters would you look for at the beginning and end?" Repeat for *dad*, and begin to involve students in the sorting. After all the words are sorted and matched to the pictures, read down each column. Ask the students how the words are alike. Children should note that they all end with the same two letters. Explain that they are in the same family (the *an* family or *ad* family) and they all rhyme.
3. Remove the words and shuffle them. Give them out to the students to match to the pictures again. Read each column and then remove the pictures to see if the students can use just the initial sound and the rime to read each word in the column.
4. Give students their own set of pictures and words to sort for seatwork. Follow up with other word family activities such as Build, Blend, and Extend, described in activities 5-12 on page 160.

Introducing mixed-vowel word families with words.   In the following procedure for sorting word families, *ig*, *ag*, and *og* are used as examples. Students should already be able to read two or more words in each family.

1. Begin by laying down a known word as a header for each family. Choose words you are sure the students can read, such as *big*, *dog*, and *bag*. Explain that the rest of the words are to be sorted under one of the headers.
2. Pick up another word such as *frog* and say, "I am going to put this word under *dog*. Listen: *dog, frog*." Continue to model one or two words in each category, always sorting first and then reading down, starting with the header.
3. Ask students to sort the next word. They should sort first and then read from the top of each column to help them identify the new word. They are not expected to sound the word out first and then sort. Instead, their sense of rhyme will support them as they read the new word by simply changing the first sound of a word they already know. The final sort might look like this:

big	dog	bag
dig	frog	wag
pig	hog	flag
wig	log	rag
	fog	tag

4. After all the words have been sorted, lead a discussion to focus students' attention on the common features (sounds and letters) in each word: "How are the words in each column alike?"
5. Provide students with individual sorts. Conclude as in the sort above with follow up activities.

During the study of word families, it is appropriate to modify one of the principles of word study described in Chapter 3: *Use words students can read*. When working with word families, students probably cannot read all the words initially. However, because the words are in rhyming families, students are supported in their reading of the words as long as the header and the first few words are familiar. Students sort visually first and then read unknown words by blending different onsets with the rime of the header. Be sure to include words with digraphs and blends as a review of those features and a chance to see them in another context. The study of the *ack* family can grow to be quite large when you include *black, clack, track, shack, quack, stack, snack,* and *crack*.

With the publication of research on onsets and rimes and renewed interest in word families, there has been a flood of reading materials for students that feature a particular family or short vowel. Some of these little books are engaging and well-written, offering students support in the form of patterned or rhyming text. Such books can be used as a starting point or as a follow-up for word study, and students can use them to go on word hunts for additional words that follow the same phonics feature. However, choose these books carefully. Stories featuring sentences such as "The tan man ran the van" change reading from the making of meaning into exercises in word calling. Some phonics readers are better done than others and should never constitute the sole reading materials used at this level.

There are lots of activities and games to use in connection with the study of word families. Follow-ups to sorting include re-sorting, blind sorts, and writing sorts, as described in Chapter 3. Board games designed to study beginning sounds can be adapted to word families. Activities like Build, Blend, and Extend, Sound Wheels, Flip Charts, and the Show Me game are favorites and are included in the activities to follow. From this point on, students are expected to spell the words they sort correctly. Word study notebooks can be used to record writing sorts and the results of word hunts or brainstorming sessions.

The study of word families can take a long time if you feel compelled to study every family in a thorough fashion, but this should not be the case. Some students quickly pick up the notion that words that sound alike probably share similar rimes and are spelled alike. They will also be able to use this knowledge to figure out new words by analogy; for example, noting the *and* in *stand*, they quickly decode it. However, these students may still make errors in spelling short vowels.

The Study of Short Vowels in the CVC Pattern

Once students are spelling perhaps approximately half of the short-vowel words correctly on a spelling inventory and working with mixed-vowel word families easily and accurately, they are ready for the study of short vowels in nonrhyming words outside of word families. This study will ask them to look at words in a new way, not as two units with various rimes (*m-ad, fl-ag, tr-ack*), but as three units with the same CVC pattern (*m-a-d, fl-a-g, tr-a-ck*), one vowel surrounded by consonants. This ability to see words as patterns is the key feature of the next stage, within word pattern. Over the course of studying the short vowels, students come to see that CVC is the basic pattern for all short vowels.

When beginning the study of short vowels, plan contrasts that are fairly distinct from each other. We recommend that students compare short -*a* to short -*i* or short -*o*. Do not try to move directly from a short -*a* to a short -*e* or from short -*e* to a short -*i*, those are the very sounds students are most likely to confuse. Most sorting for short vowels will be done with words, but you can use pictures to focus students' attention on the vowel sounds and you can use pictures for column headers. Pictures for sorting can be found in Appendix C. Consider what words your students already know from familiar texts and word banks as you select words for sorts. Lists of words spelled with short vowels can be found in Appendix E. These lists can be used to create handouts similar to those used by Mr. Perez in Figure 5-1C. Appendix D has suggested sorts.

During the study of short vowels is a good time to establish the **oddball,** or miscellaneous category, to accommodate variations in dialect and spelling. Some students may hear a short -*o* in *lost*, but others will hear a sound closer to /*aw*/. Some students hear a different vowel in *pin* and *pen*, but others consider them homophones. Rather than forcing students to doubt their own ear, the oddball category offers an alternative and acknowledges that people do not all speak quite the same way nor does spelling always match pronunciation. Good words to use for oddballs in this stage are high-frequency words students may already know as sight words. The top 200 high-frequency words, as determined by Fry (1980), are marked with asterisks in the word lists in Appendix E. It is a good idea to include these in the sorts. Some of these will be oddballs (*was, put*), but many will turn up in word families (*can, get, had, not, that*) or other short vowel sorts (*with, this, much*).

Be prepared to spend some time on short vowels, as they pose special problems for young spellers and can persist as problems beyond first grade. However, short vowels will be reviewed when they are compared to long vowels in the next stage, so do not expect 100% accuracy. Once students begin using but confusing vowel markers (e.g., *RANE* for *rain*) you may want to move on to the study of vowel patterns.

Word sorting to compare two or more short vowels.   Following is the basic procedure for sorting words by short vowels.

1. Make a collection of word cards to model the sort on a table-top, pocket chart, or overhead projector.
2. Begin by laying down a known word as a header for each vowel. Read each word and isolate the vowel: "Here is the word *cap*. Listen: *cap, ap, /a/. Cap* has the short -*a* sound in the middle. We will listen for other words that have the same vowel sound in the middle." Repeat for each category.
3. Pick up a new word such as *fast* and say: "I am going to put this word under *cap*. Listen: *ca-a-ap, f-a-a-ast.*" Continue to model one or two words in each category, reading each new word and comparing it to the header. Hold up an oddball like *for* or *was*. Ask students if they hear the same vowel sound in the middle. Model how to place it in the oddball category because it does not have the same vowel sound. Ask your students to help with the sort. They should read each word and then sort it. Once the words are sorted, read down each column and discuss how the words are alike in sound and spelling.
4. Invite students to try sorting their own words next. Correct any errors made during the first sort. The final sort might look something like this:

cap	pig	hot	oddball
fast	ship	stop	for
camp	fish	lock	ball
hat	sit	shop	
mad	hill	job	
trap	him	not	

5. After all the words have been sorted, discuss the common features in each word: "How are the words in each column alike? How are the oddballs different?" Help student identify the CVC pattern by labeling the units in *cap, pig*, and *not*. Point out that *hill* and *trap* are also CVC words because *ll* and *tr* are consonant units on each side of the single vowel.
6. Reread the words in each column and then lead the students in sorting a second time. Any mistakes should be left until the end and checked by reading down the columns.
7. Students should be given their own set of words to sort at their seats, with partners, or for homework.
8. Because it is easy to sort the words visually by attending to the vowel letters, the blind sort described in Chapter 3 is particularly important as a follow-up activity. Model this first in a small group or with an overhead projector and then let partners work together. One partner reads each word aloud while the other partner indicates where it goes without seeing the word.

If students are still making errors in the spelling of digraphs and blends, which is likely, include words that have those features in the short-vowel sorts. At this time, they have many more sight words that contain beginning and ending consonant digraphs and blends. Preconsonantal nasals can also be included in this study. You might even plan a two-way sort—first by vowel sounds and second by digraphs or blends.

First Sort by Vowel			**Second Sort by Blends**		
a	*i*	*u*	*tr*	*dr*	*cr*
trap	trick	drug	trap	drag	crack
crack	trip	crumb	track	drip	crash
drag	trim	truck	trick	drum	crumb
crash	drip	drum	trim	drill	crab
track	crib	crush	truck	drag	crib

FIGURE 5-6   Jeff's Open Sort

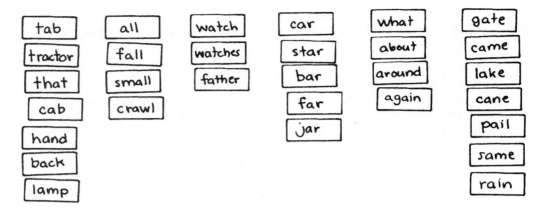

Words like *car* and *for* look as though they follow the CVC pattern, but they do not have the short sound. Because words spelled with *ar* and *or* are common in beginning reading materials, it is worthwhile to spend some time with them. *R*-controlled vowels form a major subcategory of vowels that will need to be examined closely during the next stage. Following is a special sort that might examine such words.

Short -*a ar*		**Short -*o or***		**Oddballs**
clap	car	fox	for	word
jam	star	shop	sort	work
black	park	pond	born	
sand	yard	spot	fort	
camp	jar	trot	horn	

This chapter has presented many examples of teacher-directed sorts or **closed sorts.** The teacher selects the words and leads a group sorting activity accompanied by a discussion of the features of interest. Student-centered sorts, or **open sorts,** as described in Chapter 3, allow students to establish their own categories and offer the teacher diagnostic information that will help to determine how much students understand about the orthography.

Figure 5-6 is an open sort by a student in the late letter name–alphabetic stage. Jeff was asked to go through his word bank; find the word cards that had an *a* in them, and sort them into categories. His first sort resulted in three categories: short -*a*, long -*a*, and a large pile of miscellaneous words. He was then challenged to take the miscellaneous words and sort them into a number of piles. His new categories include short -*a*, *l*-influenced, broad -*a*, *r*-influenced, schwa, and long -*a*. Figure 5-6 shows that Jeff has developed quite a good ear for vowel sounds and understands that *a* is used to represent a variety of sounds.

WORD STUDY WITH ENGLISH LANGUAGE LEARNERS IN THE LETTER NAME–ALPHABETIC STAGE

Letter-name spellers who are also English learners contrast the sounds in their primary languages as they learn the sounds of English. For example, Spanish speakers generally build on 24 sounds as they contrast and add sounds to acquire the 44 sounds of English. The assessments in Chapter 2 highlight the consonants and vowels students spell.

Consonant sounds.   In general, most other languages do not have as many single consonants or blends as we do in English. English learners may need more time to practice these sounds because they will have to learn how to hear and pronounce the sounds, segment the sounds, and learn the letter correspondences. The difficult consonant sounds in English for Spanish speakers are presented in Table 5-5. Here you can see the sounds that students may omit or mispronounce. For example, Spanish-speaking students may confuse words that begin with *d* and *th*, pronouncing *dog* with a *th* sound, more like *thog*. *Jump* may be pronounced *chump*. It will be important to create sorts that make these comparisons clear (*d* and *th* or *j* and *ch*) once the other beginning sounds are established. It is common for students to omit the ending consonant sounds in words like *hard* that may be spelled *HAR*, or *test*, which may be spelled *TES*, so final consonant picture sorts may be needed. Only five consonants occur in the final position in Spanish, so sorting words by rhyme or word families like *bag, rag, tag* can be more of a challenge for English learners. Contrasts in which the vowel and the final consonant differ (at, op, un) are a better starting place. In Spanish, the *s*-blends work differently. In a word like *Spanish* the sp blend is split into two syllables. The *s* is given a vowel (es) and *p* starts the second syllable (es-pan-ole) in *Es-pan-ole*, and the blend is given a vowel and split into two syllables.

　　Still, there are many consonants we share (*b, d, f, g, k, l, m, n, p, r, s, t, w, y*), and Spanish-speaking students can begin the study of consonants with these. Spanish picture sorts can be found in the word study program for Spanish learners on the Interactive *Words Their Way* CD. Teachers should talk explicitly about the different sounds in English and Spanish and acknowledge students' confusion as logical. Because students might not be able to name the pictures, you might pair them with an English-speaking partner who can supply the English names.

Vowels.　　As with consonants, other languages do not have as many vowels sounds as we do in English. Spanish has only one short-vowel sound (short -*o*), and it is spelled with the letter *a* as in *gracias*. Expect students to substitute vowels in their own language

TABLE 5-5　*Difficult Consonant Sounds in English for Spanish Speakers (Adapted from Helman, 2004).*

Difficult Consonant Sounds for Spanish Speakers Learning English	May Be Pronounced	May Be Spelled
d as in *den*	*then*	*DEM*
j as in *joke*	*choke*	*GOB*
r as in *race*	(rolled *r*) *race*	*WAS*
v as in *very*	*bery*	*BARY*
z as in *zoo*	*soo*	*SO*
sh as in *shine*	*chine*	*CHIN*
th as in *think*	*tink*	*TAK*
Beginning *s* blends *st, sp, sc, sk, sm, sn*	espace, esquirt, esplash	*ESPAS* for *space*
Ending blends with *r: -rd, -rt, -rl, -rs*	har (hard), cur (curl), tar (tarp)	*HAR* for *hard*
-ng as in *sing*	sin (g)	*SIN* for *sing*
Ending blends with *s:*	was (wasp), pos	*POS* for *post*
-sp, -st, -sk	(post), as (ask)	

that are close in point of articulation for these short English vowels when they say and spell English words. Short *-e* may be pronounced like long *-a* (*pet* as *pait*), short *-i* like long *-e* (*tip* as *teep*), and short *-a* and short *-u* like short *-o* (*cat* and *cut* as *cot*). Refer back to Figure 5-2 of vowels in the mouth to see the location of the vowels and the logic of these contrasts and spellings.

Watch the Letter Name–Alphabetic section on the *Words Their Way* DVD for specific ideas on organizing word study instruction with letter name–alphabetic spellers.

WORD STUDY ROUTINES AND MANAGEMENT

Word study during the letter name–alphabetic stage begins with picture sorts for initial sounds and ends with word sorts for short vowels. During this transition, there are a variety of routines and generic activities to help students explore features of study in depth (see Chapter 3). Betty Lee's schedule is particularly appropriate for students who are doing picture sorts and students can keep their materials in two-pocket folders. Once students are sorting words, other routines that involve writing sorts in word study notebooks are more effective. Table 5-6 summarizes routines for this stage. Games and activities are described in detail in the section that follows.

Assess to determine whether students need more practice or are ready to move on. Assessment can be as simple as observing how quickly and accurately students sort pictures or you can have students paste the pictures they have sorted into categories and label them. Assessment in the middle to late part of this stage may involve a brief spelling test of five to ten words.

Pacing is an important issue. There are many blends and many word families and if every one were studied for a week, it could take many months. You might want to create 2- or 3-day cycles. For example, you might introduce two word families on Monday, another two on Wednesday, and then combine them for several days. Be ready to pick up the pace by combining a number of blends or families into one sort (up to four or five) or by omitting some features. Only your own observations can dictate the particular pace appropriate for your students.

TABLE 5–6 Sample Weekly Schedules for Word Study in the Letter Name–Alphabetic Stage

	Picture Sorting	Word Sorting
Day 1	Small group sort: Demonstrate, sort and check, reflect	Small group sort: Demonstrate, sort and check, reflect
Day 2	Seatwork or center: Repeat the sort; check	Seatwork or center: Repeat the sort; check; write the sort in word study notebook
Day 3	Seatwork: Repeat the sort; draw and label	Seatwork; Partner work: Blind sort; writing sort: word study notebook extensions
Day 4	Small group or seatwork: Repeat the sort; word or picture hunts in magazines, ABC books, and familiar texts	Seatwork: Repeat the sort Small group: Word hunt in familiar texts; games
Day 5	Assessment and games; paste and label pictures used for sorting during the week	Assessment and games
	Homework: Students take pictures home to sort again and hunt for more pictures that begin with the sound	Homework throughout the week: Repeat the sort; blind sort; writing sort; word hunts

The letter name–alphabetic stage easily spans kindergarten through second grade. A handful of students in third grade and even a few students in the upper elementary grades will still need to work on the features that characterize this stage. It may be tempting to rush through this stage, but word study in the letter name–alphabetic stage helps to build a solid foundation for the study of long vowels and other vowel patterns in the next stage.

Activities for Beginning Readers in the Letter Name–Alphabetic Stage

In this section, specific activities for students in the letter name–alphabetic stage have been organized into the following categories.

 You'll find even more activities for Emergent spellers in the Letter Name–Alphabetic section of the Word Sorting Application on the *Words Their Way* CD. Create your own activities, games, and manipulatives and print them or save them to your hard drive to use again and again.

1. Development and use of personal readers and word banks
2. Review of beginning sounds, including digraphs and blends
3. Study of word families
4. Study of short vowels

Some of the games and activities are adaptable to a variety of features at different stages. These are indicated by the generic symbol.

DEVELOPMENT AND USE OF PERSONAL READERS AND WORD BANKS

Collecting Individual Dictations and Group Experience Stories 5-1

Adaptable for Other Stages

Recording students' individual or group dictations as they talk about personal or group experiences is a key feature of the language experience approach, or LEA (Stauffer, 1980). The text created makes especially good reading material for beginning readers because it is inherently familiar and easy to remember. It is ideal to have every student in a group contribute a sentence, but dictations need to be kept to a reasonable length to be sure beginning readers will be able to read them back. This activity is divided into a 4-day sequence, but it can be accomplished in fewer days with smaller groups.

Materials

You will need chart paper, an overhead projector, a computer, or another way to record dictation so that students can observe as the teacher writes.

Procedures

Day 1: Share an experience and collect dictations—Select a stimulus (a box turtle, autumn leaves, parts of a flashlight) or experience (a trip to the bakery, a classroom visitor, the first snowfall) to share with students. It should be an interesting and memorable experience that encourages students to talk. For some individual dictations, students can be prompted to just tell about a personal experience.

After a discussion that stimulates ideas and vocabulary, ask each student to tell you something to write down. Say each word as you write it and invite the group to help decide some of the letters or spellings you need. Talk about conventions such as capitals and punctuation. Reread each sentence and make any changes the speaker requests. Decide on a title at the end as a kind of summary of the ideas. When it is complete, reread the entire dictation. Reread it again as the students read along with you in a choral reading fashion. Then have them repeat after you, sentence by sentence in the manner of echo reading, as you point to each word.

Before day 2, make a copy of the dictation for each student in the group. Computers make it easy to create these copies. Select a font that has the type of letters easily recognized by young readers (Geneva or Comic Sans MS work well) and enlarge it as much as possible. It is also easy to make copies by writing neatly in your best manuscript handwriting. These copies will go into each student's personal reader and should be numbered.

Day 2: Reread dictations and underline known words—Choral read the dictation again and encourage the students to follow along on their own copies, pointing to words as they read. Individual students can be called on to read a sentence. Once students can read the dictation successfully, they are invited to underline known words for their word bank. Point to the underlined words randomly to make sure they know the words they underline. Students might make an illustration to go with the dictation.

Day 3: Choral read and harvest word cards—Students can work together or individually to read the dictation again. Make word cards for underlined words that are recognized accurately and quickly.

Day 4 and on: Choral read and review new word cards—Students continue to reread their dictations, review the words in their word banks, and complete their pictures. A new dictation or story cycle is begun when students can read their new readings with good accuracy and modest fluency.

In intervention programs staffed by a specialist or volunteers, students might have personal readers that they take with them back and forth from the tutoring sessions to their classrooms. Students also take the personal readers home, where they reread the stories, review their word banks, and sort words and pictures. (Bear, Caserta-Henry, Venner, 2004; Johnston, Invernizzi, & Juel, 1998).

Bilingual entries in the personal readers are particularly useful during the early part of the letter name–alphabetic stage (Bear & Barone, 1998). These bilingual stories are written in both the first and second languages. Initially dictations are just one or two sentences long. A school aide or parent can help with the translations.

Support Reading with Rhymes and Pattern Stories 5-2

Rhymes and jingles and predictable patterned texts make good reading materials because they provide support for beginning readers and can then be used to harvest known words for word banks.

Materials

Find a rhyme, jingle, or predictable story that students will find memorable and readable. You can focus on one major pattern or verse, such as the refrain in *The Gingerbread Man*. Find a big book or make a chart or overhead of the text for group work, and make copies of the rhymes and patterns for students' personal readers.

Procedures

Day 1: Introduce and read the text—Talk about the title and cover and look at the pictures (if applicable) with the students. Read the rhyme or story while fingerpointing the text. Read fluently and with expression, but not too fast. Stop periodically to discuss and enjoy the story. Reread the text and invite students to choral or echo read the entire text if it is short or read parts of the text. Decide which parts of the text will be compiled for personal readers. Type the text onto a single page or two pages that can be duplicated for each student. Number and date this entry.

Days 2, 3, and 4: Reread the rhyme or story and harvest words for word bank—The same procedures described in Activity 5-1 for dictations can be done as follow-ups for rhymes and predictable text. Sentences from the text can also be written on sentence strips, and the students can work to rebuild the text in a pocket chart as described in Activity 4-32 and 4-33.

In Figure 5-7 you see a sample of a rhyme adapted from the story *Caps for Sale* (Slobodkina, 1947). Kari has underlined a number of words to harvest for her word bank. In addition, Kari has made a tick mark each time she reread the rhyme. It is interesting to see that she has used a base-4 marking system.

FIGURE 5-7   Caps for Sale

<u>Caps</u> for <u>sale</u>
Caps for sale
<u>Red</u> and <u>white</u> and blue and green
The <u>finest</u> caps <u>you</u> have ever seen.

Caps for sale
Caps for sale
Red and white and blue and green
The finest caps have ever seen.

Ⅻ   Ⅻ   ⅣⅬ   Ⅻ

Harvesting Words for Word Banks 5-3

Students need to have a stock of sight words that they can read with ease. These can be harvested from books, familiar rhymes, and dictations; stored in a word bank, and reviewed over time. Many of the words will be high-frequency words (*will, this, want*), while others will be words that interest the reader (*dinosaur, chocolate, birthday*). These concrete imagable nouns are more easily learned than helping verbs or prepositions. Although word bank words are traditionally chosen by the students, teachers can also encourage them to include those high-frequency words that young readers need to learn. The following activities help students develop and maintain a word bank.

Materials

You will need copies of personal readers, dictations, familiar books, and so on. Prepare a collection of blank word cards. Tagboard and index cards can be cut to a size that is large enough to hold easily, yet small enough so that students can work with them on a desktop when sorting (4″ by 1.5″ is about right). Teachers can also create a sheet of words for a particular story or poem read by a group of students. These sheets can be reproduced and cut apart and the words can then be quickly handed out as students identify them.

Students will need to store their words in envelopes, plastic bags, small margarine containers, or small cans. Plastic and metal index card file boxes work well—words can be sorted with dividers. You can start with plastic bags for the first 50 words and then move to a box.

Procedures

Following are ways to harvest words for the word bank.

1. *From personal readers.*   If students have an individual copy of dictations, jingles, parts of stories, and so on, they can simply be asked to underline the words they know. Many students will be tempted to underline every word, but over time they will begin to understand the procedure and realize they need to be selective and underline only words they really know. Suggesting that they scan through the text backwards can help some students find known words more accurately.

   A teacher, assistant, or classroom volunteer points to the underlined words in a random fashion to check if the student can indeed name the word quickly (without rereading the sentence in which it occurs). Known words are then written on word cards. Having an adult write the word will ensure that it is neat and accurate. The student can be asked to spell it aloud as the adult writes. On each card write the number of the page in the personal reader. This will make it possible for the students to go back and use context clues to name the word if they forget it.

The students can be asked to write their initials on the back of each card in case words get mixed up during word bank activities.

2. *From familiar books.* Students can also collect sight words independently from books they have read. Some of the words from the book can be put on word cards that are stored in a library pocket in the back of the book. After reading the text, students are taught to read through the words in the pocket to see which ones they know at sight. Students write the words they know onto their own cards and place them in their word banks. Unknown words can be matched back to their counterpart in the text.

3. *From any text.* The easiest procedure for harvesting words is to simply ask the students to point to words in a book or from a chart that they would like to put in their word bank. After several words have been written on cards, the teacher or helper can hold them up to check for recognition.

Variations

To ensure that unknown words do not enter students' word banks, a short-term word bank can be developed for words that students recognize from the latest stories and dictations and stored inside their personal readers (see Figure 5-3). Periodically, teachers work with students in small groups to have them read through the words in their short-term word banks. Words they know from memory go into the permanent word bank.

The Grand Sort with Word Bank Words 5-4

Reviewing the words in the word bank regularly is important to secure those words in memory as sight words. In this sort, students simply go through their word cards, saying the words they know and putting them in one pile, and placing the unknown words to the side. The students try to move quickly through the pile. The words that students put in the "I know" pile can be used in subsequent sorts. Students can do this sort under the teacher's supervision, with a partner or classroom volunteer, or independently.

The unknown words can be discarded, but this can be a touchy point for some students who are hesitant to throw away words. There is no harm in letting a few temporarily unknown words remain, but working with a lot of unknown words makes students' work hesitant, prone to errors, and frustrating. Students in the early letter name–alphabetic stage do not have the word knowledge they need to sound out unknown words, so the teacher should show them how to figure out an unknown word by using context. Referring to the number on the card, the students return to their personal reader to find the word and figure it out. Because this procedure can be time consuming, it is important that only a small percent of words in a word bank are unknown.

Reviewing Word Bank Words 5-5

There are other ways to review and work with words in the word bank.

1. *"Pickup."* Lay out a collection of 5 to 10 words faceup. Words that the student does not know or frequently confuses are good candidates. Someone calls out the words randomly for the student to find and pick up. This simple activity requires the student to use at least partial alphabetic cues to find the words, but does not require him or her to sound out the word.

2. *"I Am Thinking Of."* This activity is similar to the pickup game, but the student is given clues instead of words: "I am thinking of a word that rhymes with pet" or "I am thinking of a word that starts like play."

3. *Concentration.* Make a second set of words and play this classic game as described in Activity 4-23. Work with ten sets of words at a time so that the activity moves quickly.

4. *Word Hunts.*   Students look through their word banks for words that have a particular feature, for example, words that start with *t*, words that end in *m*, or words that have an *o* in them.
5. *Concept Sorts.*   Students look through their word banks for words that fit given semantic categories, for example, words that name animals, words that name people, color words, or things in a house.
6. *Alphabetize Words.*   Make and laminate a large alphabet strip up to 6 feet long. Students place their words under the beginning letter. Pictures can be sorted by beginning sounds as well.

REVIEW OF BEGINNING SOUNDS INCLUDING DIGRAPHS AND BLENDS

A number of activities or games in Chapter 4 are appropriate for students in the letter name–alphabetic stage who are working to master single consonants, digraphs, and blends: Soundline (4-28), Letter Spin for Sounds (4-29), Object Sorting by Sounds (4-30), and Follow-the-Path Games (4-31). Concentration is another adaptable game. Any two pictures that begin with the same sound(s) make a match that can be claimed.

Sound Boards 5-6

Adaptable for Other Stages

Sound boards are references for letter-sound features (beginning consonants, digraphs and blends, and vowels) and can be found in Appendix B. They provide a key word and picture for each letter-sound match, helping students internalize the associations.

Procedures

1. Place a copy of the sound boards at the front of students' writing folders or personal readers. These boards make it easy for students to find letters to stand for the sounds they want to use. Reduced copies of relevant sound boards can be taped to students' desks.
2. Teachers often post charts of various letter-sound features. Recently, the new technology of chart printers has made it possible to take the individual sound boards and enlarge them to poster size. Add a little color and display them in a prominent place for reference.
3. A sound board can be kept in students' word study folders (see Figure 3-16) to serve as a record of progress. Students can lightly color the letters they have studied.
4. Sound boards can be used to generate more words to add to a word family. The rime of the family is written on a small card and slid down beside the beginning sounds. In Figure 5-8, the word family *ack* has been expanded by adding many different blends and digraphs.

FIGURE 5-8 Expanding a Word Family Using a Sound Board

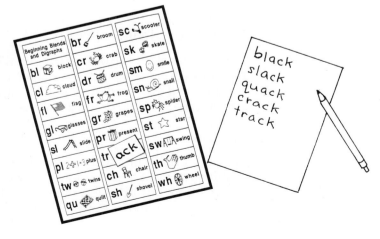

Word Hunts 5-7

Word hunts are conducted several different ways and at different times in the letter name–alphabetic stage: independently, with a partner, or in small groups.

Procedures

1. In the early letter name–alphabetic stage, students hunt for pictures that correspond to beginning sounds. Pictures can be cut from magazines or catalogs and pasted onto individual papers, group charts, or into alphabet scrapbooks. When hunting for pictures, it helps if the teacher, aide, or student helper rips out pages on which there are pictures that contain the feature being hunted. Students can be asked to label the pictures they find by spelling as best they can. Students can hunt for pictures in alphabet books and record their findings as drawings.

2. Students can also hunt for words that begin with the particular initial consonants, blends, or digraphs they are studying. They should look for words they know in familiar reading materials such as their personal reader or by going through their own word banks.

3. Students can hunt for words or pictures that sound like the short vowels they are studying. Note that hunting for additional word family words can be challenging unless you have books that have been specially written to contain a lot for certain families.

4. Word hunts can be made into a game when teams of two or three students hunt for words in a given time period. Students read the words to the teacher or group.

Initial Sound Bingo 5-8

In this version of Bingo, students discriminate among the initial sounds. This is another activity that can be adapted to single consonant, blends, digraphs, and word families.

FIGURE 5-9   Blend Bingo Boards

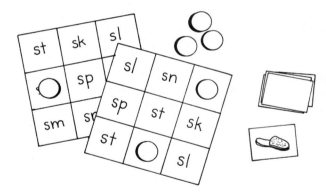

Materials

Make Bingo cards with 9 or 16 squares. In each square, write a letter(s) that features the sounds students have been studying in sorts. Figure 5-9 shows a game prepared to review the *s*-blends. You also need Bingo markers and picture cards to match sounds.

Procedures

Work with small groups of two to four students. Each student gets a Bingo card and markers. Students take turns drawing a card from the stack and calling out the picture name. Students place a marker on the corresponding square. Play continues until someone gets Bingo or the board is filled.

Gruff Drops Troll at Bridge 5-9

This is a special version of the basic follow-the-path game that reinforces *r*-blends. Easter Heatley developed this after reading Paul Galdone's *The Three Billy Goats Gruff*, which was part of a class study of books about monsters. Many of the books yielded a great crop of consonant-plus-*r* words such as *growl, groan,* and *fright.*

Materials

Prepare a game path filled in with *r*-blend letters as shown in Figure 5-10 (or whatever features you want to review). Add some artwork to create a theme. You will also need markers and pictures. Follow-the-path templates and directions for preparing the boards can be found in Appendix F.

FIGURE 5-10   Gameboard for Gruff Drops Troll at Bridge

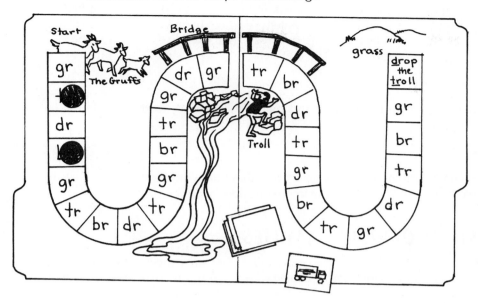

Procedures

1. Each player selects a marker. Students turn over picture cards and move the marker to the correct space.
2. In this game, the winner drops the troll from the bridge by turning up a picture that begins with *dr* (for *drop*) or *tr* (for *troll*) for the last space.

Match! 5-10

In this game, similar to the game of Slap Jack, students look for matches in beginning sounds.

Materials

Create a set of cards that feature pictures with four to eight different beginning sounds. Include at least four pictures for each sound. Pictures can be copied from Appendix C, glued on cardstock, and laminated. This can also be played with word families. When two cards are turned up from the same family they make a match.

Procedures

Each student has half the deck of pictures. Students turn a picture card faceup from their deck at the same time. If the pictures begin with the same sound, the first person to recognize and say "Match!" gets the pair. If the pictures do not match, another set is turned over until a match occurs. There can be penalties for calling out "Match" carelessly.

Beginning and End Dominoes 5-11

This activity is a picture sort to match initial and final consonants (e.g., *lamp* matches *pig*).

Materials

Pictures for these matches can be found in Appendix C. Divide a 2″ × 4″ card in half and paste a picture from each of the following pairs on each side.

Adaptable
for Other
Stages

ghost-tub	book-leg	gate-pin	nine-goat	ten-log
dishes-map	pie-bed	desk-mop	pig-nut	tent-bed
rain-dog	goat-zip	pin-sit	tie-mad	door-pear
two-hat	toes-road	doll-rock	key-lips	seal-boat
pen-bug	gas-sun	net-belt	tail-sink	kite-jeep

Procedures

Students draw a set of five pairs and match the pairs as in the traditional game of Dominoes.

Variations

Students compete to make the longest string they can with a collection of pictures (e.g., tub/book-kite/toad-doll/lip-pig/game-mad/door-rope/pen).

THE STUDY OF WORD FAMILIES

Once students begin the study of word families, they are expected to read and spell the words they sort. Many word games can be adapted as follow-up activities for word sorting. Some activities are especially designed to enhance students' understandings of how families work.

Build, Blend, and Extend 5-12

This series of teacher-led activities is designed to reinforce phoneme segmentation, phoneme blending, and the use of analogy as a spelling strategy ("If I can spell *cat*, then I can spell *fat*.") as students work with onsets and rimes. This should follow sorting lessons in which students have worked with a collection of word families.

Materials

Prepare a set of cards to be used in a pocket chart. Write the targeted onsets and rimes on these cards, keeping the letters of the rime together. For the *at* family, you would have cards with *at*, *b*, *c*, *f*, *h*, *m*, *p*, *r*, and *s*. As students study digraphs and blends, those can be added as well, such as *th*, *ch*, and *fl*. These cards will look much like the cards in Figure 5-13.

Procedures

1. *Building.*   This procedure reinforces the spelling of word families. The teacher should model how to make a word in the family by putting up two cards, such as *m* and *at*. Then students are asked what letter would be needed to make the word *sat*. The teacher would model how to replace the *m* in *mat* with the *s* to make the new word. Students could then be invited to build additional words called by the teacher by substituting beginning letters.
2. *Blending.*   This activity reinforces the reading of word families. It is similar to building except that the teacher starts with a word the students all know, such as *cat*, and then substitutes a different beginning letter. The teacher models how to blend the new onset with the familiar rime to read the word: "*Mmmmmm, aaaaaaat, mat.* The new word is *mat*." Students are then asked to use the two parts of the onset and rime to sound out the word just as the teacher has modeled.
3. *Extending.*   During the extending part of this activity, the teacher selects words that are not included in the sort to demonstrate to students that they can read and spell many more words once they know how to spell several words in a family. This is a time when you might demonstrate using unusual words like *vat* or challenging words with digraphs and blends such as *chat*, *flat*, or *scat*.

Variations

1. Students can work with small cards at their seats as the teacher leads the activity.
2. Add more digraphs and blends as they are studied. There will be many words you can make with families such as *ack* and *ick*.
3. For the study of short vowels and the CVC pattern, the vowel is separated from the rime (*at* is cut apart into *a* and *t*).
4. After working with the cards, students can be asked to write the words on paper, small white boards, or chalk boards.

Word Family Wheels and Flip Charts 5-13

Wheels and flip charts, as shown in Figure 5-11, are fun for students to play with independently or with partners. The wheels and flip charts are used to reinforce blending the onset with the rime to read words in word families they have sorted.

Materials

To make word family wheels, follow these three steps.

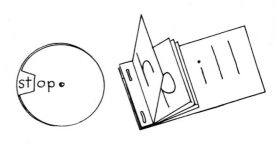

FIGURE 5-11   Word Family Wheel and Flip Chart

1. Cut two 6-inch circles from tagboard. Cut a wedge from one circle and write the vowel and ending consonants or rime to the right of it. Make a round hole in the center.
2. On the second tagboard circle, write beginning sounds that form words with that family. For example, the *op* family can be formed with *b, c, h, l, m, p, s, t, ch, sh, cl*, and *st*. Space the letters evenly around the outside edge so that only one at a time will show through the "window" wedge.
3. Cut a slit in the middle of the second circle. Put the circle with the wedge on top of the other circle. Push a brass fastener through the round hole and the slit. Flatten the fastener, making sure the top circle can turn.

To make flip charts, the steps are as follows.

1. Use a piece of tagboard or lightweight cardboard for the base of the flip book. Write the family or rime on the right half of the base.
2. Cut pages that are half the length of the base piece and staple to the left side of the base. Write beginning sounds or onsets on each one. Students can draw a picture on the backside of the pages to illustrate the word.

Show Me 5-14

This activity is a favorite with teachers who are teaching word families and short vowels.

Materials

Make each student an individual pocket to hold letter cards. To make a pocket, cut paper into rectangles about 7″ × 5″. Fold up 1-inch along the 7-inch side, then fold the whole thing into overlapping thirds. Staple at the edges to make three pockets (see Figure 5-12). Cut additional paper into cards 1.5″ × 4″ to make 14 for each student. Print letters on the top half of each card, making sure the entire letter is visible when inserted in the pocket. A useful assortment of letters for this activity includes the five short vowels and *b, d, f, g, m, n, p, r*, and *t*. Too many consonants can be hard to manage.

FIGURE 5-12   Show Me Game

Procedures

Each student gets a pocket and an assortment of letter cards. When the teacher or designated caller names a word, the students put the necessary letters in the spaces

Letter Name–Alphabetic Stage

and fold up their pockets. When "Show me" is announced, everyone opens his or her pocket at once for the teacher to see. The emphasis is on practice, not competition, but points for accuracy could be kept if desired.

Start with words having the same families, such as *bad, sad,* or *mad,* where the students focus primarily on changing the initial consonants. Move on to a different family and different vowels. For example, you could follow this sequence: *mad, mat, hat, hot, pot, pet.* Add cards with digraphs or blends to spell words such as *sh-i-p* or *f-a-st.*

Word Maker with Beginning Consonants, Digraphs, and Blends 5-15

Students match blends and digraphs with word families to make words.

FIGURE 5-13   Word Maker Cards

Materials

Create a collection of cards that have onsets on half (single consonants, blends, and digraphs) and common short-vowel rimes on the other, such as *at, an, it, ig,* and so on. For students in the later letter name–alphabetic stage, include rimes with ending blends, digraphs, and preconsonantal nasals such as *ish, ang, ast, amp,* and *all.*

Procedures

1. Each student begins by drawing five cards from the deck. With the five cards faceup, each student tries to create words as shown in Figure 5-13.
2. Once the students have made one or two words from their first five cards, they begin taking turns drawing cards from the deck. Every time they make a word, they can draw two more cards. If they cannot make a word they draw one card.
3. Play continues until all the letter cards are used up. The player with the most words is the winner.

Variations

Students can work independently with the word maker cards to generate and record as many words as possible.

Adaptable for Other Stages

Read It, Find It 5-16

This simple and fun game for two players reinforces the identification of words students have been studying in word family sorts.

Materials

You will need 30 pennies, or as many pennies as there are words on the game board. Prepare a game board by writing words from familiar word families onto a 5″ × 6″ grid or a path gameboard found in Appendix E. Prepare a set of word cards that have the same words as those on the board and place them facedown. It is okay if words repeat.

Procedures

1. One player flips a penny for heads or tails position. Each player chooses 15 pennies. One student will be heads and turn all his or her pennies to the heads side. The other will be tails and turn the pennies to the tails side.

2. The player who did not flip will begin by taking a card from the pile and reading it. The player then finds the word on the board and covers it with a penny. If the player cannot read the word or reads it incorrectly, he or she cannot cover the word. The game proceeds as each player draws one card per turn.
3. The first player to cover 15 words, using up all his or her pennies, is the winner.

Roll the Dice 5-17

This game is for two to four players and reinforces word families.

Materials

You need a cube on which to write four contrasting word families, (e.g., *an*, *ap*, *ag*, and *at*). A blank side is labeled "Lose a Turn," and another is labeled "Roll Again" (see Figure 5-14). You will also need a blackboard or paper for recording words.

FIGURE 5-14   Cube for Roll the Dice Game

Procedures

Students roll the die. If it lands on a word family, the student must come up with a word for that family and record it on the chalkboard or paper. Students keep their own lists and can use a word only once, although someone else may have used it. If a player is stumped or lands on Lose a Turn, the die is passed to the next person. If the student lands on Roll Again, he or she takes another turn. The person who records the most words at the end of the allotted time wins.

Variations

1. Play with two dice and have two teams for a relay. Each team has a recorder. The first person of each team rolls the dice and quickly calls out an appropriate word. The recorder writes the word on the board. The player hands the dice to the next player and play goes quickly to the end of the line. With this variation you would not need to lose a turn or roll again.
2. This game can also be used with blends, digraphs, and vowel patterns.

Rhyming Families 5-18

Materials

Prepare a follow-the-path gameboard as shown in Figure 5-15. You will also need a single die or a spinner, pieces to move around the board, pencils, and paper for each player. Directions for making gameboards and spinners as well as gameboard templates are in Appendix F. Write a word from each word family you have been studying in each space on the board. You can also write in special directions such as Roll Again, Go Back Two Spaces, and Write Two Words.

Adaptable for Other Stages

Procedures

The object is to make new words to rhyme with words on the gameboard that differ from the other players' words.

1. Spin to determine who goes first. The first player spins and moves the number of places indicated on the spinner. The player reads the word in the space where he or she lands. All players write a rhyming word by changing initial letter(s). Players number their words as they go. Play continues until someone reaches the end of the path.
2. Beginning with the player who reaches the end first, each player reads the first word on his or her list. Players who have a word that is different from anyone else's gets to circle that word. Continue until all words have been compared.

FIGURE 5-15   Gameboard for Word Families

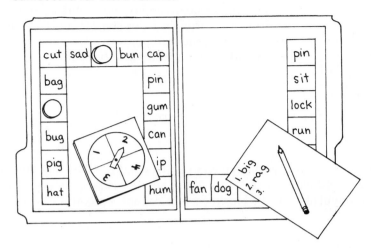

3. Each circle is worth one point; the player who reaches the end first receives two extra points. The students with the most points wins the game.

Variations

Label each space on the gameboard with the rime of a family you have studied (*at, an, ad, ack*). Use no more than five different rimes and repeat them around the path. Prepare a set of cards that have pictures that correspond to the families. Students move around the board by selecting a picture and moving to the space it matches. For example, a student who has a picture of a hat would move to the next space with *at* written on it.

Adaptable for Other Stages

Go Fish 5-19

This version of the classic game can be used as a review of word families.

Materials

Create a deck of 32 cards with four words from eight different word families written on them (e.g., *that, bat, fat,* and *hat*). Write each word at the top left of the card so that the words are visible when held in the hand, as shown in Figure 5-16.

FIGURE 5-16   Playing Cards for Go Fish

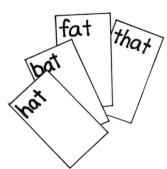

Procedures

1. Five cards are dealt to each player and the remainder are placed in the middle as a draw pile. The first player asks any other player for a match to a card in his or her hand: "Give me all your words that rhyme with *hat*." If the player receives a matching card, he or she may put the pair down and ask for another card. If the other player does not have the card requested, that player tells the first player to "Go fish," which means that the first player must draw a card from the "fish pond." The first player's turn is over when he or she can no longer make a match.
2. Play continues around the circle until one player runs out of cards. Points can be awarded to the first person to go out and to the person who has the most matching cards.

Variations

Go Fish can be adapted for beginning sounds and blends using pictures, or it can be used with vowel patterns.

STUDY OF SHORT VOWELS

After short vowels have been explored through word sorts and weekly routines, games can provide additional practice.

Hopping Frog Game 5-20

This game, created by Janet Bloodgood, is for two to four players and reviews the five short vowels.

Materials

1. Create a gameboard like the one shown in Figure 5-17. Cut green circle lily pads for each space and write CVC words students have used in word sorts on each one (e.g., *pin, get, hot, bad, leg, run, bug, wish*).
2. You will need four frog markers. The spinner is marked into five sections, with a vowel in each one. Pictures can be added to cue the sound: *a*, apple; *e*, ten; *i*, fish; *o*, frog; *u*, sun). See Appendix F for directions on how to make a spinner.

Procedures

Each student selects a frog marker. Players take turns spinning and moving their markers to the first word that matches the vowel sound on which they land (e.g., *e*, get). They then pronounce this word and must say another word with the same vowel sound to

FIGURE 5-17　Frog Marker and Hopping Frog Game

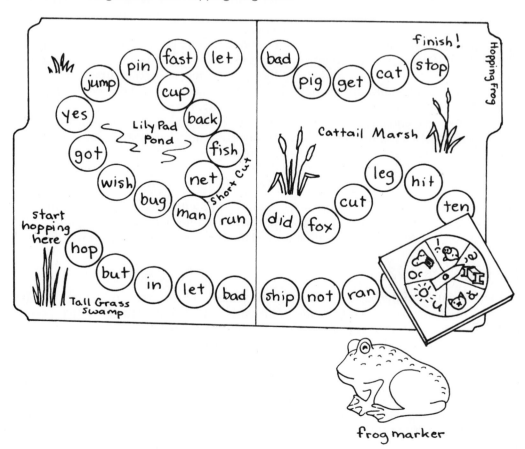

stay on that space. The next player then spins and plays. The first player who can finish the course and hop a frog off the board wins.

Variations

1. Students can write the words they land on and organize them in columns by short vowel.
2. The same game plan could be used for long-vowel patterns and inflected endings.

Making-Words-with-Cubes Game 5-21

Adaptable for Other Stages

Short-vowel words are built with letter cubes in this game. It can be used for other vowels as well.

Materials

Letter cubes that can be found in many games (Boggle and Perquackery) are needed. Playing pieces can also be made from blank wooden cubes. Write all the vowels on one cube to be sure that a vowel always lands face up. Put a variety of consonants on five or six other cubes. (Pairs like *qu* and *ck* might be written together.) The students need a sand clock or timer, paper and pencil, and a record sheet such as the one shown in Figure 5-18.

FIGURE 5-18   Making-Words-with-Cubes Game

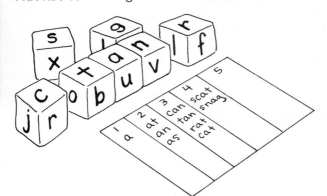

Procedures

1. In pairs, students take turns being the player and the recorder. The recorder writes the words made by the player.
2. A player shakes the letters, spills them out onto the table, and then starts the timer. Whatever letters land faceup must be used to make words. The word maker moves the cubes to create words and spells them to the recorder. The cubes can then be moved around to make more words. Errors should be ignored at this point. Write the words in columns by the number of letters in the words.
3. When the time ends, the students review the words and check for accuracy. Words are then scored by counting the total number of letters used. Students soon realize that the bigger the words they make, the greater their score.

Variations

Students in the within word pattern stage should work with two vowel cubes. On a second cube, write vowel markers such as *e* (put two or three), *a, i,* and *o.* By this time, students may be able to use multiplication to total the letters (e.g., four 3-letter words is 12).

The Bug Race 5-22

This is a variation of the basic follow-the-path game and reviews combinations of short vowels. This example uses a bug theme, but it can be adapted to many other themes such as the zoo, space travel, comic characters, or vehicles. Use stickers and cutouts to add interest to the basic path templates found in Appendix F.

Materials

Use one of the follow-the-path gameboards and label the spaces with *a, e, i, o,* or *u.* Add pictures of leaves, grass, and so on to make it resemble a bug's world. Make a collection of short-vowel pictures on tagboard using the short-vowel pictures in the Appendix. It is important that the pictures do not show through the card. On several additional cards write commands such as Skip a Turn, Go Back Two Spaces, and Move Ahead Three Spaces. Make bug-like playing pieces from bottle caps by drawing in eyes, antennae, and spots with a permanent fine-tip marker.

Procedures

1. Shuffle the picture and command cards and turn them facedown in a pile. The players move around the board by turning over a picture and moving their playing piece to the next free space on the board that has the corresponding short vowel.
2. The student who reaches the end first is the winner.

Variations

Long-vowel pictures can be used for students in the within word pattern stage.

Follow-the-Pictures Spelling Game 5-23

This variation of the basic follow-the-path game works as a follow-up to word sorts for short-vowel words.

Materials

Use one of the follow-the-path templates in Appendix F. Make reduced copies of short-vowel pictures (about half-size or 50% should work). Cut the pictures out and paste them in the spaces on the game path. Use two, three, four, or five short vowels. You will also need playing pieces to move along the path and a spinner or single die. In some spaces you can write Roll Again, Go Back Two Spaces, and other directives. Include an answer card on which all the words are written in the same order they are pasted on the board to settle any arguments about spelling.

Procedures

1. Students take turns spinning for a number. Before they can move to the space indicated by the spinner, they must correctly spell the word pictured. If they cannot spell the word, they must stay where they are for that turn.
2. The student who reaches the end first is the winner.

Variations

Any pictures can be pasted on the gameboard. Long-vowel pictures can be used for students in the within word pattern stage.

FIGURE 5-19 Slider for Slide-a-Word

Slide-a-Word 5-24

Students can be asked to list and then read all the CVC words they are able to generate using the slider created by Jeradi Cohen (Figure 5-19). As different short vowels are studied, the central vowel letter can be changed.

Materials and Procedures

Supplies include tagboard or posterboard, ruler, marker, single-edge razor blade, and scissors. Cut a piece of tagboard or posterboard into strips 8.5″ × 2.5.″ Using the razor, cut a pair of horizontal slits on each end 1.5 inches apart. Write a vowel in the center. Cut two 12″ × 1.5″ strips for each slider. Thread them through the slits at each end and print a variety of consonants, blends, or digraphs in the spaces as they appear through the slits. Turn the strips over and print additional beginning and ending sounds on the back.

Students slide the strips to generate as many words as they can, listing each word as they find it.

Put in an M or N 5-25

Materials

Create word pairs like the ones listed below on word cards.

rag	rang	rig	ring	sag	sang	tag	tang
cap	camp	rap	ramp	trap	tramp	bag	bang
dig	ding	pup	pump	hag	hang	lip	limp
rug	rung	gag	gang	bet	bent	wig	wing
sprig	spring	pin	ping	hug	hung	lap	lamp
swig	swing						

Procedures

Three or four students can play. All the word cards are shuffled and dealt. Players look for pairs (i.e., rag/rang) in their hands and lay them down before play begins. Students then take turns laying down a word from their hand. The student who has the match to the pair takes the card, matches it to the word in his or her hand, and adds the two cards to his or her pile. The student with the most cards is the winner.

Word Study for Transitional Learners in the Within Word Pattern Stage

6

Orthographic development and word study instruction during the within word pattern spelling stage helps students build on their knowledge of the sound level of English orthography and explore the pattern level. Before we discuss development, let us visit the classroom of Ms. Watanabe, a second grade teacher who is working with a group of eight students in the early part of this stage of development.

On Monday morning, after meeting with a reading group to share responses to *Fantastic Mr. Fox* by Roald Dahl, 1988, Ms. Watanabe takes small-group time to introduce a word sort. She has prepared a word study sheet like the one in Figure 6-1A as well as a collection of the words written on index cards that she will use to model the sort in a pocket chart. The students have already studied the common long -*a* patterns (CVCe in *cake*, CVV in *say*, and CVVC in *chain*), and this sort will introduce long -*e* patterns.

Ms. Watanabe begins by saying, "Let's read these words together." As each of the words is read, Ms. Watanabe places it randomly at the bottom of her pocket chart. There is some discussion of *read* when Jason points out that it can be read two ways.

They agree for now to pronounce it as "reed." She then asks, "What do you notice about these words?"

"They all have -es in them," explains Troy.

"Do they all have the same sound in the middle?" Ms. Watanabe asks. She puts up pictures of a web and a queen as keys to the sounds they are to listen for: "We'll place all the words with short -e in the middle here, under this picture of a web. We'll put words with the long -e sound under this picture of a queen. Let's place words that do not fit either under the oddball column." She places a blank word card on the right side of the pocket chart to make a third column. "Let's try a few. Jean, show us how you would figure out where to put this word."

Jean places the word bed underneath the picture of the web while she says, "Web. Bed."

"Fine, Jean. Why did you put bed under the web?"

"Because they sound alike in the middle. They both say 'eh' in the middle."

"Right. They have the short -e sound. David, where would this word go?" Ms. Watanabe hands David the word team. David takes the word card and checks out the fit as he talks himself through this sort: "Team, web. Team, queen. Team, queen." He places the word team underneath the picture of the queen.

Further into the sort, students decide that been does not fit under either picture and should go in the oddball column. After all the words have been sorted, Ms. Watanabe and the students check each category by reading the words from top to bottom. Then Ms. Watanabe poses the next important question, "How are the words in each column alike?"

David notes that the words under the web all have one e. Jean points out that the words in the second column all have two vowels. This leads to the next question: "Do you see some words in the second column that look alike or are spelled alike?" Ms. Watanabe invites Jason to come up, and he quickly pulls out all the words spelled with ee and puts them in a new column, leaving the words spelled with ea. Once more Ms. Watanabe asks the students how the words in each column are alike. She helps them come to the conclusion that short -e is spelled with a single e while long -e is spelled with two vowels—either ee or ea. Then she removes all the cards from the pocket chart, leaving only one word in each of the three categories as a key word. She mixes up the words and passes them out to the students. They then take turns coming up to sort their three words. The final sort looks like the one in Figure 6-1B.

FIGURE 6-1A Long -e and Short -e Word Study Sheet

 🕸	 🧑	Long E Short E Sort 1
web	queen	team
seat	bed	seen
yes	jeep	read
meal	tree	leg
treat	bell	sheep
jet	cream	seed
eat	been	feel

FIGURE 6-1B Long -e and Short -e Pattern Sort

web	queen	team	been
bed	seen	seat	
yes	jeep	treat	
jet	feel	read	
leg	sheep	eat	
bell	tree	meal	
	seed	cream	

Ms. Watanabe ends this lesson by giving each student a copy of the word study sheet in Figure 6-1A. The students return to their seats, cut apart the words, and sort them independently while Ms. Watanabe checks in with another group. Later, Ms. Watanabe moves among the students and asks them, "Why did you put these words together?" This prompt gets students to reflect on their sorts.

To close this word study activity, students store their word cards in plastic bags. The next day they will sort again when they convene in their group, and Ms. Watanabe will watch to see how accurately and easily they sort this second day. Later they will write the sort in their word study notebooks, work with partners to do a blind sort and a writing sort, and go on a word hunt for more words that have the same vowel sounds and patterns.

LITERACY DEVELOPMENT OF STUDENTS IN THE WITHIN WORD PATTERN STAGE

The within word pattern stage is a transitional period of development between the beginning stage when students' reading and writing are quite labored, and the intermediate stage when students can read nearly all texts that they encounter. Transitional readers read most single-syllable words accurately and with increasing fluency. They also can read many two- and three-syllable words when there is enough contextual support.

See how motivating word study can be by watching the Within Word Pattern section on the *Words Their Way* DVD.

Students in the within word pattern or transitional stage use but confuse vowel patterns (Invernizzi, Abouzeid, & Gill, 1994). They no longer spell *boat* sound by sound to produce *BOT*, but as *BOTE, BOWT, BOOT*, or even *boat* as they experiment with possible patterns for the long *-o* sound. When spellers begin including silent letters, they are ripe for instruction in long-vowel patterns. In Eduardo's early within word writing in Figure 6-2, we can see that he knows a good deal about short-vowel patterns, spelling *with, pick, on, it*, and *up* correctly and *BLANCKET* quite predictably as *BLANCKET*. But Eduardo is also experimenting with long-vowel patterns, as in *PLAED* for *played* and *TOOTHE* for *tooth*.

The orthographic development of students across the within word patterns stage is summarized in Table 6-1. Vowel knowledge distinguishes where students fall in the stage. In the early within word patterns stage, students spell short vowels correctly and are experimenting with silent letters that mark long vowels. The final silent *e* is the most common pattern and the most likely to turn up first. It might be used but confused when spelling short vowels (*job* as *JOBE*) or long vowel patterns (*FLOTE* for *float*). After administering a spelling inventory, consider your students' scores on long vowels. If they spell most short vowels correctly but score 0–2 on the long vowels, they are probably in the early part of the stage. Look at the kinds of errors as well as the numerical score. Are they using but confusing silent letters?

By the middle of this stage, students are spelling many of the most common long-vowel patterns correctly in high-frequency words, but less common and "other vowels" (ambiguous vowels and *r*-controlled vowels) will pose problems. By the end of this stage, students will have mastered nearly all the long vowel patterns and will be making only a few errors in the other vowel patterns on an inventory. Identifying whether students are in the early, middle, or late part of the stage will help you plan word study instruction. The following table highlights what features are under good control, which ones are used but confused (the place for instruction), and which features are missing.

FIGURE 6-2   Eduardo's Tooth Story

My toothe came
Out beckus I plaed tugwoure
with a blancket with botes on it
and the tooth fairy
came tw pick it up.

Characteristics of Within Word Pattern Spelling

	What Students Do Correctly	What Students Use but Confuse	What Is Absent
Early Within Word Pattern *ship, when, jump* ROBE for *rob* FLOTE for *float* TRANE for *train* BRITE for *bright*	• Consonants, blends, digraphs • Preconsonantal nasals • Short vowels in CVC words • *R*-influenced CVC words: *car, for, her* • Spell known sight words	• Silent letters in long vowel patterns • *k, ck* and *ke* endings: SMOCK for *smoke*, PEKE for *peak* • Substitutions of short vowels for ambiguous vowels: COT for *caught*	Vowels in unaccented syllable FLOWR for *flower* Consonant doubling: SHOPING for *shopping*
Middle Within Word Pattern *float, train* FRITE for *fright* TABUL for *table*	• All of the above plus: • Common long-vowel patterns (CVCe, CVVC) • -k, -ck, and -ke endings	• Less common and ambiguous vowel patterns • -ed and other common inflections: MARCHT for *marched*, BATID for *batted*	Consonant doubling E-drop: DRIVEING for *driving*
Late Within Word Pattern *bright* SPOYLE for *spoil*, CHOOD for *chewed* SURVING for *serving*	• All of the above plus: • Long-vowel patterns in one-syllable words	• Ambiguous and *r*-influenced vowel patterns • Complex consonant units: SWICH for *switch*, SMUGE for *smudge* • Vowels in unaccented syllables	Consonant doubling Changing *y* to *i*: CAREES for *carries* E-drop:

Reading and Writing in the Within Word Pattern Stage

Teachers may find transitional students in the middle-to-late part of first grade, but transitional students are found mostly in second, third, and early fourth grade classrooms. You will also find struggling readers in middle and high school who are in this stage. (Zutell, 1998).

During this stage, students move from the full alphabetic phase to the consolidated alphabetic phase (Ehri, 1997), where they begin to recognize patterns and chunks to decode unfamiliar words. Instead of processing a word like *chest* as four or five letters to match to sounds (*ch-e-s-t*), they process it as two chunks (*ch-est*). This enables them to decode and store words more readily and their sight word vocabulary grows quickly. This, in turn, enables them to read with increasing fluency compared to the disfluent, word-by-word reading in the beginning stage of literacy.

Transitional readers begin to read in phrases, pausing at the end of sentences, and they read with greater expression. Teachers observe that most of the fingerpointing characteristics of the beginning stage drop away, and transitional readers approach oral reading rates of 100 words per minute (Bear, 1992; Bear & Cathey, 1989). Transitional readers also begin to read silently during sustained silent reading (SSR) or Drop Everything and Read (DEAR). We think of transitional readers as the Wright brothers of reading: They have taken flight but have limited elevation in their reading, and it does not take much to bring them down to frustration level or to cause them to be less fluent in their reading.

Writing also becomes more fluent during this period of development; there is greater sophistication in the way transitional writers express their ideas. The physical act of writing is performed with greater speed and less conscious attention (Bear, 1991a). This added fluency gives transitional writers more time to concentrate on ideas, which may account for the greater depth and expression. Cognitively, they compose with a better sense of the reader's background knowledge and with a greater complexity in the story line.

Opportunities abound in the transitional stage for vocabulary instruction that capitalizes on spelling–meaning connections. Students will encounter many **homophones** during this stage, and these words that sound the same but are spelled differently provide rich fodder for vocabulary development. Why is *thrown*, the verb, spelled with an *ow*? Because the vowel-consonant-*e* pattern is already taken for the noun *throne*—the chair occupied by kings and queens. The spelling pattern reflects the different meaning! This insight provides a fun and interesting approach to both spelling and vocabulary instruction. Students in the transitional stage will truly become word-smiths as they collect hundreds of homophones, such as the ones on page 343 in Appendix E. Through the study of homophones, the logic of English spelling is particularly revealed to learners in the transitional stage. Most homophones are what Beck et al. (2002) would call "Tier 2" words, words that have high utility in multiple contexts. As teachers, we can never *rest* until we *wrest* every ounce of meaning from word study!

Excerpts of Katrina's two-and-a-half-page, single-spaced story about a squirrel named Nuts (see Figure 6-3) shows how much students know about written language and spelling in the later part of the within word pattern stage. Katrina, a second grader, has a rich language base and she writes with a strong voice.

In terms of orthographic knowledge, Katrina spells most long-vowel patterns and *r*-influenced words correctly (*woke, search*). But this knowledge is not stable, as seen in her later spelling of *searches* as SERCHES, and her overgeneralizing patterns (BREAKFEAST for *breakfast* and HOWL for *whole*). Later in the story, Katrina spelled

FIGURE 6-3   Katrina's Squirrel Story

Twelve year old Chistine was glad it was Fially Satarday alltow she loved school Epspshelly math she loved taking her pet Squrrle Nuts to the park even more.

(Nuts runs away and)

Christine orginizes a search. She looked evrywhere. Christine climbd a tree Nuts wasn't there.

(Nuts returns and the next day)

Christine and Nuts woke up they went down stairs and there breakfeast was ready it was all difrent kinds of pancake animals.

(Later)

Christine thought Nuts ran away but he didn't because Nuts went tawa difrent park. Christine serches the howl park.

(The story ends with Christine)

niting a sweter for Nuts the colors where red, white and blue.

thought as *TOOUGHT*, and then went back and wrote in an *h*. She also confuses homophones (*two/too, there/their*). Katrina is a late within word pattern speller who would be appropriately placed in a word study group in which students were studying diphthongs and ambiguous vowels.

Literacy Learning and Instruction

Books for transitional readers cover a wide range of levels, from late first, early second- through early fourth-grade materials. In the early part of this stage, transitional readers read and reread familiar text from several sources: basal readers, picture books, favorite poems, and three-paragraph-long individual dictations. There are many books that students can read independently, such as the *Frog and Toad* books (by A. Lobel) and *Henry and Mudge* (by C. Rylant). By the end of this stage, students's reading includes easy chapter books such as *The Time Warp Trio* (by J. Scieska), *Encyclopedia Brown* (by D. Sobol), or the *Boxcar Children* series (by G. Warner). Transitional readers also explore different genres, and informational text becomes more accessible. For example, they read informational books from the *Let's Find Out* series and magazines such as *Ranger Rick*.

Repeated and timed-repeated readings (Samuels, 1979), readers' theater, and poetry readings are good ways to promote fluent, expressive reading, which is an important goal during this stage. However, fluent, expressive reading is reliant on automatic word recognition and extensive word knowledge (Bear, 1989; Rasinski, 2003). Increasing reading rates without building the underlying word knowledge is a hollow victory.

Students in the transitional stage meet in small groups for reading, where they discuss what they read in greater depth than they did as beginning readers, partly because what they read is longer and more complex. Independently and with partners, they read books without the teacher's support. This independence makes it possible to use reading group time to conference, share, and discuss in more detail.

Lots of experience in reading and writing is crucial during this stage. Students must read for at least 30 minutes each day in instructional- and independent-level materials. They need this practice to propel them into the next stage; otherwise, they will stagnate as readers and writers.

ORTHOGRAPHIC DEVELOPMENT DURING THE WITHIN WORD PATTERN STAGE

By the time students reach the within word pattern stage, their phonemic awareness is well-developed and they can segment the elusive vowel sounds in the middle of one-syllable words. However, problems spelling those sounds still pose challenges.

The Complexities of English Vowels

The study of vowel patterns characterizes much of the word study during the within word pattern stage and accounts for the name selected to label it. As described in Chapter 5, short vowels pose a problem for letter name-alphabetic spellers. because they do not match to a letter name. However, once students have learned to associate the five common short-vowel sounds with *a, e, i, o,* and *u*, the relationship is usually one letter to one sound. In contrast, students in the within word pattern stage must employ a higher degree of abstract thinking because they face two tasks at once. They (a) must segment words into phonemes to determine the sounds they hear and need to represent, and (b) must choose from a variety of patterns that represent the same phoneme and usually involve silent letters (*cute, boat, suit*) or special consonant patterns (*lodge, itch*).

Mastery of vowels is complicated by the following factors.

1. There are many more vowel sounds than there are letters to represent them. Each designated vowel, including *y*, is pressed into service to represent more than one sound. Listen to the sound of *a* in these words: *hat, car, war, saw, father, play*. To spell such a variety of sounds, vowels are often paired (e.g., the *oa* as a long *-o* in *boat* or *ou* for the diphthong in *shout*); or a second vowel or consonant is used to mark or signal a particular sound. The silent *-e* in *ride*, the *y* in *play*, and the *w* in *snow* are examples of silent **vowel markers.**

2. Not only are there more vowel sounds than vowels, most of those sounds are spelled a number of different ways. Some of these long-vowel patterns are more frequent or common than others, as indicated in Table 6-1.

3. In addition to short and long vowels, there are many more vowel sounds, all of which are spelled with a variety of patterns. These include *r-***influenced vowels** (*car, sir, earn*), **diphthongs** (*brown, cloud, boil, toy*), and other **ambiguous vowels** that are neither long nor short (*caught, chalk, straw, thought*). These vowel patterns involve either a second vowel, or the vowel is influenced by a letter that has some vowel-like qualities. The *l, r*, and *w* are examples of consonants that influence the sound of the vowel (*bulk, bird, crowd*). These additional vowel patterns are also shown in Table 6-2.

4. The history of the English language explains why there are so many patterns. English has been enriched with the addition of vocabulary from many different languages, but it has imported diverse vowel sounds and spelling patterns as well. In addition, certain patterns represent sounds that have changed over the centuries.

TABLE 6-1 *Vowel Patterns*

Long-Vowel Patterns

Common long *-a* patterns:	*a-e (cave), ai (rain), ay (play)*
Less common:	*ei (eight), ey (prey)*
Common long *-e* patterns:	*ee (green), ea (team), e (me)*
Less common:	*ie (chief), e-e (theme)*
Common long *-i* patterns:	*i-e (tribe), igh (sight), y (fly)*
Less common:	*i* followed by *nd* or *ld (mind, child)*
Common long *-o* patterns:	*o-e (home), oa (float), ow (grow)*
Less common:	*o* followed by two consonants *(cold, most, jolt)*
Common long *-u* patterns:	*u-e (flute), oo (moon), ew (blew)*
Less common:	*ue (blue), ui (suit)*

Consonant-Influenced Vowels

R-influenced vowels

a with *r:*	*ar (car), are (care), air (fair)*
o with *r:*	*or (for), ore (store), our (pour), oar (board)*
e with *r:*	*er (her), eer (deer), ear (dear), ear (learn)*
i with *r:*	*ir (shirt), ire (fire)*
u with *r:*	*ur (burn), ure (cure)*

W influences vowels that follow: *wa (wash, warn), wo (won, word)*.
L influences the *a* as heard in *al (tall, talk)*.

Diphthongs and Ambiguous Vowels

$\overline{oo}$ *(moon)* and $\breve{oo}$ *(book)*
oy (boy), oi (boil)
ow (brown), ou (cloud)
aw (crawl) au (caught) al (tall)

For example, *igh* was once a guttural sound different from long *-i*, but over time pronunciation tends toward simplification while spelling tends to stay the same. Therefore, one long-vowel sound is spelled many different ways (Vallins, 1954).

5. English is a language of infinite dialects, and the difference between dialects is most noticeable in the pronunciation of vowels. In some regions of the United States, the long *-i* sound in a word like *pie* is really more of a vowel glide or diphthong as in *pie*. *House* may be pronounced more like *hoo-se* in some areas, and *roof* may sound more like *ruff* than *rue-f*. Sometimes the final *r*s in *r*-controlled vowels are dropped, as in Boston where you "*pahk the cah*" (park the car). In other regions, a final *r* is added to words as in the "hollers" (hollows) of southwest Virginia. Such regional dialects add color and interest to the language, but teachers may be worried about how speakers of such dialects will learn to spell if they cannot pronounce words "correctly." Rest assured that these students will learn to associate certain letter patterns with their own pronunciations (Cantrell, 2001). The value of word sorting over more inflexible phonics programs is that students can sort according to their own pronunciations, and a miscellaneous or oddball column can be used for variant pronunciations.

6. Many words in English do not match even one of the patterns listed in Table 6-2. These words have sometimes been called exceptions to the rule. We prefer to put them in the miscellaneous or **oddball** category. During word study in the within word pattern stage, the oddball category will get a lot of use. Sometimes these words are true exceptions, as with *was, build,* and *been;* at other times they are not exceptions, but rather part of a little known category. Examples of these words are *dance, prince,* and *fence,* which may look like they should have long-vowel patterns. But in these words the *e* is there to mark the /c/ sound "soft" (consider the alternative: *danc, princ,* and *fenc*). Such exceptions should not be ignored, and in fact a few such words should be deliberately included in the sorts you plan. They become memorable because they deviate from the common patterns.

7. English vowels pose special problems for English learners because English has so many more vowel sounds than most languages. This will be discussed more later.

Despite the complexity of vowels, by the end of the within word pattern stage, students have a good understanding of vowel spelling patterns. This knowledge is prerequisite to the examination of the way syllables are joined during the next stage of development, the syllables and affixes stage. For example, when students understand the patterns in words like *bet* and *beat*, they are ready to understand why *betting* has two *t*s and *beating* has one *t*.

Recall the three layers of the orthography. In this stage, students continue to rely on sound and are learning vowel patterns, but meaning also matters. The meaning connection is as critical to learning vowel patterns as is sound, and both are emphasized in the study of homophones (*meat* and *meet*) and **homographs** (*tear:* I *tear* the sheet into rags. You have a *tear* in your eye).

The Influence of Consonants on Vowels

In English, vowel patterns often consist of two vowels, one of which marks or signals a particular sound for the other vowel. Common examples are the silent *-e* in words such as *bake* and *green;* but consonants are also vowel markers, such as the *gh* in *night* and *sigh*, which signals the long *-i* sound. Students who have come to associate the CVC pattern with short vowels may be puzzled when presented with *saw, joy, hall,* or *car*. In those words, *w, y,* and *l* are no longer acting as consonants but are taking on vowel-like qualities. *R* retains its identity as a consonant in *car*, but the preceding vowel has a sound quite different from short *-a*. These words may look like they are exceptions to the CVC rule, but they are, in fact, simply additional patterns that are very regular. This is why it is so important to learn patterns at this stage rather than rules. The influence of *r* is particularly common and deserves further discussion.

R-influenced vowels.   As our friend Neva Viise says, "*R* is a robber!" The presence of an *r* following a vowel robs the sound from the vowel before it. This causes some words with different short vowels to become homophones (*fir/fur*) and makes vowel sounds spelled with *er, ir,* and *ur* indistinguishable in many cases (*herd, bird, curd*). Even long-vowel sounds before the robber *r* are not as clear as the same vowels preceding other consonants (*pair* versus *pain*).

The *r*-influenced vowel sorts draw students' attention to the location of the *r* and to the subtle difference in sound that location creates. Word study of *r*-influenced words can begin with activities that contrast initial consonant *r* blends (*grill*) with *r*-influenced vowels (*girl*).

Complex Consonants

There are several consonant issues that pose challenges for within word pattern spellers. They know many beginning and ending consonant blends and digraphs. However, lingering problems can exist in three-letter blends and digraphs such as *spr (spring), thr (throw), squ (square), scr (scream), shr (shred), sch (school), spl (splash),* and *str (string)*. Because words that contain these triplets have a variety of vowel patterns, they are specifically studied toward the end of the stage but can be included in sorts throughout the stage when appropriate. There are also several silent consonants that occur in one syllable words: *kn (knife), wr (wrong),* and *gn (gnaw)*.

What is of special interest in this stage are other characteristics of consonants. Based on Venesky's (1970) work, Henderson (1990) called these **complex consonant patterns**. For example, students in the within word pattern stage can examine words that end in *ck (kick), tch (catch),* and *dge (ledge)*. Teachers might ask, "What do you notice about the vowel sounds in these word sorts?"

tack/take	fetch/peach	fudge/huge
lick/like	notch/roach	badge/cage
rack/rake	patch/poach	ledge/siege
smock/smoke	sketch/reach	ridge/page

Contrasting these pairs will enable students to make interesting discoveries. Students see that *ck (tack), tch (fetch),* and *dge (fudge)* patterns are associated with short vowels, whereas *ke (take), ch (peach),* and *ge (huge)* are associated with long-vowel patterns.

The consonants *g* and *c* have two sounds that are determined by the vowel that follows them. When *g* and *c* are followed by *a, o,* and *u,* they have a "hard" sound, as in *gate* and *cake*. When they are followed by *i, e,* or *y,* they have a "soft" sound (/s/ or /j/) as in *ginger* or *cent*. (*C* is more regular than *g* because the *g* is hard in many words like *girl* and *gill*). In a similar fashion, words ending in *ce (dance), ge (edge), ve (leave),* and *se (sense)* have silent *e*s associated with the consonant rather than the vowel.

Homophones and Homographs

Homophones will inevitably turn up in the study of vowel patterns and can be included in the word sorts you plan even at the beginning of this stage, but an intensive look at homophones at the end of this stage is also recommended. At this point, students know most of the vowel patterns and are ready to focus on the meaning of the words. Students enjoy creating lists of homophones (*bear/bare, Mary/marry/merry*) and **homographs** (*wind up string/listen to the wind*). The different spellings of homophones may seem capricious, but they reflect their historical origins and may even make reading easier and meaning clearer (cf., Taft, 1991; Templeton, 1992). Contrast the two sentences below:

The weigh Peat cot the bare was knot fare.
The way Pete caught the bear was not fair.

Mandy Grotting helps her second graders grasp homophones and homographs in the Within Word Pattern section on the *Words Their Way* DVD.

Pairs of homographs and homophones differ grammatically as well as semantically. For example, when discussing the homophones *read* and *red*, it makes sense to talk about the past tense of the verb *to read* and the color word *red*. In the study of homophones and homographs, students are beginning to scratch the meaning layer of the orthography. A group of third graders observed that *weight* and *height* had three things in common: They were both spelled with an *ei*, they both made a vowel sound that was unexpected, and they both had to do with measurement. The study of contractions and possessives also presents a new series of patterns to examine that are rooted in the pattern and meaning layers of the orthography. We examine meaning in contractions, for example, when we compare *its* and *it's*, or *we're* and *were*.

This new emphasis on meaning is a time to build vocabulary knowledge. Students should learn how to use dictionaries and refer to them to see, for example, what the three words *vein/vane/vain* mean. Also during the within word pattern stage, students create semantic sorts that are collections of words on a particular topic (e.g., baseball words, words related to outer space, government words, and key vocabulary words from their other content area texts and studies). This focus on meaning and spelling prepares students for the next stage of spelling when the meaning of syllables is examined, the syllables and affixes stage.

Simple Prefixes and Suffixes

The study of prefixes and suffixes is explored in the next stage, syllables and affixes. Increasingly, however, the reading and language arts content standards of many states are requiring that students be taught simple prefixes and suffixes beginning in second grade when most students are developmentally in the within word pattern phase. Understanding how these affixes—prefixes and suffixes—work lays the foundation for later exploration, in grade three and up, of a wide range of prefixes and suffixes. These words are explored first as vocabulary words students encounter in their reading, and are not treated as spelling words until students know how to spell the base word on which they are built.

The most common prefixes in the English language are *un-* (meaning "not"), *re-* ("again"), *in-* ("not"), and *dis-* ("not"); these four prefixes account for about 58% of all prefixes in the language (White, Sowell, & Yanagihara, 1989). Though there is some variability across states, the prefixes that most states have mandated in grade two are *un-* and *re-*. These can be explored as vocabulary words, beginning with simple base words such as *do* and discussing what happens when *un-* and *re-* are added to *do*.

Several states mandate that the suffixes: *-ly, -ful, -y,* and the comparatives *-er/-est* be taught in grade two. Using frequently occurring and easily understood words, walk children through a discussion of, for example, *small/smaller/smallest* vs. *tall/taller/tallest*. Beginning with the word *care*, talk about being *careful* and watching over a baby brother or sister *carefully*.

Word Study Instruction for the Within Word Pattern Stage

Carefully planned word sorts are a systematic way to guide students' mastery of the complexities of vowel and consonant patterns in the within word pattern stage. Three brief reminders are instructive at this point: (a) Ensure that students are able to read the words before sorting; (b) choose sorts that match students' development and represent what they use but confuse; (c) avoid teaching rules—instead, have students find reliable patterns. Although it is common to teach students rules about silent *-e* and "when two vowels go walking," often these rules are less reliable than the categories of patterns themselves. For example, the rule about two vowels works for *oa* and *ai* in *boat* and *rain*, but not for *oy* or *oi* in *boy* or *join*, yet *oy* and *oi* are very regular spelling patterns (Johnston, 2001). The time to state a rule is when students have already observed and understand the pattern that underlies the rule. Remember that rules are useful mnemonics for something already understood; they are not teaching tools.

Two principles of word study listed in Chapter 3 have particular importance in this stage.

- *Sort by sight and sound.*   Plan sorts that first ask students to contrast vowels by how they *sound*. Long vowels should be introduced by comparing them to their corresponding short vowels, as Ms. Watanabe did in the vignette at the beginning of this chapter. R-influenced vowels (such as the *ar* in *car*) can be compared with the short CVC patterns (such as short -*a* in *cash* or *trap*). Sound sorts are important because sound is the first clue that spellers use. Long- and short-vowel pictures can be used for sound sorts, but most of these sound sorts are done with words at this stage. After sorting by sound, sort by sight—look for the different orthographic spelling patterns used to spell the sounds.

- *Don't hide exceptions.*   Include two or three oddball words when appropriate. For example, a long -*o* sort could include *love* and *some*, which look as though they fit the CVCe but whose vowel sounds are not long. However, don't overdo it. Too many oddballs placed in a sort can make it difficult for students to find the pattern. The best oddballs are high frequency words like *done* or *come* that students already know how to read or less common patterns that will be studied later, like *most* or *mind*. High frequency words (both regular and irregular) are listed in Appendix E and marked with asterisks in the word lists.

Sequence and Pacing of Word Study in the Within Word Pattern Stage

The sequence of word study in the within word pattern transitional stage begins by taking a step back with a review of short vowels as they are compared with long vowels. Then the focus shifts to common long-vowel patterns and then less common and *r*-influenced vowel patterns. Ambiguous vowels and complex consonant patterns are studied toward the end of the stage. Table 6-2 summarizes the sequence of word study in this stage. Remember to use students' spellings to determine where in this sequence to start. Observations of students' writings and the inventories described in Chapter 2 help to pinpoint the features students have learned and those that pose problems. Table 6-1 will help you identify whether students are in the early, middle, or late part of the stage.

Table 6-2 suggests contrasts and a sequence for the study of vowels under three possible pacing guides in the early middle and late part of this stage. Because there is a lot to cover in this stage, two years is not too long to address the range of features for average achieving students.

Pacing will depend on several things: developmental level, grade level, and rate of progress. For early within word pattern spellers in late first or early second grade, an introductory pace is recommended. Start with some picture sorts to focus attention on the different short- and long-vowel sounds and then study the common CVCe pattern across four long vowels (long -*e* is not studied because the CVCe pattern is rare in one syllable words). During this introductory pace, students may be using word study notebooks for the first time and learning new sorting routines.

If students in late second, early third, or later grades are in the early part of this stage, there is a greater sense of urgency to catch them up with their peers. The moderate pace is a good place to start, but careful observation and assessment are needed to determine if you can go faster or slower. The first few vowels may take more time than ones studied later. Pacing can be adjusted by adding more categories to a single sort (up to four or five) or dropping back to fewer categories when students exhibit confusion. Students in the middle within word pattern stage might benefit from the pace outlined in the last column; a quick review of long vowels before going on to *r*-influenced and ambiguous vowels.

TABLE 6-2   Pacing and Sequence Guide for Within Word Pattern

Slow Introductory Pace	Moderate Pace	Advanced Pace/Review
Use easy words with few blends or digraph. Less common patterns may be oddballs.	Use oddballs and some words with blends and digraphs.	Use more words spelled with blends and digraphs, oddballs, and less common patterns.

Early Within Word Pattern

Common and Less Common Long Vowels

Long and short vowels in picture sorts	Short *a*, *a-e*	Review all CVC vs. CVCe
Short *a*, *a-e*	Short *i*, *i-e*	*a-e*, *ai*, *ay*, *ei*, *ey*
Short *i*, *i-e*	Short *o*, *o-e*	*o-e*, *oa*, *ow*
Short *o*, *o-e*	Short *u*, *u-e*	*u-e*, *ui*, *oo*, *ew*
Short *u*, *u-e*	Combine all CVC vs. CVCe	*ee*, *ea*, *ie*
Combine all CVC vs. CVCe	Final *k*, *ck*, *ke*	*i-e*, *igh*, *y*
Final *k*, *ck*, *ke*	*a-e*, *ai*, *ay*	VCC in *ol*, *il*, *in*
Short *a*, *a-e*, *ai*	*o-e*, *oa*, *ow*	
a-e, *ai*, *ay*	*u-e*, *ui*, *oo*, *ew*	
Short *o*, *o-e*, *oa*	*ee*, *ea*	
o-e, *oa*, *ow*	Review CVVC across vowels	
Short *u*, *u-e*, *ui*	*i-e*, *igh*, *y*	
ui, *ue*, *ew*, *oo*	VCC in *ol*, *il*, *in*	
Short *e*, *ee*, *ea*		
Review CVVC across all vowels		
Short *i*, *i-e*, *igh*		
i-e, *igh*, *y*		
VCC in *ol*, *il*, *in*		

Middle Within Word Pattern

***R*-Influenced Vowels**

Short *a*, *ar*	*ar*, *are*, *air*	*ar*, *are*, *air*, *w+ar*
Long *a*, *are*, *air*	*er*, *ear*, *eer*	*er*, *ear*, *eer*
Short *e*, *er*	*ir*, *ire*, *ier*	*ir*, *ire*, *ier*
er, *ere*, *eer*, *ear*	*or*, *ore*, *oar*, *oor*	*or*, *ore*, *oar*, *w+or*
Short *i*, *ir*	*ur*, *ure*, *ur-e*	*ur*, *ure*, *ur-e*
Long *i*, *ire*, *ier*	*ar*, *or*, *ər*	
Short *o*, *or*, *w+or*	*ar*, *or*, *w+ar*, *w+or*	
Long *o*, *oar*, *ore*, *oor*		
Short *u*, *ur*		
ur, *ure*, *ur-e*, *ear*, *ar*, *or*, *ə r*		
r-blends *ar*, *ir*, (crate/cart)		
or, *ur*, *ir*		

Late Within Word Pattern

Diphthongs and Other Ambiguous Vowels

Long *o*, *oi*, *oy*	*oi*, *oy*	*oi*, *oy*, *ou*, *ow*
oo (boot, book)	*ou*, *ow*	*al*, *au*, *aw*
Short *o*, *ou*, *ow*	*oi*, *oy*, *ou*, *ow*	
oi, *oy*, *ou*, *ow*	*al*, *au*, *aw*	
Short *a*, *al*, *aw*		
al, *au*, *aw*		
Review *ow*, *ew*, *aw*		

TABLE 6-2 Continued		
Slow Introductory Pace	**Moderate Pace**	**Advanced Pace/Review**
Complex Consonants		
kn, wr, gn	*kn, wr, gn*	*shr, thr, str, squ*
sh, shr, th, thr	*thr, shr, squ*	Hard/Soft *g* and *c*
scr, str, spr	*scr, str, spr, spl*	*dge, ge, tch, ch*
spl, squ	Hard/Soft *g* and *c*	
Hard/Soft *c* and *g*	*dge, ge*	
dge, ge	*ch, tch*	
ch, tch	*ce, se, ve*	
ce, se, ve, ge		

Many teachers are expected to use their school district's adopted phonics or spelling program. Often these published programs are set at a fast pace and they cover several patterns at one time. To differentiate instruction at students' developmental levels, you can adjust the lessons by adding other words for students who need a slower pace and postponing the study of some patterns.

The study of vowel patterns in single-syllable words lays a critical foundation for the study of two-syllable words in the next stage and cannot be short-changed. Perhaps 25% of the adult population in the United States is stunted at this point of literacy proficiency. Even community college and university students who are poor spellers would benefit from beginning their word study with a review of vowel patterns. It is important to take a step back and conduct word study activities that help them cement their knowledge of vowel patterns in single-syllable words to get a running start as they study two-syllable words. For many of these students, the fast pace in the third column of Table 6-3 may be appropriate.

The Study of High-Frequency Words

A number of spelling programs feature high-frequency or high-utility words. The authors of these programs argue that spelling instruction should focus on a small core of words students need the most, words such as *said, because, there, they're, friend,* and *again*. Unfortunately, this narrow view of word study reduces spelling to a matter of brute memorization and offers students no opportunity to form generalizations that can extend to the reading and spelling of thousands of unstudied words.

Many of these high-frequency words do not follow common spelling patterns, but can be included in within word pattern sorts as oddballs. For example, the word *said* is usually examined with other words that have the *ai* pattern, such as *paid, faint,* and *wait*. It becomes memorable because it stands alone in contrast to the many words that work as the pattern would suggest. It is also likely to be spelled correctly by most students because they have seen it so often when they read. The word lists in the Appendix E contain the majority of such high-frequency words, and the words are marked with asterisks. Note that most of the top 200 most frequently occurring words (Dolch, 1942; Fry, 1980; Zeno, Ivens, Millard, & Duvvuri, 1996) are covered by the end of the within word pattern stage.

Some words in English, however, persist as problems for young writers. There are also some words students need to write frequently in the lower grades that are not included in the weekly lessons designed to meet their developmental needs. An example of this is the word *because,* which occurs often in the writings of first graders. Many teachers will accept students' inventions for such words (*BECUZ, BECALZ, BECAWS*), but some teachers grow tired and concerned about such errors, especially beyond the primary grades. Although we feel confident that such errors will be worked out over time there are good reasons to address them sooner.

Some teachers study about five high-frequency words a week as described in word wall activities (Cunningham, 2004). We suggest including a week-long unit several times a year. In either case, studying high-frequency words should not replace the developmental study of words by features, but rather should supplement such study. The words chosen should be highly functional words seen in your own students' writing and should be kept few in number. The words should also not be too far in advance of your students' developmental levels. Interesting content or theme words that students need for short periods of time such as *Thanksgiving, leprechaun,* and *tyrannosaurus* can simply be posted for easy reference and are not appropriate spelling words for students who are still learning to spell one-syllable words.

Guidelines to Study High-Frequency Words

1. Select 6 to 10 words for 1 week of each 9-week period for a total of 24 to 40 words a year. (Short weeks of 2 to 3 days might be good for these.) A list developed in a second grade class might include *know, friend, again, our, went, would,* and *once*. Students can take part in this selection by choosing words they have difficulty spelling and by choosing words from the teacher's master list. A cumulative list of these words in alphabetical order should be posted in the room for reference, with the understanding that students are expected to spell those words correctly in all their written work once they have been studied. Individual student copies of these words in alphabetical order can also be created and added to as words accumulate. Students may place the individual lists in their writing workshop folders or in a section of their word study notebooks.

2. Develop routines to help students examine and study the words carefully. Here are some suggestions.

• *Introduction and discussion.* As the teacher writes the words on the board, the students copy them on their own paper in a column. (Be sure that everyone copies correctly!) The teacher should then lead a discussion about each word. "What part of this word might be hard to remember and why?" (For the word *friend,* the discussion would focus on the fact that it has a silent -*i*.) "What might help you remember how to spell this word?" (Students might note that it ends with *end*.)

• *Self-corrected test method.* After each word has been written and discussed, students should fold their paper over so that the list is covered. The teacher calls the words aloud while the students write them again. The students then check their own work by unfolding the paper to compare what they copied to what they spelled. Any words spelled incorrectly should be rewritten. This strategy to support memorization has been well researched (Horn, 1954).

• *Self-study method.* The self-study method is a long-standing activity that appears in most published spelling books. This process can be used independently, but students need to be taught to follow these steps: (a) look at the word and say it; (b) cover the word; (c) write the word; (d) check the word; and (e) write the word again if it was spelled wrong.

• *Practice test.* The words are called aloud. Students spell the word and then immediately check it by looking at the chart posted in the room. Students become familiar with using the chart as a reference and can call the words to each other in pairs or small groups, or the teacher may lead the practice test.

• *Final test.* The chart is covered and students spell the words as they are called aloud. Because the number of words is kept low, the chance of 100% success is high. Once students have been tested they are responsible for those words from then on. The teacher will undoubtedly need to remind students often to reread a piece of written work to check for the posted words in the editing stage. Any word that continues to be a problem can reappear on the next list, but students will have about 8 weeks to work at getting it under control.

WORD STUDY AND ENGLISH LANGUAGE LEARNING IN THE WITHIN WORD PATTERN STAGE

There are three things we need to consider when planning word study with English learners: (1) compare English to the students' primary languages in terms of sounds; (2) compare the writing systems; and (3) know what language and literacy experiences students have had.

To understand their knowledge of words and the way sounds in English contrast with their primary languages, we administer spelling inventories in English and in their primary languages when available. (See *Words Their Way for English Language Learners.*) The spelling errors in uncorrected writing are also valuable to understand students' word knowledge. It is useful to know about the students' development in their primary languages because the more literate students are in their first language, the more information there is to transfer to learning to read in English (Proctor, August, Carlo, & Snow, 2006).

Many vowel sounds in English do not exist in other languages. As hard as vowels are for English-speaking children, they can be overwhelming for English learners (Helman, 2004). Spanish, for example, has only one short-vowel sound, one ambiguous vowel sound (oi) sound, and no *r*-influenced vowels or schwa. In Spanish, the letter-sound matches for the vowels are one-to-one and very regular, but the matches are not always the same as in English. Notice, for example, in Table 6-4 that the long *-a* sound is spelled with the letter *e* in the Spanish word *hecho* and the long *-i* sound is spelled with the letters *ai*. These differences explain some students' misspellings. For example, the word *reach* may be spelled *rich* because the letter *i* in Spanish has a long *-e* sound.

Some students, including many English learners, speak with a dialect in which the pronunciation of long vowels is quite different than the standard ways the vowels are pronounced. Interestingly, word and orthographic knowledge of English gained during

Examine how Alyson Wilson implements specific adaptations to word study instruction, to ensure her English learners are successful, in the Within Word Pattern section on the *Words Their Way* DVD.

TABLE 6-4 *Vowel Sounds in English and Spanish*

English Letter and Word		Spelled in Spanish	Spelling Errors
Long *a* as in	*cake*	*e* as in *hecho*	*LEK (lake)*
Long *e*	*bean*	*i* as in *ido*	*BIN (bean)*
Long *i*	*like*	*ai* as in *aire*	*NAIT (night)*
Long *o*	*hope*	*o* as in *ocho*	*FLOUT (float)*
Short *o*	*top*	*a* as in *ajo*	*JAB (job)*
Long *u*	*June*	*u* as in *usted*	*FLUT (flute)*
oy, oi	*toy*	*oy* as in *voy*	*NOYZ (noise)*

From Bear, D. R., Templeton, S., Helman L. A., & Baren, T. (2003). Orthographic development and learning to read in different languages. In G. G. Garcia, *English learners: Reaching the highest levels of English literacy*. Newark, DE: International Reading Association. Copyright by the International Reading Association.

the within word pattern stage contributes to slight changes in students' dialect and pronunciation. Cantrell (2001) found that Appalachian students' pronunciations of long vowels changed as a result of word study. The more they read in English, the more "standardized" their speech became. Eventually, students with other dialects and first languages acquire a literate register that reflects their expanded knowledge.

Some English learners memorize many words, but their strategies for spelling unknown words often indicate that their orthographic knowledge could be deeper. For example, a student memorized the spelling of *rain*, but continued to spell unknown, long -*a* words with an *e*, (train as *tren*) using the Spanish spelling of the long -*a* sound as in Table 6-4. When it seems that students' spelling of sight words is ahead of their more conceptually based orthographic knowledge, use a moderate or introductory pace when following the sequence of word study in Table 6-3.

At times a word study lesson that was meant to focus on a particular spelling pattern becomes unexpectedly focused on pronunciation and meaning. Plan additional language experiences to cement the meaning and sound layers for English learners. They will also benefit from being involved in vocabulary activities like the semantic sorts and activities described at the end of this chapter.

Teachers need to accept differences in pronunciation due to individual and regional dialectical differences. This means that some students will sort words by sound a little differently than the teacher or other classmates, but there is no harm in this. Let students sort by sound in ways that make sense to them, and observe what students do differently but consistently. After focusing on sounds in sorts, students turn to the patterns of the words. The goal is for students to associate patterns with their own pronunciations.

Occasionally, disputes arise among the students about whether words are oddballs. Some students say *again* with a long -*a*, whereas others say it with a short -*i*. *Poem* has a long -*o* to some students and an /oi/ sound to others. Some people pronounce *bear* and *bar* as homophones. Students may find these dialectical contrasts interesting and teachers should treat them as variations, not as issues of right or wrong. You will find that the fourth grade social studies curriculum in many parts of the United States is a great place to discuss dialects as students study the diverse groups that have settled the state in which they live.

WORD STUDY ROUTINES AND MANAGEMENT

Word sorts and word study notebooks are the most common and crucial activities to use during this stage. Chapter 3 describes important routines (blind sorts, writing sorts, word hunts, speed sorts, homework) and offers guidelines for organization. Figure 3-17 (p. 73) shows two schedules for students in the within word pattern stage and Figure 3-20 (p. 76) offers some variations on these.

The Word Study Lesson Plan in the Within Word Pattern Stage

Word sorts begin as a teacher-directed activity and then offer individual practice throughout the week. Most sorts will follow a standard format presented in Chapter 3 and reviewed here.

1. *Demonstrate the Sort.* When starting a sort, go over the words with students to be sure they are able to read them, and talk briefly about the meaning of unfamiliar words. Sometimes familiar words have more than one meaning and this is a good time to address them. For example, *park* means both a recreational area (noun) and the process of placing of a car (verb). If there are more than a few words students do not know, and this may be so for English language learners, continue to talk about the meaning of the words during the week. After going over the words in the sort, a simple open-ended question to ask next is, "What do you notice about these words?"

There are many ways to introduce a sort. In a teacher-directed or **closed sort,** set up the categories with **key pictures** or **key words** as Ms. Watanabe did with short -*e* and long -*e*. Closed sorts are helpful when students are new to sorting or when they start the study of a new feature. Once students understand the process, **open sorts** require more analytic thinking and encourage discovery. Students look for their own categories and are asked to explain why they sorted they way they did. After sorting, lead a discussion to focus students' attention on the distinguishing features: "How are the words in this column alike?"

2. *Sort and Check.* After a group sort, it is important for students to work independently or with a partner using their own sets of words. Some teachers create reusable sorts in manila folders with the key words or pictures at the top and the words stored in a plastic bag inside the folder. Figure 6-4 shows the student isolating the long -*e* sound in *leaf* before placing it in the column with the picture of the feet at the top. Saying the words aloud and comparing them in this way is a necessary strategy when students begin a sort. After sorting, encourage students to check their words by saying all the words aloud in each column to make sure they all fit. When errors are made, offer gentle hints such as, "One word in this column does not sound (or look) right. Can you find it?"

3. *Reflect: Declare, Compare, and Contrast.* "Why did you sort the way you did?" is the question that often starts the reflection part of a lesson. You might ask students to turn and talk to a partner as a good first step. If students do not come up with the insights needed to understand the feature, be ready to model your own thinking: "When I look at all the words in this column, I notice that. . . ." We like for students to tell us, but if they cannot, then we must be explicit in our explanations. Sometimes students do not have the language to take part in a discussion so teachers must supply the terminology they need, such as "vowel sounds" and "patterns."

FIGURE 6-4   Long-Vowel Sorts: Student Sorts by Sound

A sort is successful when students sort accurately and quickly and can discuss why they sorted the way they did. If students seem just to mimic other students, you can ask them to say it another way, or ask: "What else did you notice about the words we sorted?"

4. *Extend: Students Work Independently Across the Week.* Word study is extended beyond the small-group sessions through activities students complete at their seats, in word study notebooks, at a word study center, or at home. Blind sorts that involve students sorting words by sound as a partner reads them aloud are particularly recommended at this stage because students must not only distinguish the sound of the vowel but associate it with a particular orthographic pattern. Games give enjoyable practice in reading the words and thinking about their patterns. Many games are described in the activities section at the end of this chapter.

Word Study Notebooks in the Within Word Pattern Stage

The word study notebook is used across the week for a number of activities. It provides an organizational structure and documentation of student work for assessment and grading.

Written reflections. Students can be asked to summarize what they learn from their sorts in their own words, as Graciela has done in Figure 6-5. She has numbered each column and written a generalization for each, such as, "*Climb* is the same as *bind, wind,* and *hind.*" These written reflections help teachers assess students' progress and students can be referred back to them for review.

FIGURE 6-5   A Page from Graciela's Word Study Notebook

Graciela
10/22

I that say his name

shine	climb	sky	right	wind
bite		try	slight	find
slide		my	sigh	blind
slime	2	3	night	hind
spine				
1			4	
				5

1. This word Say i by the e at the end.

2. Climb is the same as bind, wind, and hind.

3. a i tarn's into an y.

4. The i is with gh we can not hear it.

5. This word all got an i-n-d.

Sections in word study notebooks. The word study notebook can also serve as an organized collection of words students examine for different purposes. Students can be asked to bring their notebook to small-group sessions, along with reading materials and response journals or logs. We recommend having at least two sections for transitional readers: one section devoted to vocabulary and another section devoted to phonics and spelling.

The vocabulary section of the word study notebook is where students will record words related to a particular concept derived from their reading. When reading *Stuart Little*, for example, some students might be encouraged to make lists of boat terms (*rigging, bow, stern*) or weather-related words (*squall, breeze, mist*). These words can be shared and then combined and sorted into semantic categories, or added, where possible, to the spelling sorts (e.g., *breeze* could be added to a long *-e* category of *ee* patterns). The vocabulary section of the word study notebook may also be used for subject areas. Students might create a science web on pandas, make a list of concepts related to immigration, or compare and contrast math terms related to multiplication and division (*product, multiplier, factor* vs. *dividend, divisor, quotient*).

A subsection might be an ongoing list of homophones with sentences or pictures to illustrate the different meanings of the words. Each vowel might comprise a small section set off with a tab or Post-it note. In addition to routine word hunts, students are challenged to always be on the lookout for new words that they might add to earlier sorts. In this way, sounds and patterns are constantly revisited. Word study notebooks have a long instructional life in learning and students should have ready access to their notebooks throughout the day.

Word Hunts

Word hunts (see Chapter 3) are particularly important in the within word pattern stage because they help students see the connection between word study and reading. Ask students to go through what they have recently read to find words that fit a particular sound or pattern. The common vowel patterns will turn up frequently in most reading materials while less common patterns may present a challenge. In both cases two- and three-syllable words are welcome additions (i.e., *ai* in *rainbow* or *retained*). Such words extend generalizations into more difficult vocabulary.

Occasionally you might use the kids section of a newspaper for the hunt. Words fitting desired patterns are circled in crayon or highlighted and shared with the group.

Homework in the Within Word Pattern Stage

In Chapter 3, there is a letter for parents describing homework routines for each day of the week. These routines are especially appropriate for within word pattern spellers and homework will provide much needed extra practice. A checklist such as the one in Figure 6-6 can be sent home with an extra copy of the words for the week. Everything can go into an envelope or plastic zip bag. Students might be allowed to choose two or three activities and more options can be added to the checklist occasionally, such as using a small number of words in sentences.

Guidelines for Creating Word Sorts

Create your own sorts by choosing words to drop into the templates available on the CD-ROM.

Sorts that contrast sounds and patterns are the key to effective word study in this stage. Possible contrasts are suggested in Table 6-3 and lists of words in Appendix E can be used to complete the sorts. There are also sample sorts in Appendix D ready to transfer to a template found in Appendix F. However, it is also important to look for words in your own students' writing and reading materials for words to include in sorts. The words students can already read and spell are still useful when they are looking for patterns across words to form generalizations.

FIGURE 6-6   Word Study Homework Checklist

Word Study at Home   Name _____

Check off the activities you complete and return this to your teacher.

_____ Sort the words into the same categories you did in school.

_____ Write the words into categories.

_____ Blind sort with someone at home.

_____ Write the words into categories as someone calls them aloud.

_____ Hunt for more words that fit the categories and write them here:

                          Parent's Signature _____

For closed sorts, key words for sorting can be posted at the top of the word sort page, and the key words can be highlighted with underlining, bolding, or with a star in the corner. Other teachers like the key words to be established as part of the group discussion with students then underlining them.

Be sensitive to the difficulty of words in the sort and make sure students can read the majority of them easily. Words starting with consonant blends, like *blame* or *frame*, are harder than words starting with single consonants like *came* or *name*, even though they share the same vowel-consonant-*e* spelling pattern. Likewise, words that contain triple blends (*scream, stream, squeek*) and digraph-blend combinations (*throat, shriek*) are harder to analyze and spell than two-letter blends (*steam, sneak*) or simple consonant digraphs (*sheet, these*).

Activities for Students in the Within Word Pattern Stage

In this section, three basic sorts are described first. Games and other activities are then offered as follow-ups that extend and reinforce students' understandings after they have sorted the words multiple times and reflected on the sounds and patterns. Many games from the previous chapter—particularly the ones marked with the adaptable logo—can be utilized with the features covered in this stage.

You'll find even more activities for Within Word Pattern spellers on the *Words Their Way* DVD. Create your own activities, games, and manipulatives and print them; or save them to your hard drive to use again and again.

Picture Sorts to Contrast Long and Short Vowels 6-1

This bridge activity is for students in the early part of the within word pattern stage. This sort will help to identify students who are having problems recognizing the differences in the vowel sounds.

Materials

Focus on one vowel and choose 10–14 short-vowel pictures and 10–14 long-vowel pictures from Appendix C.

Procedures

1. The teacher holds up the pictures for the students to name and supplies any words that are unknown.
2. The teacher places a picture at the top of the two columns to indicate the categories (such as *pig* and *kite*) and models how to sort several pictures: "*Chick, ick, i.* Chick has the same vowel sound in the middle as *pig.*"
3. Students sort the remaining pictures and check the sort by naming all the pictures in each column.
4. At the end, students declare the reason why they sorted as they did.

Teacher-Directed Word Sorts for Long Vowels 6-2

This basic procedure involves setting up and carrying out a sort that begins with sound and moves to pattern. This is similar to the sort done by Ms. Watanabe, but uses short and long -*a*.

Adaptable for Other Stages

Materials

Using the word lists in the Appendix, select about seven short -*a* words, seven long -*a* words that are spelled with the CVVC pattern (*rain, pail*), and seven with the CVCe pattern (*cake, tape*). Include one or two oddballs that do not fit the expected sound or pattern (*was* or *have*, for example). Short -*a* and long -*a* pictures (e.g., *cat* and *cake*) may be used as sound headers. Prepare word cards and/or write the words randomly on a word study handout template for students to cut apart for independent sorting.

Procedures

1. Introduce the sort by reading the words together and talking about any whose meaning may be unclear. Invite students to make observations about the words: "What do you notice?"
2. Model how to sort a few words by the sound of the vowel in the middle and then ask the students to help you finish the sort. Set the oddballs off to the side. Read all the words in each column to check them.
3. After discussing the sound categories, ask students to look for patterns in the long -*a* column and separate them into two categories. Talk about how the words in each column have different spelling patterns and why the oddballs do not fit. Create new headers from among the word cards and underline them or label them with CVC, CVCe, and CVVC.
4. Keep the headers in place and scramble the words to sort a second time. The categories will look something like the following sort.

Short -*a*	Long -*a*		Oddballs
CVC	CVCe	CVVC	
camp	cape	chain	have
gas	came	rain	was
back	name	pail	
has	lake	pain	

5. Ask students to sort independently. After the sort, students shuffle the words and store them for activities on subsequent days.

Variations

Study sounds and patterns for *e, i, o,* and *u* in the same manner.

Within Word Pattern Stage

Open Sort Using R-Influenced Vowels 6-3

After students are familiar with listening and looking for the vowel patterns, they can be very successful at open-ended sorts such as the one described here.

Materials

Select about 20 words that are spelled with *ar (bark)*, *are (bare)*, or *air (chair)*. Select words that your students should already know how to read. You may also include one or two oddballs that have the same sound but not the same spelling pattern (*pear* and *bear*, for example). Write the words randomly on a word study handout template for students to cut apart for independent sorting.

Procedures

1. Introduce the sort by reading the words together and talking about any whose meaning may be unclear. Invite students to make observations about the words: "What do you notice?"
2. Ask students to sort the words into categories of their own choosing. Call on different students to describe the rationale for their sorts. Accept all reasonable categories.
3. Agree on key words or headers and ask all the students to sort the same way. The categories will look something like the following sort. Discuss the categories and oddballs. Ask students to identify the homophones (*fare/fair, bare/bear, hare/hair*) and define them or use them in sentences.
4. Ask the students to scramble their words and sort a second time. Shuffle and store the words for sorting activities on subsequent days.

bark	bare	air	war	pear
chart	share	chair	warm	bear
yarn	stare	pair	warn	
large	scare	hair		
sharp	square	fair		

Variations

Any number of sounds and patterns can be explored in a similar fashion.

Adaptable for Other Stages

Train Station Game 6-4

This easy board game for up to four people is used to emphasize automaticity with common long vowels. It was created by Janet Bloodgood.

Materials

Use a basic pathway board found in Appendix F and decorated like the one shown in Figure 6-7. Write in words that have been studied in word sorts as well as additional words that share the same feature. Incorporate four special squares into the gameboard: (1) Cow on the track. Lose 1 turn. (2) You pass a freight train. Move ahead 2 spaces. (3) Tunnel blocked. Go back 1 space. (4) You lost your ticket. Go back 2 spaces.

Procedures

Each child selects a game piece. The first child then spins or rolls the die and moves the appropriate number of spaces. Players pronounce the word they land on and identify the

FIGURE 6-7   Train Station Game: Long-Vowel Patterns

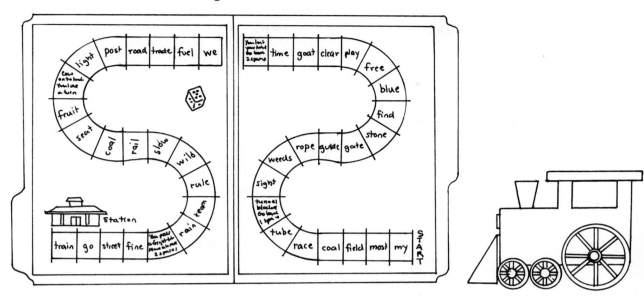

vowel. If students have studied the long-vowel patterns within each long vowel, they can be asked to say what the pattern is. For example, *"Nail is a long -a with a CVVC pattern."* In addition, the child must say another word containing the same vowel sound to stay on that space. Play continues in this fashion until someone reaches the station.

Variations

Divide a spinner into five sections and label each with a vowel. Students move to the next word with the vowel sound they spin.

Turkey Feathers 6-5

In this game created by Marilyn Edwards, two players compare patterns across a single long vowel.

Adaptable for Other Stages

Materials

You will need two paper or cardboard turkeys without tail feathers, such as the one in Figure 6-8; 10 construction paper feathers; and at least 20 word cards representing the long vowel studied (for example, for long -a: a-e, ai, and ay.

FIGURE 6-8   Turkey Feathers: Comparing Vowel Patterns

Procedures

1. One player shuffles and deals five cards and five feathers to each player. The remaining cards are placed facedown for the draw pile.
2. Each player puts down pairs that match by pattern. For example, *cake/lane* would be a pair, but *pain/lane* would not. Each time a pair is laid down, the player puts one feather on his or her turkey.
3. The dealer goes first, says a word from his or her hand, and asks if the second player has a card that has the same pattern.

4. If the second player has a card that matches the pattern, the first player gets the card and lays down the pair and a feather; if not, the first player draws a card. If the player draws a card that matches any word in his or her hand, the pair can be discarded, and a feather is earned. The next player proceeds in the same manner.

5. The player using all five feathers first wins. If a player uses all the cards before earning five feathers, the player must draw a card before the other player's turn.

Adaptable for Other Stages

The Racetrack Game 6-6

Darrell Morris (1982) developed this game, which has become a classic. It can be used for any vowel patterns and serves as a good review of the many patterns for the different vowels. Generally limit your categories to five or six patterns. A racetrack template can be found in Appendix F. A sample game board appears in Figure 6-9.

Procedures

This game for two to four players is played on an oval track divided into 20 to 30 spaces. Different words following particular patterns are written into each space, and a star is drawn in two spaces. For example, *night, light, tie, kite, like, my, fly, wish,* and *dig* could be used on a game designed to practice patterns for long and short *-i*. Prepare a collection of 40 to 50 cards that share the same patterns. A number spinner or a single die is used to move players around the track.

1. Shuffle the word cards and deal six to each player. Turn the rest facedown to become the deck. Playing pieces are moved according to the number on the spinner or die.

2. When players land on a space, they read the word and then look for words in their hand that have the same pattern. For example, a player who lands on *night* may pull *sign* and *right* to put in their point pile. If they move to a space with a star, they dispose of any oddballs they might have (such as *give*) or choose any pattern.

FIGURE 6-9   Racetrack Games Are Popular, Easy to Make, and Simple to Play

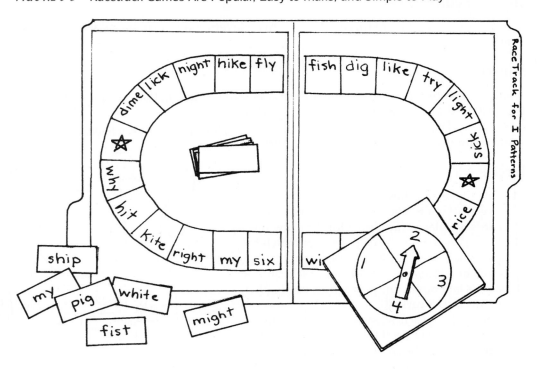

3. Any cards played are replaced by drawing from the deck. A player who has no match for the pattern must draw a card anyway.
4. The game is over when there are no more cards to play. The winner is the player with the most word cards in their point pile.

The Spelling Game 6-7

This game for two to four players can be used for any feature and is easily changed from week to week by simply replacing the word cards.

Adaptable for Other Stages

Materials

Use a follow-the-path gameboard, but leave the spaces blank except for several spaces where you may write directions such as Go Back 3 Spaces, Lose a Turn, and Go Ahead 2 Spaces. Add playing pieces and a spinner or die. Students use their own collection of words for the week.

Procedures

1. Students roll or spin. Whoever has the highest number will start and play proceeds clockwise.
2. The second player draws a card from the stack of words placed facedown. The player reads the word aloud to the first player, who must spell the word aloud. If players spell correctly, they can spin or roll to move around the path. If they misspell the word they cannot move.
3. The winner is the first one to get to the end of the path by landing on the space.

Variations

This game can be used with word families, short vowels, and multisyllabic words as well as the many one-syllable words explored in the within word pattern stage.

"I'm Out" 6-8

This card game is a favorite for two to five players; three is optimal.

Adaptable for Other Stages

Materials

Prepare a set of at least 30 cards from a unit of study such as words with *a, a-e, ay, ai*. Write the words at the top of the word card so students can easily see them in their hand.

Procedures

1. Deal all the cards so that each player gets the same number. The person to the right of the dealer begins or students may roll a die for the highest number.
2. The first player places a card down, reads the word, and designates the vowel pattern to be followed, for example, *rain, ai*.
3. The next player must place a card down with the *ai* pattern and read it aloud. If the player does not have a word with the *ai* pattern or read a word incorrectly, he or she must pass.
4. Play continues around the circle until all of the players are out of the designated pattern.
5. The player who last played the pattern card begins the new round. This player chooses a different card from his or her hand, places it in the middle, and declares what vowel pattern is to be followed.
6. The object of the game is to be the first player to play all cards.

FIGURE 6-10   Letter Spin Game: Finding Words to Match the Spinner

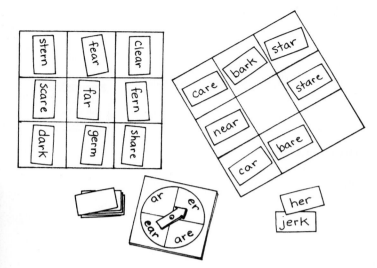

Variations

1. Students who do not have a match must draw from the remaining cards until a match is found.
2. Wild cards can be added so players can change categories in midstream.
3. Write words arranged by pattern in the word study notebooks.
4. Parts of speech could be designated along with the pattern (e.g., nouns with *ai*).

Letter Spin 6-9

Players spin for a feature and remove pictures or words from their gameboards that match the feature.

Materials

Make game boards divided like Tic-Tac-Toe as shown in Figure 6-10. The game can be played without the board by simply laying out the word cards in a three-by-three array. Make 30 or more word cards or picture cards that correspond to the feature students have been studying. You will also need a spinner divided into three to six sections and labeled with the patterns to be practiced. You can find directions for making a spinner in Appendix F.

Procedures

1. Put the cards in a deck facedown. Players draw nine cards and turn them faceup on their boards or in a three-by-three array.
2. The first player spins and removes the picture or word cards that fit the sound or pattern indicated by the spinner. The cards go into the player's "point pile." That same player draws enough cards from the pile to replace the gaps in the playing board before play moves to the next player.
3. Play continues until a player has removed all cards and there are no more to be drawn as replacements. The player who has the most cards in his or her point pile wins.

Variations

1. Following is a Tic-Tac-Toe version: Players prepare boards as described, but when they spin they can turn facedown one picture that has that feature. The winner is the one who turns down three in a row. Blackout is a longer version of Tic-Tac-Toe. Players turn over their cards. The player who turns over all of the words on the board wins.
2. A large cube (1-inch square) can be used like a die instead of a spinner. Use sticky dots to label the sides with the different features.

Sheep in a Jeep Game 6-10

This activity features *Sheep in a Jeep* (by N. Shaw, illustrated by M. Apple). In this game, created by Allison Dwier-Seldon, players examine the *ee* and *ea* pattern.

Materials

Prepare a gameboard using a follow-the-path template as shown in Figure 6-11. Write long -*e* words from the book as well as other words with the same patterns in each space. You will need a spinner with numbers 1 through 4 (see directions for spinners in

FIGURE 6-11   Board Game for *Sheep in a Jeep*

Appendix F), playing pieces to move around the board, and a pencil and small piece of paper for each player.

Procedures

1. After reading *Sheep in a Jeep* and sorting words with the *ee* and *ea* patterns, players move to the board game and place game markers at the start position.
2. One player spins and moves that number of spaces on the board. The player reads the word on the space and "adds a sheep to the jeep" by saying or writing a word that rhymes with that word. A player moves back a space if he or she reads the word incorrectly.
3. Players alternate turns. The first player to the finish wins.

Jeopardy Game 6-11

In this game contributed by Charlotte Tucker, four or five students recall and spell words that follow a particular pattern, for example, the final *ch* pattern. A poster board is divided into 5-by-5-inch sections such as the one shown in Figure 6-12, and clue cards are placed in each space.

One side of each card holds a clue about a word in that category (with the answer); the other side shows an amount (100 to 400). All the clue cards are placed on the board so that the amount shows on the back.

FIGURE 6-12   Word Jeopardy Game

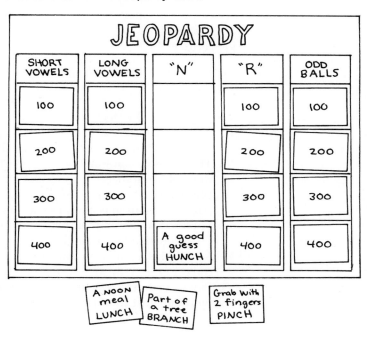

Procedures

1. One player is the moderator or game host. The others roll a die to determine who goes first.
2. The game begins when the first player picks a category and an amount for the moderator to read, for example, "I'll take short vowels for 100." The moderator reads the clue and the player must respond by phrasing a question and spelling the word. For example:

   Moderator: "When struck, it produces fire."
   Player: "What is a match? M-a-t-c-h."
3. The player receives the card if the answer is correct. This player chooses another clue. (A player can only have two consecutive turns.) If the player misses, the player to the left may answer.
4. The game continues until all the clue cards are read and won or left unanswered. Players add their points, and the one with the highest amount wins.

Word lists. Here are words that could be used for a game reviewing *ch* and *tch*.

R	N	Short Vowels	Long Vowels	Oddballs
march	bench	stitch	beach	much
perch	lunch	watch	teach	such
porch	branch	sketch	roach	rich
torch	pinch	witch	coach	which

Vowel Poker 6-12

Up to four students practice grouping short- and long-vowel words by pattern. Older students like this game because of the poker terms. Fran de Maio developed this version.

Materials

A deck of 35–45 cards is needed. A good starting combination might be five cards for each short vowel in the CVC pattern for a total of 25 cards, and five cards for each long vowel in the CVCe pattern (except for long -*e* because there are so few words in that category), for a total of 20 more cards. Wild cards can be included.

Procedures

1. Five cards are dealt to each player and the rest are turned facedown in a deck. Players look in their hands for pairs, three of a kind, four of a kind, or five of a kind.
2. Each player has one chance to discard unwanted cards and draw up to four new cards from the deck to keep a hand of five cards. For example, a player might be dealt *bone, rope, that, wet, rake.* This player may want to discard *that, wet,* and *rake,* and draw three other cards to possibly create a better hand.
3. The possible combinations are a pair (*that, camp*); two pairs (*that, camp, bone, rope*); three of a kind (*bone, rope, rode*); four of a kind (*bone, rope, rode, smoke*); three of a kind plus a pair (*bone, rope, rode, hat, rat*); or five of a kind. In poker, three of a kind plus a pair combination is a full house, and five of a kind is a flush.
4. Students lay down their hands to determine the winner of the round. The winner is determined in this order: Five of a kind (this beats everything), four of a kind, three of a kind plus a pair, two pairs, three of a kind, and one pair. In the case of a tie, players can draw from the deck until one player comes up with a card that will break the tie.
5. Play continues by dealing another set of cards to the players. The player who has won the most rounds is the winner.

Adaptable for Other Stages

Declare Your Category! 6-13

This card game for two to five players (three is optimal) works best with students who have had some experience playing games. In this game, players guess the first player's category.

Materials

Create a deck of 45 word cards with a variety of vowels and vowel patterns. Make at least four cards with any one pattern.

Procedures

1. Seven cards are dealt to each player and the remainder are placed facedown in a deck. Players lay out their seven cards faceup.
2. The first player turns up a key card from the deck (*home*, for example) and looks for a word in his or her hand to match in some way. It might have the same sound and/or spelling pattern (either *o-e* or VCe). *Soap, bone,* or *gave* might be matched to *home*, for example. The match is laid down for all to see and the player announces: "Guess my category." Play moves to the next person, who must search his or her hand for a similar match. The player who started the category keeps the sorting strategy a secret, and waits until the last player puts a card down and declares the category. Players can pass when they wish.
3. If the person who set up the category does not think the next player put down an acceptable card, he or she can send a card back and give that player another chance. Mistakes are discussed at the end of each round.
4. The player who plays the last card has to declare the category. If he or she declares it correctly, he or she is the winner and keeps all of the cards. If the player is wrong, the previous player gets a chance to declare the category.
5. At the end of each round, students are dealt enough cards to get them back to seven. The winner of the round turns up a card from the pile and makes up the next category.
6. The player with the most cards wins.

Variations

1. Add wild cards to the pile to change categories in midstream. The person who establishes a new category must guess the original category correctly. This player becomes the new judge: "Your category was by words with long -o and the silent -e. I am putting down my wild card, and laying down *loan*. Guess my category."
2. The rules of the game can be expanded to include semantic (e.g., types of birds) and grammatical (e.g., nouns) categories.

Word Study Pursuit 6-14

Adaptable for Other Stages

This game for four players was adapted from Trivial Pursuit by Rita Loyacono, and students who know that game will learn this one easily.

Materials

You will need poster board, construction paper in four different colors, four envelopes, a die or spinner, and game piece markers. To construct the gameboard, glue $1\frac{1}{2}$ inch squares of construction paper in four colors onto the poster board, alternating colors and making a trail from start to finish covering the entire board. Write words from a unit of study on cards cut from the same four colors and store them in envelopes marked by the corresponding color.

Procedures

1. Players determine the order of play by spinning or tossing the die. The winner chooses a color and goes first; each player in turn selects a color.
2. Players take the packet of word cards corresponding to their color and call these words out when another player lands on their respective color. If players land on their own color, they may take another turn. When a student lands on a space where there is already another card, the player sorts by pattern as well, placing a word that sounds alike and looks alike on top of the word or to the side if it sounds alike but does not look the same.

    For example, suppose Adam spins a five and lands on a green square. The person with the green packet calls out a word. Adam spells the word correctly, and the card is placed faceup next to the caller. Bonnie takes a turn and also lands on a green square. After successfully spelling her word, she must decide if it is to be placed on top of the first word (follows the same pattern) or beside it (is a different pattern). In this way, students spell the words as well as sort them by pattern.
3. Players who misspell the word must go back one square and try a word from that color providing it is not their own color (in which case they move back two squares). If players are unable to spell that word, they remain where they are and lose one turn. If players are unable to sort the word properly, they must move back one space (again providing it is not their color; if so, they move back two spaces), but do not lose a turn. The first player to get to the finish square is the winner and will be referee the next time.

Variations

Because neither the gameboard nor the envelopes are marked, the board can be used for any word patterns that are being studied. Having several sets of the game allows different groups of four students to play the same game while practicing different patterns.

Word Study Uno 6-15

Adaptable for Other Stages

This game is a version of the popular card game for three to four players contributed by Rita Loyacona.

Materials

Create a set of cards by writing words in the upper left corner of tagboard rectangles or blank cards. Make at least 27 word cards that include the patterns that you have been studying. For example, if students are studying long -*o* patterns, create word cards that have *o-e*, *oa*, and *ow*. Also create four wild cards and two of each of the following cards:

Skip *o-e*	Draw 2 *o-e*
Skip *ow*	Draw 2 *ow*
Skip *oa*	Draw 2 *oa*

Procedures

1. Deal five cards to each player. The remaining cards are placed in a deck facedown and the top card is turned faceup to start the discard pile.
2. Players alternate and discard a card that matches the pattern of the played card, or play one of the special cards (Skip, Draw-2, Wild). For example, if the beginning card was *boat*, the player could discard *soap*, *road*, or *goat*. A player who did not have one of those cards, or who chose not to use one of those, could discard a Skip or Draw-2 card. The Skip card indicates that the next player loses a turn. The Draw-2 card forces the next player to pick two cards from the pile, and no cards may be discarded.
3. Skip and Draw-2 cards indicate the next pattern that must be played. When a Wild card is discarded, the player can select the category. A player who cannot discard

must draw from the pile, and if the draw matches the pattern of the last discard, it can be played.

4. A player who has only one card remaining must say, "UNO." If the player forgets, another player can tell the player with one card to draw another card.
5. The first player to run out of cards wins the game.

Homophone Win, Lose, or Draw 6-16

Four or more students work in teams to draw and guess each other's words in a game that resembles charades. A list of homophones can be found in the Appendix. Barry Mahanes based this on the television show.

Procedures

1. Write homophone pairs on cards and shuffle.
2. Students divide into two equal teams, and one player from each team is selected as the artist for that round. The artist must draw a picture representing the given homophone which will elicit the homophone itself, the spelling, and the meaning.
3. A card is pulled from the deck and shown simultaneously to the artists for both teams. As the artists draw, their teammates call out possible answers. When the correct word is offered, the artist calls on someone to spell both words in a pair.
4. A point is awarded to the team that provides the correct information first. The artist then chooses the next artist and play proceeds in the same fashion.

Homophone Rummy 6-17

This activity is suitable for two to six students. The object of the game is to get the most homophone pairs.

Materials

Prepare several decks of homophone pairs (52 cards, 26 pairs). A list of homophones can be found in the Appendix. Select words with which your students have some familiarity. Write the words in the upper left corner of the cards as shown in Figure 6-13.

Procedures

1. Players are dealt seven cards and begin the game by checking their hands for already existing pairs. Once a pair is discovered, it can be laid down in front of the player. The player must give the meaning for each word or use it in a sentence that makes the meaning clear.

FIGURE 6-13   Homophone Rummy

2. The remainder of the deck is placed in a central location and the first card is turned faceup beside it to form a discard pile.
3. The person on the left of the dealer goes first. Each player draws from either the deck or the discard pile. Any new pairs are laid down and defined. The player must then discard one card to end the turn. *Note*: If a card is taken from the discard pile, all the cards below are also taken and the top card must be used to make a pair.
4. A player can be challenged by someone else disagreeing with the definitions. The person who challenges looks up the words in the dictionary. Whoever is right gets to keep the pair.

Within Word Pattern Stage

FIGURE 6-14 Hink Pinks

whale pail

sad Dad

5. The game is over when one player has no cards left. That person yells, "Rummy!" Then the pairs are counted up to determine the winner.

Hink Pinks 6-18

Hink Pinks is a traditional language game that involves a riddle answered by a pair of rhyming words, such as "What do you call a chubby kitty? (*fat cat*). What do you call an angry father? (*mad dad*). What do you call a plastic pond? (*fake lake*). Hinky Pinky usually demands two-syllable rhymes: What is a bloody tale? (*gory story*), while Hinkety Pinkety requires three-syllable answers: What is the White House? (*presidents' residence*) You can find lots more examples of all of these by searching online. Visual hink pinks are featured in the book *One Sun: A Book of Terse Verse*, by Bruce McMillan (1990).

1. Share examples of hink pinks and discuss the structure of the language or read *One Sun* with your students and talk about the riddles and photographs.
2. Brainstorm objects and possible adjectives that rhyme; for example, *pink/sink, bear/lair, sled/bed*. When students understand the concept, have them work in small groups or individually to think of their own hink pinks.
3. Challenge students to draw a picture to illustrate their hink pink as Bruce McMillan did or to write a riddle. These can be exchanged with a friend (see Figure 6-14).

Semantic Brainstorms 6-19

This small group activity focuses on the meaning of the words and serves as a great activity for content studies.

Procedures

1. Choose a topic for students to study. Topics can be chosen by students and can be related to content studies. Start with easy, familiar topics such as sports and locations (as well as countries, animal life, clothes, furniture, modes of transportation).
2. Students brainstorm related words and then record them. Using chart paper is a good way to record these sorts.
3. Students share their findings and see if they can come up with subcategories from their brainstorming. Categories can be circled by color or written over into columns.

Variations

1. Look in magazines, newspapers, and catalogs. Circle words that express feelings, color words, people's names, or parts of speech.
2. Organizing software (e.g., *Inspiration*) can be used to record these brainstorms in a chart form. Additional software, such as VISIO software for drawing graphics, can be used in the same way. You can record student responses within circles and rectangles using the drawing toolbar in PowerPoint software.

Semantic Sorts 6-20

Students work with content-related words to compare and contrast.

Procedures

1. Look through a chapter or unit in a textbook and make a list of the key terms. Often they are listed at the end of a unit. Make word cards for the words.
2. Students sort the words in an open sort, establishing their own categories. Start with easy and familiar topics.
3. The sorts are copied into word study notebooks in a separate section for that content area.

Variations

Grammatical sorts are variations in which students sort by parts of speech (see Figure 6-15). For example, students can collect nouns and then divide them into different types (e.g., things that move/animate versus stationary/inanimate nouns). When students look for differences in the concepts, they begin to debate. One could argue that *run* is both a noun and a verb.

Computer Sorts, Materials, and Games.   The wide range of phonics materials and games on the market offers a huge selection, from stand-alone electronic games to free software found on the World Wide Web. A search engine will yield many word study resources (search "word study," "phonics," or the actual feature you want to study).

Word sorts on computer.   A search of the World Wide Web provides a variety of free or for-purchase materials that teachers post. For example, the BBC has made game-oriented software available. Another site is maintained by Sadlier-Oxford.

Word Sort is a software program developed by Ed Henderson, his son, and several students that can be used independently with students in the within word pattern stage. It provides 215 timed sorts that focus on vowel patterns. The teacher's guide and disk contain a management system that provides a student report form as well as ways for teachers to compile class profiles. Mac and PC versions are available at www.hendersonedsort.com.

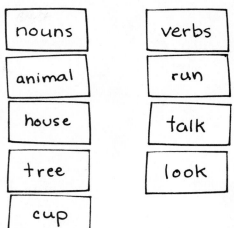

FIGURE 6-15   Grammatical Relations Can Be Examined in Semantic Sorts

7 Word Study for Intermediate Readers and Writers: The Syllables and Affixes Stage

The stages of word knowledge through which most students will move during the intermediate and middle grade years are termed *syllables and affixes* and *derivational relations*. Beginning in second and third grade for some students, and in fourth grade for most, cognitive and language growth allows children to make new and richer connections among the words they already know and the words they will learn. In this chapter addressing syllables and affixes, and the next chapter addressing derivational relations, you will learn how teachers can establish a firm foundation in spelling and in vocabulary development as they facilitate students' move into understanding the role of structure and meaning in the spelling system.

As you teach students at these levels, you will find the whole enterprise of learning about words to be fascinating as well as never ending. This awareness can nourish your own interest and delight in words and what your students will be learning about words. As in earlier stages, you will facilitate students' word explorations to help them discover the patterns of sound, spelling, and meaning that link thousands of words. This knowledge will help them read, write, and spell much more effectively.

Before we talk in detail about the features of study in this stage, let's visit Sharon Lee's fourth grade classroom in midyear. Ms. Lee has a range of abilities in her classroom that are evident in both reading levels and spelling inventory results. She has a large group of 14 students who fall into the syllables and affixes stage, four students who remain in the within word pattern stage, and five students who are in derivational relations. She makes time to meet with each group several times a week for systematic word study, while the other groups work independently. In the following vignette, Ms. Lee calls for the attention of the larger syllables and affixes group at the front of the room for a 20-minute lesson while the rest of the students find comfortable places to read and discuss in the "Book Club" format (Raphael, Pardo, Highfield, & McMahon, 1997). The syllables and affixes students are studying final *ar/er/or*. This final unaccented syllable poses a challenge for spellers because it is pronounced the same, /ər/, across different spellings.

In preparation for a directed spelling thinking activity (Zutell, 1996), Ms. Lee begins her word study unit for this week by asking her students to spell three words: *dollar, faster,* and *actor*. She then calls on several students to tell how they spelled each word as she writes their answers on an overhead transparency, encouraging a variety of answers. The results include *doller, dollor, dollar, faster, acter, actor*. Ms. Lee then "thinks aloud": "Hmmm . . . This is very interesting. We agree on how to spell the first syllable of each word, but we don't always agree about how to spell the final syllable. What makes this part hard?" Jason volunteers that the words sound the same at the end. "Do the rest of you agree?" Ms. Lee asks. "Let's say each word and listen carefully. Do they sound alike? Let's find out if this is true for other words as well."

Ms. Lee has made a transparency of the weekly word sort and cut it apart to sort on the overhead projector. She discusses *blister* and *mayor* with the students to make sure they are clear on each word's meaning, and reviews the meaning of *lunar* and *solar*, words used in their recent study of space. Then she asks, "How might we sort these words?" Sara suggests that they sort by the last two letters. "Let's do that," Ms. Lee responds, "and as we sort them, let's say them aloud and listen for the sound in the last syllable."

Ms. Lee removes all the words except *dollar, faster,* and *actor,* which she underlines to use as key words for the sort. She then places each word in turn on the overhead and calls on a student to read it and tell her where to put it. The final sort resembles the one shown in Figure 7-1. After reading the words in each column, Ms. Lee asks the students, "What have we found out about these words?" Several students offer ideas, and Ms. Lee summarizes by saying, "When we hear /ər/, the sound will not help us spell it, so we will have to concentrate on remembering whether it is spelled *-er, -or,* or *-ar*."

Ms. Lee hands out the word sort and goes over the students' word study assignments for the week. Students are expected to cut apart and sort the words independently and then write the word sort in their word study notebooks. While they do that, Ms. Lee will meet with her within word pattern group for word study. On other days they will work independently by sorting again with a buddy, sorting at home, and hunting for additional words in trade books. On Friday, Ms. Lee will give them a spelling test, but she will also call the group together to compile a large class list of the words they were able to find in their word hunts. This will be used to introduce the following week's lesson, where students will be helped to discover that *er* is the most common way to spell the final sound, that it is always used to spell comparative adjectives (*faster, smaller, longer*), and that *er* and *or* are often used to spell agents or people who do things (*teacher, worker, author, sailor*).

FIGURE 7-1 Final /ar/ Word Sort

dollar	faster	actor
sugar	blister	doctor
grammar	jogger	tractor
solar	speaker	motor
lunar	skater	favor
collar	cleaner	editor
	poster	mayor
	freezer	author
	dreamer	
	bigger	

Ms. Lee's lesson promotes two key ideas of this stage: (a) It demonstrates to students how much they already know about spelling a particular word—spelling is not an

 Watch the Syllables and Affixes section on the *Words Their Way* DVD for ideas on assessing, grouping, organizing, and implementing word study with syllables and affixes spellers.

all-or-none affair where they "get a word wrong." Usually they will get most of the word correct, and teachers need to remind and reassure students about this. (b) It demonstrates to students what they need to focus on when they look at a word. Because they already know most of the word, they need to attend to the part that is still challenging.

LITERACY DEVELOPMENT OF STUDENTS IN THE SYLLABLES AND AFFIXES STAGE

The intermediate stage is a time of expanding reading interests and fine-tuning reading strategies. In the upper elementary grades and middle school, students will be expected to read textbooks and much more informational text as classroom instruction shifts to a greater emphasis on content area subjects. In previous developmental stages, the challenges posed by reading stem more from children's ability to identify words than from their prior knowledge about the topic or genre. At the intermediate and advanced levels, however, background knowledge and vocabulary become critical elements in comprehension. Developing word knowledge allows them to read more fluently, which in turn allows them to exercise and expand their increasing level of cognitive and language sophistication.

In previous chapters, word study has been limited to single-syllable words, even though students have been reading, and even writing, polysyllabic words for some time. Knowledge of vowel and consonant patterns within single-syllable words builds a foundation for the polysyllabic words of intermediate word study in much the same way that basic math facts build a foundation for long division. Once students have this foundation, they are ready to begin the study of polysyllabic words. Major features of study at the syllables and affixes stage include the following.

1. How consonant and vowel patterns are represented in polysyllabic words
2. What occurs when syllables join together (syllable juncture)
3. How stress or lack of stress determines the clarity of the sounds in syllables
4. How simple affixes (prefixes and suffixes) change the usage, meaning, and spelling of words

In Chapter 1 we described some of the characteristic errors made by students in this stage and the spelling issues they will need to explore. Table 7-1 provides a summary of what students know, what they use but confuse, and what is still missing in the early, middle, and late syllables and affixes stage. In the spelling of *crall* for *crawl*, we can see lingering confusions with ambiguous vowel patterns. However, for the most part students know how to spell single syllable words correctly, so the focus shifts to two-syllable words and the conventions that govern spelling where syllables meet, or their **syllable juncture.** The spellings of *SHOPING* and *AMAZZING* show us that the student knows how to spell the *ing* suffix but lacks knowledge about the doubling rule where syllables join. Syllable juncture problems can also be seen in the using but confusing of doubled letters in *KEPPER* for *keeper* and *BOTEL* for *bottle*.

The syllables and affixes stage represents a new point in word analysis because there is more than one syllable to consider and each syllable may present a spelling problem. The accented second syllable in *parading* might be spelled several ways, as in *PERAIDING*. Problems with unaccented final syllables are also evident in *BOTTEL* for *bottle* and *DAMIGE* for *damage*. As the name of the stage suggests, in addition to syllables, students grapple with meaning units such as prefixes and suffixes (known collectively as **affixes**) and begin to study base words as **morphemes** or meaning units that must retain their spelling when affixes are added. In *KEPER* for *keeper*, the student may be relying on sound rather than knowledge of the **spelling meaning connection** of the base word *keep*.

The Elementary Spelling Inventory (ESI) or the Upper Level Spelling Inventory (ULI) described in Chapter 2 will help you collect information about students' spelling errors so that you can place them appropriately for word study in this stage.

Characteristics of Syllables and Affixes Spelling

	What Students Do Correctly	What Students Use but Confuse	What Is Absent
Early Syllables and Affixes *CRALL* for *crawl* *SHOPING* for *shopping* *AMAZZING* for *amazing* *BOTEL* for *bottle* *KEPER* or *KEPPER* for *keeper*	Blends, digraphs, short vowels Vowel patterns in one syllable words Complex consonant units in one-syllable words Spell known sight words correctly	Ambiguous vowels Consonant doubling and e-drop Syllable juncture: open and closed syllable patterns	Few things are completely missing Occasional deletion of reduced syllables: *DIFFRENT* for *different* Doubled consonant of absorbed prefixes
Middle Syllables and Affixes *SELLER* for *cellar* *DAMIGE* for *damage* *PERAIDING* for *parading*	All of the above plus: Doubling and e-drop with inflected endings Syllable juncture: open and closed syllable patterns	Vowel patterns in accented syllables Unaccented final syllables	Doubled consonant of absorbed prefixes
Late Syllables and Affixes *parading* *cattle, cellar* *CONFEDENT* for *confident*	All of the above plus: Vowel patterns in accented syllables Unaccented final syllables	Some suffixes and prefixes: *ATTENSION* for *attention*, *PERTEND* for *pretend* Reduced vowel in unaccented syllables	Doubled consonant of absorbed prefixes

Use the table above to determine what features they are using but confusing as a guide to planning instruction.

One of your most important responsibilities for word study instruction at this stage is to engage students in examining how important word elements—prefixes, suffixes, and base words—combine; this **structural analysis** is a powerful tool for vocabulary development, spelling, and figuring out unfamiliar words during reading. You can show students directly how to apply this knowledge by modeling the following strategy for analyzing unfamiliar words in their reading that they cannot identify.

1. Examine the word for meaningful parts—base word, prefixes, or suffixes.
   - If there is a prefix, take it off first.
   - If there is a suffix, take it off second.
   - Look at the base to see if you know it or if you can think of a related word (a word that has the same base).
   - Reassemble the word, thinking about the meaning contributed by the base, the suffix, and then the prefix. This should give you a more specific idea of what the word is.
2. Try out the meaning in the sentence; check if it makes sense in the context of the sentence and the larger context of the text that is being read.
3. If the word still does not make sense and is critical to the meaning of the overall passage, look it up in the dictionary.
4. Record the new word in your word study notebook.

Let us take a look at how Ms. Lee models this process for students, beginning with a familiar word and then extending the lesson to an unfamiliar word.

"I've underlined one of the words in this sentence: They had to <u>redo</u> the programs after they were printed with a spelling error. What does *redo* mean? Yes, Chloe?"

"When you have to do something over again?"

"Okay! So you already had done something once, right?

Now, let's cover up this first part of the word [covers *re*]. What word do we have? Right—*do*. Now, let's look at these words."

Ms. Lee writes the words *join, tell,* and *write* on the board, then the prefix *re-* in front of each base word as she pronounces the new word. "When we join the prefix *re-* to each of them, what happens? Right! We are going to be doing these things again—we can *rejoin* a group, *retell* a story, *rewrite* a paper." She then asks the students what they think the prefix *re-* means. After a brief discussion, she asks a student to look up the prefix in the dictionary to check their definitions.

Ms. Lee's next step is to model this strategy with a word she is fairly certain the students do not yet know. She shows the following sentence on the overhead:

> As they got closer to the front of the line, her friends had to <u>reassure</u> Hannah that the Big Thunder roller coaster ride was safe.

"Okay," Ms. Lee proceeds, "I've underlined this word [pointing to <u>reassure</u>]. Any ideas what this word is?" Most students shake their heads; Kaitlyn squinches up her face as she slowly pronounces "REE–sure." "Good try, Kaitlyn," Ms. Lee responds. "You're trying to pronounce it, but it doesn't sound like a word we've heard before. What about the beginning of the word, though? Could that be the prefix we've just been thinking about?"

This prompt works for the students and they start trying to pronounce the base, *assure,* without the prefix *re-.* "Right," Ms. Lee encourages. "You've taken off the prefix, *re-,* and are trying to figure out the base word. Any ideas?" Though a couple of students are pronouncing *assure* correctly, they are uncertain about its meaning.

Ms. Lee continues: "Well, we know that, whatever *assure* means, the prefix *re-* means it's being done again! Let's look back at the sentence. Do you think Hannah can't wait to go on the roller coaster—or is she beginning to be worried?" After some discussion with the students, Ms. Lee talks about the base word, *assure,* and explains that Hannah's friends had probably already talked with her about how safe the roller coaster was, that there had never been any accidents, and had helped Hannah to feel more confident—*assured* her—that Big Thunder was safe. (Most students are nodding their heads now, saying things such as "Oh, yeah, I've heard that word before.") As Hannah and her friends got closer to actually going on the roller coaster, however, they had to assure her again—*reassure* her.

Ms. Lee summarizes: "Most of the time, by looking carefully at a word you don't know—looking for any prefixes, suffixes, and thinking about the base—you can get pretty close to the actual meaning of the word. Then ask yourself if this meaning makes sense in the sentence and text that you're reading."

It is critical to model and reinforce this strategic approach to analyzing unfamiliar words in text, and students need plenty of opportunities to try it out under your guidance (Baumann, Edwards, Font, Tereshinksi, Kame'enui, & Olijnik, 2003). Encourage your students to talk about their ideas as they apply the process so that you can encourage, facilitate, and redirect as necessary. This strategy will become one of the most effective means of developing and extending students' vocabulary knowledge. It is also important, however, to model what to do when the process does not yield an appropriate meaning for the unfamiliar word—analyzing *repel* into *re* + *pel* will not be of much help to intermediate students—and then the dictionary might be consulted.

The dictionary offers opportunities for determining the precise meaning of a word students need to know in their reading as well as for understanding a word deeply. For example, based on Robyn Montana Turner's biography of Faith Ringgold, Ms. Lee focuses on the word *enhancing* in the sentence, "Faith Ringgold decided to use cloth frames as a way of enhancing her art." Pronouncing the word does not seem to help because it is not in the students' speaking/listening vocabularies and breaking the word into parts does not help. Ms. Lee talks about the context in which the word occurs; it may narrow the possibilities somewhat, but possible meanings suggested by the context might include, for example, "protecting" or "showing." This is definitely a situation in which the dictionary will be of use and strategies for looking words up should be modeled.

> Ms. Lee underlines the word *enhancing* and explains that, to check the meaning of this word in the dictionary, they would need to look up the base word, *enhance*. Reminding the students that they may need to watch out for changes in spelling when they are trying to figure out the base word for an unfamiliar word, she notes that the e is dropped when the *-ing* is added. Looking up a base word also helps to highlight the spelling of other forms of the word.
>
> The dictionary definition for *enhance* is "to make greater, as in value, beauty, or reputation." Ms. Lee has the students return to the sentence in the text and discuss which of these features they believe Faith Ringgold had in mind when she decided to use cloth frames. The students agree that, in the context of the sentence and the overall text, Faith Ringgold probably wanted to make her quilts more "beautiful."

Dictionaries can also provide helpful information about the history of a word and make explicit the interrelationships among words in the same meaning "families." A discussion of dictionary entries illustrates how one word's entry can include information about words related in spelling and meaning—the entry for *entrap*, for example, also includes *entraps* and *entrapment*. Sections labeled "Usage Notes," "Synonyms," and "Word History" provide important information about the appropriateness of particular words, and subtle but important differences among their meanings. Some entries contain stories that explain spellings and deepen understanding of important terms.

You will notice that authors of many textbooks try to provide a rich context to support new vocabulary and often highlight important new terms for the reader. Although students need to learn about bolded terms, they also need to learn the strategy of breaking words into parts (prefixes, suffixes, and base words) so that they can grow confidently and competently into independent word learners. This strategy depends critically on the students' knowledge of word structure. Adams (1990) best emphasized this importance:

> Learning from context is a very, very important component of vocabulary acquisition. But this means of learning is available only to the extent that children bother to process the spelling—the orthographic structure—of the unknown words they encounter. Where they skip over an unknown word without attending to it, and often readers do, no learning can occur. (p. 150)

ORTHOGRAPHIC DEVELOPMENT DURING THE SYLLABLES AND AFFIXES STAGE

During the syllables and affixes stage, students will learn to look at words in a new way, not as single-syllable units with CVC, CVVC, or other vowel patterns, but as two or more syllabic or meaning units. This structural analysis is more sophisticated than the phonics instruction typically offered in the primary grades that teaches students to process words using consonants, blends, digraphs, and vowel patterns—elements that students master in Ehri's full alphabetic phase. In the syllables and affixes stage students use larger chunks to decode, spell, and store words in memory as sight words as described by Ehri as the consolidated alphabetic phase (1997). For example, a word like *unhappy* can be analyzed as three syllabic chunks (*un-hap-py*) or two morphemic chunks (*un-happy*). Word study in the syllables and affixes stage helps students learn where these syllable and morphemic breaks come in words so that they can use the appropriate chunks to quickly and accurately read, spell, and determine the meaning of polysyllabic words.

Henderson (1990) referred to students in this stage of word knowledge as intermediate readers, not quite mature or advanced. He also noted the wide divergence of reading skill during this stage of development, spanning, on average, five levels, from the third to the eighth grade levels. The range of reading skill within this stage makes it imperative to revisit many of the orthographic concepts underlying syllables and affixes in light of the more complex reading vocabulary of the upper elementary and middle school years. Some of that revisiting might start with a reexamination of compound words.

Compound Words

When students explore compound words, they can develop several types of understandings. First, they learn how words can combine in different ways to form new words (*sunlight, lightweight*). This is an introduction to the combinatorial features of English words. Second, the study of compound words lays the foundation for explicit attention to syllables: very often, compound words are comprised of two smaller words, each of which is a single syllable. Third, students reinforce their knowledge of the spelling of many high-frequency, high-utility words in English because these words include so many compound words. Look in the activities section on page 221 for specific ideas such as illustrating words and brainstorming words that share the same base.

Base Words and Inflectional Endings/Suffixes

One type of suffixes, known as **inflectional endings,** includes *-s, -ed,* and *-ing.* These suffixes change the number and tense of the base word, but do not change its meaning or part of speech. While inflectional endings have been used in oral language since the preschool years, studying them in spelling will introduce students to base words and suffixes as well as the rules that govern spelling changes.

The basic doubling rule for adding inflectional suffixes is: When a suffix beginning with a vowel is added to a base word containing a short vowel followed by a single consonant, double the final consonant. This can be simplified as the one-one-one rule: One syllable, one vowel, one consonant—double. The doubling rule has few exceptions and is worth learning. It does take time, however, for students to develop a firm understanding of it. Rather than teaching rules, we suggest a series of word sorts that will allow children to discover the many principles at work. In Sort 1 of Figure 7-2, the students first sort by words that double and those that do not and are asked to underline the base word.

FIGURE 7-2   Adding Inflectional Ending to Base Words

Sort 1

			Sort 2	
resting	jogging	CVVC	CVCC	CVC
reading	running	reading	resting	jogging
feeding	shopping	feeding	walking	running
walking	winning	sleeping	jumping	shopping
sleeping	planning	waiting	smelling	winning
jumping	skipping	raining	dressing	planning
waiting	sobbing			skipping
smelling	hugging			sobbing
dressing	snapping			snapping

In Sort 2 shown in Figure 7-2, sorting by the vowel pattern in the base word helps students discover that there are two conditions when the ending is simply added (CVVC words like *read* and CVCC words like *rest*). This will help clear up the confusion of *smelling* and *dressing*, words that students may initially place in the doubled column.

Table 7–1 summarizes the conditions that govern the addition of inflectional endings. The rules can get quite complicated, but when planning instruction, begin with the most common in the early syllables and affixes stage (numbers 1–3) and expect to reinforce these throughout upper elementary school and even beyond in the case of two- and three-syllable words (where the accent can vary between the last syllable and the next to last syllable). Remember: It will take time for children to master these generalizations and they should know the spelling of the base words before they are asked to think about how to add suffixes.

One of the earliest suffixes students learn to use is the plural, adding -*s* even when the sound it represents varies, as in *cats* /s/ and *dogs* /z/. However, plurals deserve to be addressed systematically to cover additional issues.

1. Add -*es* when words end in *ch, sh, ss, s,* and *x.* When -*es* is added to a word, students can usually "hear" the difference because it adds another syllable to the word (*dish* becomes *dish-es,* unlike *spoons*).
2. Change the *y* at the end of a word to *i* before adding -*es* when the word ends in a consonant + *y* (*baby* to *babies*), but not when it ends in a vowel + *y* (*monkeys*).
3. Words may change spelling and pronunciation in the plural form. Some words with final *f* or *fe* change the *f* to *v* and add *es* (*wife* to *wives, wolf* to *wolves*). *Goose* changes to *geese* and *mouse* to *mice.* And some words remain the same (*fish, sheep, deer*).

TABLE 7-1   Changes to Base Words When Adding Inflectional Endings or Other Suffixes That Start with a Vowel

Base Words	+ *ing*	+ *ed* (or *er*)	+ *s*
1. CVVC, CVCC Ex: *look, walk*	No change Ex: *looking, walking*	No change Ex: *looked, walked*	No change Ex: *looks, walks*
2. CVC Ex: *bat*	Double final letter Ex: *batting*	Double final letter Ex: *batted, batter*	No change Ex: *bats*
3. CVCe Ex: *rake*	Drop final -*e* Ex: *raking*	Drop final -*e* Ex: *raked*	No change Ex: *rakes*
4. Words that end in a consonant + *y* Ex: *cry*	No change Ex: *crying*	Change *y* to *i* Ex: *cried, crier*	Change *y* to *i* and add *es* Ex: *cries*
5. Words that end in a vowel + *y* Ex: *play*	No change Ex: *playing*	No change Ex: *played*	No change Ex: *plays*
6. Two-syllable words accented on second syllable Ex: *admit, invite, apply, enjoy*	Follow rules for 1–5 Ex: *admitting, inviting, applying, enjoying*	Follow rules for 1–5 Ex: *admitted, invited, applied, enjoyed*	Follow rules for 1–5 Ex: *admits, invites, applies, enjoys*
7. Words that end in a *c* Ex: *panic*	Add a *k* Ex: *panicking*	Add a *k* Ex: *panicked*	No change Ex: *panics*

Note: Words ending in *x* do not double (e.g., *boxed, boxing*). Words that end in *ck* avoid having to double a final *k* (*blocked, blocking* versus *blocking*). Words that end in *ve* avoid having to double a final *v* (*loved, loving*).

Open/Closed Syllables and Syllable Patterns

Why is *Tigger*, the name of the tiger from *Winnie the Pooh*, spelled with two *g*s? How do you pronounce *Caddie Woodlawn*? Answering these questions depends on whether you are dealing with an open or a closed syllable. **Open syllables** (CV) end with a long-vowel sound: *tiger, Katy, reason*. **Closed syllables** (CVC) contain a short-vowel sound that is usually "closed" by two consonants: *Tigger, Caddie, rabbit, racket*.

Students are first introduced to the basics of open and closed syllables when they examine what happens when *-ed* and *-ing* are added to short- and long-vowel pattern words. Consider these examples:

*hop + ing = **hopp**ing hope + ing = **hop**ing*
*strip + ing = **stripp**ing stripe + ing = **strip**ing*

As Henderson (1985) explained, "The core principle of syllable juncture is that of doubling consonants to mark the short English vowel" (p. 65). Students learn that when they are uncertain about whether to double the consonants at the juncture of syllables, they should say the word and listen to the vowel sounds. If they hear a long-vowel sound, the syllable is open and will be followed by a single consonant. If they hear a short-vowel sound, the odds are likely that the syllable will need to be closed by two consonants. For example, if they are writing about how a rabbit moves along the ground (*hopping*) and do not double the *p*, they will wind up with an entirely different meaning (*hoping*). Knowledge about whether to double develops first through examining base words plus inflectional suffixes, and is later applied *within* base words: Because the vowel in the first syllable of *Tigger* is short, the *g* is doubled; because the vowel in the first syllable of *tiger* is long, the *g* is not doubled.

Another way of describing what goes on at the juncture of syllables is through syllable patterns. For example, *hopping, Tigger,* and *stripping* illustrate the VCCV syllable juncture pattern; *hoping, tiger,* and *striping* illustrate the VCV syllable juncture pattern. Table 7-2 lists the common syllable juncture patterns. The first two syllable patterns, the open V/CV pattern and the closed VC/CV pattern, are the most frequent. The third pattern, the closed VC/V pattern, with only a single consonant at the juncture after a short vowel occurs less frequently than the others. The fourth pattern, the closed VC-CCV pattern, includes words that have a consonant digraph or blend at the syllable juncture (*ath-lete, hun-dred*). The VV pattern has each vowel contributing a sound; the word is usually divided after the first long-vowel sound (*cre-ate, lion*).

Figure 7-2 shows a sort that can be used to introduce syllable juncture patterns. You might begin by sorting three to four words into each column in a Guess-My-Category activity. Start asking students to help you sort the rest of the words. After sorting, ask the students how the words in column 1 are alike. Probe by asking them if anyone noticed the vowel sounds and where the words were "divided" when you pronounced them. Then go to column 2 and guide the students' examination in the same fashion.

TABLE 7-2   Syllable Juncture Patterns

Label	Type	Examples
VCCV	Closed	*skipping, button, rubber* (doublets)
		chapter, window, garden (two different consonants)
V/CV	Open	*lazy, coma, beacon, bacon*
VC/V	Closed	*river, robin, cover, planet*
VCCCV	Closed	*laughter, pilgrim, instant, complain*
VV	Open	*create, riot, liar*

FIGURE 7-3   Introducing Syllable
Juncture Patterns

VC/C	VCCV
baby	contest
human	dinner
basic	basket
bacon	summer
music	dentist
silent	winter
	kitten

FIGURE 7-4   Different vs. Same
Consonants at Syllable Juncture

Different	Same
contest	dinner
basket	summer
dentist	kitten
winter	

After completing this first sort, the words in the second column could be sorted further by those that have different consonants at the juncture and those that have the same, as shown in Figure 7-4.

Vowel Patterns

Vowels can be reexamined in two-syllable words as a way to review those patterns and extend students' understanding of how those patterns work in polysyllabic words. For example, look at the familiar long *-a* patterns in the sort in Figure 7-5. Students in the syllables and affixes stage learn to listen for the stressed syllable and see the familiar vowel patterns (*ai, ay,* and *a-e*) they learned in the previous developmental stage, within word patterns.

There are a number of vowel patterns within single-syllable and polysyllabic words that are not sorted out until the upper elementary years. These are often called **ambiguous vowels** because they represent a range of sounds and spellings. For example, the vowel sound is the same in *cause, lawn,* and *false,* but is spelled three different ways. The *ou* spelling pattern has four different sounds in *shout, touch, your,* and *thought.* These patterns are often cited as examples of the irregularity of English spelling, but word sorting allows students to see that they nevertheless represent categories like other vowel patterns (Johnston, 2001). By paying attention to the position of ambiguous vowels, students can often determine which spelling pattern occurs most often. For example, *aw* and *oy* usually occur at the end of words or syllables (*straw, boycott*), whereas *au* and *oi* are found within syllables (*fault, voice*). If these patterns persist as problems into the syllables and affixes stage, then it is appropriate to take a step back and spend a little more time with these vowels in one-syllable words. They also can be examined, with other vowel patterns, in two-syllable words like *mouthful, counter,* and *lousy,* vs. *coward, chowder,* and *brownie.*

FIGURE 7-5   Common Long *-a* Spellings
in Two-Syllable Words

maintain	dismay	debate
raisin	crayon	bracelet
dainty	decay	parade
trainer	layer	mistake
sailor	today	escape

Accent or Stress

In most words of two or more syllables, one syllable is emphasized, stressed, or accented more than the others. Some dictionaries use bold apostrophes to show which syllables are stressed; others boldface the stressed syllable. Teach your students both systems. Determining the stressed syllable can be a challenge for teachers and students, but starting with a name sort is a good way to introduce the concept. When we pronounce a familiar name, where do we put the most emphasis?

Which syllable seems to "sound louder" than the others? Molly's name is pronounced /**moll** ee/, not /mo **lee**/. We say /**jen** ifer/, not /je **ni** fer/ or /jenni **fer**/. One way we can test for accent is to hold a hand lightly under our chin as we say a two-syllable word such as *a-round*. Our jaw probably drops more for the accented syllable.

Now try this with certain **homographs**—words that are spelled alike but whose meaning and part of speech changes with a shift in accent:

Would you pre**sent** the **pre**sent to the guest of honor?
The band hopes to re**cord** a **rec**ord.
The dump might re**fuse** the **ref**use.

Thinking about accent as it works with names and then with certain homographs should help solidify this concept.

When examining words of more than one syllable, knowing about accent helps students identify what they know about the spelling of a polysyllabic word and what they do not know, that is, what they will need to pay particular attention to. For example, when students pronounce the word *market*, they realize they know the spelling of the accented syllable (*mar*) yet may be uncertain about the vowel spelling in the final **unaccented** syllable. When students grasp the concept of an accented syllable, therefore, they also learn about the other side of this concept, the unaccented syllable. The unaccented syllable is the one in which the spelling of the vowel is not clearly long or short, so students will need to pay close attention to it. The sound in this syllable is often represented by the **schwa** sound—the upside down *e* in a dictionary pronunciation key (ə). By the middle of the syllables and affixes stage, word study can focus on these unaccented final syllables.

/ ər/ as in *super, actor,* and *sugar*
/ əl/ as in *angle, angel, metal, civil,* and *fertile*
/ ən/ as in *sudden, human, basin, apron,* and *captain*
/ch ər/ and /zhar/ as in *lecture, pitcher,* and *treasure*
/ j/ as in *village,* and *damage*

When sorting these words, you will find there is no tidy generalization that governs the spelling (except that comparative adjectives are always spelled with *er* as in *smarter, faster, taller*). However, some spellings are much more common than others. For example, -*er* is by far more common than -*or* or -*ar* and there are over 1,000 words than end in -*le*, but only about 200 that end in -*el*. An excellent follow-up to sorting these words is creating class lists that will give students insight into their frequencies. Then they might use a "best guess" strategy when spelling an unfamiliar word.

Identifying the vowel in unaccented syllables is one of the biggest challenges we all face as spellers. As our colleague Tom Gill explains to students, "You can't trust sound when your voice goes down." However, as we shall see in the next chapter, the spelling of the schwa in the unaccented syllable can sometimes be explained in terms of parts of speech or meaning.

Base Words and Derivational Affixes

While students are spending time examining and consolidating their word knowledge at the level of the syllable, part of their focus will naturally include attention to **base words** and simple **derivational affixes** (both prefixes and suffixes). Unlike inflectional suffixes that do not significantly affect the bases to which they are attached, derivational affixes affect their bases—their meaning and often their grammatical function in a sentence. It is important that students learn to read and spell words that are constructed from these meaning or morphemic elements.

The terms *base word* and *root word* are often used interchangeably. We prefer to use *base word* when referring to words that stand on their own after all prefixes and suffixes have been removed (*govern* in *government; agree* in *disagreement*). Base words such as these are also known as **free morphemes**. We want to avoid confusion with the term *word root,* which sometimes refers to the part of a word that remains after all prefixes and suffixes have been removed, but is *not* a word that can stand by itself (*vis* in *visible* and *spec* in *spectator*). These **bound morphemes** usually come from Greek or Latin and are studied extensively in the next stage. In preparation, students in the syllable and affixes stage study base words and affixes and the changes in spelling and meaning that do or do not take place in the process of affixation.

Research in vocabulary instruction (Biemiller, 2005) has underscored the critical importance of establishing a common sequence of vocabulary acquisition. The word study we describe in this chapter provides a giant step forward in this direction. We laid the groundwork for this during the within word pattern phase when we talked about simple prefixes and suffixes in reading vocabulary. At the syllables and affixes stage, students' understanding of how prefixes and suffixes combine with base words and word roots to create new words is vital. This understanding can help students analyze unknown words they encounter in their reading and leads to a rich expansion and elaboration of their vocabularies. Systematic exploration gets underway when students begin to investigate the addition of plural and inflectional endings. Later in this stage they will examine the meaning and spelling effects of combining simple derivational prefixes, suffixes, and base words. For example, Figure 7-6 shows three prefixes that are attached to base words that students are likely to understand and already able to spell. Analysis of these morphemic structures help students understand the generative nature of derivational affixes.

FIGURE 7-6   Simple Prefix Sort

unfair	retell	disagree
unable	replay	disorder
uncover	research	disobey
unplug	reuse	disarm
undress	retrain	disown
unkind	return	disappear

The sort in Figure 7-6 might be introduced by inviting the students to do an **open sort.** Many students will probably sort by the prefix, and this term can be introduced when you ask how all the words in a column are alike. Unlike most sorts, do not begin by discussing what the words and prefixes mean; insights will evolve as students talk about the meaning of the base word and how it changes with the addition of the prefix. By considering a list of words, students can determine what the prefix means for themselves. Students might be encouraged to use the words in sentences, such as "I must *obey* my parents because if I *disobey* I can get in trouble." The generative aspect of combining prefixes and bases can be explored by constructing different words through combining and recombining prefix and base word cards or tiles in various ways: *dis, re, un* can be combined with *able* and *order* to produce *disable, disorder, reorder, unable.*

Suffixes can also be introduced through sorts in which students make discoveries about how the derivational suffixes change the meanings of known words as well as parts of speech. For example, adding *y* to the noun *guilt* produces the adjective *guilty*; adding *-ly* produces the adverb *guiltily.* Some derivational suffixes to study in this stage include:

-*er* as in *quicker* and *-est* as in *quickest* (denotes a comparison of some type)
-*er* as in *farmer* and *-or* as in *professor* (both denote "agents or someone or something who does something"; words of Latin origin use the *-or* spelling)
-*y, -ly, -ful -less,* and *-ness* (these suffixes generally change the meaning and part of speech)

Students will need to revisit the rules that govern *e* drop and doubling as they add suffixes that begin with vowels to base words. *Brave* becomes *bravely* with no change; but in *flatter,* the doubling rule applies. In addition, *y* must be changed to *i* before adding suffixes (*silly* to *sillier, silliest, silliness*).

Further Exploration of Consonants

Consonants continue to be revisited in more difficult words. Consider words like *circus* or *garbage.* They might be spelled phonetically as *sirkus* and *garbij,* but generalizations about the spelling of hard and soft *g* and *c* reveal an underlying logic. As in one-syllable words, the sound of *g* and *c* depend on the vowel that follows (*a, o,* and *u* follow the hard sound, while *e, i,* and *y* follow the soft sound) and this results in some interesting spellings. Why is there a silent *u* in *tongue*? Without it, the *g* would become soft (*/tonj/*). The sound of */k/* can be spelled with *ck* (*shamrock*), *ic* (*magic*), *x* (*index*), and *qu* (*antique*), and many words contain silent consonants such as *t* (*moisten*), *w* (*wrinkle*), *k* (*knuckle*), *gh* (*daughter*), and *h* (*rhythm*). The study of silent consonants at the beginning (*honest, honour*), ending (*through, though*) and middle position (*fasten, soften*) foreshadow the in-depth study of spelling meaning connections explored in derivational relations.

WORD STUDY INSTRUCTION FOR SYLLABLE AND AFFIXES SPELLERS

Word study at the intermediate level should demonstrate to students how their word knowledge can be applied to advance their spelling knowledge, their vocabulary, and their strategies for figuring out unknown words in reading. At the intermediate and middle grades, the following principles should guide instruction.

- Students should be actively involved in the exploration of words; they are then more likely to develop a positive attitude toward word learning and a curiosity about words.
- Students' prior knowledge should be engaged; this is especially important if they are learning specialized vocabulary in different disciplines or content areas.
- Students should have many exposures to words in meaningful contexts, both in and out of connected text.
- Students need systematic instruction of structural elements and how these elements combine; elements include syllables, affixes, and the effects of affixes on the base words to which they are attached.

Exploring New Vocabulary

A quarter century of research has supported particular approaches to learning new words and/or challenging concepts. Not surprisingly, these approaches engage students' prior knowledge and get them talking with the teacher and with one another about the meanings and associations of words.

How do teachers select new vocabulary words? In addition to the words that emerge from narrative reading and writing, words from specific content areas become increasingly important as students move through the grades. You will find these words in your district and state standards and the curricula for the different content areas—social studies, science, math, and so forth. If there is a required textbook for a particular content area, it will usually reflect the important concepts and the words that represent those concepts.

Once words have been selected, the following steps should be followed in the context of engaging activities.

1. Activate background knowledge. Find out what students already know about the concept, and remind them of related concepts they have already learned.
2. Explain the concept and its relationship to other concepts.
3. Use graphic organizers, charts, or diagrams as needed to portray relationships among concepts.
4. Discuss examples and nonexamples.

A number of graphic organizer formats developed over the years have proven very effective in facilitating the types of engagements with new and/or difficult concepts that lead to understanding and deeper knowledge (Diamond & Gutlohn, 2006; Robb, 1999;

FIGURE 7-7   Sematic Maps for Fourth Grade Math Lessons

Figures	
Planes	Solids
Circle	Cube
Square	Cone
Rectangle	Prism
Triangle	Pyramid
Rhombus	Sphere

Solids	
Flat Surface	Curved Surface
Cube	Sphere
Rectangular Prism	Cone
Triangular Prism	Cylinder
Rectangular Pyramid	
Triangular Pyramid	

Stahl & Nagy, 2006; Templeton, 1997). One key to the effectiveness of graphic organizers is their visual presentation of the relationships among target vocabulary and related concepts. Two that we will address in this section are semantic maps and concept or word maps.

In both semantic maps and concept or word maps, the terms teachers have selected are presented, discussed, and related words are brainstormed. Figure 7-7 presents two simple semantic maps a fourth grade teacher prepared to move into explorations of figures and solids. In the "Figures" map, the visual arrangement represents the relationship among the superordinate category *figures* and the two types of figures: planes and solids. In turn, the types of planes and solids are listed in the second map. The teacher would present each semantic map to the students, have them discuss what they understand about each of the terms in small groups, and then come together as a whole class to share. In this fashion, understandings and misunderstandings are brought to the fore and the teacher gets a good sense of the level and depth of students' conceptual knowledge of these terms.

To kick off a unit on volcanoes, the teacher simply writes the word *volcanoes* on the board, then asks students what words or ideas they associate with volcanoes. She writes these words on a chart; afterwards, she adds a few additional terms that were not mentioned but are important terms in the unit. She talks with the students about different ways in which these words may be categorized, and then she arranges/categorizes the words, with students' input, along the appropriate "leg" of the map (see Figure 7-8). The terms that the teacher introduces are placed in parentheses and discussed with the students. As they talk and read further, they will be growing their understanding of the new terms and their relationship to more familiar words and concepts. These maps should be kept up throughout the unit of study, prominently displayed, and students may add terms to them as they move through the unit. Students may also decide that a particular term belongs to a different category, and if they can justify it, then the term may be moved to that category.

Concept or word maps focus on a specific term and visually represent its place in a conceptual hierarchy using guided questions. In Figure 7-9, the word *colony* is the focus. When the teacher first presented the map, the ovals were blank except for the headings:

FIGURE 7-8   Semantic Map for Volcano Unit

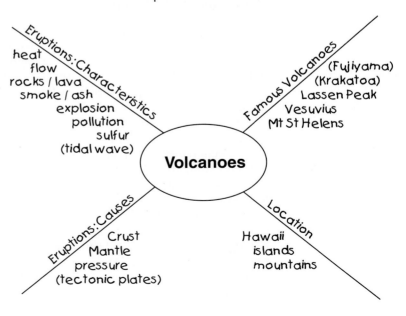

FIGURE 7-9   Concept or Word Map: *Colony*

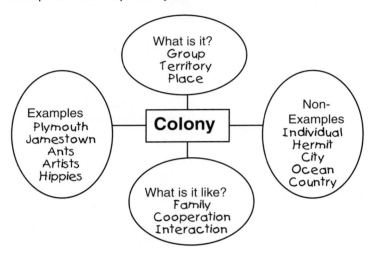

What is it? What is it like? What are some examples? What are some nonexamples? As each question was discussed, the teacher filled in ideas offered by students. It is critical to emphasize how important discussion is in the context of using graphic organizers in the classroom. As Stahl and Nagy (2006) observe, "The graphs and procedures are no more than structures to explain to students what particular words mean. It is the explanation, the talk, that is important" (p. 96).

Vocabulary activities such as these form a critical component of word study instruction for syllables and affixes spellers. It is important to remember however that not all of the words encountered and discussed when constructing these graphic organizers are appropriate for spelling words. Two-syllable words like *mantle, pressure, pumice,* and *lava,* can be added to sorts featuring syllable patterns and accent, but other words (e.g., *teutonic, bacteria*) would not be appropriate spelling words.

Sequence and Pacing

A sequence of word study during this stage is presented in Table 7-3. This sequence touches on the important patterns and features to consider, and is based on what students do developmentally. Normally achieving students in the upper elementary grades will typically take at least two years and probably more to progress through this stage. Use students' spellings as shown in Table 7-1 to determine where in this sequence to begin instruction.

As the table shows, early syllables and affixes spellers explore inflectional endings and discover the "double, drop, or nothing" rules that govern the place where base word and inflection meet. They also review ambiguous vowels in one- and two-syllable words. Students squarely in the middle of the stage will extend their understanding of doubling to syllable junctures within words as they study open and closed syllables. Vowel patterns students learned in the within word pattern stage are reviewed within the accented syllable. After studying accented syllables, students in the middle of the syllables and affixes stage look at the final unstressed syllable and two-syllable homophones and homographs. Some unusual consonant sounds and spellings are also examined. Finally, toward the end of the stage, late syllables and affixes spellers study prefixes and derivational suffixes that change the meaning of base words in straightforward ways.

TABLE 7-3   Sequence of Word Study: Syllables and Affixes

Early

Plural endings -*s* and -*es*	*books/dishes*
Unusual plurals	*goose/geese, knife/knives, fish, sheep*
Compound words	*pancake, sidewalk*
Inflectional endings:	
Sort by sound of -*ed* suffix	*walked /t/, wagged /d/, shouted /ed/*
Doubling	*stopping, stopped* (CVC)
E drop	*skating, skated* (CVCe)
No change	*walking, walked* (CVCC) and *nailing, nailed* (CVVC)
Change final *y* to *i* and add -*ed* or -*s*	*cried* (*y* after a consonant), *plays* (*y* after a vowel)
Review ambiguous vowels in one-syllable words:	
/ô/	*h**au**l, str**aw**, th**ou**ght*
/ou/	*m**ou**ntain, ch**ow**der*

Middle

Open and closed syllables:	
VCCV doublet at juncture	***butt**on, **happ**y*
VCCV different consonants at juncture	***wind**ow, **sist**er*
V/CV open with long vowel	***ba**con, **la**zy*
VC/V closed with short vowel	***riv**er, **cam**el*
VCCCV blend or digraph at juncture	
	***pil**grim, **tan**gle*
Vowel patterns in accented syllables:	
Common vowel patterns in accented syllable	***lo**nely, **toa**ster, **ow**ner*
Less common and ambiguous vowels in accented syllables	*f**ou**ntain, p**ow**der, l**au**ndry, **aw**ful, m**ar**ble, prep**are**, rep**air**, n**arr**ow*
Final unaccented syllables:	
/ər/	*begg**ar**/barb**er**/act**or***
/ən/	*capt**ain**/hum**an**/fright**en**/bas**in**/apr**on***
/əl/	*ang**el**/ab**le**/centr**al**/civ**il**/fert**ile***
/chər/ and/zhər/	*cul**ture**, mea**sure**, tea**cher***
Spelling /j/	*ba**dger**/ma**jor**/villa**ge***
Two-syllable homophones	*pedal, petal, peddle*
Two-syllable homographs	***re**bel/re**bel***
Special consonants in two-syllable words	hard and soft *g* and *c* silent consonants (***w**ritten, **k**nuckle, rhyt**h**m*) *ph (dol**ph**in), **gh** (lau**gh**ter, dau**gh**ter)* *qu (**qu**estion, anti**qu**e)*

Late

Simple prefixes and base words	*un (not–**un**lock), re (again–**re**make), dis (opposite–**dis**miss), in (not–**in**decent), non (not–**non**fiction), mis (wrong–**mis**fire), pre (before–**pre**view), ex (out–**ex**clude), uni (one–**uni**cycle), bi (two–**bi**cycle), tri (three–**tri**cycle)*
Simple suffixes	*-y (adjective–like, tending, toward: jump**y**), -ly (adverb–like: glad**ly**), -er, -est (comparatives), -ful (full of, like: grace**ful**), -less (without: penni**less**), -ness (condition–happi**ness**)*

*There are other meanings for *in*, but this is the most frequent and occurs more often in words at this level of reading.

This serves as an introduction to the spelling meaning connection that is the focus in the derivational relations stage.

WORD STUDY FOR ENGLISH LEARNERS

For English learners in the syllables and affixes stage, it is especially important to make word study a language-learning event. Words that are featured due to spelling issues must also become vocabulary words, and should be used and analyzed in conversational speech and connected text as a part of every lesson. English learners will feel more comfortable speaking up if you make oral discussions about words part of your daily routine in word study.

There will be many features in the syllables and affixes stage that may present some conceptual difficulty for English learners. Verb forms may be constructed differently in the native language, particularly inflected verbs (*ing, ed*). In Spanish, for example, the corresponding equivalent to the English *ing* is often an infinitive used as an abstract noun (e.g., To sleep is good for you). As a result, English learners may have difficulty understanding English sentences that use the *ing* form as the subject of the sentence (e.g., Sleeping is good for you) or perceiving the pronunciation of *-ing* or *-ed* at the end of English words (Swan & Smith, 2001). Spelling changes in the base word add a layer of complexity to this process. Plurals may also be formed differently in the native language. Perceiving and producing the pronunciations of *-s* and *-es* at the end of a word may require explicit attention. Learning the small subset of English nouns, verbs, and adjectives that involve an internal sound/spelling change (*knife, knives; leave, left; child, children*) may not be as simple as they seem. Comparatives may also be constructed differently. Instead of being signaled by spelling changes or different words altogether, comparatives may be signaled by tonal changes. In addition, the compounding aspect of English vocabulary may not occur in the native language, making compound words like *outsmart* or *windfall* seem quite strange to English learners. Similarly, the use of affixes and base words which is very common in English may be rare in other languages. All of these things point to the importance of connecting word study to the English language arts—especially to the study of grammar and vocabulary at the syllables and affixes stage of development.

WORD STUDY ROUTINES AND MANAGEMENT

Watch the Syllables and Affixes section on the *Words Their Way* DVD to see how Ryan Ichanberry organizes for instruction with his syllables and affixes spellers.

At the intermediate and middle grade levels, word study should take place in two important ways: (a) It should continue to be systematic as teachers identify stages of development and features students need to study, and (b) it should also be serendipitous, taking place whenever the teacher sees an opportunity to draw students' attention to words that arise in reading, writing, and content areas. Word study instruction takes place all day long in incidental discussions with small groups and large groups, but most students will need in-depth systematic attention to features at their developmental level as well.

Word Study Lesson Plan

The basic word study lesson plan described in detail in Chapters 3 and 6 is recommended for this stage as well: (1) Teachers begin with demonstrations in small groups and discussion of the generalizations revealed by the sort; (2) students sort their own set of words and check their sorts; (3) oral and written reflections encourage students to clarify and summarize their understandings; and (4) extension activities across the week reinforce and broaden students' understandings. It is very important to model and talk about the sorts with students as Ms. Lee did at the beginning of this chapter. Sorting the weekly words, not once but four times or more, is the most valuable routine for students and should be at the heart of systematic, developmental word study. Teachers are often skeptical about using word sorts with older students, but experience proves the value of sorts at this level. Even adults who are poor spellers enjoy and benefit from hands-on sorting activities (Massengill, 2006).

Organizing instructional-level groups for word study is a challenge but will best serve the needs of students, especially those who might be below grade level. The key to finding time to meet with small groups is establishing routines. When students learn weekly word study routines, they become responsible for completing much of their work independently (both in class and at home) or with partners, and this leaves teachers free to work with other small groups.

Word Study Notebooks

The use of word study notebooks in this stage continues to be an easy way to help students and teachers manage the routines and organization of word study (see Chapters 3 and 6). Tamara Baren has her students divide their word study notebooks into two sections. The first section is titled "Word Study" and contains the assigned sorts. This section includes weekly records of sorts, word hunts, lists generated in small groups, written reflections of sorts, and sorts assigned for homework. The second section is called "Looking into Language" and contains lists of words related to themes and units, words categorized by parts of speech, and semantic webs of content area studies. Other teachers add a section called a "Personal Dictionary," where students record words they frequently need to use in writing. Because these notebooks will be used constantly, we recommend stiff-backed, stitched composition books.

In addition to basic word sorting routines, you may want to develop a list of additional word study notebook activities from which students select when they work independently or for homework. Some of these may be more appropriate at times than others, and some can be done to review previous lessons.

1. Find words that have base words and underline the base word.
2. Break words into syllables and underline the accented syllables.
3. Make appropriate words on your lists plural or add *-ing* or *-ed*.
4. Circle any prefixes or suffixes you find in the words on your list.
5. Add a prefix and/or suffix, when possible, to words on your list.
6. Select five words and use them in sentences.
7. Sort your words by parts of speech or subject areas and record your sort.
8. Go for speed. Sort your words three times and record your times.
9. Select five words to look up in the dictionary. Record the multiple meanings you find for each word.

GUIDELINES FOR CREATING SORTS IN THE SYLLABLES AND AFFIXES STAGE

In earlier stages teachers were urged to exercise caution when selecting words for sorts to be sure students can read the words. However, students in the upper elementary grades in the syllables and affixes stage have extensive reading vocabularies that are typically far in advance of their spelling ability. This means that students can often read words whose meanings elude them. It is important to consider the semantic difficulty of the words as much as the spelling challenge when selecting words and features to study. For example, the old saying, "*I* before *e* except after *c* or when sounded like *a* as in *neighbor* and *weigh*" is worthwhile to teach, but many of the words that follow the saying may not be in the speaking vocabulary of elementary students (*conceive, perceive, conceited, receipt*).

It is fine to select a few words that students might not know the meaning of, or words that they only know tenuously, but do not overburden sorts with these words. Looking a few words up in a dictionary as part of the initial demonstration lesson is a good way to encourage regular dictionary use for an authentic reason. Keep dictionaries handy for students in this stage and the next, but avoid assigning students to look up long lists of words and remember the limitations of dictionaries. Sometimes you can offer a better definition than the dictionary because you know what your students are likely to understand. While it is important to have unabridged dictionaries available in the classroom, it is also important to have dictionaries that are published for intermediate students available; for example, the *American Heritage Children's Dictionary* (grades 4–6) and the *American Heritage Student's Dictionary* (grades 5–9) are also very helpful at this stage. Attractive in format, they present definitions, word histories, and usage information in student-friendly language.

There are sample sorts in Appendix D that can be written into the template in Appendix F to create sorts for your students. Appendix E offers lists of words for other sorts or to modify the lists that are suggested. Games and other activities are another way to engage students in further exploration and review of the features they are learning in their sorts.

Create your own sorts by choosing words to drop into the templates available on the CD-ROM.

Activities for Students in the Syllables and Affixes Stage

You'll find even more activities for Syllables and Affixes spellers on the *Words Their Way* CD. Create your own activities, games, and manipulatives and print them or save them to your hard drive to use again and again.

This section outlines activities and games for readers and writers in the syllables and affixes stage. The activities and games are designed to reinforce word study introduced first in word-sorting activities.

ADAPTABLE GAMES

There are many games described in previous chapters that are adaptable for use with the features studied in this stage.

1. The Spelling Game (6-7) can be used with any feature, as it involves asking a player to spell a word before moving on the board. The word cards from any sort can be used as the playing cards for the game.
2. Go Fish (5-19), Race Track (6-6), "I'm Out" (6-8), Jeopardy (6-11), Card Categories (6-12), Declare Your Category (6-13), Word Study Pursuit (6-14), Word Study Uno (6-15), and Homophone Rummy (6-17) work well with the many features that have three or more categories: syllable patterns, vowel patterns in stressed syllables, unaccented final syllables, silent consonants, hard and soft *g* and *c*, prefixes, suffixes, and so on.

Compound Word Activities 7-1

When examining compound words, consider the difficulty of the base words that make them up. *Cupcake* and *outfit* are made up of two words that have common one-syllable patterns mastered in the within word pattern stage, but *cheeseburger* and *grandparent* are made up of two-syllable words that students may find challenging to spell (*burger* and *parent*). Following are ways you can explore these words.

1. Share some common compound words with the students (e.g., *cookbook* and *bedroom*). Discuss their meaning, pointing out how each word in the compound contributes to the meaning of the whole word. You might ask students to draw pictures to illustrate these. For example, a student might draw a horse and a shoe and then a horseshoe.

2. Prepare word sorts with the words presented in Appendix E that can be sorted in a variety of ways. The sort can focus on shared words (**head**light, **head**band, **head**ache, **head**phone versus **foot**ball, **foot**hill, **foot**print, **foot**step). You might also conduct concept sorts, for example, words that have to do with people (*anyone, someone, somebody, nobody, anybody*) or things we find outdoors (*sunshine, airplane, campfire, airport*).

3. Have students cut a set of compound words apart. Then challenge them to create as many new compound words as they can. Some words will be legitimate words (*mailbox*); others will be words that do not yet exist, but could (*bookbox*). Have students share and discuss their words. Students might then write sentences using these pseudo-words, and draw a picture that illustrates the meaning of each.

4. Students can be given a word such as *fire, man, head, book,* or *rain* and challenged to see how many related compound words they can brainstorm (*fireplace, firefighter, cookbook, bookmark, rainbow, raincoat*). Teams compete to see who can come up with the longest list. To add another twist, let the team with the longest list read it aloud. Everyone crosses out any word that two or more teams thought of. Only words that no other team thinks of earn points. Repeat until every team has had a chance to read the words left on their list. Remember that each part of the word must stand alone as a free morpheme. *Mankind* is a compound but *foreman* is not.

5. Create a yearlong class collection of compound words. This collection can include hyphenated words (*good-bye, show-off, push-up,* etc.).

Double Scoop 7-2

This board game created by Marilyn Edwards will help children review and master consonant doubling and *e* drop when adding inflectional endings. It is appropriate for small groups of two to four students.

Materials

Prepare a gameboard as shown in Figure 7-10 and write sentences like the ones below on small cards to go into a deck. You will also need playing pieces, a spinner or die, and a small whiteboard or paper on a clipboard for writing answers under the categories of *E drop, Double,* and *No Change.*

The bunny was <u>hopping</u> down the road. I enjoy <u>trading</u> baseball cards.
The cat is <u>sunning</u> herself on the chair. He is <u>diving</u> into the pool.
Brittany <u>shopped</u> at her favorite store. She <u>glided</u> across the ice.
We go <u>swimming</u> in the summer. I like <u>riding</u> bikes.
Danny <u>flopped</u> down on his bed. I <u>hoped</u> you would come.
The child went <u>running</u> out the door. I like <u>sliding</u> down water slides.
I don't like people who go around <u>bragging</u>. We went <u>skating</u> last winter.
I <u>slipped</u> on the ice. He <u>wasted</u> his time at the movie.
Jerry was so tired he felt like <u>quitting</u>. Will you please stop your <u>whining</u>.
The kite string became <u>knotted</u>. The paint was <u>flaking</u> off.

FIGURE 7-10   Double Scoop Gameboard

Procedures

1. Players put their pieces on the sun to start. Player 2 (the reader) reads a sentence card and repeats the underlined word.
2. Player 1 (the writer) then writes the underlined word under the correct heading on the board without seeing it.
3. Player 2 checks player 1's answer by comparing it with the sentence card. If it is correct, player 1 spins and moves that number of spaces on the playing board.
4. Play then moves to the next student who must spell and sort the underlined word given them by the next player. If there are only two players, they simply switch roles.
5. The first player to reach the double scoop of ice cream wins.

Freddy, the Hopping, Diving, Jumping Frog 7-3

In this board game for two to four players, students review generalizations for adding -ing.

Materials

Create a game board using one of the follow-the-path templates in the Appendix or by arranging green circles in a path to represent lily pads much like the game board for the Hopping Frog game in Chapter 5. On each space, write either *Double*, *E Drop*, or *Nothing*. Prepare playing cards by writing a variety of words with -ing added, an equal number for each rule (i.e., *hopping*, *diving*, *jumping*). Use words that students have been sorting and add more words from the word list in the Appendix. You can also add penalty or bonus cards such as the following.

> You have the strongest legs. Jump ahead to the next lily pad.
> You are the fastest swimmer. Skip 2 spaces.

Your croaking made me lose sleep. Move back 2 spaces.
You ate too many flies. Move back 2 spaces.

Procedures

1. Place playing cards facedown and put playing pieces on the starting space.
2. Each player draws a card, reads the card aloud, and moves to the closest space that matches. For example, if the card says *hopping*, the player moves to the nearest space that says double.
3. A player who draws a penalty or bonus card must follow the directions on the card.
4. The winner is the first to reach the home lily pad.

Variations

1. Players draw for each other, read the word aloud, and the player whose turn it is must spell the word correctly before moving to the appropriate space.
2. Write uninflected forms on cards (*hop, jump, dive*), and have players write how the word should be spelled before moving to the appropriate place. Include an answer sheet with words in alphabetical order to check if there is disagreement.

Slap Jack 7-4

Adaptable for Other Stages

This card game for two people may be used to contrast open- and closed-syllable words as represented by any of the syllable spelling patterns (V/CV with VCCV; V/CV with VC/V). The object of the game is for one player to win all 52 cards.

Materials

On 52 small cards, write the words that you want to be contrasted. For example, 26 words would follow the open-syllable VCV pattern (*pilot, human*) and 26 would follow the closed-syllable VCCV pattern (*funny, basket*). See word lists in the Appendix E. Write the word on both ends of the cards so that neither player has to read the words upside down.

Procedures

1. The cards are dealt one at a time until the deck is gone. Players keep their cards facedown in a pile in front of them.
2. Each player turns a card faceup in a common pile at the same time. When two words with either open syllables or closed syllables are turned up together, the first player to slap the pile takes all the cards in the common pile and adds them at the bottom of his or her pile.
3. Turning cards and slapping must be done with the same hand.
4. A player who slaps the common pile when there are not two open- or closed-syllable words must give both cards to the other player.
5. Play continues until one player has all the cards. If time runs out, the winner is the player with the most cards.

Variations

1. Once students are comfortable contrasting two-syllable patterns, an additional pattern may be added to the deck, for example, closed-syllable VCV (*cabin, water*).
2. Word cards could be prepared for any feature that has two or three categories; for example, inflected forms with *-ed* could be used and players would slap when the words both represented *e* drop, double, or no change.

Syllables and Affixes Stage

Double Crazy Eights 7-5

This activity is designed to review consonant doubling and *e* drop, and at the same time to reexamine the various spellings of /k/ in two-syllable words. On the basis of the traditional card game Crazy Eights, students can play in groups of two or three. The object of the game is to get rid of all the cards in your hand. This is a good follow-up to Sort 74 in Appendix D.

Materials

Prepare 52 word cards comprised of four suits: (1) V-*ck* pattern (*tacking*), (2) V-*k-e* pattern (*baking*), (3) VV-*k* pattern (*looking, speaking*), (4) VC-*k* pattern (*asking*). Use 13 words per suit. Four Crazy Eight cards are designated by the words *eight* and *ate*, or the numeral *8*.

Procedures

1. The dealer gives each player eight cards. The remaining cards become the draw pile. The dealer turns the top card of the draw pile over and places it beside the deck. This card becomes the starter card and is the first card in the discard pile.
2. The player to the left of the dealer begins by placing a card that matches the starter card onto the discard pile. Matches may be made in three ways:
   a. By sound—long, short, or neither
   b. By pattern—V-*ck* (*lick*), V-*k-e* (*like*), VV-*k* (*leak*), or VC-*k* (*drank*)
   c. By rule—whether the consonant *s* doubled, the *e* dropped, or no change made
3. With a Crazy Eight card, the player can change the suit to anything the player chooses.
4. If the player does not have a match, he or she must draw from the draw pile until one is found.
5. If all the cards in the draw pile are used up, reserve the top card from the discard pile, shuffle the rest of the cards, and place them facedown on the table as the new draw pile.
6. Play continues until one player has discarded all cards.

Variations

This game can be adapted simply by making up a new deck using words that focus on another spelling feature. Remember that the deck must have four suits and allow for matching by at least two different elements. For example, long-vowel patterns in two-syllable words could be matched by pattern (*debate* and *bracelet*), by sound (long *u* in both *include* and *human*), or by stress (*explain* and *include*).

You're Up 7-6

The purpose of the game, which should be played with five students, is to contrast the spellings for the /ure/ sound: *ure* as in *picture* and *cher* as in *preacher*, as well as other incidents of the suffix *ure*. Charlotte Tucker adapted this from the television show password.

FIGURE 7-11   Cover for You're Up

Materials

You will need a scoring pad and pencil, a stopwatch, and window cards such as the one in Figure 7-11.

Procedures

1. One student is designated as the recorder, while the other four pair up into two teams of two players. Each team decides who is player A and player B. The recorder flips a coin to see which team will go first.
2. Both players are given the window card with the first word to be played showing through the window. (Both teams are given the same word.) See Figure 7-11.

3. Player A from the team that won the coin toss begins by giving player B (on the same team) a one-word clue as to the word on the card. This clue may not be any part of the word to be guessed, or contain the word in any form. For example, if the word is *pasture*, the clue might be *meadow* or *field*. If player B does not guess the correct word on the first attempt, the other team has a chance.

4. Play moves back and forth between teams until one team guesses the word. If both teams have given five clues and the word is still not guessed, the referee throws the word out. Player Bs are given the second word, and the second team's player B leads off with a one-word clue to his or her partner.

5. Each time a team successfully guesses a word, they receive one point. If the same player that guessed the word can also spell the word, the team receives another point (total of two). If the player cannot spell the word, the opposing team has a chance to do so with whichever player was guessing the clues. The team with the most points wins.

6. For the teacher to assess students' knowledge of the targeted feature, and in the interest of fairness, the recorder is to write down the given clues on a sheet provided with the words played. The recorder also acts as referee and timekeeper, making sure only one-word clues are given and that those clues are in keeping with the rule. Keeping time involves allowing each team 15 seconds total for giving clues and guessing the word during each round, as well as a 15-second limit to spell the word.

Variations

1. Have students create their own window cards with this feature, or another, for their fellow students to use.
2. This game could also be played with *ant/ent* words, providing an engaging way to practice spelling these words as well as sharpen vocabulary (see Chapter 8).

Pair Them Up 7-7

In this version of Memory or Concentration, students match up unusual plurals.

Adaptable for Other Stages

Materials

Create 11 sets of cards using word pairs such as the ones that follow: *wife/wives, leaf/leaves, life/lives, wolf/wolves, knife/knives, man/men, woman/women, mouse/mice, goose/geese, tooth/teeth, child/children*. Make one card each of *fish, sheep*, and *deer*.

Procedures

1. Shuffle the cards and lay them all out facedown in a 5 × 5 array.
2. Each player turns over two cards at a time. If the cards make a match, the player keeps them and turns over two more.
3. If *fish, sheep*, or *deer* are turned over, there is no match and the player automatically gets to keep the card and go again.

Variations

Create a similar game for two syllable homophones (*berry, bury*) or for irregular past-tense pairs: *sleep/slept, slide/slid, shine/shone, freeze/froze, say/said, think/thought, and so on.*

The Apple and the Bushel 7-8

The purpose of this board game created by Charlotte Tucker, is to give students added practice in differentiating between *-le* and *-el* endings.

FIGURE 7-12   Apple and Bushel Gameboard

Materials

Prepare the Apple and Bushel gameboard (see Figure 7-12) and word cards with words that end in -el and -le (*bushel, angel, apple, angle*).

Procedures

1. Players draw for each other and read the word aloud.
2. Players must spell the word correctly and then move the marker to the nearest -le or -el ending that spells the word.
3. The game continues until one player reaches the bushel. (*Note*: To get in the bushel, an -el word must be drawn. A player who draws an -le word must move backwards and continue playing from that space.)

Variation

Add words that end with -il (*pencil*) and -al (*pedal*).

Prefix Spin 7-9

This game for two to four players reinforces the idea that prefixes and base words can be combined in different ways. Let students play this after they have sorted words with the featured prefixes.

Materials

Make a spinner using the directions in Appendix F. Divide the spinner into six sections and write each of these prefixes in a section: *mis, pre, un, dis,* and *re* (use *re* twice because it can be used in twice as many words as the others). Prepare a deck of 24 cards with the following base words written on them: *count, judge, match, take, use, set, test, view, charge, pay, able, like, form, place, wrap, order, cover,* and *pack* (you can duplicate the last five to enlarge the deck; each can combine with three of the prefixes, for example, *misplace, replace,* and *displace*). Include paper and pencil for each player to record their matches. You may also want to include a list of allowable words to solve disputes. Matches include the ones listed here.

Adaptable for Other Stages

miscount, misjudge, mismatch, misplace, mistake, misuse, prejudge, preset, pretest, preview, preorder, prepay, recount, rematch, replace, retake, reuse, reset, retest, review, recharge, reform, reorder, repay, recover, repack, rewrap, unable, uncover, unlike, unpack, unwrap, discount, displace, discharge, disorder, disable, discover, dislike

Procedures

1. Turn the base word cards facedown in a deck in the center of the playing area. Turn one card up at a time.
2. The first player spins for a prefix (such as *un*). If the prefix can be added to the base word to form a real word (such as *unwrap*), the player takes the card and records the whole word on paper.
3. If the first player spins a prefix that cannot be added (such as *mis*), the next player spins and hopes to land on a prefix that will work with the base word. This continues until someone can form a word.
4. A new base word is turned up for the next player and the game continues.
5. The winner is the player who has the most base word cards at the end of the game.

Variations

1. Two spinners could be used with suffixes written on the second one, such as *-s, -ed, -ing*, and *-able*. A bonus point could be assigned when a player can use both the prefix and suffix with a base word, as in *replaceable* or *discovering*.
2. Make two sets of cards with the base words and pass out four words to each player that are laid out faceup. When each player spins, he or she tries to match the prefix with one of the words he or she has. This word can be turned over in a point pile and another card drawn so the player always has four cards for possible matches. This works well with other prefixes that might not be as common.

Homophone Solitaire 7-10

Building on the traditional game of Solitaire, this simple card game requires flexible thinking and versatile attention to words. Word cards are matched by homophone, syllable pattern, or whether the homophonic spelling change is in the stressed or unstressed syllable. The object of the game is to end up with all the words in one pile.

Materials

You will need 52 word cards using two-syllable homophones. The cards are comprised of two suits: (a) homophones in the stressed syllable and (b) homophones in the unstressed syllable. There are 13 pairs of matching homophones from each suit. (See the homophone list in Appendix D.)

Procedures

1. Shuffle the deck; then turn one card over at a time. Say the word, observe the pattern, and place the card down, faceup.
2. Turn over the next card. Place it on top of the previously placed card if it matches by any of the following three features:
   a. Exact homophone (e.g., *alter-altar*).
   b. Syllable pattern: VCCV doublet (e.g., *mussel* could be placed on *lesson*); VCCV different (e.g., *canvas* could be placed on *incite*); open V/CV (e.g., *miner* could be placed on *rumor*); closed VC/V (e.g., *baron* could be placed on *profit*).
   c. Spelling change in the stressed or unstressed syllable. For example, suppose *sender* was the last card played; the homophone for *sender* is *cinder*—the spelling change in the *sender/cinder* homophone pair occurs in the stressed syllable. If a

student is holding the card *morning,* she could place it on *sender* because the homophone for *morning* is *mourning,* which also has the spelling change in the stressed syllable. Alternately, if the student is holding the card *presents,* he could play it on *miner* because the homophone for *presents* is *presence* and the homophone for *miner* is *minor*—the spelling change occurs in the *un*stressed syllables.

3. If there is no match, place the card to the right of the last card played.
4. Continue play in this way, placing cards with no matches to the right of the last card played. Stacks may be picked up and consolidated at any time. The top card played on a stack determines the movement.
5. Players may move back no more than four stacks for play.
6. Play continues until the entire deck is played. Then shuffle and play again!

Stressbusters 7-11

The purpose of this board game is to practice discriminating the accented or stressed syllable in a given word. Students can play the game in pairs after they have been introduced to the idea of accent and know how to determine it. Brenda Reibel contributed this game.

Materials

Create a Stressbusters gameboard using a template from Appendix F or using circles as shown in Figure 7-13. Prepare game cards with familiar two- and three-syllable words. (You might start with names of students in the class.) You will also need playing pieces and a dictionary (to verify placement of stress or accent).

Procedures

1. As students correctly identify the placement of stress, they will do the following: If the accent falls in the beginning syllable, the player moves one space; if the accent

FIGURE 7-13 Stressbusters Gameboard

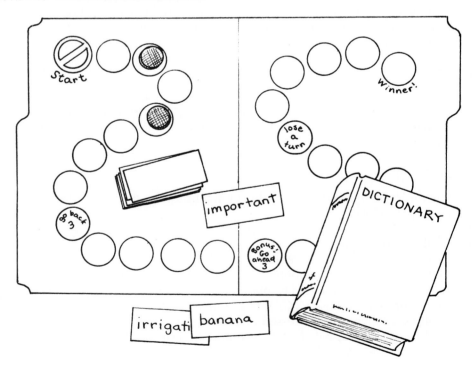

falls in the second syllable, the player moves two spaces; if the accent is on the third syllable, the player moves three spaces.

2. The game continues until one player reaches the finish circle.

3. Challenging answers: Players may challenge the acceptability of accent answers by looking the word up in the dictionary to determine the accented syllable. If correct, the challenger gets to move his or her gamepiece forward one, two, or three places, depending on where the accent falls. If the player is correct and the challenger is wrong, the challenger must move back one space.

Words that are accented on the third syllable are also accented on the first syllable. These words may be challenged. If a player moves one space for the word *constitution*, for example, not realizing it is also accented on the third syllable, then the other player could challenge. An incorrect challenge, however, costs the challenger the corresponding number of spaces. If the challenger thinks the word is accented on the second syllable and is incorrect, he or she must move back two spaces; if the challenger thinks the accent is on the third syllable and is incorrect, he or she moves back three spaces.

Semantic Chart Sorts 7-12

Use a bulletin board to create an interactive word wall related to content studies. As with the semantic sorts in Chapter 6, students arrange words conceptually. As an ongoing activity, students look for words that are tied to their content studies.

1. Students collect words from a unit of study on a bulletin board. Words selected for the board are defined and reviewed as an ongoing class activity.

2. These words are given to groups to sort into meaning- or association-based groups. Students write the groups on chart paper with an explanation for each grouping. Charts may remain posted for the duration of particular units of study.

Vocabulary Jeopardy 7-13

Students enjoy the familiar Jeopardy game after brainstorming terms related to a unit of study.

1. Students generate vocabulary cards from a unit of study. Tamara Baren starts with the vocabulary students generate on their own, followed by a scan through texts and materials.

2. With these cards, students make a Jeopardy game. (A sample gameboard can be found in Activity 6-11.) Students write questions on cards that relate to facts and concepts studied. Answers are written on the back side. The cards are sorted into categories.

3. Teams of students play the game as a whole-class vocabulary review of the unit.

Syllables and Affixes Stage

8 Word Study for Advanced Readers and Writers: The Derivational Relations Stage

The term **derivational relations** is used to describe the type of word knowledge that more advanced readers and writers possess. The term emphasizes how spelling and vocabulary knowledge at this stage grow primarily through processes of *derivation*—from a single base word or word root, a number of related words are *derived* through the addition of prefixes and suffixes. Students begin to explore these processes at the syllables and affixes stage, but their understanding expands and becomes much more elaborate at the derivational relations stage. In contrast to the syllables and affixes stage, exploration of words at the derivational relations stage draws upon more extensive experience in reading and writing: There is reciprocity between growth in vocabulary and spelling knowledge and the amount of reading and writing in which students are engaged (e.g., Carlisle, 2000; Cunningham & Stanovich, 2003; Mahony, Singson, & Mann, 2000; Smith, 1998).

We will visit the eighth grade classroom of Jorge Ramirez several times in this chapter. Here he illustrates how a teacher can guide students to understand how thinking about the root word and its meaning can be a clue to spelling the word.

Writing the misspelled word *compisition* on the board, Mr. Ramirez begins: "I'd like to point something out to you: Words that are related in meaning are often related in spelling as well. For example [pointing to *compisition*], everything is correct in this word except for the letter *i* in the second syllable. However, there's a word that is related in spelling and meaning that actually provides a clue to the correct spelling. Any ideas what this word might be?"

No one responds. Mr. Ramirez continues. "Well, let's look at this word [writes *compose* directly above *compisition*]. Are *compose* and *composition* related in meaning? Yes, they are! Can you hear the long -*o* sound in *compose*? You know how to spell this sound, and because *compose* and *composition* are related in meaning, the *o* in *compose* is the clue to the spelling of what we call the schwa sound in *composition*.

"Keeping this fact in mind can help you spell a word you may not be sure of, like *composition*. Why? Because schwas don't give you any clue to the spelling—they can be spelled with any of the vowel letters. You've got a powerful strategy you can use, though: By thinking of a related word, like *compose*, you can get a clue.

"Let's try another one. Here's a misspelling I've seen a lot." He writes *oppisition* on the board. "Is there a word that is related in meaning and spelling that can give you a clue about how to spell the schwa sound?" He points to the *i* in the second syllable of *oppisition*.

There are a few seconds of silence, then a student tentatively responds, "*Oppose?*"

"Could be! Let's check it out." He writes *oppose* directly above *oppisition*. "We can clearly hear the sound that *o* in the second syllable of *oppose* stands for, and sure enough, *opposition* comes from *oppose*—they're similar in meaning—so Darci is right! *Oppose* gives us the clue for remembering the spelling of *opposition*. Remember: Words that are related in meaning are often related in spelling as well. So by thinking of a word that is related to one you're trying to spell, you will often discover a helpful clue to the spelling."

LITERACY DEVELOPMENT IN THE DERIVATIONAL RELATIONS STAGE

Students in the derivational relations stage will be found in upper elementary, middle school, high school, and well into adulthood. Students at this level are fairly competent spellers, so the errors they make are "high level," requiring a more advanced foundation of spelling and vocabulary. However, misspellings such as *INDITEMENT, ALLEDGED, IRELEVANT,* and *ACCOMODATE* do occur among highly skilled and accomplished readers and writers. (Indeed, the persistence of such misspellings leads many adults to lament that, though they are good readers, they are "terrible" spellers!) Exploring the logic underlying the correct spellings of these words not only helps individuals learn and remember their correct spelling but, more importantly, leads to a deeper understanding and appreciation of how words work. This understanding and appreciation leads in turn to the growth and differentiation of concepts—to vocabulary development.

Watch the Derivational Relations section on the *Words Their Way* DVD for word study ideas that benefit advanced readers and writers.

The Upper Level Spelling Inventory (USI) is useful for collecting spelling errors for analysis and the table on the next page summarizes some of the characteristics of spellers in this stage. At first glance, misspellings at the derivational relations stage appear similar in type to those at the syllables and affixes stage: Errors occur at the juncture of syllables and with the vowel in unaccented or unstressed syllables.

Specific spelling errors characteristic of this stage fall into three main categories. (1) In polysyllabic words there are often unstressed syllables in which the vowel is **reduced** to the schwa sound, as in the second syllable of *opposition*. Remembering the root from which this word is derived (*oppose*) will often help the speller choose the correct vowel. (2) Suffixes like the *-tion* in *opposition* also pose challenges for spellers because they are easily confused with *-ian* (*clinician*) and *-sion* (*tension*), which sound the same. (3) Other errors occur in the feature known as an **absorbed** or **assimilated** prefix.

Characteristics of Derivational Relations Spelling

	What Students Do Correctly	What Students Use but Confuse	What Is Absent
Early Derivational Relations *trapped, humor, sailor* CONFUDENSE for *confidence,* OPISISION for *opposition*	Spell most words correctly Vowel patterns in accented syllables Doubling and *e* drop at syllable juncture	Unstressed vowels in derivationally related pairs—*CONFUDENT* Suffixes and prefixes Other spelling meaning connections *CRITISIZE*/critic	Note: No features are completely absent
Middle Derivational Relations CLOROFIL for *chlorophyl* MEDISINAL for *medicinal*	All of the above Common Latin suffixes and prefixes	Some silent letters: *emfasize* for *emphasize* Greek and Latin elements	
Late Derivational Relations OPOSITION for *opposition* DOMINENCE for *dominance*	All of the above	Absorbed prefixes: *SUCESSION, ILITERATE* Advanced Latin suffixes: DEPENDANCE Foreign borrowing: *CROKAY* for *croquet*	

The prefix in *opposition* originally comes from *ob,* but because the root word starts with the letter *p (pos),* the spelling changed to reflect an easier pronunciation (*obposition* or *opposition?*).

Reading and Writing in the Derivational Relations Stage

The type of word knowledge that underlies advanced reading and writing includes an ever-expanding conceptual foundation and the addition of words that represent this foundation. Advanced readers are able to explore the Greek and Latin word elements that are the important morphemes out of which thousands of words are constructed. Linguists refer to this process as *generative* and estimate that 60% to 80% of English vocabulary is created through the combination of roots, prefixes, and suffixes. Students who understand these processes will be in position to analyze and understand the unfamiliar words they will encounter in the content area reading materials of middle school and high school. Reading is the primary means by which students gain access to these words; they simply do not occur with nearly as great a frequency in oral language.

During reading, this additional layer of word knowledge makes it possible to add a morphological layer to the perception of polysyllabic words: While the intermediate reader (syllables and affixes) picks up syllabic chunks in such words, the advanced reader (derivational relations) picks up **morphemic** chunks as well (Taft, 1991; Templeton, 1992). For example, an intermediate reader attempting to read the word *morphology* would most likely analyze it syllable by syllable, picking up the letter sequences *mor-pho-lo-gy.* The advanced reader would most likely pick up morphemic letter sequences *morph-ol-ogy,* which cross syllable boundaries.

The Spelling-Meaning Connection

The **spelling-meaning connection** is another way of referring to the significant role that morphology plays in the spelling system. As we begin to explore spelling-meaning relationships, we help students become explicitly aware of this principle as it applies in English: Words that are related in meaning are often related in spelling as well, despite changes in sound (Chomsky, 1970; Templeton, 1983). This in turn supports the spelling strategy: If you are unsure how to spell a word, try to think of a word that is similar in meaning that you **do** know how to spell. This consistency presents an excellent opportunity to integrate spelling and vocabulary instruction.

The awareness that there are logical spelling-meaning connections that apply to most words in the English language results in far more productive and reassuring word learning than the traditional one-word-at-a-time approach. For example, *paradigmatic* will be better learned, understood, and retained when related to *paradigm*, as well as providing a helpful clue to remembering the silent -*g* in *paradigm*; *mnemonic* will be related to *amnesia* and *amnesty*.

A number of sound changes may occur in a group of related words whose spelling remains the same, and so we guide students first to notice particular changes that represent an increasing order of difficulty and abstractness. Templeton (1979, 1983, 1989, 1992) and Templeton and Scarborough-Franks (1985) originally identified this order of difficulty and abstractness; recent work by Leong (2000) further substantiates this sequence. Let us examine each in turn.

WORD STUDY INSTRUCTION DURING THE DERIVATIONAL RELATIONS STAGE

The principles for instruction listed for intermediate readers and writers (Chapter 7, page 214) also guide our instruction at the advanced level. As at the intermediate level, word study for advanced readers emphasizes active exploration of words and the application of word knowledge to spelling, vocabulary development, and the analysis of unknown words encountered in reading. We can initiate word study for advanced readers by observing, "You know, when you first learned to read you had to learn how spelling stands for sounds. Now you're going to be learning how spelling stands for meaning."

See how word study is implemented with advanced readers and writers in the Derivational Relations section on the *Words Their Way* DVD.

Sequence and Pacing

Table 8-1 presents a general sequence for word study in the derivational relations stage. It begins with a straightforward exploration of the spelling-meaning connection in consonant and vowel alternations, then moves to Greek and Latin word roots and affixes, to predictable spelling changes in related words, and then on to another look at prefixes that become absorbed by the first letter of the base word. Study of Greek and Latin word roots begins with those that occur with the greatest frequency. Importantly, you will emphasize how these elements combine within words—this knowledge provides a powerful foundation and productive strategy for continuing vocabulary and spelling growth. It extends the basic understandings developed during the syllables and affixes stage when students examined how simpler prefixes, suffixes, and base words combined. This more advanced word knowledge will help tremendously when students realize how many of these elements occur in the vocabulary terms that represent core concepts in science, social studies, and math.

As in the syllables and affixes stage, decisions about what features to teach are often restricted by the difficulty of the word meanings rather than the difficulty of

TABLE 8-1   Sequence of Word Study in the Derivational Relations Stage

Consonant and Vowel Alternations

1. Consonant Alternations

silent/sounded	*si**g**n/si**g**nal, condem**n**/condem**n**ation, softe**n**/soft*
/t/ to /sh/	*conne**ct**/conne**ct**ion, sele**ct**/sele**ct**ion*
/k/ to /sh/	*musi**c**/musi**c**ian, magi**c**/magi**c**ian*
/k/ to /s/	*criti**c**/criti**c**ize, politi**c**al/politi**c**ize*
/s/ to /sh/	*prejudi**c**e/prejudi**c**ial, offi**c**e/offi**c**ial*

2. Vowel Alternations

Long to short	*cr**i**me/cr**i**minal, ign**i**te/ign**i**tion, hum**a**ne/hum**a**nity*
Long to schwa	*comp**e**te/comp**e**tition, def**i**ne/def**i**nition, g**e**ne/g**e**netic,*
Schwa to short	*loc**a**l/loc**a**lity, leg**a**l/leg**a**lity, ment**a**l/met**a**llic*

3. Suffix Study
Explore the addition of *-sion, -tion, -ian* to basewords.

Greek and Latin Word Elements

1. Start with Greek number prefixes *mono-* (one), *bi-* (two), *tri-* (three), and move to the Greek roots *tele-* (far, distant), *therm-* (heat), *photo-* (light), and *astr-* (star). (See lists in Appendix E.)

2. Move to frequent Latin roots with the aim of gaining a working understanding of a few frequently occurring roots with relatively concrete and constant meanings: *-tract-* (draw, pull), *-spect-* (look), *-port-* (carry), *-dict-* (to say), *-rupt-* (to break), and *-scrib-* (to write). (See lists in Appendix E.)

3. Explore additional Latin and Greek prefixes, building on those already taught at the syllables and affixes stage.

Prefix	Meaning	Prefix	Meaning
inter-	between	*sub-*	under
intra-	within	*pre-*	before
super-	over; greater	*anti-*	against
counter-	opposing	*demi-*	half
ex-	out	*semi-*	half
fore-	before	*quadr-*	four
post-	after	*pent-*	five
pro-	in front of, forward		

4. Explore common Greek suffixes

Suffix	Meaning
-crat/-cracy	rule: *democracy*—rule by the *demos*, people
-emia	condition of the blood: *leukemia*—the blood has too many white (*leuk*) blood cells
-ician	specialist in: *dietician*
-ine	chemical substance: *chlorine, Benzedrine*
-ism/-ist	belief in; one who believes: *communism/communist, capitalism/capitalist*
-logy/-logist	science of; scientist: *geology*—science of the earth, studying the earth; *geologist*—one who studies the earth
-pathy/-path	disease; one who suffers from a disease: (*sociopath;* someone with a personality disorder)
-phobia	abnormal fear: *claustrophobia*—fear of being closed in or shut in (*claus*)

Predictable Spelling Changes in Consonants and Vowels

1. /t/ to /sh/	*permi**t**/permi**ss**ion, transmi**t**/transmi**ss**ion*
2. /t/ to /s/	*silen**t**/silen**ce***
3. /d/ to /zh/	*explo**d**e/explo**s**ion, deci**d**e/deci**s**ion*
4. /sh/ to /s/	*fero**ci**ous/fero**ci**ty, preco**ci**ous/preco**ci**ty*
5. Long to short	*v**ai**n/v**a**nity, rec**ei**ve/rec**e**ption, ret**ai**n/ret**e**ntion*
6. Long to schwa	*expl**ai**n/expl**a**nation, excl**ai**m/excl**a**mation*

Table 8-1 Continued	
Advanced Suffix Study	
1. -able/-ible	respectable, favorable versus visible, audible
2. -ant/-ance	fragrant/fragrance, dominant/dominance
-ent/-ence	dependent/dependence, florescent/florescence
3. Consonant doubling and accent	occurred, permitted versus traveled, benefited
Absorbed Prefixes	
1. Prefix + base word	in + mobile = immobile; ad + count = account
2. Prefix + word root	ad + cept = accept, in + mune = immune

reading the words. Absorbed prefixes, for example, are left to the end because many of the words that contain them will not occur with much frequency in the reading materials or be in the speaking vocabulary of most upper elementary or middle school students (i.e., *immunity* or *innumerable*). While some new vocabulary words can be included in every sort at this level, there should still be a good number of familiar words from which students can begin to make generalizations, moving from the known to the unknown.

In the letter name alphabetic stage and the within-word pattern stage there is a sense of urgency in moving students along at a steady pace and working to help struggling spellers catch up with their peers. There is less sense of urgency in this stage because students will be in this stage for a long time. Word study for derivational relations is typically spread out over the middle school and high school years and never really ends! Nevertheless, the study of spelling-meaning connections is of paramount importance in boosting students' vocabulary, which is "needed if children are to read well" (Biemiller, 2003).

Consonant Alternation

Consonants that are silent in one word are sometimes "sounded" in a related word, as in the words *sign, signal*, and *signature*. This phenomenon is known as **consonant alternation.** It occurs in related words where the spelling of consonants remains the same despite an alternation or change in the sound represented by the spelling. We begin the examination of consonant alternation with silent/sounded pairs such as these: *bomb/bombard, crumb/crumble, muscle/muscular, hasten/haste, soften/soft*. There are not many words in which consonants alternate in this way, but it provides a good introduction to the basic concept of spelling-meaning connections. As students move through the grades, they will encounter more words that follow this pattern, thereby expanding their vocabulary: *column/columnist, solemn/solemnity, assign/assignation*. Rather than trying simply to remember the spelling of one silent consonant in one word, students learn the following strategy: To remember the spelling of a word with a silent consonant, try to think of a word related in spelling and meaning. You may get a clue from the consonant that is sounded.

The next consonant alternation pattern to be studied involves alternations in which the consonant sound alternates with a different sound as endings are added. For example, when *-ian* is added to *clinic (clinician)*, the final /k/ sound changes to /sh/. In other words that end in *-ic*, the /k/ sound changes to /s/, as in *critic* to *criticize* and *public* to *publicize*.

Vowel Alternation

In the pair *revise/revision*, the long *-i* in the base word (*re-vise*) changes to a short *-i* in the derived word (*revision*). **Vowel alternation** occurs in many related words where the spelling of the vowels remains the same despite an alternation or change in the sound represented by the spelling. These alternations occur as affixes are added and the accented syllables change (e.g., *im-pose' / im po si' tion*). Students benefit most from the study of vowel alternation patterns when these patterns are presented in a logical sequence. Begin with the study of related words containing simple vowel alternations that change from long-to-short vowel sounds as suffixes are added, as in *nature* to *natural*, *sane* to *sanity*, or *divine* to *divinity*.

Next, students may explore in depth the spelling of the schwa, or least-accented vowel sound where the vowel is reduced from the long sound to the schwa sound: *reside* to *resident*, *oppose* to *opposition*, *invite* to *invitation*. In other words, the vowel is reduced from the short sound to the schwa: *allege* to *allegation*, *excel* to *excellent*, *habit* to *habitat*. Again as affixes are added to words, the accented syllables change—*re side'* to *res' i dent*—and this reduction in stress influences the sound of the vowel.

Sorts to explore vowel alternations begin by pairing derived words and then grouping the pairs by the changes in the vowel sounds and stressed syllables. Pairing words in this way will help students discover that vowels are heard most clearly in the accented syllables. The pairing of related words also illustrates a primary spelling strategy for spellers in the derivational relations stage: To remember the spelling of the schwa in an unaccented syllable, think of a related word in which that syllable is accented.

Adding -ion to Words

The suffix /*shun*/ as in *protection, invasion,* and *musician* can be spelled several ways and also affects the base word in interesting ways. It sometimes may cause a final consonant sound to alternate (as in *detect/detection*, where the /*t*/ becomes /*sh*/) or a vowel to alternate (as in *decide/decision*). Hundreds of words in English end with this suffix, which means "action" or "process" (or "person," in the case of *ian: clinician, dietician*). Usually a verb is changed to a noun with the addition of *-ion*, as in *elect* to *election* or *create* to *creation*. The generalizations that govern changes in spelling when this suffix is added are rather complex but can be addressed early in the derivational relations stage because there are so many familiar words to examine. In order to spell the /*shun*/ suffix, the ending of the base word must be considered. Here is a summary of the generalizations and the order in which they can be introduced.

- Base words that end in *-ct* or *-ss* just add *-ion* (*traction, expression*).
- Base words that end in *-ic* add *-ian* (*magician*).
- Base words that end in *-te* drop the *e* and add *-ion* (*translation*).
- Base words that end in *-ce* drop the *e* and add a *tion* (*reduce/reduction*).
- Base words that end in *-de* and *-it* drop those letters and add *-sion* or *-ssion* (*decide/decision, admit/admission*).
- Sometimes *-ation* is added to the base word but causes little trouble for spellers because it can be heard (*transport/transportation*).

In Figure 8-1, students first pair the base word (the verb) with its derivative (the noun), and then group the pairs by the spelling patterns to determine the generalization. Students should also look for the type of vowel or consonant alternations that have occurred.

FIGURE 8-1   **Word Sort to Explore -ion Ending**

divide	division	produce	production
delude	delusion	reduce	reduction
deride	derision	introduce	introduction
allude	allusion	reproduce	reproduction

Help your students notice that very often *multiple* alternations are occurring in a group of related words. This insight leads to an investigation of how many vowel and consonant alternations students can find within a group of words, as follows.

ferocious	*ferocity*
diplomatic	*diplomacy*
specific	*specificity*
pugnacious	*pugnacity*

In *ferocious* and *ferocity*, for example, there is a long-to-short *o* vowel alternation and a /sh/-/s/ consonant alternation.

In summary, the spelling-meaning connection explored through consonant and vowel alternations plays a very important role in fine-tuning spelling knowledge and in expanding students' vocabularies. Once students understand how the principle operates in known words, we show them how it applies in unknown words. For example, let us say a student understands, but misspells, the word *solemn* as *solem* in his writing. You would then show him the related word *solemnity*. In so doing, you have the opportunity to address two important objectives: First, the reason for the so-called silent *-n* in *solemn* becomes clear—the word is related to *solemnity*, in which the *n* is pronounced. Second, because students already know the meaning of *solemn*, they are able to understand the meaning of the new but related word *solemnity*. You have just used the spelling system, in other words, to expand this student's vocabulary!

Greek and Latin Elements

The study of Greek roots and Latin stems offers an incredibly rich terrain of **word elements** that remain at the core of the word after all prefixes and suffixes have been removed. Usually these roots or stems do not stand alone like base words, for example, *chron* ("time") in *chronology* and *struc* ("build") in *restructure*. It is important to note that, over the years, educators and linguists have used different terms to refer to these elements and to make distinctions between roots of Greek origin or stems of Latin origin (Dale, O'Rourke, & Bamman, 1971; Henry, 2003; Moats, 2000; Templeton, 1996). For example, roots of Greek origin are often labeled "combining forms" and those of Latin origin simply "stems." This is to distinguish the flexibility of Greek elements from Latin elements: Greek roots such as *photo* and *graph* may combine in different places in words—at the beginning, middle, or end (*telephoto*, *graphic*, *photograph*). Latin stems, on the other hand, tend to stay in one place, have prefixes and suffixes attach to them, and do not move around (*credible*, *credence*, *incredible*). Word root is a single term that we use to introduce the concept of Greek and Latin word parts. Later, after students understand these word parts and how they work, it may be helpful—as well as interesting—to point out this distinction between Greek roots and Latin stems. As with so much of word study, we need to know the various terms and usages but must use them judiciously with our students so as not to overwhelm them with labels when they are first learning a concept.

In the following lesson, Jorge Ramirez shows his students how Latin word roots function within words. He begins by passing out a sheet of words and asks students for ideas about how to sort them. The students quickly discover that the words contain similar word parts, *struct* and *fract*. Mr. Ramirez writes the key words *fracture* and *construct* and then writes the rest into categories as students call them out.

> Mr. Ramirez points out *fracture* and *fraction* on the board. "We know what these two words are and what they mean. What happens when you *fracture* your arm?"
>
> Students respond, "You break it."
>
> "What do you do when you divide something into *fractions*?" Mr. Ramirez elicits from the students that you break whole numbers down into fractions.
>
> "Good! Now, both words *fracture* and *fraction* have *fract* in them. Is *fract* a word?"
>
> Students respond, "No."

"It's a very important part of the words *fracture* and *fraction*, however. We call *fract* a word root. It comes from a word in Latin that means 'to break.' Remember our discussion about the history of English and how so many words and word parts in English come from the Greek and Latin languages? *Fract* lives on in the words *fracture* and *fraction*. Word roots are everywhere! Let's look at these words."

Mr. Ramirez points to the words under *construct: construction, structure*. "What's the same in these three words?"

Students point out *struct*.

"Good! You've found the word root! Now, let's think about what this word root might mean. Think about what happens when construction workers construct a building or structure." Students engage in a brief discussion in which the meaning "to build" emerges. "Right! *Construct* means 'to build something,' and *structure* is another term we often use to refer to a building or something that has been built."

Next, Mr. Ramirez points to the word *instruct* and asks the students how the meaning of "build" might apply to the word. Through discussion, students come to the realization that *instruct* refers to how learning or knowledge is "built."

Mr. Ramirez assigns his students the task over the next few days of finding more words with the -fract- and -struct- roots. Students brainstorm, use the class dictionary, and consult an online dictionary to develop a long list of words including **fract**ious, **fract**als, in**fract**ion, re**fract**ion, super**struct**ure, recon**struct**ion, un**struct**ured, de**struct**ion, inde**struct**ible, ob**struct**ion, and in**struct**ional. Students will record the words they find in the vocabulary section of their word study notebooks and come together to compare their findings.

Word roots nestle within a word and are the meaningful anchor to which prefixes and suffixes may attach. These roots also follow the basic spelling-meaning premise that words with similar meanings are usually spelled similarly, and it is important to point out to students that spelling *visually* represents the meaning of these elements and preserves the meaning relationships among words that at first may appear quite different. Notice, for example, the consistent spelling -jud- in the words *judge, prejudice*, and *adjudicate*.

Because roots are usually not base words or affixes, they are at first more challenging to locate. Their consistent spelling, however, is the best clue to identifying them and examining how they function within words. Usually their spelling remains the same (*inspect, spectator; predict, indict*), although some roots have several spellings. Both *vid* (in *video* and *evident*) and *vis* (in *visible* and *television*) come from the Latin word *videre*, meaning "to see." Students may already have noted some of these variations in their exploration of spelling-meaning relationships, as, for example, thinking about how *receive* and *reception* are related in meaning; they can now examine them while attending to the meaning of the root within the related words (*ceiv* and *cep* both mean "take").

At the derivational relations stage, exploration of Greek and Latin elements begins with those that occur with greatest frequency in the language and should be sequenced according to the abstractness of their meaning, from concrete to more abstract. For example, the Greek roots *phon* (sound) and *graph* (writing) and the Latin roots *spect* (to look), *rupt* (to break, burst), and *dic* (to speak, say) are introduced and explored early in the sequence; more abstract roots such as the Latin *fer* (to carry) and *spir* (to breathe) are explored later.

Table 8-1 lists the roots that occur most frequently in the reading material that intermediate and middle grade students encounter. Because of this frequency of occurrence, these roots warrant students' direct attention and exploration (Becker, Dixon, & Anderson-Inman, 1980; Templeton, 2004). More Greek and Latin roots can be found in Appendix E. Choosing which ones to study may depend on the number of words that will be at least partially familiar to your students. You may also select roots on the basis of content areas of study. If you are studying forms of government, words like *democracy, monarchy*, and *plutocracy* suggest a study of the common roots. The resources listed in Table 8-2 provide lists of more words. The study of word roots should begin in the upper elementary and

TABLE 8-2 Resources for Word Study

Greek and Latin Elements

For Students and Teachers

Crutchfield, R. (1997). *English vocabulary quick reference: A comprehensive dictionary arranged by word roots.* Leesburg, VA: LexaDyne Publishing, Inc.

Danner, H., & Noel, R. (2004). *Discover it! A better vocabulary the better way, Second Edition.* Occoquan, VA: Imprimis Books.

Fine, E.H. (2004). *Crytomanial: Teleporting into Greek and Latin with the cryptokids.* Berkeley, CA: Tricycle Press. Illustrated by K. Donner.

Kennedy, J. (1996). *Word stems: A dictionary.* New York: Soho Press.

Moore, B., & Moore, M. (1997). *NTC's dictionary of Latin and Greek origins: A comprehensive guide to the classical origins of English words.* Chicago: NTC Publishing Group.

For Teachers

Ayers, D. M. (1986). *English words from Latin and Greek elements* (2nd ed., revised by Thomas Worthen). Tucson: The University of Arizona Press.

Fry, E. (2004). *The vocabulary teacher's book of lists.* San Francisco: Jossey-Bass.

Johnston, F., Bear, D. R., & Invernizzi, M. (2006). *Words their way: Word sorts for derivational relations spellers.* Upper Saddle River, NJ: Merrill/Prentice-Hall.

Nilsen, A. P., & Nilsen, D. L. F. (2004). *Vocabulary plus high school and up: A source-based approach.* Boston: Allyn & Bacon.

Schleifer, R. (1995). *Grow your own vocabulary.* New York: Random House.

Word Origins

For Students and Teachers

Asimov, I. (1961). *Words from the myths.* Boston: Houghton Mifflin. (The most readable and most interesting resource of this kind.)

Ayto, J. (1993). *Dictionary of word origins.* New York: Arcade.

D'Aulaire, I., & D'Aulaire, E. (1980). *D'Aulaires' book of Greek myths.* New York: Doubleday. (Of interest to third graders and up; upper intermediate reading level.)

Fisher, L. (1984). *The Olympians: Great gods and goddesses of ancient Greece.* New York: Holiday House (Of interest to third graders and up; third grade reading level.)

Gates, D. (1983). *Two queens of heaven: Aphrodite and Demeter.* NY: Puffin. (Of interest to fourth graders and up; upper intermediate reading level.)

Jones, C.F. (1999). *Eat your words: A fascinating look at the language of food.* NY, NY: Delacorte Press. Illustrated by J. O'Brian.

Kingsley, C. (1980). *The heroes*: or Greek fairy tales for my children (1980), Lititz; PA: BiblioBazaar (Of interest to third graders and up; intermediate reading level). The stories behind many present-day words that come from myths and legends help students remember the meanings of the terms and their spellings.

Merriam-Webster new book of word histories. (1995). Springfield, MA: Merriam-Webster Inc.

For Teachers

Shipley, J. (2001). *The origins of English words.* Baltimore: Johns Hopkins University Press. (For truly dedicated wordsmiths, Shipley's book is the ultimate source. A delightful read!)

middle grades and extend throughout high school and beyond. It is almost endless in terms of possibilities because there are so many roots and meaning connections to discover.

Predictable Spelling Changes in Vowels and Consonants

After students have systematically explored word roots and their derivational relatives that share the same spelling, they can begin to examine related words in which both the sound *and* the spelling changes. Fortunately, this change is predictable or occurs regularly in families. For example, although the spelling of the long *-a* in *explain* changes from *ai* to *a* in the derived word *explanation*, these are not the only words in which this change occurs; it also occurs in *exclaim/exclamation, detain/detention, receive/reception,* and *deceive/deception.* Students learn that, if the base word has the *ai* or *ei* spelling, the derived word's spelling is simply *a* or *e.* Students are ready to examine these words because they understand the spelling-meaning patterns presented earlier. Students first do a sort in which each base word is paired with its derivative and then sort the word pairs according to the specific spelling change that occurs. The following sort illustrates this feature.

receive/reception	*exclaim/exclamation*	*detain/detention*
conceive/conception	*proclaim/proclamation*	*retain/retention*
deceive/deception	*reclaim/reclamation*	
perceive/perception	*acclaim/acclamation*	

Advanced Suffix Study

A handful of suffixes present occasional challenges even for advanced readers and writers. The adjective-forming suffix *-able/-ible* seems to be a classic for misspelling. There is a generalization that usually helps determine whether this suffix is spelled *-able* or *-ible.* Consider the sort below and look for the root or baseword from which each word is derived.

dependable	credible
profitable	audible
agreeable	edible
predictable	visible

A fairly powerful generalization emerges: If the suffix is attached to a base word that can stand alone (*depend*), it is usually spelled *-able;* if it is attached to a word root (*cred*), it is usually spelled *-ible.* Base words that end in *e* will usually drop the *e* and add *-able* (*desire/desirable*); however, soft *c* or *g* endings may be followed by *-ible* as in *reducible* and sometimes a final *e* is retained to keep the soft sound, as in *noticeable* and *manageable.*

The connection between the suffixes *-ant/-ance* and *-ent/-ence* can be also understood when pairs are examined: *brillant/brillance, confident/confidence.* Sound is no clue, but if you know the spelling of a word that ends in one of these suffixes, that word is a clue to the spelling of the suffix in the related word (Templeton, 1980). At this level, most individuals know how to spell one of the words in such pairs correctly; making this spelling-meaning relationship explicit is extremely helpful for the learner.

The addition of inflected endings and consonant doubling in words like *committed* and *benefited* is revisited in the derivational relations stage as it applies to words of more than one syllable. Jorge Ramirez provides a collection of words that double and words that don't and challenges his students to figure out why.

"Okay, we've got a few words here to sort. What do you notice about these words? That's right, they all end in *-ed.* What do you notice about the base words?" He and his students discuss the fact that in some cases the final consonant has been doubled before adding *-ed,* and in others it has stayed the same. He has them sort the words into two columns by those features:

excelled	edited
occurred	limited
submitted	orbited
referred	conquered

Mr. Ramirez asks the students to work in pairs to talk about what they see and hear when they contrast the words in both columns. He encourages them to read the base words in each column several times. If no one brings up "accent" as a possible explanation, he asks them to listen as he reads the base words in each column emphasizing the accented syllable: *excel, occur, submit, refer*. Then he reads *edit, limit, orbit, conquer*.

"I get it, I get!" yells Silvio. "The accent is on a different syllable! When it is on the last syllable you have to double!"

The generalization toward which Mr. Ramirez is working with the students is this: If the last syllable of the base word is accented, double the final consonant before adding *-ed* (and *-ing* as well). If the last syllable is not accented, then do not double the final consonant. Mr. Ramirez follows up the sort by pointing out the following bit of history:

"Remember when Daire brought in the British copy of *Harry Potter and the Goblet of Fire* that her grandma bought for her in England and we noticed how the spelling of some of the words was different than in American English? For example, there were a lot of doubled consonants that we don't have—*benefited* had two *t*s at the end. Actually, in just about every situation where we in the United States do not double the final consonant, people in other English-speaking countries do. Do you know who we can blame for making it so that Americans have to think about whether or not to double? Would you believe it was Noah Webster? Yes! The man who brought us our dictionary!

"Actually, what Webster wanted to do was make English spoken and written in the United States different in many ways from English spoken in Britain. When he did this, our country wasn't getting along too well with Britain—after all, we had fought a war to become independent not long before! So, in his dictionary of American English—the first of its kind—Webster decided to change many spellings. One of the most obvious ways was to take out the *u* in words such as *honour* and *behaviour*." Mr. Ramirez writes these words on the board. "He also switched the *re* in words such as *theatre* and *centre*." He writes these on the board.

When students notice exceptions to this principle—when they see the spelling *traveled* or *benefitted*, for example—ask them to check the dictionary: Though they will see the correct spelling they will also see the so-called incorrect spelling listed. In other words, over time, if enough people misspell a word, the misspelling will work its way into the dictionary as an accepted—if not the preferred—spelling!

Absorbed Prefixes

Prefixes are first studied in the syllable and affixes stage and then throughout the derivational relations stage. Prefixes are often obvious visual and meaning units that are easy to see and understand, as in *unlikely* or *inaccurate*. However, there is a group of prefixes that are somewhat disguised, as in the word *illegal*. The only clue to the prefix is the doubled letters. These prefixes are known as absorbed or assimilated prefixes and pose the most difficult spelling challenge for students because they depend on considerable prior knowledge about other basic spelling-meaning patterns, processes of adding prefixes to base words, and simple Greek and Latin roots. Most adults are unaware of this feature but it can resolve many spelling dilemmas—such as how to spell *accommodate*, the most frequently misspelled word in the English language.

Below is a sort that might be used by a middle or high school English teacher to explore the idea of absorbed prefixes. The words are first presented in a random list and the students are asked to discuss their meanings. The students are likely to conclude that they all seem to mean "not" or "the opposite of." When asked how they might sort the words, the following categories emerge.

ineffective	illiterate	immature	irregular	impossible
inorganic	illegal	immobile	irrational	impatient
inactive	illogical	immortal	irrelevant	improper
infinite	illegible	immodest		

The students might then be asked what they notice about the base words in each column. The particular spelling of the prefix *in-* sometimes depends on the first letter of the base word, taking on the same spelling (i.e., being "absorbed"). You might ask your students to try saying *inmobile* or *inrelevant*. We can say them, but we have to stress the prefix in order to do so (in most words the accent does not fall on the prefix). If they go to the dictionary to look up the prefixes or the words, they will be referred back to the original prefix *-in*. Here is how Mr. Ramirez describes this process.

> "Let's take the word *immobile*. The word is constructed from the prefix *in-*, meaning 'not,' and the base word *mobile*, which means 'capable of moving.' When we put *in-* and *mobile* together, two things happen. First, the word parts combine to mean 'not mobile, not capable of moving.' Second, notice that the spelling of the prefix *in-* has changed to *im*. A long time ago, someone combined the prefix *in-* with the word *mobile* to create a new word that meant 'not mobile.' Now, try pronouncing the word like it was pronounced when it first came into existence: *inmobile*. Does that feel kind of weird? Does your tongue kind of get stuck on the beginning of *mobile*? Mine sure does! Over time it became easier for people to leave out the /n/ sound when pronouncing the word. The sound of the *n* became 'absorbed' into the /m/ sound at the beginning of the base word *mobile*. Before long, the spelling of the *n* changed to indicate this change in pronunciation—but it's important to remember that this letter didn't disappear. They knew it was necessary to keep the two letters in the prefix to indicate that it was still a prefix. If the last letter of the prefix had been dropped, then the meaning of the prefix would have been lost."

Absorbed or assimilated prefixes are primarily Latin in origin and are widespread in English. An extensive list of assimilated prefixes can be found in Appendix E. Although the prefix *ad-* is the most common, it is also the most abstract, so explore others first. By the way, *accommodate* has two assimilated prefixes: The *d* in the prefix *ad-* is absorbed into the first letter/sound of the second prefix *con-*, and the *n* in *con-* is absorbed into the first letter/sound of the word root *modate*.

Content Area Vocabulary

In addition to the systematic study of orthographic and derivational features, students in this stage will need to master many words from content areas. Ideas about activating background knowledge and the use of graphic organizers are described in chapter 7. More ideas can be found in books that deal specifically with vocabulary such as *Bringing Words to Life* (Beck, McKeown, & Kucan, 2002), *Teaching Word Meanings* (Stahl & Nagy, 2006), and the *Vocabulary Handbook* (Diamond and Gutlohn, 2006).

Word Origins

Exploring the origins of words and the processes of word creation provides a powerful knowledge base for learning spelling and vocabulary, as well as for facilitating more effective reading and writing. **Etymology,** the study of word origins (from the Greek *etumon,* meaning "true sense of a word"), may develop into a lifelong fascination for many students. As you engage students in examining word roots and affixes, you are laying the groundwork for more focused exploration of etymology. Students develop a real sense of how words work at this level as well as a general sense of how words can move through history.

Many times the spelling of a word may appear odd, but an understanding of its origin provides the most powerful key to remembering the spelling. Knowing that so many words have come from mythology, literature, and historical events and figures provides important background knowledge for students' reading in the various content areas. Table 8-3 provides a list of resource books. To stimulate students' curiosity about word origins you might read aloud excerpts from such books when you have a few extra minutes.

Another way to add interest to the study of word origins is to talk about words we have imported from other countries. A significant number of words have recently come into American English from other contemporary languages, primarily Spanish (*quesadilla, chili con carne*), but some French (*bistro, a la carte*). A popular classroom activity is to post a large world map on the wall and display words according to their country of origin. Where would you post the word *segue*?

WORD STUDY WITH ENGLISH LEARNERS

English Language Learners students have the potential to be *more* sensitive to words than monolingual speakers simply because they must be more analytical—of their home language as well as of English—in order to negotiate the nature of spelling/sound/meaning relationships.

The study of cognates seems particularly fruitful at the derivational relations stage and can also benefit native English speakers who might be learning Spanish, French, or German as a foreign language.

Many words in English are derived from Latin but this is true for other languages as well. You can see the spelling meaning connection in *mater* (Latin), *madre* (Spanish), *mere* (French), *mutter* (German), and *mother* (English). **Cognates** are words in different languages that share similar structures and similar meanings because they share similar origins. Attention to cognates help English learners see morphological similarities between English and their home language. Just as with our word sorts in English, sorting English and Spanish cognates offers opportunities for examining spelling-meaning relationships and grammatical features. For example, students may be guided to notice the common suffixes and their spellings that key different parts of speech (Nash, 1997):

	Nouns	**Adjectives**	**Verbs**	**Adverbs**
English	alphabet	alphabetic	alphabetize	alphabetically
Spanish	alfabeto	alfabético	alfabetizar	alfabéticamente
English	favor	favorable	favor	favorably
Spanish	favor	favorable	favorecer	favorablemente

Word roots also offer a very rich terrain for exploring cognates in other languages: *nocturno* and *extensor* in Spanish have very similar meanings to *nocturnal* and *extensive* in English. Make it a point to look for cognates as you study the different Latin roots—*port* shows up in Spanish *importar* and *exportar* and means the same thing as *export* and *import*. You may want to start a chart in your classroom of cognates as students discover them. It is important to bear in mind, however, that some spelling-meaning connections that seem obvious in Spanish and English can lead to some embarrassing "false friends." For example, the Spanish word *suburbia/suburbi* looks a lot like the English word *suburbia*, or *suburbs*, but the Spanish word *suburbio* actually refers to the slums, not *suburbia* as we know it at all (Swan & Smith, 2001, p. 110)! Likewise, the Spanish word *éxito/éxit*, doesn't correlate with *exit* at all. *Éxito* means "success"! To avoid embarrassment, it might be wise to explore some "false cognates" at the same time.

WORD STUDY ROUTINES AND MANAGEMENT

There are three basic points to keep in mind regarding students' word study at this level (Templeton, 1989, 1992):

1. Words and word elements selected for study should be *generative*, which means that, when possible, we teach about words in "meaning families." This highlights the awareness that particular patterns of relationships can be extended or generalized to other words. For example, an awareness of the long-to-short vowel alternation pattern that was introduced during the syllables and affixes stage with words such as *please* and *pleasant* can generalize to words such as *compete/competitive*.

2. The words that we initially select for exploration by our students should be selected based on how obvious their relationship is. For example, we will teach clearly related words such as *represent/misrepresent* before teaching about words that are less clearly related, such as *expose/exposition*.

3. There should be a balance of teacher-directed instruction with students' exploration and discussion.

Dictionaries

In the derivational relations stage, dictionaries will get a lot of use. Students should be taught about the features of dictionaries such as pronunciation guides, multiple definitions, parts of speech, and so on. Have at least one dictionary in the classroom that has etymological information about the word. This information is usually in brackets at the end of main entries. Online dictionaries, such as *American Heritage, yourdictionary.com*, and *onelook.com*, are also useful. The following materials should always be readily available to students.

- Intermediate and collegiate dictionaries; enough copies for six to eight students to work in a small group
- Thesaurus collection, enough for six to eight students in small-group work
- Several word history (etymological) dictionaries and root books (see Table 8-3 on page 239 for an annotated list)

Teacher-Directed Word Study Instruction

Word study should take place all day long and in all content areas as teachers pause to examine words, to talk about unusual spellings (*pneumonia*), to look for clues to meaning in the word and in context, and to look up and discuss words in the dictionary. But, as in other stages, students in the derivational relations stage still need in-depth systematic attention to features at their developmental level. We emphasize the importance of word study at this developmental level for middle and secondary students, especially if these students have not experienced this type of systematic word study in school prior to this time.

Teachers who use the upper-level spelling inventory described in Chapter 2 will be able to identify what features to address in instruction. Typically there is a plateau effect with upper-level assessments, which suggests that students in homogeneous classes may all benefit from similar instruction. Small-group differentiated instruction is less important if students are all advanced readers and spellers. This may be reassuring for secondary teachers who only have their students for short periods of time each day.

Chapter 3 describes a variety of routines and word study notebook activities, but they need to be carefully considered at this stage. The categorization of words through sorting is still a powerful learning activity; however, some teachers rely more on writing words into categories than on cutting out words and sorting them physically. Blind sorts still work well when spelling is an issue (as in *-able* and *-ible* sorts or when working with the /*shun*/ ending) but will not pose much of a challenge when the sort features prefixes and roots.

Word hunts should extend over longer periods of time because the words and features at this level are less common, especially in fiction. Don't expect students to find words with Greek and Latin roots in Hemingway's *The Old Man and the Sea!* They are more likely to occur in textbooks. However, brainstorming additional words (word hunts in the head) sometimes works well and dictionaries can become a place for word hunts. Students can be taught to search online dictionaries by using an asterisk before and/or after the word part to get a list of words (e.g., **cian* will give you words that end with *-cian*). Ongoing classroom displays of words provide continual review as words turn up in reading and class discussions that can be added to categories started weeks before.

FIGURE 8-2 Illustrating Words Relationships

Throughout the derivational relations stage, it is particularly important to include routines that focus on the meaning of words. Students can be asked to use the dictionary to look up and record definitions and word origins of selected words (**not** 20 at a time, however!). They can be asked to use words in sentences to demonstrate their understanding of meaning, but invite them also to try illustrations or cartoons. These visual representations can be powerful mnemonics, as shown in Figure 8-2. Having students work cooperatively and letting them share their sentences or drawings can be engaging.

Games are still a valuable way to review words not only for a test, but also over time. At this level students can create many games themselves based on popular games like Concentration, Rummy, War, Slap Jack, Uno, Trivial Pursuit, and Jeopardy. Give them blank game board templates from Appendix F or card stock for playing cards and they can do the rest. In the process of creating games they will remember the words and come to understand the feature better.

Because there is less classroom time in middle school and high school, some teachers adopt a two-week schedule that includes a word study contract (see Chapter 3 for an example). Students are given a collection of 20–40 words and complete a selection of routines independently in school or for homework. Testing is done every two weeks and often includes an assessment of mastery of meaning as well as of spelling. For example, students are asked to explain the meaning of a prefix, root, or particular words.

Preparing Sorts

There are a number of word sorts in Appendix D that are appropriate for more advanced derivational relations students. Additional words can be found in the lists in Appendix E and the word lists will suggest other sorts as well. Middle school and high school English/language arts teachers should find this section to be helpful, as it extends the types of word knowledge that are possible to develop at this level. In particular, it presents avenues of word study that will be engaging and quite rewarding for students who are verbally advanced.

 Create your own sorts by choosing words to drop into the templates available on the CD-ROM.

This type of exploration and curiosity about words will unavoidably become part of students' learning repertoires. Indeed, it is more a mindset than a strategy per se. Students become lifelong wordsmiths and almost automatically wonder about the relationships among words in general and about a particular word specifically; for example, does the similarity in spelling between *applaud/plaudit* and **mordant/morsel** capture underlying meaning relationships? (Yes!) This type of awareness and curiosity leads to the continual nourishment and growth of underlying conceptual networks.

Activities for Students in the Derivational Relations Stage

You'll find even more activities for Derivational Relations spellers on the *Words Their Way* CD. Create your own activities, games, and manipulatives and print them or save them to your hard drive to use again and again.

Here we present routines, activities, and games for students in the derivational relations stage.

Vocabulary Notebooks 8-1

Vocabulary notebooks are an integral part of students' word learning at the derivational relations phase (Gill & Bear, 1989). They are used, for example, to record word sorts and add words to the sorts after going on word hunts. To begin, divide the notebooks into two sections:

> *Word Study:* A weekly record of sorts, explanations of sorts, and homework
> *Looking into Language:* Records of whole group word study of related words, semantic sorts, interesting word collections, investigations, and theme study words

Following is a description of how to facilitate older students' collections of "interesting" words.

1. *Collect the word.* While reading, mark words you find difficult. When you are through reading or studying, go back to these words. Read around the word, and think about its possible meaning.
2. *Record the word and sentence.* Write the word, followed by the sentence in which it was used, the page number, and an abbreviation for the title of the book. (At times the sentence will be too long. Write enough of it to give a clue to meaning.) Think about the word's meaning.
3. *Look at word parts and think about their meaning.* Look at the different parts of the word—prefixes, suffixes, and base word or root word. Think about the meaning of the affixes and base or root.
4. *Record related words.* Think of other words that are like this word, and write them underneath the part of the word that is similar.
5. *Use the dictionary.* Look the word up in the dictionary, read the various definitions, and in a few words record the meaning (the one that applies to the word in the book you are reading) in your notebook or on a card. Look for similar words (both in form and meaning) above and below the target word and list them as well. Look at the origin of the word, and add it to your entry if it is interesting.
6. *Review the words.* A realistic goal is to collect 10 words a week. These words may be brought up in class and shared. In addition, record words that consistently present spelling challenges in the notebook or on the cards. For each word, think of words that are related to this particular word again, as in Step 4.

Let us summarize the process with an example.

1. Collect the word: *orthography*.
2. Record the word and sentence: "English *orthography* is not crazy, and it carries the history of the word with it." p. 22, *Sounds of Language*.
3. Look at word parts and think about their meaning: *ortho/graph* (may have something to do with writing).

Note: The third definition fits most nearly the meaning of *orthography* as it was used in the sentence. The first two meanings are: 1. the art or study of standard spelling; and 2. the aspect of language study concerned with letters and spelling (*The American Heritage College Dictionary* (1993), p. 965).

4. Record possible related words: *orthodontist, orthodox, graphics, orthographer.*
5. Study the word in the dictionary, and record interesting information: "A method of representing the sounds of a language by letters; spelling." Origin: *ortho*: correct graph, something written.

You Teach the Word 8-2

Students need to learn many vocabulary words for content areas. One way to handle these is to assign each student in the class one word and make him or her responsible for teaching that word to the rest of the class. Ask each student to create a small poster to add to a class word wall, such as the one in Figure 8-3, that includes a definition, a synonym and/or antonym, an etymology, a sentence, or an illustration. Students can share their poster but can also be encouraged to think of creative ways to help each other learn the word, such as by acting it out.

FIGURE 8-3   Poster for Laissez Faire

laissez faire
/lay-zay fair/
definition: noninterference, lack of government intervention
origin: French laisser - to let + faire - to do
example: The teacher had a laissez faire attitude about chewing gum in school.

We Think (with tion/sion) 8-3

This activity will involve students in small groups or two teams of two each, examining words to determine clues for spelling the *-tion* or *-sion* suffixes.

Materials

Each team or group needs a sheet divided into two columns. The left column is labeled "We Think" and the right column is labeled "Because."

Procedures

1. Each team gets a stack of cards to sort (e.g., *act, action, separate, separation, express, expression*) that contain several categories and three to four words in each category. The same words are in each stack; to keep word cards for each team separate, one stack is printed in black letters and the other in red.
2. Each team pairs up the base words and derived words and then sorts them into categories.
3. After looking closely at the words sorted, each team individually fills out their "We Think" sheets with generalities that they notice when words took the *-tion* or the *-sion* ending.
4. After the teams have filled out their "We Think" sheets and supported their generalized rules under the "Because" section, the teams have a meeting of the minds to compare findings.

Variations

This activity will work with other base words, word roots, and derivatives.

Words That Grow from Base Words and Word Roots 8-4

In this whole-class or small-group activity, students see directly how words "grow." It builds on and extends the understanding, begun during the syllables and affixes stage, of how word elements combine.

FIGURE 8-4   Word Tree: Words that Grow from Base Words and Roots

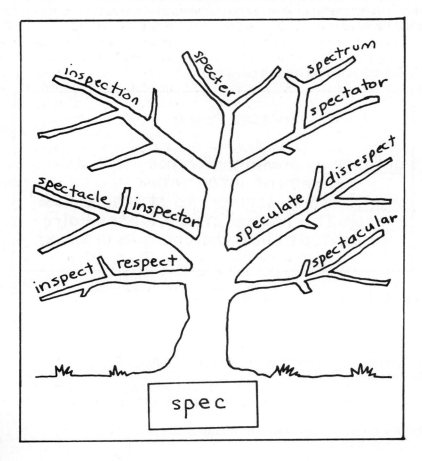

Materials

You will need a drawing of a tree (see Figure 8-4).

Procedures

1. Decide on a base word or a word root to highlight. Begin with more frequently occurring ones; over time, move to less frequently occurring roots.
2. Write the base word or word root at the bottom of the tree, and think of as many forms as possible.
3. Write the different forms on individual branches.
4. Display the word tree in the classroom for several days and encourage students to think of, find, and record more derived words. At the end of the week wipe them off and begin again with the introduction of a new base or word root.

Variations

After making the words, students may use them individually in sentences and/or discuss their meanings. Confirm with the dictionary.

Latin and Greek Jeopardy 8-5

At least three students are needed for this game (a host and scorekeeper as well as two players), but lots more can play as well. The whole class can be divided into two teams.

Materials

Create a grid with five columns and six rows. Make headers to indicate the categories. Make a clue card by writing the points on one side and the answer on the other. Turn over the square that is requested during the playing of the game so the answer can be read. An alternative for a large group is to make an overhead transparency of the Latin Root Jeopardy and Double Latin Root Jeopardy boards shown in Figures 8-5 and 8-6 and project it on a screen. Cover the clues with sticky notes on the transparency. On a chalkboard use tape to fix squares of paper in the correct order.

Procedures

The game consists of two rounds: Jeopardy and Double Jeopardy.

1. The game is modeled after the *Jeopardy* television game. The clue is in the form of an answer and players must phrase their response in the form of a question:

FIGURE 8-5   Latin Root Jeopardy Board

LATIN ROOT JEOPARDY				
SPECT (to look)	FORM (shape)	PORT (to carry)	TRACT (draw or pull)	DICT (to say, speak)
100 One who watches; an onlooker	100 One "form" or style of clothing such as is worn by nurses	100 Goods brought into a country from another country to be sold	100 Adjective: having power to attract; alluring; inviting	100 A book containing the words of a language explained
200 The prospect of good to come; anticipation	200 One who does not conform	200 One who carries burdens for hire	200 A powerful motor vehicle for pulling farm machinery, heavy loads, etc.	200 A speaking against, a denial
300 To regard with suspicion and mistrust	300 To form or make anew; to reclaim	300 To remove from one place to another	300 The power to grip or hold to a surface while moving, without slipping	300 A blessing often at the end of a worship service
400 Verb: to esteem Noun: regard, deference Literally: to look again	400 To change into another substance, change of form	400 To give an account of	400 An agreement: literally, to draw together	400 An order proclaimed by an authority
500 Looking around, watchful, prudent	500 Disfigurement, spoiling the shape	500 A case for carrying loose papers	500 To take apart from the rest, to deduct	500 To charge with a crime

Answer clue: Coming from the Latin root *tract*, it means "a machine for pulling heavy loads."

Question response: What is *tractor*?

2. Determine who will go first. The player will select the first category and point value. The host uncovers the clue and reads it aloud.
3. The first player responding correctly adds the point amount of the question to his or her total or gets to keep the card that was turned over. He or she then chooses the next category and point amount. An incorrect answer means that the points are subtracted.
4. The winner is the one with the most points.

"Questions" for Latin Root Jeopardy

	100	200	300	400	500
spect	spectator	expectation	suspect	respect	circumspect
form	uniform	nonconformist	reform	transform	deformity
port	import	porter	transport	report	portfolio
tract	attractive	tractor	traction	contract	subtract
dict	dictionary	contradiction	benediction	edict	indict

FIGURE 8-6   Double Latin Root Jeopardy Board

DOUBLE LATIN ROOT JEOPARDY				
CRED (to believe)	DUCT (to lead)	FER (to bear, carry)	PRESS (to press)	SPIR (to breathe)
200 A system of doing business by trusting that a person will pay at a later date for goods or services	200 A person who directs the performance of a choir or an orchestra	200 (Plants) able to bear fruit; (Animals) able or likely to conceive young	200 A printing machine	200 An immaterial intelligent being
400 A set of beliefs or principles	400 To train the mind and abilities of	400 To carry again; to submit to another for opinion	400 Verb: to utter; Noun: any fast conveyance	400 To breathe out: to die
600 Unbelievable	600 To enroll as a member of a military service	600 To convey to another place, passed from one place to another	600 To press against, to burden, to overpower	600 To breathe through; to emit through the pores of the skin
800 Verb, prefix meaning "not"; word means to damage the good reputation of	800 The formal presentation of one person to another	800 Endurance of pain; distress	800 State of being "pressed down" or saddened	800 To breathe into; to instruct by divine influence
1000 An adjective, prefix ac, word means officially recognized	1000 An artificial channel carrying water across country	1000 Cone bearing, as the fir tree	1000 To put down, to prevent circulation	1000 To plot; to band together for an evil purpose

"Questions" for Double Latin Root Jeopardy

	200	400	600	800	1000
cred	credit	creed	incredible	discredit	accredited
duct	conductor	educate	induct	introduction	aqueduct
fer	fertile	refer	transfer	suffering	coniferous
press	press	express	oppress	depression	suppress
spir	spirit	expire	perspire	inspire	conspire

Variations

1. A round of Final Jeopardy can be added if you wish. When it is time for the Final Jeopardy question, players see the category, but not the answer. They then decide how many of their points they will risk. When they see the answer, they have 30 seconds to write the question. If they are correct, they add the number of points they risked to their total; if incorrect, that number of points is subtracted from their total.

2. Play can alternate from one player to the next or from one team to the next rather than be based on who shouts out the response first. If one player misses, the other team gets a chance to respond. If they are correct, they also get another turn.

Derivational Relations Stage

3. Daily Doubles may be included, if desired. (The number of points for an answer is doubled and, if correct, added to the player's score; if incorrect, the doubled number of points is subtracted from the player's score.)
4. Develop a Vocabulary Jeopardy to accompany a unit of study.
   - Generate vocabulary cards from a unit of study that fit into four or five categories (for example, "Food Groups" or "Habitats").
   - Write questions that relate to facts and concepts studied on cards.
   - Teams of students play the game as a whole class vocabulary review of unit.

Quartet 8-6

Many games can be played with a deck of word cards made into suits of four. This game is much like the game Go Fish, in which the object is to collect and lay down a suit of four cards (or a quartet).

Materials

Create 10–12 suits of four cards composed of words that share a common root. For example: *biology, biography, biome, antibiotic*. Write the words at the top left so the words can be read when they are held in the hand.

Procedures

1. Each player is dealt seven cards; the rest are put in a deck. Each player looks through his or her cards for words in the same suit.
2. The first player turns to the next and asks for a particular root: "Give me any cards with the *bio* root." (The player must have at least one card in his or her hand with the root he or she asks for.) The next player must give up any words he or she has; the first player gets to go again. If the player who was asked does not have any matches, he or she responds, "Draw one" and the first player draws from the deck.
3. Play proceeds in a clockwise fashion. When a player has a complete suit of four cards, he or she may lay them down. The player who has the most suits at the end—when someone runs out of cards—is the winner.

It's All Greek to Us 8-7

In this card game, the deck is composed of words derived from Greek roots. Three to five players may participate, one of whom will serve as game master and hold and read definition cards.

Materials

Prepare 10 definition cards that consist of a root and definition such as *"derm"*—"skin." For each root, create four or more word cards (*epidermis, dermatology, taxidermist, hypodermic, pachyderm*). Write these words at the top so they can be seen when held in the hand. A collection of roots, meanings, and words can be found in Appendix E.

Procedures

1. The game master shuffles the word cards, deals 10 cards per player, and places the remaining word cards facedown.
2. The game master reads a definition card and lays it down faceup. All players who are holding a card that matches the definition read it and place it below the corresponding Greek root. If no player can respond to the definition, the game

master places the definition card on the bottom of his or her cards for rereading later in the game.

3. To begin the next round, a new definition card is laid down.
4. The player who discards all 10 word cards first is the winner and becomes the next game master.

Brainburst 8-8

In this game, players compete to brainstorm as many words as they can that are derived from the same root. Only unique words will earn points.

Materials

Write different roots on cards such as *graph, phon, scope, aud, dict, port, tract, struct, spect,* and so on. Choose roots that have a wide variety of possible derivations. Each team or player needs a pencil and sheet of paper. A timer is needed, as well as a standard dictionary (condensed dictionaries may not have enough words).

Procedures

1. A card is turned over and the timer is set for 2–3 minutes. Each player or team tries to think of as many words as possible derived from that root.
2. When the timer goes off, players draw a line under their last word and count the number they have.
3. The player with the longest list reads the list aloud. If another player has the same word, it is crossed off of everyone's list. Any words that are not on another list are checked.
4. Each player in turn reads aloud any words that no one else has called to determine if he or she has a unique word. Disputes should be settled with the help of a dictionary.
5. The player or team with the most unique words is the winner of the round.

Variations

This game can also be played with prefixes (*ex-, sub-, pre-, post-,* etc.) and suffixes (*-ible, -able, -ant, -ent,* etc.).

Joined at the Roots 8-9

This word sort is an effective extension of students' exploration of Latin and Greek word roots. It is appropriate for individuals, partners, or small groups.

Materials

You will need a word sort board, word cards, and word study notebook.

Procedures

1. The teacher begins by modeling how to place words with appropriate roots under a particular category, for example, "Speaking and Writing," "Building/Construction," "Thinking and Feeling," and "Movement." The teacher then involves the students in the categorization.
2. Once students have grasped how this categorization scheme works, they can work in small groups or in pairs. Each group or pair will take a different category and sort words whose roots justify their membership in that category.
3. Lists can be written in word study notebooks and brought back to the larger group to share and discuss. (*Note:* Several of the words to be sorted may be placed under

different categories.) Following are some examples of categories and a few illustrative words.

Sample Categories

Building/Construction	*Thinking and Feeling*	*Movement*	*Travel*
technology	philanthropy	synchrony	astronaut
construct	philosophy	fracture	exodus
tractor	attraction		

Government	*Speaking and Writing*		
economy	autobiography		
demagogue	photograph		
politics	catalogue		
	emphasis		

Root Webs 8-10

Root webs like the one in Figure 8-7 are a graphic way to represent the links between words derived from a common root.

1. Choose a set of common roots, such as *photo-, geo-, aqua-, astro-*.
2. The teacher should first model on an overhead, as students complete their own web in their word study notebooks. Once students understand how to create the root webs, they can do them independently or in small groups.
3. Brainstorm related words. Students should use dictionaries to locate roots, verify their meaning, find their origin, and search for related words.
4. Eliminate words that do not fit the meaning of root. Honor all suggestions. Lead students to examine parts and meaning.

FIGURE 8-7   "Root Web" in Student's Vocabulary Notebook

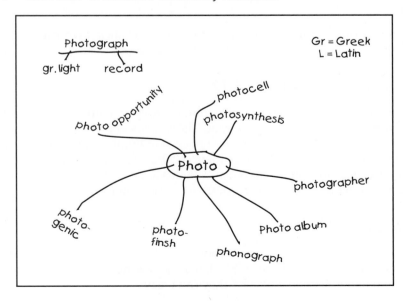

Derivational Relations Stage

Identifying the Meaning of Word Roots 8-11

Given a series of words that share the same root, students analyze the words to determine the meaning of the root. Each group of three words can be finished with one of the words provided. For example, in #1 of the first grouping below, students would look for which of the three words—*introspection, interrupt,* or *distract*—contains the same root as *spectator, inspect,* and *prospector* (*introspection*). In the sentence that follows this, they would then write what they believe the root *spect* means. In the next sentence, they would decide which of the remaining words—*interrupt* or *distract*—contains the same root as *corrupt, disrupt,* and *eruption*—and so on. This is an excellent activity for students to work on in pairs.

   introspection   interrupt   distract

   1. spectator, inspect, prospector, _____
      The root *spect* means _____. (look, count, divide)
   2. corrupt, disrupt, eruption, _____
      The root *rupt* means _____. (speak, break, fall)
   3. tractor, attract, extract, _____
      The root *tract* means _____. (place, look, pull)

   audience   refract   contradict

   1. audible, auditory, audio, _____
      The root *aud* means _____. (throw, hear, touch)
   2. fraction, fracture, infraction, _____
      The root *fract* means _____. (stretch, eat, break)
   3. dictate, diction, predict, _____
      The root *dict* means _____. (say, touch, fight)

   dermatologist   nominative   invaluable

   1. nominate, nominal, nominee, _____
      The root *nom* means _____. (write, figure, name)
   2. value, valor, devalue, _____
      The root *val* means _____. (money, to be strong/to be worth, truth)
   3. hypodermic, epidermis, dermatology, _____
      The root *derm* means _____. (skin, medicine, platform)

Variations

Following this format, groups of students can construct their own exercises and then swap with other groups. Appendix E has additional roots.

Combining Roots and Affixes 8-12

In a matrix such as the one in Figure 8-8, students indicate with an x words that can be made by combining the prefix and the root. Then they write the words below. A variation is to indicate with a "?" words that do not exist in English, but could. Students may write these words in a special section of their vocabulary notebooks, create a definition for each, and use each in a sentence. When students are uncertain about whether a word is an actual word in English, they may check it in the dictionary.

Word Building 8-13

Write prefixes (*re-, in-, ex-, pre-, trans-*), roots (*tract, dict, cred, gress, port*), and suffixes (*-ion, -able, -ible, -ant*) on a set of cards. Students see how many real words they can construct and how many "possible words" they can create.

FIGURE 8-8   Matrix of Roots and Prefixes

	duce/duc/duct	port	spect	dict	tract
in/im		x			
trans					
ex					
pre					
		import			

Procedure

Students get their own set of cards to move around to create as many words as they can. Students can compete to see who can get the most words in a certain period of time.

From Spanish to English—A Dictionary Word Hunt 8-14

Purpose

Expand vocabularies through finding relations among languages. These words are known as *cognates*.

Procedures

1. Look through a Spanish-English dictionary to find words in Spanish that remind you of words in English. Briefly note the definition or synonym (see Nash, 1997).
2. With an English dictionary, find words that share the same root or affix. Write these related words in your word study notebook.
3. Record findings in the word study notebook and create a class chart.

Following are sample entries on a class chart of cognates that one group of students collected in this activity.

Spanish (Translation)	*English Relations*	*Spanish Relations*
presumir (*boast*)	presume, presumption, presumptuous	presunción presumido
extenso (*extensive*)	extend, extension	extensivo, extender
nocturno (*nightly*)	nocturnal, nocturne	noche, noctámbulo
polvo (*powder*)	pulverize (from Latin, *pulvis*, dust)	polvillo, polvorear

The Synonym/Antonym Continuum 8-15

This activity encourages students to think about the subtle differences between word meanings as they work with antonyms and synonyms.

Materials

Think of opposites like *hot/cold, brave/frightened, old/young, lazy/energetic,* and so on. Use a thesaurus to find synonyms for each word in the pair and write them on cards or in a list.

Procedure

Have students arrange the words along a continuum. At the ends of the continuum will be the antonyms (words that are most opposite in meaning). Next to each of these words students will decide where to place synonyms (words that are closest to the meaning of the opposite words) and so on until all words have been used.

For example, the words *balmy, frigid, chilly, boiling, frozen, tepid, hot, cool,* and *warm* could be arranged this way:

frigid   frozen   chilly   cool   tepid   balmy   warm   **hot**

First, students might work individually. Then they compare their continua with one another. They should discuss differences and provide rationale for why they arranged particular words the way they did. The dictionary will be the final judge of any disagreements.

Variations

1. Encourage students to add other words like *sweltering, steamy, balmy,* and so on by brainstorming or using a thesaurus or dictionary.
2. Give students a word pair of opposites and send them to a thesaurus to create a list of words. They can then order them as above or present them to another team to order.

FIGURE 8-9   Semantic Web

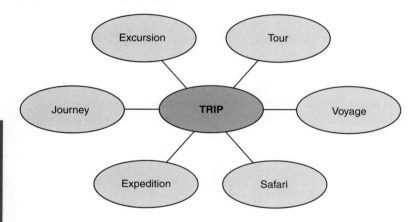

Semantic Webs 8-16

Semantic webs are graphic aids that may be used to (a) fine-tune students' understanding of words/concepts in the same semantic "family," and (b) expand students' vocabulary by presenting new terms. The example in Figure 8-9 elaborates and expands the concepts associated with *trip*. All the words except *excursion* are familiar to the students.

Procedures

1. When introducing semantic webs, present a completed web. Later, students will help you create them.
2. Have students discuss their understandings of the familiar words (as with the synonym/antonym activity, this discussion requires them to make finer distinctions among the concepts). As they discuss meanings, encourage them to use the words in sentences. As always, the dictionary can resolve uncertainties.
3. Ask students if they have heard or seen the unfamiliar word (*excursion*) before. Discuss its possible meanings. Check the dictionary.
4. Ask students if they can think of any other words that could be added to the web.

Variations

When students are used to this format, involve them in generating a web. Present your "core" word/concept, and then have students brainstorm other words that occur to them. You may then add one or two of your own words that will extend students' vocabulary.

Semantic Feature Analysis 8-17

This analysis (Anders & Bos, 1986) engages students in the examination of words/ definitions in relation to each other.

FIGURE 8-10   Semantic Feature Analysis

	Cannot Stand Alone	Comes Before a Base Word or Root Word	Usually Comes from Greek or Latin	Can Stand Alone	Comes After Base Word or Word Root
Prefix	+	+	+	-	-
Base word	-	-	?	+	-
Affix	+	?	+	-	?
Suffix	+	-	+	-	+
Word root	+	-	+	-	-

Following is a description of how the semantic feature analysis is constructed and taught.

- Write the words to be examined down the left margin of a matrix. (In this example, the words are *prefix, base word, affix, suffix,* and *word root.*) Then write the features of these words across the top. When you introduce this activity to students, list these features yourself. Later, after students understand how the analysis works, they can be involved in suggesting the features that will be listed.
- Discuss the matrix with the whole class or with small groups. Students will mark each cell with one of the following symbols: a plus sign (+) indicates a definite relationship between the word and a feature; a minus sign (−) indicates the word does not have that feature; and a question mark (?) indicates that students feel they need more information before responding.
- After students complete the matrix, point out (1) they now *really* know how much they know about each word; and (2) they also know what they still need to find out (Templeton, 1997).

Figure 8-10 illustrates a semantic feature analysis completed by a group of sixth grade students under the teacher's guidance to clarify the meanings of word study terms.

Which Suffix? 8-18

This activity is an excellent follow-up to previous work with base words, word roots, and suffixes. It is appropriate for individuals, buddies, or small groups. The suffixes included are: *-ible/-able, -tion/-sion, -ence/-ance, -ary/-ery.*

Materials

You will need a word sort board, word cards, and word study notebook.

Procedures

1. The teacher decides how many suffix pairs to place at the top of the word sort board. (Note that several of the words to be sorted may be placed under different suffixes, for example, *permit: permissible, permission.*) Each card has the base word written on one side and the same word with allowable suffixes on the other side.
2. The teacher mixes up the word cards and places the deck with base words faceup. The students in turn choose the top card and decide in which suffix category it belongs.

3. After all the cards are placed, the students record in their word study notebooks what they think is the correct spelling of the word.
4. After recording all the words, students turn the cards over to self-check the correct spelling.

Variations

Students can work as buddies to explore a particular suffix "team" (e.g., *-tion* and *-sion*) to see what generalization(s) may underlie the use of a suffix.

Defiance or Patience? 8-19

The game Defiance (if using the *ant/ance/ancy* family) or Patience (if using the *ent/ence/ency* family) is for three to five players. The object of the game is to make as many groups of two, three, or four cards of the same derivation and to be the first to run out of cards.

Materials

You will need to create a deck of 52 cards with suits of two, three, or four words (e.g., *attend*, *attendance*, and *attendant* is a set of three, while *radiate*, *radiant*, *radiance*, and *radiancy* is a set of four). Use words from the lists in Appendix E. Write each word across the top of a card, and your deck is prepared.

Procedures

1. Each player is dealt five cards from the deck. The player to the left of the dealer begins the game. The player may first lay down any existing groups of two, three, or four held in hand. This player then may ask any other player for a card of a certain derivation in his or her own hand: "Matthew, give me all of your *resistance*." (This could result in gaining *resistance*, *resistant*, *resistancy*, or *resist*.)
2. If a player does not have cards with the feature being sought, he or she responds, "Be Defiant" or "Be Patient," depending on which game is being played.
3. At this point, the asking player must draw another card from the deck. If the card is of the same family being sought, the player may lay down the match and continue asking other players for cards. If the card is not of the correct derivational group, play passes to the person on the left and continues around the circle in the same manner. If the drawn card makes a match in the asking player's hand, but was not that which was being sought, he or she must hold the pair in hand until his or her turn comes up again. Of course, this means there is a risk of another player taking the pair before the next turn.
4. Play ends when one of the students runs out of cards. The player with the most points wins.
5. Players may play on other people's card groups, laying related cards down in front of themselves, not in front of the player who made the original match.
6. Scoring is as follows.

Singles played on other people's matches	1 point
Pairs	2 points
Triples	6 points
Groups of four	10 points
First player to run out of cards	10 points

Variations

1. The game Defy My Patience could be the version that mixes sets of words from both lists to create an *ent/ant* deck.

2. **Challenge My Patience or Defy My Challenge:** In this version, during scoring, before everyone throws down his or her hand, students should secretly write additional words for groups they have laid down that have not been played. Before hands are revealed, these lists should be shared, and an additional point added to every player's score for each related word he or she wrote. If other players doubt the authenticity of a word claimed by an opponent, someone may challenge the word. The challenger loses a point if the word is valid, or gains a point if it is not. The player, likewise, counts the word if it is valid, or loses a point if the challenger proves him or her wrong.

3. Students should be encouraged to develop their own derivational families to be added to this game or another feature to be substituted for the *ant/ent* contrast.

Assimile 8-20

This game can be played by two to six players. It was created by Telia Blackard.

Materials

Gameboard modeled after Monopoly (see Figure 8-11); dice; game playing pieces; a deck of prefixes that can be assimilated (*ad-, sub-, in-, ex-, com-, ob-*); a deck of base words that can take assimilated prefixes (e.g., base words such as *company (accompany)* or *mortal (immortal)*; and a set of chance cards. The chance cards are similar to the base word cards but should be written on cards of a different color. Players will need a sheet of paper and pencil or pen to use in spelling words.

Procedures

This game is modeled after Monopoly.

1. Place base words facedown around the board, one in each space. A particular prefix is chosen as the focus, and placed faceup in the center of the board. Chance cards are also placed in the middle.

2. Players roll the dice to see who goes first. The player with the highest number rolls again and moves that number of spaces on the board.

FIGURE 8-11   Assimile Gameboard

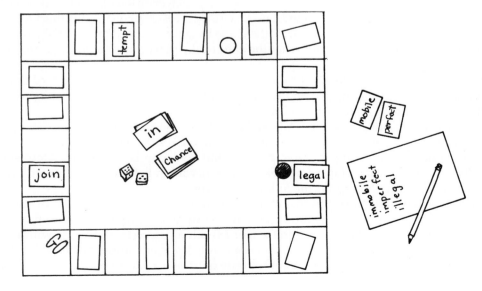

3. Upon landing on a particular space, the player turns up a word card and must determine whether this word can be assimilated to the prefix in the center of the board. If the card can be made into a word, the player attempts to both say the word and correctly spell it. A player who is able to correctly spell the word gets to keep the card. If the word cannot be assimilated, it is kept on the board faceup (this word will not be played again). However, if the word can be assimilated, but the player misspells the word, the card is turned back over to be played later in the game.
4. A player who is unable to come up with a word (for whatever reason) forfeits a turn, and play moves to the next player.
5. When a player passes "Go" or lands on a card that is faceup, he or she can draw from the chance pile. Chance cards provide players a chance to think of their own assimilated prefix word using the base word on the card and any assimilated prefix.
6. The game is over when all cards that can be played are played. The winner is the player with the most correctly spelled words.

Variations

A separate set of Community Chest cards using all of the original assimilated prefixes can be placed in the middle of the board, from which players can draw after each round of turns. This ensures that all prefixes are studied. (Community Chest cards will have the prefixes *ad-, in-, com-, ob-, sub-, ex-, per-,* and *dis-.*) With this method, the word cards that cannot be played with one particular prefix are turned back over until they are able to be played.

Rolling Prefixes 8-21

Players must be familiar with all types of assimilated prefixes to play this card game.

Materials

Create a deck of 32 word cards of assimilated prefixes (eight sets of four). Each group of four should consist of a mixed sort from each of the seven sets of assimilated prefixes: *ad-, in-, com-, ob-, sub-, ex-,* and *dis-.* One set will have to be a "wild set" (words with the aforementioned prefixes).

Procedures

1. Each player is dealt eight cards—three cards to each player on the first round, two cards to each player on the second round, and three cards to each player on the third round.
2. The player on the dealer's left starts the game by putting a card faceup in the center of the table. It does not matter what the card is; the player must read the word and state the prefix.
3. The next player to the left and the others that follow attempt to play a card of the same suit as the first one put on the table ("suit" meaning having the same prefix). Players must read their word and state the prefix.
4. If everybody follows suit, the cards in the center of the table are picked up after all the players have added their cards, and are put to the side. No one scores.
5. The game continues in the same fashion until someone is unable to follow suit. When this occurs, the player can look through his or her hand for a "wild card" and play it, changing the suit for the following players.
6. A player may change suit in this manner at any point in the game if he or she so chooses. For example, a player may play the word *collide* (prefix *com-*), and the next player may either play a *com-* prefix word (such as *concoct*) or a word with *com,* elsewhere in the word, such as *accommodate.* If the player chooses *accommodate,* the prefix the following player must concentrate on is *ad-* or a form of *ad-.*

7. A player who is unable to follow suit must pick up the center deck of cards. The player who picks up the cards begins the next round. The game continues this way until someone runs out of cards.

Variations

1. At first, players may not wish to state the original prefix of the words.
2. Multiple decks of assimilated prefixes can be made, allowing for variation.
3. Instead of ending the game after one person runs out of cards, the game can continue by the winner of the first round receiving one point for each card that the other players hold in their hands at the end of the game.

Eponyms: Places, Things, Actions 8-22

Eponyms are words that refer to places, things, and actions that have been named after an individual (from Greek *epi-*, after, + *noma*, name). Students' interest in word origins is often sparked by finding out where such words originate. As these words are discovered, they can be recorded in a special section of the word study notebook and/or displayed on a bulletin board.

Following is a sampler of common eponyms.

bloomers	Amelia Bloomer, an American feminist in the late 19th century
boycott	Charles Boycott, whose servants and staff refused to work for him because he would not lower rents
diesel	Rudolph Diesel, a German engineer who invented an alternative engine to the slow-moving steam engine
Ferris wheel	G. W. C. Ferris, designer of this exciting new ride for the 1893 World's Fair in Chicago
guillotine	Joseph Guillotin, a French physician and the inventor of the device
leotard	Jules Leotard, a French circus performer who designed his own trapeze costume
magnolia	Pierre Magnol, French botanist
pasteurize	Louis Pasteur, who developed the process whereby bacteria are killed in food and drink
sandwich	John Montagu, the Earl of Sandwich, who requested a new type of meal
sax	Antoine Joseph Sax, Belgian instrument maker, designer and builder of the first saxophone

The following resources include lists and information about eponyms:

Dale, D., O'Rourke, J., & Bamman, H. (1971). *Techniques of teaching vocabulary*. Palo Alto, Calif.: Field Educational Enterprises.

Terban, M. *Guppies in tuxedos: Funny eponyms*. New York: Clarion.

Derivational Relations Stage

Appendices

This section of the text contains seven segments, or Appendices. Appendix A provides the materials you will need for assessments. (Printable versions of these materials are also on the Assessment CD-ROM along with other assessments described in Chapter 2). Other Appendices contain pictures, sample sorts, word lists, and templates that you can use to create your own word study activities.

APPENDIX A

Assessment Materials

General Directions for Administering the Inventories

Students should not study the words in advance of testing. Assure students that they will not be graded on this activity, and that they will be helping you plan for their needs. Following is a possible introduction to the assessment.

> *I am going to ask you to spell some words. Spell them the best you can. Some of the words may be easy to spell; some may be difficult. When you do not know how to spell a word, spell it the best you can.*

Ask students to number their paper (or prepare a numbered paper for kindergarten or early first grade). Call each word aloud and repeat it. Say each word naturally, without emphasizing phonemes or syllables. Use it in a sentence, if necessary, to be sure students know the exact word. Sample sentences are provided along with the words. After administering the inventory, use a Feature Guide, Class Composite Form, and, if desired, a Spelling-by-Stage Classroom Organization Chart to complete your assessment. An Error Guide form is available on the Assessment CD-ROM.

Scoring the Inventory Using the Feature Guides

1. Make a copy of the appropriate Feature Guide (PSI p. 267, ESI p. 271, USI p. 274) for each student. Draw a line under the last word called if you called fewer than the total number and adjust the possible total points at the bottom of each feature column.
2. Score the words by checking off the features spelled correctly that are listed in the cells to the left of each word. For example, if a student spells *bed* as *bad*, he gets a check in the initial *b* cell and the final *d* cell, but not for the short vowel. Write in the vowel used (*a*, in this case), but do not give any points for it. If a student spells *train* as *trane*, she gets a check in the initial *tr* cell and the final *n* cell, but not for the long vowel pattern. Write in the vowel pattern used (*a–e* in this case), but do not give any points for it. Put a check in the "Correct" column if the word is spelled correctly. Do not count reversed letters as errors but note them in the cells. If unnecessary letters are added, give the speller credit for what is correct (e.g., if *bed* is spelled *bede*, the student still gets credit for representing the short vowel), but do not check "Correct" spelling.
3. Add the number of checks under each feature and across each word, double-checking the total score recorded in the last cell. Modify the ratios in the last row depending on the number of words called aloud.

 Use the Assessment CD-ROM to fill in feature guides. Totals and a class composite will be created for you.

Interpreting the Results of the Spelling Inventory

1. Look down each feature column to determine instructional needs. Students who miss only one (or two, if the features sample 8 to 10 words) can go on to other

features. Students who miss two or three need some review work; students who miss more than three need careful instruction on this feature. If a student did not get any points for a feature, earlier features need to be studied first.

2. To determine a stage of development, note where students first make two or more errors under the stages listed in the shaded box at the top of the Feature Guide. Circle this stage.

Using the Class Composite and Spelling by Stage Form

1. Staple each Feature Guide to the student's spelling paper and arrange the papers in rank order from highest total points to lowest total points.
2. List students' names in this rank order in the left column of the appropriate Classroom Composite (PSI p. 268, ESI p. 272, USI p. 275) and transfer each student's feature scores from the bottom row of the individual Feature Guides to the Classroom Composite. If you do not call out the total list, adjust the totals on the bottom row of the Classroom Composite.
3. Highlight cells where students make two or more errors on a particular feature to get a sense of your groups' needs and to form groups for instruction.
4. Many teachers find it easier to form groups using the Spelling-by-Stage Classroom Organization Chart. List each student under the appropriate spelling stage (the stage circled on the Feature Guide) and determine instructional groups.

NOTE: See Chapter 2 for more detailed directions for choosing, administering, scoring, interpreting, and using the inventories to form instructional groups.

Primary Spelling Inventory (PSI)

The Primary Spelling Inventory (PSI) is used in kindergarten through third grade. The 26 words are ordered by difficulty to sample features of the letter name–alphabetic to within word pattern stages. Call out enough words so that you have at least five or six misspelled words to analyze. For kindergarten or other emergent readers, you may only need to call out the first five words. In late kindergarten and early first grade classrooms, call out at least 15 words so that you sample digraphs and blends; use the entire list for late first, second, and third grades. If any students spell more than 20 words correctly, you may want to use the Elementary Spelling Inventory.

1. fan I could use a fan on a hot day. *fan*
2. pet I have a pet cat who likes to play. *pet*
3. dig He will dig a hole in the sand. *dig*
4. rob A raccoon will rob a bird's nest for eggs. *rob*
5. hope I hope you will do well on this test. *hope*
6. wait You will need to wait for the letter. *wait*
7. gum I stepped on some bubble gum. *gum*
8. sled The dog sled was pulled by huskies. *sled*
9. stick I used a stick to poke in the hole. *stick*
10. shine He rubbed the coin to make it shine. *shine*
11. dream I had a funny dream last night. *dream*
12. blade The blade of the knife was very sharp. *blade*
13. coach The coach called the team off the field. *coach*
14. fright She was a fright in her Halloween costume. *fright*
15. chewed The dog chewed on the bone until it was gone. *chewed*
16. crawl You will get dirty if you crawl under the bed. *crawl*
17. wishes In fairy tales wishes often come true. *wishes*
18. thorn The thorn from the rosebush stuck me. *thorn*
19. shouted They shouted at the barking dog. *shouted*
20. spoil The food will spoil if it sits out too long. *spoil*
21. growl The dog will growl if you bother him. *growl*
22. third I was the third person in line. *third*
23. camped We camped down by the river last weekend. *camped*
24. tries He tries hard every day to finish his work. *tries*
25. clapping The audience was clapping after the program. *clapping*
26. riding They are riding their bikes to the park today. *riding*

Words Their Way Primary Spelling Inventory Feature Guide

Student's Name _____   Teacher _____   Grade _____   Date _____

Words Spelled Correctly: ____ / 26   Feature Points: ____ / 56   Total: ____ / 82   Spelling Stage: _____

SPELLING STAGES →	EMERGENT LATE		LETTER NAME–ALPHABETIC			WITHIN WORD PATTERN		SYLLABLES AND AFFIXES		
			EARLY / MIDDLE	MIDDLE / LATE	LATE	EARLY / MIDDLE	MIDDLE	EARLY		
	Consonants									
Features →	Initial	Final	Short Vowels	Digraphs	Blends	Long Vowel Patterns	Other Vowels	Inflected Endings	Feature Points	Words Spelled Correctly
1. fan	f	n								
2. pet	p	t								
3. dig	d	g								
4. rob	r	b								
5. hope	h	p				o-e				
6. wait	w	t				ai				
7. gum	g	m								
8. sled			e		sl					
9. stick			i		st					
10. shine				sh		i-e				
11. dream					dr	ea				
12. blade					bl	a-e				
13. coach				-ch		oa				
14. fright					fr	igh				
15. chewed				ch			ew	-ed		
16. crawl					cr		aw			
17. wishes				-sh				-es		
18. thorn				th			or			
19. shouted				sh			ou	-ed		
20. spoil							oi			
21. growl							ow			
22. third				th			ir			
23. camped								-ed		
24. tries					tr			-ies		
25. clapping								-pping		
26. riding								-ding		
Totals	/7	/7	/7	/7	/7	/7	/7	/7	/56	/26

Words Their Way Primary Spelling Inventory Classroom Composite

Teacher _____   School _____   Grade _____   Date _____

SPELLING STAGES →	EMERGENT	LETTER NAME–ALPHABETIC			WITHIN WORD PATTERN			SYLLABLES AND AFFIXES		
	LATE	EARLY	MIDDLE	LATE	EARLY	MIDDLE	LATE	EARLY		
Students' ↓ Name	Consonants	Short Vowels	Diagraphs	Blends	Long Vowels	Other Vowels	Inflected Endings	Correct Spelling	Total Rank Order
	Initial	Final								
Possible Points	7	7	7	7	7	7	7	7	26	82
1.										
2.										
3.										
4.										
5.										
6.										
7.										
8.										
9.										
10.										
11.										
12.										
13.										
14.										
15.										
16.										
17.										
18.										
19.										
20.										
21.										
22.										
23.										
24.										
25.										
26.										
Highlight for instruction*										

*Highlight students who miss more than 1 on a particular feature; they will benefit from more instruction in that area.

Spelling-by-Stage Classroom Organization Chart

SPELLING STAGES →	EMERGENT			LETTER NAME–ALPHABETIC			WITHIN WORD PATTERN			SYLLABLES AND AFFIXES			DERIVATIONAL RELATIONS		
	EARLY	MIDDLE	LATE	EARLY	MIDDLE	LATE	EARLY	MIDDLE	LATE	EARLY	MIDDLE	LATE	EARLY	MIDDLE	LATE

CHAPTERS IN *WORDS THEIR WAY*	CHAPTER 4	CHAPTER 5	CHAPTER 6	CHAPTER 7	CHAPTER 8

Elementary Spelling Inventory (ESI)

The Elementary Spelling Inventory (ESI) covers more stages than the PSI. It can be used as early as first grade, particularly if a school system wants to use the same inventory across the elementary grades. The 25 words are ordered by difficulty to sample features of the letter name–alphabetic to derivational relations stages. Call out enough words so that you have at least five or six misspelled words to analyze. If any students spell more than 20 words correctly, use the Upper Level Spelling Inventory.

1.	bed	I hopped out of bed this morning.	*bed*
2.	ship	The ship sailed around the island.	*ship*
3.	when	When will you come back?	*when*
4.	lump	He had a lump on his head after he fell.	*lump*
5.	float	I can float on the water with my new raft.	*float*
6.	train	I rode the train to the next town.	*train*
7.	place	I found a new place to put my books.	*place*
8.	drive	I learned to drive a car.	*drive*
9.	bright	The light is very bright.	*bright*
10.	shopping	She went shopping for new shoes.	*shopping*
11.	spoil	The food will spoil if it is not kept cool.	*spoil*
12.	serving	The restaurant is serving dinner tonight.	*serving*
13.	chewed	The dog chewed up my favorite sweater yesterday.	*chewed*
14.	carries	She carries apples in her basket.	*carries*
15.	marched	We marched in the parade.	*marched*
16.	shower	The shower in the bathroom was very hot.	*shower*
17.	bottle	The bottle broke into pieces on the tile floor.	*bottle*
18.	favor	He did his brother a favor by taking out the trash.	*favor*
19.	ripen	The fruit will ripen over the next few days.	*ripen*
20.	cellar	I went down to the cellar for the can of paint.	*cellar*
21.	pleasure	It was a pleasure to listen to the choir sing.	*pleasure*
22.	fortunate	It was fortunate that the driver had snow tires.	*fortunate*
23.	confident	I am confident that we can win the game.	*confident*
24.	civilize	They wanted to civilize the forest people.	*civilize*
25.	opposition	The coach said the opposition would be tough.	*opposition*

Words Their Way Elementary Spelling Inventory Feature Guide

Student's Name _____ Teacher _____ Grade _____ Date _____

Words Spelled Correctly: ____ /25 Feature Points: ____ /62 Total: ____ /87 Spelling Stage: _____

Features →	Consonants Initial	Consonants Final	Short Vowels	Digraphs	Blends	Long Vowels	Other Vowels	Inflected Endings	Syllable Junctures	Unaccented Final Syllables	Harder Suffixes	Bases or Roots	Feature Points	Words Spelled Correctly
1. bed	b	d												
2. ship		p		sh										
3. when			e	wh										
4. lump	l		u		mp									
5. float		t			fl	oa								
6. train		n			tr	ai								
7. place					pl	a-e								
8. drive		v			dr	i-e								
9. bright					br	igh								
10. shopping			o	sh				pping						
11. spoil					sp		oi							
12. serving							er	ving						
13. chewed				ch			ew	ed						
14. carries							ar	ies	rr					
15. marched				ch			ar	ed						
16. shower				sh			ow			er				
17. bottle									tt	le				
18. favor							or		v	or				
19. ripen									p	en				
20. cellar									ll	ar				
21. pleasure											ure	pleas		
22. fortunate											ate	fortun		
23. confident											ent	confid		
24. civilize											ize	civil		
25. opposition											tion	pos		
Totals	/7		/5	/6	/7	/5	/7	/5	/5	/5	/5	/5	/62	/25

Words Their Way Elementary Spelling Inventory Classroom Composite

Teacher _____ School _____ Grade _____ Date _____

| SPELLING STAGES → | EMERGENT | LETTER NAME–ALPHABETIC | | | WITHIN WORD PATTERN | | | SYLLABLES AND AFFIXES | | | DERIVATIONAL RELATIONS | | |
| | EARLY LATE | MIDDLE LATE | | | EARLY MIDDLE LATE | | | EARLY MIDDLE LATE | | | EARLY MIDDLE | | |
Students' Name ↓	Consonants	Short Vowels	Digraphs	Blends	Long Vowels	Other Vowels	Inflected Endings	Syllable Junctures	Unaccented Final Syllables	Harder Suffixes	Bases or Roots	Correct Spelling	Total Rank Order
Possible Points	7	5	6	7	5	7	5	5	5	5	5	25	87
1.													
2.													
3.													
4.													
5.													
6.													
7.													
8.													
9.													
10.													
11.													
12.													
13.													
14.													
15.													
16.													
17.													
18.													
19.													
20.													
21.													
22.													
23.													
24.													
25.													
26.													
Highlight for instruction*													

Note: *Highlight students who miss more than 1 on a particular feature; they will benefit from more instruction in that area.

Upper-Level Spelling Inventory (USI)

The Upper-Level Spelling Inventory (USI) can be used in upper elementary, middle, high school, and postsecondary classrooms. The 31 words are ordered by difficulty to sample features of the within word pattern to derivational relations spelling stages. With normally achieving students, you can administer the entire list, but you may stop when students misspell more than eight words and are experiencing noticeable frustration. If any students misspell five of the first eight words, use the ESI to more accurately identify within word pattern features that need instruction.

1. switch — We can switch television channels with a remote control. *switch*
2. smudge — There was a smudge on the mirror from her fingertips. *smudge*
3. trapped — He was trapped in the elevator when the electricity went off. *trapped*
4. scrape — The fall caused her to scrape her knee. *scrape*
5. knotted — The knotted rope would not come undone. *knotted*
6. shaving — He didn't start shaving with a razor until 11th grade. *shaving*
7. squirt — Don't let the ketchup squirt out of the bottle too fast. *squirt*
8. pounce — My cat likes to pounce on her toy mouse. *pounce*
9. scratches — We had to paint over the scratches on the car. *scratches*
10. crater — The crater of the volcano was filled with bubbling lava. *crater*
11. sailor — When he was young, he wanted to go to sea as a sailor. *sailor*
12. village — My Granddad lived in a small seaside village. *village*
13. disloyal — Traitors are disloyal to their country. *disloyal*
14. tunnel — The rockslide closed the tunnel through the mountain. *tunnel*
15. humor — You need a sense of humor to understand his jokes. *humor*
16. confidence — With each winning game, the team's confidence grew. *confidence*
17. fortunate — The driver was fortunate to have snow tires on that winter day. *fortunate*
18. visible — The singer on the stage was visible to everyone. *visible*
19. circumference — The length of the equator is equal to the circumference of the earth. *circumference*
20. civilization — We studied the ancient Mayan civilization last year. *civilization*
21. monarchy — A monarchy is headed by a king or a queen. *monarchy*
22. dominance — The dominance of the Yankee's baseball team lasted for several years. *dominance*
23. correspond — Many students correspond through e-mail. *correspond*
24. illiterate — It is hard to get a job if you are illiterate. *illiterate*
25. emphasize — I want to emphasize the importance of trying your best. *emphasize*
26. opposition — The coach said the opposition would give us a tough game. *opposition*
27. chlorine — My eyes were burning from the chlorine in the swimming pool. *chlorine*
28. commotion — The audience heard the commotion backstage. *commotion*
29. medicinal — Cough drops are to be taken for medicinal purposes only. *medicinal*
30. irresponsible — It is irresponsible not to wear a seat belt. *irresponsible*
31. succession — The firecrackers went off in rapid succession. *succession*

Words Their Way Upper-Level Spelling Inventory Feature Guide

Student's Name _____ Teacher _____ Grade _____ Date _____

Words Spelled Correctly: _____ /31   Feature Points: _____ /68   Total: _____ /99   Spelling Stage: _____

SPELLING STAGES →	WITHIN WORD PATTERN			SYLLABLES AND AFFIXES			DERIVATIONAL RELATIONS			Feature Points	Words Spelled Correctly
	EARLY — MIDDLE — LATE			EARLY — MIDDLE — LATE			EARLY — MIDDLE — LATE				
Features →	Blends and Digraphs	Vowels	Complex Consonants	Inflected Endings and Syllable Juncture	Unaccented Final Syllables	Affixes	Reduced Vowels in Unaccented Syllables	Greek and Latin Elements	Assimilated Prefixes		
1. switch	sw	i	tch								
2. smudge	sm	u	dge								
3. trapped	tr			pped							
4. scrape		a-e	scr								
5. knotted		o	kn	tted							
6. shaving	sh			ving							
7. squirt		ir	squ								
8. pounce		ou	ce								
9. scratches		a	tch	es							
10. crater	cr			t	er						
11. sailor		ai			or						
12. village				ll	age						
13. disloyal		oy			al	dis					
14. tunnel				nn	el						
15. humor				m	or						
16. confidence						con	fid				
17. fortunate					ate			fortun			
18. visible						ible		vis			
19. circumference						ence		circum			
20. civilization							liz	civil			
Subtotals	/5	/9	/7	/8	/7	/4	/2	/4	/0	/46	/20

(Continued)

Words Their Way Upper-Level Spelling Inventory Feature Guide (Continued)

Student's Name _____ Grade _____ Date _____

Words Spelled Correctly: ____ / 31   Feature Points: ____ / 68   Total: ____ / 99   Spelling Stage: ____

Features →	WITHIN WORD PATTERN			SYLLABLES AND AFFIXES			DERIVATIONAL RELATIONS			Feature Points	Words Spelled Correctly
	Blends and Digraphs	Vowels	Complex Consonants	Inflected Endings and Syllable Juncture	Unaccented Final Syllables	Affixes	Reduced Vowels in Unaccented Syllables	Greek and Latin Elements	Assimilated Prefixes		
	EARLY — MIDDLE	MIDDLE — LATE	LATE	EARLY	MIDDLE	LATE	EARLY	MIDDLE	LATE		
21. monarchy								arch			
22. dominance						ance	min				
23. correspond							res		rr		
24. illiterate					ate				ll		
25. emphasize						size	pha				
26. opposition							pos		pp		
27. chlorine						ine		chlor			
28. commotion						tion			mm		
29. medicinal					al			medic			
30. irresponsible						ible	res		rr		
31. succession						sion			cc		
Subtotals	/ 0	/ 0	/ 0	/ 0	/ 2	/ 6	/ 5	/ 3	/ 6	/ 22	/ 11
Totals	/ 5	/ 9	/ 7	/ 8	/ 9	/ 10	/ 7	/ 7	/ 6	/ 68	/ 31

Words Their Way Upper-Level Spelling Inventory Classroom Composite

Teacher _____ School _____ Grade _____ Date _____

SPELLING STAGES →	WITHIN WORD PATTERN			SYLLABLES AND AFFIXES			DERIVATIONAL RELATIONS			
	EARLY / MIDDLE	MIDDLE / LATE	LATE	EARLY	MIDDLE / LATE	LATE	EARLY / MIDDLE	MIDDLE	LATE	
Students' Names	Blends and Digraphs	Vowels	Complex Consonants	Inflected Endings and Syllable Juncture	Unaccented Final Syllables	Affixes	Reduced Vowels in Unaccented Syllables	Greek and Latin Elements	Assimilated Prefixes	Total Rank Order
Possible Points	5	9	7	8	9	10	7	7	6	99
1.										
2.										
3.										
4.										
5.										
6.										
7.										
8.										
9.										
10.										
11.										
12.										
13.										
14.										
15.										
16.										
17.										
18.										
19.										
20.										
21.										
22.										
23.										
24.										
25.										
26.										
27.										
Highlight for instruction*										

*Highlight students who miss more than 1 on a particular feature if the total is between 5 and 8. Highlight those who miss more than 2 if the total is between 9 and 10.

Soundboards

Sound Board for Beginning Consonants and Digraphs

Beginning Consonants	**j** 🍶 jug	**s** ☀️ sun
b 🔔 bell	**k** 🔑 key	**t** ⛺ tent
c 🐱 cat	**l** 💡 lamp	**y** 🧶 yarn
d 🐕 dog	**m** 🐭 mouse	**w** ⌚ watch
f 🐟 fish	**n** 🥅 net	**v** 🚐 van
g 👻 ghost	**p** 🐷 pig	**z** 🤐 zip
h ✋ hand	**r** 💍 ring	

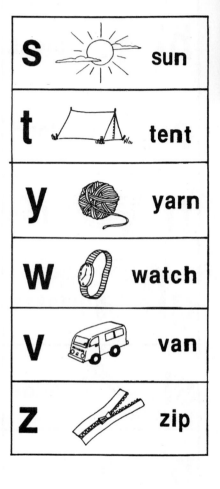

Beginning Digraphs

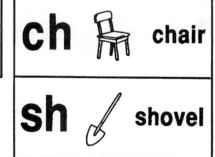

ch 🪑 chair
sh 🪏 shovel

th ✋ thumb
wh ☸️ wheel

Sound Board for Beginning Blends

Beginning Blends	br broom	sc scooter
bl block	cr crab	sk skate
cl cloud	dr drum	sm smile
fl flag	fr frog	sn snail
gl glasses	gr grapes	sp spider
sl slide	pr present	st star
pl 2+1=3 plus	tr tree	sw swing
tw twins	qu quilt	

Words Their Way: Word Study for Phonics, Vocabulary, and Spelling Instruction © 2008 by Pearson Education, Inc.

Sound Board for Long and Short Vowels

Short Vowels		Long Vowels			
a	cat	**a**	cake	**a**	tray
				a	rain
e	bed	**e**	feet	**e**	leaf
i	pig	**i**	kite	**i**	light
o	sock	**o**	bone	**o**	soap
u	cup	**u**	tube		

Pictures for Sorts and Games

The pictures that follow can be used in a number of ways. They can be used like clip art to create picture sorts. Suggested contrasts for picture sorts can be found in Chapters 4 and 5 or you can create your own. Simply make copies of the pictures you need (combining two, three, or four sounds) and glue them randomly onto a template such as the one on page 375. Create headers in the small boxes at the top of the template. (You can use the labels from the sound board boxes as headers.) You may also want to make a complete set of pictures to use for modeling, small-group work, or centers. Pictures can be copied on cardstock or glued to cardstock and perhaps colored and laminated for durability. Pictures can be used for games and other activities as well.

Pictures are grouped by beginning consonants, digraphs, blends, short vowels, and long vowels. The following list will help you find pictures for rhyme sorts, word families, additional short vowels, and long vowels. The pictures in bold type are in either the short- or long-vowel picture section while the others can be found by their beginning sound.

Long-Vowel Picture Rhymes

tape	game	**peas**	**beach**	deer	**slide**	fire
cape	frame	**cheese**	**peach**	spear	**bride**	tire
vine	**bone**	**soap**	**toad**	pear	moon	stool
nine	**cone**	rope	**road**	chair	spoon	spool
suit	gate	**tray**	snake	**glue**	jeep	**three**
fruit	plate	**hay**	**cake**	shoe	sleep	**bee**
flute	skate	pray	rake	zoo	sweep	tree
					sleep	key
hive	**rose**	**coat**	**cane**	**pie**	**whale**	
five	hose	boat	**rain**	tie	**snail**	
dive	nose	goat	**chain**	fly	**mail**	
drive	toes	float	plane	cry	**sail**	
			train	fry	**pail**	
					nail	
					scale	

Note: More long-vowel pictures found among initial sounds: paint, vase, shave, blade, grapes, leaf, seal, key, wheel, sleeve, queen, dream, dice, kite, pipe, smile, prize, climb, price, globe, snow, comb, ghost

Short-Vowel Picture Rhymes

glass	lamp	**vest**	pin	**wig**	switch	mitten
grass	stamp	nest	chin	**pig**	witch	kitten
pot	four	bus	trunk	duck	hook	**box**
dot	door	plus	skunk	truck	book	**fox**
						socks
bag	car	**net**	leg	**cut**	**sun**	wall
flag	jar	**jet**	egg	**hut**	**bun**	saw
tag	star	**pet**	peg	nut	**run**	claw
hen	**bed**	kick	**gum**	**hill**	bell	dog
men	shed	stick	drum	**mill**	well	log
ten	bread	chick	plum	spill	yell	jog
pen	sled	brick	thumb	drill	smell	frog
cap	**can**	**cat**	king	**sock**	**mug**	
map	**man**	**bat**	ring	**rock**	**bug**	
trap	fan	mat	wing	**lock**	**jug**	
clap	pan	hat	sting	**clock**	rug	
snap	van	bat	swing	block	plug	
mop	**zip**	**jack**	jump			
hop	**lip**	**sack**	stump			
top	ship	**pack**				
chop	whip	shack				
shop	skip	quack				
stop	clip	track				
	drip	crack				

Note: Bolded words may be found in vowel pictures and more short-vowel pictures found among initial sounds: gas, ham, mask, match, glass, crab, desk, check, dress, fish, six, bridge, swim, crib, cup, gum, tub, brush

Bb

Words Their Way: Word Study for Phonics, Vocabulary, and Spelling Instruction © 2008 by Pearson Education, Inc.

Appendix C

Cc

Dd		Ff

Words Their Way: Word Study for Phonics, Vocabulary, and Spelling Instruction © 2008 by Pearson Education, Inc.

Gg

Words Their Way: Word Study for Phonics, Vocabulary, and Spelling Instruction © 2008 by Pearson Education, Inc.

Appendix C

Kk

Words Their Way: Word Study for Phonics, Vocabulary, and Spelling Instruction © 2008 by Pearson Education, Inc.

Nn

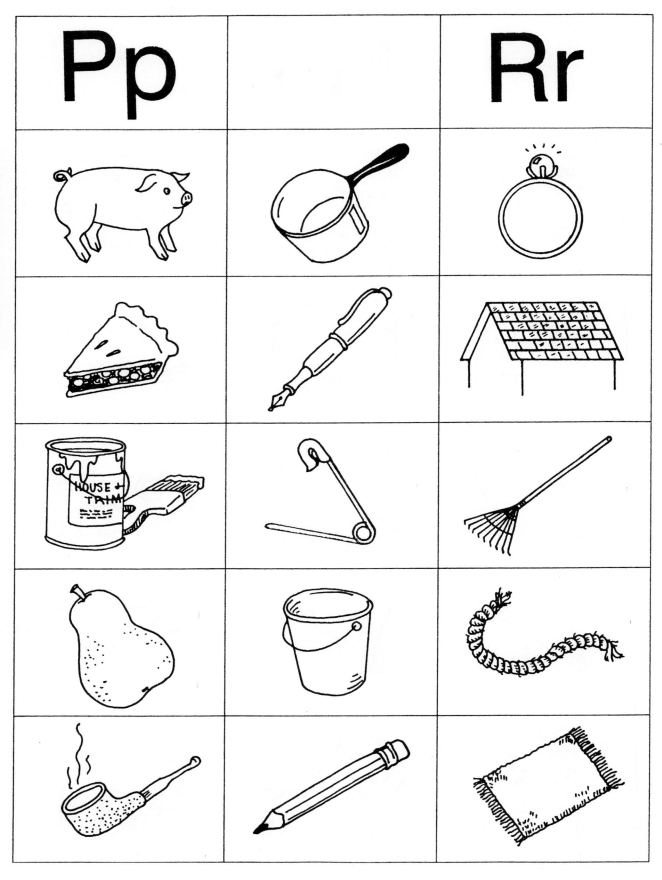

Pp		Rr

Ss

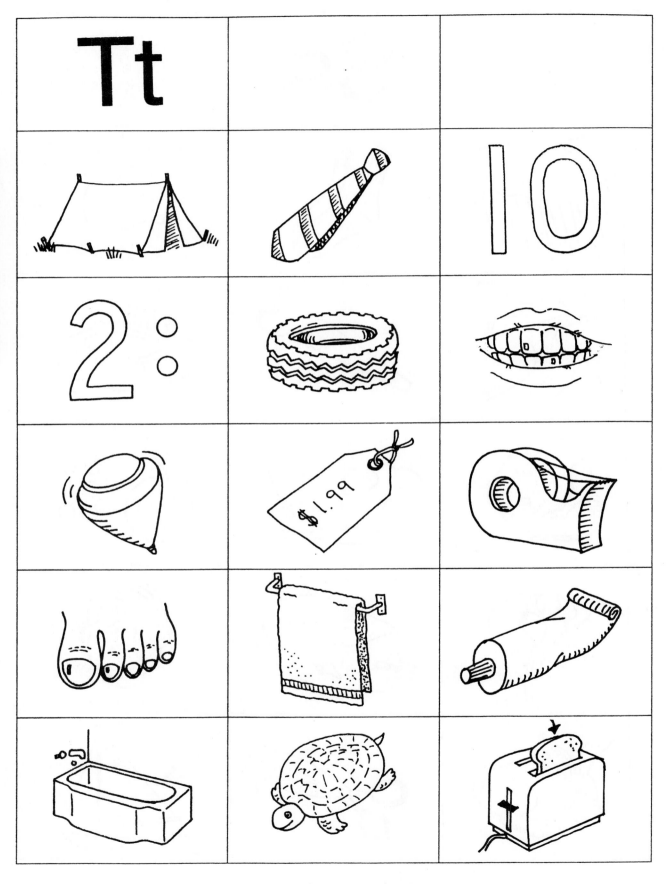

Words Their Way: Word Study for Phonics, Vocabulary, and Spelling Instruction © 2008 by Pearson Education, Inc.

Words Their Way: Word Study for Phonics, Vocabulary, and Spelling Instruction © 2008 by Pearson Education, Inc. **293**

Words Their Way: Word Study for Phonics, Vocabulary, and Spelling Instruction © 2008 by Pearson Education, Inc.

ch		sh

wh

Words Their Way: Word Study for Phonics, Vocabulary, and Spelling Instruction © 2008 by Pearson Education, Inc.

th		br
13		

Words Their Way: Word Study for Phonics, Vocabulary, and Spelling Instruction © 2008 by Pearson Education, Inc.

Appendix C

bl		cl

Words Their Way: Word Study for Phonics, Vocabulary, and Spelling Instruction © 2008 by Pearson Education, Inc.

cr		dr

Appendix C

gl	gr	fl

Words Their Way: Word Study for Phonics, Vocabulary, and Spelling Instruction © 2008 by Pearson Education, Inc.

	fr	**pr**

pl		**qu**

Words Their Way: Word Study for Phonics, Vocabulary, and Spelling Instruction © 2008 by Pearson Education, Inc.

Appendix C

| sc | | sk |

sl	sm	sn

Words Their Way: Word Study for Phonics, Vocabulary, and Spelling Instruction © 2008 by Pearson Education, Inc.

sp		sw

st		tw

Words Their Way: Word Study for Phonics, Vocabulary, and Spelling Instruction © 2008 by Pearson Education, Inc.

tr		

Words Their Way: Word Study for Phonics, Vocabulary, and Spelling Instruction © 2008 by Pearson Education, Inc.

a		e
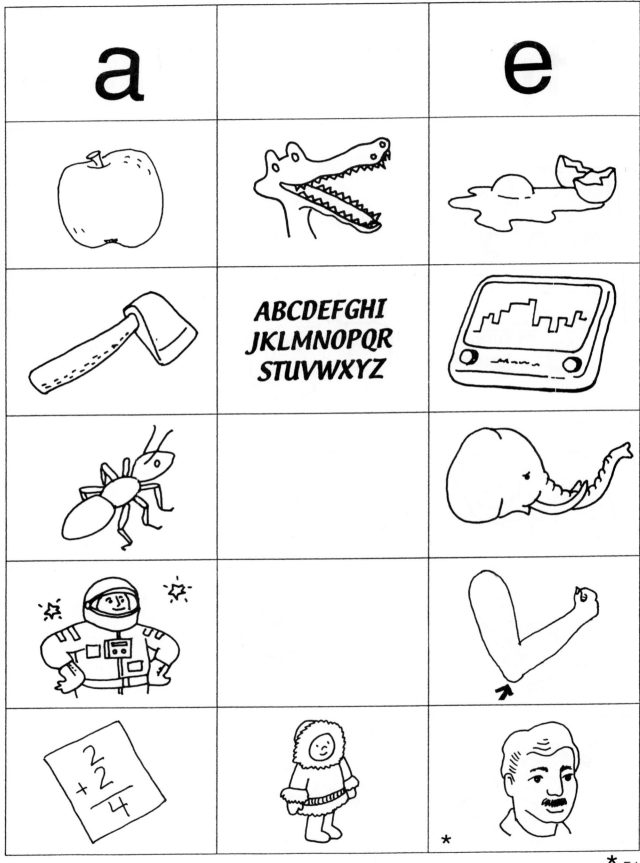		

ABCDEFGHI
JKLMNOPQR
STUVWXYZ

*

* Ed

Words Their Way: Word Study for Phonics, Vocabulary, and Spelling Instruction © 2008 by Pearson Education, Inc.

i	o	u

Words Their Way: Word Study for Phonics, Vocabulary, and Spelling Instruction © 2008 by Pearson Education, Inc.

ĕ

Words Their Way: Word Study for Phonics, Vocabulary, and Spelling Instruction © 2008 by Pearson Education, Inc.

Words Their Way: Word Study for Phonics, Vocabulary, and Spelling Instruction © 2008 by Pearson Education, Inc.

ā

ē

Words Their Way: Word Study for Phonics, Vocabulary, and Spelling Instruction © 2008 by Pearson Education, Inc.

Words Their Way: Word Study for Phonics, Vocabulary, and Spelling Instruction © 2008 by Pearson Education, Inc.

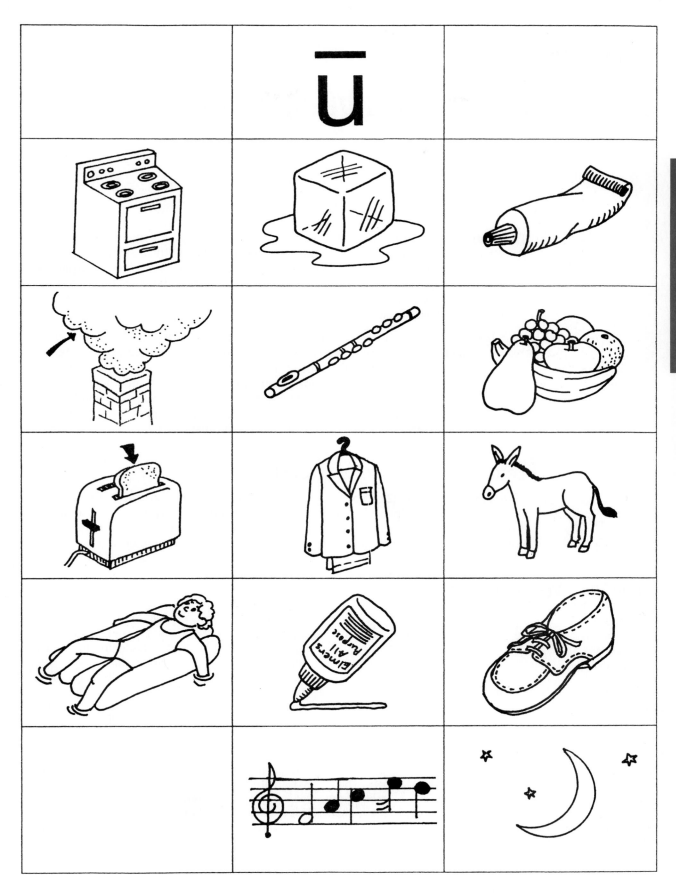

$\bar{u}$

Sample Word Sorts by Spelling Stage

The sample word sorts on the following pages are arranged sequentially by spelling stage and can be used with many of the activities described in the instructional chapters. Prepare word sorts to use with your students by writing the words on a template such as the one on page 376. Be sure to write the words on the template randomly so students can make their own discoveries as they sort. Several points need to be made considering the use of these sorts.

- These sorts are not intended to be a sequence for all students. Chapters 2 will help you match your students to the stages of spelling. There are additional suggestions in each instructional chapter about the pacing and sequencing of word study for each stage. Choose appropriate sorts from among those presented here.
- This is not an exhaustive list of sorts, but it does give you a starting point for creating your own. You can adapt these sorts by adding, deleting, or substituting words that are more appropriate for your students. Word lists are provided in Appendix E.

Letter Name–Alphabetic Sorts

Words from sorts 1 to 22 can be used in connection with games and activities in Chapter 5, but letter name–alphabetic spellers will also need to study initial consonants, digraphs, blends, and short vowels with picture sorts. Use the pictures in the previous section to create these sorts and refer to Table 5-3 for a scope and sequence.

Same Short-Vowel Families

1. Short -a

cat	man
bat	can
sat	pan
fat	ran
mat	fan
rat	van
hat	tan

2. More Short -a's

sad	cap	bag
mad	tap	rag
dad	map	wag
had	nap	tag
pad	lap	flag
	rap	

3. Short -i

sit	big
bit	wig
hit	pig
fit	dig
kit	fig
quit	

4. More Short -i's

pin	pill	rip	sick
win	will	lip	pick
fin	fill	hip	lick
thin	hill	zip	kick
chin	mill	dip	tick
	bill		chick
	kill		

5. Short -o

not	hop
got	pop
hot	mop
lot	cop
pot	stop
dot	shop
shot	

6. More Short -o's

job	lock	dog
rob	rock	log
cob	sock	frog
mob	dock	fog
blob	clock	jog
sob	block	

7. Short -e

pet	ten	bed	bell
net	hen	red	tell
met	pen	fed	well
set	men	led	fell
jet	then	sled	shell
bet	when		
get			

8. Short -u

cut	tub	bug	fun	duck
nut	rub	rug	bun	luck
hut	cub	dug	run	suck
but	club	jug	sun	truck
shut		hug	gun	tuck
		tug		

Mixed Short-Vowel Families

9. Short -a, -i, -u

man	pin	fun
can	win	run
fan	fin	sun
ran	thin	bun
than	grin	gun
plan	chin	
van	skin	

10. Short -a, -i, -o, -u

cat	sit	not	cut
mat	fit	hot	mut
hat	hit	got	nut
sat	kit	pot	but
rat	bit	rot	hut
that	pit	cot	shut
	quit	dot	

11. Short -a, -i, -e

bag	big	pill	bell
rag	wig	will	sell
wag	pig	hill	tell
flag	jig	fill	well
tag	dig	bill	fell
snag	fig	spill	shell
		drill	smell

12. Families with ck

back	sick	lock	duck	neck
sack	lick	rock	suck	peck
tack	pick	sock	tuck	deck
jack	tick	dock	truck	speck
pack	kick	clock		
black	chick	block		

13. Preconsonantal Nasals

camp	jump	band	sink
lamp	dump	hand	pink
ramp	hump	sand	think
stamp	stump	land	wink
damp	lump	stand	
drink			

14. Families Ending in sh

mash	fish	mush
cash	dish	hush
trash	wish	rush
rash	swish	gush
dash		brush
crash		
flash		

Short Vowels, CVC

15. Short -a and Short -o

cat	not	*
bag	job	was
mad	top	for
pan	fox	
pat	pop	
cab	got	
jam	top	

16. Short -e and Short -u

pet	but	*
bell	sun	put
red	cup	push
yes	mud	
let	cut	
ten	hug	
beg	duck	
	gum	

17. Short -a, Short -i, and Short -o

hat	big	pop
fan	six	rock
cab	lip	box
tax	did	mom
bat	dig	stop
back	zip	not
	will	hop
	win	hot

18. All Short Vowels

can	let	hit	rock	hug
that	fed	fish	mop	luck
lap	met	fill	dot	run
last	web	six	box	bus
sack	fell	this	rob	pup
	wet	sick		bun
		wig		rug

19. Short Vowels with Digraphs

that	ship	when
chat	chill	check
than	whip	shed
shall	this	shell
shack	whiz	then
chap	chip	them
wham	thin	
	thick	

20. Two-Step Sort with Blends and Short Vowels

a. Initial consonant and blends

rack	tack	dug	trick	drum
rag	tag	dip	track	drill
rash	tap	duck	trash	drag
rug	tick		trap	drug
rip			trip	drip
			truck	

b. Short-vowels

tack	tick	truck
tap	trip	drum
trash	drill	dug
drag	dip	rug
rack	rip	duck
rag	trick	drug
rash	drip	
trap		

21. Two-Step Sort with Blends and Short Vowels

a. Blends

cram	slip	spill
crab	slid	spin
crash	slap	spot
crib	clock	snap
brag	blob	
brat	flag	
grip	flop	
	flock	

b. Vowels

crab	clip	trot
cram	slid	drop
brag	spill	spot
brat	grip	flop
slap	slip	clock
crash	spin	blob
flag	crib	flock
snap	twig	

22. Two Step Sort with Presconsonantal Nasals

a. Preconsonantal Nasals

sang	camp	pant	pink	sand
king	lamp	plant	think	land
sing	stamp	print	junk	
swing	limp	hunt	trunk	
sting	jump	want		
sung	bump			

b. Short Vowels

sang	king	jump	*
camp	limp	sung	want
sand	print	bump	
lamp	pink	junk	
pant	sing	hunt	
land	think	trunk	
plant	swing	skunk	
stamp	sting		

*Note: Odd balls are marked asterisk.

Within Word Pattern Sorts

Words from sorts 23 to 65 can be used in connection with games and activities in Chapter 6. The asterisk marks the oddball category.

23. Short/Long -*a*

hat	name	*
jack	date	have
ask	race	what
slap	plane	
fast	cape	
lap	page	
flag	same	
pass	safe	
path	gave	
glad	gate	

24. Short/Long -*a*

cap	lake	rain
last	wave	wait
plan	late	nail
sat	tape	gain
flat	bake	fail
tax	base	pail
	shade	plain
	made	sail
	maze	
	sale	

25. Long -*a* Patterns

same	mail	day	*
whale	pain	say	said
flake	train	play	have
grape	paid	may	
stage	brain	pay	
grade	snail	stay	
chase	chain	clay	
shave	tail		
tale	waist		
waste			

26. Short/Long -*e*

well	week	she
step	peel	he
west	weed	we
men	peek	me
bed	speed	
help	keep	
belt	pee	

27. Short/Long -*e*

best	green	mean	*
left	wheel	team	been
neck	sheet	deal	head
bell	need	reach	
bled	bleed	beach	
yet	teeth	steam	
	creep	clean	
	speed	bean	

28. Short/Long -*e*

mess	head	neat
rest	dead	meal
bell	deaf	speak
kept	breath	meat
nest	death	treat
shell	dread	sneak
vest	bread	heat

29. Short/Long -*i*

dish	hike	*
chip	ride	give
king	ripe	live
whip	nice	
twin	white	
miss	dime	
pink	fine	
rich	life	

30. Short/Long -*i*

clip	mine	try	*
win	price	fly	eye
trick	spine	shy	buy
gift	lime	why	bye
list	wife	sky	
mitt	vine	dry	
thick	five		
swim			

31. Short/Long -*o*

lock	home	*
odd	slope	move
crop	note	gone
shot	hose	some
clock	vote	
shock	joke	
knob	smoke	
slot	hope	
	choke	

32. Long -*o* Patterns

rope	road	blow	*
woke	boat	grow	now
close	soap	know	cow
stone	soak	slow	
bone	moan	throw	
phone	loaf	snow	
broke	coach	low	
hole	load	bow	
vote	toast	flow	

33. Short/Long -*u*

bun	June	blue	*
fuss	cute	glue	truth
luck	rule	clue	
lump	tube	due	
trust	tune	true	
plum	huge		
crust	cube		

34. Long -*u* Patterns

rude	fruit	new	*
crude	suit	chew	fuel
flute	juice	drew	build
mule	bruise	knew	
fume	cruise	stew	
chute		few	
dune		dew	
use		brew	

35. Less Common Long -*a*

hay	prey	eight	break
tray	they	weigh	great
stray	obey	vein	steak
pray	hey	veil	
sway		freight	
play		sleigh	
		neigh	

36. *R*-influenced *a*

car	care	chair	*
star	share	pair	bear
bark	bare	hair	
card	mare	air	
far	rare		
dark	scare		
arm	hare		
start			

37. Less Common Long -*e*

greed	chief	these	*
speech	field	scene	vein
greet	brief	theme	friend
creek	grief	eve	seize
fleet	shriek		
geese	piece		
cheese	thief		
	niece		

38. *R*-influenced *e*

her	near	cheer	bear	*
fern	clear	deer	pear	heart
germ	dear	sneer	wear	
jerk	year	queer	swear	
herb	spear	peer		
herd	beard			
perch				

39. Long -*i* Patterns

kite	might	mind
bride	night	wild
write	right	kind
spice	bright	blind
hide	light	find
wipe	tight	child
mice	sight	mild
		grind

40. *R*-blends/
R-influenced *i*

grin	third	hire
bring	shirt	tire
drip	dirt	fire
grill	bird	wire
trick	skirt	tired
drink	girl	
brick		
crib		

41. Ambiguous/Long -*o*

soft	roll	ghost	*
moth	cold	most	son
cost	stroll	host	from
cross	mold	post	
cloth	scold		
lost	fold		
toss	told		
frost	folk		
long			

42. *R*-influenced *o*

for	more	door	*
born	store	poor	your
short	chore	floor	
porch	tore		
storm	shore		
north	score		
fort	wore		
torch	swore		

*Note: Odd balls are marked asterisk.

Words Their Way: Word Study for Phonics, Vocabulary, and Spelling Instruction © 2008 by Pearson Education, Inc.

43. *Other Long -u*

gloom	new	who
bloom	grew	to
roost	crew	too
smooth	flew	two
scoop	blew	
school	stew	
mood	dew	
pool	knew	

44. *R-influenced u*

hurt	cure	heard
turn	pure	learn
church	sure	earn
burst	lure	pearl
curl		yearn
purr		earth
purse		search

45. *R-blends/Vowels*

grill	girl
trap	tarp
crush	curl
fry	first
price	purse
track	dark
brag	bark
drip	dirt
frog	fort

46. *R-influenced Vowels*

car	her	for
shark	first	short
farm	bird	corn
hard	burn	horn
card	word	scorn
yard	worm	torn
scar	world	
march	dirt	
	jerk	

47. *ck, k, ke*

lick	leak	like
lack	seek	lake
tack	soak	take
snack	sleek	snake
stuck	weak	stake
stick	week	strike
whack	croak	wake

48. CVCe Sorts Across Vowels

cave	drive	drove	huge
crane	while	those	fume
taste	smile	throne	prune
stage	twice	phone	chute
trade	crime	wrote	flute
waste	guide	quote	mule

49. Sorts Across Long Vowels

day	team	fine	rope	rule
gate	seat	light	post	fruit
mail	free	pie	gold	blue
trade	field	wild	coal	tube
stay	street	time	stone	
eight	she	shy	throw	

50. CVVC Across Vowels

road	team	rain	*
boast	stream	strain	board
coach	sweet	claim	great
groan	queen	waist	
throat	peach	faith	
toast	thief	praise	
roast	peace	strain	
		trail	

Ambiguous Vowels and Complex Consonants

51. Diphthongs

toy	coin	town	sound
boy	foil	clown	mouth
joy	boil	brown	scout
	spoil	gown	round
	noise	frown	couch
	point	howl	loud

52. More Diphthongs

row	owl	out
snow	growl	found
blown	drown	shout
flown	crown	cloud
grown	plow	south
thrown	fowl	foul
	prowl	doubt

53. Ambiguous Vowels

salt	hawk	fault	*
bald	draw	caught	fought
chalk	lawn	cause	ought
stall	raw	taught	
false	crawl	sauce	
small	claw	haul	
walk	paw	pause	

54. Words Spelled with *w*

watch	war	wrap
swamp	warn	wreck
swan	warm	write
wand	dwarf	wrist
swat	swarm	wren
wash	wart	wrong

55. Complex Consonants

scram	straight	shrank	square
scrape	strange	shrink	squawk
scratch	stretch	shred	squint
screech	strict	shrunk	squash
screw	string	shriek	squeeze
screen	strong	shrimp	squirt
scrap			

56. *ch* and *tch*

catch	reach	*
witch	coach	rich
patch	peach	such
fetch	roach	
hutch	screech	
itch	beach	
switch	pouch	
ditch		
latch		

57. *ge* and *dge*

badge	page
ridge	stage
edge	huge
fudge	rage
bridge	cage
judge	
hedge	
lodge	

58. Hard and Soft *c* and *g* Across Vowels

cave	coat	cute	cent	cyst
camp	coast	cup	cell	gym
cast	cost	cue	cease	
gave	gold	gum	gem	
gain	golf	gush	germ	
gasp	goof			

59. *ce, ge, ve, se*

dance	charge	glove	cheese
chance	large	give	please
prince	wedge	curve	tease
fence	dodge	shove	loose
since	ridge	live	choose
voice	edge	above	
juice	change	have	

Concept Sorts

60. What Lives in Water?

Yes	No
frog	toad
fish	lizard
whale	zebra
sea turtle	tortoise
clam	elephant
crab	horse

61. Edible Plants

Grain	Fruit	Vegetable
wheat	apples	carrots
oats	peaches	beans
rice	berries	lettuce
rye	pears	cucumber
barley	bananas	cabbage
	oranges	beets

62. Animal Attributes

Fish	Bird	Mammal
scale	feather	hair
eggs	eggs	born alive
gills	lungs	lungs
heart	heart	heart
no legs	two legs	legs
fins	wings	

63. States

East	West	North	South
Virginia	California	Maine	Florida
North Carolina	Nevada	Vermont	Mississippi
Maryland	Utah	New York	Texas
Delaware	Arizona		Alabama

64. Geometry Terms

Shapes	Lines	Measurements
triangle	ray	perimeter
rhombus	angle	degrees
square	line	diameter
rectangle	right angle	circumference
parallelogram	obtuse angle	area
isosceles triangle		radius

65. Solar System Concept Sort

Planets	Other Bodies	Events	Movements
Mercury	asteroid	eclipse	revolution
Uranus	meteorite	lunar eclipse	axis
Jupiter	satellite	solar eclipse	orbit
Mars	meteor		rotation
Venus	comet		
Neptune			
Saturn			

Syllables and Affixes Sorts

Words from sorts 66 to 107 can be used in connection with games and activities in Chapter 7. The asterisk heads the oddball category.

Inflected Endings (ed and ing), Consonant Doubling, and Plurals

66. Sort for Sound of *ed*

trapped	waited	played
mixed	dotted	mailed
stopped	patted	boiled
chased	treated	raised
cracked	traded	tried
walked	ended	filled
asked	handed	seemed
jumped	needed	yelled

67. Plural Words (*s* and *es*)

cows	boxes	buses	dishes
chicks	mixes	glasses	benches
farms	axes	dresses	watches
fences	foxes	passes	lashes
gates		gases	churches
horses		guesses	ashes
			brushes

68. Plurals with *y*

babies	plays
carries	monkeys
ponies	boys
bodies	trays
pennies	donkeys
worries	enjoys
daddies	turkeys
berries	valleys
parties	

69. Base Words + *ed* and *ing*

jump	jumped	jumping
hike	hiked	hiking
dress	dressed	dressing
wait	waited	waiting
stop	stopped	stopping
pass	passed	passing
live	lived	living
wag	wagged	wagging

70. Adding *ing* (double and e-drop)

batting	baking
shopping	skating
bragging	biting
hopping	hoping
humming	sliding
begging	waving
skipping	moving
swimming	caring

71. Adding *ing* (double, *e*-drop, nothing)

trimming	diving	pushing	floating	*
running	riding	jumping	raining	mixing
popping	sliding	finding	sleeping	taxing
dragging	driving	kicking	boating	
wagging	wasting	wanting	waiting	
quitting	whining	munching	cheering	

72. Past Tense Verbs

kneel	knelt	chase	chased
teach	taught	mix	mixed
bring	brought	walk	walked
deal	dealt	bake	baked
sweep	swept	shop	shopped
send	sent		
think	thought		
lend	lent		
drink	drank		

73. Adding *ed* (double, nothing)

slipped	picked	traded
grabbed	called	baked
stopped	tracked	wasted
wagged	peeled	liked
tripped	watched	stared
knotted	cheered	waved
rubbed	talked	skated
whizzed	dreamed	tasted

74. Adding *ing* to *k* words (*ck, e*-drop, CVVC, VCk)

tacking	baking	leaking	asking
sticking	flaking	speaking	spending
tracking	shaking	croaking	shrinking
plucking	smoking	squeaking	drinking
wrecking	stroking	hooking	marking
clucking	making	looking	working
quacking	raking	cooking	frisking

Use with Double Crazy Eights Game.

Syllable Juncture Sorts, Open and Closed Syllables (VCCV, VCV)

75. Compound Words

landfill	downtown	backyard	homework
homeland	downstairs	backbone	homemade
wasteland	lowdown	backpack	hometown
landlord	downcast	backward	homeroom
landslide	downfall	bareback	homesick
landscape	downpour	flashback	
landmark	breakdown	piggyback	
mainland	countdown	paperback	

76. VCCV at Juncture (same/different)

button	market
sunny	garden
yellow	signal
happy	member
happen	basket
sitting	center
fellow	plastic
matter	tablet

77. Syllable Juncture (VCCV, open VCV)

tablet	baby
napkin	human
happen	music
winter	fever
foggy	silent
tennis	duty
sudden	writer
fossil	rival

78. VCV Open and Closed

meter	petal	*
human	rapid	water
secret	punish	busy
paper	magic	
lazy	shiver	
even	comet	
major	river	
climate	clever	
crater	proper	
clover	liquid	
bacon		

Use with Slap Jack Activity.

Appendix D

79. Closed VCCV/Open VCV

funny	picture	pilot
summer	expert	navy
pretty	until	nature
dollar	forget	music
butter	napkin	spoken
gossip	canyon	frozen
letter	sister	spider
pattern	army	student
	number	

80. Closed/Open with Endings

sadden	dusting	sliding
chipped	rented	shining
matted	helping	named
scarred	sifted	scaring
winner	faster	rider
biggest	longest	tamest
running	walker	moping

81. VCC/CV, VC/CCV, and V/V

athlete	pilgrim	create *
pumpkin	control	poet cruel
English	complete	riot
Kingdom	children	trial
mushroom	monster	lion
halfway	kitchen	diet
	hundred	

Unaccented Syllable Sorts

82. le and el

fable	camel	*
angle	angel	pencil
little	model	journal
rattle	gravel	
settle	motel	
cattle	bushel	
nibble	level	
turtle	pretzel	
table	travel	
middle	smaller	

83. er, ar, or

bigger	burglar	doctor
freezer	grammar	favor
dreamer	collar	author
faster	dollar	editor
blister	lunar	tractor
jogger	solar	motor
speaker		mayor
skater		
smaller		

84. er, ar, or

Comparatives	Agents	Things
sweeter	worker	cellar
thinner	teacher	meter
smarter	waiter	river
slower	voter	pillar
younger	actor	anchor
gentler	beggar	vapor
steeper	director	trailer
cheaper	barber	mother
		flower

85. or, ar, er and Parts of Speech

Noun	Adjective	Comparative Adjective
doctor	lunar	cooler
anchor	solar	cleaner
mirror	proper	braver
motor	similar	slower
tractor		quicker
freezer		older
lumber		lighter
ladder		stronger

86. Final en/on/in/ain

broken	dragon	cousin	mountain
hidden	weapon	cabin	captain
heaven	apron	napkin	fountain
chosen	ribbon	pumpkin	curtain
children	gallon		certain
eleven	cotton		

87. Unaccented First Syllables

again	decide	beyond
away	design	begin
another	defend	between
aloud	debate	behave
agree	depend	before
afraid		beside
awoke		

88. /j/ Sound

carriage	budget	magic
voyage	agent	engine
message	angel	region
postage	gorgeous	fragile
village	danger	margin
storage	legend	logic
sausage	pigeon	
savage	dungeon	
courage	gadget	

89. Changing y to i

cry	cries	cried
hurry	hurries	hurried
party	parties	partied
empty	empties	emptied
baby	babies	babied
reply	replies	replied
supply	supplies	supplied
carry	carries	carried
fry	fries	fried

90. y Words by Part of Speech

Long -i		Long -e	
Verb	Noun	Adjective	Adverb
try	celery	happy	happily
certify	candy	pretty	correctly
apply	gypsy	guilty	clearly
occupy	quarry	angry	safely
rely	country	silly	horribly
	cemetery		hourly
	category		certainly
	copy		sensibly

Words Their Way: Word Study for Phonics, Vocabulary, and Spelling Instruction © 2008 by Pearson Education, Inc.

Appendix D

Sorts to Explore Stress

91. Stress in Homographs

re'cord n.	re cord' v.
protest n.	protest v.
conduct n.	conduct v.
subject n.	subject v.
extract n.	extract v.
permit n.	permit v.
insert n.	insert v.
desert n.	desert v.
rebel n.	rebel v.
combat n.	combat v.
conflict n.	conflict v.

92. Stress in VCCV Words

per'son	at tend'
welcome	perform
offer	support
expert	survive
harvest	escape
fellow	allow
barber	disturb
tender	suppose
common	hello
urgent	raccoon

93. Stress in VCV words

bi'son	a lone'
major	relay
pirate	amaze
climate	remote
agent	away
fever	obey
rated	refuse
dozing	salute
raven	erase

94. Long -u in Stressed Syllable

bu' gle	a muse'
future	compute
ruby	confuse
rumor	reduce
tulip	perfume
tuna	pollute
tutor	salute
super	excuse
pupil	abuse
ruler	include

Revisiting Patterns in Longer Words

95. Short -a/ Long -a

canvas	agent
lantern	basic
package	cradle
tragic	fatal
attic	labor
bandage	vapor
candle	sacred
cannon	April

96. Patterns for Long -a

debate	explain	layer
mistake	dainty	dismay
amaze	trainer	payment
parade	complain	crayons
engage	acquaint	hooray
bracelet	raisin	decay
estate	refrain	betray
escape	painter	

97. Patterns for Long -u and -o patterns

rooster	useful	toaster	suppose
cartoon	refuse	oatmeal	decode
scooter	amuse	approach	remote
balloon	reduce	loafer	erode
noodle	conclude	rowboat	tadpole
	pollute	goalie	lonesome
	perfume		explode

98. Patterns for Long -e and -i

needle	reason	polite	highway	*
succeed	eager	decide	lightning	sweater
fifteen	increase	advice	delight	believe
thirteen	defeat	invite	tonight	
canteen	season	surprise	resign	
steeple	conceal	survive		

99. Diphthongs in Two Syllables

moisture	joyful
appoint	boycott
poison	royal
turquoise	soybean
moisten	oyster
pointless	voyage
broiler	annoy
embroider	enjoy
rejoice	destroy
noisy	employ
avoid	
pointed	

100. More Dipthongs in Two Syllables

county	flower	*
council	allow	double
lousy	brownie	
fountain	vowel	
mountain	shower	
scoundrel	towel	
counter	tower	
around	chowder	
bounty	coward	
foundry	drowsy	
mouthful	powder	
rowdy	prowler	
	power	

101. Spelling the /er/ Sound in Stressed and Unstressed Syllables

cer′tain	re verse′	sur prise′	lan′tern
person	observe	perhaps	concert
thirsty	alert	survive	modern
service	prefer	surround	western
hurry	emerge		govern
turkey			

102. Words with *ure* and *er* (*ture, sure, cher*)

capture	measure	archer	*
creature	treasure	butcher	injure
fracture	pleasure	preacher	failure
mixture	closure	stretcher	
pasture	leisure	teacher	
texture		rancher	
future			
nature			

103. Advanced Homophones

Spelling Change in Stressed Syllable		Spelling Change in Unstressed Syllable	
aloud	allowed	patience	patients
cinder	sender	accept	except
morning	mourning	alter	altar
berry	bury	miner	minor
roomer	rumor	council	counsel
kernel	colonel	hanger	hangar
vary	very	profit	prophet
censor	sensor	lesson	lessen
incite	insight	presence	presents

104. Prefixes

unfair	retell	disagree
unable	replay	disappear
uncover	retrain	disgrace
unkind	return	disarm
undress	reuse	disorder
unplug	research	disobey
unequal	regain	disable
uneven	reword	displaced
unpack	rebuild	disloyal
unusual	remodel	dishonest

105. More Prefixes

preschool	explode	misspell
preview	exceed	mistreat
prevent	expose	misplace
preheat	explore	misuse
prefix	exile	misbehave
prepare	expand	mistake
predict	exclaim	

106. Number Prefixes

unicycle	bicycle	tricycle
unison	biweekly	trilogy
unicorn	bisect	triangle
unique	bilingual	tripod
uniform	biplane	triple
universe	bifocals	trio
		triplets

107. Suffixes

darkness	harmless	colorful
kindness	fearless	faithful
illness	homeless	dreadful
weakness	restless	thankful
freshness	ageless	thoughtful
hardness	mindless	painful
blindness	helpless	

Derivational Relations Sorts

Words from sorts 108 to 123 can be used in connection with games and activities in Chapter 8.

Adding Suffixes

108. Adding *-ion*

ct + *-ion*		*ss* + *-ion*	
act	action	express	expression
distinct	distinction	impress	impression
select	selection	process	procession
extinct	extinction	depress	depression
predict	prediction	success	succession
subtract	subtraction	profess	profession
contract	contraction	discuss	discussion
affect	affection		

109. E-drop + *-ion*

te + *-ion*		*ce* + *-ion*		*se* + *-ion*	
educate	education	induce	induction	expulse	expulsion
congratulate	congratulation	introduce	introduction	convulse	convulsion
create	creation	produce	production	repulse	repulsion
decorate	decoration	deduce	deduction		
generate	generation	reproduce	reproduction		
imitate	imitation	reduce	reduction		
fascinate	fascination				
complicate	complication				
separate	separation				

Words Their Way: Word Study for Phonics, Vocabulary, and Spelling Instruction © 2008 by Pearson Education, Inc.

110. -sion and Spelling Changes

t to s + -sion		de-drop, + -sion	
commit	commission	explode	explosion
transmit	transmission	collide	collision
permit	permission	conclude	conclusion
emit	emission	persuade	persuasion
omit	omission	erode	erosion
regret	regression	delude	delusion
remit	remission	include	inclusion
		divide	division
		intrude	intrusion

111. E-drop + -ation or -ition

e-drop + -ation		e-drop + ition	
admire	admiration	compose	composition
determine	determination	define	definition
explore	exploration	dispose	disposition
combine	combination	oppose	opposition
declare	declaration	expose	exposition
inspire	inspiration	decompose	decomposition
organize	organization		
examine	examination		
perspire	perspiration		

112. -ible and -able

base + -able	root + -ible
dependable	audible
expendable	edible
breakable	visible
agreeable	feasible
predictable	terrible
remarkable	possible
readable	legible
profitable	plausible
perishable	horrible
punishable	tangible
laughable	credible

113. -able after e

e-drop	soft ce/ge	hard c/g
presumable	changeable	navigable
desirable	manageable	amicable
usable	peaceable	despicable
lovable	serviceable	impeccable
deplorable	noticeable	applicable
comparable		
excusable		

114. Related words + -able and -ible

-ation to -able		-sion or -tion to -ible	
toleration	tolerable	collection	collectible
separation	separable	contraction	contractible
education	educable	reduction	reducible
vegetation	vegetable	exhaustion	exhaustible
application	applicable	repression	repressible
observation	observable	expression	expressible
navigation	navigable	production	producible

115. Assimilated Prefix Sort

com-	ad-	in-
compound	adverse	inactive
conform	affair	irresponsible
colleague	affront	immature
compact	assemble	irrational
context	affirm	immortal
correlate	arrange	illogical
constrain	acclaim	innumerable
	admit	illegal

Vowel Alternations

116. Vowel Alternations in Related Pairs

Long -a to Short -a	Long -a to Schwa
cave/cavity	major/majority
humane/humanity	narrate/narrative
nation/national	relate/relative
volcano/volcanic	famous/infamous
grave/gravity	able/ability
nature/natural	native/nativity
insane/insanity	educate/educable

117. Vowel Alternations in Related Pairs

Long -e to Short -e	Long -e to Schwa
serene/serenity	compete/competition
brief/brevity	repeat/repetition
proceed/procession	remedial/remedy
recede/recession	
succeed/succession	
conceive/conception	
receive/reception	

118. Vowel Alternations in Related Pairs

Long -*i* to Short -*i*	Long -*i* to Schwa
resign/resignation	invite/invitation
sign/signal	define/definition
divine/divinity	reside/resident
divide/division	recite/recitation
revise/revision	deprive/deprivation
deride/derision	admire/admiration
	inspire/inspiration
	preside/president

119. Vowel Alternations in Related Pairs

Long -*u* to Short -*u*	Long -*o* to Schwa
induce/induction	compose/composition
seduce/seduction	propose/proposition
misconstrue/misconstruction	impose/imposition
conduce/conduction	expose/exposition
reduce/reduction	harmonious/harmony
produce/production	

120. Vowel Alternation Patterns in Related Words

Long to Short	Long to Schwa	Schwa to Short
prescribe/prescription	compose/composition	metal/metallic
sage/sagacity	proclaim/proclamation	brutal/brutality
profane/profanity	stable/stability	local/locality
criticize/criticism	preside/president	spiritual/spirituality
telescope/telescopic	impose/imposition	vital/vitality
microscope/microscopic		fatal/fatality
cone/conic		total/totality
flame/flammable		normal/normality
arise/arisen		final/finality
		original/originality

Sorting by Roots

121. Latin Stems (contrast 3 or 4 at a time)

judge	traction	suspect	visual	formulate	credit	portable	dictate
adjudicate	contract	spectator	visionary	uniform	incredible	porter	dictate
judgment	attract	inspect	vision	reform	discredit	reporter	contradict
judicial	intractable	respect	vista	transform	creed	portfolio	prediction
prejudice	subtraction	spectacular	visible	deformed	credulous	export	verdict
judicious	tractor	inspector	revise	nonconformist	accredit	import	dictionary
prejudicial	contraction	spectacles	television				dictator
judiciary	protractor	disrespect	supervise				diction
	distraction	expectation					
		circumspect					

conduct	fertile	pressure	respiration
induct	refer	express	spirit
educate	transfer	depression	expire
introduction	suffer	suppress	perspire
produce	conifer	impression	inspiration
reduce	conference	oppressive	conspire
induction			

Words Their Way: Word Study for Phonics, Vocabulary, and Spelling Instruction © 2008 by Pearson Education, Inc.

Appendix D

122. Greek Roots

autograph	telegram
automatic	telepathy
autobiography	telegraph
autonomy	televise
automobile	telephone
autonomous	teleconference

123. Greek and Latin Science Vocabulary Sort

astro	astronomer, astronaut, astrology, astrolabe
bio	biology, biome, biosphere, biotic
chlor	chlorophyll, chloroplast, chlorine, chlorella
eco	ecology, economy, ecosystem, ecotype
hydro	hydrophobia, hydrology, hydrogen
hypo	hypodermis, hypodermic, hypothermia, hypotension
photo/phos	phosphorescent, photography, telephoto
vor	voracious, omnivore, carnivore

Appendix D

Word Lists

Creating Your Own Word Sort Sheets

The following lists of words are organized by features students need to study in the letter–name alphabetic through derivational relations stages. Under each feature the words are generally grouped by frequency and complexity. For example, under short -*a*, the early part of the list contains words most likely encountered by first graders (*am*, *ran*, *that*). The latter part of the list contains words that may be obscure in meaning and spelled with blends or digraphs (*yam*, *brass*, *tramp*).

The following lists include possible exceptions or oddballs that can be added to sorts. Sometimes the oddballs you include will be true exceptions (such as *said* in a sort with long -*a* patterns), but other times oddballs may represent a less common spelling pattern, such as *ey* representing long -*a* in *prey* and *grey*.

Prepare word sorts to use with your students by writing the selected words on a template such as the one on page 376. We recommend that you enlarge it about 5–8% before writing in the words neatly. Be sure to write the words randomly so students can make their own discoveries as they sort. Many people find it easy to create computer-generated word sort sheets using the "table" function in a word processing program. First set the margins all around at .5, and then insert a table that is three columns by six to eight rows. Type in words in each cell, leaving a blank line before and after each word. After typing in all words, "select" the entire table and click on the "center" button. Select a simple font (Ariel and Geneva work well) and a large font size (26 works well). After creating the sort, save it using a name that defines the features such as "Short Vowels: a, o, e." You can contrast sounds, spelling patterns, word endings, prefixes, root words, and so on. Create a template that you use each time.

Here are some reminders and tips about creating your own word sorts.

1. Create sorts that will help your students form their own generalizations about how words work. Use a collection of 15 to 25 words so that there are plenty of examples to consider.
2. Contrast at least two and up to four features in a sort. There are many sample sorts in Appendix D to give you ideas.
   Examples of sound sorts:
   Contrast short -*o* and long -*o*.
   Contrast the sound of *ear* in *learn* and in *hear*.
   Contrast the sound of *g* in *guest* and *gym*.
   Examples of pattern sorts:
   Contrast long -*o* spelled with *oa*, *o-e*, and *ow*.
   Contrast words that end with *or*, *er*, and *ar*.
   Contrast words that double a consonant before -*ing* with those that do not.

Fry's 300 Instant Sight Words

First Hundred

a	can	her	many	see	us
about	come	here	me	she	very
after	day	him	much	so	was
again	did	his	my	some	we
all	do	how	new	take	were
an	down	I	no	that	what
and	eat	if	not	the	when
any	for	in	of	their	which
are	from	is	old	them	who
as	get	it	on	then	will
at	give	just	one	there	with
be	go	know	or	they	work
been	good	like	other	this	would
before	had	little	our	three	you
boy	has	long	out	to	your
but	have	make	put	two	
by	he	man	said	up	

Second Hundred

also	color	home	must	red	think
am	could	house	name	right	too
another	dear	into	near	run	tree
away	each	kind	never	saw	under
back	ear	last	next	say	until
ball	end	leave	night	school	upon
because	far	left	only	seem	use
best	find	let	open	shall	want
better	first	live	over	should	way
big	five	look	own	soon	where
black	found	made	people	stand	while
book	four	may	play	such	white
both	friend	men	please	sure	wish
box	girl	more	present	tell	why
bring	got	morning	pretty	than	year
call	hand	most	ran	these	
came	high	mother	read	thing	

Third Hundred

along	didn't	food	keep	sat	though
always	does	full	letter	second	today
anything	dog	funny	longer	set	took
around	don't	gave	love	seven	town
ask	door	goes	might	show	try
ate	dress	green	money	sing	turn
bed	early	grow	myself	sister	walk
brown	eight	hat	now	sit	warm
buy	every	happy	o'clock	six	wash
car	eyes	hard	off	sleep	water
carry	face	head	once	small	woman
clean	fall	hear	order	start	write
close	fast	help	pair	stop	yellow
clothes	fat	hold	part	ten	yes
coat	fine	hope	ride	thank	yesterday
cold	fire	hot	round	third	
cut	fly	jump	same	those	

Appendix E

Examples of meaning sorts:
> Contrast words derived from *spect* and *port*.
> Contrast words with prefixes *sub*, *un*, and *trans*.

The best sorts are those that combine a sound sort with a pattern sort. For example, a long *-o* and short *-o* sort can begin with a sound sort and then proceed to sort the long vowels by patterns—CVVC and CVCe.

3. In most sorts, include up to three oddballs—words that have the same sound or pattern but are not consistent with the generalization that governs the other words. For example, in a long *-o* sort, with words sorted by the *oa*, *o-e*, and *ow* patterns, the exceptions might include the words *now* and *love* since they look like they would have the long *-o* sound but do not. The best oddballs are high-frequency words students already know from reading. These are marked with asterisks under "oddballs" in the word lists in Appendix E and a list of Fry's top 300 words is on page 333.

4. Words in a sort can be made easier or harder in a number of ways.
   - Common words like *hat* or *store* are easier than uncommon words like *vat* or *boar*. It is important to use words students know from their own reading in the letter name–alphabetic and within word pattern stages to make sorts easier. This is less important when you get to syllables and affixes and derivational relations where words sorts can help to extend a student's vocabulary.
   - Add words with blends, digraphs, and complex consonant units (i.e., *ce*, *dge*, or *tch*) to make words harder. *Bat* and *blast* are both CVC words, but *blast* is harder to read and spell.
   - Adding more oddballs to a sort makes the sort harder. Oddballs should never, however, constitute more than about 20% of the words in a sort or students might fail to see the generalizations that govern the majority of words. Don't use oddballs children are not likely to know (like *plaid* in a long *-a* sort for students early in the within word pattern stage).

a Families

at	*ad*	*ag*	*an*	*ap*	*ab*	*am*	*all*	*ar*	*art*
at*	had*	bag	man*	cap	cab	am**	all*	bar	cart
cat	bad	rag	than**	lap	dab	dam	ball*	car	dart
bat	dad	sag	ran**	gap	jab	ham	call*	far	mart
fat	mad	wag	can	map	nab	ram	tall**	jar	part
hat	pad	nag	fan	nap	lab	jam	fall	par	tart
mat	sad	flag	pan	rap	tab	clam	hall	star	start
pat	rad	brag	tan	yap	blab	slam	mall		chart
rat	glad	drag	van	tap	crab	cram	wall		smart
sat	lad	shag	plan	zap	scab	wham	small		
that*		snag	clan	clap	stab	swam	stall		
flat		lag	scan	flap	grab	yam			
brat		tag		slap	slab	gram			
chat				trap					
gnat				chap					
				snap					
				wrap					
				strap					

*occurs in first 100 high frequency words

**occurs in second 100 high frequency words

Words Their Way: Word Study for Phonics, Vocabulary, and Spelling Instruction © 2008 by Pearson Education, Inc.

and	*ang*	*ash*	*ack*	*ank*	*amp*	*ast*	*ant*	*atch*	*ass*
hand**	bang	bash	back**	bank	camp	fast	ant	batch	mass
band	fang	cash	pack	sank	damp	cast	pant	catch	pass
land	hang	dash	jack	tank	lamp	past	chant	hatch	class
sand	sang	gash	rack	yank	ramp	last	slant	latch	grass
brand	rang	hash	lack	blank	champ	mast	grant	match	brass
grand	clang	mash	sack	plank	clamp	vast	plant	patch	glass
stand**		rash	tack	crank	cramp			snatch	bass
strand		sash	black**	drank	stamp			scratch	
		lash	quack	prank	tramp				
		trash	crack	spank	scamp				
		crash	track	thank					
		smash	shack						
		slash	snack						
		clash	stack						
		flash							

More Short -*a* Words

as*	wax	bath	fact	draft	ranch	*Oddballs*	
has*	ask	path	mask	shaft	grasp	want**	saw**
gal	yak	task	bask	craft	plant	what*	laugh
pal	tax	calf	raft	staff	shall*	was*	
gas	math	half	lamb	graph	branch		

e Families

et	*en*	*ed*	*ell*	*eg*	*ess*	*eck*	*est*	*end*	*ent*
get*	men**	red**	tell*	beg	less	deck	best**	end**	bent
let**	den	bed	bell	peg	mess	neck	nest	bend	dent
bet	hen	fed	cell	leg	guess	peck	pest	lend	cent
met	ten	led	fell	keg	bless	wreck	rest	mend	lent
net	pen	wed	jell		dress	speck	test	send	rent
pet	then*	bled	sell		press	check	vest	tend	sent
set	when*	fled	well		stress	fleck	west	blend	tent
wet	wren	sled	shell				chest	spend	vent
vet	Ben	shed	smell				jest	trend	went
fret	Ken	shred	spell				chest		scent
jet			swell				crest		spent
yet			dwell				guest		

More Short -*e*

								Spelled ea	
yes	gem	pep	left**	melt	self	etch	clench	read	death
web	them*	step	kept	pelt	shelf	fetch	drench	head	breath
egg	hem	held	slept	knelt	fresh	sketch	tempt	bread	dread
elm	stem	help	wept	lens	flesh	wretch	tenth	dead	deaf
	next**	desk	swept			stretch	debt	lead	

*occurs in first 100 high frequency words

**occurs in second 100 high frequency words

Appendix E

Short -*i* Families

it	*id*	*ig*	*in*	*ill*	*im*	*ip*	*ick*	*ink*	*int*	*itch*	*ing*
it*	did*	big**	in*	will*	dim	dip	lick	link	mint	itch	king
bit	hid	dig	fin	dill	him	hip	kick	mink	lint	pitch	ping
fit	lid	fig	pin	fill	Jim	lip	pick	pink	hint	ditch	sing
hit	kid	jig	tin	hill	Kim	nip	sick	sink	print	pitch	ring
lit	bid	pig	din	kill	rim	rip	tick	rink	glint	hitch	wing
pit	rid	rig	win	gill	Tim	sip	slick	wink	flint	witch	thing**
sit	slid	wig	bin	mill	trim	tip	quick	think**		switch	bring**
kit	skid	zig	thin	pill	brim	zip	trick	blink			sling
wit		twig	twin	till	swim	whip	chick	drink			sting
skit			chin	bill	slim	clip	flick	stink			swing
spit			shin	drill	whim	flip	brick	clink			spring
slit			spin	grill	grim	slip	stick	shrink			string
quit			grin	chill	skim	skip	thick				cling
				skill		drip	click				fling
				spill		trip	prick				wring
				still		chip					
				thrill		ship					
				quill		snip					
						strip					

More Short -*i*

											Oddballs
if*	him*	mix	mitt	crib	cliff	rich	film	risk	swift	disc	child
is*	his*	six	hiss	fish	stiff	wind	tilt	brisk	inch	sixth	mind
with*	this*	fix	kiss	dish	lift	fist	limp	sift	pinch	fifth	find
wish*	which*	whiz	milk	swish	gift	inn	limb	shift			climb

o Families

ot		*ob*	*og*	*op*	*ock*	*ong*	*oss*
not**	blot	bob	dog	cop	cock	long*	boss
got**	slot	cob	bog	hop	dock	bong	toss
hot	plot	job	fog	pop	lock	gong	moss
jot	shot	rob	hog	mop	mock	song	loss
lot	spot	gob	jog	top	rock	strong	gloss
pot	knot	mob	log	slop	sock	throng	cross
cot	trot	sob	clog	flop	tock		
dot		snob	frog	drop	block		
		blob		shop	clock		
		glob		stop	flock		
		knob		crop	smock		
		throb		plop	shock		
				prop	stock		

*occurs in first 100 high frequency words

**occurs in second 100 high frequency words

Words Their Way: Word Study for Phonics, Vocabulary, and Spelling Instruction © 2008 by Pearson Education, Inc.

More Short -o Words

					Ambiguous Sounds of o*			Oddballs	
box**	rod	prod	fond	notch	on*	lost	moth	of*	for*
ox	sod	odd	bond	romp	off	cost	cloth	won	from*
fox	god	mom	blond	stomp	loft	frost	broth	son	cold
pox	plod	con	gosh	prompt	soft	doll	golf	front	post

*These words do not have a short -o in some dialects, but instead are pronounced as /aw/.

u Families

ut	ub	ug	um	un	ud	uck	ump	ung
but*	cub	bug	bum	run*	bud	buck	bump	sung
cut	hub	dug	gum	fun	mud	duck	jump	rung
gut	rub	hug	hum	gun	stud	luck	dump	hung
hut	tub	jug	sum	bun	thud	suck	hump	lung
nut	club	mug	plum	sun		tuck	lump	swung
rut	grub	rug	slum	spun		yuck	pump	clung
jut	snub	tug	scum	stun		pluck	rump	strung
shut	stub	slug	chum			cluck	plump	slung
strut	scrub	plug	drum			truck	stump	sprung
	shrub	drug	strum			stuck	thump	wrung
		snug					clump	flung
							slump	stung
							grump	

uff	unk	ush	ust	unch	umb
buff	bunk	gush	must*	bunch	dumb
cuff	hunk	hush	just*	hunch	numb
huff	junk	mush	gust	lunch	crumb
muff	sunk	rush	dust	munch	thumb
ruff	chunk	blush	bust	punch	plumb
puff	drunk	brush	rust	crunch	
fluff	flunk	crush	crust	brunch	
stuff	skunk	flush	trust		
snuff	shrunk	slush			
scuff	stunk				
gruff	slunk				
bluff	trunk				

More Short u Words

					ul*	ou = u	o = u	o-e = u	Oddballs
up*	much*	buzz	gull	hunt	gulp	tough	of*	come	put*
us*	such*	fuzz	dull	grunt	bulge	rough	does	some	push
pup	plus	tusk	mutt	stunt	bulk	touch	son	none	bush
cup	thus	dusk	butt	shucks	gulf	young	ton	done	truth
bus	fuss	husk	tuft	gruff	sulk		won	love	
					pulse		from*	dove	
							front	glove	

*These words have a slightly different u sound before the l.

*occurs in first 100 high frequency words

**occurs in second 100 high frequency words

Long -a Words

CVCe

a-e

made*	ate	wake	tame	ape	pane
name*	gate	fake	fame	gape	vane
same	hate	shake	flame	grape	mane
came*	late	brake	blame	drape	slate
make*	date	flake	lame	trace	scale
take*	sale	base	lane	grace	stale
bake	male	vase	plane	space	gaze
cake	tale	chase	cane	waste	daze
lake	whale	race	crane	paste	blaze
age	pale	lace	rate	taste	graze
cage	fade	place	fate	haste	haze
page	wade	pace	crate	sake	range
face	shade	state	grate	quake	change
gave	grade	plate	bathe	drake	strange
save	trade	skate	cave	phase	
wave	shape	rage	grave	jade	*Oddballs*
tape	cape	stage	slave	blade	
safe	mate				

CVVC

ai

rain	wait	snail
pain	bait	frail
tail	gain	praise
nail	vain	trail
mail	main	strait
sail	plain	saint
pail	chain	quaint
rail	stain	strain
fail	drain	faith
jail	grain	straight
gain	brain	
main	aim	
train	claim	
aid	ail	
paid	aide	*Oddballs*
maid	raid	said*
laid	paint	again*
braid	waist	their*
have		
dance		
chance		

CVV-open

ay

day
jay
may
play
say
stay
way
clay
gray
pray
tray
slay

ey

they*
prey
grey
hey

CVVC

ei

eight
neigh
rein
weigh
weight
eighth
freight
reign
veil
sleigh
weigh
beige

ea

break
great
steak

Long -e Words

CVCe

e-e

eve
scene
scheme
theme
these

open

me*
he*
we*
be*
the*

she*

CVVC

ea

read**	beak	east	leave
sea	leak	feast	weave
eat	weak	least	flea
beat	peak	clean	peace
seat	lean	steal	please**
meat	heal	knead	cease
mean	real	sneak	crease
bean	deal	creak	grease
seal	meal	steam	squeal
tea	heap	dream	league
pea	leap	cream	breathe
bead	seam	scream	squeak
neat	each**	stream	
team	teach	plead	*Oddballs*
beam	beach	knead	*head*
lead	reach	beast	*dead*
ear**	peach	treat	steak
			great
			break

ee

see*	deep	tree**	sheep
seem*	beep	flee	sleep
bee	seep	glee	creep
feed	jeep	knee	steep
feel	keep	free	sweep
feet	seek	three**	creek
beet	week	kneel	cheek
meet	beef	steel	sleek
seen	reef	wheel	speech
week	deep	speed	teeth
peek	eel	bleed	sleet
wee	heel	greed	greet
free	reel	breed	sheet
seed	peel	keen	sweet
need	deed	green	fleet
tree	weed	queen	street
peep	knee		three

spree
geese
cheese
sneeze
breeze
freeze
sleeve
screen
preen

Oddballs
been*
seize
weird
vein
suite

ie

thief
chief
grief
brief
yield
field
shield
niece
piece
shriek
priest
grieve
fierce
fiend
siege
pier

Oddballs
friend**

*occurs in first 100 high frequency words

**occurs in second 100 high frequency words

Words Their Way: Word Study for Phonics, Vocabulary, and Spelling Instruction © 2008 by Pearson Education, Inc.

Long -*i* Words

CVCe						CV open		iCC	
i-e						*ie*	*y/ye*	*igh*	
like*	five**	while**	wide	white**	tribe	lie	my*	high**	find**
bike	mine	ice	slide	quite	scribe	pie	by*	night**	kind**
dime	fine	mice	pride	write	stride	tie	why**	right**	mind
time	nine	nice	tide	spite	stripe	die	fly	light	climb
hide	vine	rice	glide	site	strike		cry	might	child
ride	shine	mile	wipe	lice	spine	*Oddballs*	sky	bright	wild
side	drive	file	pipe	spice	whine	buy	try	fight	blind
line	dive	pile	swipe	slice	prime	guy	dry	sigh	grind
live	hive	smile	spike	twice	chime	live**	shy	tight	hind
kite	life	wise	lime	price	fife	give*	sly	flight	sign
size	ripe	rise	crime	guide	knife	prince	spry	fright	bind
bite	hike	wife	pine	prize	thrive	since	dye	sight	wind
							lye	slight	hind
							rye	thigh	rind

Long -*o* Words

CVCe				CVVC			Open	CVV	VCC	
o-e				*oa*			*o*	*ow*	*oCC*	
home*	wove	rove	slope	boat	foam	float	go*	bow	old*	both**
nose	drove	cove	lope	coat	roam	coach	no*	know*	gold	most**
hole	dome	stove	lone	goat	goal	roach	so*	show	hold	folk
rope	globe	whole	stroke	road	coal	throat	ho	slow	cold	roll
robe	cone	sole	throne	toad	loaf	toast	yo-yo	snow	told	poll
note	zone	wrote	quote	load	coax	coast		crow	fold	stroll
hose	role	choke	clothe	soap	whoa	boast	*Oddballs*	blow	mold	scroll
hope	stole	broke		oat	loan	roast	to*	glow	sold	post
vote	doze	poke		oak	moan	cloak	do*	grow	bold	ghost
code	froze	smoke		soak	groan	croak	who*	sow	scold	host
mole	pose	yoke		whoa	moat	loaves	two*	low	bolt	
pole	chose	spoke						tow	colt	
joke	those	tone		*Oddballs*				flow	jolt	
stone	close	shone		one*	love	some*	broad	own**	volt	
	owe	phone		done*	dove	come*	sew	flown		
				none	glove	move		throw		
				gone	prove	lose		thrown		
				once	shove	whose		blown		
								grown		
								bowl		

*occurs in first 100 high frequency words

**occurs in second 100 high frequency words

Long -*u* Words

CVCe			CVVC	CVV		CVV		See also: *oo* words
u-e			*ui*	*ue*		*ew*		*Oddballs*
use**	cube	fume	fruit	blue	sue	new*	brew	do*
cute	duke	chute	suit	due	fuel	dew	stew	you*
rude	huge	mute	bruise	clue	cruel	chew	crew	to*
rule	dude	plume	cruise	glue		drew	whew	two*
mule	nude	prune	juice	true		few	screw	build
tune	crude	muse		flue		flew	threw	built
June	dune	spruce		hue		knew	shrewd	guide
tube	flute			cue		grew	strewn	truth
								through

Ambiguous Vowels: *ô* sound

al	*au*	*aw*		*o*		*ough*		*w + a*
tall	caught	saw	gnaw	on	loss	cough		was*
wall	taught	paw	thaw	off	cross	ought		want**
mall	pause	law	caw	dog	gloss	fought		wash
talk	sauce	draw	bawl	frog	cloth	bought		wand
walk	fault	claw	awe	log	moth	thought		wasp
calm	haunt	dawn	drawn	fog	broth	brought		watt
palm	launch	lawn	crawl	bog	soft	trough		swap
bald	because**	yawn	shawl	hog	loft			swat
halt		fawn	sprawl	lost	golf			watch
salt	*Oddballs*	hawk	squawk	cost	bong	*Oddballs*		
small	aunt	raw	straw	frost	song	through	could**	
stall	laugh			boss	long	tough	would*	
stalk				toss	strong	rough	should**	
chalk				moss	throng	touch		
						young		

Ambiguous Vowels/Diphthongs (*ou*/*ow* and *oi*/*oy*)

ow		*ou*			*oo*	*oo - u*			*oi*	*oy*
how*	drown	out*	house**	*Oddballs*	book**	too**	soon**	school**	coin	boy*
now*	frown	our*	about*	could**	look**	zoo	noon	spoon	join	toy
cow	crown	loud	mouse	would*	good*	moo	moon	tooth	oil	joy
down*	crowd	pout	foul	should**	cook	boot	room	shoot	foil	enjoy
bow	fowl	ouch	mouth	touch	took	root	zoom	smooth	soil	soy
wow	scowl	cloud	shout	young	foot	food	boom	roost	boil	ploy
town	prowl	proud	pout	cough	wood	mood	loom	proof	coil	
gown	growl	count	scout	tough	hook	tool	bloom	stool	point	
brown	vow	round	snout	ought	shook	cool	gloom	spook	joint	
clown		sound	stout	bought	stood	fool	loop	brood	hoist	
owl		found**	sprout	through	wool	pool	troop		moist	
howl		pound	pouch		crook	roof	whoop	*Oddballs*	toil	
sow		mound	couch		hood	goof	scoop	two*	broil	
plow		bound	crouch		hoof			blood	voice	
		hound	drought		soot				noise	
		wound	doubt		brook				choice	
		ground								

*occurs in first 100 high frequency words

**occurs in second 100 high frequency words

Words Their Way: Word Study for Phonics, Vocabulary, and Spelling Instruction © 2008 by Pearson Education, Inc.

R-influenced Vowels

ar	ar	ar + e	are	air	ear	eer	er	ear	Oddballs
far**	dart	carve	care	fair	ear*	deer	her*	heard	very*
car	start	large	bare	hair	near*	cheer	fern	earth	their*
jar	bark	starve	dare	pair	hear*	steer	herd	learn	there*
star	shark	barge	share	stair	dear**	queer	jerk	earn	were*
card	lark	charge	stare	flair	year**	jeer	term	search	here*
hard	scar		mare	chair	fear	sneer	germ	pearl	where**
yard	mar	Oddballs	flare	lair	tear	steer	stern	yearn	heart
art	barb	are*	glare		clear	peer	herb		bear
part	harp	war	rare		beard		per		wear
cart	sharp	warm	scare		gear		perk		swear
bar	snarl		hare		spear		perch		pear
arm	scarf		snare				clerk		
harm	charm		blare				nerve		
dark	arch		fare				verse		
park	march		square				swerve		
spark	smart								
yarn	chart								

ur	ir	ire	or		ore	our	oar	w + ar	w + or
burn	girl**	fire	or*	storm	more**	your*	roar	warm	work*
hurt	first**	tire	for*	porch	store	four*	soar	war	word
turn	bird	wire	born	torch	shore	pour	boar	ward	world
curl	dirt	hire	corn	force	bore	mourn	coarse	wharf	worm
curb	stir	sire	horn	north	chore	court	hoarse	quart	worth
burst	sir		worn	horse	score	fourth			worse
church	shirt	ure	cord	forth	sore	gourd			
churn	skirt	sure**	cork	scorn	before*	source			
surf	third	cure	pork	chord	wore	course			
purr	birth	pure	fort	forge	tore				
burr	firm	lure	short	gorge	swore	Oddballs			
blur	swirl		nor			our*			
lurch	twirl		ford		oor	flour			
lurk	chirp		lord		door	hour			
spur	squirt				poor	scour			
hurl	thirst				floor	sour			
blurt	squirm								

*occurs in first 100 high frequency words

**occurs in second 100 high frequency words

Appendix E

Complex Consonants

ch	tch	Cch		Hard *g*		Soft *g*	*dge*	C*ge*
teach	catch	ranch	arch	frog	guide	huge	edge	range
reach	patch	branch	march	drug	guard	cage	ledge	change
beach	hatch	lunch	starch	twig	guilt	age	hedge	barge
peach	latch	bunch	search	flag	guess	page	wedge	charge
coach	match	munch	perch	shrug	guest	stage	pledge	large
speech	watch	punch	lurch	gave	ghost	rage	badge	forge
couch	ditch	bench	church	game		orange	ridge	gorge
crouch	pitch	clench	birch	gain	*Oddballs*	gauge	bridge	surge
pouch	witch	trench	torch	gone	get*	gem	lodge	bulge
screech	switch	wrench	porch	goat	girl**	germ	dodge	strange
	fetch	drench	scorch	gold	gift	gene	judge	
Oddballs	sketch	pinch		goose	gear	gym	budge	
rich	clutch	finch		goof	geese	gyp	fudge	
such	scratch	hunch		golf		giant	smudge	
much*	stretch	mulch		gulp		gist	trudge	
	stitch	gulch		gull			grudge	
	twitch	launch		gust				
	blotch							

Hard *c*	Soft *c*	-*ce*	-*Vse*	-*se*	-*ze*	-*z*	-*ve*	Voiceless *th*	Voiced *th*
card	cell	rice	wise	cause	size	buzz	love	bath	bathe
cave	cent	face	chase	cease	haze	fizz	dove	cloth	clothe
cast	cease	place	chose	dense	doze	jazz	shove	booth	soothe
cause	cinch	brace	close	false	prize	frizz	glove	loath	loathe
caught	cyst	slice	phase	geese	froze	quiz	have*	teeth	teethe
couch	cite	price	muse	goose	graze	quartz	give*		
core	truce		those	loose	blaze	waltz	move		
coin	trace		these	moose	gauze		weave		
coast	since		prose	mouse	seize		leave		
cost	fence			noise	freeze		curve		
coach	peace			nurse	sneeze		nerve		
cough	juice			pause	snooze		serve		
curb	niece			purse	breeze				
curl	voice			raise	maize				
curve	sauce			sense	bronze				
cult	once			tense	wheeze				
cuff	hence			tease					
	force			rinse					
	ounce			cheese					
	dance			verse					
	chance								
	prince								

*occurs in first 100 high frequency words

**occurs in second 100 high frequency words

Homophones

be/bee	hey/hay	serial/cereal	Mary/mary/merry	bred/bread
blue/blew	made/maid	cheap/cheep	great/grate	tred/tread
I/eye/aye	male/mail	days/daze	seem/seam	guessed/guest
no/know	nay/neigh	dew/do/due	knew/new	rest/wrest
here/hear	oh/owe	doe/dough	stair/stare	beech/beach
to/too/two	pail/pale	gray/grey	hour/our	real/reel
hi/high	pair/pear/pare	heel/heal	rough/ruff	peel/peal
new/knew/gnu	peek/peak/pique	horse/hoarse	poor/pour	team/teem
see/sea	reed/read/Reid	ho/hoe	haul/hall	leak/leek
there/they're/their	so/sew/sow	in/inn	piece/peace	sees/seas
bear/bare	root/route	need/kneed/knead	ant/aunt	sheer/shear
by/buy/bye	shone/shown	lone/loan	flair/flare	feet/feat
deer/dear	aid/aide	we/wee	mist/missed	hymn/him
ate/eight	add/ad	ring/wring	mane/main	whit/wit
for/four/fore	break/brake	peddle/petal/pedal	wail/whale/wale	scents/cents/sense
our/hour	cent/sent/scent	straight/strait	died/dyed	tents/tense
red/read	flee/flea	pole/poll	manor/manner	gilt/guile
lead/led	creak/creek	earn/urn	pier/peer	knit/nit
meat/meet	die/dye	past/passed	Ann/an	tic/tick
plane/plain	fair/fare	sweet/suite	tacks/tax	sight/site/cite
rode/road/rowed	hair/hare	ore/or	cash/cache	rye/wry
sail/sale	heard/herd	rain/reign/rein	rap/wrap	style/stile
stare/stair	night/knight	role/roll	maze/maize	might/mite
we'd/weed	steel/steal	sole/soul	air/heir	climb/clime
we'll/wheel	tail/tale	seller/cellar	bail/bale	fined/find
hole/whole	thrown/throne	shoo/shoe	ail/ale	side/sighed
wear/ware/where	fir/fur	soar/sore	prays/praise	tide/tied
one/won	waist/waste	steak/stake	base/bass	vice/vise
flower/flour	week/weak	some/sum	faint/feint	awl/all
right/write	we've/weave	tow/toe	wade/weighed	paws/pause
your/you're	way/weigh	vein/vane/vain	wave/waive	born/borne
lye/lie	wait/weight	medal/metal/meddle	knave/nave	chord/cord
its/it's	threw/through	wrote/rote	whet/wet	foul/fowl
not/knot	vail/veil/vale	forth/fourth	sell/cell	mall/maul
gate/gait	aisle/I'll/isle	tea/tee	bell/belle	mourn/morn
jeans/genes	ball/bawl	been/bin	bowled/bold	rot/wrought
time/thyme	beat/beet	sox/socks	bough/bow	bomb/balm
son/sun	bolder/boulder	board/bored		bald/balled
boy/buoy	course/coarse			browse/brows

Compound Words by Common Base Words

We have limited the list here to words that have base words across a number of compound words.

aircraft	checkbook	foothold	homesick	snowman	raincoat
airline	cookbook	footlights	homespun	fireman	raindrop
airmail	scrapbook	footnote	homestead	gentleman	rainfall
airplane	textbook	footprint	homework	handyman	rainstorm
airport	buttercup	footstep	horseback	policeman	roadblock
airtight	butterfly	footstool	horsefly	salesman	roadway
anybody	buttermilk	barefoot	horseman	nightfall	roadwork
anymore	butterscotch	tenderfoot	horseplay	nightgown	railroad
anyone	doorbell	grandchildren	horsepower	nightmare	sandbag
anyplace	doorknob	granddaughter	horseshoe	nighttime	sandbar
anything	doorman	grandfather	racehorse	overnight	sandbox
anywhere	doormat	grandmother	sawhorse	outbreak	sandpaper
backboard	doorstep	grandparent	houseboat	outcast	sandpiper
backbone	doorway	grandson	housefly	outcome	sandstone
backfire	backdoor	haircut	housewife	outcry	seacoast
background	outdoor	hairdo	housework	outdated	seafood
backpack	downcast	hairdresser	housetop	outdo	seagull
backward	downhill	hairpin	birdhouse	outdoors	seaman
backyard	download	hairstyle	clubhouse	outfield	seaport
bareback	downpour	handbag	doghouse	outfit	seasick
feedback	downright	handball	greenhouse	outgrow	seashore
flashback	downsize	handbook	townhouse	outlaw	seaside
hatchback	downstairs	handcuffs	landfill	outline	seaweed
paperback	downstream	handmade	landlady	outlook	snowball
piggyback	downtown	handout	landlord	outnumber	snowflake
bathrobe	breakdown	handshake	landmark	outpost	snowman
bathroom	countdown	handspring	landscape	outrage	snowplow
bathtub	sundown	handstand	landslide	outright	snowshoe
birdbath	touchdown	handwriting	dreamland	outside	snowstorm
bedrock	eyeball	backhand	farmland	outsmart	somebody
bedroom	eyebrow	firsthand	homeland	outwit	someone
bedside	eyeglasses	secondhand	highland	blowout	someday
bedspread	eyelash	underhand	wasteland	carryout	somehow
bedtime	eyelid	headache	wonderland	cookout	somewhere
flatbed	eyesight	headband	lifeboat	handout	something
hotbed	eyewitness	headdress	lifeguard	hideout	sometime
sickbed	shuteye	headfirst	lifejacket	workout	underline
waterbed	firearm	headlight	lifelike	lookout	undergo
birthday	firecracker	headline	lifelong	overall	underground
birthmark	firefighter	headlong	lifestyle	overboard	undermine
birthplace	firefly	headmaster	lifetime	overcast	underwater
birthstone	firehouse	headphones	nightlife	overcome	watercolor
childbirth	fireman	headquarters	wildlife	overflow	waterfall
blackberry	fireplace	headstart	lighthouse	overhead	watermelon
blackbird	fireproof	headstrong	lightweight	overlook	waterproof
blackboard	fireside	headway	daylight	overview	saltwater
blackmail	firewood	airhead	flashlight	playground	windfall
blacksmith	fireworks	blockhead	headlight	playhouse	windmill
blacktop	backfire	figurehead	moonlight	playmate	windpipe
bookcase	bonfire	homeland	spotlight	playpen	windshield
bookkeeper	campfire	homemade	sunlight	playroom	windswept
bookmark	football	homemaker	mailman	playwright	downwind
bookworm	foothill	homeroom	doorman	rainbow	headwind

Plurals

ch + es	sh + es	ss + es	x + es	y + s	change y to i + es				f>ves
arches	bushes	bosses	foxes	plays	flies	babies	daisies	stories	wives
watches	dishes	classes	boxes	stays	fries	berries	guppies	buddies	knives
coaches	flashes	bonuses		trays	cries	bodies	ladies	sixties	leaves
crashes	brushes	glasses	s + es	donkeys	tries	bunnies	parties		loaves
couches	ashes	crosses	gases	monkeys	skies	cities	pennies	*Oddballs*	lives
inches	wishes	guesses	buses	jockeys	spies	copies	ponies	goalies	wolves
peaches	crashes	kisses		turkeys	dries	counties	supplies	taxies	calves
notches	leashes	passes		volleys		fairies	puppies	movies	elves
lunches	lashes	dresses		valleys		duties	bullies	cookies	scarves

Verbs for Inflected Ending Sorts

VCC		CVVC	E-drop		CVC Words That Double			Don't Double	Miscellaneous Verbs
help	act	need	live	dance	stop	drip	grab	level	see/saw
jump	add	wait	time	glance	pat	fan	hug	edit	fall/fell
want	crash	boat	live	hike	sun	flop	jam	enter	feel/felt
ask	crack	shout	name	hire	top	grin	kid	exit	tell/told
back	block	cook	bake	serve	hop	grip	log	limit	grow/grew
talk	bowl	head	care	score	plan	mop	map	suffer	know/knew
call	count	meet	close	solve	pot	plod	nap	appear	draw/drew
thank	brush	peek	love	sneeze	shop	rob	nod	complain	blow/blew
laugh	bump	bloom	move	trace	trip	shrug	pin	explain	throw/threw
trick	burn	cool	smile	trade	bet	sip	dip	repeat	find/found
park	climb	cheer	use	vote	cap	skin	dim	attend	drink/drank
pick	camp	clear	hate	drape	clap	skip	rub	collect	sink/sank
plant	curl	dream	hope	fade	slip	slam	beg		hear/heard
rock	dash	float	ice	graze	snap	slap	blur	**Double**	break/broke
start	dust	flood	joke	praise	spot	snip	bud	admit	hold/held
bark	farm	fool	paste	scrape	tag	sob	chip	begin	stand/stood
work	fold	oil	phone	shave	thin	strip	chop	commit	build/built
walk	growl	join	prove	shove	trap	wrap	crop	control	ring/rang
yell	hunt	lean	race	snare	trot	zip	strum	excel	sing/sang
wish	kick	mail	scare	cause	tug	brag	swap	forbid	sweep/swept
guess	land	nail	share	cease	wag	char	swat	forget	sleep/slept
turn	learn	moan	skate	pose	drop	chug		omit	keep/kept
smell	nest	scream	stare	quote	drum	hem		permit	drive/drove
track	lick	pour	taste	rove	whiz	jog		rebel	shine/shone
push	lock	sail	taste	blame	flap	mob		refer	feed/fed
miss	melt	trail	wave		flip	plot			bleed/bled
paint	point	zoom	carve		scar	prop	*Oddballs*	**E-drop**	lay/laid
wash	print				skim	blot	box	arrive	pay/paid
wink	quack				slug	chat	fix	escape	say/said
rest	reach				stab	scan	wax	excuse	speak/spoke
					throb	slop	row	nibble	send/sent
							chew	rattle	buy/bought
							sew	refuse	bring/brought
							show	amuse	tear/tore
							snow	ignore	wear/wore
								retire	

Appendix E

Syllable Juncture

VCCV Doublet	VCCV		VCV Open	VVCV Open	VCV Closed	VV	VCCCV
pretty*	after*	public	over**	season	never**	create	constant
better**	under**	signal	open**	reason	present**	riot	dolphin
blizzard	number	sister	baby	peanut	cabin	liar	laughter
blossom	chapter	subject	hoping	leader	planet	fuel	pilgrim
button	pencil	Sunday	writer	sneaker	finish	poem	instant
cabbage	picnic	temper	basic	easy	robin	diary	complain
copper	basket	thunder	even	floated	magic	cruel	hundred
cottage	cactus	trumpet	waving	waiter	limit	trial	monster
dipper	canyon	under	bacon	needed	manage	diet	orchard
fellow	capture	twenty	chosen	reading	prison	neon	orphan
foggy	center	umpire	moment		habit	lion	purchase
follow	window	walnut	raking	*Oddballs*	punish	idea	complete
common	compass	thunder	human	cousin	cover	video	athlete
funny	contest	welcome	pilot	water	promise	meteor	kitchen
happen	costume	whimper	silent	busy	closet	violin	children
mammal	doctor	seldom	vacant		camel	annual	inspect
message	picture	winter	navy		cavern	casual	pumpkin
office	plastic	wonder	music		comet	radio	english
pattern	public	plastic	female		dozen		kingdom
sudden	problem	fellow	stolen		finish		bottle
tennis	reptile	lumber	robot		habit		mumble
traffic	rescue	index	crater		honest		
tunnel	sentence	insect	climate		level		
valley	seldom	injure	duty		lever		
village	fabric	after	famous		lizard		
hollow	helmet	elbow	female		modern		
dessert	husband	enter	fever		never		
butter	lumber	velvet	final		oven		
hammer	master	chimney	flavor		palace		
attic	napkin		humid		timid		
	dentist		labor		panic		
			legal		rapid		
			local		robin		
			music		visit		
			pirate		solid		
			private		wagon		
			program		vanish		
			recent		topic		
			rumor		travel		
			siren				
			solar				
			spiral				

*occurs in first 100 high frequency words

**occurs in second 100 high frequency words

Appendix E

a Patterns in Stressed Syllables

Long -*a* VCV open Accent in 1st	Long -*a* Accent in 1st	Long -*a* Accent in 2nd	Short -*a* in VCCV Accent in 1st	Short -*a* in VCV Accent in 1st	*ar* Accent in 1st	*air* Accent in 1st	*are* Accent in 1st
baby	rainbow	complain	attic	wagon	artist	stairway	marry
nation	painter	contain	hammer	cabin	marble	fairway	parrot
vapor	raisin	explain	batter	planet	garden	airport	narrow
skater	railroad	remain	happen	magic	party	dairy	carrot
cradle	daisy	terrain	mammal	habit	carpet	haircut	sparrow
lazy	dainty	exclaim	valley	camel	pardon	fairy	narrate
bacon	sailor	refrain	cabbage	habit	market	airplane	barrel
wafer	straighten	campaign	traffic	rapid	tardy	chairman	carry
fable	sprained	regain	pattern	panic	harvest	prairie	parent
raven	maintain	obtain	scatter	panel	parka		careful
famous	failure	detail	ballot	palace	charter	**Accent in 2nd**	barely
fatal	tailor	maintain	daddy	cavern	larva	repair	barefoot
ladle	waiter	decay	gallop	manage	garland	despair	
navy	traitor	dismay	massive	vanish	parcel	unfair	**Accent in 2nd**
basic	mailbox	delay	attach	travel	barber	impair	despair
flavor	maybe	subway	napkin	satin	starchy	affair	repair
data	player	portray	basket	tragic	charter		prepare
crater	crayon	mistake	fabric	falcon	garlic		compare
savor	mayor	parade	plastic	shadow	margin		beware
raking	payment	amaze	master		hardly		aware
labor	prayer	vibrate	cactus		partner		declare
vacant	layer	replace	chapter		bargain		airfare
April	crayfish	dictate	canyon		carbon		fanfare
radar	bracelet	crusade	capture		farther		hardware
	pavement	debate	tadpole		jargon		nightmare
	basement	behave	ambush		scarlet		software
	baseball	cascade	lantern		parlor		warfare
	grateful	escape	scamper		sharpen		
	graceful	disgrace	canvas		sparkle		*Oddballs*
	safety	erase	package		target		toward
	statement	essay	tablet		tarnish		lizard
		foray	walnut		harbor		
		garbage	chocolate		partial		
Oddballs	*Oddballs*				marshal		
any*	again*				martyr		
many*	captain						
water	bargain						
	postage						

*occurs in first 100 high frequency words

**occurs in second 100 high frequency words

Appendix E

o Patterns in Stressed Syllables

Long -*o* VCV open Accent in 1st	Long -*o* Accent in 1st	Long -*o* Accent in 2nd	Short -*o* in VCCV Accent in 1st	Short -*o* in VCV Accent in 1st	*or* Accent in 1st	*wor* Accent in 1st	*ore/oar/our* Accent in 1st
robot	lonely	alone	foggy	robin	morning**	worker	boredom
pony	lonesome	explode	follow	closet	forty	worry	shoreline
chosen	hopeful	erode	copper	comet	stormy	worthy	scoreless
donate	homework	awoke	blossom	promise	story	worship	hoarsely
motor	closely	decode	cottage	honest	corner		coarsely
soda	goalie	enclose	common	modern	border	*war/quar*	hoarding
notice	loafer	dispose	office	solid	torment	warning	sources
sofa	coaster	suppose	hollow	topic	forest	warden	fourteen
frozen	toaster	compose	nozzle	volume	fortress	warrior	pouring
local	coastal	remote	bottle	body	shortage	wardrobe	mournful
moment	soapy	unload	comma	novel	torrent	wardrobe	foursome
rodent	roadway	approach	cotton	profit	tortoise	quarrel	courtroom
cobra	owner	afloat	hobby	promise	portrait		
grocer	bowling	below	yonder		forfeit		**Accent in 2nd**
potion	rowboat	bestow	popcorn	*Oddballs*	morning		before*
ocean	snowfall	aglow	contest	wonder	shorter		ignore
rotate	lower	disown	costume	dolphin	order		restore
program	mower	enroll	doctor	dozen	forest		before
hoping	slowly	behold	bonfire	oven	normal		explore
stolen	towboat	revolt	bother	shovel	northern		galore
solar	soldier	almost	cobweb	stomach	forward		aboard
poem	poster		conquer	Europe	corncob		ashore
	hostess		problem	sorry	chorus		adore
Oddball	postage		posture		florist		
hotel	smolder		monster		boring		
only**	molten		congress		sporty		
	molding						
	folder				**Accent in 2nd**		
					report		
					record		
					perform		
					inform		
					afford		
					reform		
					absorb		
					abhor		
					adorn		

*occurs in first 100 high frequency words

**occurs in second 100 high frequency words

Words Their Way: Word Study for Phonics, Vocabulary, and Spelling Instruction © 2008 by Pearson Education, Inc.

Appendix E

i Patterns in Stressed Syllables

Long -*i* VCV open Accent in 1st	Long -*i* Accent in 1st	Long -*i* Accent in 2nd	Short -*i* in VCCV Accent in 1st	Short -*i* in VCV Accent in 1st	*ir* Accent in 1st	*ire* Accent in 1st	*y* = *i* Accent in 1st
pilot	ninety	polite	little*	finish	thirty	tiresome	typist
silent	driveway	surprise	into**	limit	firmly	firefly	dryer
diner	sidewalk	decide	kitten	river	dirty	direful	flyer
writer	iceberg	advice	dipper	lizard	birthday		tyrant
tiger	lively	survive	slipper	timid	thirsty	**Accent in 2nd**	hydrant
siren	ninety	combine	mitten	visit	birdbath	require	bypass
pirate	mighty	arrive	dinner	given	circle	rehire	nylon
private	slightly	invite	silly	city	circus	attire	stylish
spiral	frighten	describe	skinny	sliver	stirring	inquire	rhyming
biker	lightning	divide	ribbon	civil	firmly	expire	python
spider	highway	excite	pillow	digit	virtue	desire	cycle
visor	brightly	provide	dizzy	prison	stirrup	perspire	tryout
minus	higher	reptile	chilly	wizard	twirler	admire	cyclone
title	nightmare	confide	bitter	quiver	skirmish	inspire	hybrid
rival	tighten	recline	minnow	exist	circuit	entire	hyphen
bridle	fighter	ignite	blizzard	figure	irksome	acquire	stylish
bison	highlight	despite	tissue		whirlpool	entire	tyrant
item	sightsee	oblige	mixture	*Oddballs*	chirping	retire	skyline
Friday	blindfold	divine	fifty	machine	flirting		hygiene
sinus	climber	tonight	picnic	forgive			
slimy	wildcat	resign	picture	liter		**Accent in 2nd**	
icy	wildlife	design	chimney	mirror		defy	
climax		delight	frisky	pizza		July	
		remind	windy	guitar		apply	
VV		rewind	signal	spirit		rely	
lion		unkind	sister			imply	
dial			whimper			supply	
diet			finger			reply	
riot			winter				
pliers			kidnap				
diary			jigsaw				
vial			window				

*occurs in first 100 high frequency words

**occurs in second 100 high frequency words

Appendix E

u Patterns in Stressed Syllables

Long -*u* VCV open Accent in 1st	Long -*u* Accent in 1st	Long -*u* Accent in 2nd	Short -*u* in VCCV Accent in 1st	Short -*u* in VCV Accent in 1st	*ur* Accent in 1st	*ure* Accent in 2nd	VV
super	useful	amuse	supper	upon*	sturdy	secure	fuel
music	Tuesday	misuse	button	under**	purpose	assure	cruel
ruby	juicy	confuse	funny	punish	further	endure	annual
tuna	chewy	reduce	sudden	suburb	hurry	impure	casual
truly	dewdrop	conclude	tunnel	pumice	purple	mature	
pupil	jewel	dilute	puppet	public	turtle	unsure	
rumor	pewter	exclude	buddy	study	furnish	obscure	
human	skewer	include	butter		Thursday	manure	
bugle	sewage	pollute	fuzzy		blurry	brochure	
humid	poodle	excuse	guppy		turkey	unsure	
future	rooster	resume	puzzle		current		
tutor	moody	compute	ugly		purchase		
tumor	doodle	abuse	husband		burger		
futile	noodle	perfume	lumber		furry		
student	scooter	protrude	number		murky		
tuba	toothache	salute	public		mural		
tulip		dispute	Sunday		surfer		
unit	*Oddballs*	askew	thunder		burden		
ruler	cougar	cartoon	trumpet		bureau		
July	beauty	raccoon	umpire		burrow		
	cousin	lagoon	under		curfew		
		shampoo	hundred		hurdle		
		balloon	mumble		jury		
		baboon	lucky		murmur		
		cocoon	hungry		turnip		
		maroon	bucket		burner		
		tattoo	bundle		gurgle		

*occurs in first 100 high frequency words

**occurs in second 100 high frequency words

Appendix E

e Patterns in Stressed Syllables

Long -*e* VCV open Accent in 1st	Long -*e* Accent in 1st	Long -*e* Accent in 2nd	Long -*ie* Accent in 1st	Short -*e* in VCCV Accent in 1st	Short -*e* in VCV Accent in 1st	*er* = *ur* Accent in 1st	*eer/ear/ere* Accent in 1st
even	needle	succeed	briefly	better	select	person	eerie
female	freedom	indeed	diesel	letter	medal	perfect	deerskin
fever	freezer	fifteen		fellow	metal	nervous	cheerful
zebra	breezy	thirteen	**Accent in 2nd**	tennis	level	sermon	earache
legal	cheetah	canteen	believe	message	lever	serpent	fearful
meter	steeple	agree	achieve	penny	never	hermit	earmuff
recent	tweezers	degree	retrieve	beggar	debit	thermos	spearmint
depot	beetle	between	relief	effect	denim	kernel	yearbook
cedar	feeble	proceed	besiege	respect	lemon	perky	dreary
detour	greedy	asleep	apiece	pencil	melon	permit	bleary
veto	sweeten	delete	relieve	dentist	memo	serene	clearly
prefix	beaver	supreme	belief	center	pedal	sherbet	nearby
tepee	eager	trapeze		helmet	petal	gerbil	hearsay
decent	easy	compete	**Long *ei* Accent in 1st**	reptile	seven	mermaid	teardrop
preview	easel	extreme	either	rescue	clever	certain	weary
prefix	season	stampede	ceiling	seldom	credit	merchant	merely
evil	reason	deplete	leisure	sentence		version	
even	reader	recede	seizure	temper	*Short ea*		**Accent in 2nd**
	feature	convene	neither	twenty	feather	*ear = ur*	reindeer
VV	creature	mislead		welcome	heavy	early	career
neon	meaning	disease		velvet	steady	earnings	appear
create	eastern	increase	**Accent in 2nd**	pesky	ready	earthworm	overhear
	bleachers	defeat	receive		leather	pearly	nuclear
	cleaner	repeat	perceive	*Oddballs*	weather	earnest	endear
	eager	conceal	receipt	people	pleasant	yearning	adhere
	treaty	ideal	deceive	hearty	sweater	rehearse	austere
	neatly	reveal	receipt	pretty	healthy	research	cashmere
	peanut	ordeal	conceive	cherry	weapon	clearing	revere
	weasel	appeal	caffeine		sweaty	dearest	severe
	greasy	mislead			heaven	spearmint	sincere

*occurs in first 100 high frequency words

**occurs in second 100 high frequency words

Appendix E

Ambiguous Vowels in Stressed Syllables

oy/oi	ow	ou	ou = short -u	au	aw	al
Accent in 1st						
voyage	powder	county	trouble	saucer	awful	also**
loyal	power	counter	double	author	awkward	always
joyful	flower	thousand	southern	August	lawyer	almost
boycott	prowler	fountain	couple	autumn	awesome	already
royal	coward	mountain	cousin	laundry	awfully	although
soybean	tower	council	touched	caution	gnawing	halter
oyster	drowsy	lousy	younger	faucet	gawking	salty
moisture	brownie	scoundrel	youngster	sausage	flawless	balky
poison	rowdy	bounty	moustache	auction	drawing	balmy
noisy	chowder	boundary		haunted	jawbone	calmly
pointed	vowel	founder	*ou = long u*	cauldron	lawless	falter
toilet	dowdy	doubtful	coupon	gaudy	tawny	halting
	towel	southeast	routine	daughter	yawning	hallway
Accent in 2nd	shower	voucher	toucan	jaunty	clawed	waltzing
annoy	cowboy	cloudy	youthful	naughty		
enjoy	powwow	flounder	cougar	slaughter		*Oddballs*
employ	drowning	trousers	crouton	trauma		laughed
destroy			acoustics	pauper		all right
ahoy						balloon
appoint		**Accent in 2nd**		**Accent in 2nd**		gallon
avoid		about*		because**		
exploit		without				
rejoice		around				
		announce				
		amount				
		profound				

*occurs in first 100 high frequency words

**occurs in second 100 high frequency words

Appendix E

Final Unstressed Syllables

-al	-il/ile	-el	-le		-et	-it
central	April	angel	little*	people**	basket	audit
crystal	civil	barrel	able	hurdle	blanket	bandit
cymbal	council	bagel	ample	hustle	bucket	credit
dental	evil	bushel	angle	juggle	budget	digit
fatal	fossil	camel	ankle	jungle	carpet	edit
feudal	gerbil	cancel	apple	kettle	closet	exit
final	lentil	channel	battle	knuckle	comet	habit
focal	nostril	chapel	beagle	maple	cricket	hermit
formal	pencil	diesel	beetle	middle	faucet	limit
global	peril	flannel	bottle	needle	fidget	merit
journal	pupil	funnel	bramble	noodle	gadget	orbit
legal	stencil	gravel	bridle	noble	hatchet	profit
mammal	tonsil	hazel	bubble	paddle	helmet	rabbit
medal	docile	jewel	buckle	pebble	hornet	spirit
mental	facile	kennel	bundle	pickle	jacket	summit
metal	fertile	kernel	bugle	purple	locket	unit
nasal	fragile	label	candle	puzzle	magnet	visit
naval	futile	level	castle	riddle	midget	vomit
neutral	hostile	model	cattle	saddle	planet	
normal	missile	morsel	cable	sample	poet	
oval	mobile	nickel	chuckle	scribble	puppet	
pedal	sterile	novel	circle	settle	racket	
petal		panel	cradle	single	scarlet	
plural		parcel	cripple	steeple	secret	
rascal		quarrel	cuddle	struggle	skillet	
rival		ravel	cycle	stumble	sonnet	
royal		satchel	dimple	tackle	tablet	
rural		sequel	doodle	tickle	target	
sandal		shovel	double	title	thicket	
scandal		shrivel	eagle	triple	toilet	
signal		squirrel	fable	trouble	trumpet	
spiral		swivel	fiddle	twinkle	velvet	
tidal		tinsel	freckle	turtle	wallet	
total		towel	fumble	waffle		
vandal		travel	gamble	whistle		
vital		tunnel	gargle	wrinkle		
vocal		vessel	gentle			
		vowel	grumble			
			handle			

*occurs in first 100 high frequency words

**occurs in second 100 high frequency words

Appendix E

er			er Agents	er Comparatives	ar	or	
other*	poster	bother	jogger	bigger	beggar	color**	rumor
under**	printer	center	dreamer	cheaper	burglar	actor	mirror
better**	shower	copper	dancer	cleaner	scholar	author	horror
never**	timber	drawer	speaker	farther	cellar	doctor	humor
over**	toaster	finger	teacher	quicker	cedar	editor	meteor
mother**	trouser	prayer	skater	slower	cheddar	mayor	motor
another**	ladder	power	marcher	younger	collar	neighbor	razor
banner	counter	powder	shopper	older	cougar	sailor	scissors
blister	prefer	proper	racer	flatter	dollar	tailor	splendor
border	crater	quiver	grocer	plainer	grammar	traitor	sponsor
clover	cancer	roller	barber	lighter	hangar	tutor	terror
cluster	cider	rubber	peddler	darker	lunar	visitor	tractor
fiber	scorcher	sander	plumber	weaker	solar	donor	tremor
freezer	ledger	saucer	ranger	stronger	molar	armor	vapor
liter	stretcher	scooter	soldier	wilder	polar	error	cursor
litter	pitcher	shaver	usher	sweeter	sugar	favor	honor
lumber	answer		voter	cooler	nectar	anchor	
manner	blender		catcher	braver	pillar		

/chər/			/shoor/	/yoor/	/zhər/	/jər/	
culture	nurture	mature	assure	endure	leisure	conjure	
capture	rapture	mixture	ensure	failure	measure	injure	
creature	sculpture	moisture	insure	obscure	closure	procedure	
denture	stature	picture	pressure	secure	pleasure		
feature	stricture	pasture	fissure	manicure	treasure		
fixture	texture	posture	brochure	insecure	pressure		
fracture	tincture	puncture	enclosure	figure			
future	torture	nature	exposure				
gesture	venture	furniture	reassure		*Oddballs*		
juncture	adventure	miniature	composure		senior		
lecture	departure	premature	disclosure		danger		
injure	immature	signature					

ain	an	en-verb	en-noun	en-adj	in	on	
again*	human	frighten	chicken	golden	basin	apron	bacon
captain	organ	listen	children	often	cabin	button	carton
certain	orphan	sharpen	garden	open**	cousin	cannon	cotton
curtain	slogan	shorten	kitten	rotten	margin	common	gallon
fountain	urban	sweeten	mitten	spoken	pumpkin	dragon	lemon
mountain	woman	thicken	women	sunken	raisin	wagon	lesson
villain		widen	heaven	swollen	robin	pardon	prison
bargain		deafen	oxygen	wooden	dolphin	person	poison
chieftain		flatten	siren	broken	muffin	reason	ribbon
		lengthen	linen	hidden	penguin	season	weapon
		open**	heaven	chosen	satin	salmon	weapon

Words Their Way: Word Study for Phonics, Vocabulary, and Spelling Instruction © 2008 by Pearson Education, Inc.

/j/		/is/		ey	ie	y	
voyage	sausage	justice	furnace	chimney	cookie	very*	berry
bandage	cabbage	practice	surface	donkey	movie	pretty**	body
village	rummage	service	palace	turkey	brownie	early	beauty
message	savage	office	necklace	jockey	genie	crazy	drowsy
cottage	passage	crevice	menace	valley	goalie	candy	empty
wreckage	image	notice	grimace	volley	sweetie	daisy	guilty
courage	marriage	novice	terrace	journey	zombie	forty	tidy
storage	manage	bodice		honey	birdie	envy	treaty
luggage	sewage	crisis		money	eerie	worry	carry
damage	language	tennis	*Oddballs*	jersey	bootie	gravy	bossy
postage		axis	lettuce	pulley	rookie	sorry	trophy
garbage	*Oddballs*	basis	porpoise	hockey	pinkie	dizzy	stingy
hostage	knowledge	iris	tortoise	galley	prairie	cherry	bury
	cartridge						

Prefixes and Suffixes

mis-	*pre-*	*re-*	*un-*	*dis-*	*in-* "not"	*non-*
misbehave	precook	rebound	unable	disable	incomplete	nonsense
misconduct	predate	recall	unafraid	disagreeable	incorrect	nonstop
miscount	prefix	recapture	unarmed	disappear	indecent	nonfiction
misdeed	pregame	recharge	unbeaten	disarm	indirect	nonfat
misfit	preheat	reclaim	unbroken	discharge	inexpensive	nonprofit
misgivings	prejudge	recopy	uncertain	disclose	inflexible	nondairy
misguide	premature	recount	unclean	discolor	informal	nonstick
misjudge	prepay	recycle	unclear	discomfort	inhuman	nonviolent
mislay	preschool	reelect	uncommon	discontent	injustice	nonskid
mislead	preset	refill	uncover	discover	insane	nonstandard
mismatch	preteen	refinish	undone	dishonest	invalid	
misplace	pretest	reform	unequal	disinfect	invisible	
misprint	preview	refresh	unfair	dislike		
misspell	prewash	relearn	unkind	disloyal	*in-* "in"	
mistake	predict	remind	unlike	disobey	or "into"	
mistreat	precede	remodel	unlock	disorder	income	
mistrust	prehistoric	renew	unpack	displace	indent	
misuse	prepare	reorder	unreal	disregard	indoor	
	prevent	repay	unripe	disrespect	inset	
	precaution	reprint	unselfish	distaste	insight	
	preschool	research	unstable	distrust	inside	
		restore	unsteady	different	inlaid	
		retrace	untangle	diffuse	inmate	
		return	untie	diffident	ingrown	
		review	unwrap		inboard	
		rewrite			inland	
					infield	

Appendix E

uni-	*bi-*	*tri-*	*fore-*	*sub-*	*ex-*	*en-*
unicorn	biceps	triangle	forearm	subset	expel	enable
unicycle	bicycle	triple	forecast	subtract	express	endanger
uniform	bifocals	triceps	foretell	subdivide	explore	enact
unify	bilingual	triceratops	foresee	subgroup	exceed	enclose
union	binoculars	tricycle	foresight	submerge	excerpt	encourage
unique	bisect	trilogy	forehand	submarine	exclaim	enforce
unison	biweekly	trio	forehead	submerse	exclude	enjoy
universal		trivet	foreman	submit	excrete	enslave
universe		triplets	forethought	subway	exhale	enlarge
		tripod	foreshadow	subtotal	exile	enlist
		triad	forepaw	subtitle	expand	enrage
		trinity	foremost	sublet	explode	enrich
		trident		subsoil	exit	enroll
		triathalon		subject		entrust

-ly	*-y*	*-er/-est*	*-less*	*-ful*	*-ness*
badly	breezy	blacker/blackest	ageless	careful	awareness
barely	bumpy	bigger/biggest	breathless	cheerful	closeness
bravely	chilly	bolder/boldest	careless	colorful	coolness
closely	choppy	braver/bravest	ceaseless	fearful	darkness
coarsely	cloudy	calmer/calmest	endless	graceful	firmness
constantly	dirty	closer/closest	helpless	harmful	goodness
costly	dusty	cheaper/cheapest	homeless	hopeful	openness
cowardly	easy	cleaner/cleanest	lawless	lawful	ripeness
cruelly	floppy	cooler/coolest	painless	peaceful	sickness
deadly	frosty	colder/coldest	powerless	playful	sharpness
directly	gloomy	smaller/smallest	priceless	powerful	stiffness
eagerly	greasy	thinner/thinnest	reckless	tasteful	stillness
finally	grouchy	fewer/fewest	spotless	thoughtful	thinness
frequently	gritty	finer/finest	tasteless	truthful	weakness
loudly	noisy	hotter/hottest	painless	useful	moistness
loyally	rainy	harder/hardest	speechless	wasteful	vastness
proudly	sandy	sadder/saddest	thankless	wonderful	dullness
really	soapy	newer/newest	cloudless	youthful	
smoothly	snowy	quicker/quickest	fruitless	beautiful	
kindly	stormy	lighter/lightest	jobless	armful	
nicely	sweaty	louder/loudest	scoreless	dreadful	
nightly	thirsty	larger/largest	sleeveless	respectful	
safely	windy	meaner/meanest			
	dressy				
Change y to i	skinny	*Change y to i*	*Change y to i*		*Change y to i*
noisily	speedy	funnier/funniest	penniless		dizziness
lazily	floppy	noisier/noisiest	pitiless		emptiness
angrily		prettier/prettiest	merciless		laziness
busily		dirtier/dirtiest			readiness
easily		easier/easiest			fussiness
happily		juicier/juiciest			happiness
		lazier/laziest			ugliness

Special Consonants

Hard *g*	Soft *g*	Hard *c*	Soft *c*	Final *c*	*que*	*k / Ke*	*ck*	*Silent Letters*
gadget	genie	cabin	city	attic	antique	namesake	attack	wrinkle
gallon	genius	cafe	cider	music	unique	cupcake	carsick	wreckage
gallop	genre	cactus	civil	topic	clique	earthquake	gimmick	wrestle
gamble	general	campus	cinder	zodiac	opaque	forsake	haddock	answer
garage	gentle	candle	circle	clinic	critique	keepsake	hemlock	knuckle
gully	gerbil	canyon	circus	comic	physique	mistake	potluck	knowledge
golden	gesture	cavern	citric	cynic	mystique	pancake	hammock	honest
gossip	giant	carpet	cedar	toxic	brusque	provoke	ransack	honor
guilty	ginger	cable	celery	panic		slowpoke	padlock	rhyme
gorilla	giraffe	comma	cement	picnic		turnpike		rhythm
gopher	gyro	copy	census	classic	*x*	evoke		shepherd
gather	gypsy	cozy	center	critic	relax	homework		castle
gutter	gyrate	cocoa	cereal	elastic	complex	embark		whistle
guitar		comet	ceiling	exotic	index	landmark		fasten
gobble		coffee	certain	frantic	perplex	network		listen
goggles		corner	cycle	graphic		berserk		often*
gaily		county	cynic	hectic	*ck*			moisten
gallery		cubic	cymbal	garlic	attack			daughter
		cuddle	cyclist	fabric	gimmick			naughty
Oddballs		culprit	cyclone	frolic	hammock			height
giggle		curtain	cylinder	logic	ransack			weight
geyser		custom		drastic	padlock			freight
gecko		curtain		scenic	potluck			design
					hemlock			resign
					carsick			gnaw
					haddock			gnarl
								gnome
								gnostic
								gnu

Alternations

Silent to Sounded Consonant	Long to Short	Long to Schwa	Short to Schwa
bomb/bombard	cave/cavity	able/ability	metallic/metal
column/columnist	flame/flammable	famous/infamous	academy/academic
soften/soft	grave/gravity	major/majority	malice/malicious
crumb/crumble	nature/natural	native/nativity	periodic/period
debt/debit	athlete/athletic	prepare/preparation	emphatic/emphasis
damn/damnation	please/pleasant	relate/relative	celebrate/celebrity
design/designate	crime/criminal	stable/stability	democratic/democracy
fasten/fast	decide/decision	compete/competition	excel/excellent
haste/hast	revise/revision	combine/combination	perfection/perfect
hymn/hymnal	wise/wisdom	define/definition	critic/criticize
malign/malignant	know/knowledge	divide/division	habit/habitat
moisten/moist	episode/episodic	invite/invitation	mobility/mobile
muscle/muscular	assume/assumption	recite/recitation	prohibit/prohibition
resign/resignation	produce/production	reside/resident	geometry/geometric
sign/signal	convene/convention	compose/composition	
condemn/condemnation	volcano/volcanic	expose/exposition	
	serene/serenity	custodian/custody	
	ignite/ignition	pose/position	
	humane/humanity	social/society	

Appendix E

Adding /shun/ to base words

ct + ion	ss + ion	t + ion	de > sion	e-drop + ion	it > ission
subtraction	expression	assertion	explosion	creation	admission
distinction	oppression	digestion	decision	decoration	omission
election	possession	invention	division	generation	permission
prediction	profession	suggestion	invasion	imitation	submission
extinction	confession	adoption	conclusion	illustration	transmission
detection	compression	insertion	intrusion	indication	
selection	obsession	congestion	protrusion	translation	**e-drop + tion**
rejection	digression	prevention	allusion	congratulation	production
reaction	impression	distortion	collision	frustration	introduction
connection	discussion	exhaustion	suspension	operation	reduction
distraction	aggression	eruption	evasion	location	reproduction
objection	depression	exception	erosion	vibration	deduction
infection	procession	desertion	seclusion	circulation	seduction
instruction	recession		allusion	pollution	
protection		**t + ation**	expansion	dictation	**be > p + tion**
conviction	**c + ian**	adaptation	persuasion	hesitation	description
correction	magician	temptation	ascension	donation	prescription
detection	musician	presentation		devotion	inscription
abstraction	optician	indentation		graduation	subscription
inspection	logician	plantation		migration	transcription
injection	clinician	infestation		navigation	
reflection	diagnostician	lamentation		isolation	
	electrician	confrontation		translation	

Vowel Alternations with Change in Accent When Adding Suffixes

Schwa to Short with ity	*Long to Short with cation*	*Long to Schwa with ation*
mental/mentality	apply/application	declare/declaration
general/generality	certify/certification	degrade/degradation
moral/morality	clarify/clarification	prepare/preparation
brutal/brutality	classify/classification	admire/admiration
central/centrality	gratify/gratification	combine/combination
eventual/eventuality	imply/implication	define/definition
personal/personality	notify/notification	deprive/deprivation
neutral/neutrality	purify/purification	derive/derivation
original/originality	modify/modification	incline/inclination
normal/normality	unify/unification	invite/invitation
mental/mentality	simplify/simplification	recite/recitation
formal/formality	multiply/multiplication	compile/compilation
equal/equality	magnify/magnification	perspire/perspiration
vital/vitality	specify/specification	explore/exploration
legal/legality	verify/verification	
local/locality	qualify/qualification	
hospital/hospitality	identify/identification	
personal/personality		

Words Their Way: Word Study for Phonics, Vocabulary, and Spelling Instruction © 2008 by Pearson Education, Inc.

Adding the Suffix *able/ible*

Root Word + *ible*	Base Word + *able*	*e-drop* + *able*	*y to i* + *able*
audible	affordable	achievable	variable
credible	agreeable	admirable	reliable
edible	allowable	adorable	pliable
eligible	avoidable	advisable	pitiable
feasible	breakable	believable	justifiable
gullible	comfortable	comparable	identifiable
horrible	dependable	conceivable	deniable
invincible	expandable	consumable	enviable
legible	favorable	debatable	remediable
plausible	laughable	deplorable	
possible	payable	desirable	Drop *ate* in Base
terrible	preferable	disposable	tolerable
visible	predictable	excitable	vegetable
indelible	profitable	lovable	operable
intangible	punishable	notable	navigable
compatible	reasonable	pleasurable	abominable
combustible	refillable	recyclable	negotiable
	remarkable	valuable	educable
	respectable		estimable
	transferable	*ce/ge* + *able*	irritable
		manageable	appreciable
		enforceable	
		noticeable	
		changeable	

Adding *ant/ance/ancy* and *ent/ence/ency*

hesitant/hesitance/hesitancy
abundant/abundance/abundancy
relevant/relevance/relevancy
hesitant/hesitance/hesitancy
extravagant/extravagance/extravagancy
malignant/malignance/malignancy
petulant/petulance/petulancy
radiant/radiance/radiancy
brilliant/brilliance/brilliancy
defiant/defiance
reluctant/reluctance
exuberant/exuberance
fragrant/fragrance
instant/instance
elegant/elegance
vigilant/vigilance
resistant/resistance
significant/significance
tolerant/tolerance
observant/observance
relevant/relevance

competent/competence/competency
dependent/dependence/dependency
emergent/emergence/emergency
equivalent/equivalence/equivalency
excellent/excellence/excellency
expedient/expedience/expediency
lenient/lenience/leniency
resident/residence/residency
resilient/resilience/resiliency
convenient/convenience
different/difference
diligent/diligence
evident/evidence
impatient/impatience
independent/independence
patient/patience
innocent/innocence
intelligent/intelligence
obedient/obedience
indulgent/indulgence
violent/violence

Using *ary,* *ery,* and *ory*

ary = /ary/	*ery = /ary/*	*ary = /ǝry/*	*ery = /ǝry/*	*ory = /ory/*	*ory = /ǝry/*
customary	very	anniversary	artery	allegory	compulsory
fragmentary	cemetery	boundary	bribery	auditory	cursory
extraordinary	stationery	documentary	celery	category	directory
hereditary	confectionery	elementary	discovery	dormitory	memory
imaginary		glossary	gallery	explanatory	satisfactory
legendary		salary	grocery	inventory	theory
literary		summary	imagery	observatory	victory
military		burglary	machinery	territory	history
missionary		diary	mystery	circulatory	memory
necessary		infirmary	nursery	derogatory	accessory
ordinary		auxiliary	scenery	laboratory	compulsory
revolutionary		documentary	surgery	mandatory	victory
secretary		rudimentary	drapery	respiratory	
solitary			forgery		
stationary			misery		
temporary					
vocabulary					

Accent in Polysyllabic Words

First Syllable		*Second Syllable*		*Third Syllable*
anything	cantaloupe	December	asparagus	constitution
somebody	comedy	November	attorney	population
beautiful	customer	October	computer	planetarium
families	engineer	September	election	Sacramento
grandfather	evidence	uncommon	endurance	Tallahassee
January	forestry	unusual	executive	understand
libraries	generator	unwanted	erosion	imitation
Wednesday	improvise	protection	ignition	regulation
wonderful	iodine	reduction	judicial	California
populate	meteorite	romantic	mechanic	definition
acrobat	navigator	unable	banana	diagnosis
amateur	average	providing	department	hippopotamus
aptitude	camera	vacation	important	irrigation
architect	carpenter	whoever	deliver	Mississippi
artery	everything	accountant	remember	declaration
avalanche	colorful	agility	whenever	exclamation
calculator	gasoline	amphibian	tomorrow	
	everywhere	apprentice	abilities	
	hamburger		apartment	
			companion	
			condition	

Appendix E

Prefixes

anti "against"	auto "self"	circum "around"	inter "between"		mal "bad"
antifreeze	autograph	circumference	interact	international	malice
antidote	automation	circumvent	intercede	interlocking	malignant
antitoxin	autobiography	circumstance	interfere	intermission	maltreated
antibiotic	automobile	circumspect	interloper	international	malpractice
anticlimactic	autocrat	circumscribe	interchange	intermural	maladjusted
antisocial	autonomy	circumlocution	interject	*intra* "within"	malnutrition
antigen	autopsy	circumnavigate	interrupt	intramural	malcontent
antipathy			intercede	intravenous	malfunction
antiseptic			intercom	intrastate	malady

peri "around"	post "after"	pro "before," "forward"		super "higher"	trans "across"
perimeter	posterior	proceed	profile	superpower	transfer
period	posterity	propel	promotion	supervision	transport
periphery	posthumous	produce	prohibit	supermarket	transmit
periscope	postpone	progress	procreate	supernatural	transplant
peripatetic	postscript	provide	propitious	superman	translate
periodontal	postmortem	program	pronounce	supersede	translucent
	postgraduate	projector	promulgate	supersonic	transparent
	postmeridian	protective	propensity	superstition	transform
		proclaim	proficient	superficial	transient
		profess	protracted	supercilious	transcend

Number-Related Prefixes (see *uni, bi,* and *tri* under easier prefixes on page 356)

mon, mono	cent	mil	oct	poly	semi	multi
monarchy	centigrade	million	octagon	polygon	semiannual	multitude
monastery	centimeter	millimeter	octopus	polygamy	semicolon	multiply
monogram	centipede	milligram	October	polychrome	semicircle	multicolored
monologue	centennial	millennium	octave	polyhedron	semisolid	multipurpose
monorail	century	millionaire	octahedron	polyglot	semiconscious	multicultural
monotone	percent		octogenarian	polyester	semifinal	multimedia
monotonous	bicentennial	*deca*		polygraph	semiweekly	multiplex
monolith		decade	*pent*	polymath	semiprecious	multifaceted
monopoly		December	pentagon	polymers		multivitamin
monochrome		decahedron	pentameter	polyp		multifarious
monogamy		decagon	pentacle	polytechnic		multiplication

Assimilated or Absorbed Prefixes

in ("not")	il	im	ir	im
inaccurate	illogical	immature	irrational	impure
inefficient	illegal	immaterial	irreconcilable	impaired
inoperable	illiterate	immobile	irreparable	impartial
insecure	illegible	immodest	irregular	impossible
innumerable	illicit	immoderate	irrelevant	impediment
inactive	illustrious	immoral	irreplaceable	imperfect
inappropriate	illegitimate	immortal	irresistible	impersonal
incompetent	illuminate	immovable	irresponsible	improper
indecent		immigrant	irreversible	impractical
		immediate	irradiate	
		immerse	irreligious	

Appendix E

ex ("out" or "without")

			ef	
extract	extension	excrete	effort	effluent
excavate	exclude	excursion	effigy	effusion
exceed	exhaust	exhume	effervescent	
excerpt	exclaim	exile	effront	
expand	explosion	extinct	efferent	

sub ("under" or "lower")

		suf	*sup*	*sur*
subversion	subatomic	suffix	supplant	surreal
subterranean	subcommittee	suffuse	suppliant	surrender
suburban	subdivision	suffer	support	surrogate
substitute	submarine	suffice	supposition	surreptitious
substandard	subconscious	sufficient	suppress	
subsidize	subcontractor	suffocate	supplicant	*suc*
subclass	subjugate		supplement	succumb
sublease	subscribe			succeed
subscript	subscription			success
subtract	submarine			succinct
subdue	submit			successive

com ("with" or "together")

	col	*con*	*cor*	*co*
common	collection	conspire	correlate	coagulate
community	collide	concert	corroborate	coexist
combination	collision	connect	correct	coalition
committee	collage	congress	correspond	coauthor
company	collaborate	congestion	corrupted	coeducational
comply	colleague	congregation	corrugated	cohabit
compress	collapse	conclude		cohesion
compound	collusion	condense		cohort
companion	collate	construct		coincide
compact	collateral	constellation		cooperate
complete	colloquial	connote		coordinate
comrade	collect			
combine				

ad ("to" or "toward")

	at	*ac*	*af*	*al*	*ap*	*as*	*ar*
adjacent	attend	accompany	affinity	alliance	approach	assemble	arrange
adjoining	attune	acceptable	affable	alliteration	approximate	associate	arrest
addicted	attract	access	affection	allowance	appropriate	assimilate	array
adhesive	attach	accident	affluence	allusion	apprentice	assent	arrive
adjacent	attack	accommodate	affiliate	alleviate	apprehend	assault	arrogant
adaptation	attain	accomplish	affricative	allotment	appreciate	assertion	
additional	attention	accumulate	affirmation		application	assessment	
adjective	attempt	accomplish		*an*	applause	assume	
adjust	attitude	accelerate	*ag*	annex	appetite	assiduous	
admire	attribute	acquisition	aggregate	annihilate	appendix	assistance	
admission	attrition	acquire	aggravate	announce	appear	assuage	
advocate		acquisitive	aggression	annul	appeal	assumption	
			aggrieved	annotate			

dis ("not" or "opposite of" or "apart")

		dif	*ex* ("out" or "from")	*ef*
disadvantage	disarray	difficult	extract	efface
dissatisfied	disconcerted	diffusion	excavate	effect
disillusioned	discharged	different	exceed	efferent
disaster	disclaimer	diffidence	exception	efficiency
disability	disconsolate		excerpt	effrontery
disagreeable	discouraged		excursion	effusive
disseminate	disregard		exhale	
disappoint	disenchanted		exile	*ec*
discern	disillusioned		expansion	ecstasy
disdain	disoriented		expenditure	eccentric
				ecclesiastical

ob ("to," "toward," or "against")

			op	*of*	*oc*
oblong	obscure	obscure	opponent	offend	occurrence
objection	observant	oblique	opposite	offensive	occasion
obligation	obstruction	obstacle	opportunity	offering	occupation
obliterate	obstreperous	obsolete	opposition	offense	occupy
oblivious	obstinate	obnoxious	oppress	officious	occlude

Greek Roots

aer	"air" aerate, aerial, aerobics, aerodynamic, aeronautics, aerosol, aerospace
arch	"chief" monarchy, anarchy, archangel, archbishop, archetype, architect, hierarchy, matriarch, patriarch
aster, astr	"star" aster, asterisk, asteroid, astrology, astronomy, astronaut, astronomical, astrophysics, disaster
bi, bio	"life" biology, biography, autobiography, biopsy, symbiotic, biodegradable, antibiotic, amphibious, biochemistry
centr	"center" center, central, egocentric, ethnocentric, centrifuge, concentric, concentrate, eccentric
chron	"time" chronic, chronicle, chronological, synchronize, anachronism
cosm	"world" cosmic, cosmology, cosmonaut, cosmopolitan, cosmos, microcosm
crat	"rule" democrat, plutocrat, bureaucrat, idiosyncratic, plutocrat, technocrat
crit	"judge" critic, criticize, critique, criterion, diacritical, hypocrite
cycl	"circle" cycle, bicycle, cyclone, tricycle, unicycle, recycle, motorcycle, cyclical, encyclopedia
dem	"people" demagogue, democracy, demographics, endemic, epidemic, epidemiology
derm	"skin" dermatologist, epidermis, hypodermic, pachyderm, taxidermist, dermatitis
geo	"earth" geology, geophysics, geography, geothermal, geocentric, geode
gram	"to write" diagram, program, telegram, anagram, cryptogram, epigram, grammar, monogram
graph	"to write" graph, paragraph, autograph, digraph, graphics, topography, biography, bibliography, calligraphy, choreographer, videographer, ethnography, phonograph, seismograph, lexicographer
homo	"same" homophone, homograph, homosexual, homogeneous
hydra	"water" hydra, hydrant, hydrate, hydrogen, hydraulic, hydroelectric, hydrology, hydroplane, hydroponics, anhydrous, hydrangea, hydrophobia
logo	"word, reason" logic, catalogue, dialogue, prologue, epilogue, monologue
logy	"study" biology, geology, ecology, mythology, pathology, psychology, sociology, theology, genealogy, etymology, technology, zoology
meter	"measure" centimeter, millimeter, diameter, speedometer, thermometer, tachometer, altimeter, barometer, kilometer
micro	"small" microscope, microphone, microwave, micrometer, microbiology, microcomputer, microcosm
ortho	"straight, correct" orthodox, orthodontics, orthography, orthodontists, orthopedic
pan	"all" pandemic, panorama, pandemonium, pantheon, Pan-American
path	"suffer" sympathy, antipathy, apathetic, empathize, pathogen, pathologist, pathetic, pathos, osteopath
ped	"child" (see Latin ped for foot) pedagogy, pediatrician, pedophile, encyclopedia
phil	"loving" philosophy, philharmonic, bibliophile, Philadelphia, philanderer, philanthropy, philatetic, philter
phobia	"fear" phobia, acrophobia, claustrophobia, xenophobia, araeniphobia, xenophobia

Appendix E

phon	"sound" phonics, phonograph, cacophony, earphone, euphony, homophone, microphone, telephone, xylophone, saxophone, phoneme, symphony
photo	"light" photograph, telephoto, photocopier, photographer, photosynthesis, photocell
phys	"nature" physics, physical, physician, physiology, physique, astrophysics, physiognomy, physiotherapy
pol	"city" politics, police, policy, metropolis, acropolis, cosmopolitan, megalopolis, Minneapolis
psych	"spirit, soul" psyche, psychology, psychoanalyst, psychiatry, psychedelic, psychosis, psychosomatic, psychic
scope	"see" microscope, periscope, scope, telescope, stethoscope, gyroscope, horoscope, kaleidoscope, stereoscope
sphere	"ball" sphere, atmosphere, biosphere, hemisphere, ionosphere, stratosphere, troposphere
tech	"art, skill" technical, technician, technology, polytechnic
tele	"far" telecast, telegraph, telegram, telescope, television, telethon, teleconference, telepathy
therm	"heat" thermal, geothermal, thermometer, thermonuclear, thermos, thermostat, thermodynamic, exothermic
typ	"to beat, to strike" typewriter, typist, typographical, archetype, daguerreotype, prototype, stereotype, typecast
zo	"animal" zoo, zoology, protozoan, zodiac, zoologist

Latin Stems

aud	"hear" audio, auditorium, audience, audible, audition, inaudible, audiovisual
bene	"well" benefactor, benevolent, beneficial, benefit, benign, benefactress, benediction
cand, chand	"shine" candle, chandelier, incandescent, candelabra, candid, candidate
cap	"head" captain, capital, capitol, capitalize, capitulate, decapitate, per capita
cide	"cut, kill" incise, incision, concise, circumcise, excise, fungicide, herbicide, pesticide, insecticide, suicide, homicide, genocide
clud, clos, clus	"shut" close, closet, disclose, enclose, foreclose, conclude, exclude, exclusive, preclude, occlude, seclude, seclusion, recluse
cogn	"know" recognize, incognito, cognizant, cognition, recognizance
corp	"body" corpse, corporal, corporation, corpus, corpulent, incorporate, corpuscle
cred	"trust, believe" credit, credible, credentials, incredible, accredited, credulous
dent, dont	"tooth" dentist, dentures, orthodontist, indent
dic, dict	"speak" dictate, diction, dictionary, predict, verdict, benediction, contradict, dedicate, edict, indict, jurisdiction, valedictorian dictation
doc	"teach" documentary, indoctrinate, doctorate, doctor, docent, docile, doctrine
duc, duct	"lead" abduct, conductor, deduct, aqueduct, duct, educate, educe, induct, introduction, reduce, reproduce, viaduct
equa, equi	"equal" equal, equality, equation, equator, equity, equivalent, equilibrium, equivocate, equidistant, equinox
fac, fact, fect	"do" factory, manufacture, factory, faculty, artifact, benefactor, confection, defect, effect, facile, facilitate, facsimile, affect, affection
fer	"carry" ferry, transfer, prefer, reference, suffer, vociferous, inference, fertile, differ, conifer, conference, circumference
fid	"trust" fidelity, confidant, confidence, diffident, infidelity, perfidy, affidavit, bona fide, confidential
fin	"end" final, finale, finish, infinite, definitive
flex, flect	"bend, curve" flex, flexible, inflexible, deflect, reflection, inflection, circumflex, genuflect
flu	"flow" fluid, fluent, influx, superfluous, affluence, confluence, fluctuate, influence
form	"shape" conform, deform, formal, formality, format, formation, formula, informal, information, malformed, platform, reform, transform, uniform
grac, grat	"thankful" grace, gratuity, gracious, ingrate, congratulate, grateful, gratitude, ingrate, ingratiate, persona non grata, gratify
grad, gress	"step" graduate, gradual, gradient, grade, retrograde, centigrade, degraded, downgrade, digress, aggressive, congress, egress, ingress, progress, regress, transgression
ject	"throw" eject, injection, interject, object, objection, conjecture, abject, dejected, interject, projection, projectile, projector, reject, subjective, trajectory
jud	"judge" judge, judgment, prejudice, judiciary, judicial, adjudge, adjudicate, injudicious
junct	"join" junction, juncture, injunction, conjunction, adjunct, disjunction
langu, lingu	"tongue" language, bilingual, linguistics, linguist, linguine, lingo
lit	"letter" literature, illiterate, literal, literacy, obliterate, alliteration, literary
loc, loq	"speak" elocution, eloquent, loquacious, obloquy, soliloquy, ventriloquist, colloquial, interlocutor
manus	"hand" manual, manufacture, manicure, manuscript, emancipate, manacle, mandate, manipulate, manage, maneuver

Words Their Way: Word Study for Phonics, Vocabulary, and Spelling Instruction © 2008 by Pearson Education, Inc.

mem	"mindful" remember, memory, memorize, memorial, memorandum, memento, memorabilia, commemorate
min	"small" diminish, mince, minimize, minute, minuscule, minus, minor, minnow, minimum
miss, mit	"send" transmission, remission, submission, admit, transmit, remit, submit, omit, mission, missile, demise, emission, admission, commission, emissary, intermission, intermittent, missionary, permission, promise
mob, mot	"move" mobile, motion, motor, remote, automobile, promote, motivate, motion, motel, locomotion, immobile, emotion, demote, commotion
pat	"father" paternal, patrimony, expatriate, patron, patronize
ped	"foot" pedal, pedestal, pedicure, pedigree, biped, centipede, millipede, moped, impede, expedite, orthopedic, pedestrian, quadruped
pens, pend	"hang" appendage, appendix, pending, pendulum, pension, suspended, suspense, compensate, depend, dispense, expend, expensive, pensive, stipend, impending, pendant
port	"carry" porter, portfolio, portage, portable, export, import, rapport, report, support, transport, comportment, deport, important, portmanteau
pos, pon	"put, place" pose, position, positive, a propos, compose, composite, compost, composure, disposable, expose, impose, imposter, opposite, postpone, preposition, proponent, proposition, superimpose, suppose
prim, princ	"first" prime, primate, primer, primeval, primitive, prima donna, primal, primary, primogeniture, primordial, primrose, prince, principal, principality, principle
quir, ques	"ask" inquire, require, acquire, conquer, inquisition, quest, question, questionnaire, request, requisite, requisition
rupt	"break" rupture, abrupt, bankrupt, corrupt, erupt, disrupt, erupt, interrupt, irruption
sal	"salt" salt, saline, salary, salami, salsa, salad, desalinate
sci	"know" science, conscience, conscious, omniscience, subconscious, conscientious
scrib, script	"write" scribble, script, scripture, subscribe, transcription, ascribe, describe, inscribe, proscribe, postscript, prescription, circumscribe, nondescript, conscription
sect, seg	"cut" bisect, dissect, insect, intersect, section, sector, segment
sent, sens	"feel" sense, sensitive, sensory, sensuous, sentiment, sentimental, assent, consent, consensus, dissent, resent, sensation
sequ, sec	"follow" seque, sequel, sequential, consequence, consecutive, non sequitor, persecute, second, sect, subsequent
son	"sound" sonic, sonnet, sonorous, unison, ultrasonic, assonance, consonant, dissonant, resonate, sonate
spec, spic	"see" spectacle, spectacles, spectacular, specimen, prospect, respect, retrospective, speculate, suspect, suspicion, aspect, auspicious, circumspect, inspector, introspection
spir	"breathe" spirit, respiration, perspire, transpire, inspire, conspire, aspirate, dispirited, antiperspirant
sta, stis	"stand" stable, state, station, stationary, statistic, statue, stature, status, subsist, assist, consistent, desist, insistent, persistent, resist
stru	"build" construct, instruct, destruction, reconstruction, obstruct
tain	"hold" detain, obtain, pertain, retain, sustain, abstain, appertain, contain, entertain, maintain
tang tact	"touch" tangible, intangible, tangent, contact, tactile
ten	"stretch" distend, tendon, tendril, extend, intend, intensify, attend, contend, portend, superintendent
term	"end" term, terminal, terminate, determine, exterminate, predetermine
terra	"earth" terrain, terrarium, terrace, subterranean, terrestrial, extraterrestrial, Mediterranean, terra cotta, terra firma
tort, torq	"twist" contort, distort, extort, torture, tortuous, torque
tract	"pull" tractor, traction, contract, distract, subtract, retract, attract, protracted, intractable, abstract, detract
vac	"empty" vacant, vacuum, evacuate, vacation, vacuous, vacate
val	"strong, worth" valid, valiant, validate, evaluate, devalue, convalescent, valedictorian, invalid
ven, vent	"come" vent, venture, venue, adventure, avenue, circumvent, convention, event, intervene, invent, prevent, revenue, souvenir, convenient
vers, vert	"turn" revert, vertex, vertigo, convert, divert, vertical, adverse, advertise, anniversary, avert, controversy, conversation, extrovert, introvert, inverse, inverted, perverted, reverse, subvert, traverse, transverse, universe, versatile, versus, vertebra
vid, vis	"see" video, vista, visage, visit, visual, visa, advise, audiovisual, envision, invisible, television, supervise, provision, revision, improvise
voc	"call" vocal, vociferous, evoke, invoke, advocate, avocation, convocation, equivocal, invocation, provoke, revoke, vocabulary, vocation
vol, volv	"roll" revolve, evolve, involve, volume, convoluted, devolve

Games and Templates for Sorts

Gameboards

Figures F-1 through F-8 are gameboard templates that can be used to create some of the games described throughout the book. Note that there are two sides for each gameboard. When the two sides are placed together, they form a continuous track or path. These games can be adapted for many different features and for many different levels. Here are some general tips on creating the games.

1. The gameboards can be photocopied (enlarge slightly) and mounted on manila file folders (colored ones are nice), making them easy to create and store. All the materials needed for the game, such as spinners, word cards, or game markers, can be put in plastic bags or envelopes labeled with the name of the game and stored in the folder. You might mark the flip side of word cards in some way so that lost cards can be returned to the correct game. Rubber stamp figures work well.

2. When mounting a gameboard in a folder, be sure to leave a slight gap (about an eighth of an inch) between the two sides so that the folder will still fold. If you do not leave this gap the paper will buckle. Trim the gameboards to line up neatly or cut out of the entire path.

3. A variety of objects (buttons, plastic discs, coins, and bottle caps) can be used for game markers or pawns that the children will move around the board. Flat objects store best in the folders or you may just want to put a collection of game markers, dice, and spinners in a box. This box can be stored near the games, and students can take what they need.

4. Add pizazz to games with pictures cut from magazines or old workbooks, stickers, comic characters, clip art, and so on. Rubber stamps, your drawings, or children's drawings can be used to add interest and color. Create catchy themes such as Rabbit Race, Lost in Space, Through the Woods, Mouse Maze, Rainforest Adventure, and so forth.

5. Include directions and correct answers (when appropriate) with the game. They might be stored inside along with playing pieces or glued to the game itself.

6. Label the spaces around the path or track according to the feature you want to reinforce, and laminate for durability. If you want to create open-ended games that can be adapted to a variety of features, laminate the path before you label the spaces. Then you can write in letters or words with a washable overheard pen and change them as needed. Permanent marker can also be used and removed with hairspray or fingernail polish remover.

7. Add interest to the game by labeling some spaces with special directions (if you are using a numbered die or spinner) or add cards with special directions to the deck of words. Directions might offer the students a bonus in the form of an extra turn or there might be a penalty such as lose a turn. These bonus or penalty directions can tie in with your themes. For example, in the Rainforest Adventure the player might forget a lunch and be asked to go back to the starting space. Keep the reading ability of your children in mind as you create these special directions.

Spinners

Many of the word study games described in this book use a game spinner. Figure F-8 provides simple directions for making a spinner.

FIGURE F-1 Racetrack Gameboard (left and right)

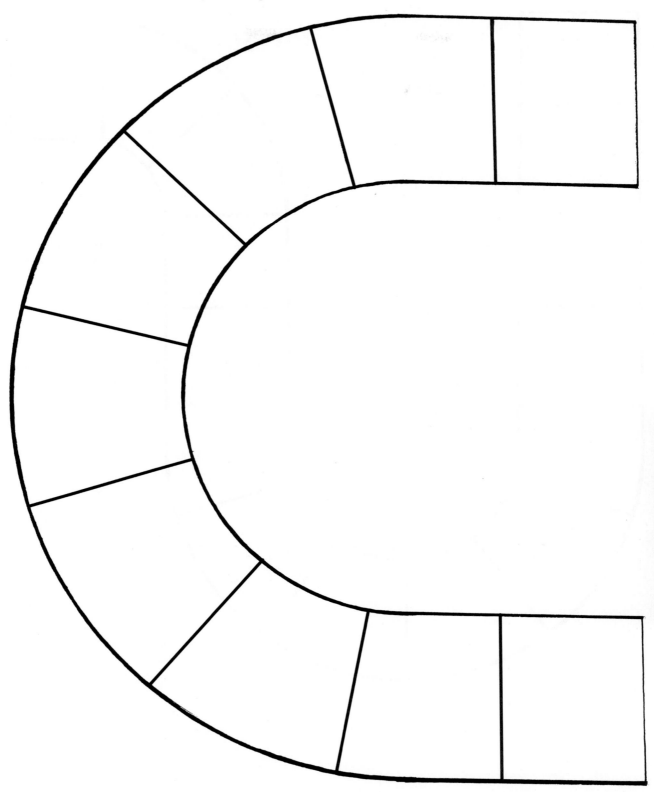

Appendix F

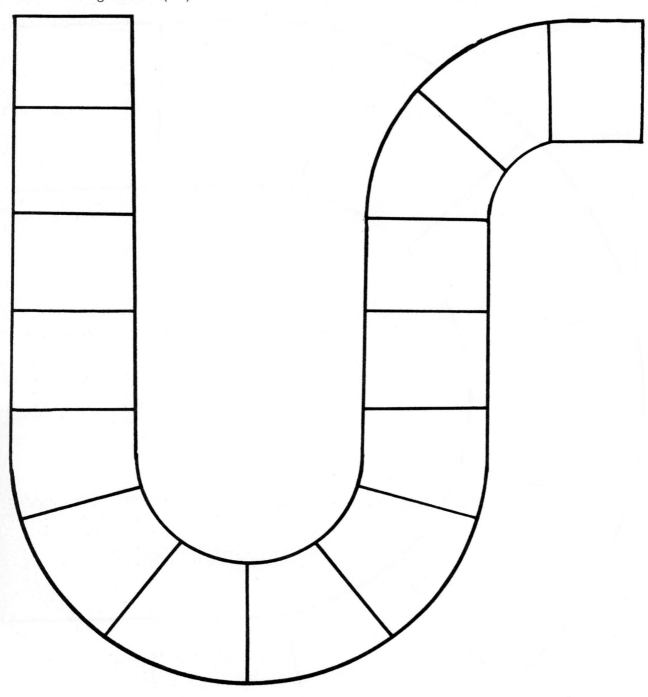

FIGURE F-3　U-gameboard (right)

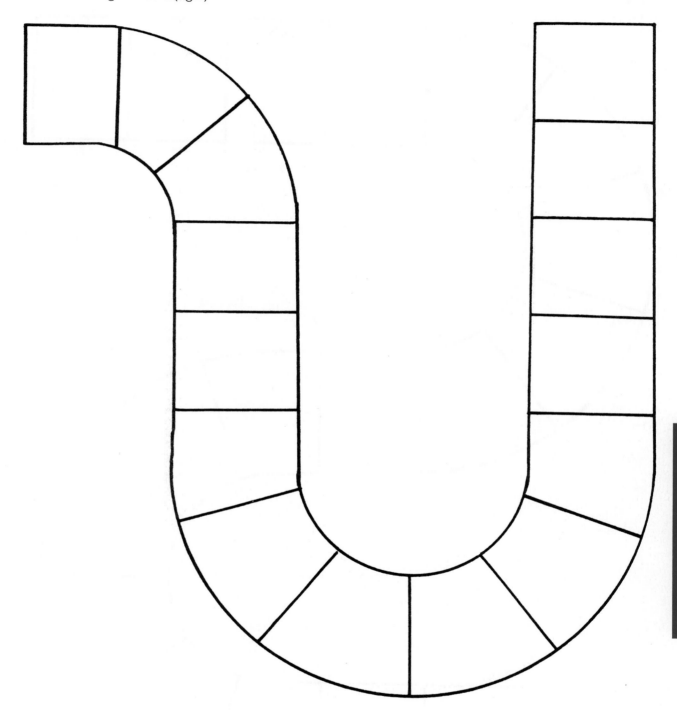

FIGURE F-4 S-gameboard (left)

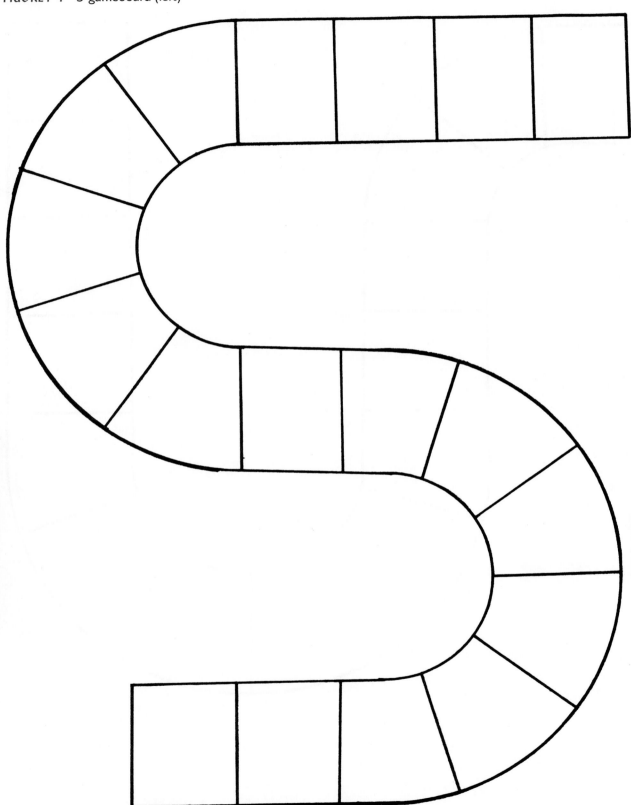

Words Their Way: Word Study for Phonics, Vocabulary, and Spelling Instruction © 2008 by Pearson Education, Inc.

Appendix F

FIGURE F-5   S-gameboard (right)

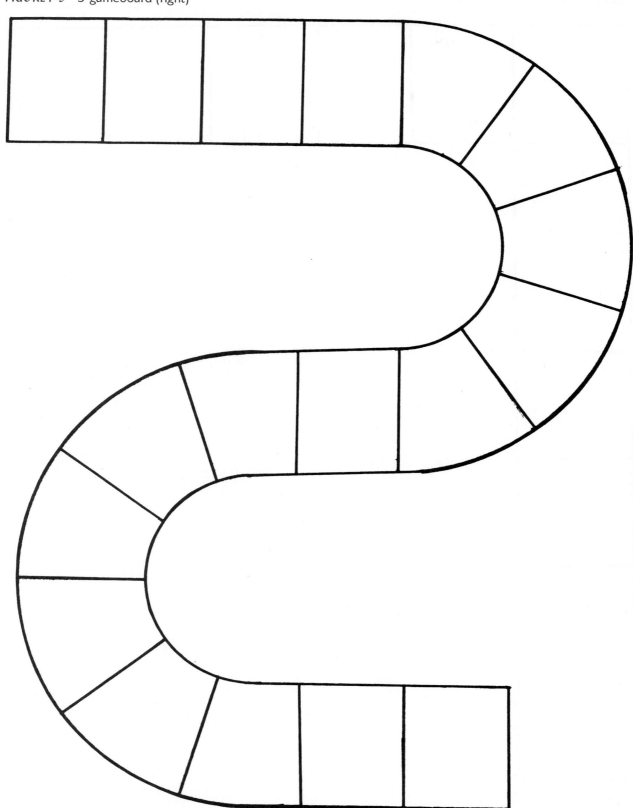

FIGURE F-6   Rectangle Gameboard (left)

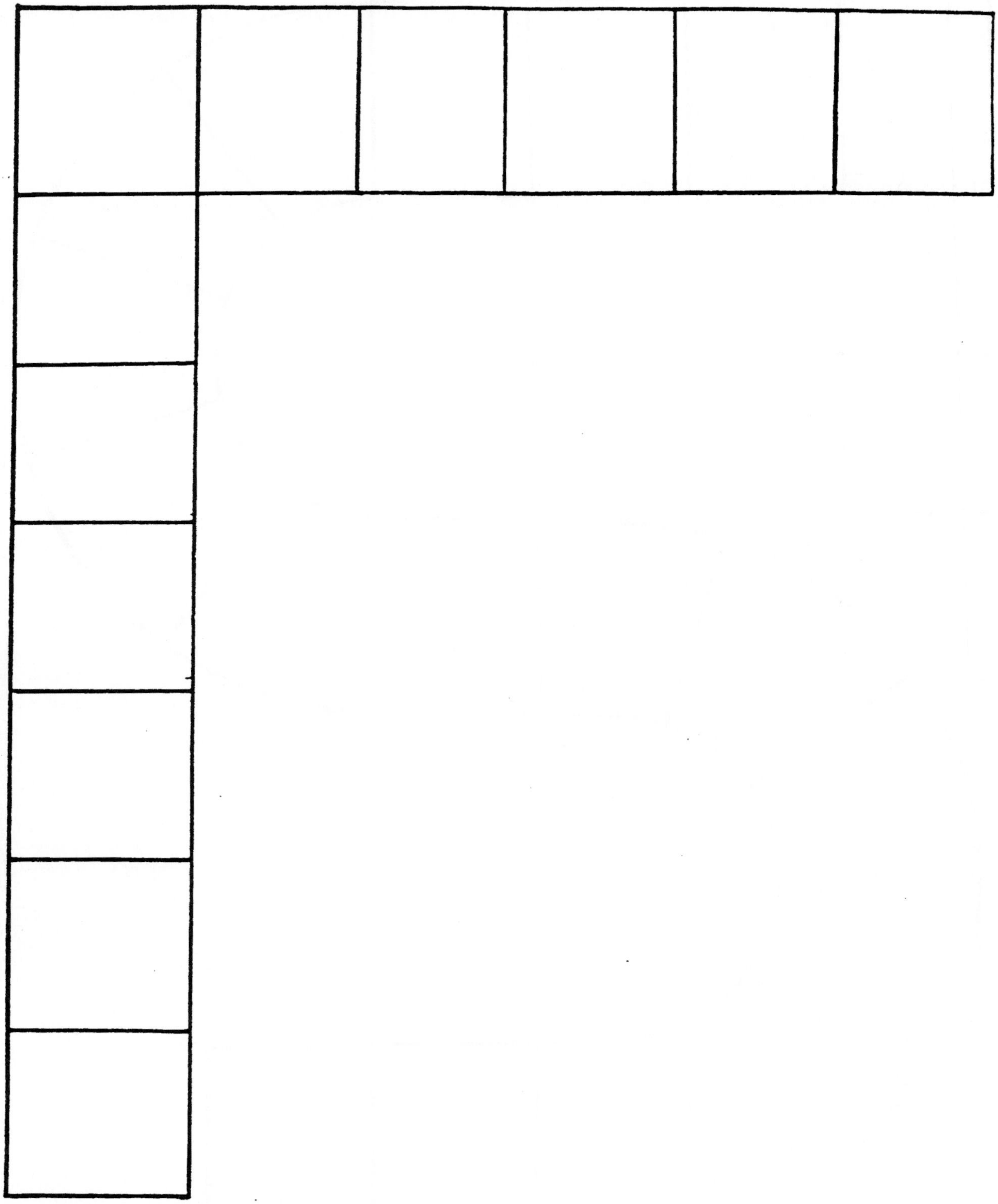

Words Their Way: Word Study for Phonics, Vocabulary, and Spelling Instruction © 2008 by Pearson Education, Inc.

FIGURE F-7 Rectangle Gameboard (right)

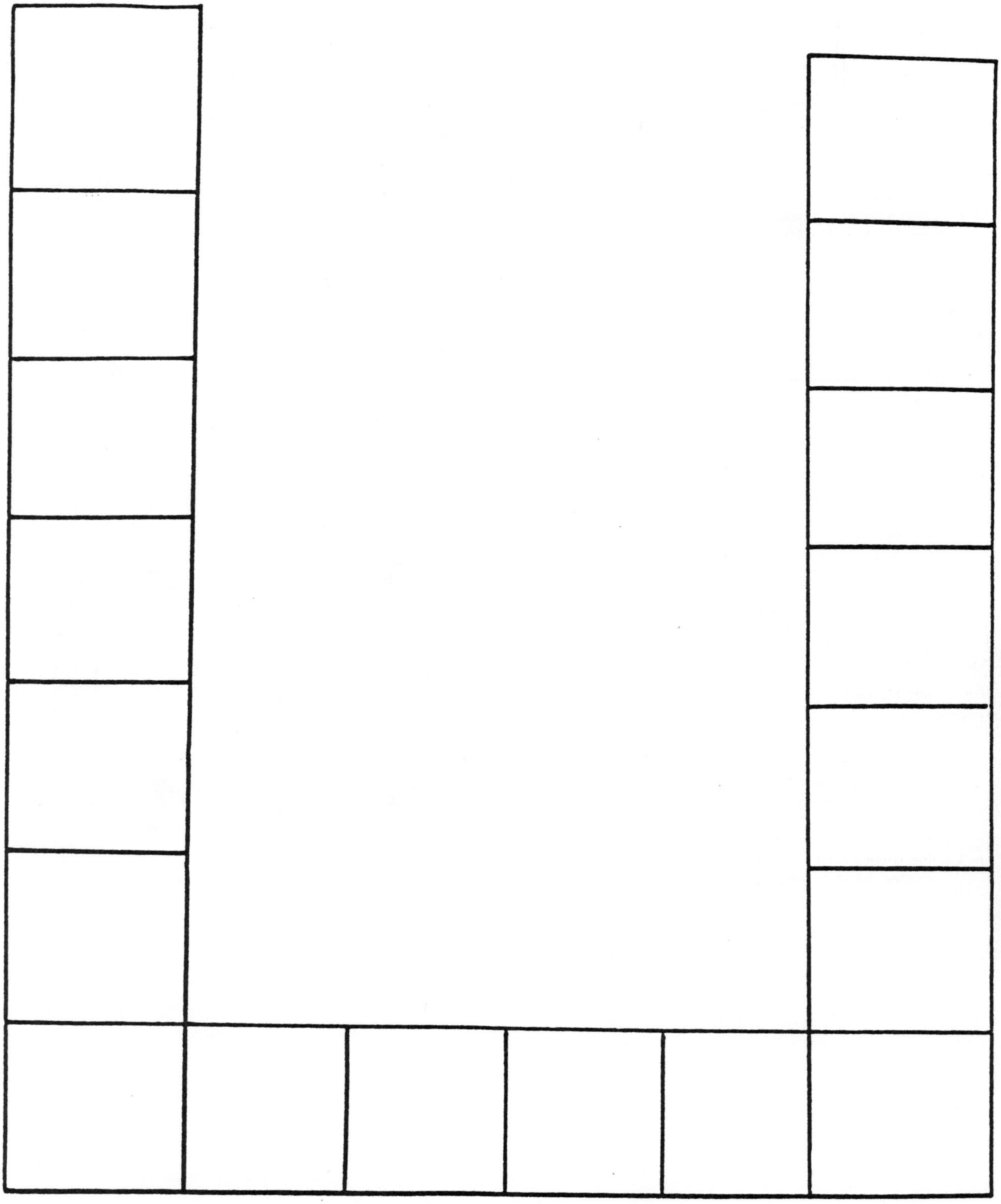

FIGURE F-8 Directions for Making a Game Spinner

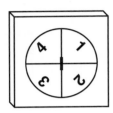

1. Glue a **circle** (patterns or cutouts to the right) onto a square of **heavy cardboard** that is no smaller than 4" x 4". Square spinner bases are easier to hold than round bases.

2. Cut a narrow slot in the center with the point of a sharp pair of scissors or a razor blade.

pointer pattern

3. Cut the pointer from **soft plastic** (such as a milk jug) and make a clean round hole with a **hole punch**.

4. A **washer,** either a metal one from the hardware store or one cut from cardboard, helps the pointer move freely.

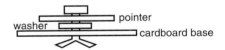

washer pointer cardboard base

5. Push a **paper fastener** through the pointer hole, the washer, and the slot in the spinner base. Flatten the legs, leaving space for the pointer to spin easily.

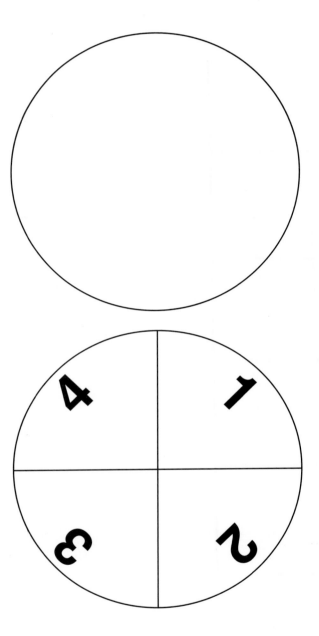

Templates for Sorts

Template for Picture Sorts

Appendix F

Sample Word Sorts

Within Word Pattern Sort 1

Short-e CVC
Long-e CVVC EE
Long-e CVVC EA
1 pair of homophones

feel	fell	see
meat	fed	tree
leak	bee	read
seen	leap	sled
sea	jeep	free
bleed	seat	neck
treat	feet	mess
help	team	sweet

Word Family Sort for *et* and *en*

pet	wet	jet
ten	pen	net
hen	men	vet

Syllables & Affixes Sort

Sort by *ic* and *ick*
Sort by Syllables and Compounds

brick	panic	picnic
music	limerick	flick
cowlick	trick	basic
homesick	arctic	attic
quick	classic	chopstick
comic	fabric	drastic
fantastic	yardstick	garlic
gimmick	magic	Pacific

Within Word Pattern Sort 2

Long-a CVVC *ai*   L-controlled *al*
Long-a CVV *ay*   1 oddball

rain	may	call
small	pail	pain
play	say	mail
tail	hay	said
wall	clay	gray
day	tall	talk
walk	stay	sail
fall	snail	train

Words Their Way: Word Study for Phonics, Vocabulary, and Spelling Instruction © 2008 by Pearson Education, Inc.

Resources

Children's Literature*

Brett, J. (2003). *Town mouse, country mouse*. New York, NY: Putnam.

Carle, E. (1974). *My very first book of shapes*. New York: HarperCollins.

Carle, E. (1987). *Have you seen my cat?* Picture Books LTD.

Christelow, E. (1989). *Five little monkeys jumping on the bed*. Boston: Clarion Books.

Crews, D. (1995). *Ten black dots*. New York: Harper Trophy.

Dahl, R. (1988). *Fantastic Mr. Fox*. New York: Puffin Books.

Galdone, P. (1973). *The three billy goats gruff*. New York: Clarion Books.

Heller, R. (1993). *Chickens aren't the only ones*. New York: Putnam.

Hoban, T. (1978). *Is it red? Is it yellow? Is it blue?* New York: Greenwillow Books.

Langstaff, J. (1974). *Oh, a hunting we will go*. New York: Atheneum.

Lionni, L. (1969). *Alexander and the wind-up mouse*. New York: Pantheon.

Martin, B., & Archambault, J. (1989). *Chicka chicka boom boom*. New York: Simon & Schuster.

Parish, P. (1981). *Amelia Bedelia*. New York: Avon.

Raffi. (1976). *Singable songs for the very young*. Universal City, CA: Troubadour Records.

Raffi. (1985). *One light, one sun*. Universal City, CA: Troubadour Records.

Scieska, J. (2001). *The time warp trio series*. New York: Viking.

Seuss, Dr. (1974). *There's a wocket in my pocket*. New York: Random House.

Sharmat, M. (1980). *Gregory the terrible eater*. New York: Four Winds Press.

Shaw, N. (1986). *Sheep in a jeep*. Boston: Houghton Mifflin.

Slepian, J., & Seidler, A. (1967). *The hungry thing*. New York: Follet.

Slepian, J., & Seidler, A. (1990). *The hungry thing returns*. New York: Scholastic.

Slobodkina, E. (1947). *Caps for sale*. New York: Harper Trophy.

Steig, W. (1978). *Amos and Boris*. New York: Farrar, Straus and Giroux.

Wallner, J. (1987a). *City mouse–country mouse*. New York: Scholastic.

Wallner, J. (1987b). *The country mouse and the city mouse and two more mouse tales from Aesop*. New York: Scholastic.

Wells, N. (1980). *Noisy Nora*. New York: Dial Press.

White, E. B. (1945). *Stuart Little*. New York: Harper Row.

Wildsmith, B. (1982). *The cat on the mat*. New York: Oxford Press.

*See Chapter 4 for rhyme and ABC books.

Bibliography of Word Study Books

Allen, M. S., & Cunnigham, M. (1999). *Webster's new world rhyming dictionary*. New York: Simon & Schuster.

Almond, J. (1995). *Dictionary of word origins: A history of the words, expressions, and cliches we use*. New Jersey: Carol Publishing Group.

Asimov, I. (1959). *Words of science, and the history behind them*. Boston: Houghton Mifflin.

Asimov, I. (1961). *Words from the myths*. Boston: Houghton Mifflin.

Asimov, I. (1962). *Words on the map*. Boston: Houghton Mifflin.

Ayers, D. M. (1986). *English words from Latin and Greek elements* (2nd ed). Tucson: University of Arizoria.

Ayto, J. (1990). *Dictionary of word origins*. New York: Arcade Publishing.

Balmuth, M. (1992). *The roots of phonics: An historical introduction*. Austin, TX: Pro-Ed.

Black, D.C. (1988). *Spoonerisms, sycophants and sops; A celebration of fascinating facts about words*. New York: Harper & Row.

Byson, B. (1990). *The mother tongue: English and how it got that way*. New York: Morrow.

Byson, B. (1994). *Made in America: An informal history of the English language in the United States*. New York: Morrow.

Ciardi, J. (1980). *A browser's dictionary: A compendium of curious expressions and intriguing facts*. New York: Harper & Row.

Collis, H. (1981). *Colloquial English*. New York: Regents Pub.

Collis, H. (1986). *101 American English idioms*. New York: McGraw Hill.

Crystal, D. (1987). *The Cambridge encyclopedia of language*. New York: Cambridge University Press.

Cummings, D.W. (1988). *American English spelling*. Baltimore: Johns Hopkins University Press.

Folsom, M. (1985). *Easy as pie: A guessing game of sayings*. New York: Clarion.

Franlyn, J. (1987). *Which is witch?* New York: Dorset Press.

Fry, E. B., & Kress, J. E. (2006). *The reading teacher's book of lists* (5th ed.). Jossey-Bass.

Funk, C.E (1948). *A hog on ice and other curious expressions*. New York: Harper & Row.

Funk, C. E. (1955). *Heavens to Betsy and other curious sayings*. New York: Harper & Row.

Funk, W. (1954). *Word origins and their romantic stories*. New York: Grosset & Dunlap.

Gwynne, F. (1970). *The king who rained*. New York: Simon & Schuster.

Gwynne, F. (1976). *A chocolate moose for dinner*. New York: Simon & Schuster.

Gwynne, F. (1980). *A sixteen hand horse.* New York: Simon & Schuster.

Gwynne, F. (1988). *A little pigeon toad.* New York: Simon & Schuster.

Harrison, J. S. (1987). *Confusion reigns.* New York: St. Martin's Press.

Heacock, P. (1989). *Which word when?* New York: Dell Pub.

Heller, R. (1987). *A cache of jewels and other collective nouns.* New York: Grosset & Dunlap.

Heller, R. (1988). *Kites sail high.* New York: Grosset & Dunlap.

Heller, R. (1989). *Many luscious lollipops: A book about adjectives.* New York: Grosset & Dunlap.

Heller, R. (1990). *Merry-go-round: A book about nouns.* New York: Grosset & Dunlap.

Heller, R. (1991). *Up, up and away: A book about adverbs.* New York: Grosset & Dunlap.

Heller, R. (1995). *Behind the mask: A book about prepositions.* New York: Grosset & Dunlap.

Hoad, T. F. (1986). *The concise Oxford dictionary of English etymology.* New York: Oxford University Press.

Jones, C. F. (1999). *Eat your words: A fascinating look at the language of food.* New York: Delacorte Press.

Kennedy, J. (1996). *Word stems.* New York: Soho Press.

Kinsley, C. (1980). *The heroes.* New York: Mayflower.

Kress, J. E. (2002). *The ESL teacher's book of lists.* John Wiley & Sons.

Lewis, N. (1983). *Dictionary of correct spelling.* New York: Harper & Row.

Maestro, G. (1983). *Riddle romp.* New York: Clarion.

Maestro, G. (1984). *What's a frank frank? Easy homograph riddles.* New York: Clarion.

Maestro, G. (1985): *Razzle-dazzle riddles.* New York: Clarion.

Maestro, G. (1986). *What's mite might? Homophone riddles to boost your word power.* New York: Clarion.

Maestro, G. (1989). *Riddle roundup: a wild bunch to beef up your word power.* New York: Clarion.

Nash, R. (1991). *NTC's dictionary of Spanish cognates thematically organized.* Chicago: NTC Publishing Group.

Partridge, E. (1984). *Origins: A short etymological dictionary of modern English.* New York: Greenwich House.

Pei, M. (1965). *The story of language.* Philadelphia: Lippincott and Company.

Presson, L. (1996). *What in the world is a homophone?* Hauppauge, NY: Barron's.

Presson, L. (1997). *A dictionary of homophones.* New York: Barrons.

Randall, B. (1992). *When is a pig a hog? A guide to confoundingly related English words.* New York: Prentice Hall.

Room, A. (1992). *A NTC's dictionary of word origins.* Lincolnwood, IL: National Textbook.

Safire, W. (1984). *I stand corrected: More on language.* New York: Avon.

Sarnoff, J., & Ruffins, R. (1981). *Words: A book about word origins of everyday words and phrases.* New York: Charles Scribner's Sons.

Schleifer, R. (1995). *Grow your own vocabulary: By learning the roots of English words.* New York: Random House.

Scragg, D. G. (1974). *A history of English spelling.* Manchester, England: Manchester University Press.

Shipley, J. T. (1967). *Dictionary of word origins.* Lanham, MD: Rowman & Littlefield.

Shipley, J. (1984). *The origins of English words.* Baltimore: Johns Hopkins University Press.

The Oxford English Dictionary on CD-ROM. (1994). Oxford: Oxford University Press.

The American heritage book of English usage: A practical and authoritative guide to contemporary English. (1996). Boston: Houghton Mifflin.

The Scholastic dictionary of synonyms, antonyms, homonyms. (1965). New York: Scholastic.

Terban, M. (1982). *Eight ate: A feast of homonym riddles.* New York: Clarion.

Terban, M. (1983). *In a pickle and other funny idioms.* New York: Clarion.

Terban, M. (1984). *I think I thought and other tricky verbs.* New York: Clarion.

Terban, M. (1986). *Your foot's on my feet! And other tricky nouns.* New York: Clarion.

Terban, M. (1987). *Mad as a wet hen! and other funny idioms.* New York: Clarion.

Terban, M. (1988a). *The dove dove: Funny homograph riddles.* New York: Clarion.

Terban, M. (1988b). *Guppies in tuxedoes: Funny eponyms.* New York: Clarion.

Terban, M. (1988c). *Too hot to hoot: Funny palindrome riddles.* New York: Clarion.

Terban, M. (1991). *Hey, hay! A wagonful of funny homonym riddles.* New York: Clarion.

Terban, M. (1992). *Funny you should ask: How to make up jokes and riddles with wordplay.* New York: Clarion.

Venesky, R. (1970). *The Structure of English orthography.* The Hague: Mouton.

Venezky, R. L. (1999). *The American way of spelling: The structure and origins of American English orthography.* New York: Guilford Press.

Webster's dictionary of word origins. (1992). New York: Smithmark.

Weiner, S. (1981). *Handy book of commonly used American idioms.* New York: Regents Pub.

Yopp, H. K., & Yopp, R. E. (2000). *Oo-pples and boo-noo-noos.* Posrtsmouth, NH: Heineman.

Young, S. (1994). *Scholastic rhyming dictionary.* New York: Scholastic.

Glossary

absorbed/assimilated prefixes   The spelling and sound of the consonant in a prefix has been absorbed into the spelling and sound at the beginning of the base or root to which the prefix is affixed (e.g., *ad + tract = attract*).

advanced readers   Highly skilled readers and writers capable of reading different genres of texts for different purposes with speed, accuracy, and comprehension. Advanced readers acquire an advanced Greek- and Latin-derived vocabulary particular to specific fields of study. See also *specialized readers; derivational relations spelling stage*.

affix   Most commonly a suffix or prefix attached to a base word, stem, or root.

affixation   The process of attaching a word part, such as a prefix or suffix, to a base word, stem, or root.

affricate   A speech sound produced when the breath stream is stopped and released at the point of articulation, usually where the tip of the tongue rubs against the roof of the mouth just behind the teeth when pronouncing the final sound in the word *clutch* or the beginning sound in the word *trip*.

alliteration   The occurrence in a phrase or line of speech of two or more words having the same beginning sound.

alphabetic   A writing system containing characters or symbols representing individual speech sounds.

alphabetic layer of instruction   The first layer of word study instruction focusing on letters and letter–sound correspondences.

alphabetic principle   The concept that letters and letter combinations are used to represent phonemes in orthography. See *phoneme; orthography*.

alternation   See *consonant alternation* or *vowel alternation*.

ambiguous vowels   A vowel sound represented by a variety of different spelling patterns, or vowel patterns that represent a wide range of sounds.

analytic   Word study that divides words into their elemental parts through phonemic, orthographic, and morphological analysis.

articulation   How sounds are shaped in the mouth during speech. Some confusions are made in spelling based on similarities in articulation (e.g., *tr* for *dr*).

assimilated   Prefixes See *absorbed prefixes*.

automaticity   Refers to the speed and accuracy of word recognition and spelling. Automaticity is the goal of word study instruction and frees cognitive resources for comprehension.

base word   A word to which prefixes and/or suffixes are added. For example, the base word of *unwholesome* is *whole*.

beat-the-teacher speed sorts   Students practice their word sorts all week to increase the speed of their categorization processes. Their speed and accuracy are "tested" by trying to beat the teacher who also sorts the same set of words into the same categories. Beat-the-teacher speed sorts encourage automaticity. See *automaticity; speed sorts*.

beginning period of literacy development   A period of literacy development that begins when students have a concept of word and can make sound-symbol correspondences. This period is noted for disfluent reading and writing, and letter name–alphabetic spelling.

blends   An orthographic term referring to two- or three-letter sequences that are blended together. There are *l*-blends (*bl, cl, fl, gl, pl, sl*), *r*-blends (*br, cr, dr, fr, gr, pr, tr*), and *s*-blends (*sc, scr, sk, sp, st, squ, sw*). Although the letter sounds are blended together quickly, each one is pronounced. Consonant blends occurring at the beginning of words are *onsets*, and as such, are treated orthographically as a unit. See *onset*.

blind sort   A picture or word sort done with a partner in which students who are responsible for sorting cannot see the word. They must instead attend to the sounds and sometimes visualize the spelling pattern to determine the category.

blind writing sort   A variant of a blind sort in which one student (or teacher) names a word without showing it to another student who must write it in the correct category under a key word.

bound morphemes   Meaning units of language (morphemes) that cannot stand alone as a word. *Respected* has three bound morphemes: *re+spect+ed*. See free morphemes.

center time   Work completed independently in prepared areas within a classroom.

choral reading   Oral reading done in unison with another person or persons.

circle time   Group work conducted under the teacher's direction.

classroom composite   A classroom profile that organizes children into instructional groups by features to be taught within each stage.

closed sorts   Word sorts based on predetermined categories.

closed syllable   A closed syllable ends with or is "closed" by a consonant sound. In polysyllabic words, a closed syllable contains a short vowel sound that is closed by two consonants (*rabbit, racket*). See *open syllable.*

cloze   An activity in which children supply a single missing word in the middle or end of a sentence, as in, "the cat sat on the _____."

cognates   Words in different languages derived from the same root.

complex consonant patterns   Consonant units occurring at the end of words determined by the preceeding vowel sound. Final *tch* follows the short vowel sound in *fetch* and *scotch*, while final *ch* follows the long-vowel sound in *peach* and *coach*. Other complex consonant patterns include final *ck* (*pack* vs. *peak*) and final *dge* (*badge* vs. *cage*).

compound words   Words made up of two of more smaller words. A compound word may or may not be hyphenated, depending on its part of speech.

concept of word   The ability to match spoken words to printed words as demonstrated by the ability to point to the words of a memorized text while reading including two-syllable words.

concept sorts   A categorization task in which pictures, objects, or words are grouped by shared attributes or meanings to develop concepts and vocabulary.

consonant alternation   The process in which the pronunciation of consonants changes in the base or root of derivationally related words, while the spelling does not change. For example, the silent-to-sounded g in the words *sign* and *signal*; the /k/ to /sh/ pattern in the words *music* and *musician.*

consonant blend   See *blends.*

consonant digraph   See *digraph.*

consonant-vowel-consonant (CVC)   Refers to the pattern of consonants and vowels within a syllable. The spelling pattern for the word *mat* would be represented as a *CVC* pattern, while the spelling pattern for the word *mail* would be represented as a *CVVC* pattern.

consonants   Students often learn what consonants are by what they are not: they are not vowels (*a, e, i, o,* and *u*). Where vowel sounds are thought of as musical, consonant sounds are known for their noise and the way in which air is constricted as it is stopped and released or forced through the vocal tract, mouth, teeth, and lips.

continuant sound   A consonant sound, such as /s/ or /m/, that can be prolonged as long as the breath lasts without distorting the sound quality.

cut-and-paste activities   A variation of picture sorting in which students cut out pictures from magazines or catalogs and paste them into categories.

derivational affixes   Affixes added to base words that affect the meaning (sign, **re**sign; break, break**able**) and/or part of speech (beauty, beau**tiful**). Compare to inflected endings.

derivational relations spelling stage   The last stage of spelling development in which spellers learn about derivational relationships preserved in the spelling of words. *Derivational* refers to (a) the process by which new words are created from existing words, chiefly through affixation; and (b) the development of a word from its historical origin. *Derivational constancy* refers to spelling patterns that remain the same despite changes in pronunciation across derived forms. *Bomb* retains the *b* from *bombard* because of its historical evolution.

developmental level   One of five stages of spelling development: emergent, letter name–alphabetic, within word pattern, syllables and affixes, or derivational relations.

digraph   Two letters that represent one sound. There are consonant digraphs and vowel digraphs, though the term most commonly refers to consonant digraphs. Common consonant digraphs include *sh, ch, th,* and *wh.* Consonant digraphs at the beginning of words are *onsets.*

diphthong   A complex speech sound beginning with one vowel sound and moving to another within the same syllable. The *oy* in *boy* is a diphthong as is the *ou* in *cloud.*

directed reading-thinking activities (DRTAs) A strategy for developing comprehension processes during reading. The strategy is a variation of a predict-read-prove routine.

directionality   The left-to-right direction used for reading and writing English.

draw and label activities   A variation of picture sorting in which students draw pictures of things that begin with the sounds under study. The pictures are drawn in the appropriate categories and labeled with the letter(s) corresponding to that sound.

echo reading   Oral reading in which the student echoes or imitates the reading of the teacher or partner. Echo reading is used with very beginning readers as a form of support. Echo reading can also be used to model fluent reading.

emergent   A period of literacy development ranging from birth to beginning reading. This period precedes the letter name–alphabetic stage of spelling development.

eponyms   Places, things, and actions that are named after an individual.

error guide   A sample of spelling errors arranged by spelling stages that enables teachers to place children in instructional groups.

etymology   The study of the origin and historical development of words.

feature analysis   More than scoring words right and wrong, feature analyses provide a way of interpreting children's spelling errors by taking into account their knowledge of specific orthographic features such as consonant blends or short vowels. Feature analyses inform teachers what spelling features to teach.

feature guide   A tool used to classify students' errors within a hierarchy of orthographic features. Used to score spelling inventories to assess students' knowledge of specific spelling features at their particular stage of spelling development and to plan word study instruction to meet individual needs.

fingerpoint reading   Refers to the kind of reading in which emergent and beginning readers use a finger to point to each word as it is spoken.

free morpheme   Meaning units of language (morphemes) that stand alone as words (*workshop* has two free morphemes, *work* and *shop*). See *bound morphemes*.

frustration level   A dysfunctional level of instruction where there is a mismatch between instruction and what an individual is able to grasp. This mismatch precludes learning and often results in frustration.

generative   An approach to word study that emphasizes processes that apply to many words, as opposed to an approach that focuses on one word at a time.

homographs   Words that are spelled alike, but have different pronunciations and different meanings, e.g., "*tear* a piece of paper" and "to shed a *tear*"; "*lead* someone along" and "the element *lead*."

homonyms   Words that share the same spelling but have different meanings (tell a *yarn*, knit with *yarn*). See *homophones* and *homographs*.

homophones   Words that sound alike, are spelled differently, and have different meanings, e.g., *bear* and *bare, pane* and *pain*, and *forth* and *fourth*.

independent level   That level of academic engagement in which an individual works independently, without need of instructional support. Independent-level behaviors demonstrate a high degree of accuracy, speed, ease, and fluency.

inflected endings   Suffixes that change the verb tense (walk**s**, walk**ed**, walk**ing**) or number (dog**s**, box**es**) of a word.

instructional level   A level of academic engagement in which instruction is comfortably matched to what an individual is able to grasp. See *zone of proximal development*.

intermediate readers   Intermediate readers are fluent readers and writers whose word recognition of one- and two-syllable words is automatic. Intermediate readers are grappling with a more advanced vocabulary involving meaning units such as prefixes and suffixes. Intermediate readers negotiate unfamiliar genres and expository texts typical of the upper elementary and middle grades. Intermediate readers are spellers learning about syllables and affixes.

invariance   Spelling features that do not vary, but remain constant.

invented spelling   A term coined by Charles Read referring to children's phonetic spelling. Spellings generated by any speller when the word is not stored in memory.

juncture   Syllable juncture refers to the transition from one syllable to the next. Sometimes this transition involves a spelling change such as consonant doubling or dropping the final *-e* before adding *ing*.

key pictures   Pictures placed at the top of each category in a picture sort. Key pictures act as headers for each column and can be used for analogy.

key words   Words placed at the top of each category in a word sort. Key words act as headers for each column and can be used for analogy.

kinetic reversal   An error of letter order (pte for pet).

language experience   An approach to the teaching of reading in which students read about their own experiences recorded in their own language. Experience stories are dictated by the student to a teacher who writes them down. Dictated accounts are reread in unison, in echo fashion, and independently.

lax   Lax vowels are commonly known as the short-vowel sound.

letter name–alphabetic spelling stage   The second stage of spelling development in which students represent beginning, middle, and ending sounds of words with phonetically accurate letter choices. Often the selections are based on the sound of the letter name itself, rather than abstract letter-sound associations. The letter name *h* (aitch), for example, produces the /*ch*/ sound, and is often selected to represent that sound (HEP for chip).

liquids   The consonant sounds for /*r*/ and /*l*/ are referred to as liquids because, unlike other consonant sounds, they do not obstruct air in the mouth. The sounds for /*r*/ and /*l*/ are more vowel-like in that they do not involve direct contact between the lips, tongue, and the roof of the mouth as other consonants do. Instead, they sort of roll around in the mouth, as if liquid.

long vowels   Every vowel (*a, e, i, o,* and *u*) has two sounds, commonly referred to as "long" and "short." The long-vowel sound "says its letter name." The vocal cords are tense when producing the long-vowel sound. Because of this, the linguistic term for the long-vowel sound is *tense*.

meaning layer of information   The third layer of English orthography including meaning units such as prefixes, suffixes, and word roots. These word elements were acquired primarily during the Renaissance when English was overlaid with many words of Greek and Latin derivation.

meaning sorts   A type of word sort where the categories are determined by semantic categories or by spelling-meaning connections.

memory reading   An accurate recitation of text accompanied by fingerpoint reading. See *fingerpoint reading*.

mock linear   Writing characteristic of the emergent stage of spelling development in which the linear arrangement of written English is mimicked in rows of letterlike shapes and squiggles.

morphemic   Refers to morphemes, or meaning units in the spelling of words, such as the suffix *-ed* which signals past tense, or the root *graph* in the words *autograph* or *graphite.*

morphology   The study of word parts related to syntax and meaning (see *morphemic*).

nasals   A sound produced when the air is blocked in the oral cavity but escapes through the nose. The first consonants in the words *mom* and *no* represent nasal sounds.

oddballs   Words that do not fit the targeted feature in a sort.

onset   The onset of a single syllable or word is the initial consonant(s) sound. The onset of the word *sun* is /s/. The onset of the word *slide* is /sl/.

open sorts   A type of picture or word sort in which the categories for sorting are left open. Students sort pictures or words into groups according to the students own judgment. Open sorts are useful for determining what word features are salient for students.

open syllable   An open syllable ends with a long-vowel sound (*labor, reason*). See *closed syllable.*

orthography/orthographic   Refers to the writing system of a language, specifically, the correct sequence of letters, characters, or symbols.

pattern   Letter sequences that function as a unit and are related to a consistent category of sound. Frequently these patterns form rhyming families, as in the *ai* of *Spain, rain,* and *drain.*

pattern layer   The second layer or tier of English orthography in which patterns of letter sequences, rather than individual letters themselves, represent vowel sounds. This layer of information was acquired during the period of English history following the Norman Invasion. Many of the vowel patterns of English are of French derivation.

pattern sort   A word sort in which students categorize words according to similar spelling patterns.

personal readers   Individual books of reading materials for beginning readers. Group experience charts, dictations, and rhymes comprise the majority of the reading material.

phoneme   The smallest unit of speech that distinguishes one word from another. For example, the *t* of *tug* and the *r* of *rug* are two phonemes.

phoneme segmentation   The process of dividing a spoken word into the smallest units of sound within that word. The word *bat* can be divided or segmented into three phonemes: /b/a/t/.

phonemic awareness   Refers to the ability to consciously manipulate individual phonemes in a spoken language. Phonemic awareness is often assessed by the ability to tap, count, or push a penny forward for every sound heard in a word like *cat*: /c/a/t/.

phonetic   Representing the sounds of speech with a set of distinct symbols (letters), each denoting a single sound. See *alphabetic principle.*

phonics   The systematic relationship between letters and sounds.

phonics readers   Beginning reading books written with controlled vocabulary that contain recurring phonics elements.

phonograms   Often called *word families*, phonograms end in high frequency rimes that vary only in the beginning consonant sound to make a word. For example, back, sack, black, and track are phonograms.

phonological awareness   An awareness of various speech sounds such as syllables, rhyme, and individual phonemes.

picture sort   A categorization task in which pictures are sorted into categories of similarity and difference. Pictures may be sorted by sound or by meaning. Pictures cannot be sorted by pattern.

preconsonantal nasals   Nasals that occur before consonants, as in the words *bump* or *sink*. The vowel is nasalized as part of the air escapes through the nose during pronunciation. See *nasals.*

predictability   The degree to which a story, text passage, or word sort may be anticipated or foretold based on familiarity and/or prior knowledge.

prefix   An affix attached at the beginning of a base word or word root.

preliterate stage   Henderson (1990) called the emergent stage preliterate because students are not yet reading or writing conventionally. Students in the preliterate stage have not discovered the alphabetic principle. (See *alphabetic principle.*)

prephonetic   Writing that bears no correspondence to speech sounds; literally, "before sound." Prephonetic writing occurs during the emergent stage and typically consists of random scribbles, mock linear writing, or hieroglyphic-looking symbols. See *mock linear.*

pretend reading   A paraphrase or spontaneous retelling told by children as they turn the pages of a familiar story book.

prosody/prosodic   The musical qualities of language, including intonation, expression, stress, and rhythm.

reduced vowel   A vowel occurring in an unstressed syllable (see schwa).

rimes   A rime unit is composed of the vowel and any following consonants within a syllable. For example, the rime unit in the word *tag* would be *ag.*

r-influenced vowels   (or r-controlled) In English, *r* colors the way the preceding vowel is pronounced. For example, compare the pronunciation of the vowels in *bar* and *bad.* The vowel in *bar* is influenced by the *r.*

root word/roots   Refers to Greek roots or word parts of Greek origin that are often combined with other roots to form words such as *telephone* (*tele* and *phone*).

salient sounds   A prominent sound in a word or syllable that stands out because of the way it is made or felt in the mouth, or because of idiosyncratic reasons such as being similar to a sound in one's name.

scaffold A form of support. The familiar structures of oral language offer a form of support for beginning readers.

schwa A vowel sound in English that often occurs in an unstressed syllable, such as the /uh/ sound in the first syllable of the word *above.*

seat work School work that is completed at the student's own desk. Seat work is usually on a student's independent level and is usually assigned for practice. See *independent level.*

semiphonetic Writing that demonstrates *some* awareness that letters represent speech sounds. Literally, "part sound." Beginning and/or ending consonant sounds of syllables or words may be represented but medial vowels are usually omitted (ICDD for *I see Daddy*). Semiphonetic writing occurs at the end of the emergent stage or the very outset of the early letter name–alphabetic stage.

short-term word banks Words that are not consistently recognized out of context; words are promoted to word bank status when consistently recognized out of context or, conversely, are discarded if they remain problematic. Compare with *word bank.*

short vowels Every vowel (*a, e, i, o,* and *u*) has two sounds, commonly referred to as "long" and "short." The vocal cords are more relaxed when producing the short-vowel sound, as opposed to the long-vowel sound. See *long vowels.* Because of this, short-vowel sounds are often referred to as *lax.* The five short vowels can be heard at the beginning of these words: *apple, Ed, igloo, octopus,* and *umbrella.*

sight words Words recognized and pronounced immediately "at first sight." The term *sight words* does not necessarily mean high frequency words or phonetically irregular words. A sight word is simply any *known* word, regardless of its frequency or phonetic regularity.

sound board Charts used by letter name–alphabetic spellers that contain pictures and letters for the basic sound-symbol correspondences (e.g., the letter *b*, a picture of a bell, and the word *bell*).

sound sort Sorts that ask students to categorize pictures or words by sound as opposed to visual patterns.

specialized readers Proficient readers whose reading speeds exceed 250 to 300 words per minute and vary thereafter according to interest and background knowledge. Specialized readers encounter derivational vocabulary of Greek and Latin origin. Vocabulary growth begins to specialize according to academic discipline, personal interest, or profession.

speed sorts Pictures or words that are sorted under a timed condition. Students try to beat their own time.

spelling-by-stage classroom organization chart A classroom composite sheet used to place children in a developmental spelling stage and form groups.

spelling-meaning connections Words that are related in meaning often share the same spelling despite changes in pronunciation from one form of the word to the next. The word *sign*, for example, retains the *g* from *signal* even though it is not pronounced, thus "signaling" the meaning connection through the spelling.

static reversal A handwriting error that is the mirror image of the intended letter (**b** for **d** or **p** for **d**).

stems Word parts, usually of Latin origin, that cannot stand alone, but are used in combination with other word parts in words related in meaning. Latin stems carry consistent though abstract meanings and can appear in various positions in words. For example, the Latin stem *spect* means roughly "to look at" or "to watch" and occurs at the beginning of the word *spectator*, the end of the word *inspect*, and the middle of the word *respectable.*

structural analysis The process of determining the pronunciation and/or meaning of a word by analyzing word parts including syllables, base words, and affixes.

suffix An affix attached at the end of a base word or word root.

syllable patterns The alternating patterns of consonants (C) and vowels (V) at the point where syllables meet. For example, the word *rabbit* follows a VCCV syllable pattern at the point where the syllables meet.

syllables Units of spoken language that consist of a vowel that may be preceded and/or followed by several consonants. Syllables are units of sound and can often be detected by paying attention to movements of the mouth. Syllabic divisions indicated in the dictionary are not always correct since the dictionary will always separate meaning units regardless of how the word is pronounced. For example, the proper syllable division for the word *naming* is *na-ming*; however, the dictionary divides this word as *nam-ing* to preserve the *ing.*

syllables and affixes stage The fourth stage of spelling development which coincides with intermediate reading. Syllables and affixes spellers learn about the spelling changes which often take place at the point of transition from one syllable to the next. Frequently this transition involves consonant doubling or dropping the final *-e* before adding a suffix.

synchrony Occurring at the same time. In this book, stages of spelling development are described in the context of reading and writing behaviors occurring at the same time.

synthetic phonics instruction that begins with individual sounds and the blending of sounds to form words.

tense A vowel sound that is commonly known as the long-vowel sound. Long-vowel sounds are produced by tensing the vocal cords.

tracking   The ability to fingerpoint read a text, demonstrating concept of a word.

transitional stage of literacy development   A period of literacy development when learners are becoming fluent in reading easy materials. Silent reading becomes the preferred mode of reading. There is some expression in oral reading. This stage is between the beginning and intermediate stages of literacy development. The transitional period corresponds to the within word pattern stage of spelling development.

unaccented   Unstressed syllables. The final unstressed syllable in words such as *label* and *doctor* have no distinct vowel sound.

unvoiced   A sound that, when produced, does not necessitate the vibration of the vocal cords.

voiced   A sound that, when produced, vibrates the vocal cords. The letter sound *d*, for example, vibrates the vocal cords in a way that the letter sound *t* does not. See *unvoiced*.

vowel   A speech sound produced by the easy passage of air through a relatively open vocal tract. Vowels form the most central sound of a syllable. In English, vowel sounds are represented by the following letters: *a, e, i, o, u*, and sometimes *y*. See *consonants*.

vowel alternation   The process in which the pronunciation of vowels changes in the base or root of derivationally related words, while the spelling does not change. For example, the long-to-short vowel change in the related words *crime* and *criminal*; the long-to-schwa vowel change in the related words *impose* and *imposition*.

vowel digraphs   See *digraph*.

vowel marker   A silent letter used to indicate the sound of the vowel. In English, silent letters are used to form patterns associated with specific vowel sounds. Vowel markers are usually vowels as the *i* in *drain* or the *a* in *treat*, but they can also be consonants, as the *l* in *told*.

within word pattern spelling stage   The third stage of spelling development that coincides with the transitional period of literacy development. Within word pattern spellers have mastered the basic letter-sound correspondences of written English, and they grapple with letter sequences that function as a unit, especially long-vowel patterns. Some of the letters in the unit may have no sound themselves. These silent letters, such as the silent *-e* in *snake* or the silent *-i* in *drain*, serve as important markers in the pattern.

word   A unit of meaning. A word may be a single syllable or a combination of syllables. A word may contain smaller units of meaning within it. In print, a word is separated by white space. In speech, several words may be strung together in a breath group. For this reason, it takes a while for young children to develop a clear concept of word: See *concept of word*.

word bank   A collection of known words harvested from frequently read texts such as little leveled books, dictated stories, basal preprimers, and primers. Word bank words are written on small cards. Words students can recognize with ease are used in word study games and word sorts.

word cards   Words written on 2-by-1-inch pieces of cardstock or paper.

word consciousness   An attitude of curiosity and attention to words critical for vocabulary development.

word families   Phonograms or words that share the same rime (ex: *fast, past, last, blast*, all share the *ast* rime). In the derivational relations stage word families refer to words that share the same root or origin, as in *spectator, spectacle, inspect, inspector*. See *rime, phonogram*.

word hunts   A word study activity in which students go back to texts they have previously read to hunt for other words that follow the same spelling features examined during the word or picture sort.

word root   A Greek or Latin element to which affixes are attached, for example, *cred, dict, fract, phon*. A word root usually cannot stand alone as a word. See *stems*.

word sort   A basic word study routine in which students group words into categories. Word sorting involves comparing and contrasting within and across categories. Word sorts are often cued by key words placed at the top of each category.

word study   A learner-centered, conceptual approach to instruction in phonics, spelling, word recognition, and vocabulary.

word study notebooks   Notebooks in which students write their word sorts into columns and add other words that follow similar spelling patterns throughout the week. Word study notebooks may also contain lists of words generated overtime such as new vocabulary, homophones, cognates, and so on.

writing sorts   A writing sort often follows a word sort. Students write words under headings of columns.

zone of proximal development (ZPD)   A term coined by the Russian psychologist Vygotsky referring to the ripe conditions for learning something new. A person's ZPD is that zone which is neither too hard nor too easy. The term is similar to the concept of *instructional level*.

References

Adams, M. J. (1990). *Beginning to read: Thinking and learning about print*. Cambridge, MA: MIT Press.

Adams, M. J., Foorman, B. R., Lundberg, L., & Beeler, T. (1998). The elusive phoneme: Why phoneme awareness is so important and how to help children develop it. *American Educator, 22*, 18–29.

Allington, R. L. (1983). The reading instruction provided readers of differing abilities. *Elementary School Journal, 83*, 548–559.

Anders, P., & Bos, C. (1986). Semantic feature analysis: An interactive strategy for vocabulary development and text comprehension. *Journal of Reading, 29*, 610–616.

Armbruster, B. B., Lehr, F., & Osborn, J. (2001). *Put reading first: The research building blocks for teaching children to read*. Washington, DC: The Partnership for Reading.

Ball, E. W., & Blachman, B. A. (1988). Phoneme segmentation training: Effect on reading readiness. *Annals of Dyslexia, 38*, 208–225.

Balmuth, M. (1992). *The roots of phonics: A historical introduction*. Austin, TX: Pro-Ed.

Baretta-Lorton, M. L. (1968). *Math their way*. Reading, MA: Addison-Wesley.

Barrentine, S. J. (1996). Engaging with reading through interactive read-alouds. *The Reading Teacher, 50*, 36–42.

Baumann, J. F., Edwards, E. C., Font, G., Tereshinski, C. A., Kame'enui, E. J., & Olejnik, S. (2003). Teaching morphemic and contextual analysis to fifth-grade students. *Reading Research Quarterly, 37*(2), 150–176.

Bear, D. (1982). *Patterns of oral reading across stages of word knowledge*. Unpublished manuscript, University of Virginia, Charlottesville.

Bear, D. (1989). Why beginning reading must be word-by-word. *Visible Language, 23*(4), 353–367.

Bear, D. (1991a). Copying fluency and orthographic development. *Visible Language, 25*(1), 40–53.

Bear, D. (1991b). "Learning to fasten the seat of my union suit without looking around": The synchrony of literacy development. *Theory into Practice, 30*(3), 149–157.

Bear, D. (1992). The prosody of oral reading and stage of word knowledge. In S. Templeton & D. Bear (Eds.), *Development of orthographic knowledge and the foundations of literacy: A memorial Festschrift for Edmund H. Henderson* (pp. 137–186). Hillsdale, NJ: Lawrence Erlbaum.

Bear, D., & Barone D. (1989). Using children's spellings to group for word study and directed reading in the primary classroom. *Reading Pyschology, 10*, 275–292.

Bear, D., & Barone, D. (1998). *Developing literacy: An integrated approach to assessment and instruction*. Boston: Houghton Mifflin.

Bear, D., & Cathey, S. (1989, November). *Reading fluency in beginning readers and expression in practiced oral reading: Links with word knowledge*. Paper presented at National Reading Conference, Austin, TX.

Bear, D., Helman, L., Invernizzi, M., Templeton, S., & Johnston, F. (2007). *Words Their Way with English Learners*. Upper Saddle River NJ: Merrill Prentice Hall.

Bear, D., & Templeton, S. (1998). Explorations in developmental spelling: Foundations for learning and teaching phonics, spelling and vocabulary. *The Reading Teacher, 52*, 222–242.

Bear, D., Templeton, S., Helman, L., & Baren, T. (2003). Orthographic development and learning to read in different languages. In G. Garcia (Ed.), *English learners: Reaching the highest level of English literacy* (pp. 71–95). Newark, DE: International Reading Association.

Bear, D., Templeton, S., & Warner, M. (1991). The development of a qualitative inventory of higher levels of orthographic knowledge. In J. Zutell & S. McCormick (Eds.), *Learner factors/teacher factors: Issues in literacy research and instruction: Fortieth yearbook of the National Reading Conference* (pp. 105–110). Chicago: National Reading Conference.

Bear, D., Truex, P., & Barone, D. (1989). In search of meaningful diagnoses: Spelling-by-stage assessment of literacy proficiency. *Adult Literacy and Basic Education, 13*(3), 165–185.

Bear, D. R., & Helman, L. (2004). Word Study for Vocabulary Development: An Ecological Perspective on Instruction during the Early Stages of Literacy Learning. In J. F. Baumann and E. J. Kame'enui, Eds. *Vocabulary Instruction: Research to Practice* (pp. 139–158). New York: Guilford Press.

Bear, D. R., Caserta-Henry, C., Venner, D. (2004). *Personal Readers and Literacy Instruction with Emergent and Beginning Readers*. Berkeley, CA: Teaching Resource Center.

Beck, I. L., McKeown, M. G., & Kucan, L. (2002). *Bringing words to life: Robust vocabulary instruction*. New York: Guilford Press.

Becker, W. C., Dixon, R., & Anderson-Inman, L. (1980). *Morphographic and root word analysis of 26,000 high frequency words*. Eugene, OR: University of Oregon Follow Through Project. (Technical Report 1980-1).

Beers, J. W., & Henderson, E. H. (1977). A study of developing orthographic concepts among first grade children. *Research in the Teaching of English, 11*, 133–148.

Berninger, V. W., Vaughn, K., Abbott, R. D., Brooks, A., Abbott, S. P., Rogan, L., Reed, E., & Graham, S. (1998). Early interventions for spelling problems: Teaching functional spelling units of varying size with a multiple-connections framework. *Journal of Educational Psychology, 90*, 587–605.

Biemiller, A. (1970). The development of the use of graphic and contextual information as children learn to read. *Reading Research Quarterly, 6*, 1, 75–96.

Biemiller, A. (2001). Teaching vocabulary: Early, direct, sequential. *American Educator, 25*(1), 24–28.

Biemiller, A. (2003). Vocabulary: Needed if more children are to read well. *Reading Psychology, 24*(3-4), 323–335.

Biemiller, A. (2004). Teaching vocabulary in the primary grades: Vocabulary instruction needed. In J. F. Baumann & E. J. Kame'enui (Eds.), *Vocabulary instruction: Research to Practice* (pp. 28–40). New York: Guilford Press.

Biemiller, A. (2005). Size and sequence in vocabulary development: Implications for choosing words for primary grade vocabulary instruction. In E. H. Hiebert & M. L. Kamil (Eds.), *Teaching and learning vocabulary: Bringing research to practice* (pp. 223–242). Mahwah NJ: Lawrence Erlbaum.

Biemiller, A., & Slonim, N. (2001). Estimating root word vocabulary growth in normative and advantaged populations: Evidence for a common sequence of vocabulary acquisition. *Journal of Educational Psychology, 93,* 498–520.

Bissex, G. L. (1980). *Gnys at wrk.* Cambridge, MA: Harvard University Press.

Blachman, B. A. (1994). What we have learned from longitudinal studies of phonological processing and reading, and some unanswered questions: A response to Torgeson, Wagner, and Rashotte. *Journal of Learning Disabilities, 27,* 287–291.

Brown, K. (2003). What do I say when they get stuck on a word?: Aligning teacher's prompts with student's level of development. *The Reading Teacher, 56,* 720–734.

Bryant, P., Nunes, T., & Bindman, M. (1997). Backward readers' awareness of language: Strengths and weaknesses. *European Journal of Psychology of Education, 12*(4), 357–372.

Button, K., Johnson, M. J., & Furgeson, P. (1996). Interactive writing in a primary classroom. *The Reading Teacher, 49,* 446–454.

Cantrell, R. J. (2001). Exploring the relationship between dialect and spelling for specific vocalic features in Appalachian first-grade children. *Linguistics and Education, 12*(1), 1–23.

Carey, S. (2001). On the very possibility of discontinuities in conceptual development. In E. Dupoux (Ed.), *Language, brain, and cognitive development: Essays in honor of Jacques Mehler* (pp. 303–324). Cambridge, MA: The MIT Press.

Carlisle, J. F. (2000). Awareness of the structure and meaning of morphologically complex words: Impact on reading. *Reading and Writing: An Interdisciplinary Journal, 12,* 169–190.

Cathey, S. S. (1991). *Emerging concept of word: Exploring young children's abilities to read rhythmic text.* Doctoral dissertation, University of Nevada. Reno, UMI #9220355.

Cataldo, S., & Ellis, N. (1988). Interactions in the development of spelling, reading, and phonological skills. *Journal of Research in Reading, 11,* 86–109.

Chall, J. S. (1983). *Stages of reading development.* New York: McGraw-Hill.

Chomsky, C. (1970). Reading, writing, and phonology. *Harvard Educational Review, 40*(2), 287–309.

Chomsky, C. (1971). Write first read later. *Childhood Education, 47,* 296–299.

Chomsky, N., & Halle, M. (1968). *The sound pattern of English.* New York: Harper & Row.

Clarke, L. K. (1988). Invented versus traditional spelling in first graders' writing: Effects on learning to spell and read. *Research in the Teaching of English, 22,* 281–309.

Clay, M. (1975). *What did I write?* Exeter, NH: Heinemann.

Clay, M. M. (1991). Introducing a new storybook to young readers. *The Reading Teacher, 45,* 264–273.

Cunningham, A. E., & Stanovich, K. E. (2003). Reading matters: How reading engagement influences cognition. In J. Flood, D. Lapp, J. Squire, & J. Jensen (Eds.), *Handbook of Research on Teaching in the English Language Arts,* (*vol. 2,* pp. 857–867). Mahwah, NJ: Lawrence Erlbaum.

Cunningham, P. (2005). *Phonics they use: Words for reading and writing* (4th ed.). Boston: Allyn & Bacon.

Dale, E., O'Rourke, J., & Bamman, H. (1971). *Techniques of teaching vocabulary.* Palo Alto, CA: Field Educational Publications.

Daniels, H. (2002). Literature circles: Voice and choice in book clubs and reading groups. Portland ME: Stenhouse Publishers.

Delpit, L. D. (1988). The silenced dialogue: Power and pedagogy in educating other people's children. *Harvard Educational Review, 58,* 280–298.

Diamond, L., & Gutlohn, L. (2006). *Vocabulary handbook.* Berkeley, CA: Consortium on Reading Excellence.

Dolch, E. W. (1942). *Better spelling.* Champaign, IL: The Garrard Press.

Edwards, W. (2003). *Charting the orthographic knowledge of intermediate and advanced readers and the relationship between recognition and production of orthographic patterns.* Unpublished doctoral dissertation. University of Nevada, Reno, NV.

Ehri, L. (1992). Review and commentary: Stages of spelling development. In S. Templeton & D. Bear (Eds.), *Development of orthographic knowledge and the foundations of literacy: A memorial Festschrift for Edmund H. Henderson* (pp. 307–332). Hillsdale, NJ: Lawrence Erlbaum.

Ehri, L. C. (1997). Learning to read and learning to spell are one and the same, almost. In C. A. Perfetti, L. Rieben, & M. Fayol (Eds.), *Learning to spell: Research, theory, and practice across languages* (pp. 237–269). Mahwah, NJ: Lawrence Erlbaum.

Ehri, L. C. (1998). Grapheme-phoneme knowledge is essential for learning to read words in English. In J. L. Metsala & L. C. Ehri (Eds.), *Word recognition in beginning literacy* (pp. 3–40). Mahwah, NJ: Lawrence Erlbaum Associates.

Ehri, L. C. (2000). Learning to read and learning to spell: Two sides of a coin. *Topics in Language Disorders, 20,* 19–36.

Ehri, L. C. (2006). Alphabetics instruction helps children learn to read. In. R. M. Joshi & P. G. Aaron (Eds.) *Handbook of orthography and literacy* (pp. 649–678). Mahwah, NJ: Lawrence Erlbaum.

Ehri, L., & McCormick, S. (1998). Phases of word learning: Implications for instruction with delayed and disabled readers. *Reading and Writing Quarterly: Overcoming Learning Difficulties, 14,* 135–164.

Ehri, L. C., & Roberts, T. (2006). The roots of learning to read and write: Acquisition of letters and phonemic awareness. In D. K. Dickinson & S. B. Neuman (Eds.), *Handbook of early literacy research (vol. 2)* (pp. 113–131). New York: The Guilford Press.

Ehri, L. C., & Wilce, L. S. (1980). Do beginning readers learn to read function words better in sentences or lists? *Reading Research Quarterly, 15,* 675–685.

Elkonin, D. B. (1973). U.S.S.R. In J. Downing (Ed.), *Comparative reading.* New York: Macmillan.

Ellis, N., & Cataldo, S. (1992). Spelling is integral to learning to read. In C. M. Steriing & C. Robson (eds). *Psychology, spelling, and education* (pp 112–142). Clevedon, UK: Multilingual Matters.

Estes, T., & Richards, H. (2002). Knowledge of orthographic features in Spanish among bilingual children. *Bilingual Research Journal, 26,* 295–307.

Fashola, O., Drum, P. A., Mayer, R.E., & Kang, S. J. (1996). A cognitive theory of orthographic transitioning: Predictable errors in how Spanish-speaking children spell English words. *American Educational Research Journal, 33,* 825–843.

Ferreiro, E., & Teberosky, A. (1982). *Literacy before schooling.* Portsmouth, NH: Heinemann.

Flanigan, K. (2006). "Daddy, where did the words go?" How teachers can help emergent readers develop a concept of word in text. *Reading Improvement, 46,* 37–49.

Frith, U. (1985). Beneath the surface of developmental dyslexia. In K. Patterson, J. Marshall, & M. Coltheart (Eds.), *Surface dyslexia: Neuropsychological and cognitive studies of phonological reading* (pp. 301–330). London: Lawrence Erlbaum Associates.

Fry, E. (1980). The new instant word list. *The Reading Teacher, 34,* 284–289.

Ganske, K. (1994). Developmental spelling analysis: A diagnostic measure for instruction and research (University of Virginia). *Dissertation Abstracts International, 55*(05), 1230A.

Ganske, K. (1999). The developmental spelling analysis: A measure of orthographic knowledge. *Educational Assessment, 6,* 41–70.

Gentry, J. (1980). Learning to spell developmentally. *Reading Teacher, 34,* 378–381.

Gibson, E. J. (1965). Learning to read. *Science, 148,* 1006–1072.

Gibson, J. J., & Yonas, P. M. (1968). A new theory of scribbling and drawing in children. In *The analysis of reading skill: A program of basic and applied research* (Final Report, Project No. 5–1213, Cornell University and the U.S. Office of Education, pp. 335–370). Ithaca, NY: Cornell University.

Gill, C. (1980). An analysis of spelling errors in French. Unpublished doctoral dissertation. University of Virginia.

Gill, J., & Bear, D. (1988). No book, whole book, and chapter DR-TAs: Three study techniques. *Journal of Reading, 31*(5), 444–449.

Gillet, J. W., & Kita, M. J. (1979). Words, kids, and categories. *The Reading Teacher, 32,* 538–542.

Goswami, U. (1990). A special link between rhyming skill and the use of orthographic analogies by beginning readers. *Journal of Child Psychiatry, 31,* 301–311.

Goswami, U., & Mead, F. (1992). Onset and rhyme awareness and analogies in reading. *Reading Research Quarterly, 27,* 153–162.

Gough, P. B., & Hillinger, M. L. (1980). Learning to read: An unnatural act. *Bulletin of the Orton Society, 20,* 179–196.

Goulandris, N. K. (1992). Alphabetic spelling: Predicting eventual literacy attainment. In C. M. Sterling & C. Robson (Eds.) *Psychology, Spelling, and Education* (pp. 143–158). Clevedon, UK: Multilingual Matters.

Graham, S., Harris, K. R., & Chorzempa, B. F. (2002). Contribution of spelling instruction to the spelling, writing, and reading of poor spellers. *Journal of Educational Psychology, 94,* 669–686.

Hall, M. (1980). *Teaching reading as a language experience.* Columbus, OH: Merrill.

Hanna, P. R., Hanna, J. S., Hodges, R. E., & Rudorf, H. (1966). Phoneme-grapheme correspondences as cues to spelling improvement. Washington, DC: United States Office of Education Cooperative Research.

Harste, J. C., Woodward, V. A., & Burke, C. L. (1984). *Language stories and literacy lessons.* Portsmouth, NH: Heinemann.

Hart, B., & Risley, T. R. (1995). *Meaningful differences in the everyday experience of American children.* Baltimore: Paul C. Brookes.

Helman, L. (2004). Building on the sound system of Spanish. *The Reading Teacher, 57,* 452–460.

Henderson, E. H. (1981). *Learning to read and spell: The child's knowledge of words.* DeKalb: Northern Illinois Press.

Henderson, E. H. (1985). *Teaching spelling.* Boston: Houghton Mifflin.

Henderson, E. H. (1990). *Teaching spelling* (2nd ed.). Boston: Houghton Mifflin.

Henderson, E. H. (1992). The interface of lexical competence and knowledge of written words. In S. Templeton & D. R. Bear (Eds.), *Development of orthographic knowledge and the foundations of literacy: A Memorial Festschrift for Edmund H. Henderson* (pp. 1–30). Hillsdale, NJ: Lawrence Erlbaum Associates.

Henderson, E. H., & Beers, J. (Eds.), (1980). *Developmental and cognitive aspects of learning to spell.* Newark, DE: International Reading Association.

Henderson, E. H., Estes, T., & Stonecash, S. (1972). An exploratory study of word acquisition among first graders at midyear in a language experience approach. *Journal of Reading Behavior, 4,* 21–30.

Henderson, E. H., & Templeton, S. (1986). The development of spelling ability through alphabet, pattern, and meaning. *Elementary School Journal, 86,* 305–316.

Henry, M. (1988). Beyond phonics: Integrated decoding and spelling instruction based on word origin and structures. *Annals of Dyslexia, 38,* 258–275.

Henry, M. (1993). Morphological structure: Latin and Greek roots & affixes as upper grade code strategies. *Journal of Reading & Writing, 5,* 227–241.

Henry, M. (2003). *Unlocking literacy: Effective decoding and spelling instruction.* Baltimore: Paul H. Brookes.

Horn, E. (1954). *Teaching spelling.* Washington, DC: National Education Association.

Invernizzi, M. (1985). *A cross-sectional analysis of children's recognition and recall of word elements.* Unpublished manuscript, University of Virginia, Charlottesville.

Invernizzi, M. (1992). The vowel and what follows: A phonological frame of orthographic analysis. In S. Templeton & D. Bear (Eds.), *Development of orthographic knowledge and the foundations of literacy: A memorial Festschrift for Edmund H. Henderson* (pp. 106–136). Hillsdale, NJ: Lawrence Erlbaum.

Invernizzi, M. (2002). Concepts, sounds, and the ABCs: A diet for a very young reader. In D. M. Barone & L. M. Morrow (Eds.), *Literacy and young children.* New York: Guilford Publications.

Invernizzi, M. (May, 2005). *The History and Technical Adequacy of Qualitative Spelling Inventories.* Presentation for the Special Interest Group on English Orthography. International Reading Association (IRA), San Antonio, TX.

Invernizzi, M., Abouzeid, M., & Gill, T. (1994). Using students' invented spellings as a guide for spelling instruction that emphasizes word study. *Elementary School Journal, 95*(2), 155–167.

Invernizzi, M., & Hayes, L. (2004). Developmental-spelling research: A systematic imperative. *Reading Research Quarterly, 39,* 2–15.

Invernizzi, M., Juel, C., Swank, L., & Meier, J. (2006). *Phonological Awareness Literarcy Screening for Kindergartners* (PALS-K). Charlottesville, VA: University Printing Services.

Invernizzi, M., Justice, L., Landrum, T., & Booker, K. (Winter, 2005). Early literacy screening in kindergarten: Widespread implementation in Virginia. *Journal of Literacy Research, 36,* 479–500.

Invernizzi, M., Meier, J., & Juel, C. (2003). *PALS 1-3 Phonological Awareness Literacy Screening* (4th ed.). Charlottesville, Va.: University Printing Services.

Invernizzi, M., & Worthy, J. W. (1989). An orthographic-specific comparison of the spelling errors of LD and normal children across four levels of spelling achievement. *Reading Psychology, 10,* 173–188.

James, W. (1958). *Talks to teachers on psychology and to students on some of life's ideals*. New York: Norton. (Original work published 1899.)

Johnston, F. R. (1998). The reader, the text, and the task: Learning words in first grade. *The Reading Teacher, 51*, 666–675.

Johnston, F. R. (2000). Word learning in predictable text. *Journal of Education Psychology, 92*, 248–255.

Johnston, F. R. (2001). The utility of phonic generalizations: Let's take another look at Clymer's conclusions. *The Reading Teacher, 55*, 132–143.

Johnston, F. R. (2003, December). *The Primary Spelling Inventory: Exploring its validity and relationship to reading levels*. Paper presented at the National Reading Conference, Scottsdale, AZ.

Johnston, F. R., Invernizzi, M., & Juel, C. (1998). *Book buddies: Guidelines for volunteer tutors of emergent and beginning readers*. New York: Guilford Press.

Juel, C. (1991). Beginning reading. In R. Barr, M. Kamil, P. Mosenthal, & P. D. Pearson (Eds.), *Handbook of reading research* (Vol. II, pp. 759–788). New York: Longman Press.

Juel, C., & Minden-Cupp, C. (2000). Learning to read words: Linguistic units and instructional strategies. *Reading Research Quarterly, 35*, 458–492.

Juel, C., & Roper-Schneider, D. (1985). The influence of basal readers on first grade reading. *Reading Research Quarterly, 18*, 306–327.

Justice, L. M. (2006). *Communication Sciences and Disorders: An Introduction*. Upper Saddle River, NJ: Pearson/Merrill/Prentice Hall.

Justice, L. M., Invernizzi, M., Geller, K., Sullivan, A. K., & Welsch, J. (2005). Descriptive-Developmental performance of at-risk preschoolers in early literacy. *Reading Psychology, 26*(1), 1–25.

Kaderavek, J., & Justice, L. M. (2004). Embedded-explicit emergent literacy: II Goal selection and implementation in the early childhood classroom. *Language, Speech, and Hearing Services in Schools, 25*, 212–228.

Leong, C. K. (2000). Rapid processing of base and derived forms of words and grades 4, 5, and 6 children's spelling. *Reading and Writing: An Interdisciplinary Journal, 12*, 277–302.

Liberman, I., & Shankweiler, D. (1991). Phonology and beginning reading: A tutorial. In L. Rieben & C. Perfetti (Eds.), *Learning to read: Basic research and its implication*. Hillsdale, NJ: Lawrence Erlbaum.

Lundberg, I., Frost, J., & Peterson, O. (1988). Effects of an extensive program for stimulating phonological awareness in preschool children. *Reading Research Quarterly, 23*, 267–284.

Mahony, D., Singson, M., & Mann, V. (2000). Reading ability and sensitivity to morphological relations. *Reading and Writing: An Interdisciplinary Journal, 12*, 191–218.

Malinowski, B. (1952). The problem of meaning in primitive languages. In C. K. Ogden & I. A. Richards (Eds.), *The meaning of meaning* (10th ed.). New York: Harcourt.

Marzano, R. J. (1992). A different kind of classroom: Teaching with dimensions of learning. Alexandria, VA: ASCD.

Massengill, D. (2006). Mission accomplished . . . it's learnable now: Voices of mature challenged spellers using a word study approach. *Journal of Adolescent and Adult Literacy, 49*, 420–431.

Mathews, M. (1967). *Teaching to read: historically considered*. University of Chicago Press.

McCabe, A. (1996). *Chameleon readers: All kinds of good stories*. New York: Webster-McGraw-Hill.

McCandliss, B., Beck, I., Sandak, R., & Perfetti, C. (2003). Focusing attention on decoding for children with poor reading skills: Design and preliminary tests of the word building intervention. *Scientific Studies of Reading, 7*, 75–103.

McKenzie, M. G. (1985). Shared writing: Apprenticeship in writing. *Language Matters, 1–2*, 1–5.

Mesmer, H. A. E. (2006). Text decodability and the first-grade reader. *Reading & Writing Quarterly, 21*, 61–86.

Moats, L. (2000). *Speech to print: Language essentials for teachers*. Baltimore, MD: Paul H. Brookes Publishing Co.

Morais, J., Cary, L., Alegria, J., & Bertelson, P. (1979). Does awareness of speech as a sequence of phonemes arise spontaneously? *Cognition, 7*, 323–331.

Morris, D. (1980). Beginning readers' concept of word. In E. Henderson & J. Beers (Eds.), *Developmental and cognitive aspects of learning to spell* (pp. 97–111). Newark, DE: International Reading Association.

Morris, D. (1981). Concept of word: A developmental phenomenon in the beginning reading and writing process. *Language Arts, 58*(6), 659–668.

Morris, D. (1982). "Word sort": A categorization strategy for improving word recognition ability. *Reading Psychology, 3*, 247–259.

Morris, D. (1999). *The Howard Street tutoring manual*. New York: Guilford Press.

Morris, D., Blanton, L., Blanton, W., & Perney, J. (1995). Spelling instruction and achievement in six elementary classrooms. *The Elementary School Journal, 96*, 145–162.

Morris, D., Blanton, L., Blanton, W. E., Nowacek, J., & Perney, J. (1995). Teaching low achieving spellers at their "instructional level." *Elementary School Journal, 92*, 163–177.

Morris, D., Bloodgood, J. W., Lomax, R. G., & Perney, J. (2003). Developmental steps in learning to read: A longitudinal study in kindergarten and first grade. *Reading Research Quarterly, 38*, 302–328.

Morris, D., Nelson, L., & Perney, J. (1986). Exploring the concept of "spelling instructional level" through the analysis of error-types. *Elementary School Journal, 87*, 181–200.

Morris, D., & Perney, J. (1984). Developmental spelling as a predictor of first-grade reading achievement. *The Elementary School Journal, 84*, 441–457.

Murray, B. A. (1998). Gaining alphabetic insight: Is phonemic manipulation skill or identity knowledge causal? *Journal of Educational Psychology, 90*, 461–475.

Nash, R. (1997). *NTC's dictionary of Spanish cognates thematically organized*. Chicago: NTC Publishing Group.

Nathenson-Mejia, S. (1989). Writing in a second language: Negotiating meaning through invented spelling. *Language Arts, 66*, 515–526.

National Reading Panel (NRP). (2000). *Teaching children to read: An evidence-based assessment of the scientific research literature on reading and its implications for reading instruction*. Washington, DC: National Institute of Child Health and Human Development.

Nessel, D., & Jones, M. (1981). *The language-experience approach to reading*. New York: Teachers College Press.

Perfetti, C. A. (1997). The psycholinguistics of spelling and reading. In C. A. Perfetti, L. Rieben, & M. Fayol (Eds.), *Learning to spell: Research, theory, and practice across languages* (pp. 21–38). Mawah, NJ: Lawrence Erlbaum Associates.

Perfetti, C., Beck, I., Bell, L., & Hughes, C. (1987). Phonemic knowledge and learning to read are reciprocal. *Merrill-Palmer Quarterly, 33*, 283–319.

Phenix, J. (1996). *The spelling teacher's book of lists*. Ontario: Pembroke.

Pressley, M. (2006). *Reading instruction that works: The case for balanced teaching* (3rd ed.). New York: Guilford Publications.

Proctor, C. P., August, D., Carlo, M. S., Snow, C. (2006). The intriguing role of Spanish language vocabulary knowledge in predicting English reading comprehension. *Journal of Educational Psychology, 98,* 159–169.

Purcell, T. (2002). *Linguistic influences on letter sound learning: Considering manner, place, and voicing.* Unpublished Doctoral Dissertation. University of Virginia, Charlottesville.

Raphael, T. E., Pardo, L. S., Highfield, K., & McMahon, S. I. (1997). *Book club: A literature-based curriculum.* Littleton, MA: Small Planet Communications, Inc.

Rasinski, T. V. (2003). *The Fluent Reader: Oral Reading Strategies for Building Word Recognition, Fluency, and Comprehension.* New York City, NY: Scholastic.

Rayner, K., Foorman, B. R., Perfetti, C. A., Pesetsky, D., & Seidenburg, M. S. (2001). How psychological science informs the teaching of reading. *Psychological Science in the Public Interest, 2,* 31–74.

Read, C. (1971). Pre-school children's knowledge of English phonology. *Harvard Educational Review, 41*(1), 1–34.

Read, C. (1975). *Children's categorization of speech sounds in English.* Urbana, IL: NCTE Research Report No. 17.

Richgels, D. J. (1995). Invented spelling ability and printed word learning in kindergarten. *Reading Research Quarterly, 30,* 96–109.

Richgels, D. J. (2001). Invented spelling, phonemic awareness, and reading and writing instruction. In S. B. Neuman & D. K. Dickenson (Eds.), *Handbook of Early Literacy Research* (pp. 142–155). New York: The Guilford Press.

Robb, L. (1999). *Easy mini-lessons for building vocabulary.* New York: Scholastic.

Roberts, B. S. (1992). The evolution of the young child's concept of word as a unit of spoken and written language. *Reading Research Quarterly, 27*(2), 125–138.

Sawyer, D. J., Lipa-Wade, S., Kim, J., Ritenour, D., & Knight, D. F. (1997). *Spelling errors as a window on dyslexia.* Paper presented at the 1997 annual convention of the American Educational Research Association, Chicago.

Samuels, S. (1979). The method of repeated readings. *The Reading Teacher, 32,* 403–408.

Samuels, S. J. (1988). Decoding and automaticity: Helping poor readers become automatic at word recognition. *The Reading Teacher, 41,* 756–760.

Sawyer, D. J., Wade, S., & Kim, J. K. (1999). Spelling errors as a window on variations in phonological deficits among students with dyslexia. *Annals of Dyslexia, 49,* 137–159.

Schlagal, R. (1989). Constancy and change in spelling development. *Reading Psychology, 10,* 207–232.

Schlagal, R. (1992). Patterns of orthographic development into the intermediate grades. In S. Templeton & D. Bear (Eds.), *Development of orthographic knowledge and the foundations of literacy: A memorial Festschrift for Edmund H. Henderson* (pp. 31–52). Hillsdale, NJ: Lawrence Erlbaum.

Shen, H., & Bear, D. R. (2000). The development of orthographic skills in Chinese children. *Reading and Writing: An Interdisciplinary Journal, 13,* 197–236.

Smith, M. L. (1998). Sense and sensitivity: An investigation into fifth-grade children's knowledge of English derivational morphology and its relationship to vocabulary and reading ability. University Microfilms No. AAM9830072. *Dissertation Abstracts International, 59* (4-A), 1111.

Smith, S. B., Simmons, D. C., & Kame'enui, E. J. (1995). *Synthesis of research on phonological awareness: Principles and implications for reading acquisition* (Tech. Rep. No. 21). Eugene, OR: University of Oregon, National Center to Improve the Tools of Educators.

Smith, N. B. (2002). *American Reading Instruction* (special edition). Newark. DE: International Reading Association.

Snow, C. E. (1983). Literacy and language: Relationships during the preschool years. *Harvard Educational Review, 53*(2), 165–189.

Snow, C. E., Burns, M. S., & Griffin, P. (Eds.), (1998). *Preventing reading difficulties in young children.* Washington, DC: National Academy Press.

Spear-Swerling, L., & Sternberg, R. J. (Contributor) (1997). *Off track: When poor readers become "learning disabled."* Boulder, CO: Westview Press.

Stahl, S. A., & McKenna, M. C. (2001, August). The concurrent development of phonological awareness, word recognition, and spelling. CIERA Technical Report No. 01-07. Available at http://www.ciera.org/library/archive/index.html.

Stahl, S. A., & Nagy, W. (2006). *Teaching word meanings.* Mahwah, NJ: Lawrence Erlbaum Associates.

Stanovich, K. (1986). Matthew effects in reading: Some consequences of individual differences in the acquisition of literacy. *Reading Research Quarterly, 21,* 360–406.

Stauffer, R. (1980). *The language-experience approach to the teaching of reading* (2nd ed.). New York: Harper & Row.

Strickland, D., & Morrow, L. (1989). Environments rich in print promote literacy behavior during play. *Reading Teacher, 43,* 178–179.

Sulzby, E. (1986). Writing and reading organization. In W. H. Teale & E. Sulzby (Eds.), *Emergent literacy: Writing and reading* (pp. 50–89). Norwood, NJ: Abex.

Swan, M., & Smith, B. (2001). *Learner English: A teacher's guide to interference and other problems* (2nd ed.), Cambridge: University Press.

Swank, L. (1991). A two-level hypothesis of phonological awareness (Doctoral dissertation, University of Kansas). *Dissertation Abstracts International, 53–08A* (2754).

Taft, M. (1991). *Reading and the mental lexicon.* London: Lawrence Erlbaum Associates.

Temple, C. S. (1978). *An analysis of spelling errors in Spanish.* Unpublished doctoral dissertation. University of Virginia.

Templeton, S. (1979). Spelling first, sound later: The relationship between orthography and higher order phonological knowledge in older students. *Research in the Teaching of English, 13,* 255–264.

Templeton, S. (1980). Logic and mnemonics for demons and curiosities: Spelling awareness for middle- and secondary-level students. *Reading World, 20,* 123–130.

Templeton, S. (1983). Using the spelling/meaning connection to develop word knowledge in older students. *Journal of Reading, 27*(1), 8–14.

Templeton, S. (1989). Tacit and explicit knowledge of derivational morphology: Foundations for a unified approach to spelling and vocabulary development in the intermediate grades and beyond. *Reading Psychology, 10,* 233–253.

Templeton, S. (1991). Teaching and learning the English spelling system: Reconceptualizing method and purpose. *Elementary School Journal, 92,* 183–199.

Templeton, S. (1992). Theory, nature, and pedagogy of higher-order orthographic development in older children. In S. Templeton & D. Bear (Eds.), *Development of orthographic knowledge and the foundations of literacy: A memorial Festschrift for Edmund H. Henderson* (pp. 253–278), Hillsdale, NJ: Lawrence Erlbaum.

Templeton, S. (1996). *Children's literacy: Contexts for meaningful learning.* Boston: Houghton Mifflin.

Templeton, S. (1997). *Teaching the integrated language arts* (2nd ed.). Boston: Houghton Mifflin.

Templeton, S. (2002). Effective spelling instruction in the middle grades: It's a lot more than memorization. *Voices from the Middle, 9*(3), 8–14.

Templeton, S. (2003). Spelling. In J. Flood, D. Lapp, J. R. Squire, & J. M. Jensen (Eds.), *Handbook of research on teaching the English language arts* (2nd ed., pp. 738–751). Mahwah, NJ: Lawrence Erlbaum Associates.

Templeton, S., & Bear, D. (Eds.). (1992a). *Development of orthographic knowledge and the foundations of literacy: A memorial Festschrift for Edmund H. Henderson.* Hillsdale; NJ: Lawrence Erlbaum.

Templeton, S., & Morris, D. (1999). Questions teachers ask about spelling. *Reading Research Quarterly, 34,* 102–112.

Templeton, S., & Morris, D. (2000). Spelling. In M. Kamil, P. Mosenthal, P. D. Pearson, & R. Barr (Eds.), *Handbook of reading research: Vol. 3* (pp. 525–543). Mahwah, NJ: Lawrence Erlbaum Associates.

Templeton, S., & Scarborough-Franks, L. (1985). The spelling's the thing: Older students' knowledge of derivational morphology in phonology and orthography. *Applied Psycholinguistics, 6,* 371–389.

Templeton, S., & Spivey, E. M. (1980). The concept of "word" in young children as a function of level of cognitive development. *Research in the Teaching of English, 14*(3), 265–278.

Treiman, R. (1985). Onsets and rimes as units of spoken syllables: Evidence from children. *Journal of Educational Psychology, 77*(4), 417–427.

Tunmer, W. E. (1991). Phonological awareness and literacy acquisition. In L. Rieben & C. A. Perfetti (Eds.), *Learning to read: Basic research and its implications* (pp. 105–120). Hillsdale, NJ: Lawrence Erlbaum Associates.

Vallins, G. H. (1954). *Spelling.* Andre Deutsch.

Viise, N. (1994). *Feature word spelling lists: A diagnosis of progressing word knowledge through an assessment of spelling errors,* Unpublished doctoral dissertation. University of Virginia.

Viise, N. (1996). A study of the spelling development of adult literacy learners compared with that of classroom children. *Journal of Literacy Research, 28*(4), 561–587.

Vygotsky, L. S. (1962). *Thought and language.* Cambridge, MA: MIT Press.

White, T. G., Sowell, J., & Yanagihara, A. (1989). Teaching elementary students to use word-part clues. *The Reading Teacher, 42,* 302–308.

Worthy, M. J., & Invernizzi, M. (1989). Spelling errors of normal and disabled students on achievement levels one through four: Instructional implications. *Bulletin of the Orton Society, 40,* 138–149.

Worthy, M., & Viise, N. M. (1996). Morphological, phonological and orthographic differences between the spelling of normally achieving children and basic literacy adults. *Reading and Writing: An Interdisciplinary Journal, 8,* 138–159.

Wylie, R. E., & Durrell, D. D. (1970). Teaching vowels through phonograms. *Elementary English, 47,* 787–791.

Yang, M. (2005). Development of orthographic knowledge among Korean children in grades 1 to 6. (Doctoral Dissertation, University of Virginia). *Dissertation Abstracts International, 66/05,* 1697.

Yopp, K. K. (1988). The validity and reliability of phoneme awareness tests. *Reading Research Quarterly, 23,* 159–177.

Zeno, S. M., Ivens, S. H., Millard, R. T., & Duvvuri, R. (1996). *The educator's word frequency guide.* New York: Touchstone Applied Science Associates.

Zutell, J. (1992). An integrated view of word knowledge: Correlational studies of the relationships among spelling, reading, and conceptual development. In S. Templeton & D. Bear (Eds.), *Development of Orthographic Knowledge and the Foundations of Literacy: A Memorial Festscrift for Edmund H. Henderson* (pp. 213–230). Newark, DE: International Reading Association.

Zutell, J. (1994). Spelling instruction. In A. C. Purves, L. Papa, & S. Jordan (Eds.), *Encyclopedia of English studies and language arts* (Vol. 2, pp. 1098–1100). New York: Scholastic.

Zutell, J. (1996). The directed spelling thinking activity (DSTA): Providing an effective balance in word study instruction. *The Reading Teacher, 50,* 98–107.

Zutell, J. (1998). Word sorting: A developmental spelling approach to word study for delayed readers. *Reading & Writing Quarterly, 14,* 219–238.

Zutell, J., & Allan, V. (1988). The English spelling strategies of Spanish-speaking bilingual children. *TESOL Quarterly, 22,* 333–340.

Zutell, J., & Rasinski, T. (1989). Reading and spelling connections in third and fourth grade students. *Reading Psychology, 10,* 137–156.

Index